Consumer Behavior

Marketing Strategy Perspectives

The Irwin Series in Marketing
Consulting Editor:
Gilbert A. Churchill, Jr.,
University of Wisconsin

Consumer Behavior

Marketing Strategy Perspectives

J. Paul Peter
University of Wisconsin, Madison

Jerry C. Olson
Pennsylvania State University

1987

IRWIN

Homewood, Illinois   60430

ISBN 0-256-03177-0

Library of Congress Catalog Card No. 86–81801

Printed in the United States of America

3 4 5 6 7 8 9 0 K 4 3 2 1 0 9 8

Rose and Angie
Becky, Matt, and Seth

Preface

Although writing a textbook is never easy, we undertook this task because we saw a need for a new text with a more integrative, strategic marketing approach to consumer behavior. There are several reasons why we believe such an approach is necessary.

First, while the consumer behavior course is typically housed in marketing departments, often it is not well integrated into marketing curricula. Consumer behavior usually stands alone as a course in applied psychology with little attention paid to using the information to develop marketing strategies. Although courses in psychology are useful for marketing students and psychology provides a useful background for consumer analysis, students need a text that more clearly analyzes consumers from the perspective of marketing strategy.

Second, a basic problem with the consumer behavior course is that it often becomes a review of the consumer research literature rather than an action-oriented, strategic marketing course. A history of consumer research and psychological theory can be fascinating, but a strategic approach is more valuable for undergraduate and master's students training for jobs in marketing management.

Third, we wanted to offer our own ideas on the field using our own organization. Both of us have taught the consumer behavior course for many years and conducted research and studied theoretical developments in the field. Based on our own experiences, we have omitted or deemphasized dated topics and research. In addition, we have included topics and research that are not covered in traditional consumer behavior texts but have useful implications for developing marketing strategies. We also include new ideas and frameworks that we developed specifically for educating future marketing managers about consumer behavior.

Finally, we wanted to develop an integrated view of consumer analysis. Too often students leave a consumer behavior course with little knowledge of how all of the topics fit together and how the information can be used to develop marketing strategies. So we developed the model shown below; it divides consumer analysis into four interrelated elements. Each of these four elements—cognition, behavior, environment, and marketing strategy—is equally important for analyzing and understanding consumers and for developing successful marketing strategies.

The four major sections of our text offer detailed discussions of each of these model elements. In Section Two, cognition is analyzed. By *cognition* we mean the psychological processes that go on inside consumers' minds. In Section Three, behavior is analyzed. By *behavior* we mean all of the overt actions that consumers perform. In Section Four, the environment is analyzed. By the *environment* we mean all of the stimuli external to consumers that influence their cognitions and behaviors. In Section Five, marketing strategy is analyzed. By *marketing strategy* we mean the

The Wheel of Consumer Analysis

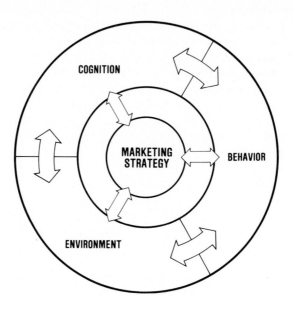

processes by which marketing stimuli (such as products, advertisements, stores, and price information) are created and placed in consumer environments. As shown by the arrows in the model, each of these elements both influences and is influenced by the others in a dynamic, reciprocal manner. By considering all of these elements and relationships, students can gain better understanding of consumers and thus devise better marketing strategies.

Overall, we believe we have created an interesting and useful book for educating future marketing managers about consumers. Our major purposes are (1) to offer students a simple, comprehensive framework and appropriate tools for analyzing consumers and (2) to offer students a way to *think about* and analyze consumer behavior/marketing strategy relationships. To the degree we have achieved these objectives, we think we have made a valuable contribution to marketing education. To the degree we have failed to achieve these objectives, we can only promise to work diligently to improve the text. In fact, we would greatly appreciate receiving criticisms, comments, and suggestions from readers.

There are many people connected with this text to whom we offer our sincere thanks. First, we would like to thank our students for *their* contributions to *our* education. Second, we would like to thank Gilbert A. Churchill, Jr., Irwin Consulting Editor, for his encouragement and constructive criticism throughout the preparation of this text. Third, we would like to thank the reviewers of this text for the time, effort, and insights they offered. They include Mickey Belch (San Diego State), Russell Belk (University of Utah), Ray Burke (University of Pennsylvania), Ellen Day (Indiana University), Mike Etzel (University of Notre Dame), Bill Gaidis (Arizona State University), Meryl Gardner (New York University), Walter Nord (Washington University), and Tommy Whittler (University of Kentucky). We also thank Janet Christopher for her skilled typing and production efforts.

J. Paul Peter

Jerry C. Olson

Contents

Conceptual Issues in Pricing: *Money. Time. Cognitive Activity. Behavior Effort. Value.* Pricing Strategy: *Analyze Consumer/Product Relationships. Analyze the Environmental Situation. Determine the Role of Price in Marketing Strategy. Estimate Relevant Production and Marketing Costs. Set Pricing Objectives. Develop Pricing Strategy and Set Prices.* Price Environment. Price Cognitions: *Price Perceptions and Attitudes.* Price Behaviors: *Funds Access. Transaction.*

Channel Strategy Issues: *Commodity. Conditions. Competition. Costs. Coverage. Competence. Control. Characteristics of Middlemen.* Store Environment: *Store Location. Store Layout. In-Store Stimuli.* Store-Related Cognitions: *Store Image. Store Atmosphere.* Store-Related Behaviors: *Store Contact. Store Loyalty.*

Section Six
Societal Influences on Marketing Practices

The Rights of Marketers and Consumers: *Legal Influences. Political Influences. Competitive Influences. Ethical Influences.*

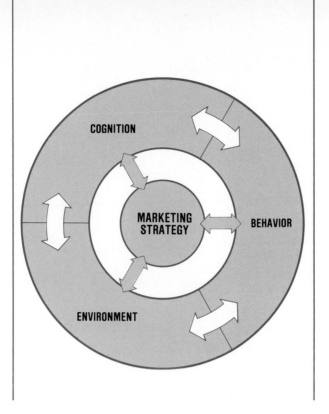

Section One

Introduction and Overview

Chapter One

Consumer Behavior and Marketing Strategy

Is Consumer Behavior Big Business?

It may be difficult for many people to appreciate how much Americans purchase and consume. For example, did you know that *in an average day,* Americans . . .

Eat 5.8 million pounds of chocolate candy.

Use 550,000 pounds of toothpaste and gargle 69,000 gallons of mouthwash.

Buy 190,000 watches, about half of which are for gifts.

Eat 228,000 bushels of onions.

Buy 120,000 new radios and 50,000 new television sets.

Eat 47 million hot dogs.

Buy almost 5 million books.

Spend $200,000 to buy roller skates.

Spend $40 million for automobile repairs and replacements caused by rust.

Wear more than 3 million pounds of rubber off their tires, enough to make 250,000 new tires.

Buy 38,000 Ken and Barbie dolls.

Buy about 35 million paper clips and 4 million eraser-tipped wooden pencils.

Buy 12,000 new refrigerators and 10,000 new kitchen ranges.

And last but not least, snap up 82,000 mousetraps?

Source: Excerpted from Tom Parker (1984), In One Day, *Boston: Houghton Mifflin.*

We believe that a course in consumer behavior is one of the most important in business education. This is because, as Professor Theodore Levitt of the Harvard Business School has so clearly stated, "The purpose of a business is to create and keep a customer."[1] Customers are developed and maintained through marketing strategies. In other words, the success of a business depends on the quality of its marketing strategies, and the quality of marketing strategies depends on knowing, serving, and influencing consumers to achieve organizational objectives.

In their best-seller, *In Search of Excellence*, Peters and Waterman reported on a study of highly successful corporations. One of their major conclusions was that

> All business success rests on something labeled a sale, which at least momentarily weds the company and the customer. A simple summary of what our research uncovered on the customer attribute is this: the excellent companies *really are* close to their customers. That's it. Other companies talk about it; the excellent companies do it.[2]

It is interesting to note that this best-selling book had only a single chapter on customers; yet in a follow-up book, *A Passion for Excellence*, Peters and Austin included five full chapters on customers and their importance for successful corporations.[3]

One interesting phenomenon in popular business literature is the discussion of marketing and how major corporations have recently "discovered" or "rediscovered" it.[4] Certainly, these firms had always produced products, and priced, promoted, and distributed them. What then, did these firms really discover? What they really discovered is *consumers*—and that by knowing as much as possible about their consumers and potential consumers, superior marketing strategies could be developed.

This suggests that a knowledge of consumers is critical for developing successful marketing strategies. Consumer behavior is an important business course because it provides this knowledge and challenges you to *think about* and *analyze* the relationships between marketing strategy and consumer behavior. Rather than simply telling you to "analyze consumers,"

[1]Theodore Levitt (1983), *The Marketing Imagination*, New York: Free Press, p. 5.

[2]Thomas J. Peters and Robert H. Waterman, Jr. (1982), *In Search of Excellence*, New York: Harper & Row, p. 156.

[3]Thomas J. Peters and Nancy K. Austin (1985), *A Passion for Excellence*, New York: Random House, chapters 4–8.

[4]For examples, see "Marketing: The New Priority," *Business Week* (November 21, 1983), pp. 96–102; Bill Saporito (1984), "Hewlett-Packard Discovers Marketing," *Fortune* (October 1), pp. 50–56; "A Leaner Consolidated Foods Rediscovers Marketing," *Business Week* (August 29, 1983), pp. 58–59; "The Consumer Drives R. J. Reynolds Again," *Business Week* (June 4, 1984), pp. 92–99; Maggie McComas (1985), "Quaker Is Feeling Its Oats," *Fortune* (June 10), pp. 54–64.

HIGHLIGHT 1–1   **What Is a Customer?**

From a marketing management perspective, there is no important difference between the terms *customer* and *consumer.* On posters displayed prominently around the very successful L. L. Bean Company in Freeport, Maine, employees are constantly reminded of what a customer is to them:

- A Customer is the most important person ever in this office . . . in person or by mail.

- A Customer is not dependent on us . . . we are dependent on him.

- A Customer is not an interruption of our work . . . he is the purpose of it. We are not doing a favor by serving him . . . he is doing us a favor by giving us the opportunity to do so.

- A Customer is not someone to argue or match wits with. Nobody ever won an argument with a Customer.

- A Customer is a person who brings us his wants. It is our job to handle them profitably to him and ourselves.

Source: Adapted from Thomas J. Peters and Nancy K. Austin (1985), A Passion for Excellence, *New York: Random House, p. 95.*

this course provides a comprehensive framework and a variety of concepts for doing so.

In the remainder of this chapter we will offer definitions for and briefly discuss some of the critical dimensions of marketing, marketing strategies, and consumer behavior. We hope this discussion will convince you of the importance of consumer behavior in developing marketing strategy and of the value of this course for a successful marketing career.

What Is Marketing?

Many definitions of marketing have been suggested over the years. These definitions, and the debate surrounding them, focused on various marketing functions, institutions, and processes. Although no definition has been accepted completely, the American Marketing Association has developed a very good one: **Marketing** is the process of planning and executing the conception, pricing, promotion, and distribution of ideas, goods, and services to create exchanges that satisfy individual and organizational objectives.[5]

---

[5]"AMA Board Approves New Marketing Definition," *Marketing News* (March 1, 1985), p. 1.

While many aspects of this definition could be discussed at length, two key phrases are of interest here. First is the idea that marketing *creates exchanges*. This is important because it indicates that marketing is not a passive activity which simply reacts to the environment and consumers. Rather, marketing is a proactive process that attempts to change the environment and consumers so that exchanges occur.

The second key phrase concerns *satisfying individual and organizational objectives*. Marketing organizations are encouraged to develop quantitative, measurable, realistic objectives that are often expressed in terms of sales, profits, and market share. These objectives can only be met by influencing consumers to purchase and repurchase the market offering. Similarly, individual consumers may have specific needs and objectives they are attempting to satisfy through purchase/consumption. However, relatively little is known about the degree to which consumers actually develop purchase/consumption objectives or goals or about the influence of marketing in creating such consumer goals.

Nonetheless, this discussion highlights one of our own basic assumptions about marketing: we believe that marketing, particularly as practiced

Fred Leavitt: Click/Chicago

Marketing creates environments for exchange.

The marketing imagination is the starting point of success in marketing. It is distinguished from other forms of imagination by the unique insights it brings to understanding customers, their problems, and the means to capture their attention and their custom. By asserting that people don't buy things but buy solutions to problems, the marketing imagination makes an inspired leap from the obvious to the meaningful. "Meaning" resides in its implied suggestion as to what to do—in this case, find out what problems people are trying to solve. It is represented by Charles Revson's famous distinction regarding the business of Revlon, Inc.: "In the factory we make cosmetics. In the store we sell hope." It is characterized by Leo McGinneva's clarification about why people buy quarter-inch drill bits: "They don't want quarter-inch bits. They want quarter-inch holes." It leads to Professor Raymond A. Bauer's point that when buyers select a known vendor or known brand over another it is more meaningful to think of the choice as an act of risk reduction rather than as the expression of a brand preference.

Each of these reconceptualizations found a deeper meaning in customer behavior, thus causing marketing programs to be reshaped in ways that better attract and hold customers. To attract a customer, you must ask him to do something different from what he would have done in the absence of the programs you directed at him. He has to change his mind and his actions.

Source: Adapted from Theodore Levitt (1983), The Marketing Imagination, *New York: Free Press, pp. 128–129.*

by successful corporations, is a powerful force in society. We believe that marketing strategies not only adapt to consumers, but also change what consumers think and feel about themselves, about various market offerings, and about the appropriate situations for product purchase and use. This does not mean that marketing is unethical or an inappropriate activity. However, the power of marketing and the ability of marketing research and consumer analysis to gain insight into consumer behavior should not be discounted or misused.

What Are Marketing Strategies?

We define **marketing strategies** as managerial decisions designed to affect the probability or frequency of exchanges in order to achieve marketing objectives. Ordinarily, in a business context, this translates into increasing the probability or frequency of consumer purchasing behaviors by developing and presenting marketing mixes directed at selected target markets.

Don Smetzer: Click/Chicago

Marketing strategies influence exchanges.

FIGURE 1–1   **Examples of Consumer Issues Involved in Developing Marketing Strategy**

Strategy	Consumer Issues
Segmentation	Which consumers are the prime prospects for our product?
	What consumer characteristics should we use to segment the market for our product?
Product	What products do consumers use now?
	What benefits do consumers want from this product?
Promotion	What promotion appeal would influence consumers to purchase and use our product?
	What advertising claims would be most effective for our product?
Pricing	How important is price to consumers in various target markets?
	What effects will a price change have on purchase behavior?
Distribution	Where do consumers buy this product?
	Would a different distribution system change consumers' purchasing behavior?

A **marketing mix** consists of product, promotion, distribution, and pricing strategies.

In Figure 1–1 we present some consumer behavior issues involved in developing various aspects of marketing strategy. Issues such as these can be addressed through formal marketing research, informal discussions with consumers, or intuition and thinking about the relationships between marketing strategy and consumer behavior.

Courtesy T. J. Lipton Co. and General Mills

This ad incorporates several marketing strategy elements.

Figure 1–1 shows that understanding consumers is a critical element in developing marketing strategies. There are very few—if any—strategy decisions that do not involve a consideration of consumer behavior. For example, analysis of the competition requires an understanding of what consumers think and feel about competitive brands, which consumers buy these brands and why, and in what situations consumers purchase and use competitive products. In sum, the more you learn about consumers (and approaches to analyzing them), the better your chances for developing successful marketing strategies.

What Is Consumer Behavior?

It might seem easy to define consumer behavior. However, this is not the case, because many different perspectives, constituencies, and contexts are involved in the study of this phenomenon. We will briefly review these in order to position our text and our definition of consumer behavior.

Different Perspectives

A variety of perspectives has been used to study consumer behavior. Frameworks and ideas from anthropology, sociology, psychology, economics, and marketing have been employed, as well as ideas from other fields. Overall, most consumer research is based on a variety of psychological theories that are applied to marketing problems. This is the primary focus taken here, although we do employ concepts from other fields to analyze particular aspects of consumer behavior.

Different Constituencies

A variety of constituencies is also interested in consumer behavior. For example, Figure 1–2 presents a macro view of consumer behavior and shows three major groups and the relationships among them. The first group is marketing organizations. These include not only what are conventionally thought of as business firms, but also other organizations such as hospitals, museums, law firms, and universities. Thus, marketing organizations include all groups that have a market offering and are seeking exchanges with consumers. While the focus of our text is on relationships between marketing strategy and consumers primarily in the context of business firms, the ideas we present can also be applied to other marketing organizations, such as the American Cancer Association or your college or university.

The second group in Figure 1–2 comprises various government and political organizations. These include government agencies such as the Federal Trade Commission and the Food and Drug Administration. The major concern of these organizations is monitoring and regulating exchanges between marketing organizations and consumers. This is accomplished through the development of public policy, which affects marketing strategies and consumer activities. Political constituencies include activists such as Ralph Nader or the members of Students against Drunk Driving. While these relationships are not the major concern of our text, they are considered, particularly in Chapter 21.

The third group in Figure 1–2 includes both individual and industrial consumers who exchange resources (typically money) for various goods and services. Although the major concern of our text is with the ultimate consumers, the logic presented here can be applied in the industrial market, and several examples of industrial buyer behavior are included.

Overall, each of the groups and relationships shown in the figure can be considered part of the field of consumer behavior.

Different Contexts

In addition to the variety of theoretical perspectives on consumer behavior and the variety of constituencies concerned with consumer behavior, the

FIGURE 1–2   **A Macro View of Consumer Behavior**

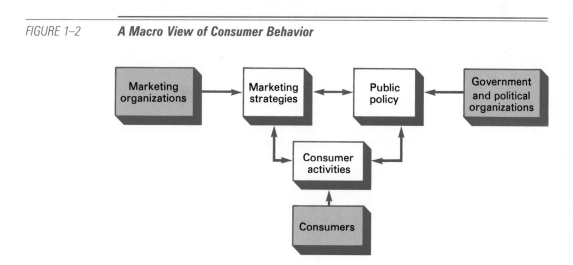

Courtesy Air National Guard

Governmental agencies also use marketing strategies to achieve their objectives.

term is used in a variety of contexts and can be defined in a variety of ways. For example, *consumer behavior* is used to refer to the college course you are taking, to a field of academic study, to every aspect of the exchange process from the consumer's point of view, and to the specific overt actions of consumers. In other words, consumer behavior is a somewhat ambiguous term that has no fully accepted definition.

Despite the ambiguity about what exactly "consumer behavior" means, we believe it is important to offer a working definition of the topic of our text. Recognizing that no one definition is likely to satisfy the re-

William Means: Click/Chicago

The interaction of cognition, behavior, and environment determines exchanges.

quirements of every perspective and person involved in the field, we define consumer behavior as follows: **consumer behavior** involves the dynamic interaction of cognition, behavior, and environmental events by which human beings conduct the exchange aspects of their lives. It includes the relationships among what people think, feel, and do in various consumption situations and environments, as well as the role of marketing strategies in this process. A more detailed discussion and overview of these processes and their relationships is provided in Chapter 2.

Back to the Case

This case demonstrates that many products you may purchase only rarely, are purchased by many other consumers each day, and tremendous amounts of money are involved. Thus, while a drop in market share of 1 or 2 percent may not sound like much, it often translates into millions of dollars in lost sales. For example, 1 percent of the U.S. soft-drink industry is worth about $300 million in retail sales. The U.S. consumer market is certainly big business!

You can also see from this case that consumer behavior accounts for the success or failure of products and firms. Sales, profits, and market-share objectives are achieved by successfully knowing, serving, and influencing consumers. Thus, in every sense of the phrase, consumer behavior *is* big business.

Reprinted with permission of PepsiCo. Inc.

If this promotion strategy has even a small effect on market share, it would still be significant.

Summary

In this chapter, we argued that consumer behavior is an important topic of study because achieving marketing objectives depends on knowing, serving, and influencing consumers. We defined and discussed three key terms: marketing, marketing strategy, and consumer behavior. We hope that after reading this chapter, you can now appreciate the relevance and importance of consumer behavior for many constituencies. Finally, we hope that you will learn something about yourself by considering how the analytic framework and information in our text applies to you as a potential marketing manager, as a consumer, and as a human being.

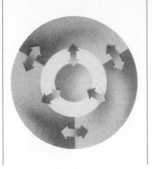

Chapter Two

Consumer Behavior: A Framework for Marketing Analysis

Buying a Peugeot

"The doctor says I need to get more exercise. My blood pressure is up, and I'm 20 pounds overweight," lamented Carl Perkins to his wife, Betty. "I hate jogging—and besides, it's hard on your knees and joints. I think I'll buy a bike. Biking is good aerobic exercise, and it would be fun to peddle around the neighborhood."

"That's a super idea," said Betty. "Let's check the phone book and go visit some bike shops."

A few minutes later they were in the car. They had found two bike shops within a few miles of home. Because Carl and Betty both realized they knew little about bikes, they agreed to get some pamphlets and information from the stores and study them before buying.

In the first store, they were greeted by an attractive young salesperson. Carl related that they planned to purchase a bike eventually, but for now they were just looking and collecting some information.

"That's fine," said the salesperson. "Let's start with the Raleigh bikes, which are our best line. You are probably looking for the middle range of their line, so let's look at the Raleigh Pursuit. This is a 12-speed recreational bike. It has a Suntour derailleur, alloy frame, 14 to 30 free wheel, and 90-pound pressure tires. It costs $186.95 and comes in either red or blue. It's a very popular bike, and Raleigh is rated very well in the bike magazines."

"What's the difference between this one and the cheaper Raleigh bikes?" asked Carl.

"Well . . . this one is made with better components, so there will be a lot less maintenance on it," said the salesperson.

"Okay. Give us some literature on these bikes, and we'll be back," said Carl.

Back on the road, Carl confessed to Betty that he just learned more about bikes than he wanted to know. "I hope the next place is of more help."

In the next store, the Perkins' were greeted by a slender, bearded chap wearing biking shorts. "Can I help you?" he asked.

"Sure . . . uh, we're interested in some information about bikes," said Carl.

"Fine. My name is Warren Nesterrink. Could I ask what type of biking you plan to do?"

"Mainly riding around the neighborhood or in the park for some exercise and fresh air. Probably won't ride over an hour a day," reported Carl.

"Now let me ask you one more question . . . uh, about what price range are you considering?" asked Warren.

"I really haven't thought about that. I just want a bike that is efficient to ride and works well. I don't know much about bike prices, but about $200 would be all right."

"Thanks. That helps a lot. We carry five major bike lines. In your price range, you can get a great bike for your purposes in any of them. Personally, I ride a lot and I like the Peugeots. Let me show you one.

"This is the Peugeot P-8. Let's see if this 23-inch frame is right for you. You can try it out in the parking lot," offered Warren.

Carl test-rode the P-8 and enjoyed it. He thought it was very smooth and efficient, and it looked great. Compared to the bikes he rode as a youngster, this was some machine!

"How much is the P-8?" asked Carl after his test ride.

"It sells for $230, but that includes maintenance for the first year. It's really a quality bike, and we don't discount Peugeots, so it'll hold its resale value if you ever want to trade," explained Warren.

"Well, what's the advantage of purchasing a more expensive model?" asked Carl.

"To be honest, for your use, there's little advantage to spending more. Sure, you could trim a pound or two off the weight of the bike and get a bit better components. But unless you're going to race competitively or go on long trips, why spend more money? The P-8 is a dandy bike, and you can't beat it for the money," Warren explained.

Carl purchased the P-8 and charged it on a VISA card. A week later, he bought one for Betty. On returning for a free 100-mile check, they each bought a set of toe clips and an Huret odometer. They were very pleased with their purchases and recommended biking and Warren's Bike Shop to all their friends.

Many theories, models, and concepts have been borrowed from other fields as well as developed by marketing researchers in attempts to understand consumer behavior. In many cases, these ideas overlap and even compete with each other as viable descriptions of consumers. To date, no single approach is fully accepted; nor is it likely that a single, grand theory of consumer behavior can be devised that all researchers would agree on.

For these reasons, neither this chapter nor the text itself should be viewed as a theory of consumer behavior. Rather, it is a *framework* for studying, analyzing, and understanding consumers to help you develop successful marketing strategies.

This chapter introduces the general framework on which our text is organized. The chapter is divided into two major parts. In the first section, we introduce three of the major elements of our framework: cognition, behavior, and the environment. We then discuss the nature of the relationships among these elements.

In the second part of the chapter, we discuss the fourth element of our framework: marketing strategy. In addition, we illustrate one approach to developing marketing strategy based on this overall model.

Consumer Behavior: A Conceptual Framework

Figure 2–1 presents three of the four major elements of our model: cognition, behavior, and the environment. In the following section, we provide an overview of these elements and the special relationships among them.

Cognition

In this text, we use the term **cognition** in a broad sense to refer to everything that goes on inside consumers' minds, including rational, emotional, and subconscious processes. For example, attention, comprehension, memory, knowledge, meaning, belief, attitude, and intention are cognitive factors that describe consumers' internal, mental processes and mental states.

This subject will be dealt with at greater length in Section Two, which is devoted to a discussion of cognition. In Chapter 3, we provide a general model of the cognitive processes involved in consumer decision making. The remaining five chapters in the section provide detailed discussions of each element of this general cognitive model. Chapters 4 and 5 detail current approaches to consumer memory, in particular, to consumers' knowledge of products and brands. Chapter 6 concerns the processes by which consumers interpret marketing information from their environment. Chapter 7 discusses consumer attitudes and intentions. Finally, Chapter 8 describes the information integration processes involved in consumer decision making.

Behaviors

In this text, **behavior** refers to overt acts—actions of consumers that can be directly observed. Although the field is called "consumer behavior," relatively little attention has been given to what consumers actually *do*.

FIGURE 2–1   *A Reciprocal Model for Analyzing Consumers*

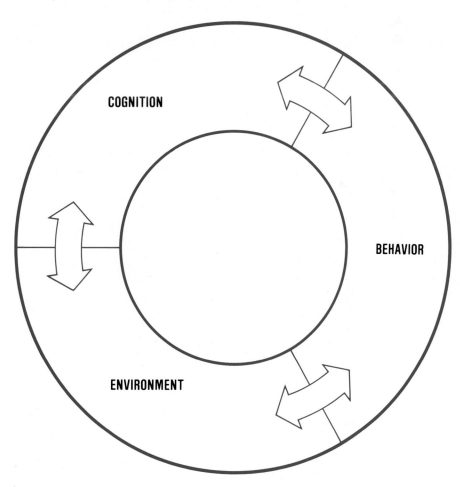

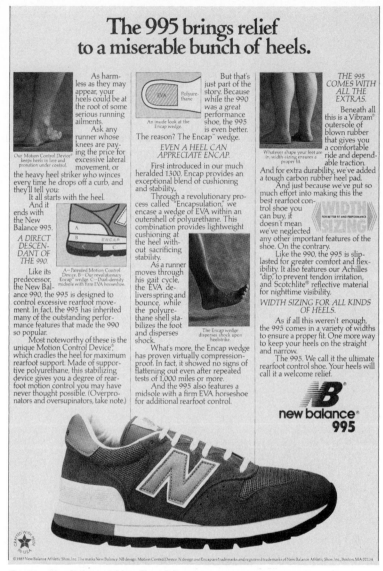

Courtesy New Balance Athlete Shoe, Inc.

Some marketing strategies encourage considerable cognitive activity.

Instead, the focus has been on what they *say* they think and feel, or what they *report* that they do. Overt behavior is seldom measured in spite of its relevance to understanding consumers and to developing marketing strategy.

Section Three of this text is devoted to a further discussion of con-

Although many competing theories and ideas about consumer cognitions have been proposed, no single theory completely describes the workings of the consumer's mind. However, carefully studying and thinking about the information in Section Two of this text should help you develop informed answers to questions about cognition such as:

1. How do consumers interpret information about marketing stimuli such as products, stores, and advertising?

2. How do consumers choose from among alternative product classes, products, and brands?

3. How do consumers form attitudes about products and brands?

4. How does memory affect consumer decision making?

5. How do cognitions affect behavior and environments?

6. How do behavior and environments affect cognitions?

7. How do consumers interpret the benefits of marketing offerings?

8. Why are consumers more interested or involved in some products or brands than others?

9. How do marketing strategies affect consumer cognitions?

10. How cognitively active and rational are consumers?

sumer behavior and techniques designed to maintain or change it. Chapter 9 offers a basic discussion of how behavior-oriented researchers differ in their viewpoint from those studying cognitive processes. A variety of examples is included to demonstrate the approach. Chapter 10 is devoted to conditioning processes and their use in marketing strategies designed to influence consumer behavior. Chapter 11 discusses vicarious learning or modeling—a useful approach for describing certain aspects of consumer behavior and for modifying behavior. The last chapter in Section Three, Chapter 12, applies behavior modification techniques to designing marketing strategies. Overall, the section is designed to encourage the analysis of overt behavior in developing marketing strategies.

Environment

In this text, **environment** refers to the complex of physical and social stimuli in the external world of consumers. Section Four is devoted to discussing these stimuli. In Chapter 13, we provide an overview of environmental influences on consumer behavior. Chapters 14 and 15 are devoted to ex-

Although little attention has been given to studying the overt behavior of consumers, many behavior influence techniques seem to be commonly used by marketing practitioners. Carefully studying and thinking about the information in Section Three of the text should help you develop informed answers to questions about behavior such as:

1. How do behavior approaches differ from cognitive approaches to studying consumer behavior?

2. What is respondent conditioning, and how is it used by marketers to affect consumer behavior?

3. What is operant conditioning, and how is it used by marketers to affect consumer behavior?

4. What is vicarious learning, and how is it used by marketers to affect consumer behavior?

5. What consumer behaviors are of interest to marketing management?

6. How much control does marketing have over consumers' behavior?

7. How do cognitions and environments affect behavior?

8. How does behavior affect cognitions and environments?

9. How can behavior theory be used by marketing managers?

10. Does the frequency and quality of consumer behavior vary by individuals, products, and situations?

© George W. Gardner

Learning to use a complex product may be a long-term process.

Environmental psychology seeks to extend knowledge about the relationships between environmental stimuli and human behavior. In consumer research, the major environmental factors examined have been concerned with the impact of various societal aspects. Carefully studying and thinking about the information in Section Four of the text should help you develop informed answers to questions about the environment such as:

1. In what physical environments do consumer behaviors occur?

2. How do environments affect consumer cognitions and behavior?

3. How do consumer cognitions and behavior affect the environment?

4. What effect does culture have on consumers?

5. What effect does subculture have on consumers?

6. What effect does social class have on consumers?

7. What effect do reference groups have on consumers?

8. What effect do families have on consumers?

9. In what ways do consumers influence each other concerning marketing offerings?

10. How powerful are interpersonal influences on consumer behavior?

amining five aspects of the social environment and their influences on consumer behavior. These aspects of the social environment include culture, subculture, social class, reference groups, and families.

Relationships among Model Elements

Perhaps the major difference between our model and other approaches to describing consumer behavior involves **causality.** In general, most approaches are concerned with one-way cause-and-effect relationships. For instance, some cognitive researchers focus only on the causal impact of cognitive factors on behavior, whereas some behavior-oriented researchers focus only on the causal impact of the environment on behavior.

While such one-way causal approaches have value, they may lead consumer researchers and marketing strategists to overlook important relationships among cognition, behavior, and environments. To overcome this problem, we believe it is useful to view the relationships among these elements as a continuous set of interactions, called *reciprocal determinism.* **Reciprocal** refers to a mutual action of events, and **determinism** indicates

Alan Carey/The Image Works
Store environments influence consumers.

the effects caused by these events. Thus, **reciprocal determinism** means that each element in the model both causes the other elements and in turn, is caused by them, usually in a continuous fashion, over a period of time.

Bandura illustrates reciprocal determinism as follows:

Television-viewing behavior provides an everyday example. Personal preferences influence when and which programs, from among the available alternatives, individuals choose to watch on television. Although the potential televised environment is identical for all viewers, the actual televised environment that impinges on given individuals depends on what they select to watch. Through their viewing behavior, they partly shape the nature of the future televised

FIGURE 2–2　　**What Affects What in TV Viewing?**

1. Do consumer preferences for TV shows affect which shows they view? If so, cognitions affect behavior.

2. Do consumer preferences and perceptions affect what they see when they watch a TV show? If so, cognitions affect the environment.

3. Do consumer viewing behaviors affect consumer preferences for watching the same show again? If so, behavior affects cognitions.

4. Do consumer viewing behaviors affect what shows remain and what shows are canceled? If so, behavior affects the environment.

5. Does the availability of various TV shows affect consumer preferences for them? If so, the environment affects cognitions.

6. Does the availability of various TV shows affect consumer viewing behavior? If so, the environment affects behavior.

environment. Because production costs and commercial requirements also determine what people are shown, the options provided in the televised environment partly shape the viewer's preferences. Here, all three factors—viewer preferences, viewing behavior, and televised offerings—reciprocally affect each other.[1]

In this example, personal preference is a cognition; TV viewing is behavior; and TV shows and their availability are parts of the television environment. Figure 2–2 presents a series of six questions, based on this example, which illustrate six possible one-way relationships between cognitions, behaviors, and environments. If the answer to all six questions is yes—and we believe that yes is the appropriate answer—it should be clear that each element in the model affects and is affected by the other elements; i.e., they are reciprocally determined. Thus, simple one-way cause-and-effect relationships are incapable of providing a complete explanation of even simple events. There are always a variety of causal interactions involved.

Reciprocal Determinism and the Elements in the Model

There are three important points to be made about reciprocal determinism and the relationships among the elements in the model. First, any comprehensive analysis of consumer behavior must *consider all three elements*. De-

---

[1]Albert Bandura (1978), "The Self System in Reciprocal Determinism," *American Psychologist* (April), p. 346.

scriptions of consumer behavior in terms of only one or two of the elements are incomplete. For example, to assume that cognitions cause behavior and to ignore the influence of the environment underestimates the dynamic nature of consumer behavior and may lead to a less effective marketing strategy.

Second, it is important to recognize that any of the three elements may be the *starting point* for consumer analysis. In the example above, the analysis began with consumer preferences; yet this was arbitrary. We could have begun with television viewing behavior or with the television programming environment.

Third, the model is *dynamic;* it views consumer behavior as a process of continuous change. While we may offer a good description of consumers in terms of these elements at a particular time, any or all of these elements can change over time. Thus, the results of consumer research often become quickly outdated. For this reason, we have chosen not to emphasize specific research findings that are more than a few years old. The results of much of that work, even if valid in its day, may have little relevance in today's market.

Marketing Strategy

The fourth element in our framework is marketing strategy. From the consumer's viewpoint, marketing strategies are part of the environment and consist of a variety of physical and social stimuli. These stimuli include products and services, promotional materials (advertisements), places for exchange (retail stores), and price information (price tags attached to products). Implementing marketing strategies involves placing these marketing stimuli in consumers' environments in order to affect their cognitions and behaviors.

To highlight its importance in this text, we represent marketing strategy as a separate element in our framework, as shown in Figure 2–3. Marketing strategy can affect each of the other elements—cognition, behavior, and the environment—and in turn, can be affected by each of these factors. For example, placing a service station sign next to an interstate highway changes the *landscape* (the environment) and may change consumer *intentions* (a cognition) to stop for gas with the result of *stopping and purchasing* from the station (behavior). The success of using the sign may lead to placing more signs along highways, thus changing other environments, cognitions, and behaviors. Eventually, research may show that many consumers dislike having too many signs cluttering the landscape and a new strategy may have to be developed, and so on. In other words, marketing strategies interact reciprocally with cognitions, behaviors, and environments across time. Marketing strategies may change the other elements and be changed by them.

Of course, not every consumer is equally likely to be influenced by a particular marketing strategy. For example, married couples without children are less likely to be heavy consumers of Mattel toys than are parents of small children. Therefore, marketers are encouraged to segment markets on the basis of the probability that various consumers will purchase, use, and continue to repurchase their products.

FIGURE 2–3   **The Wheel of Consumer Analysis**

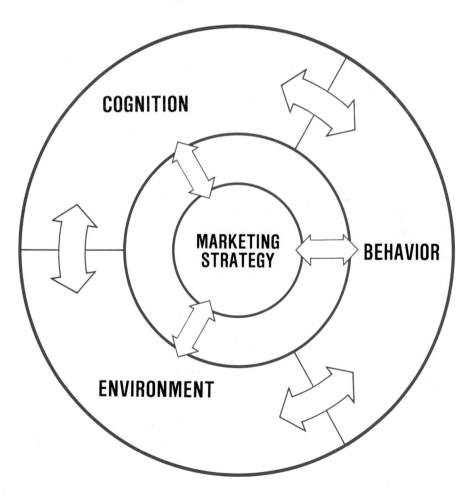

HIGHLIGHT 2–4   **Some Basic Questions about Marketing Strategy and Consumers**

Consumers are the focal point in developing successful marketing strategies. According to the principle of reciprocal determinism, marketing strategies both affect and are affected by consumers' cognitions, behaviors, and environments. Carefully studying and thinking about the information in Section Five of the text should help you develop informed answers to questions about marketing strategies such as:

1. What are some effective ways to segment markets?

2. How can products be effectively positioned?

3. What are the relationships between products and consumers?

4. What are the relationships between promotions and consumers?

5. What are the relationships between channels of distribution and consumers?

6. What are the relationships between pricing variables and consumers?

7. What consumer variables affect the success of a marketing strategy?

8. How can a firm develop brand-loyal consumers?

9. What is the role of consumer satisfaction in developing successful market offerings?

10. How important is image in successful marketing strategies?

Section Five of our text is devoted to marketing strategy. In Chapter 16, market segmentation and product positioning are discussed, and a sequential model is presented to facilitate the segmentation process. The next four chapters of the section present the elements of the marketing mix: product strategy (Chapter 17), promotion strategy (Chapter 18), pricing strategy (Chapter 19), and channels of distribution strategy (Chapter 20). While these chapters are concerned with approaches to developing marketing strategies, the consumer remains the focal point for strategy development.

The wheel of consumer analysis in Figure 2–3 implies that marketing is a powerful force in society. For this reason, we think it is critical for marketing managers to carefully consider their social responsibility and not abuse their abilities to influence consumers. Section Six of our text discusses four societal influences on marketing practice: legal, political, competitive, and ethical. All readers of the text are encouraged to carefully review this section and consider this information when designing marketing strategies.

Many people feel that marketing is a very powerful force in society. In fact, it is considered so powerful that society has developed a number of checks on marketing practices, and these checks need to be seriously considered. Carefully studying and thinking about Section Six of the text should help you develop informed answers to questions such as:

1. What is the relative power of marketers and of consumers?

2. How important are legal influences, and what is their effect on marketing strategy?

3. How important are political influences, and what is their effect on marketing strategy?

4. How important are competitive influences, and what is their effect on marketing strategy?

5. How important are ethical influences, and what is their effect on marketing strategy?

An Illustration of a Strategy Development Approach

The more marketers know about consumers' cognitions, behavior, and environments, the more likely they are to develop successful marketing strategies. In the final part of this chapter, we present a simple approach for designing marketing strategies based on our framework. Because our discussion is designed only to illustrate the general logic of our approach, we will keep it simple by ignoring many of the variables that would be included in a complete analysis.

Initial Consumer Analysis

The first step in developing a marketing strategy involves performing an initial consumer analysis. While many cognitions, behaviors, and environments could be considered, we focus on two basic cognitive elements and one behavior.

The first cognitive element is *awareness*, which is simply whether consumers know about the existence of our brand. For example, most consumers are aware of Tide laundry detergent, one of the oldest brands on the market. The second element is *attitude* or *evaluation*, which refers to consumers' feelings about our brand—do they like it or dislike it? For example, given that Tide is the market leader, many consumers probably like it. With only these two cognitive variables, consumers could be classified into three basic groups: (1) consumers who are aware of but dislike our brand, (2) consumers who are unaware of our brand or are aware of it but have no feelings about it, and (3) consumers who are aware of our brand and like it.

In terms of behavior, we consider only *purchase behaviors.* Again, three groups or segments of consumers can be distinguished. The first group consists of consumers who do not purchase our brand, but purchase a competing brand instead. For example, if we were analyzing the market for Tide detergent, regular purchasers of Wisk would be classified in the nonpurchasing group. The second group consists of people who do not purchase the product at all. For example, consumers who have their laundry and dry cleaning done outside the home may not purchase any brand of laundry detergent. The third group consists of consumers who regularly purchase our brand—in this example, loyal Tide users.

Construct a Matrix

One approach to strategy development would be to cross-classify each of the three cognitive groups in relation to each of the three behavior groups. Doing so results in the matrix shown in Figure 2–4, which has nine basic cells. These cells represent the entire market, broken down into the various combinations of positive (+), neutral (0), and negative (−) cognitions and behaviors relative to our brand.

FIGURE 2–4   **A Marketing Strategy Matrix**

Behaviors

	B_-	B_o	B_+
C_-	**Cell 1** Consumers in this cell dislike our brand and purchase competing brands.	**Cell 2** Consumers in this cell dislike our brand but do not buy the product.	**Cell 3** Consumers in this cell dislike our brand but purchase it.
C_o	**Cell 4** Consumers in this cell are either unaware of or have no feeling about our brand and purchase competing brands.	**Cell 5** Consumers in this cell are either unaware of or have no feeling about our brand but do not purchase the product.	**Cell 6** Consumers in this cell are aware of our brand, have no strong feelings about it, but do purchase it.
C_+	**Cell 7** Consumers in this cell like our brand but purchase competing brands.	**Cell 8** Consumers in this cell like our brand but do not purchase the product.	**Cell 9** Consumers in this cell like our brand and purchase it.

Cognitions

Analyze the Matrix Cells

In this stage, there are two basic steps. First, we must determine the size of each of the market cells. This is important, for it helps to focus the strategy development process so that those cells which contain a large number of people will be the first to be considered as potential target markets. In fact, the cells can be ranked based on the number of people in each, as a guide to initial market selection. Some cells may have so few people that they can be eliminated from further consideration.

The second step involves investigating the reasons for our brand's success or failure in each of the remaining cells. Simply knowing that people don't like our brand or don't purchase it is not sufficient. We want to understand the consumer/brand relationships in each cell. We want to know *why* consumers aren't aware of our brand, or *why* they feel the way they do about it. In addition, we want to know *why* they purchase it, purchase another brand, or do not purchase the product at all.

Figure 2–5 provides some basic examples of consumer/brand relationships in each cell of the matrix. By further investigating these relationships, insights can be gained for developing marketing strategies. For example, consider the consumers in Cell 1. If this is a large segment of the

FIGURE 2–5   **Examples of Consumer/Brand Relationships in Each Strategy Cell**

		Behaviors	
	B_-	B_o	B_+
C_-	**Cell 1** Consumers previously tried our brand, didn't like it, and now buy a different brand.	**Cell 2** Consumers previously tried our brand, didn't like it, but no longer purchase the product.	**Cell 3** Consumers dislike our brand but purchase it because it is the only brand available in their market.
C_o	**Cell 4** Consumers never heard of our brand or have heard of it but already have a satisfactory alternative.	**Cell 5** Consumers don't purchase the product and pay no attention to brands of it.	**Cell 6** Consumers are not involved with the product and purchase our brand out of habit only.
C_+	**Cell 7** Consumers like our brand but do not purchase it because it is too expensive.	**Cell 8** Consumers previously tried our brand and liked it, but it is not available in their market.	**Cell 9** Consumers are involved with and very satisfied with our brand.

(Cognitions — row label at left: C_-, C_o, C_+)

market, then further research is necessary to determine the reasons these consumers did not like our brand when they tried it.

In sum, the study of consumer/product relationships is a key aspect of consumer analysis. This step is the crux of any consumer analysis designed to develop marketing strategies.

Develop Strategies

With the knowledge gained in the previous stage, we can now consider strategy alternatives for each group of consumers we have selected as influence targets. We may have eliminated some cells because they are too small to be served profitably. We may eliminate other cells at this stage because they cannot be reached or influenced efficiently. For example, if consumers in Cell 1 are highly brand loyal to a competing brand and we cannot offer a clear advantage to attract them, we may choose to ignore this segment and seek opportunities in other cells.

Alternatively, we may choose to modify our brand to attempt to attract this market. Coke, for example, modified its formula primarily to attract Pepsi drinkers, while Tide developed a different product form, Liquid Tide, to attract users of Wisk liquid detergent.

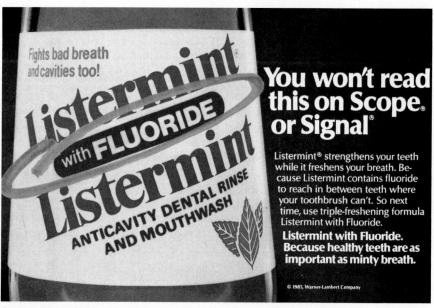

Courtesy Warner-Lambert Company

Warner-Lambert developed Listermint for consumers who didn't like the taste of Listerine.

Another possibility is to develop a new brand or model for this market to avoid the difficulties of trying to change consumers' cognitions from negative to positive attitudes. Warner-Lambert developed Listermint for people who didn't like Listerine and used Procter & Gamble's Scope. Changes in other elements of the marketing mix probably could not get these people to like the taste of Listerine.

Select Strategy Elements

A final point to be noted concerns the fact that any of the marketing mix elements may be used to influence consumers in a specific target market. Consider Ford Motor Company's promotion tag line, "Have you driven a Ford lately?" This promotion is directed to consumers who have previously tried a Ford and were dissatisfied with it—primarily consumers in Cell 1 of Figure 2–5. In addition to the promotion, Ford also improved the quality of its models in an attempt to develop more loyal consumers and keep them from switching to other brands. Moreover, for some models such as the Ford Thunderbird, the price was reduced considerably to attract consumers in Cell 7 of Figure 2–5, who liked the model but did not purchase it because they felt it was too expensive.

An example of a distribution change can be found in the market expansion undertaken by Coor's beer. In the 1970s, Coor's enjoyed a fabulous national brand image, but was not distributed in very many states. Consumers traveling through "Coor's territory" would even smuggle the beer home. In this case, consumers liked the brand but usually could not purchase it because it was not available in their market. Thus, Coor's market expansion strategy could be viewed as an attempt to influence consumers in Cell 8 of the matrix—consumers who liked the brand but did not purchase it because it was not available in their market (environment). Interestingly, Coor's brand image became less positive after the brand was readily available in many markets; perhaps it lost its mystique once it could be purchased in the eastern United States. This illustrates how cognitions about the brand can change with a change in the environment.

A final example illustrates how powerful the promotion element of the marketing mix can be. For many years, Arm & Hammer baking soda had one primary use, as an ingredient used in baking. Because so little baking soda is used in recipes, and people were doing less baking, brand sales were limited. The strategy of promoting the brand as a product to freshen refrigerators, rugs, and toilets drastically changed consumer *perceptions* of the uses of this product, as well as their actual *uses* of it. This promotion also affected frequency of purchase, as demand increased dramatically.

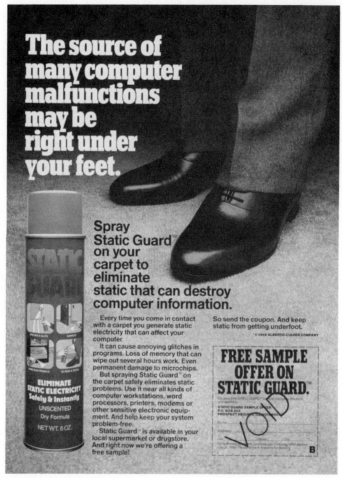

Courtesy Alberto-Culver Company

This marketing strategy attempts to change perceptions of appropriate product use and stimulate product trial.

Note that nothing about the Arm & Hammer product was changed, nor was it priced or distributed any differently. Its marketing success was brought about simply by changing what consumers thought about the product and how to use it (product meanings). This strategy probably affected consumers in several of the cells in Figure 2–5.

Back to the Case

This case provides a simple description of the purchase of bikes and accessories. We hope it is written in such a manner that you can easily understand the sequence of events. However, imagine how difficult it would be to try to describe this incident by considering *only* cognitive *or* behavioral *or* environmental factors.

Cognitive factors such as awareness, problem recognition, perception, information overload, information processing, product knowledge, and satisfaction are useful—but they cannot describe overt behaviors and environmental factors efficiently. Overt behaviors such as information search and contact, verbal behavior, store contact, product contact, trial, purchase, and use are also helpful—but they are incomplete for capturing the meaning and contexts in which these events occurred. Environmental factors such as the doctor's report, phone book ads, stores, salespeople, and products and their components are necessary for understanding the case—but they are quite sterile when discussed independently.

Thus, even for simple descriptions of consumers, all three elements—cognition, behavior, and environment—work together to provide efficient, useful knowledge of consumer behavior. This is also true for academic attempts at explanation or management attempts to develop marketing strategies. Analysis of all three elements is superior to any one or two of the elements taken in isolation.

Finally, you may be curious as to why the second salesperson was successful in making a sale to a customer who only wanted information. Why did Warren's marketing strategy work so effectively?

The first salesperson clearly provided a lot of product information. Unfortunately, it was too much information and of the wrong kind for this potential buyer, because it focused on technical product attributes. If the salesperson had considered more carefully what Carl was saying and how he looked, and had asked him the right questions, perhaps a better approach could have been developed.

The second salesperson asked but two questions and easily segmented this consumer and devised an appropriate marketing strategy. The answers to Warren's questions suggested that this consumer would be a casual user of the product and was looking for a good-quality bike in the middle price range. The consumer was not concerned with technical specifications but would appreciate a good riding bike. The experience of test-riding in the parking lot would likely be the primary decision criterion.

While a number of other tactics and relationships could be analyzed, the key point is that this successful marketing strategy involved (1) inferences about consumer information needs and prior knowledge (cognitions), (2) encouraging product trial (behavior) in (3) an appropriate environment (one similar to the stated use location). A cognitive view might suggest that this is a clear example of satisfying consumer needs, while a behavior view might suggest that this is a clear example of increasing the probability of a behavior by arranging the appropriate contingencies.

Summary

In this chapter, we presented our overall framework for the analysis of consumer behavior. We also described a general approach to developing marketing strategies intended to affect consumer cognitions, behaviors, and environments. We believe that this conceptual framework can help you understand many of the complexities of consumer behavior. However, other concepts related to consumer behavior must be considered. Later in this text, we will present many of these concepts and discuss how they can be used to develop, select, and evaluate marketing strategies.

Additional Reading

Albert Bandura (1977), *Social Learning Theory,* Englewood Cliffs, N.J.: Prentice-Hall.
_____(1983), "Temporal Dynamics and Decomposition of Reciprocal Determinism: A Reply to Phillips and Orton," *Psychological Review* (April), pp. 166–170.
D. C. Phillips and Rob Orton (1983), "The New Causal Principle of Cognitive Learning Theory: Perspectives on Bandura's Reciprocal Determinism," *Psychological Review* (April), pp. 158–165.
Girish N. Punj and David W. Stewart (1983), "An Interaction Framework of Consumer Decision Making," *Journal of Consumer Research* (September), pp. 181–196.

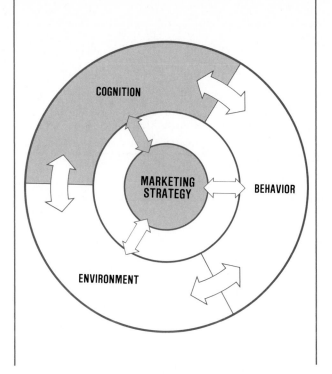

Section Two

Cognitive Theory and Marketing Strategy

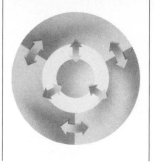

Chapter Three

Consumers' Cognitive Processes

"Everyday" Cognition

As do millions of other consumers, Bruce Macklin makes a weekly trip to a local supermarket to buy groceries. On this sunny Saturday morning, Bruce has driven to the Giant supermarket with his three-year-old daughter, Angela. As he walks through the front doors of the store, Bruce enters one of the most complex information environments a consumer can face.

A supermarket is loaded with information. The average grocery store stocks some 10,000 items, but some very large stores may carry as many as 20,000. Large supermarkets offer many alternatives in each product category. For instance, one large store offers 18 different brands of mustard in a variety of sizes. Moreover, most product packages contain lots of information. The average package of breakfast cereal, for example, contains some 250 individual pieces of information!

Despite this complexity, Bruce (like most of us) feels no particular uneasiness or anxiety about grocery shopping, for this is familiar territory. During the next 50 minutes (the average time consumers spend in the store on a major shopping trip), Bruce will process a great deal of information. He will make numerous decisions during the time it takes to fill his grocery cart. Most of his choices will be made easily and quickly, seemingly with little effort. Some choices, though, will involve noticeable cognition (thinking) and may require a few seconds of time. And a few of his choices may require substantial cognitive processing and many seconds, perhaps even minutes. How does Bruce Macklin move through this complex informational environment so easily, buying tens, perhaps hundreds, of products? The cognitive processes that make this possible are the subject of this chapter.

Components of the Wheel of Consumer Analysis

In Chapter 2 we saw that consumer behavior can be thought of as an interactive function of the environment, behavior, and cognition. In this chapter, we begin our examination of the cognition component of our overall model. In particular, we consider a number of ideas about and models of human cognitive processing. These will help us understand how consumers interpret information from their environments and use it to behave in a manner that satisfies their consumption goals.

We begin by reviewing Bruce Macklin's grocery shopping situation from the perspective of our wheel of consumer analysis (refer back to Figure 2–3). The model contains four interrelated components—environment, behavior, marketing strategies, and cognition—each of which influences the others in a reciprocal, interactive manner. All four components are important for understanding Bruce's supermarket shopping situation.

Environment

What is the supermarket environment like? Well, on a Saturday morning, the market is likely to be *busy*, with many people *crowding* the aisles. The store is likely to be somewhat *noisy*. Because Bruce is shopping with Angela, her *chattering* adds to the commotion. These social aspects of the environment will influence Bruce's cognitions and his overt behavior. The store *layout*, the *width* of the aisles, the special sale *signs* on the shelves, the product *displays* at the ends of the aisles and elsewhere in the store, the *lighting*, and other physical aspects of the supermarket environment may also have an effect. Even environmental factors such as the *temperature*, background *music* playing, and the *wobbly wheel* on his shopping cart may have important effects on Bruce's cognitions and behaviors.

Behavior

What kinds of behaviors occur in this situation? Bruce is engaged in a large number, including *walking* down the aisles, *looking* at products on the shelves, *picking up* and *examining* packages, *talking* to Angela and a friend he met in the store, *steering* the wobbly cart, and so on. Although some of these behaviors may not seem to be of much interest to a marketing manager, many have important effects on cognitions and other behaviors. For example, unless Bruce *walks* down the aisle containing breakfast foods, he cannot *notice* and *buy* a package of Kellogg's Raisin Squares. Typically, marketers are most concerned about purchase behavior. In the supermarket environment, this means *picking up* a package, *placing* it in the cart, and *paying* for it at the checkout counter.

Marketing Strategies

Much of the in-store environment Bruce experiences is due to marketing strategy decisions made by the retailer and the manufacturers whose products are carried by the store. In fact, a grocery store is a very good place to observe marketing strategies in action. The huge number of products sold in such stores requires an equally huge number of marketing strategies. For instance, a firm's *distribution* strategy (place products only in up-scale stores) determines whether that product is even present in a particular store. A variety of *pricing* strategies (reduced price on Oreo cookies) and *promotion* strategies (free samples of cheese) are evident in a supermarket environment. *Package designs* (easy-opening milk containers) and specific *product characteristics* (low-calorie frozen entrées) are also marketing strategies. Finally, specific environmental details such as *point-of-purchase displays* (a stack of Pepsi six-packs near the store entrance) are important aspects of marketing strategy. All of these environmental stimuli are meant to influence consumers' cognitions and behaviors.

Cognition

Our primary concern in this chapter is **consumer cognition.** Bruce's cognitive system was active in the supermarket environment. Indeed, our cognitive systems are active in every environment, but some of this cognitive activity is conscious and involves effort, while other activity may occur without much conscious awareness. For instance, Bruce will *pay attention* to certain aspects of the store environment and *ignore* other parts. Some products will *catch his eye*, while others will not. He must *interpret* a large amount of information in the store environment—from aisle signs to brand names to price tags to nutrition labels. In addition, he must *evaluate* whether the considered products are useful in meeting his needs and those of his family. He must *remember* what products he still has on hand at home and what he has run out of and needs to replace. He must *make choices* from among some of the 10,000 to 20,000 items available in the store. In addition, he must *make decisions* about many other specific behaviors. Should he go down aisle 3 or skip it this week? Should he stock up on canned peaches or just buy one can? Should he give Angela a cookie for being good? Should he take the wobbly cart back and get another one? Should he pay with cash or by check?

In sum, Bruce's grocery purchasing behavior on this particular Saturday morning is a complex function of his social and physical environ-

Alan Carey/The Image Works

Consumer information processing—a last-minute check for bargains.

ment, the marketing strategies intended to influence him, the processes of his cognitive system, and his own behaviors. Each factor interacts with and reciprocally influences the others.

About an hour after entering the Giant supermarket, Bruce emerges with five bags of groceries containing 48 different products. Given our analysis of his shopping situation, we might be somewhat surprised to find that he has a smile on his face and does not feel at all tired. In fact, he is already looking forward to his 11:00 A.M. tennis match. How did Bruce's cognitive system accomplish so much, so quickly, with such apparent ease? How do we all perform similar cognitive feats while shopping?

Consumer Cognition

In this and the next five chapters, we will consider many useful concepts and models of how the human cognitive system interprets and uses environmental information to make decisions that guide behaviors. Many of these ideas are based on psychological theories of human cognition. When you understand these ideas, you will be able to analyze and describe how consumers like Bruce Macklin think, what they think about in specific situations, and how that thinking affects their consumption-related behavior. We also believe you will find these concepts and ideas useful for developing effective marketing strategies to influence consumers' choices.

It is worth reminding ourselves that marketing strategies involve creating or changing aspects of the physical or social environment. For instance, *advertising strategies* create advertisements on television, in magazines, etc.; *pricing strategies* are communicated to consumers through signs and labels; and *product strategies* often involve creating or changing product characteristics. *Distribution strategies* often involve changes in the physical environment (new stores, in-store displays). Finally, *public-policy strategies* may involve environmental stimuli such as the warning labels on the packaging for diet soft drinks, antacids, and cigarettes.[1] For these marketing strategies to be effective, consumers must come in contact with the environmental stimuli, interpret them, and then use the resulting knowledge to choose between alternative behaviors.

In sum, an understanding of consumers' cognition can be used by marketing managers in developing, selecting, implementing, and evaluating marketing strategies. Unfortunately, many marketing and public-policy strategies do not successfully affect consumers' behaviors, frequently because of problems with consumer cognition.[2]

---

[1] James R. Bettman (1975), "Issues in Designing Consumer Information Environments," *Journal of Consumer Research* (December), pp. 169–177; Raymond E. Schucker, Raymond C. Stokes, Michael L. Stewart and Douglas P. Henderson (1983), "The Impact of the Saccharin Warning Label on Sales of Diet Soft Drinks in Supermarkets," *Journal of Public Policy and Marketing*, Vol. 2, pp. 46–56.

[2] Jacob Jacoby (1984), "Perspectives on Information Overload," *Journal of Consumer Research* (March), pp. 432–435; Michael B. Mazis and Richard Staelin (1982), "Using Information Processing Principles in Public Policymaking," *Journal of Marketing & Public Policy*, Vol. 1, pp. 3–14.

HIGHLIGHT 3–1   **Information versus Knowledge, Meanings, and Beliefs**

Researchers often find big differences between the objective physical environment (information) and the consumer's interpretation of those cues (knowledge, meanings, and beliefs). Marketers, of course, are interested in both, because they create many of the features in the physical environment through their marketing strategies. Moreover, marketers have to understand how consumers will interpret these strategies. Here are a few examples of the differences between information and knowledge or meanings.

Objective, Environmental Information	Subjective, Cognitive Knowledge, Meanings, and Beliefs
Ratings of microwave ovens by *Consumer Reports*	"Amana RadarRange is best."
Price tag on grocery shelf	"$.89 is too expensive."
A product claim that 7UP has no caffeine	"7UP won't help keep me alert."
A new McDonald's opens for business at a local mall	"That would be a good place to have lunch next Saturday."

What Is Information?

More than 10 years ago, it was pointed out that "information . . . is a vague term that could encompass many possible influences on consumers' conceptual and behavioral activities."[3] A consensus on the meaning of information still has not emerged. Some marketing researchers treat information as *environmental stimuli* involving brands and their attributes. For instance, *Consumer Reports* presents this kind of "information" in their comparative ratings of the attributes and performance characteristics of different brands of microwave ovens. In this view, information is an objective, tangible aspect of the consumer's environment.

In contrast, other researchers consider information as *consumers' cognitive interpretations* of environmental stimuli. "Information" in this sense is subjective and varies from consumer to consumer. For instance, not every consumer will understand *Consumer Reports'* microwave oven ratings in the same way.

In this book, we use the term information in the former sense. **Information,** then, refers to objective, physical aspects of the marketing envi-

---

[3]William L. Wilkie (1975), "How Consumers Use Product Information," Report prepared for National Science Foundation, Washington, D.C.

ronment. Sometimes we use the term **cue** or **informational cue** to indicate that we are concerned with a specific aspect of the social or physical environment. In contrast, we use the terms **knowledge, meanings,** and **beliefs** to refer to the consumer's mental representations of environmental information.

What Is Cognition?

Cognition means "thinking" to most people. Human beings have evolved highly sophisticated cognitive systems by which they perceive, believe, feel, remember, and think. People often experience elaborate and vivid mental states. We use the term **cognition** to refer to all of these mental states and processes. As emphasized in our wheel of consumer analysis (see Figure 2–3), cognition has important reciprocal relationships with overt behavior and environmental factors. In this chapter, we consider cognition in terms of *cognitive processing*.

What Is Cognitive Processing?

In a very basic sense, **cognitive processing** concerns how external information in the environment is transformed into *meanings* or patterns of thought, and how these meanings are combined to form judgments about behavior.[4] As you know, marketers are particularly interested in consumers' purchasing behaviors. Because of marketing's concern with purchase, consumer researchers have emphasized the cognitive processes involved in consumers' decisions about which products and brands to buy.[5]

However, we must recognize that cognitive processes are also involved in a wide range of behaviors besides purchasing products. For instance, consumers not only use the products they buy but also dispose of them.[6] In addition, consumers read magazines and watch TV, talk to sales personnel and to friends, go shopping, watch other consumers use prod-

---

[4]David E. Rumelhart (1977), *Introduction to Human Information Processing,* New York: John Wiley & Sons.

[5]James R. Bettman, Harold H. Kassarjian and Richard J. Lutz (1978), "Consumer Behavior," in *Review of Marketing,* G. Zaltman and T. Bonoma (eds.), Chicago: American Marketing Association, pp. 194–229.

[6]For interesting discussions of possession, use, and disposal behaviors see Russell Belk (1984), "Manifesto for a Consumer Behavior of Consumer Behavior," in *Scientific Method in Marketing,* P. Anderson and M. Ryan (eds.), Chicago: American Marketing Association, pp. 163–167; and Jacob Jacoby, Carol K. Berning and Thomas F. Dietvorst (1977), "What About Disposition?" *Journal of Marketing,* Vol. 41, pp. 22–28.

HIGHLIGHT 3–2   **"Higher" Mental Processes**

What do we mean by higher mental processes? Consider the following general capabilities of the human cognitive system and the cognitive activities that are involved in each.

- Understanding — Interpreting specific aspects of one's environment, especially determining the meaning of those environmental features in terms of personal relevance.

- Evaluating — Judging whether an aspect of the environment, or one's own behavior, is good or bad, positive or negative, favorable or unfavorable.

- Planning — Determining how to achieve a solution to a problem.

- Deciding — Comparing alternative solutions to a problem in terms of information about each one and selecting the best (or a satisfactory) alternative.

- Thinking — The cognitive activity that occurs during all of the above processes.

Source: Adapted from John R. Anderson (1980), Cognitive Psychology and Its Implications, *San Francisco: W. H. Freeman.*

ucts, try to understand *Consumer Reports* articles, and so on. Many of these "other" behaviors are relevant for understanding purchase decisions. Moreover, all of these behaviors involve cognitive processes.

By taking a cognitive processing approach we do not mean that every purchase requires extensive, highly elaborate cognitive processing. Many purchases involve minimal cognition. In some cases, the cognition may be mostly unconscious—that is, the consumer may not be aware of any cognitive activity. Marketers must recognize that the intensity of consumers' cognitive processing varies widely across different consumers, environments, products, and purchase contexts. The majority of voluntary behaviors do require at least some cognitive processing, however.

The study of consumer behavior is currently dominated by a concern with cognition. In fact, the emphasis on cognitive processing is so strong that relatively little attention is given to the actual behavior of consumers (beyond their purchase of products) or to the effects of specific environmental factors on consumers' behavior or cognitive processes. Given the awesome capabilities of the human cognitive system, the current fascination with cognition is understandable. Consumers can understand, learn, remember, evaluate, decide, and plan. However, studying these "higher" cognitive processes is quite difficult. Therefore, many consumer researchers have considered consumer cognition from a simpler **information processing** perspective.

An Information Processing Approach to Consumer Cognition

In an information processing model, the complex mental activities involved in cognition are divided into separate **cognitive processes** and arranged as a sequence of **stages.** Each process refers to a set of cognitive operations by which information is "processed."[7] These information processing operations transform or recode information, by adding to it, subtracting from it, or otherwise modifying the information. Each processing stage receives the informational output of the preceding stage, and in turn, processes (transforms) the information and passes the output on to the next stage for further processing.

Information Processing Models

Researchers often express their theories about these information processing operations in the form of **flowcharts,** which graphically represent the "flow" of information through an information processing system. Flowchart models identify several important elements: the processing operations that occur, the flow or path of information through these processes, and the form of the information as it is transformed by one operation after another. The scientist's goal is to specify as completely as possible what happens between exposure to information and an observed behavior.

Figure 3–1 presents a simple information processing model, called the **hierarchy of effects model.** Note how this model (at least partially) accounts for the flow of information from exposure to environmental stimuli (not shown) to purchase behavior. Information processing begins with *awareness*, when the consumer learns that the product exists. This is followed by the acquisition of *knowledge* about the product and the formation of an attitude toward the product (*liking* or disliking). Here, the consumer begins to perceive some relevance or use for the product in his/her life. The *preference stage* follows in which the consumer begins to want this particular product rather than alternatives. The *conviction stage* occurs when the consumer decides to purchase the product. Finally, the consumer reaches the *purchase stage* and engages in behaviors associated with purchasing the chosen product (traveling to the store, finding the product, and paying for it).

In sum, an information processing model breaks down a complex process such as decision making into subparts that are more easily under-

---

[7]For an early model of human information processing see Alan Newell and Herbert Simon (1972), *Human Problem Solving*, Englewood Cliffs, N.J.: Prentice-Hall.

stood and measured. We give up something by using such models, how-ever, because they are likely to oversimplify the overall process. Thus, although we may be able to see certain aspects of cognitive processing more clearly, we may lose sight of how the whole cognitive system functions.

Criticisms of Information Processing Models

The information processing approach to consumer decision making has been criticized on several grounds. Perhaps the dominant criticism is that information processing models make consumer decision making seem too

FIGURE 3–1   **A Hierarchy of Effects Model of Advertising Effects**

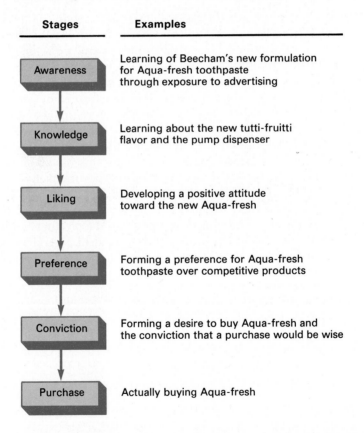

Stages	Examples
Awareness	Learning of Beecham's new formulation for Aqua-fresh toothpaste through exposure to advertising
Knowledge	Learning about the new tutti-fruitti flavor and the pump dispenser
Liking	Developing a positive attitude toward the new Aqua-fresh
Preference	Forming a preference for Aqua-fresh toothpaste over competitive products
Conviction	Forming a desire to buy Aqua-fresh and the conviction that a purchase would be wise
Purchase	Actually buying Aqua-fresh

Source: Adapted from Robert J. Lavidge and Gary A. Steiner (1961), "A Model for Predictive Measurements of Advertising Effectiveness," Journal of Marketing *(Octo-ber), pp. 59–62.*

Since the ancient Greeks, the dominant technology of the times has provided a model for cognitive functioning. Today, the electronic computer is the dominant metaphor for mental activity. Earlier, the telephone exchange provided a source of inspiration for researchers trying to understand the cognitive system—information entered the system and was routed to the appropriate places by a central controller that functioned much like a switchboard operator. Much earlier mechanical metaphors for the cognitive system include a network of "pipes" that were thought to carry "fluids" to various parts of the "mind."

Most information processing models are based on the assumption that the human cognitive system functions much like a digital computer. Like a computer, these models have a processor (a central processing chip), a memory (chips or disk storage), and input (keyboard) and output (monitor screen, plotter, or printer) devices.

You may feel that the discussion of information processing in this chapter gives the impression that a consumer's cognitive system operates like a machine, or actually is a machine. In fact, information processing models do tend to be mechanistic. Most models are similar to the way a computer operates using multiple subroutines or programs. That is, the specific cognitive subprocesses are similar to subroutines in a computer program which engage in certain information processes and then "send" the output to other subroutines for further processing.

Information processing research and theory has this mechanical tone because machines were used as analogies or metaphors by the creators of the models. The computer (and other mechanical devices such as the telephone switchboard or holograph) continue to provide an analogy for much of the research and theoretical development in human information processing.

However, virtually no one seriously suggests that the human mind operates exactly like a computer, or that the brain is "wired" like a computer or a switchboard. The point is only that it is sometimes useful to think about something as complex as human cognitive activity in terms of something we know more about, such as how computers operate. But we have to watch out that a machine metaphor doesn't come to dominate our thinking and blind us to other possibilities.

---

reasoned and rational. Factors such as emotion and general mood tend to be ignored. This criticism is based partly on the perception that consumer information processing models are too linear and mechanical—they make consumer decision making seem like a sequence in a computer program (see Highlight 3–3). Another aspect of this criticism is that nonverbal factors such as visual images,[8] emotions and moods,[9] and experiential aspects

---

[8]Julie A. Edell and Richard Staelin (1983), "The Information Processing of Pictures in Print Advertisements," *Journal of Consumer Research* (June), pp. 45–61.

[9]Meryl Paula Gardner (1985), "Mood States and Consumer Behavior: A Critical Review," *Journal of Consumer Research* (December), pp. 281–300.

of products such as simple enjoyment or fantasy[10] are not often included in information processing models. Yet another criticism is that information processing explanations tend to characterize consumers' decisions as due only to internal, cognitive factors, while behavior and aspects of the environment have little or no impact.

Most of these criticisms of information processing models are well taken. Note, however, that the major problem is not with the concept of cognition per se, but with the excessively narrow view of cognition in much information processing research. In this text, we take a broader view of cognition. We consider cognition to include rational, information processing types of activities as well as affective/emotional and even unconscious mental states and processes. Consumers' cognition involves all of these factors. (This point is discussed more thoroughly in Chapter 4.)

A final problem with most information processing models is that they do not give sufficient attention to the effects of knowledge consumers have acquired through their previous experiences.[11] This is a critically important point. Because many information processing models are hierarchical and linear, they have not emphasized the interactions between cognitive processes and existing knowledge in memory.

In the following section, we present a less linear and more flexible model of consumers' cognitive processes. Keep in mind that in some circumstances, these processes may be extensive and involve effort, while in other cases, they may occur quickly with minimal effort.

A Cognitive Processing Model of Consumer Decision Making

Figure 3–2 presents a model of the cognitive processes involved in consumer decision making. This model contains two basic processes that correspond to the two main functions of the human cognitive system. One

---

[10]Morris B. Holbrook and Elizabeth C. Hirschman (1982), "The Experiential Aspects of Consumption: Consumer Fantasies, Feelings, and Fun," *Journal of Consumer Research* (September), pp. 132–140.

[11]For a discussion of the importance of existing knowledge in information processing, see Merrie Brucks (1985), "The Effects of Product Class Knowledge on Information Search Behavior," *Journal of Consumer Research* (June), pp. 1–16; and Jerry C. Olson (1978), "Theories of Information Encoding and Storage: Implications for Consumer Research," in *Effects of Information on Consumer and Market Behavior*, A.A. Mitchell (ed.), Chicago: American Marketing Association.

concerns how consumers *interpret* the information they encounter in their physical and social environment. These processes produce a set of **subjective meanings,** also called **knowledge** or **beliefs.** The other type of cognitive process concerns how consumers **integrate** relevant knowledge, meanings, and beliefs to **evaluate** objects in the environment (form attitudes) or to *decide* among alternative behaviors (decision making/intention formation).

Knowledge, meanings, and beliefs in memory have a powerful effect on both types of processes. As shown in Figure 3–2, interpretive processes draw on the knowledge activated from memory to recognize and perceive environmental stimuli and to create new knowledge, meanings, and beliefs. Integration processes combine knowledge, meanings, and beliefs from memory with new knowledge derived from the immediate environment. Each of these processes and stages is discussed in separate chapters in this section of the text. For now, we will work through this model, paying special attention to the interactions between cognitive processes and activated knowledge, meanings, and beliefs.

FIGURE 3–2   *A Cognitive Processing Model of Consumer Decision Making*

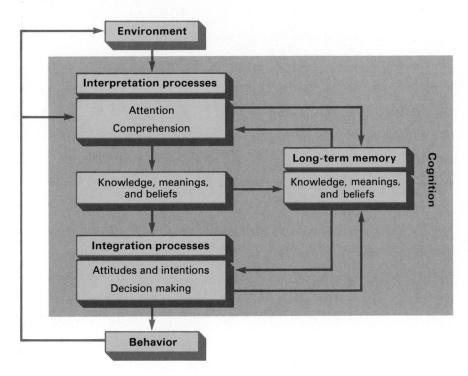

William Means: Click/Chicago

Consumers must interpret marketing information.

Exposure to Environmental Information

Cognitive processing begins when a consumer is exposed to information in the environment. Of course, consumers are continually exposed to information; therefore, cognitive processes occur continuously. However, when marketers consider the effects of an actual marketing strategy (an advertisement, a 25-cents-off coupon, or a new product attribute) they

---

HIGHLIGHT 3–4   **Racing to Meet the Demand for Mini Vans**

You may remember the van craze of the 1970s when young, blue-collar workers bought vans (full-sized), loaded them with furry carpets, mattresses, and loud stereo equipment, and painted surrealistic murals on the side. In the mid-1980s, the boom was back, but this time the hottest demand was for mini vans. These cars were quite different from the "sin bins" of the mid-1970s. Buyers wanted vans again, but for more practical reasons this time. The new vans offered several advantages over the older, larger vehicles. For one thing, they were cheaper. A mere $10,000 would get you a fully equipped Chevy Sportwagon in 1984. A Chevy Caprice Classic Wagon, on the other hand, started at $10,200. Mini vans have about twice the interior space of a full-size station wagon and provide up to 26 mpg, better economy than most four-year-old cars. Their popularity soared in 1984 and 1985.

Note that consumers were able to fully understand and appreciate the desirable features of mini vans only in terms of the knowledge they acquired through their past experiences with cars and full-sized vans. Without these existing knowledge structures in memory, the special product features of the mini vans would not have been so meaningful. And mini vans would not have been so desirable.

Source: Adapted from Jeff Blyskal (1984), "Wide-Open Spaces," Forbes (June 18), p. 124.

usually begin their analysis of consumer cognition when exposure to that stimulus occurs.

Knowledge, Meanings, and Beliefs

Earlier in this chapter you learned that consumers' cognitive systems create knowledge, meanings, and beliefs that represent stimuli in their physical and social environment. This knowledge may be retrieved or *activated* from memory and used in interpretive and/or integration processes. In Chapters 4 and 5, we discuss several concepts and models describing consumers' knowledge, meanings, and beliefs concerning products and brands.

Interpretive Processes

When they are exposed to information in the environment, consumers must interpret its meaning in terms of their own interests, values, and past experiences. **Interpretation** involves two highly related cognitive processes: attention and comprehension. (We discuss interpretation processes further in Chapter 6.)

Initial exposure to the incoming information "automatically" activates relevant knowledge, meanings, and beliefs in memory which then affect further **attention processes.** For instance, you might pass by a bicycle shop one day and notice an unusual bike in the window—a fat-tired mountain bike. The unusual stimulus makes you attend a little more closely, and you recognize the object as some type of bicycle.

As interpretation processing becomes increasingly focused on the stimulus, **comprehension processes** occur, that is, deeper and more complete interpretations are formed—meanings are assigned to the environmental information. Again, the knowledge, meanings, and beliefs that are activated from memory strongly influence how the new information is comprehended. In a sense, the activated knowledge structures "drive" the comprehension processes. For instance, your existing knowledge about bicycles, accumulated from your past experience, affects your comprehension of the contraption in the store window with its straight handlebars, cantilever brakes, and knobby tires. If you know very little about this style of bike, you may perceive only that it is a bicycle. If you are more familiar with this product form, you may develop a number of more complex and more accurate meanings or beliefs about the types and quality of the components, the Schwinn brand name, its likely performance, and so on. Finally, note that whatever knowledge, meanings, and beliefs are produced by the comprehension process are *stored* in long-term memory.

Integration Processes

Knowledge, meanings, and beliefs may be activated from memory at some later time and combined or *integrated* with additional information acquired from the immediate environment. The cognitive system engages in **knowledge integration** to accomplish some objective. We are concerned with two types of integration processes: attitude formation and decision making. Knowledge may be integrated to produce an overall *evaluation* of a product or brand—you may form a positive **attitude** toward mountain bikes in general or toward this brand in particular. (Attitudes are discussed further in Chapter 7.)

Integration processes are also involved in **decision making.** Here, consumers combine knowledge about the characteristics of products or brands in selecting an appropriate alternative. The outcome is a **choice** of a product or brand—you may form an **intention** to purchase a Schwinn High Sierra mountain bike. Note that the outcomes of integration processes—attitudes and intentions/decisions—are stored in long-term memory. (Consumer decision-making processes are discussed more fully in Chapter 8.)

Behavior

Finally, consumers' intentions, whether formed on the spot or activated from memory, produce **behaviors.** (The relationship between intentions and behavior is discussed in Chapter 7, and the formation of intentions through decision-making processes is discussed in Chapter 8.) In our bike example, a variety of behaviors could be affected, including going on a shopping trip to look at mountain bikes; actual purchase behaviors such as traveling to the store, negotiating for the best price, writing a check for a Schwinn High Sierra mountain bike, and returning to the store the next day to pick it up; or recommending the Schwinn High Sierra to a friend.

Implications

A major implication of our cognitive processing approach to consumer decision making is that any single cognitive process cannot be studied in isolation. To understand what happens during comprehension, for instance, we must also know something about exposure and attention. To understand how activated knowledge affects integration processes, it would be useful to know how knowledge is activated, as well as something about the original comprehension processes that created the knowledge in the first place. In sum, we must keep in mind that the components of our cognitive processing model are interacting, interrelated parts in a functioning cognitive system.

Basic Characteristics of Consumer Cognition

One of the best ways to understand a concept, model, or theory at a fundamental level is to examine its *basic characteristics.* In the following section, we identify and discuss eight key features of the human cognitive system. Our model of the cognitive processes involved in consumer decision making is based on these characteristics.[12] By appreciating how these basic characteristics influence consumer cognition, you should gain a deeper understanding of the cognitive processing model.

---

[12]A number of authors have influenced our thinking about these ideas, among them Roy Lachman, Janet Lachman and Earl Butterfield (1979), *Cognitive Psychology and Information Processing: An Introduction,* Hillsdale, N.J.: Lawrence Erlbaum; Jerry C. Olson (1978), "Theories of Information Encoding and Storage: Implications for Consumer Research," in *Effects of Information on Consumer and Market Behavior,* A.A. Mitchell (ed.), Chicago: American Marketing Association; Wayne A. Wickelgren (1979), *Cognitive Psychology,* Englewood Cliffs, N.J.: Prentice-Hall.

1. Sense Making

Our model of cognitive processing reflects the fundamental purpose of consumers' cognitive systems—namely, to create a set of meanings that make sense of significant aspects of their environments.[13] Consumers' cognitive systems enable them to understand their physical and social environments (including marketing stimuli) and decide on appropriate behaviors to reach their goals. In short, consumers' cognitive systems form knowledge or meanings that they use to get along in the world.

2. Representation

Perhaps the most basic characteristic of the human cognitive system is that it creates and operates on **symbolic representations** of stimuli in the environment, not the stimuli themselves. Some cognitive scientists call these representations **codes.**[14] The idea of **coded representations** comes from considering the computer as a symbol-manipulating machine. Computers operate on symbolic codes (in binary form) that represent things of interest to the computer programmer or user. The important analogy is that the human cognitive system also represents the meanings of relevant environmental stimuli in symbolic codes. These coded meanings are stored in long-term memory.

Marketers also use symbols, in the form of words and pictures, to convey important meanings to consumers. Advertisements, for instance, are miniature symbol systems that attempt to convey certain meanings to consumers. Or consider the symbolic meanings conveyed by certain brand names (Brut cologne) or company trademarks (Prudential's Rock of Gibraltar). In sum, the meanings consumers associate with products, brands, stores, and events (such as a sale) are cognitive representations that are stored in memory.

3. Cognitive Processes

Our cognitive systems are constantly active, dealing with the flow of stimulation from the senses. The mental activities involved in interpreting stimuli within and outside of our bodies and integrating meanings in making judgments are called **cognitive processes.** Cognitive processes ac-

---

[13]Gordon H. Bower (1975), "Cognitive Psychology: An Introduction," in *Handbook of Learning and Cognitive Processes,* vol. I, W.K. Estes (ed.), Hillsdale, N.J.: Lawrence Erlbaum.

[14]Wickelgren, *Cognitive Psychology.*

Courtesy The Prudential Insurance Company of America

Prudential's famous Rock conveys symbolic meaning.

tivate symbolic meanings and beliefs from memory and manipulate this knowledge in various ways to interpret new information, form attitudes, or make choices.

4. Knowledge Structures

Another important characteristic of consumer cognitive processing concerns how meanings are stored in memory. Our model of consumer cognition is based on the assumption that memory representations are associated to form **organized structures of knowledge.** A set of associated memory representations constitutes a *network of meanings* that can be used by the cognitive system in various processes.[15] Cognitive theorists have developed a variety of models of such knowledge structures; we will consider them in the next two chapters.

5. Activation of Knowledge

A key characteristic of consumers' cognitive processes concerns how representations stored in memory become available for use by the cognitive system. Consumers are never conscious of all the meanings they have stored in their memories. Occasionally consumers may think about Hoover vacuum cleaners, Levi's blue jeans, or going to a movie, but usually they do not. This shows that meanings in memory have at least two possible states: either they are *activated* and experienced as conscious thoughts, or they are not activated and remain *stored* in long-term memory.

The way meanings in memory are activated depends partially on the *type* of meaning. Some represent physical characteristics—the **sensory meanings** of an object—such as the color, size, or shape of an automobile. Such codes tend to be activated by exposure to the appropriate environmental cues, such as seeing the car in an advertisement or driving by on the street. For instance, the meaning codes for a friend can be activated by hearing or reading her name, seeing her face, or perhaps merely by catching a glimpse of the back of her head in a crowd. Once the code or representation is activated, you experience a sense of familiarity and recognition. In sum, exposure to the appropriate cue automatically activates the relevant meanings—you do not exert any noticeable effort; the meanings just "come to mind."

Other memory codes represent more abstract levels of meaning, called **semantic meanings.** For instance, a consumer may represent a BMW automobile as "a rich person's car." Such semantic meaning codes have no "direct" physical referent—i.e., "a Yuppie's car" is not a physical characteristic of a BMW in the same way that a BMW's distinctive grill is. Therefore, semantic meanings are not activated merely by exposure to a cue in

---

[15]Many cognitive psychologists agree that memory is most usefully conceptualized as a network of associated concepts. For instance, see John R. Anderson (1984), *The Architecture of Cognition,* Cambridge, Mass.: Harvard University Press; James R. Bettman (1979), *An Information Processing Theory of Consumer Choice,* Reading, Mass.: Addison-Wesley Publishing; Alan M. Collins and Elizabeth F. Loftus (1975), "A Spreading Activation Theory of Semantic Memory," *Psychological Review,* Vol. 82, pp. 407–428; Wayne Wickelgren (1979), "Human Learning and Memory," in *Annual Review of Psychology,* Vol. 32, pp. 21–52.

the environment; they frequently are activated through the thinking process. That is, thinking about (activating) other meanings leads to the activation of associated semantic meanings. This is the *spreading activation* process, which we will discuss more fully below. As an example, thinking first about expensive, high-status cars may lead you to think about BMWs.

Finally, a third type of memory code involves **episodic meanings,** that is, they represent aspects of actual events that have occurred in a person's life. Because episodic meanings represent a consumer's interpretation of an event (such as watching a TV commercial), they may be incomplete and only partially accurate. Episodic meanings are often activated by thinking about some related concept. Seeing a commercial for Levi's 501 blue jeans might activate an episodic memory for a similar event in your own life, for instance. Some ads are intended to activate such meanings.

One of the most important implications of activation is that the same environmental stimulus can and often does activate completely different meanings in different consumers. The cartoon in Highlight 3–5 illustrates this. The different meanings that consumers associate with marketers' products and brands could be used as a basis for segmenting a market.

To summarize, meanings in memory can be activated either (*a*) directly, by exposure through one of the senses to an appropriate stimulus cue in the environment, or (*b*) indirectly, by first thinking about a related meaning. Once activated, these meanings are available for use by cognitive processes. However, this does not mean that a consumer is necessarily consciously aware of every meaning that has been activated in memory. The idea of activation from memory is one of the most important aspects of consumer cognition.

6. Spreading Activation

The proposition that meaning codes are interconnected and organized into networklike structures can be combined with the concept of activation. We assume that activation of one meaning in a knowledge structure tends to activate other meanings that are associated with it. This process is known as **spreading activation.**[16] For instance, an entire cognitive structure of meanings associated with Jell-O might become activated by seeing an ad for Jell-O or by noticing packages of Jell-O on a supermarket shelf. The package cues might first activate the Jell-O brand name and then related meanings (jiggly, tastes sweet, good for a quick dessert, Bill Cosby likes it) as the activation spreads throughout the consumer's knowledge

---

[16]Alan M. Collins and Elizabeth F. Loftus (1975), "A Spreading Activation Theory of Semantic Memory," *Psychological Review,* Vol. 82, pp. 407–428.

HIGHLIGHT 3–5   **Automatic Activation of Meanings from Memory**

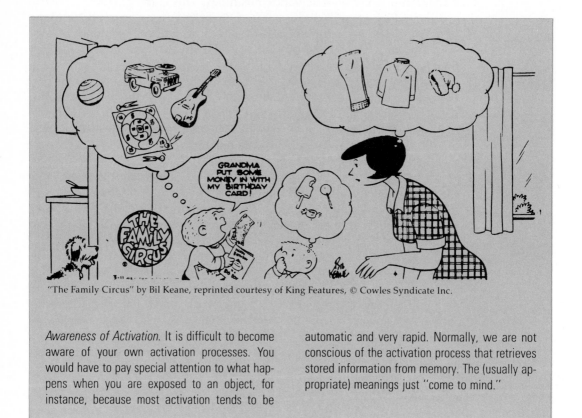

"The Family Circus" by Bil Keane, reprinted courtesy of King Features, © Cowles Syndicate Inc.

Awareness of Activation. It is difficult to become aware of your own activation processes. You would have to pay special attention to what happens when you are exposed to an object, for instance, because most activation tends to be automatic and very rapid. Normally, we are not conscious of the activation process that retrieves stored information from memory. The (usually appropriate) meanings just "come to mind."

network. Through the spread of activation, entire structures of knowledge may be activated from memory and made available for cognitive processes. Moreover, as activation spreads across multiple meanings in a knowledge network, we experience the flow of thoughts that occurs during thinking, decision making, or even daydreaming.

7. Capacity Limits

Another important characteristic of human cognition concerns the **limited capacity** of the cognitive system. Consumers' cognitive systems are restricted in the number of meanings that can be activated and processed at any one time. For instance, not all of a consumer's stored knowledge about

Ruffles potato chips or Guess? jeans—or even a product such as this text-book—can be activated and thought about at a given moment. In fact, only a tiny fraction of our stored knowledge can be considered at any one time.

8. Automaticity

A final characteristic of consumer cognitive processing, called **automaticity,** is related to the notion of capacity limits. We can think of the total amount of available cognitive capacity as a roughly fixed resource. Cognitive processes draw on this capacity to operate. You might imagine cognitive capacity as a "pool of power" (like electricity) that can be used by various processes. If too many cognitive processes are operating at once, the pool is depleted, and cognitive processing may suffer. (With electricity, the lights may dim.) When your cognitive capacity is fully used, additional processing activities cannot be undertaken without performance becoming impaired in some way.

Our cognitive system gets around the problem of capacity limits by developing automatic processes. As a cognitive process (such as deciding what brand of pen to buy) becomes more familiar through frequent repetitions, the amount of cognitive capacity it requires tends to decrease. Highly familiar, well-practiced processes tend to be quite automatic; whereas dealing with new, unfamiliar situations or stimuli requires controlled cognitive processes and thus, uses a greater proportion of one's cognitive capacity. For instance, because it is so familiar and routine for many consumers, grocery shopping involves a great deal of automatic processing. Highlight 3–6 presents another example that is probably familiar to you.

Figure 3–3 summarizes the key characteristics of consumer cognition. Each has influenced our model of consumer cognitive processing. These characteristics provide the basis for understanding how cognition interacts with behavior and the environment.

Implications of the Cognitive Processing Model

The cognitive processing model shown in Figure 3–2 divides the very complex cognitive processes in consumer decision making into smaller, simpler, more manageable "pieces." This relatively simple, yet fairly complete model of consumer cognitive processing contains just two broad cognitive processes: **interpretation processes** and **integration processes.** The third major component of the model is the **knowledge, meanings,** and **beliefs** that are activated from memory and/or produced by interpretation processes.

HIGHLIGHT 3–6   ***Increasing Automaticity—Learning to Drive a Car***

Practiced subjects can do what seems impossible to both the novice and the theorist. People can achieve dramatic improvements in skills with practice. For instance, consider your experience in learning to drive a car. When you first learned to drive, you probably couldn't drive and talk at the same time. The task of driving seemed difficult and was probably physically and mentally tiring. Today, if you are a skilled driver, you can probably drive in moderate traffic, listen to music on the radio, and carry on a casual conversation with a friend. Could you have done this when you first started driving? Probably then you kept the radio off. If anyone tried to talk to you, you ignored them or told them to shut up. Of course, even today you will probably stop talking if something unfamiliar occurs such as an emergency situation on the road up ahead. At least, we hope you do!

Learning to drive a car illustrates how cognitive processes become increasingly automatic as they are learned through practice. However, even highly automatic skills such as eating seem to require some "capacity." Perhaps you like to munch on something while you study. You might eat pretzels (as this author does) or an apple while you read this chapter. But if you come upon a difficult passage that requires greater thought, you probably will stop chewing or your hand with the pretzel may pause in midair.

By identifying these three important aspects of cognition and by specifying how they interact, we can begin to understand the complex processes of consumer decision making.[17] In turn, this gives us a basis for analyzing how cognition interacts with the environment and overt behavior. Finally, our understanding of all of these relationships is useful for developing and evaluating marketing strategies.

Another advantage of our cognitive processing model is that it helps marketers consider the interactions of consumer cognitions, behavior, and the environment as a *process* that occurs over time. The interrelationships between these three components are constantly changing. This contrasts with the more usual static approach in which researchers merely describe consumers' characteristics or behaviors in a particular environment, at a given point in time. Another important aspect of our process perspective is the interaction between cognitive processes and activated knowledge.

---

[17]Of course, we give up something by breaking up cognition into separate information processing elements. We sometimes lose our perspective on the "whole" of consumer cognition. However, given the primitive state of our current knowledge about cognitive processes, the "breakdown method" seems our only alternative.

As consumers select goals, make plans, choose courses of action, and engage in overt behavior within their environments, knowledge is continually being activated and processed. Thus, a process approach focuses marketers' attention on understanding how consumers got into a particular state and what they will do next—issues that are at least as important as describing the current situation.

Finally, *marketing strategies* have a place in this system. By developing and implementing various marketing strategies, marketers attempt to influence the outcome and direction of the continuous stream of interactions between cognition, behavior, and the environment and, ultimately, affect consumers' purchase behavior.

FIGURE 3–3   **Basic Characteristics of Consumers' Cognitive Systems**

Basic Characteristics	Explanation
1. Sense making	The basic purpose of the consumer's cognitive system is to create a consistent, coherent understanding of the person's environment.
2. Representation	The consumer's cognitive system creates symbolic codes that represent the meanings of environmental stimuli for the person.
3. Cognitive processes	The cognitive system contains processes that operate to transform information into symbolic meanings.
4. Knowledge structures	The meanings are interrelated and stored in memory in knowledge or cognitive structures.
5. Activation	Stored representations of meanings can be activated from memory and thus made available for cognitive processing.
6. Spreading activation	Activation of one meaning will spread to other concepts to which it is associated.
7. Capacity limits	The consumer's cognitive system is limited in the amount of knowledge that can be addressed at once.
8. Automaticity	As cognitive processes become more practiced, they require less conscious control and less capacity—they become more automatic.

Back to the Case

To summarize what we have covered in this chapter and to review the cognitive processing model, let's return to our friend Bruce Macklin, who is still doing his weekly grocery shopping. Consider what happened as Bruce walked down the aisle containing breakfast cereal. We have divided this purchase occasion into smaller, discrete events and related each one to the appropriate part of our cognitive processing model. As you work through this example, consider how the various pieces and parts of the model fit together to help explain each event. (You may want to refer to Figure 3–2.)

Environmental/Behavioral Event	Cognitive Processes
• Bruce noticed a bright orange shelf tag with an arrow and the words "Unadvertised Special."	Exposure to information and initial attention
• The sign reminded him that the supply of breakfast cereal at his house is getting low.	Activation of stored knowledge
• He looked at the package more closely.	More attention
• He saw that the product was a Kelloggs' cereal, Raisin Squares.	Simple comprehension—interaction with stored knowledge
He thought to himself that he likes most Kelloggs' cereals and that his wife likes raisins.	Activation of additional stored knowledge
He picked up a package and read "provides 11 essential vitamins and minerals."	Comprehension—interaction with activated knowledge
As he turned the package around, he noticed more nutrition information. This "reminded" him of things he knows about nutrition.	Attention and more activated knowledge
Bruce quickly noticed that Raisin Squares has the standard 25 percent RDA of most vitamins and minerals and that it has no added salt. He understood what most of this nutritional information meant.	Attention and comprehension; interaction with activated knowledge
Based on this information Bruce was favorably disposed toward Raisin Squares.	Integration and attitude formation
He then looked at the price on the shelf—$1.99 for 16.5 ounces.	Attention and comprehension
Bruce considered all this information . . .	Integration processes
and decided to buy a package . . .	Form intention to buy
to see whether his wife would like it.	Purchase goal
He tossed a package of Raisin Squares into the grocery cart and continued shopping.	Choice behavior
When Bruce got to the checkout counter, he paid for the Raisin Squares and the other products.	Purchase behavior

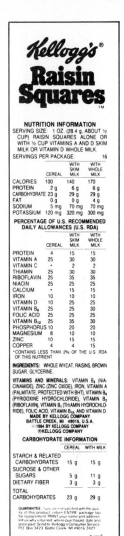

Packaging often includes a great deal of product information.

Discussion

We want to emphasize several points about this example and our model of cognitive processing.

Time

First, note that even though Bruce's entire decision process took only 42 seconds, quite a bit of cognition and behavior was involved. Because consumers' cognitive systems process information at a rapid rate, a great deal of cognitive processing can occur in a very short period of time.

Interaction

The example also illustrates the extensive interaction between Bruce's activated knowledge, meanings, and beliefs, and his interpretation and integration processes (attention/comprehension and attitude formation and decision making). This complex, back-and-forth interaction between cognitive processes and knowledge in memory is typical of naturally occurring cognitive processing episodes.

Nonlinear

Finally, note that this cognitive processing episode did not proceed in a rigid step-by-step sequence. Bruce's cognitive processing often doubled back on itself, moving from exposure to attention to comprehension and back to exposure (to new information), to more attention and additional comprehension. This complex, recursive interaction is the primary reason the linear hierarchy of effects models can not capture many of the details of natural, everyday cognitive processing episodes.

Summary

In this chapter, we introduced the cognitive processing approach to understanding consumer behavior. Two primary functions of human cognition are interpretation and integration. Through cognitive processes, consumers form symbolic representations of the environment and use the resulting knowledge and meanings to get along in their environment.

We presented a model of the key cognitive processes in consumer decision making. An important aspect of this model is the reciprocal interaction between knowledge stored in memory and the cognitive processes that both use and create this knowledge. Key cognitive processes of interpretation (attention, comprehension) and integration (attitude and intention formation and decision making) were identified and briefly described. Each of these processes is discussed in greater detail in subsequent chapters. Finally, we also reviewed the basic characteristics of human cognition that form the foundation for this model.

Additional Reading

Bobby J. Calder, Thomas S. Robertson and John R. Rossiter (1975), "Children's Consumer Information Processing," *Communication Research* (July), pp. 307–316.

Robert Chestnut and Jacob Jacoby (1977), "Consumer Information Processing: Emerging Theory and Findings," in *Consumer and Industrial Buying Behavior,* A. Woodside, J.N. Sheth and P.D. Bennett (eds.), New York: Elsevier-North Holland Publishing, pp. 119–133.

Harold H. Kassarjian (1982), "The Development of Consumer Behavior Theory," in *Advances in Consumer Research,* Vol. 9, A.A. Mitchell (ed.), Ann Arbor, Mich.: Association for Consumer Research, pp. 20–22.

P. H. Lindsay and Donald A. Norman (1972), *Human Information Processing: An Introduction to Psychology,* New York: John Wiley & Sons.

William J. McGuire (1976), "Some Internal Psychological Factors Influencing Consumer Choice," *Journal of Consumer Research* (March), pp. 302–319.

Andrew A. Mitchell (1978), "An Information Processing View of Consumer Behavior," in *Research Frontiers in Marketing: Dialogues and Directions,* S.C. Jain (ed.), Chicago: American Marketing Association.

Ulrich Neisser (1967), *Cognitive Psychology,* New York: Appelton-Century-Crofts.

John Palmer and Jean-Phillipe Faivre (1973), "The Information Processing Theory of Consumer Behavior," *European Research* (November), pp. 231–240.

Thomas K. Srull (1983), "The Role of Prior Knowledge in the Acquisition, Retention, and Use of New Information," in *Advances in Consumer Research,* Vol. 10, R.P. Bagozzi and A.M. Tybout (eds.), Ann Arbor, Mich.: Association for Consumer Research, pp. 572–576.

Alice M. Tybout, Bobby J. Calder and Brian Sternthal (1981), "Using Information Processing Theory to Design Marketing Strategies," *Journal of Marketing Research* (February), pp. 73–79.

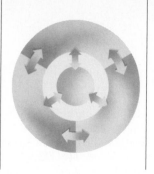

Chapter Four

Consumers' Knowledge, Meanings, and Beliefs

LA Beer—A New Category of Meaning?

First there was low-priced beer. Then came low calorie. Now, it's low-alcohol beer, beers that contain about half of regular beer's 5 percent alcohol content. American brewers are watching to see how beer-drinking consumers react to low-alcohol beer.

In 1984, giant brewer Anheuser-Busch rushed its LA brand (the initials stand for "low alcohol," not Los Angeles) to market after only six weeks of test marketing. Why did A-B forego its customary careful market analyses? Because if a market for low-alcohol beer does develop, A-B doesn't want to leave it to anyone else. According to marketing director Michael Roarty, "We have no intention if a new category emerges of waiting years to get into it."

Part of A-B's concern stemmed from their misreading of how the light beer category (beers with about one-third fewer calories) developed. A-B was among the skeptics who initially thought beer drinkers would consider the light beers as "diet beer" and "sissy." They waited until it was obvious that consumers had more favorable perceptions. Now, even with three light-beer brands, A-B has only 20 percent of the market, while Miller Lite has about a 50 percent share.

The growing number of competitors entering the low-alcohol beer market creates a consumer knowledge problem for A-B. Heileman, Stroh, and other brewers are using the initials "LA" as part of the brand names of the beers they are selling. Does this confuse consumers? A-B thought so and has brought suit against several of these companies.

Some analysts suggest that low-alcohol beers appeal most to drivers who want to cut down before leaving the bar. Roarty says, "Most beer drinkers think of LA as watered-down beer." If so, the companies may try to develop communication strategies to create more favorable meanings and beliefs.

The marketing success of LA beer largely depends on the knowledge, meanings, and beliefs formed by millions of beer drinkers. What kinds of knowledge will consumers develop regarding these products? Will consumers consider LA to be a different type of beer? What will they call the product category? What are the meanings of low-alcohol beers?

Source: Adapted from Russell Shaw and Susan Garland (1984), "Light Audience So Far for 'LA'," Advertising Age (August 23), pp. 3 and 54; Monci J. Williams (1984), "Betting on a Beer without Buzz," Fortune (June 25), p. 76.

In this chapter, we begin to examine the components in our model of consumers' cognitive processes (refer back to Figure 3–2). We start with a consideration of consumers' knowledge, meanings, and beliefs, because existing knowledge in memory has powerful and pervasive effects on the cognitive processes that create and use that knowledge. The chapter covers three broad topics. First, we examine several aspects of consumers' knowledge, including content, types of meanings, levels of abstraction, and organization. Then, we discuss levels of consumers' product knowledge. Finally, we discuss the learning processes by which knowledge is acquired.

Aspects of Consumers' Knowledge

In this section, we identify and discuss four aspects of consumers' knowledge. First are the types of things consumers have knowledge about. Then, we consider the types of meanings that consumers have stored in memory. Following this, we examine how meanings vary by level of abstraction, and describe the categorization processes by which these meanings are formed. Finally, we consider how these meanings are organized in memory to form associative networks of propositions as well as larger structures of knowledge called schemas and scripts.

Consumers' Knowledge about What?

We can begin to think about the *content* of consumers' knowledge by considering the four elements in our wheel model of consumer analysis (refer back to Figure 2–3). Figure 4–1 presents several examples of consumers' knowledge in each category. The bulk of consumers' knowledge is about

FIGURE 4–1   **Types of Consumer Knowledge Stored in Memory**

- The Physical Environment
  Locations of familiar retail outlets, such as the nearest McDonald's.

- The Social Environment
  Who among your friends is the best source of information on stereo equipment and movies.
  Which bars have the best social scene on Friday nights.

- Marketing Strategy Variables
  What the package of your favorite shampoo looks like.
  The brands of breakfast cereal you normally consider buying.
  The price of the new tennis racket you saw at the store on Saturday.
  The power and distortion specs on your stereo receiver.
  A television commercial you saw last night for a denture cleanser.
  The restaurants that offer the best pizza specials.

- Your Own Behavior
  The brand of coffee you bought last week.
  What you said to the rude salesclerk at the drug store.
  Recommendations you gave a friend who asked about where to buy used records and tapes.

- Your Own Cognitive States
  The brands of toothpaste, soda, and pens you prefer.
  Your intention to buy a new hair dryer this week.

stimuli in their physical and social environment, including aspects of marketing strategies. In addition, consumers have knowledge about their own behavior. Finally, consumers have at least some knowledge of the cognitive outcomes (meanings, beliefs, attitudes, or intentions to behave in certain ways) produced by earlier cognitive processes. Usually, however, consumers have little or no knowledge of the processes that produced those cognitive states.[1]

In a broad sense, people have two types of knowledge—episodic and semantic.[2] **Episodic knowledge** refers to the mental representations that

---

[1]K. Anders Ericsson and Herbert A. Simon (1980), "Verbal Reports as Data," *Psychological Review* (May), pp. 215–251.

[2]Endel Tulving (1972), "Episodic and Semantic Memory," in *Organization of Memory*, Endel Tulving (ed.), New York: Academic Press, pp. 382–404.

HIGHLIGHT 4–1   ***Questions Requiring Semantic and Episodic Knowledge***

Requires Episodic Knowledge	Requires Semantic Knowledge
What ads for light beer do you remember seeing?	How much did you like the Grace Jones Honda advertisement?
Which brand of soda pop did you buy last time?	What do you like best about Diet Pepsi?
How much did you pay for your new lawn mower?	What characteristics of stereo receivers are most important to you?
When did the salesperson say to check back to see whether the camera had come in?	What store carries the widest assortment of video cassettes?

people have of the specific events in their lives. **Semantic knowledge** refers to the general meanings that people have acquired about their world. For instance, your cognitive representation that you bought a Snickers candy bar from a vending machine yesterday afternoon is part of your episodic knowledge. In contrast, your general representations about Snickers bars— the peanuts and caramel they contain, the wrapper design, the aroma, and the taste—is part of your semantic knowledge. Typically, marketers are more often interested in consumers' general, semantic knowledge than in their specific, episodic knowledge.

Knowledge As Meanings

The human cognitive system is an amazingly efficient "meaning machine." A primary function of our cognitive systems is sense making—creating symbolic representations or **meanings** that stand for relevant aspects of our environment.[3] These meanings, in turn, are used in various cognitive processes by which we interpret our environment and make decisions about behaviors to achieve our goals (refer again to Figure 3–2).

---

[3]F. C. Bartlett (1932), *Remembering*, Cambridge: Cambridge University Press; Walter B. Weimer (1974), "Overview of a Cognitive Conspiracy: Reflections on this Volume," in *Cognition and the Symbolic Processes*, W. B. Weimer and D. S. Palermo (eds.), New York: John Wiley & Sons.

Types of Meanings

Consumers' cognitive systems are capable of creating many different types of meanings. Figure 4–2 presents several examples of the meanings that consumers may have in their memories. Because a great deal of the information in consumers' environments is in verbal form (signs, newspaper ads, brochures), much of consumer research has focused on these "verbal," linguistic representations. However, *visual information* is also very common, and **visual meanings** (images) also have been investigated (see Highlight 4–2). Other types of meanings such as olfactory (smell) and

---

FIGURE 4–2   **Types of Meanings Represented in Consumers' Memories**

Type of Meaning	Examples
Cognitive	Product judgments: stylish, high quality
Visual	Scenes in television commercials Brand trademarks—swoosh symbol for Nike Product spokesperson—Bill Cosby for Jell-O Package or label of favorite product
Affect	I like Diet Coke Crest toothpaste is good
Emotion	Anger, fear, joy Feelings of warmth created by AT&T's "reach out and touch someone" commercials
Mood	Relaxed, mellow, anxious, uptight Diffuse feelings created by in-store atmosphere
Auditory	A tune or jingle on the radio Sound of a soft drink being opened and poured
Taste	Sweetness of chocolate chip cookies Cola flavor of Diet Pepsi Bitterness of favorite brand of imported beer
Smells	Fresh baked bread Favorite cologne
Tactile	Feel of favorite pair of Levi's jeans Pressure from too-tight shoes
Motor	How to tie your shoes How to open a box of breakfast cereal

---

Consumers have visual images in memory which represent the important pictorial and spatial features of their environment. These visual images can be activated from memory and used in cognitive processes.

For instance, consumers may be able to retrieve a visual image of the package, which helps them identify the product in the store. Consider the case of John Smith who steps up to the bar and promptly draws a complete blank when the bartender asks him what he'd like to drink. Not normally a Scotch drinker, he settles on that product form and tries to remember the name of the brand he tried a month ago. "You know," he tells the bartender, "it's the one in the triangular bottle." The bartender promptly pours a jigger of Glenfiddich Single Malt. A distinctive liquor package has made another sale. In fact, the shape of the Glenfiddich bottle is such a distinctive visual image that marketers, in a recent product "redesign," changed only the label; they left the bottle as it is.

Source: Kate Bertrand (1984), "Shaping Packaging for Impact," Advertising Age *(July 26), p. 43.*

---

tactile (feel) are also represented in memory, but they have hardly been studied.

Although some of these meanings may not be easily translated into verbal language (can you describe the taste of freshly baked bread or the smell of old sneakers?), they can have important influences on consumer behavior. For instance, a consumer's mood can influence cognitions and behaviors in different situations. (A **mood** is a general, pervasive affective feeling,[4] which through spreading activation, can activate other evaluatively consistent meanings.) Thus, consumers in a good mood tend to think of positive meanings; the opposite is true if they are in a bad mood. In turn, these activated meanings can affect cognitive processes and behaviors. For instance, consumers who are in a good mood tend to be easier to deal with in service situations such as a restaurant. Marketing strategies can often influence consumers' moods, and thus their behavior. For instance, many soft-drink advertisements try to create a happy, exciting mood which is appropriate for thinking about that product.

---

[4]Meryl Paula Gardner (1985), "Mood States and Consumer Behavior: A Critical Review," *Journal of Consumer Research* (December), pp. 281–300.

Courtesy Estée Lauder

Some ads are designed to influence consumers' moods.

Cognitive versus Affective Meanings

Some researchers draw a sharp distinction between **cognitive meanings** (e.g., beliefs about the features of a sweater) and **affective or emotional meanings** (e.g., how the sweater makes you feel). Some researchers believe that "affect" and "cognition" are relatively independent "meaning systems."[5] Others have criticized this position, and a major controversy currently is raging on the issue.[6]

Our position recognizes that the human cognitive system creates many different types of symbolic meanings, including cognitive and affective meanings. Both cognitive and affective meanings are useful ways of representing environmental stimuli; and probably more often than not, consumers form both types of meanings to represent a product or brand. For our purposes in this text, it is not particularly important whether emotional/affective meanings are created before or after cognitive meanings, whether different brain subsystems are involved, or whether these meanings are stored in different "forms" in memory. However, marketers do need to understand both the cognitive and affective meanings that consumers may have for their products.

Symbolic Meanings

Thirty years ago, during the heyday of motivation research, marketers were very interested in the **symbolic meaning** of products.[7] Recently, there has been increasingly renewed interest in the symbolic meanings consumers associate with products.[8] The basic idea is that products often mean far more to consumers than just their functional qualities. As Levy has noted,

> The things people buy are seen to have personal and social meanings in addition to their functions. Modern goods are recognized as psychological things, as symbolic of personal attributes and goals, as symbolic of social patterns and strivings. In this sense, all commercial objects have a symbolic character, and making a purchase involves

---

[5]See Robert Zajonc (1980), "Feeling and Thinking: Preferences Need No Inferences," *American Psychologist* (February), pp. 151–175; and Robert B. Zajonc and Hazel Markus (1982), "Affective and Cognitive Factors in Preferences," *Journal of Consumer Research* (September), pp. 123–131.

[6]See critiques of the Zajonc position by Richard S. Lazarus (1982), "Thoughts on the Relation between Emotion and Cognition," *American Psychologist* (September), pp. 1019–1024; and Yehoshua Tsal (1985), "On the Relationship between Cognitive and Affective Processes: A Critique of Zajonc and Markus," *Journal of Consumer Research* (December), pp. 358–362; and a rebuttal by Robert B. Zajonc and Hazel Markus (1985), "Must All Affect Be Mediated by Cognition?" *Journal of Consumer Research* (December), pp. 363–364.

[7]Sidney J. Levy (1959), "Symbols for Sale," *Harvard Business Review* (July–August), pp. 117–124.

[8]See Sidney J. Levy (1981), "Interpreting Consumer Mythology: A Structural Approach to Consumer Behavior," *Journal of Marketing* (Summer), pp. 49–61; Michael R. Solomon (1983), "The Role of Products as Social Stimuli: A Symbolic Interactionism Perspective," *Journal of Consumer Research* (December), pp. 319–329.

Courtesy Bloomingdale's and Swatch Watch USA, Inc.

Consumers grade products as to the appropriate age of the wearer.

an assessment—implicit or explicit—of this symbolism, to decide whether or not it fits.[9]

For instance, some products are seen as more appropriate for men or women, although many of these distinctions seem to be breaking down.

---

[9]Sidney J. Levy (1977), "Symbols by Which We Buy," in *Classics in Consumer Behavior*, Louis Boone (ed.), Tulsa, Okla.: Petroleum Publishing, p. 4.

Styles of clothing are quite carefully graded as to the age of the wearer. Marketing strategies are also intended to create symbolic meanings for products. Consider, for example, the symbolic meanings that have become established for Marlboro (rugged individual, independent, macho) or Barclay (sophisticated, debonair, aloof) cigarettes.

Certain objects can acquire a wealth of symbolic meanings with use. A well-worn pair of blue jeans, a favorite record album, or an automobile may come to have a great deal of symbolic meaning for the owner. Personal-care and grooming products may be imbued with special "miraculous" properties by consumers and often are promoted as such by marketing strategies.[10] For instance, some consumers may feel that a special hair-styling mousse or a cologne can enhance their sexual desirability. Highlight 4–3 describes a study that attempts to measure some of these symbolic meanings.

In sum, all meanings formed by consumers' cognitive systems are legitimate *types of knowledge* that consumers have acquired through their experiences. Each type of knowledge represents a different meaning of the stimulus. No matter what its form, each meaning can be activated from memory and used in cognitive processing operations. For instance, seeing a perfume advertisement may cause the consumer to not only retrieve the representation of its scent, but also activate a number of other meanings such as emotions, moods, past events in one's life, and various visual and tactile images, perhaps including sexual imagery.[11]

Unique Meanings

The meanings created by each consumer's cognitive system are *unique* to each person. Differences in interpretation occur because meanings are heavily·influenced by each consumer's prior knowledge structures. Because no two consumers have had exactly the same past experiences, they will not have identical knowledge structures in memory and are not likely to form identical meanings. Even a simple marketing strategy such as a manufacturer's rebate of $5 on a Black & Decker toaster oven is likely to be interpreted differently by different consumers. Some may think the product has problems, because the marketer is trying to "get rid of it" through price reductions; other consumers will be delighted to get a "good deal."

---

[10]See a discussion of this point by Dennis W. Rook (1985), "The Ritual Dimension of Consumer Behavior," *Journal of Consumer Research* (December), pp. 251–264.

[11]Elizabeth C. Hirschman and Morris B. Holbrook (1982), "Hedonic Consumption: Emerging Concepts, Methods and Propositions," *Journal of Marketing* (Summer), pp. 92–101.

HIGHLIGHT 4–3   **Measuring Consumers' Symbolic Meanings**

A recent study attempted to measure the symbolic, and perhaps largely unconscious, meanings associated with consumers' personal grooming rituals. This research found that hair-care activities dominated the grooming behavior of the young adults, 18- to 25-years-old, in the sample. For instance, most of these consumers shampooed their hair nearly every day, and many felt frustrated and emotional about this activity. For instance, one 20-year-old woman said: "Fixing my hair is the most difficult. I spend hours—actually hours—doing my hair. It drives me crazy!"

Because many of the meanings associated with hair care were thought to be relatively unconscious, direct questioning could not be used to tap into these deeper, more symbolic meanings; consumers might just offer rationalizations for their behavior. So the researcher showed male and female consumers pictures of a young man using a blow dryer and a young woman in curlers applying makeup. Each consumer was asked to write a detailed story about the person in the picture. Their stories give some insights into the meanings of these grooming rituals.

For many consumers, hair grooming with the blow dryer seemed to symbolize an active, take-charge personality who is preparing to go on the "social prowl." For example, one 20-year-old man said, "Jim is supposed to stay home and study tonight, but he's getting ready to go out, anyway. He's hoping to meet some hot chicks, and he wants his hair to look just right."

Symbolic meanings about work and success were prominent in other stories, as the following excerpt from a 21-year-old woman illustrates: "Susan is getting ready for her first presentation, and she's very nervous. If it goes well, maybe her boss will help with a down payment on a new car."

Uncovering consumers' deep, symbolic meanings for certain products can be quite difficult. However, the knowledge may give marketers useful insights into consumers' reactions to their strategies.

Source: Dennis W. Rook (1985), "The Ritual Dimension of Consumer Behavior," Journal of Consumer Research *(December), pp. 251–264.*

Commonality of Meanings

Although each consumer's knowledge is unique, marketers usually can find enough *commonality of meanings* so that segments of consumers with relatively similar knowledge structures can be identified. This allows marketers to develop efficient strategies that appeal to large groups of consumers, or to target segments, rather than having to treat each consumer individually.

For instance, a high-status image for certain brands means that many consumers have similar meanings for the brand: upper class, distinctive, tasteful, people will look up to me, etc. Aprica Kassai baby strollers have

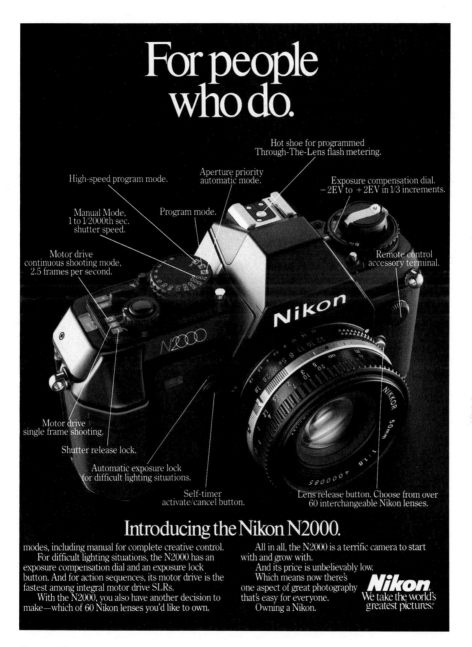

For people who do.

Hot shoe for programmed Through-The-Lens flash metering.

Aperture priority automatic mode.

High-speed program mode.

Exposure compensation dial. – 2EV to + 2EV in 1/3 increments.

Manual Mode, 1 to 1/2000th sec. shutter speed.

Program mode.

Motor drive continuous shooting mode, 2.5 frames per second.

Remote control accessory terminal.

Nikon

N2000

NIKKOR 50mm 1:1.8

Motor drive single frame shooting.

Shutter release lock.

Automatic exposure lock for difficult lighting situations.

Self-timer activate/cancel button.

Lens release button. Choose from over 60 interchangeable Nikon lenses.

Introducing the Nikon N2000.

modes, including manual for complete creative control.

For difficult lighting situations, the N2000 has an exposure compensation dial and an exposure lock button. And for action sequences, its motor drive is the fastest among integral motor drive SLRs.

With the N2000, you also have another decision to make—which of 60 Nikon lenses you'd like to own.

All in all, the N2000 is a terrific camera to start with and grow with.

And its price is unbelievably low.

Which means now there's one aspect of great photography that's easy for everyone.

Owning a Nikon.

Nikon
We take the world's greatest pictures.

Courtesy Nikon

Creating consumer knowledge about product benefits.

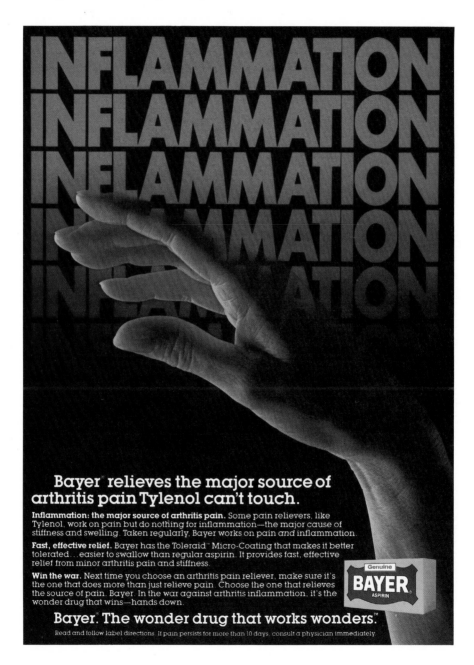

Courtesy Sterling Drug, Inc.

Creating consumer knowledge about the values satisfied by the product.

Courtesy Skil Corporation

This ad attempts to convey the sensory meanings of the product.

HIGHLIGHT 4–4   ***Idiosyncratic Meanings***

Even a simple marketing strategy such as a 20 percent price reduction or the offer of a rebate will be interpreted differently by different consumers.

Below are some possible idiosyncratic meanings and behaviors in response to receiving a 15-cents-off coupon for a new brand of mustard.

Consumer	Existing Knowledge	Interpretation
Mary K.	Likes deals and coupons very much. Heavy user of deals.	"This is a good deal." She puts the coupon in her purse and plans to redeem it on the next shopping trip.
Susan R.	Moderately favorable toward deals, coupons. Occasional user.	"This one isn't worth redeeming." She throws it in her drawer where it sits for six months until she throws it out.
Judy S.	Thinks coupons are a waste of her time. Almost never uses deals.	"Another worthless coupon." She throws it in the trash.

many of these high-status meanings, at least among Yuppies.[12] Imported from Japan, this well-made product has several clever features, such as "anatomically correct" seats and a slick, modern look. It sells for $100 to $300. The status and quality meanings associated with Aprica Kassai strollers have made them a big hit with the up-scale baby boomers who are having their children later in life. In fact, since Aprica entered the U.S. market in 1980, they have become the top seller at the higher price levels and have captured an 8 percent share of the overall market. (In Japan they command two thirds of the total market!)

Marketing Implications

Sometimes consumers' meanings create problems for marketing strategies. Many expensive marketing failures can be traced to the meanings consum-

---

[12]Larry Armstrong and Judith H. Dobrzynski (1985), "Aprica Kassai: A Fast Ride into the U.S. with Status-Symbol Strollers," *Business Week* (January 21), p. 117.

ers had for the product. For example, Paramount Pictures lost millions of dollars in 1980 by failing to recognize a meaning problem with the release of their film, *Urban Cowboy*.[13] The picture seemed to have everything going for it, including sex, violence, country and western music, and John Travolta, then a big box-office attraction. One of the reasons for the poorer-than-expected ticket sales was the title. Apparently, many young people (the prime segment of moviegoers) were confused about what the film was about. Some did not know what the word *urban* meant. Others associated the movie with the 1969 film, *Midnight Cowboy*, and thought it was about homosexuals. As one theater manager said, "Who wants to see a movie called *The Gay Cowboy*?"

Marketers need to understand the meanings consumers associate with their products and services, as well as with the other elements of their marketing strategy. In some cases, marketers may have to develop special strategies to overcome meaning problems. Consider the recent attempt by Honda and Yamaha to interest American consumers in motor scooters. Honda pursued the youth market through ads featuring rock singers Grace Jones and Adam Ant, while Yamaha sought to appeal to the over-30, white-collar crowd. Despite the differences in their target segments, both companies had similar marketing strategies regarding consumers' meanings. Both attempted to disassociate scooters from motorcycles.[14] Their marketing strategies were intended to create a distinctive set of meanings about motor scooters and avoid the negative meanings many people have for motorcycles.

Levels of Abstraction in Consumers' Knowledge

Meanings exist at different levels of abstraction. For example, we can describe a product like a tennis racquet at several levels.[15] At a very concrete level of meaning, the racquet could be described in terms of its composition—graphite fibers, nylon strings, leather grip. At a somewhat higher level of abstraction, we can characterize the racquet in terms of its size, shape, or weight. At an even more abstract level of meaning, we could describe the racquet in terms of its performance—the responsiveness or

[13]Lisa Ballner-Bear (1981), "Miscomprehension of Print Advertising," *Marketing Communications*, pp. 12 and 110.

[14]"Motor Scooters Finally Make a Dent in the U.S. Market" (1984), *BusinessWeek* (July 16), pp. 31 and 35.

[15]This example was adapted from Roy Lachman, Janet L. Lachman and Earl C. Butterfield (1979), *Cognitive Psychology and Information Processing: An Introduction*, Hillsdale, N.J.: Lawrence Erlbaum, p. 108.

power it provides. Finally, we could describe a tennis racquet in terms of very abstract meanings, such as the enjoyment one might gain from owning or using it.

Several points need to be made about **levels of abstraction** of meanings. First, no one level of abstraction captures *all* the possible meanings of an object or an event. For instance, we have seen that a tennis racquet requires multiple levels of abstraction to account for its important meanings. Second, each level of meaning is particularly suited for certain purposes, but may not be at all useful for other purposes. Finally, the different levels of abstraction are related to each other in a hierarchical fashion. Meanings at higher levels of abstraction can subsume (include or incorporate) meanings at lower levels. For example, the responsiveness of a tennis racquet subsumes or encompasses the materials used to produce it, the shape of the head, the type of strings, and so on. Thus, concepts at different levels of abstraction vary in terms of their inclusiveness. The notion of levels of abstraction is a very important concept, and we will use it throughout this book.

The Categorization Process

The cognitive process by which meanings at different levels of abstraction are formed is called categorization. Note in the following definitions that **categorization** is an integral part of the sense-making process of cognition.

> The world consists of a virtually infinite number of discriminably different stimuli. One of the most basic functions of all organisms is the cutting up of the environment into classifications by which nonidentical stimuli can be treated as equivalent.[16]

> To categorize is to render discriminably different things equivalent, to group the objects and events and people around us into classes, and to respond to them in terms of their class membership rather than their uniqueness.[17]

To interpret the stimuli in their environments, consumers must recognize similarities (and differences) between separate objects and events.

---

[16]Eleanor Rosch, Carolyn B. Mervis, Wayne D. Gray, David M. Johnson and Penny Boyes-Braem (1976), "Basic Objects in Natural Categories," *Cognitive Psychology* (July), pp. 382–439.

[17]J.S. Bruner, J. Goodnow and G.A. Austin (1956), *A Study of Thinking*, New York: John Wiley & Sons, p. 1.

HIGHLIGHT 4–5   *Chunking*

In 1859, the Scottish philosopher Sir William Hamilton wrote, "If you throw a handful of marbles on the floor, you will find it difficult to view at once more than six, or seven at most, without confusion; but if you group them in two's or three's or five's, you can comprehend as many groups as you can units because the mind considers these groups as units—it views them as 'wholeness.' "

A century later, cognitive psychologist George Miller introduced the idea of *chunking* in a classic article about the "magic number seven, plus or minus two." Miller was trying to establish the approximate number of meaningful items that could be retained in short-term memory at one time. He suggested that immediate memory could be expanded beyond seven or so items by combining information into *chunks* of "enriched," more abstract units of meaning. Other cognitive scientists such as Herbert Simon have made similar suggestions.

A *chunk* is an abstract meaning with "psychological significance" to the person. For instance, consider the following list of words: Lincoln, milky, criminal, differential, address, way, lawyer, calculus, Gettysburg. Although familiar, they are hard to learn after one reading. But through a chunking or categorization process these nine separate words could be combined into four "larger," more meaningful phrases or chunks—

Lincoln Gettysburg Address, milky way, criminal lawyer, and differential calculus—which are easily learned and remembered.

As in categorization, chunking produces more inclusive meanings that stand for many lower-level meanings. The informational capacity of short-term memory is increased by using these "larger," more abstract chunks of meaning. Although the same number of meanings can be considered at one time, the more abstract chunks contain more meaning.

In summary, the formation of meanings at different levels of abstraction is an extremely important and powerful aspect of our cognitive system. Your ability to categorize, abstract, and generalize enables you to represent meanings beyond the physical stimuli in your environment. And more meaningful chunks are easier to remember. For this reason alone, you should try to form larger, more abstract chunks of meaning while you read this text and while you take notes in class.

Sources: Alma S. Wittlin (1984), "Are The Limits of the Mind Expandable?" Behavioral Science, *Vol. 29, pp. 51–60; George A. Miller (1956), "The Magical Number Seven, Plus or Minus Two: Some Limits on Our Capacity for Processing Information,"* Psychological Review (March), pp. 81–97; Herbert A. Simon (1974), "How Big Is a Chunk?" Science (February), pp. 482–488.*

Individual concepts that are perceived to be similar in some relevant way are grouped or **chunked** together by consumers' cognitive processing systems.[18] Then a new meaning concept is created to stand for the previously

---

[18]George A. Miller (1956), "The Magical Number Seven, Plus or Minus Two: Some Limits on Our Capacity for Processing Information," *Psychological Review* (March), pp. 81–97; Herbert A. Simon (1974), "How Big Is a Chunk?" *Science* (February), pp. 482–488.

HIGHLIGHT 4–6   **What's a "California Cooler"?**

When a company introduces a dramatically different product, consumers have to figure out how to categorize it within their knowledge structures. What products is it similar to? Which products does it compete with?

California Cooler, Inc. introduced such a product in 1981. The company touched off a flurry of reactions in the wine industry by introducing a wine cooler, with the brand name California Cooler. Since then, the popularity of coolers has soared (sales have increased about 50 percent each year). By 1985, some 40 cooler brands were on the market. A major shakeout of the market is expected, as industry giants such as Gallo and Seagrams decide whether coolers are a fad, a seasonal beverage, or are here to stay. In the meantime, Gallo brought out its own brand, called Bartles & Jaynes.

What kind of product is a wine cooler? Most coolers contain about 50 percent white wine and 50 percent citrus juices, which yields a 5 to 6 percent alcohol level. Buyers tend to be the same young, affluent men and women who are turning their backs on hard liquor. In what product class do consumers think it belongs? Do consumers see coolers as a unique product form in the wine category? If so, do coolers compete with regular wine or with low-alcohol wines (light wines)?

Maybe coolers are a new product category altogether. If so, what product classes do they compete with? Perhaps coolers compete with beer, which has about the same alcohol content. Coolers tend to be distributed and guzzled like beer. Do consumers see them as a product form in the beer product class? Some experts think beer is losing sales to coolers. Perhaps some consumers consider coolers as an alternative to soft drinks. After all, most coolers are promoted as thirst-quenching, warm-weather beverages, rather similar to many of the promotions for soft drinks.

Obviously, marketers need answers to these categorization questions, but they are difficult to come by. Consumers' perceptions of such new products often develop over a period of time. The meanings of wine coolers will evolve as consumers try them and learn about their characteristics. We may have to wait to see how consumers will eventually come to perceive wine coolers in the context of other beverages.

Eventually, most consumers will form a stable knowledge structure for wine coolers. Marketers will try to monitor this process and understand consumers' categories of meaning for wine coolers. Those who can do so will have a distinct advantage in the marketplace.

Source: Ruth Stroud (1984), "Cooler's Rising Star Rocks Wine Market,"Advertising Age (September 17), pp. 2 and 86; "Stroh Gets Cool," Fortune (April 15, 1985), p. 10.

unrelated elements. This new concept is a more abstract category of meaning—a "larger" chunk of meaning—in that it subsumes its separate component parts. Then, when using the abstract category, the consumer's cognitive processing system responds to each member of the category *as if they were the same concept*, even though the category members are not identical.

Consider, for instance, the up-scale fast food restaurants that have been opening up around the country.[19] Companies such as Texas-based Chili's and Fuddruckers, or Flakey Jake's and Victoria Station are serving up hamburgers costing $3.50 and more. Will consumers create a special category of meaning, such as "fancy fast-food hamburger place," to represent these new objects in their environments? If so, they may develop special behaviors for these restaurants that differ from how they respond to the regular fast-food hamburger emporiums such as McDonald's. Highlight 4–6 presents another example of a new-product introduction, the success of which depends on consumers' categorization processes.

Advantages of Categorization

The process of categorization has many functional advantages, not the least of which is the *cognitive economy* it provides. By combining specific concepts into fewer, more abstract meanings, consumers simplify their complex environments. Rather than deal with separate concepts representing myriad environmental stimuli, consumers' cognitive systems can operate on fewer, but more inclusive concepts (more abstract categories of meaning).

Categorization is also useful because a consumer can tell a great deal about an object merely by knowing which general category of meaning it belongs to. For example, assigning a new shoe to the "running shoe category" allows most consumers to predict many of its characteristics, depending on the content of their knowledge structures for running shoes.

Organization of Consumers' Knowledge

In Chapter 3 you learned that consumers' symbolic representations are organized into associative networks or **knowledge structures.** Each cognitive representation is a separate meaning or node in a memory network. Each meaning node is associated with other meanings via *links* to form an **associative network** of interconnected meanings.[20] Figure 4–3 presents a highly simplified associative network for Nike running shoes.

---

[19]Roger Neal (1984), "Fancyburgers," *Forbes* (June 18), p. 92.

[20]Many other types of memory structures have been proposed, but most can be reduced to the more general associative network model. See James R. Bettman (1979), "Memory Factors in Consumer Choice: A Review," *Journal of Marketing* (Spring), pp. 37–53; Edward E. Smith (1978), "Theories of Semantic Memory," in *Handbook of Learning and Cognitive Processes,* Vol. 6, W.K. Estes (ed.), Hillsdale, N.J.: Lawrence Erlbaum.

FIGURE 4–3   **An Associative Network of Knowledge**

Meaning Nodes

Each **node** in an associative network represents a unique idea or meaning.[21] That is, every idea, concept, word, image, mood, or motor action that a consumer can think of is represented as a separate meaning node in his/her knowledge structure. Note that Figure 4–3 contains several different types of knowledge, including episodic representations of past events,

---

[21]Wayne A. Wickelgren (1981), "Human Learning and Memory," in *Annual Review of Psychology*, M.R. Rosenzweig and L.W. Porter (eds.), Palo Alto, Calif.: Annual Reviews Inc., pp. 21–52.

affective feelings, moods and emotions, and general semantic knowledge about the characteristics of Nike shoes.

Links

An associative network is built of **links** or simple associations between meaning nodes. For instance, links connect a product concept with its associated meanings, as shown in Figure 4–3. Links vary in the strength of the association they represent. For instance, a consumer may strongly believe that Nike shoes are long wearing, but feel less confident that they will prevent injuries.

Levels of Abstraction in an Associative Network

Each unique meaning, whatever its level of abstraction, is represented in memory as a separate node in an associative network.[22] Through categorization (the chunking processes), new, more inclusive, more abstract meanings may be created that represent or stand for an entire associative network of less abstract meanings. Figure 4–4 shows three chunks of meaning at different levels of abstraction in one consumer's knowledge structure for automobiles. Note that each chunk is itself a meaning node in a larger, more abstract chunk.

Activation of Meanings

You learned in Chapter 3 that meaning is often activated directly, upon exposure to the appropriate physical stimulus. For instance, seeing a Nike shoe or just the swoosh symbol in a Nike advertisement, will usually activate the Nike representation in memory. Thus, you recognize the stimulus as Nike virtually instantly.

Meaning nodes can also be activated indirectly, as the activation energy *spreads* from one meaning node to others at the same or different levels of abstraction. This spread of activation allows consumers' thinking to shift between more or less abstract levels of meaning. For instance, the consumer with the knowledge structure in Figure 4–4 might begin thinking about buying a used Mazda RX-7 sports car by considering its general performance. But to evaluate the car's handling (an aspect of performance at a lower level of abstraction), the contents of the handling chunk must be activated. Then the consumer can think about the tires, suspension system, and other handling-related features of the Mazda RX-7. Because spreading activation typically occurs automatically, consumers usually are

---

[22]Ibid.

FIGURE 4–4   **_Levels of Abstraction in an Associative Network_**

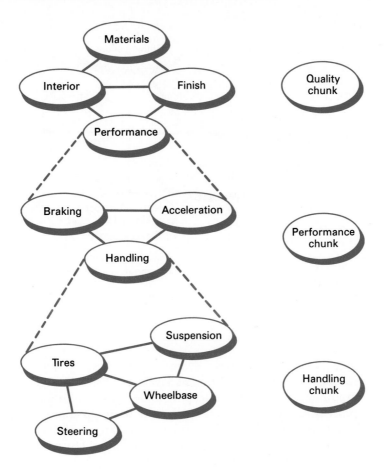

unaware of how their knowledge structures are activated and used in cognitive processes. Meanings simply "come to mind" while we are "thinking." The automatic activation of appropriate meanings at different levels of abstraction enables our cognitive processes to operate very efficiently.

Structures of Knowledge

Cognitive scientists have identified three types of knowledge units—concepts, propositions, and schemas—which encode different levels of mean-

FIGURE 4–5   **Concepts, Propositions, and Schemas of Knowledge**

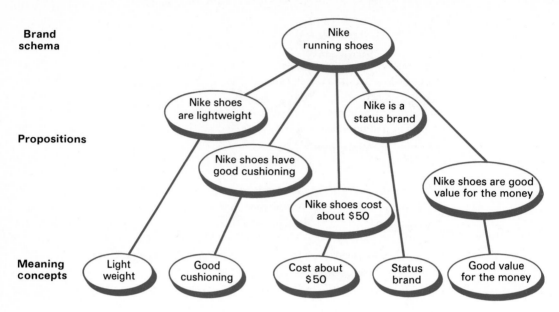

ing.[23] Thus far, we have examined the first of these meaning units—meaning concepts at different levels of abstraction. In this section, we examine how separate concepts can be combined to form propositions and procedures. Then we will examine how propositions and procedures are combined to form larger structures of knowledge called schemas and scripts. Figure 4–5 illustrates the relationship between these three types of knowledge units for Nike running shoes.

Propositions and Beliefs. Individual meaning nodes may be combined into larger units of meaning called **propositions** or **beliefs.** A *proposition* links two concept nodes together to represent a more complex meaning—for instance, "Nike running shoes are well cushioned," or "Nike is a status brand." Propositions or beliefs vary in the strength of the association. Once formed, a proposition can be treated as a single meaning node that

---

[23]This section borrows several ideas from John R. Anderson (1980), "Concepts, Propositions, and Schemata: What Are the Cognitive Units?" in *1980 Nebraska Symposium on Motivation,* H.E. Howe and J.H. Flowers (eds.), Lincoln: University of Nebraska Press, pp. 121–162.

can be activated and used as a chunk in cognitive processes. (We will discuss beliefs and belief strength in more detail in Chapter 7.)

Schemas. Propositions, in turn, can be combined to form even larger and more complex units of knowledge called **schemas.**[24] Schemas are networks of interrelated propositions. As Figure 4–5 shows, the set of propositions about Nike running shoes constitutes a brand schema. Even more abstract schemas might be formed by combining lower-level schemas. For instance, the Nike schema could be subsumed in a more abstract schema representing the product form—sports shoes—which in turn, is subsumed in the product class schema, shoes.

Like concepts and propositions, a schema can be activated and treated in cognitive processes as a single meaning node, even though the schema may represent a complex structure of knowledge.[25] However, each knowledge unit/structure, from single concepts to propositions to very abstract schemas, can be decomposed into their less abstract components, if necessary, for some cognitive process. By activating different knowledge units at the appropriate levels of abstraction, consumers' cognitive systems are able to adapt to virtually any situation and process information in a flexible, effective manner.

Procedures. Some knowledge structures also contain a special type of proposition called a **procedure.** Procedures link representations of a *concept or event* and an *appropriate action or behavior.* For instance, through their past experiences, most consumers have acquired procedural representations for how to act in a "good" restaurant. One such procedure might be:

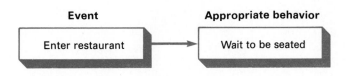

---

[24]Daniel G. Bobrow and Donald A. Norman (1975), "Some Principles of Memory Schemata," in *Representation and Understanding: Studies in Cognitive Science,* D.G. Bobrow and A.M. Collins (eds.), New York: Academic Press; Jerry C. Olson (1978), "Theories of Information Encoding and Storage: Implications for Consumer Research," in *The Effect of Information on Consumer and Market Behavior,* A.A. Mitchell (ed.), Chicago: American Marketing Association, pp. 49–60; D.E. Rumelhart and Anthony Ortony (1977), "The Representation of Knowledge in Memory," in *Schooling and The Acquisition of Knowledge,* R.C. Anderson, R.J. Spiro and W.E. Montague (eds.), Hillsdale, N.J.: Lawrence Erlbaum.

[25]Wickelgren, "Human Learning and Memory"; Anderson, "Concepts, Propositions, and Schemata."

Alan Carey/The Image Works

Chapman/Topham/The Image Works

Different scripts may be activated in different restaurant environments.

Of course, procedures will vary according to the circumstances of the situation. For example, most consumers' procedures for restaurant behavior are likely to vary according to the type of restaurant they find themselves in. For example, eating in a fast food restaurant activates a different set of procedures:

Scripts. Like schemas, **scripts** are abstract structures of general, semantic knowledge, but scripts contain organized sequences of procedures. For instance, a "fine-restaurant" script would contain a number of procedures representing the appropriate actions for the events that are most likely in that situation. Figure 4–6 presents an example of a restaurant script.

Consumers, through their extensive experiences with their environments, have formed many scripts. For instance, a consumer who is experi-

---

FIGURE 4–6   ***A Hypothetical Script of Appropriate Procedures for Dining at a "Fancy" Restaurant***

- Enter restaurant
- Give reservation name to maitre d'
- Wait to be shown to table
- Walk to table and sit down
- Order drinks when waiter asks
- Select dinner items from menu
- Order meal when waiter returns
- Drink drinks and talk until first course arrives
- Eat soup or salad when it arrives
- Eat main course when it arrives
- Order dessert when finished with dinner
- Eat dessert when it arrives
- Talk until bill arrives
- Examine bill for accuracy
- Give waiter credit card to pay for bill
- Add tip to credit card form and sign
- Leave restaurant

Source: Adapted from Arno J. Rethans (in press), "Consumer Scripts: A Tool for Teaching Process," Journal of Consumer Affairs; *and Gordon H. Bower, John B. Black and Terrence J. Turner (1979), "Scripts in Memory for Text,"* Cognitive Psychology *(April), pp. 177–220.*

enced in buying cars may have formed a generalized script of appropriate behaviors when negotiating with the salesperson about the price of a new car. When activated, these knowledge structures guide and direct the consumer's cognitive processes and behaviors.

Influence of Schemas and Scripts. Because they represent or subsume rather large amounts of knowledge, schemas and scripts often have substantial effects on cognitive processes. Schemas and scripts contain much of the knowledge on which consumers base their expectations, inferences, perceptions, and interpretations. Once activated, schemas and scripts influence the course of cognitive processes such as attention, comprehension, and integration processes (refer back to Figure 3–2). How they do so is discussed in Chapters 6, 7, and 8.

Levels of Product Knowledge

Marketers are especially interested in consumers' knowledge about the products and services they produce. It is important to recognize that consumers have product knowledge at several levels of abstraction. For instance, consumers may have knowledge about a **product class,** various **forms** of a product class, alternative **brands** within each product form, and different **models** of each brand.[26] Figure 4–7 presents several examples that illustrate how these four levels fit together. Taken as a whole, such meanings form a hierarchical structure of product knowledge in which the more abstract levels of meaning subsume (stand for) the "lower" levels of meaning.

Brand Knowledge

Most consumers possess substantial knowledge about specific brands, such as Taster's Choice and Folgers coffee, or Toyota and BMW automobiles. Marketers are particularly interested in brand-level knowledge, be-

---

[26]Others have proposed similar schemes; for example: Elizabeth C. Hirschman and Susan P. Douglas (1981), "Hierarchical Cognitive Content: Towards a Measurement Methodology," in *Advances in Consumer Research,* Vol. 8, K.B. Monroe (ed.), Ann Arbor, Mich.: Association for Consumer Research, pp. 100–105; Tony Lunn (1972), "Segmenting and Constructing Markets," in *Consumer Market Research Handbook,* R.M. Worcester (ed.), Maidenhead, Berkshire: McGraw-Hill.

cause most marketing strategies are brand oriented. That is, the typical marketing strategy is intended to make consumers aware of a particular brand, to promote a certain brand, or to increase the sales of a specific brand. Strategies designed to promote a product class or a certain product form are less common. Thus, most marketing research focuses on consumers' knowledge and beliefs about brands.

Knowledge of Models with Specific Product Features

As Figure 4–7 shows, the brand level of product knowledge is itself an abstract level of meaning. A **brand name** is an abstract category or chunk that may subsume a number of different models, each composed of different product attributes and features. For example, a BMW can be purchased in several models—318i, 535e, 735—each with unique features and different option packages, such as air conditioning, stereo radio, and fancy wheels. Although the configuration of features and options for each model is literally a different car, all are the same brand, BMW. Even a simple brand such as Folgers ground coffee is sold in 3-, 1-, and 1/2-pound con-

FIGURE 4–7   **Levels of Product Knowledge**

More Abstract			Less Abstract
Product Class	**Product Form**	**Brand**	**Model/Feature**
Coffee	Ground	Folgers	3-pound can
	Instant	Maxwell House	8-ounce jar
Automobiles	Sedan	Chevrolet	Caprice, with air and power steering
	Sports car	Porsche	Model 928, with air and 5-speed
	Sports sedan	BMW	Model 318i, with air and automatic transmission
Pens	Ball point	Bic	$.79 model, regular tip
	Felt tip	Pilot	$.99 model, extra-fine tip
Beer	Imported	Heineken	Dark
	Light	Miller Lite	Kegs
	Low alcohol	Budweiser LA	12-ounce cans

tainers; yet these different "models" are considered to be the Folgers brand and usually are treated similarly by consumers.

Can you see the economy of developing cognitive representations, categories, or meanings at higher levels of abstraction? Responding to the many different models of Nikon cameras merely as "Nikon" (brand level) is more efficient for many purposes than having to deal with each model as a separate concept.

Product-Form Knowledge

Consumers also have product-related knowledge at levels that are more abstract than brand names. Brands which are perceived to be similar on certain important characteristics may come to be classified together and treated as a more abstract category, called a **product form.** The basis for creating a product-form category varies, of course, for different types of products. Sometimes the primary basis is a dominant physical characteristic of the chunked brands—such as the freeze-dried, instant, ground, and whole-bean product forms of coffee. Different product forms of automobiles might include sedans, sports sedans, station wagons, sports cars, pickups, and vans. In other cases, a more abstract meaning will be the basis for grouping different brands, such as a product form category of soda pop brands that are "good for dieting."

Product-Class Knowledge

The most abstract level of consumer product knowledge in our scheme is the **product class.** A product-class category subsumes several product forms that the consumer perceives as similar in some important way. Concepts at the product-class level tend to have relatively few features in common. For example, perhaps the only feature that defines the product class *coffee* is that all the various product forms are made from coffee beans.

Finally (although this is not shown in Figure 4–7), consumers may form increasingly abstract categories of meaning that subsume several product classes. These might be categories of **generic competition,** in which the basis for the meaning category is the underlying need served by the different product classes. For instance, a consumer who drinks caffeinated beverages for the "lift" they give, might create an abstract category of meaning, "stimulating drinks," that includes the product classes coffee, tea, caffeinated soft drinks, and hot chocolate. In fact, consumers' categorization processes could create even more abstract categories of meaning— e.g., "beverages," "foods," and "objects."

HIGHLIGHT 4–7   **Product Knowledge Structures for Pasta**

Consumers do not have a complete hierarchical knowledge structure encompassing different product forms, brands, and models (feature combinations) for every product category. Consumers' knowledge structures for some products are much less complex.

Consider pasta. With $1.3 billion in annual sales in 1983, pasta is one of the fastest-growing products on the grocery shelves. Over the next several years, sales in the pasta product category are expected to increase at 5 percent per year, about three to four times faster than those of the average food product.

What kind of product knowledge structures do consumers have for the pasta product class? What are the dominant *product forms*? Pasta certainly comes in many forms—including amorini (little cupids), ricciolini (little curls), and vermicelli (little worms), as well as the more familiar spaghetti and fettucini shapes. But these are not product forms as we are considering them. Basically, pasta is pasta. It is hard to create a different product form for a simple product made mainly from flour and water. Says one industry executive, "There's not a lot you can do to flour to make it different."

Pasta is not clearly differentiated at the *brand level*, either. In fact, there are relatively few brands of pasta and no strong national brand to date. Most of the major companies are powerful only in regional markets. For example, Muller is sold chiefly in the East; Creamette is mainly a Midwest and South brand, and Golden Grain is a major competitor in the far West.

Despite the difficulties, the Prince Company of Lowell, Massachusetts, is developing different product forms of pasta and trying to differentiate their brands from the competition. The company has introduced Prince Light, a pasta with one-third fewer calories, and Superoni, a high-protein product marketed as a meat substitute. Other companies, such as General Foods–owned Ronzoni, are also planning to "bring some differentiation to the world of pasta."

Whether these marketing strategies can create more complex, hierarchical knowledge structures for pasta remains to be seen.

Source: Eleanor Johnson Tracy (1984), "Pasta: On The Road to a National Noodle," Fortune (May 28), p. 93.

Implications for Marketers

These four levels of product knowledge have important implications for marketing strategies. First, it is important to recognize that consumers make decisions at each of these levels. In many cases, consumers may choose from among alternative product classes or different forms of a product. Of course, many decisions occur at the brand level, which is the prime focus of most marketing research. But consumers also make choices from among different models of the same brand. It is quite likely that different types of knowledge are relevant for decisions at these different levels.

In sum, consumers' product knowledge is organized in a hierarchical arrangement of concepts at different levels of abstraction, from specific models to brands to product forms to product classes. This is not to say that every consumer possesses a complete knowledge structure for every product. Some products are so simple that all four levels may not be present. Highlight 4–7 describes such a product category, pasta. In other cases, inexperienced consumers may not be familiar enough with a product category to know about all the forms, brands, and models that are available. Such naive consumers probably have a very simple knowledge structure for that product category.

Learning: Acquiring Knowledge, Meanings, and Beliefs

In this section, we discuss how consumers acquire knowledge, meanings, and beliefs about products and brands. They get some of this knowledge early in life through **socialization processes.** But learning about products is a lifelong process of **cognitive learning,** as existing knowledge in memory is modified by the introduction of new knowledge. Both types of learning occur over time as a function of consumers' experiences in their environments. Later in the text, we will discuss another type of learning—behavioral learning.

Consumer Socialization

Although most analyses of consumer behavior focus on adults, who do the vast majority of buying, adults do not suddenly become consumers. Children begin to learn at a very early age about how the marketplace works, how to earn and spend money, types of marketing strategies, and alternative products and brands that are available for sale. This knowledge is acquired through **socialization processes** as children observe their parents buying and using products and services, as they see advertisements, and as they use products and brands.[27] Children gain much of their marketing information from television. In the late 1970s, the average child aged 2 to 5 watched about 25 hours of television per week—about 3 and 2/3rds hours

---

[27]A thorough discussion of consumer socialization is provided by Thomas S. Robertson, Joan Zielinski and Scott Ward (1984), *Consumer Behavior,* Glenview, Ill.: Scott, Foresman, chap. 7, pp. 141–165.

per day—while 6- to 11-year-olds watched slightly more.[28] It has been estimated that the average child sees about 20,000 TV commercials each year.[29] Parents and peers are also prime sources of information. Recent studies have found that even young children possess a great deal of knowledge about the marketplace and products and brands.[30]

Implications for Marketing

Certain types of products—breakfast cereal, some types of candy, toys—are heavily purchased by children, or else children exert strong influences on adult purchasers. Marketers of these products must pay special attention to socialization processes by which children acquire knowledge, meanings, and beliefs about such products.

Sources of Information

Consumers acquire new meanings and modify existing knowledge structures throughout their lives, largely through their behavioral interactions with their environment. Basically, changes in consumers' knowledge structures result from three types of interactions. First, consumers often learn about products and services through **direct behaviors.** Personal use of products is a very important source of knowledge. Marketers use a variety of strategies (such as in-store trial and free samples) to enable consumers to learn about their products through direct behavioral interaction. For instance, car dealers encourage consumers to take "a spin around the block"; clothing stores provide changing rooms for customers to try on garments; and cheese shops provide bite-sized samples. Bedding retailers nearly always have beds set up in their stores so customers can lie down and experience the "feel" of a mattress before buying. Of course, marketers tend to use such strategies when they are confident that their product will be evaluated favorably.

Consumers also acquire knowledge about products and services through indirect, **vicarious interactions** with the product. That is, consumers may acquire new meaning nodes in memory by observing other people using a product. Most vicarious experiences happen accidentally as a consumer randomly comes into contact with people who are using a product.

---

[28]A.C. Nielsen Co. (1979), *The Television Audience,* Chicago: A.C. Nielsen.

[29]Richard P. Adler, ed. (1980), *The Effects of Television Advertising on Children,* Lexington, Mass.: Lexington Books.

[30]Russell Belk, Robert Mayer and Amy Driscoll (1984), "Children's Recognition of Consumption Symbolism in Children's Products," *Journal of Consumer Research* (December), pp. 306–312.

Brands with higher market shares have an advantage over less-popular brands, because consumers are more likely to have vicarious interactions with a widely used brand. Fads, such as the latest clothing fashion on campus, can spread rapidly as consumers vicariously experience the product through observing increasing numbers of users. Marketers sometimes develop strategies that create opportunities for consumers to have vicarious interactions with a product. For instance, skiing and windsurfing shops may show videotapes of people using the product. Procter & Gamble is well known for using slice-of-life TV commercials that attempt to portray "ordinary" consumers in "natural situations" using the product and demonstrating its effectiveness (e.g., two women discussing Bold laundry detergent over a pile of dirty laundry).

Finally, much of consumers' product knowledge is learned through **interactions with product-related information** conveyed by mass media (news stories and advertising) and by personal sources (friends and family members). Frequently, this information is in the form of a direct product statement or a product claim. These messages are interpreted by consumers' cognitive processes, and the resulting meanings may affect behavior (refer back to Figure 3–2). We will discuss these cognitive processes and related issues in Chapter 6.

Levels of Learning

The various types of behavioral interactions that consumers have with their environments can result in three broad types, or levels, of learning—accretion, tuning, and restructuring.[31] As shown in Figure 4–8, the three **levels of learning** involve different types of changes in consumers' knowledge structures over time.

Accretion

Learning by **accretion** involves adding new meanings to existing knowledge structures. A vast amount of consumer learning, especially of simple information, occurs through accretion processes. Consumers are continually exposed to new information about products, brands, stores, etc. through their interactions with the environment. As this information is interpreted by cognitive processes, it is represented as new meanings and added to existing knowledge structures. Most research in cognitive psychology and consumer behavior has focused on learning single facts or beliefs through accretion processes. Although this simple level of learning

[31]David E. Rumelhart and Donald A. Norman (1978), "Accretion, Tuning and Restructuring: Three Modes of Learning," in *Semantic Factors in Cognition*, J.W. Cotton and R.L. Klatsky (eds.), Hillsdale, N.J.: Lawrence Erlbaum, pp. 37–53.

FIGURE 4–8   *Three Levels of Learning*

Type of cognitive learning

Changes in knowledge structure

Accretion
   Consumer begins to acquire knowledge, meanings, and beliefs about Nike shoes. With various experiences, new meaning nodes are connected to the "Nike shoes" concept.

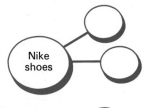

Consumer continues to add new meanings and beliefs to the knowledge structure for Nike shoes.

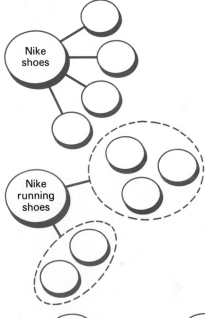

Tuning
   Consumer forms an overall meaning for entire knowledge structure that summarizes all the meanings and beliefs: "Nike shoes are running shoes." Various attributes are interpreted in terms of overall meaning. Knowledge becomes "chunked." More abstract categories are formed.

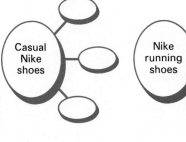

Restructuring
   As consumer accumulates more experience, he/she learns that "Nike running shoes are highly variable. Not all Nike shoes are suitable for running." A restructuring of knowledge takes place. Separate knowledge structures, each with its own unique set of knowledge, meanings and beliefs, are formed for the different types of Nike shoes that the consumer perceives.

is critically important, there is much more to learning than the accumulation of isolated bits of knowledge. More complex learning involves changes in the structure of the knowledge network.

Tuning

As consumers gain experience with a product, they may "adjust" their knowledge representations, bringing them into better correspondence with the environment, as well as making them more generalizable. This process is known as **tuning.** Knowledge structures at various levels of abstraction are probably continually undergoing minor changes in meaning (fine tuning) as a function of consumers' ongoing interactions with the environment. As shown in Figure 4–8, as a consumer learns more about a product, the overall meaning of the product may change, sometimes subtly.

Restructuring

Learning through restructuring is a more effortful type of learning with potentially far-reaching consequences. Consequently, restructuring is less

Courtesy Nike.

This ad is designed to restructure consumers' knowledge about Nike shoes.

common than accretion or tuning processes. As shown in Figure 4–8, **restructuring** involves creating entirely new meaning structures and/or imposing new organizations on old knowledge structures. The new knowledge structures provide new meanings and fresh interpretations to a once-familiar domain of knowledge. Although restructuring occurs only infrequently, when it does, the results can have significant effects on cognitive processes and behavior.

Although accretion, and some tuning processes, can occur without much cognitive effort (that is, essentially automatically), restructuring involves controlled cognitive processes that may require substantial time (perhaps hours or days) and substantial thinking/reasoning effort. Thus, restructuring tends to occur only when existing knowledge structures have become so unwieldy and inaccurate that the consumer must do something about it. Sometimes the introduction of a new product that is quite different from existing products forces adopters to restructure their existing knowledge to accommodate the new information. For instance, many consumers had to restructure their knowledge about cooking techniques when using microwave ovens.

In sum, consumers' acquisition of knowledge, meanings, and beliefs is an evolutionary process that begins with accretion processes and may end with restructuring. Although all three levels of learning have behavioral implications, tuning and restructuring have a greater potential for causing significant changes in consumption behavior.

Back to the Case

The ultimate success of low-alcohol beer depends on the meanings and knowledge structures that consumers acquire through their behaviors, such as trying the product, seeing others using the product, and seeing advertising and other promotion strategies tried by the marketers of low-alcohol beer. Over time, consumers will acquire product meanings that are organized into a structure of interrelated knowledge. These knowledge structures, along with aspects of the general environment and marketers' continuing strategies, will affect consumers' future behaviors involving these products.

At this point, predicting the eventual success of low-alcohol beers is impossible. However, after reading this chapter, you know enough to ask relevant questions about the problems of consumer knowledge and meaning faced by Anheuser-Busch management in marketing their low-alcohol beer, LA. For instance, are consumers likely to form a new category of meaning within the beer product class that includes LA and its several competitors? This would make low-alcohol beer a separate product form, like light beer. If the various LA brands generate sufficient sales to stay on the market, it seems likely that consumers will eventually acquire a special product-form meaning, which might be labeled "low-alcohol beer." Other relevant questions that you might generate include: What knowledge structures do consumers have for the Anheuser-

Busch brand, LA? What does the special attribute "low-alcohol content" mean to consumers? Answering these questions requires that A-B conduct marketing research to measure the content of consumers' knowledge structures.

The concepts discussed in this chapter can help you (or the A-B management) think about such issues and research them. In the next chapter, we will examine consumers' product knowledge in more detail and consider alternative marketing strategies for dealing with consumers' knowledge structures.

Summary

Consumers' knowledge, meanings, and beliefs have powerful effects on the cognitive processes involved in consumer decision making, on the outcomes of those processes, and on overt purchasing behaviors. In this chapter, we discussed several aspects of consumers' knowledge, including types of meanings and their content, levels of abstraction, and organization of knowledge. We also discussed the important processes of categorization, chunking, and abstraction by which meanings are created and organized. We also described two larger knowledge structures, schemas and scripts, and briefly considered how they affect cognitive processes and behaviors. We made a distinction between four levels of abstraction of consumers' product knowledge—product class, product form, brand, and model knowledge. We concluded by discussing how knowledge, meanings, and beliefs are acquired through socialization processes and the cognitive learning processes of accretion, tuning, and restructuring. In sum, this chapter provides a general overview of consumers' knowledge. In the next chapter, we will examine consumers' knowledge, meanings, and beliefs concerning products and brands in greater detail.

Additional Reading

Raymond R. Burke (1985), "A Model of Consumer Cognition," Working Paper #85-015, The Wharton School, University of Pennsylvania (February), 91 pages.

Michael D. Johnson and Jolita Kisielius (1985), "Concreteness-Abstractness and the Feature-Dimension Distinction," in *Advances in Consumer Research*, Vol. 12, E.C. Hirschman and M.B. Holbrook (eds.), Ann Arbor, Mich.: Association for Consumer Research, pp. 325–328.

Rajesh Kanwar, Jerry C. Olson and Laura S. Sims (1981), "Toward Conceptualizing and Measuring Cognitive Structures," in *Advances in Consumer*

Research, Vol. 8, Kent B. Monroe (ed.), Ann Arbor, Mich.: Association for Consumer Research, pp. 122–127.

John R. Rossiter (1980), "Representation of Information in Memory: Some General Issues," in *Advances in Consumer Research*, Vol. 7, J.C. Olson (ed.), Ann Arbor, Mich.: Association for Consumer Research, pp. 429–430.

Thomas K. Srull (1982), "The Representation of Consumer Information in Memory," in *Advances in Consumer Research*, Vol. 9, A.A. Mitchell (ed.), Ann Arbor, Mich.: Association for Consumer Research, pp. 499–501.

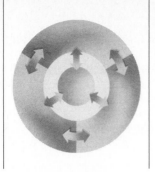

Chapter Five

Consumers' Product Knowledge and Involvement

What Do You Call This Thing?

What's the difference between a micro, a mini, a supermini, a minisuper, and a mainframe computer? Don't feel bad if you don't know; neither do the experts.

This may not be just an esoteric semantic issue. It could be a serious meaning problem which some industry analysts think was partly to blame for the dramatic slowdown in 1985 computer sales. Consumers seem to be confused about the computer product category and the various product forms and brands; and confused consumers tend not to buy. What types of product knowledge do consumers have about computers?

Some people focus on the nuts and bolts of the machines—the machine's physical *attributes*—in trying to distinguish between them. According to Henry Kee, manager of personal computing for Chemical Bank, one simple definition is based on circuitry—the arithmetical logic of the central processing unit (CPU). On a micro, the CPU is on a chip; on a mini, it is on a board; and the CPU is on a series of boards in a mainframe. But there are numerous exceptions. For instance, one micro has two CPU chips; what is it—a supermicro?

Other "experts" like to consider word length—the amount of data a computer can handle in a single operation—as the key distinction. But some micros can handle the same word lengths as many mainframe computers—up to 32 bits.

Perhaps a more reasonable suggestion is to think about computers in terms of what they can do . . . the *benefits* they offer the consumer. If you only have small amounts of data to process and you are the only user, then a micro computer is probably the right one for you. If you have more data and need to share it with a few other people, then a mini is probably appropriate. If you have huge amounts of data to be shared with many people, you probably need a mainframe. The key meanings concern what is to be accomplished. As Kee says, "People buy computers for what they can do, not for what they are."

Source: Owen Davies (1985), "What Do You Call the Damned Thing?" Forbes *(July 1), p.108.*

Consumers have knowledge about a great many aspects of their environments. However, most of these aspects of consumers' knowledge have not been studied extensively, because marketers have been most interested in consumers' **product knowledge.** In particular, marketers are concerned with what consumers think about specific *brands* within a product class. Thus, the bulk of marketing research has been focused on consumers' product and brand knowledge.

We begin this chapter by examining three types or levels of consumers' meanings for products and brands, which have been considered in past marketing research. Consumers can represent products and brands in terms of physical attributes, the benefits they provide, or the values they help satisfy (see Figure 5–1). The next section in the chapter shows how these levels can be linked together to form a simple associative network or schema of product knowledge, called a means-end chain. Finally, we examine how means-end chains of product knowledge can help marketers understand consumers' involvement with products and brands.

Products and Brands as Bundles of Attributes

Decisions about product characteristics or attributes are important elements of marketing strategy. Within the limits imposed by production capabilities and financial resources, marketing managers can add new attributes to a product ("Now, Diet 7UP contains 100% NutraSweet"), *remove* old attributes ("caffeine-free Diet Pepsi"), or *modify* existing attributes (in 1985, Coca-Cola managers modified the century-old secret recipe for Coke). By changing brand attributes, marketers hope to make their products more appealing to consumers. For instance, chemists at Procter & Gamble created a new molecule and included twice as many active ingre-

FIGURE 5–1   **What Is a Product?**

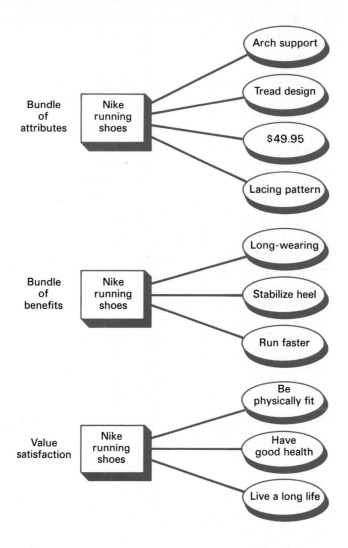

dients as competitive brands to give Liquid Tide its cleaning power.[1] The 400,000 hours of research and development time seemed to pay off; Liquid Tide's initial sales skyrocketed.

[1]Zachary Schiller and Mark N. Varmos (1984), "Liquid Tide Looks Like Solid Gold," *Business Week* (December 24), p. 32.

Perhaps because they spend so much time considering the physical characteristics of their products and brands, many marketers act as if consumers do, too. In fact, consumers have been characterized as thinking about products and brands as **bundles of attributes.**[2] Of course, products do have attributes. Even simple products such as pencils have quite a few tangible attributes (shape, color, lead density, softness of eraser). And complex products such as automobiles and stereo receivers have a great many attributes (see Highlight 5–1).

From a cognitive processing perspective, we might wonder whether consumers have knowledge about all of these attributes, and whether consumers actually consider them when thinking about the products or brands. Given the limited capacity of the human cognitive processing system, we know that consumers can consider only a few product attributes at a time, as when making a purchase decision. This raises questions such as which product attributes are most important to consumers, how knowledge about those attributes is represented in memory, and how different brands are rated on each attribute. An immense amount of marketing research has attempted to answer questions like these.

Levels of Abstraction

Our discussion of **levels of abstraction** in Chapter 4 suggests that consumers have knowledge about product attributes at different levels of abstraction. To date, however, few marketing research studies have addressed this idea.[3] In one exception, three levels of product attributes were identified:[4]

- The "A" level includes *abstract, multidimensional, difficult-to-measure,* more *subjective* attributes, such as the quality of a blanket or the style of a car. These attributes are abstract chunks that subsume

---

[2]Jonathan Gutman (1977), "Uncovering the Distinctions People Make Versus the Use of Multi-Attribute Models: Do a Number of Little Truths Make Wisdom?" in *Proceedings of the Twenty-Third Annual Conference of the Advertising Research Foundation,* New York: Advertising Research Foundation, pp. 71–76; William L. Wilkie and Edgar A. Pessemier (1973), "Issues in Marketing's Use of Multi-Attribute Attitude Models," *Journal of Marketing Research* (November), pp. 428–441.

[3]See Elizabeth C. Hirschman (1980), "Attributes of Attributes and Layers of Meaning," in *Advances in Consumer Research,* Vol. 7, Jerry C. Olson (ed.), Ann Arbor, Mich.: Association for Consumer Research, pp. 7–12.

[4]Lyle V. Geistfeld, George B. Sproles and Susan B. Badenhop (1977), "The Concept and Measurement of a Hierarchy of Product Characteristics," in *Advances in Consumer Research,* Vol. 4, H.K. Hunt (ed.), Ann Arbor, Mich.: Association for Consumer Research, pp. 302–307.

HIGHLIGHT 5–1   **New Attributes for Automobiles**

After a decade of down sizing and economizing, automakers are delighted to be up scaling again. They are adding fancy attributes to cars to make them more fun, more carefree, safer, and more costly. As always, affluent drivers—those with more than $15,000 to spend—will have the most exotic features to select from. Between now and the early 1990s, you will find many new attributes on the cars in your dealer's showroom.

In fact, some of the attributes are already here. For an extra $1,000 or so, you can get a turbocharger to knock a few seconds off your zero-to-speeding-ticket time. Of course, expensive car stereo systems have been around for a long time. By 1987 or so, car makers will be offering digital disk players for the most avid audiophiles.

What else is coming? Cadillac already has computerized rearview mirrors that automatically adjust to day and night driving. Audi has developed computerized "memory seats" that automatically assume the settings preferred by up to four different drivers. Trip computers are becoming common. Nissan offers a hood-raindrop-detector option for about $40. By the mid-1990s, your car might be able to recognize your approach from your infrared key. The car would automatically open the door and adjust the climate control, the seat, the mirrors, and the handling to suit you—and then start the engine.

Not all the new attributes are so frivolous. Antilock brakes are now available on some cars. They offer a driver rapid stopping with the ability to maneuver while braking. Many more companies are expected to offer four-wheel drive, among them Porsche, BMW, and Ford. For a more exotic attribute, consider four-wheel steering being developed by several Japanese companies. A computer adjusts the direction and amount of steering to be applied to the rear wheels, according to the car's speed. Changing lanes at highway speeds is an uncanny experience. The car seems to move sideways with disconcerting smoothness and ease. And think of how easy it will be to parallel park!

Some of the new attributes, such as more than two valves per cylinder and changing the spark-plug location, will increase fuel efficiency, perhaps as much as another 15 percent over the next five years. New, variable-speed automatic transmissions, plastic and aluminum bodies, and—of course—many more computerized functions are among the new attributes you can look forward to learning about on your next new car.

Source: Peter Petre (1985), "The High-Tech Car Hits the Road," Fortune *(April 29), pp. 204–224.*

less abstract concepts. These A-level meanings are probably most relevant at the product-class and product-form levels.

■ The "B" level contains *less abstract,* still multidimensional, but *more easily measured,* more *objective* attributes, such as the warmth of a blanket or the comfort of a car. These attributes are somewhat more tangible, in that they can be experienced in a fairly direct way; however, they are not physical characteristics of the product. These moderately abstract meanings seem most relevant to the product-class or product-form levels.

■ The "C" level includes *concrete,* one-dimensional, *directly measurable, objective* attributes, such as the type of fiber in a blanket or the front-seat leg room in a car. These are simple, physical attributes of the product. They are tangible, in that consumers can directly experience them through the various senses, or they can be directly measured through standardized procedures. These concrete attributes seem most relevant to the brand or model/feature levels.

Products and Brands as Bundles of Benefits

A number of marketers have criticized the production-oriented emphasis on product attributes (see Highlight 5–2). Theodore Levitt was among the first to suggest that consumers tend to think about products and brands in terms of their positive *consequences,* not their physical attributes.[5] When a consumer buys a product or brand and begins to use it, a number of different outcomes or consequences may occur. The product might work well, or it might be harmful. It might require assembly or repair. Perhaps other consumers will think the buyer is foolish or clever, and so on. *Positive* consequences of product purchase and use are called **benefits,** while potential negative consequences are **perceived risks** of product use.

Gradually, marketers have come to see that many consumers are buying a **bundle of benefits** (not attributes) when they purchase a product.[6] This perspective lead to the idea of **benefit segmentation,** by which marketers divide consumers into homogeneous subgroups or segments based on their knowledge about the perceived benefits stemming from product use.[7] For example, some consumers emphasize the cosmetic benefits of toothpaste (white teeth), while other consumers are more concerned with medicinal benefits such as preventing tooth decay.

---

[5]Theodore Levitt (1960), "Marketing Myopia," *Harvard Business Review* (July/August), pp. 45–56.

[6]For instance, see Paul E. Green, Yoram Wind and Arun K. Jain (1972), "Benefit Bundle Analysis," *Journal of Advertising Research* (April), pp. 32–36.

[7]Russell I. Haley (1972), "Benefit Segmentation: A Decision-Oriented Research Tool," *Journal of Marketing* (July), pp. 30–35.

In 1980, Frazier Purdy, then chairman of the board of Young & Rubicam, currently the largest advertising agency in the world, made a speech titled "Attributes of Benefits." His main point was the same as Theodore Levitt's—consumers don't buy attributes, they buy benefits. According to Purdy, consumers "don't buy technology or engineering. They buy products to make them healthier, more esteemed, more attractive, thinner, prettier, wiser, manlier, shrewder, younger, richer, more desirable, happier, etc., etc., etc. Consumers don't give a damn how a car works. What they want to know is how it will work for them. Consumers don't care what's in cat food or dog food. They want to be loved by their pets."

Purdy told a story about Samuel Johnson, the great 18th century British critic and lexicographer who happened to be in charge of auctioning off the old Anchor Brewery in London. In introducing the auction, Johnson showed his intuitive understanding of the power of benefits. He ignored the attributes of the brewery, such as its location, equipment, fixtures, and capacity. Instead he used this appeal: "We are not here to sell boilers and vats, but the potentiality of growing rich beyond the dreams of avarice."

According to Purdy, "That's what [advertising's] all about. Holding out to the consumers the potentiality of gain, of advantage, of benefit."

Source: Based on Frazier Purdy (1980), "Attributes of Benefits," a speech given to the General Foods Creative Seminar (September), Harrison Inn.

Types of Consequences

A number of schemes have been developed to organize and categorize benefits. One distinction mentioned above is between *positive consequences* (or benefits) and *negative consequences* (or perceived risk) of product use. The importance of this distinction is considered in Chapter 8, which deals with consumer decision making.

Another useful distinction is between the direct, functional consequences of product use, and the less tangible, more abstract psychological and social consequences of product use. **Functional consequences** include the immediate physiological outcomes of product use (a Hershey candy bar satisfies your hunger; a Pepsi satisfies your thirst). Functional consequences also include the direct, tangible outcomes that occur from using (consuming) the product. Hair dryers get your hair dry, toasters brown your toast, and pens write smoothly without skipping. In contrast, **psychological consequences** involve intangible, personal, and less direct outcomes of product use, such as how the product makes you feel. Using Nexxus shampoo might make you feel more attractive or confident; a Cal-

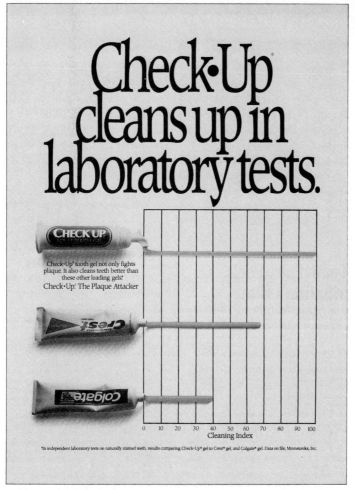

Courtesy Minnetonka, Inc.

This ad focuses on product benefits—reduced plaque and clean teeth.

vin Klein designer suit might make you feel younger or older or more important; an ice cream cone from Baskin-Robbins might make you feel happier. **Social consequences** are also less tangible, personal, indirect outcomes that involve our perceptions of other peoples' reactions to us. (My friends will like /respect /envy me if I buy this Pioneer stereo system; my mother will think I am a smart shopper if I buy this jacket on sale.) Psychological and social consequences can be grouped together and called psychosocial consequences.

Products and Brands as Value Satisfiers

Consumers may perceive products and brands as providing consequences that are even more abstract than functional and psychological/social benefits. These very abstract outcomes are called **values.** Values are the abstract consequences associated with such questions as, "What do you want out of life?"; whereas functional and psychosocial **benefits** are consequences at the more immediate and concrete level of, "What do you want from this product?" This distinction between the less abstract benefits and the more abstract values that accrue from product use is important, as both levels of meaning have important marketing implications.

What Are Values?

Values are the cognitive representations of consumers' most basic and fundamental *needs and goals*. Stated differently, values are consumers' mental representations of the important **end states** they are trying to achieve in their lives.

Instrumental and Terminal Values

The ideas of Milton Rokeach have had a great influence on consumer value research.[8] Rokeach identified two types of values, instrumental and terminal, at two levels of abstraction. **Instrumental values** represent a *preferred mode of conduct* or a preferred pattern of behavior. For example, one consumer may have a strong instrumental value (goal/need) characterized as "having a good time." Another consumer might have the instrumental values of "independence" and "self-reliance." Possessing these values means that both consumers will strive, in general, to behave in accordance with these objectives. **Terminal values** represent *preferred end states of being.* Terminal values (such as happiness or wisdom) are the symbolic representations of goals and objectives that are somewhat more abstract than instrumental values. Terminal values are the major, global goals (*ends*) that consumers are trying to achieve in their lives. The basic values in consumers' knowledge structures have a powerful and pervasive influence on their cognitive processes and their overt behaviors. For instance, we would expect consumers with different value structures to buy different products to achieve those values, or to buy the same product for different reasons.

---

[8]Milton J. Rokeach (1968), *Beliefs, Attitudes and Values,* San Francisco: Jossey-Bass; Milton J. Rokeach (1973), *The Nature of Human Values,* New York: Free Press.

Courtesy Etonic, Inc.

This ad appeals to consumer values—social recognition and sense of accomplishment.

Rokeach's Values

Rokeach identified 18 instrumental and 18 terminal values.[9] Figure 5–2 lists these values organized into broad categories based on the results of a

---

[9]According to Russell A. Jones, John Sensenig and Richard D. Ashmore (1978), "Systems of Values and Their Multidimensional Representations," *Multivariate Behavioral Research* pp. 255–270, Rokeach based these values on his study of the research literature, personal introspection, and interviews with graduate students and a small sample of adults.

consumer survey.[10] Although they have been widely used in consumer research, the Rokeach values should not be considered as the definitive set of values held by all American consumers. In fact, other researchers have developed different categorizations.[11] Indeed, it is questionable whether a standard set of values can ever be identified for a market as diverse as the American population. The Rokeach values are suggestive of the basic values and held by many—but certainly not all—American consumers.

Values and Consumers' Self-Concepts

As you look over the values in Figure 5–2, consider which values are most influential in your life. Are they different from the dominant values in your parents' lives? Can you identify specific values at both the instrumental and terminal levels that are especially important to how you think about yourself and what you want out of life? These are your **central** or **core values**—the most basic needs you are trying to satisfy through your behaviors. Perhaps some of your values are somewhat vague and shadowy, particularly if you seldom think about your major goals and needs.

Core values, goals, and needs constitute the major part of consumers' **self-concepts**—their self-schemas or knowledge structures about themselves. Because of their central importance, the core values in self-schemas have a major influence on consumers' purchasing behavior, as Highlight 5–3 illustrates. Products that consumers closely associate with their self-schemas are considered to be high in involvement, a topic discussed later in this chapter.

Marketing Implications

Marketers know that subgroups of consumers may vary considerably in terms of the values they consider important. Therefore, the value structure of a specific target group of consumers should be determined directly, because differences in consumers' values are likely to create differences in purchasing behaviors.

It should also be noted that although consumers' values are reason-

---

[10]Donald E. Vinson, J. Michael Munson and Masao Nakanishi (1977), "An Investigation of the Rokeach Value Survey for Consumer Research Applications," in *Advances in Consumer Research,* Vol. 4, W.D. Perreault (ed.), Atlanta, Ga.: Association for Consumer Research, pp. 247–252.

[11]For instance, see Jonathan Gutman and Donald E. Vinson (1979), "Value Structures and Consumer Behavior," *Advances in Consumer Research,* Vol. 6, W. L. Wilkie (ed.), Ann Arbor, Mich.: Association for Consumer Research, pp. 335–339; Jones, Sensenig and Ashmore, "Systems of Values and their Multidimensional Representations"; Janice G. Hanna (1980), "A Typology of Consumer Needs," in *Research in Marketing,* Vol. 3, J.N. Sheth (ed.), Greenwich, Conn: JAI Press, pp. 83–104.

ably stable, they are not fixed. These values can and do gradually change over time as consumers mature and society changes. For instance, consider how the values of millions of American consumers have changed over the past few years as concern for personal health and fitness has grown and spread. These value changes have created many new markets. As an ex-

---

FIGURE 5–2   *Instrumental and Terminal Values*

Instrumental Values
(Preferred Modes of Conduct)

Competence
   Ambitious (hardworking)
   Independent (self-reliant)
   Imaginative (creative)
   Capable (competent)
   Logical (rational)
   Courageous

Compassion
   Forgiving (pardon others)
   Helpful (work for others)
   Cheerful (joyful)
   Loving (affectionate)

Sociality
   Polite (courteous)
   Obedient (dutiful)
   Clean (neat, tidy)

Integrity
   Responsible (reliable)
   Honest (sincere)
   Self-controlled

Terminal Values
(Preferred End States of Being)

Social harmony
   World at peace
   Equality (brotherhood)
   Freedom (independence)
   National security
   Salvation (eternal life)

Personal gratification
   Social recognition
   Comfortable life
   Pleasure (enjoyable life)
   Sense of accomplishment

Self-actualization
   Beauty (nature and arts)
   Wisdom (understanding)
   Inner harmony (no conflict)
   Self-respect (self-esteem)
   Sense of accomplishment

Security
   Taking care of family
   Salvation (eternal life)

Love and affection
   Mature love (sexual and spiritual intimacy)
   True friendship (close companionship)

Personal contentedness
   Happiness (contentment)

Source: The values (boldfaced headings) are from Milton J. Rokeach (1973), The Nature of Human Values, *New York: Free Press. The italicized headings are the category labels for groupings of Rokeach's values identified by Donald E. Vinson, J. Michael Munson and Masao Nakanishi (1977), "An Investigation of the Rokeach Value Survey for Consumer Research Applications," in* Advances in Consumer Research, *Vol. 4, W. D. Perreault, (ed.), Atlanta, Ga.: Association for Consumer Research, pp. 247–252.*

HIGHLIGHT 5–3   **What Makes Johnny and Mary Run . . . Such a Long Way?**

Among the many Americans who have come to value physical fitness over the past decade, tri-atheletes are among the most extreme. In 1985, some 1.1 million Americans are expected to sweat their way through about 2,100 grueling three-way competitions, usually involving swimming, bicycling, and running. According to *Triathlon Magazine,* the average triathelete is a 34-year-old college graduate earning about $45,000 a year. Many of these participants train up to 30 hours per week, on top of their regular, often time-consuming jobs. And they spend millions to acquire the equipment for the sport—fancy swimming goggles, high-priced bicycles, and state-of-the-art running gear. What values influence these driven consumers? Of course, triatheletes value fitness (in the extreme). At the instrumental value level, triatheletes probably seek exciting activities and adventure. At the terminal value level, they may strive for achievement, courage, and self-esteem.

Source: Teresa Carson (1985), "The Spartan Sport that Draws Big Spenders," Business Week *(February 18), p. 148.*

ample, demand has increased dramatically for exercise equipment, more healthful foods such as pasta, fish, and vegetables, and low-calorie beers and sugar-free soft drinks. In contrast, market demand for products such as beef and liquor are shrinking, partly because of these changes in consumers' basic values.

In sum, values are a critically important influence on consumers' behavior. Figure 5–3 summarizes several important points about consumers' values. Given the pervasive influence of values on consumer behavior and the rapid changes in the dominant values of several population segments over the past 20 or 30 years, many marketers are monitoring such changes and trends to develop and maintain effective marketing strategies. They often use commercial services, such as the *Yankelovich Monitor,* which regularly collect data about the values held by specific populations and identify changes and trends. This information is sold to subscribing companies.

Linking Attributes, Consequences, and Values

Thus far, you have seen that consumers have knowledge about product attributes, consequences, and values. These product meanings represent three different levels of abstraction. Most marketing research has focused on only one level of consumers' product knowledge—typically the attrib-

---

FIGURE 5–3   ***Important Aspects of Consumers' Values***

- Values are *subjective,* not objective "truth."
- Values are *idiosyncratic* to each consumer. They are person-centered, not object-centered.
- Values have *intrinsic worth.* Terminal values, at least, lead nowhere else. They are *ends.*
- The worth or importance of a value may be *personal* (for the person holding the value), or the person may see the importance as broader, perhaps even for society as a whole.
- Values are *formed from personal experiences,* many of them develop during infancy and early childhood. Family and reference groups have a major socializing role in creating values in consumers.
- Values tend to be *enduring* and *stable.* However, values can change, sometimes gradually over time, sometimes more dramatically as a function of a major life event.
- Some values may be *widely held* by persons in a group or a subculture. Certain values may even be shared by most people in a society. In fact, most human beings in the world share certain values, such as family security.
- Values function as a *focal point* in many cognitive tasks, such as attitude formation or decision making about a brand purchase.
- Values serve to *organize* the meaning representations for products and brands stored in consumers' knowledge structures.

ute level, occasionally the benefit/consequence level. Unfortunately, as we noted earlier, attention to a single level of meaning gives marketers only a partial understanding of consumers' product knowledge. In this section, we will see how consumers combine these cognitive representations of attributes, consequences, and values into propositions and organize them into a hierarchical associative network or **schema.**

Several researchers have developed conceptual models of consumers' knowledge structures that combine different levels of consumers' product meanings.[12] Although different terminology is used, each model includes

---

[12]See Shirley Young and Barbara Feigen (1975), "Using the Benefit Chain for Improved Strategy Formulation," *Journal of Marketing* (July), pp. 72–74; James H. Myers and Alan D. Shocker (1981), "The Nature of Product-Related Attributes," in *Research in Marketing* J.N. Sheth (ed.), Greenwich, Conn.: JAI Press, pp. 211–236; Jon Gutman and Thomas J. Reynolds (1979), "An Investigation of the Levels of Cognitive Abstraction Utilized by Consumers in Product Differentiation," in *Attitude Research under the Sun,* J. Eighmey (ed.), Chicago: American Marketing Association, pp. 128–150; Joel B. Cohen (1979), "The Structure of Product Attributes: Defining Attribute Dimensions for Planning and Evaluation," in *Analytic Approaches to Product and Marketing Planning,* A.D. Shocker (ed.), Cambridge, Mass.: Marketing Science Institute, pp. 54–86.

Courtesy Nabisco Brands, Inc.

This ad focuses on product attributes—high fiber, low sugar, and low salt.

the three basic components of consumers' product knowledge identified above—attributes, consequences, and values. Each model proposes a simple, hierarchically organized schema of consumers' product knowledge, ranging from product meanings at the attribute level to higher-order, more abstract consequences of product use, to values. The resulting knowledge schema is called a **means-end chain.**[13] That is, the attributes are the *means* by which the product or brand provides more abstract consequences, which are the *ends*. The ends could be benefit consequences or values.[14]

Means-End Chains of Product Knowledge

The basic means-end chain is a simple hierarchical knowledge structure or schema containing attribute, consequence, and value nodes connected by propositional links. A more complex and complete means-end chain can be produced by dividing each basic level into two sublevels that differ in level of abstraction.[15]

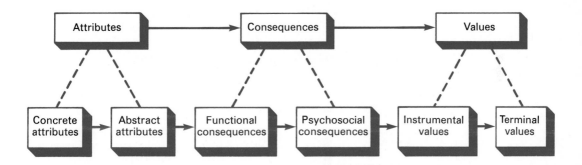

Figure 5–4 presents examples of this means-end chain and a definition of each of the six levels of product meaning. Although each level of meaning has been examined in marketing research studies, they seldom

---

[13]The basic idea of a means-end chain can be traced back at least to Edward C. Tolman (1932), *Purposive Behavior in Animals and Men,* New York: Century Company. Among the first to suggest its use in marketing was John A. Howard (1977), *Consumer Behavior: Application and Theory,* New York: McGraw-Hill. More recently, Jon Gutman, Tom Reynolds and Jerry Olson have been active proponents of means-end chain models. For example, see Jonathan Gutman and Thomas J. Reynolds (1979), "An Investigation of the Levels of Cognitive Abstraction Utilized by Consumers in Product Differentiation," in *Attitude Research under the Sun,* J. Eighmey (ed.), Chicago: American Marketing Association, pp. 125–150, and Jonathan Gutman (1982), "A Means-End Chain Model Based on Consumer Categorization Processes," *Journal of Marketing* (Spring), pp. 60–72; Jerry C. Olson and Thomas J. Reynolds (1983), "Understanding Consumers' Cognitive Structures: Implications for Marketing Strategy," in *Advertising and Consumer Psychology,* L. Percy and A.G. Woodside (eds.), Lexington, Mass.: Lexington Books, pp. 77–90.

[14]A similar model has been proposed by Donald E. Vinson, Jerry E. Scott and L.M. Lamont (1977), "The Role of Personal Values in Marketing and Consumer Behavior," *Journal of Marketing* (April), pp. 44–50.

[15]Olson and Reynolds, "Understanding Consumers' Cognitive Structures."

have been linked together and investigated as a single knowledge structure. Compared to the simple, three-stage, means-end chain, the more complex means-end chain allows a more detailed analysis of the hierarchical structure of meanings consumers may have for a product. Although this extra specificity can be useful for certain consumer analyses, the simple, three-element means-end chain shown above is sufficiently detailed for many marketing purposes.

Examples of Means-End Chains

Figure 5–5 presents part of one consumer's product and brand knowledge in terms of several means-end chains. Note that means-end chains have been produced for three different levels of product knowledge. The first

---

FIGURE 5–4   **A Means-End Chain Model of Consumers' Product Knowledge**

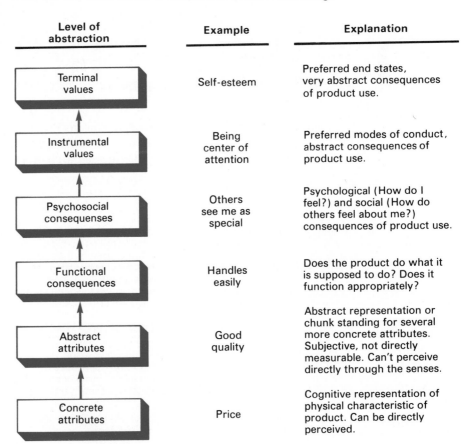

Level of abstraction	Example	Explanation
Terminal values	Self-esteem	Preferred end states, very abstract consequences of product use.
Instrumental values	Being center of attention	Preferred modes of conduct, abstract consequences of product use.
Psychosocial consequenses	Others see me as special	Psychological (How do I feel?) and social (How do others feel about me?) consequences of product use.
Functional consequences	Handles easily	Does the product do what it is supposed to do? Does it function appropriately?
Abstract attributes	Good quality	Abstract representation or chunk standing for several more concrete attributes. Subjective, not directly measurable. Can't perceive directly through the senses.
Concrete attributes	Price	Cognitive representation of physical characteristic of product. Can be directly perceived.

set of means-end chains represents knowledge at the *product-class* level, hair spray. The second set of means-end chains is for a specific *product form,* flavored potato chips. And the third set of means-end chains represents meanings for a specific *brand*, Scope mouthwash. These examples illustrate that consumers can have means-end knowledge schemas at different levels of product knowledge. We will use means-end chains to model consumers' product knowledge at the product class, product form, and brand levels.

Variations in Means-End Chains

Note that several of the examples shown in Figure 5–5 are means-end chains whose ends are at the most abstract level of terminal values. Not every means-end chain goes all the way to terminal values, however. In

---

FIGURE 5–5   **Examples of Means-End Chains**

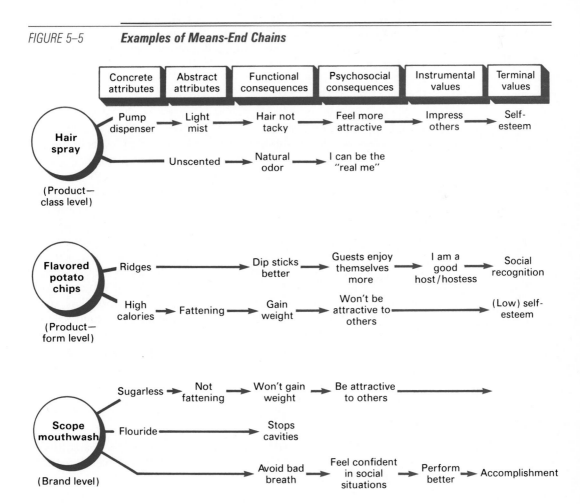

fact, the end in a means-end chain can be a consequence at any level of abstraction—from a functional consequence ("this toothpaste will give me fresh breath"), to a psychosocial outcome ("my friends will like being close to me"), to an instrumental value ("I will be clean"), to a terminal value ("I will be happy").

The length and content of a means-end chain depend on the content and organization of the semantic knowledge structures consumers have learned through their past experiences. Consumers do not necessarily perceive that every product attribute leads to a terminal or instrumental value. When product attributes are not connected to values, the means-end chains are short. In fact, some product attributes have virtually no connections to abstract consequences. These attributes have little meaning, because the consumer does not know what they are good for. Basically, the end level of a means-end chain reflects the extent to which consumers perceive the product or brand attribute as personally relevant to their self-concepts. Finally, note that some means-end chains in Figure 5–5 are incomplete. Sometimes levels of meaning are skipped. That is, consumers do not necessarily represent all six levels of product knowledge in each means-end chain.

Distinguishing between Levels

You should be aware that the differences between adjacent levels in the six-element means-end chain are often somewhat *fuzzy*. For instance, it can be difficult to tell whether a concept is a psychosocial consequence or an instrumental value. Fortunately, such fine distinctions are not critical for most marketing strategy purposes. Marketers seldom find it necessary to unambiguously categorize a product meaning into one of the six means-end levels. We have presented the complete means-end chain model to (a) demonstrate the subtlety with which product meanings can vary in abstraction, and (b) show that, at least in some circumstances, consumers may possess finely articulated, hierarchical schemas of product knowledge. For many purposes, the simple means-end chain model is sufficiently detailed. Fortunately, the three-element means-end chain seldom causes difficulties of interpretation, as the distinctions between attributes, consequences, and values are reasonably clear-cut.

Basic Assumptions Concerning Means-End Chains

The means-end chain approach to consumers' knowledge structures is based on several assumptions about consumer behavior. Several of these

FIGURE 5–6	***Basic Assumptions Underlying Means-End Chains***

- Consumers buy products primarily *to do something.* That is, consumers are interested in the ability of products to solve important problems or achieve important ends.

- Consumers' product knowledge is organized in terms of what products *do*—their *consequences.*
  Product attributes per se have relatively little meaning to consumers. Attribute meaning stems from the consequences attributes lead to.

- Consequences vary in *level of abstraction.*
  Some consequences concern functional outcomes of product use. Positive outcomes are called *benefits.*
  Some consequences involve psychosocial outcomes.
  Yet other consequences involve more abstract outcomes, such as the achievement of a value important to the consumer.

- The attribute, consequence, and value levels of product meanings are linked to form a special associative network of knowledge called a *means-end chain.*

- Means-end chains are knowledge structures by which consumers represent the connections between products and brands and their own personal needs, goals, and values—i.e., their self-concepts.

- Consumers' product knowledge exists at different levels of abstraction. Consumers may know about the attributes, consequences, and values provided by a product class, alternative product forms, different brands, and specific models.
  Consumers may have *several* means-end knowledge structures for a particular product class, product form, brand, or model.

assumptions are listed in Figure 5–6. Perhaps the most basic idea behind means-end chains is that the meaning of any concept is largely a function of the other concepts to which it is linked in an associative network of knowledge. That is, the dominant meaning of an attribute is based on the consequences the consumer perceives are associated with it.

For example, Gillette recently added a new feature, a lubricating strip, to their popular Atra razor.[16] But what does this attribute mean to consumers? Not much, until they can figure out the consequences of the strip for the shaving experience. The strip is intended to give users a

---

[16]Gay Jervey (1985), "Gillette and Bic Spots Taking on Sensitive Subject," *Advertising Age* (March 18), p. 53.

FIGURE 5–7   **A Desired Means-End Chain of Brand Knowledge**

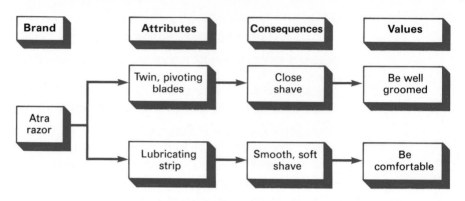

smooth and soft shave, rather than just a close shave. Gillette's strategy in adding the lubricating strip to their product is to provide an extra benefit to Atra users, and thus enhance overall attitudes toward the product. The schema that Gillette marketers hope consumers will learn can be diagrammed in the form of a means-end chain as shown in Figure 5–7.

In sum, the means-end chain approach is consistent with our emphasis on consumers' knowledge schemas as the set of meanings that consumers have formed and stored in their memories. We believe that means-end knowledge structures are particularly useful for marketing purposes. Thus, we will use means-end chains throughout this section to help us understand consumers' knowledge of the products and brands offered by marketers.

Applications of Means-End Chains

Using means-end chains to model consumers' knowledge structures for products and brands has many applications for marketing. For one, means-end chains permit a more detailed analysis of consumers' product knowledge. Marketing managers who are familiar with consumers' perceptions of attributes, benefits, and values as separate meanings find it useful to see how these meanings *fit together* to form hierarchical means-end knowledge structures.

Means-end chains also show how knowledge of product or brand attributes is related to consumers' basic values, goals, and needs, whether at the level of functional outcomes of product use or achieving the basic values inherent in consumers' self-concepts. Consider, for instance, the following means-end chain for Liquid Tide laundry detergent:

This hypothetical consumer interprets the chemical composition of Liquid Tide in terms of the more abstract attribute, "cleaning power." Cleaning power, in turn, is seen as providing the functional benefit of "clean clothes for the kids," which, in turn, helps achieve the instrumental value of

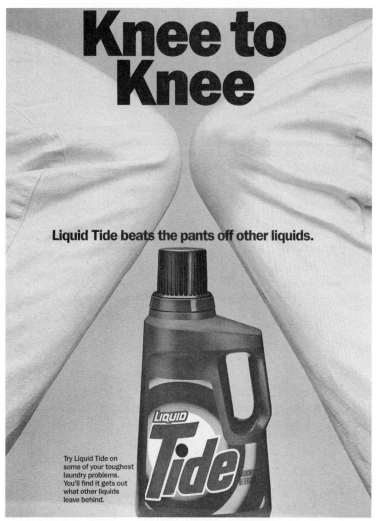

Courtesy Procter & Gamble Co.

In marketing Liquid Tide, P&G emphasized the abstract attribute of "cleaning power."

"being a good parent," which finally leads to the terminal value of "feeling good about myself" or "self-esteem."

By examining consumers' product knowledge in terms of means-end chains, marketers can develop a deeper understanding of consumers' meanings regarding product attributes and consequences. By identifying the links between meanings at different levels of abstraction, marketers can see much more clearly what consumers "mean" when they are thinking about an attribute or consequence. The means-end chain approach also facilitates developing marketing strategies. Because marketers can see where an attribute leads, they can devise more effective advertising strategies, for instance, to try to change the means-end chain. Understanding consumers' means-end chains is also useful in developing marketing strategies involving price, product, and distribution factors. We will not discuss specific marketing strategies here, as many are presented later in the text.

Product and Brand Involvement

Why do consumers seem to care about some products and brands and not about others? Why are consumers sometimes highly motivated to seek information, to learn about products, or to use products in certain situations? Why do other consumers seem not to be motivated at all? Why did some loyal Coke drinkers make such a big fuss when Coca-Cola managers made a minor change in an inexpensive, simple, and seemingly unimportant product such as a soft drink? (See Highlight 5–4.) These questions concern consumers' involvement with products and brands. In this section, we define the concept of product and brand involvement, examine two types of involvement, and consider some of the factors that affect consumers' involvement. In later chapters, we will explore its effects on the cognitive processes of interpretation and integration.

What Is Involvement?

Involvement has been a major concept in descriptions of consumer behavior for the past 20 years, and researchers have proposed many different definitions of it.[17] All of these emphasize the importance of the product to the

---

[17]A number of authors have reviewed the literature on consumer involvement, including John H. Antil (1984), "Conceptualization and Operationalization of Involvement," in *Advances in Consumer Research*, Vol. 11, T.C. Kinnear (ed.), Ann Arbor, Mich.: Association for Consumer Research, pp. 203–209; Peter H. Bloch (1981), "An Exploration into the Scaling of Consumers' Involvement With a Product Class," in *Advances in Consumer Research*, Vol. 8, K.B. Monroe (ed.), Ann Arbor, Mich.: Association for Consumer Research, pp. 61–65;

HIGHLIGHT 5–4   ***Coca-Cola Learns about Consumer Involvement***

In the spring of 1985, Coca-Cola shocked American consumers and other soft-drink manufacturers by announcing that the 99-year-old formula for Coke would be changed. The "new" Coke was a bit sweeter, and marketing research showed that it was preferred to Pepsi-Cola. The original Coke formula was to be retired to a bank vault and never again produced.

What happened then was the beginning of Coke's lesson in consumer involvement. Outraged U.S. consumers complained bitterly to the Atlanta-based company about the loss of "a great American tradition." In Seattle, a group of strident loyalists calling themselves "Old Coke Drinkers of America" laid plans to file a class-action suit against Coca-Cola. They searched out shop owners, vending-machine owners, and others willing to claim that the company's formula change had cost them business. Then, when June sales didn't pick up as expected, the bottlers also joined in the demand for old Coke's return—and fast.

Although Coca-Cola had spent some $4 million in testing the new formula, they had missed one important factor. Millions of consumers had a strong *emotional involvement* with the original Coke. They drank it as kids, and still did as adults. Many consumers had a personal attachment to Coke. Says a Coke spokesman, "We had taken away a little part of them and their past. They [consumers] said, 'You have no right to do that. Bring it back.' "

Coca-Cola had learned a costly lesson. Although consumers preferred the new taste in blind taste tests, Coca-Cola did not measure consumers' emotional reactions to removing the original Coke from the marketplace. Coca-Cola learned that a product is more than a production formula. "Extra meanings" such as emotions and strong connections to self-image may also be present.

Source: Adapted from Anne B. Fisher (1985), "Coke's Brand-Loyalty Lesson," Fortune (August 5), pp. 44–46.

consumer.[18] We define **involvement** as *degree of personal relevance,* which is a function of the extent to which the product or brand is perceived to help achieve consequences and values of importance to the consumer. The more important and central these desired consequences and values, the higher

---

Michael J. Houston and Michael L. Rothschild (1978), "Conceptual and Methodological Perspectives on Involvement," in *1978 Educators Proceedings,* S.C. Jain (ed.), Chicago: American Marketing Association, pp. 184–187; Gilles Laurent and Jean-Noel Kapferer (1985), "Measuring Consumer Involvement Profiles," *Journal of Consumer Research* (February), pp. 41–53; Andrew A. Mitchell (1981), "The Dimensions of Advertising Involvement," in *Advances in Consumer Research,* Vol. 8, K. Monroe (ed.), Ann Arbor, Mich.: Association for Consumer Research, pp. 25–30; Robert Stone (1984), "The Marketing Characteristics of Involvement," in *Advances in Consumer Research,* Vol. 11, T.C. Kinnear (ed.), Ann Arbor, Mich.: Association for Consumer Research, pp. 210–215.

[18]Peter H. Bloch and Marsha L. Richins (1983), "A Theoretical Model of the Study of Product Importance Perceptions," *Journal of Marketing* (Summer), pp. 69–81.

the consumer's level of personal involvement. Although marketing researchers often treat involvement as either high or low, it is actually a *continuum* that can vary from very low through moderate levels to very high degrees of personal relevance.

Involvement and Means-End Chains

Earlier in this chapter, you saw that consumers tend to perceive the attributes of products and brands in terms of their consequences. These meanings are organized into means-end chains of product knowledge (refer back to Figure 5–4). Means-end chains are also useful for analyzing consumers' involvement with products and brands. From a means-end perspective, involvement with a product or brand reflects the extent to which consumers' product knowledge is related to their self-knowledge about desirable values and goals. Thus, the more closely connected product knowledge about attributes and functional consequences is to more abstract psychosocial and value consequences, the more involved the consumer is with the product or brand.

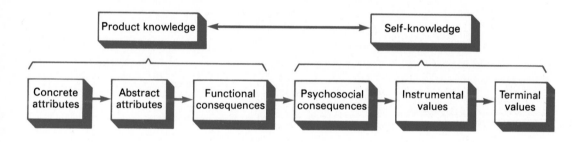

It is important to recognize that only a part of consumers' product knowledge is likely to be strongly linked to psychosocial consequences and values. For instance, consumers probably perceive relatively few products to be directly related to their terminal values. Probably, most products and brands are strongly linked to functional or psychosocial ends. This would mean that more products are moderate rather than high in involvement. In sum, for most consumers, a few products (automobiles, living-room furniture, business suits) are higher in involvement; more products (shampoo, shoes, cameras, sports equipment) are moderate in involvement; and quite a few products (toothpicks, chewing gum, facial tissues) are low in involvement. Of course, consumers vary considerably in terms of their relationships with any given product. Some may see a product or brand as rather closely tied to their values and goals, whereas others do not. Thus, marketers need to carefully evaluate the level of involvement in their target markets.

Involvement with What?

It is critically important that marketers clearly identify the *object* or *focus* of consumers' involvement. Marketers need to know exactly what it is that consumers find to be personally relevant. In a broad sense, consumers can be involved with *objects* (products, brands, stores, advertisements) in their environments or *behaviors* or *activities* in which they might engage.

Involvement with Products

Marketers are particularly interested in consumers' involvement with the products or services they sell. As you learned in Chapter 4, consumers may have product knowledge at four related levels—product class, product form, brand, and model. Thus, consumers may be "involved" with products at any or all of these levels. For instance, some consumers are involved with the product class or category, as is the teenager who is "into" cars. Cars in general are linked to important consequences (respect and envy of peers) and values (self-esteem) for such consumers. Other consumers may have substantial involvement with a particular product form, such as sports cars or mini vans. Still other consumers may be involved with a particular brand—Chevrolet or Toyota. Finally, some consumers may be involved with a specific model that represents a particular combination of product features, such as a turbocharged Ford Mustang SVO.

The various combinations of involvement with the product category and brand have different implications for marketing strategy. Figure 5–8 summarizes these relationships. Marketers may find it useful to segment consumers by the degree and level of their product and brand involvement and then develop special strategies for these different consumer/product relationships.

Involvement with Other Objects

Consumers may also be involved with other aspects of marketing strategy besides products and brands. For instance, consumers occasionally may become involved with an advertising campaign or a particular ad. Many consumers form a personal relationship with particular stores, such as a clothing store where they especially like to shop, or a favorite restaurant. As with products, consumers' involvement with other objects means that they perceive the characteristics of these objects as instrumental for achieving important consequences and values. Consumers may form emotional attachments to these objects and enjoy interacting with them.

Involvement with Behaviors

Consumers may also be involved with specific activities or particular behaviors. For instance, some people are involved in fairly sedentary activities such as needlework, painting, watching TV, or reading, whereas other people are involved in more vigorous activities such as skiing, playing golf or tennis, or jogging. Involvement with an activity means that consumers perceive characteristics of the activity as instrumental for achieving important consequences and values in their lives. For instance, the triatheletes described in Highlight 5–3 exemplify a high level of involvement with the physical activities listed (and probably also with a related set of products and brands).

FIGURE 5–8   **Consumer Segments Defined in Terms of Their Involvement with Product Category and Brand**

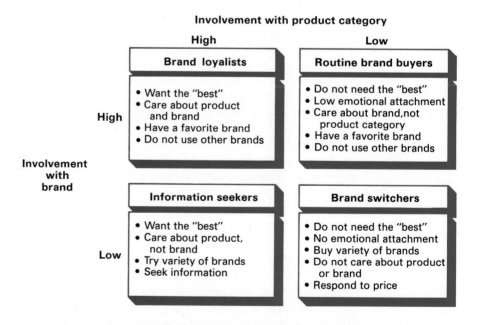

Source: Adapted from Peter Cushing and Melody Douglas-Tate (1985), "The Effect of People/Product Relationships on Advertising Processing," in Psychological Processes and Advertising Effects, Linda Alwitt and Andrew A. Mitchell (eds.), Hillsdale, N.J.: Lawrence Erlbaum, pp. 241–259.

Basis for Involvement

The level of involvement that a consumer experiences in a particular situation depends on the importance of the consequences, values, and goals that are activated in that situation. This is, the level of a consumer's felt involvement is a function of the end states in the means-end chains that are activated in a particular situation. The level of involvement a consumer feels in a situation reflects two types or sources of involvement: *enduring involvement* and *situational involvement.* Figure 5–9 presents a model of involvement that illustrates how these two factors combine to create the state of felt involvement that is experienced by consumers in a particular situation.

FIGURE 5–9   **A Basic Model of Consumer Involvement**

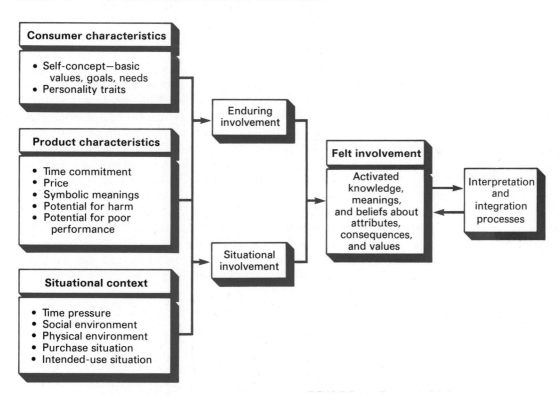

Source: Adapted from Peter H. Bloch and Marsha L. Richins (1983), "A Theoretical Model for the Study of Product Importance Perceptions," Journal of Marketing (Summer), pp. 69–81.

Enduring Involvement

Enduring involvement refers to the general personal relevance of a product or an activity. It is represented by means-end chains that link the attributes or characteristics of a product or activity with important consequences, values, and goals. These means-end relationships have been acquired (learned and stored in long-term memory) through past experiences as the consumer comes to see the product or activity as instrumental for achieving certain important consequences and value satisfactions. For example, over time, some consumers come to associate certain highly valued consequences with owning and using a high-quality stereo system. The knowledge structures that represent this enduring involvement may be activated in various situations and will affect subsequent cognitive processes (see Figure 5–9).

A key point to remember is that consumers' enduring involvement is based on their knowledge about consequences of *possessing, using,* or *consuming* the product. Consumption encompasses a wide range of consequences that may be important to consumers. For example, merely *possessing* a particular car, stereo system, or work of art may satisfy important values and goals of some consumers.[19] *Possession* tends to be an important component of the enduring involvement of avid collectors of stamps, antiques, wine, and similar products.

For other products, the consumption experiences of *using* certain products provide important affective and emotional consequences and value satisfactions. For instance, the experience (fun, pleasure, and enjoyment) of using products such as sports and recreational equipment (sailing your boat, driving your car, fishing, skiing, playing tennis or golf) can be substantial.[20] Many consumers have fairly high levels of enduring involvement with such hobby products. In addition, a variety of use activities called *product nurturing*—polishing your car, tinkering with your boat, or organizing your record collection—can provide pleasurable consequences and emotional satisfactions that help create and maintain the high levels of enduring involvement some consumers have for such products.[21]

In general, consumers have high levels of enduring involvement for relatively few objects and activities. Most consumers are not intensely interested in very many things. More products and activities are seen by

---

[19]See Russell W. Belk (1983), "Worldly Possessions: Issues and Criticisms," in *Advances in Consumer Research*, Vol. 10, R.P. Bagozzi and A.M. Tybout (eds.), Ann Arbor, Mich.: Association for Consumer Research, pp. 514–519.

[20]Morris B. Holbrook and Elizabeth C. Hirschman (1982), "The Experiential Aspects of Consumption: Consumer Fantasies, Feelings, and Fun," *Journal of Consumer Research* (September), pp. 132–140.

[21]See Peter H. Bloch and Marsha L. Richins (1983), "A Theoretical Model of the Study of Product Importance Perceptions," *Journal of Marketing* (Summer), pp. 69–81.

David S. Strickler: Click/Chicago

Product nurturing.

consumers as moderate in involvement and many are probably low in enduring involvement.

The level of enduring involvement with a product and brand is not fixed, however. Enduring involvement can change over time, as consumers' awareness and evaluations of the consequences of product use change. Consumers may lose interest in once-involving products and become increasingly interested (more involved) with others. For example, many teenagers perceive the symbolic meanings associated with certain clothing styles as extremely important for achieving consequences (peer recognition) and values (self esteem) that are important at that time of their lives. Thus, clothing may acquire a high level of enduring involvement. However, in later life stages, this perception may change, and clothing may become less involving, although probably not low in enduring involvement.

In sum, most products are not so central to one's self-concept that they have high levels of enduring involvement across many different situation and contexts. This does not mean, however, that consumers never care at all about most products and brands. In fact, under certain circumstances (such as a purchase decision), consumers tend to become at least somewhat involved with products that are low in enduring involvement. Some of these products can achieve moderate to high levels of felt involvement in particular situations.

Situational Involvement

The consequences and values that are of immediate importance to a consumer are highly sensitive to the situational context. In a particular situation and environment, relevant self-knowledge (values, goals, and psychosocial consequences) is activated from long-term memory and becomes associated with product knowledge (attributes and functional consequences) appropriate for that situation. Because the knowledge represented by these means-end chains depends on specific aspects of the situation and immediate context, this is called **situational involvement.**

Consider the rather common situation in which a consumer becomes involved in the activity of buying a relatively unimportant product (with a low level of enduring involvement). For instance, the average consumer has a low level of enduring involvement with hot-water heaters; few people have strong connections between their important central values and this object. However, if Sam's hot-water heater suddenly develops a leak, it must be replaced within a day or two. Sam may then find that choosing and buying a new hot-water heater is fairly involving, at least during the short time it takes to make the decision. Note that Sam's felt involvement is largely due to the situation—failure of the old product and pressure to replace it quickly.

It is extremely important that marketers understand the *focus* of consumers' involvement. Sam was involved with *buying* a hot-water heater, not with *possessing* or *using (consuming)* hot-water heaters. Thus, the dominant consequences and values in his activated knowledge structure concerned aspects of purchasing the product—store selection, price, delivery and installation, energy efficiency, etc. Each of these attributes and functional consequences might be connected to important higher-ordered consequences, but not necessarily. To the extent they are, the purchase of the hot-water heater takes on greater degrees of personal relevance or involvement. However, once the product choice is made, the situational involvement tends to fade away quickly. From then on, whenever Sam thinks about his hot-water heater, few higher-order consequences are activated—unless it breaks or malfunctions (another specific situation).

Another type of situational involvement occurs when the purchase of a product is highly focused on specific aspects of a particular usage situation. For example, certain products may be rather low in enduring involvement but can become quite involving during the decision process if they are being considered as a gift.[22] As another example, some products may have important consequences when used in certain social situations, but not otherwise. For instance, shopping for a suit to be worn on a special occasion such as a wedding or a job interview may activate certain values and goals that are not relevant in other use situations.

In sum, consumers' felt involvement with many products and brands is transient and is largely induced by the particular situation. Enduring involvement is low or moderate for many products and brands and, therefore, has little effect on consumers' felt involvement in many situations. Whatever level of felt involvement is experienced by consumers is due largely to situational factors.

Interaction

As shown in Figure 5–9, both enduring involvement and situational involvement affect the level of felt involvement in the knowledge structures that are activated in any given situation. That is, the level of involvement experienced by consumers is a function of the base level of enduring involvement (low to moderate for many products) *plus* the level of situational involvement caused by the physical and social context in the immediate situation. In turn, the resulting level of felt involvement and the activated knowledge, meanings, and beliefs affect both interpretation and integration cognitive processes. These influences are discussed in Chapters 6 and 8, respectively. A variety of situational, consumer, and product factors affect both enduring and situational involvement. Figure 5–10 identifies several of these factors, and their effects are discussed in greater detail in later chapters.

Marketing Implications

Marketers often try to develop strategies to increase consumers' levels of involvement with a given product or brand. In the short run, marketers

---

[22]Russell W. Belk (1982), "Effects of Gift-Giving Involvement on Gift Selection Strategies," in *Advances in Consumer Research*, Vol. 9, A.A. Mitchell (ed.), Ann Arbor, Mich.: Association for Consumer Research, pp. 408–412.

have limited ability to modify the enduring relationships between consumers and products. Over longer periods of time, however, the levels of enduring involvement that a significant segment of the market has for a product can be influenced by various marketing strategies, especially advertising. However, this process may be long and is somewhat uncertain, because marketing strategies are only one of many influences on consumers' enduring involvement.

On the other hand, marketers can and do develop many strategies to create or modify the level of consumers' situational involvement with products, most commonly in a purchase situation. For instance, the annual clearance sale on summer clothing may temporarily raise consumers' involvement with and motivation to buy such products. Premiums such as stickers or small toys placed in cereal boxes may temporarily increase childrens' involvement with a brand. Sweepstakes contests are attempts to modify consumers' short-term involvement with a product. Finally, special pricing strategies, such as the rebates on certain new cars (get $1,000 back

FIGURE 5–10   **Factors that Influence Consumers' Involvement with Products and Brands**

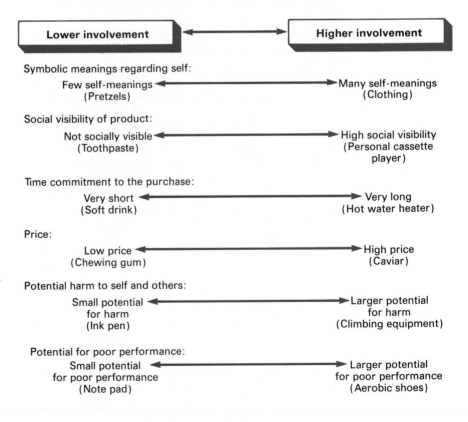

Courtesy USA Network

A marketing strategy to increase situational involvement with USA Network.

if you buy within the next 30 days), may create a temporary increase in some consumers' involvement with buying the brand.

Back to the Case

So, what is a computer? In this chapter you learned that consumers could have knowledge about computers at several levels of abstraction, including knowledge about product attributes, the functional consequences provided by those attributes, and even the psychosocial consequences and values that the computer might help achieve. To understand the meanings consumers have for any one of these levels—such as an attribute like the amount of memory storage capability (RAM)—marketers have to determine the other meanings with which it is associated. A means-end knowledge structure represents these linkages. Marketers must determine, through research, what functional consequences consumers think are provided by certain amounts of RAM and what higher-order outcomes (value states) are attained through those benefits. By investigating the entire means-end chain of meanings, marketers can gain a deeper understanding of how consumers perceive their products and brands. The deeper and more complete the marketers' understanding, the easier it is to develop and implement effective marketing strategies.

You also learned in this chapter that consumers are likely to vary widely in how involved they are with computers. Computer enthusiasts are likely to have high levels of enduring involvement. We would expect to find that they spend a great deal of time, effort, and money "fooling around" with their computers. Like auto enthusiasts who "soup up" their cars, some consumers delight in tinkering with their computers, making them more powerful or able to run at faster speeds. The majority of computer users, however, probably have only moderate levels of enduring involvement with computers. They are mostly concerned with the functional consequences of computers. Most nonusers, of course, tend to have very low levels of enduring involvement with computers. However, when any consumer is considering buying a computer, that situation is likely to create a temporary state of situational involvement that will affect their cognitive processes and their overt behaviors.

Summary

Consumers' product knowledge has a critical influence on their perceptions and thoughts about products and brands, as well as their behaviors. Thus far in the book, we have considered consumers' knowledge as the meanings which are created by consumers' cognitive systems and are stored in memory. We identified various types of meanings, including linguistic representations, visual images, and emotional, auditory, and motor representations. These meanings are represented as linked nodes in associative networks of knowledge.

Throughout this and the previous chapter we emphasized the abstraction processes of categorization or chunking, which create meanings at different levels of abstraction or inclusiveness. These meanings are organized into hierarchical associative networks of knowledge. We examined several hierarchies, including concepts, propositions, and schemas, as well as model, brand, product form, and product class.

In this chapter, we examined another multilevel scheme. We saw that consumers can consider a product class, product form, or brand in terms of three broad levels of meaning—as sets of attributes, bundles of consequences or benefits, or as the means of satisfying basic values and goals. We presented a special associative network of knowledge, a means-end chain, which organizes and connects these meanings. We described how means-end chains can help marketers understand consumers' involvement with products and brands. (In the Appendix to this chapter, we identify some basic methods for measuring means-end chains.)

In the next chapter, we will consider how consumers acquire new information from their environments, comprehend its meaning, and thus create new knowledge structures, including means-end chains. We will also consider how consumers' level of involvement affects their interpretation processes.

Additional Reading

Russell W. Belk (1985), "Materialism: Trait Aspects of Living in the Material World," *Journal of Consumer Research* (December), pp. 265–280.

Joel B. Cohen (1983), "Involvement and You: 1,000 Great Ideas," in *Advances in Consumer Research*, Vol. 10, R.P. Bagozzi and A.M. Tybout (eds.), Ann Arbor, Mich.: Association for Consumer Research, pp. 325–328.

Jonathan Gutman and Scott D. Alden (1985), "Adolescents' Cognitive Structures of Retail Stores and Fashion Consumption: A Means-End Chain Analysis of Quality," in *Perceived Quality: How Consumer View Stores and Merchandise*, Jacob Jacoby and Jerry C. Olson (eds.), Lexington, Mass.: Lexington Books, pp. 99–114.

John A. Howard (1977), *Consumer Behavior: Application of Theory*, New York: McGraw-Hill.

Harold H. Kassarjian (1981), "Low Involvement: A Second Look," in *Advances in Consumer Research*, Vol. 8, K.B. Monroe (ed.), Ann Arbor, Mich: Association for Consumer Research, pp. 31–34.

Thomas J. Reynolds, Jonathan Gutman and John A. Fiedler (1985), "Understanding Consumers' Cognitive Structures: The Relationship of Levels of Abstraction to Judgments of Psychological Distance and Preference," in *Psychological Processes and Advertising Effects: Theory, Research and Practice*, Linda Alwitt and Andrew A. Mitchell (eds.), Hillsdale, N.J.: Lawrence Erlbaum, pp. 261–272.

Milton Rokeach (1973), *The Nature of Human Values*, New York: Free Press.

Mark E. Slama and Armen Tashchian (1985), "Selected Socioeconomic and Demographic Characteristics Associated with Purchasing Involvement," *Journal of Marketing* (Winter), pp. 72–82.

Judith L. Zaichkowsky (1985), "Measuring the Involvement Construct," *Journal of Consumer Research* (December), pp. 341–352.

Appendix: Measuring Consumers' Means-End Chains

In this appendix, we describe several procedures for measuring means-ends chains of consumers' product knowledge. All have in common the requirement that consumers respond freely, in their own words. A free-response approach is necessary if marketers are to identify the unique meanings consumers associate with given products and brands.

The first step is to *specify the knowledge domain of interest.* You have seen that consumers can have means-end knowledge structures at the product category, product form, brand, or model level. Once the appropriate domain is identified, the measurement procedure must (*a*) *identify the basic categories of meaning* that consumers use to distinguish between objects or concepts in this domain, and (*b*) *determine the links to other meanings* at different levels of abstraction.

Identifying the Consumers' Basic Distinctions

The **basic meaning distinctions** that consumers use when processing information about the product or brands of interest are the entry into the means-end knowledge structure. These distinctions are often at fairly low levels of abstraction—at the physical or abstract attribute level.[23] Below we describe three general procedures for identifying the basic meanings consumers consider when thinking about products or brands: direct elicitation, free sort, and triad task. Figure 5–11 presents brief examples of each.

Direct Elicitation

The easiest procedure is to directly ask consumers what things they think about when evaluating, considering, or choosing among product classes, product forms, brands, or models. The question can be made more specific by asking consumers to state the product attributes (or consequences) they would consider. Most consumers mention two to five concepts. For example, a researcher might ask consumers to state what "things" they consider when buying a pair of jeans, and a consumer might say, "fit, price, style,

---

[23]Jonathan Gutman and Thomas J. Reynolds (1979), "An Investigation of the Levels of Cognitive Abstraction Utilized by Consumers in Product Differentiation," in *Attitude Research under the Sun,* J. Eighmey (ed.), Chicago: American Marketing Association, pp. 125–150.

and location of store." These concepts are presumed to be the most important categories of meaning for that consumer in that situation.

Free Sort

In this procedure, the researcher first identifies a large set of objects that represent the product class, product forms, brands, or models of interest. The name of each object is written on an index card, and the entire deck is given to a consumer. First, the consumer removes any unfamiliar objects—those he/she has never heard of or used before—and sets these cards aside. Next, the consumer sorts or groups the remaining objects using any concept or meaning he or she wishes. Following the sorting, the consumer describes each group of objects and discusses the meanings underlying

---

FIGURE 5–11   ***Methods of Identifying Key Distinctions Made by Consumers***

Direct Elicitation

Researcher: "Please tell me what characteristics you usually consider when deciding which brand of ball-point pen to buy."

Consumer: "I think about the *price,* the *color* of the ink, the *fineness* of the tip, and *how the pen feels* in my hand."

Free-Sort Task

Researcher: "Here are several brands of running shoes. Assume that you are thinking of buying a pair of running shoes. I want you to sort them into groups so that the shoes in each pile are alike in some important way to you, and are different from the shoes in the other piles."

or . . .

Researcher: "Here are several brands of running shoes. I want you to sort them into groups using any basis you wish."

Researcher: "Now, please describe what each pile means to you. Why are these brands together?"

Consumer: "Well, these shoes are all *high-tech* and *expensive.* These are *cheaper* and have *fewer fancy features.* And these brands are 'in between.' "

Triad Task

Researcher: "Here are three brands of running shoes. Assume that you were thinking of buying a pair of running shoes. In what important way are two of these similar and different from the third? Are there any other ways?"

Consumer: "Hmmm. Well, these two shoes have *special construction features* to keep your heel stable and solid. This one doesn't. And these two have a *staggered lacing system,* while this one has a traditional lacing pattern."

each category. Consumers often use more than one meaning distinction to categorize the objects. For instance, a set of breakfast cereal brands might be sorted as follows: "These are hot, these are sugar coated, these are for adults, these aren't sugar coated, these are crunchy, these are healthful/ they're good for you."

Triad Task

In this procedure, consumers do not deal with all the product or brand concepts at once. Rather they are given three concepts at a time—say, Levi, Wrangler, and Guess? jeans. Typically, consumers are asked to state how two of the concepts are similar to each other and different from the third. The consumer might say, "These two are more traditional, and this one is more contemporary." Thus, the traditional/contemporary distinction is identified as a basic meaning that the consumer uses when thinking about buying jeans.

Management Decision

A fourth way to gain entry into consumers' means-end chains does not involve measuring their responses. In this approach, marketing managers simply specify the meaning concepts or distinctions of interest. This approach is useful for several reasons. In some cases, management may be interested in certain product attributes, irrespective of whether any consumer would mention the attribute or not. For instance, General Electric has conducted research to see how consumers respond to different product attributes such as glass versus wire shelves in refrigerators.[24] GE could probe consumers' means-end chains related to these attributes. In other cases, management has previous research experience with how consumers answer the types of questions just described, so they may feel they already know what concepts will be produced. Thus, marketers may feel that this first step can be skipped.

Identifying Means-End Chains

The next step is to identify the different meanings that are linked to the initial distinctions. The basic procedure involves forcing consumers to

---

[24]Sunil Mehrotra and John Palmer (1985), "Relating Product Features to Perceptions of Quality: Appliances," in *Perceived Quality: How Consumers View Stores and Merchandise,* Jacob Jacoby and Jerry C. Olson (eds.), Lexington, Mass.: Lexington Books, pp. 81–96.

identify the higher-ordered concepts linked to each of the basic distinctions identified in the first stage. The technique used for this purpose is called **laddering,** because it attempts to push consumers up the "ladder of abstraction."[25] Although laddering is a relatively new procedure in consumer research, it has been used successfully to identify consumers' means-end chain structures of knowledge in a number of marketing studies.[26]

Laddering

The basic laddering procedure is simple to describe, but somewhat subtle in operation. To do laddering well requires finesse and a sensitivity to the consumer's point of view. The researcher must be willing to enter into the consumers' world to understand how they have construed reality. Because consumers' perspectives may be quite different from the interviewers', researchers must try to maintain a nonjudgmental tone. The goal, after all, is to understand the *consumers'* meanings for the product or brands of interest, not to validate the marketers' preconceived view of the product. Figure 5–12 presents an example of a laddering interview. In its simplest form, laddering is just repeatedly asking the question, "Why?"

First, consumers are asked why the elicited distinction is important to them. Their answer to that question forms the basis for the next question: "Why is that important to you?" This "why" probing continues until the consumer cannot go further. Sometimes the end is at the level of a terminal value, but in other cases the consumer stops at lower levels in the means-end chain (see example in Figure 5–5).

Typically, laddering proceeds upward, seeking to identify meaning concepts at higher levels of abstraction. But laddering can also proceed downward by identifying linked meanings at lower levels of abstraction. For instance, a marketer might wish to know what specific product attributes consumers perceive as leading to a particularly important benefit/consequence.

In sum, laddering procedures can be used to produce several means-end chains for each consumer. To keep the interview manageable, the number is usually restricted to say, three or five, by only laddering the three, four, or five most important initial distinctions.

[25]See Jonathan Gutman (1982), "A Means-End Chain Model Based on Consumer Categorization Processes," *Journal of Marketing* (Spring), pp. 60–72.

[26]See Darrel Edwards and Susan Johnson (1986), "The Meanings of Products in Consumers' Lives: The Grid Approach," and Jonathan Gutman and Thomas Reynolds (1986), "Integrating Advertising Assessment with Strategy Development: The MECCAs Approach," both in *Advertising and Consumer Psychology,* Vol. 3, Jerry Olson and Keith Sentis (eds.), New York: Praeger Publishers.

FIGURE 5–12   **An Example of a Laddering Interview**

Researcher: "You said that a shoe's lacing pattern is important to you in deciding what brand to buy. Why is that important to you?"

Consumer: "A staggered lacing pattern makes the shoe fit more snugly on my foot." **[physical attribute and functional consequence]**

Researcher: "Why is it important that the 'shoe fit more snugly on your foot'?"

Consumer: "Because it gives me better support." **[functional consequence]**

Researcher: "Why is better support important to you?"

Consumer: "So I can run without worrying about injuring my feet." **[psychosocial consequence]**

Researcher: "Why is it important for you not to worry while running?"

Consumer: "So I can relax and enjoy the run." **[psychosocial consequence]**

Researcher: "Why is it important that you can relax and enjoy your run?"

Consumer: "Because it gets rid of tension I have built up at work during the day." **[psychosocial consequence]**

Researcher: "Why is it important for you to get rid of tension from work?"

Consumer: "So when I go back to work in the afternoon, I can perform better." **[instrumental value—high performance]**

Researcher: Why is it important that you perform 'better'?"

Consumer: "I feel better about myself." **[terminal value—self-esteem]**

Researcher: Why is it important that you feel better about yourself?"

Consumer: "It just is!" **[the end!]**

Creating Aggregate Means-End Structure Maps

Once a sufficient number of individual consumers have been interviewed (say, 40 or 50 to as many as 150 to 200), the means-end chains for all individuals can be combined or aggregated to produce a knowledge structure for the entire group. The goal is to identify a general knowledge structure that incorporates the most relevant and common means-end chains of individual consumers. Figure 5–13 presents an example of an aggregate means-end knowledge structure. This is sometimes called a **hierarchical value structure map.**[27]

---

[27]Thomas J. Reynolds and Linda F. Jamieson (1985), "Image Representations: An Analytic Framework," in *Perceived Quality: How Consumer View Stores and Merchandise*, Jacob Jacoby and Jerry C. Olson (eds.), Lexington, Mass.: Lexington Books.

To generate aggregate knowledge structure maps, the unique idiosyncratic concepts mentioned by only one or a few consumers must be eliminated. For example, in one study of consumers' knowledge structures for breakfast cereal, an elderly lady identified a distinction between a presweetened cereal and two other cereals—she couldn't feed the presweetened brand to her parakeet. When asked "Why?" she answered, "That

FIGURE 5–13   ***An Aggregate Means-End Knowledge Structure for a Mineral Water Product***

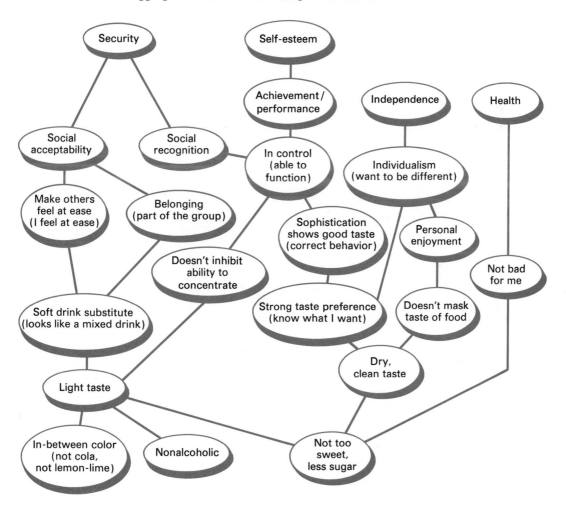

Source: Jerry C. Olson and Thomas J. Reynolds (1983), "Understanding Consumers' Cognitive Structures: Implications for Advertising Strategy," in Advertising and Consumer Psychology, L. Percy and A. G. Woodside, (eds.), Lexington, Mass.: Lexington Books, pp. 77–90.

brand sticks to his beak" (obviously a functional consequence!).[28] Although such meanings may be amusing, they are too unique to be included in the aggregate means-end knowledge structure for a segment of consumers. Marketers should focus on the most frequently mentioned means-end chains.

The basic procedure is to conduct a thorough content analysis of all the elicited concepts. All the concepts mentioned must be translated into a common language that captures their basic meaning. Then the concepts/meanings mentioned by only a few consumers are eliminated. This leaves those means-end chains that have been mentioned by at least several consumers. These common means-end chains are combined into an aggregated knowledge structure, a network of salient means-end chains, which accurately reflects many (but obviously not all) of the relevant product meanings for a group of consumers. Some errors and loss of information are unavoidable in this process, as subtle differences in the unique meanings of individual consumers may be lost or misinterpreted in the attempt to create a set of common meanings. However, the ability to study the knowledge structure of a group of consumers, such as an important market segment, usually makes the trade-off worthwhile.

---

[28]W.A.K. Frost, and R.L. Braine (1967), "The Application of the Repertory Grid Technique to Problems in Market Research," *Commentary* (July), pp. 161–175.

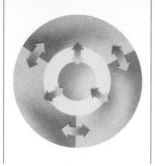

Chapter Six

Interpretation Processes: Attention and Comprehension

General Electric Pursues the Youth Market

What do consumers think of the youth-oriented audio products made by General Electric, the Fairfield, Connecticut, company that brings good things to life? Most of the under-30 crowd, the segment that accounts for most of the headphone, cassette, and boom-box sales, wouldn't be caught dead with a GE product. As Richard Costello, GE's marketing communications manager for consumer electronics, puts it, "These kids simply didn't want to buy a radio from someone who makes refrigerators and light bulbs."

The company verified this problem in a series of intensive interviews with consumers. When GE demonstrated its portable audio products next to those of chief rivals Sony and Panasonic, most people preferred the latter brands. Yet when the labels were removed, GE became the preferred choice.

GE assigned their New York advertising agency, BBDO, the difficult job of changing consumers' knowledge structures about GE. As Costello put it, "BBDO's task is to make us relevant, make the youth market know we have these products, and make them believe our goods are high performance."

In other words, the advertising BBDO was to create had to change consumers' knowledge, meanings, and beliefs about GE audio equipment. What kind of advertisements did BBDO creatives come up with to generate the appropriate meanings?

First, they scoured the history books looking for an event in which music played a powerful role. They picked the biblical tale of Joshua who ordered his men to blow rams' horns to shatter the walls of Jericho.

That idea eventually developed into a $500,000 commercial. The *Star Wars*–like fantasy depicted a group of four all-American heroes, led by a hunk chewing on a toothpick. The adventurers pass through a hazy blue cave into a bizarre land strewn with rocks. Magenta laser beams shoot from the sky. A group of slaves in silver helmets pass by, hauling a cart carrying a giant crystal. Trapped inside the crystal is a beautiful princess. The leader slips a cassette into a tape player, and rock music blasts from the machine. The crystal shatters, the slaves are liberated, and the princess is freed.

As the ad ends, the visitors and slaves are enjoying the music while the leader and the princess gaze lustfully into each other's eyes. Only a short closing tag line and the familiar blue-circle logo revealed that the commercial is for General Electric.

What kinds of interpretation processes do you think occurred when consumers were exposed to this ad?

Source: Susan Spillman (1985), "BBDO Aims to Blast GE-riatric Image," Advertising Age *(March 21), p. 4.*

The everyday environment of American consumers contains huge amounts of information, a large part of which is created and controlled by marketers. Although marketers are not able to directly control consumers' behaviors or cognitions, they can modify consumers' environments by creating advertisements, building stores, producing and distributing products, hiring salespersons to contact consumers, and so on. These marketing strategies create information that consumers may interpret if they come into contact with it.

In this chapter, we examine the interpretation processes by which consumers understand the information in their environments. First, we examine how consumers are exposed to the information. Then we discuss the *attention and comprehension processes* by which consumers construct meanings and beliefs to represent this information, organize these representations into knowledge structures, and store them in memory. In sum, we are concerned with the first part of our model of consumer cognitive processes, as shown in Figure 6–1.

It is important to recognize that the distinction between attention and comprehension processes is *not clear-cut* or *absolute*. Although we will discuss the two processes separately, the point at which attention ends and comprehension begins is not distinct. Instead, attention processes shade off into comprehension processes. In fact, both processes serve the same basic function in the human cognitive system—to construct coherent, useful interpretations of relevant aspects of the environment that enable consumers to "get along" in their world.

FIGURE 6–1   **Consumers' Cognitive Processes Involved in Interpretation**

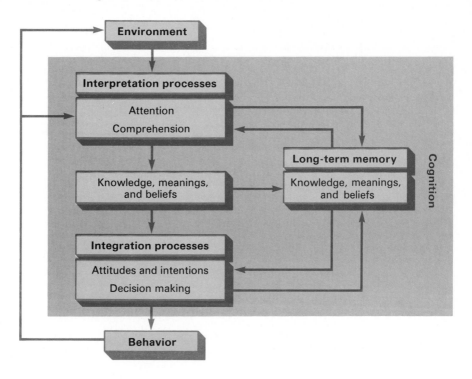

Before we examine these attention and comprehension processes, we will briefly review several of the basic characteristics of human cognition that are particularly important for understanding consumers' interpretation processes. (You may wish to refer back to Figure 3–3.) First, cognitive processes are complex *interactions* between the knowledge, meanings, and beliefs that are activated from memory and "incoming" information from the environment (see Figure 6–1).[1] Second, the activation of one meaning node can spread through an associative network of knowledge and activate other related meanings, including schemas and scripts. This activated knowledge in turn, influences the direction and intensity of attention and

---

[1]John Howard and Jagdish N. Sheth (1969), *The Theory of Buyer Behavior,* New York: John Wiley & Sons; James J. Jenkins (1974), "Remember that Old Theory of Memory? Well, Forget It!" *American Psychologist* (November), pp. 785–795; Jerry C. Olson (1978), "Theories of Information Encoding and Storage: Implications for Consumer Research," in *The Effect of Information on Consumer and Market Behavior,* Andrew A. Mitchell (ed.), Chicago: American Marketing Association, pp. 49–60.

HIGHLIGHT 6–1   **Automatic Attention and Comprehension Processes**

It is becoming widely recognized in cognitive psychology and in consumer behavior that "most of the memory and attention factors that affect our judgments are simply unavailable to consciousness."[a] That is, "Most of what we do goes on unconsciously . . . It is the exception, not the rule, when thinking is conscious."[b] This means that many interpretation processes require little or no cognitive capacity, conscious awareness, or control.

Actually, cognitive processes *must* become more automatic over time.[c] If they do not, people would expend all of their limited cognitive capacity, time, and effort on a few tasks that would never become easier. Fortunately, though, as we acquire new knowledge about our environments and become familiar with using it, that knowledge tends to be activated and used in cognitive processes in increasingly automatic ways.[d] Thus, much of **learning** is the development of increasingly automatic cognitive processes. Interestingly, consumers may be aware of the *outcomes* of the cognitive processes—that is, the *meanings* that are *constructed* by the cognitive processes—but they usually are not aware of the automatic cognitive operations that took place.[e]

Automaticity has the obvious advantage of keeping our limited cognitive capacity free for other cognitive processing tasks that require our conscious effort and control.[f] But in some circumstances, automaticity has disadvantages, in that our lack of control sometimes leads to inappropriate meanings such as misinterpretations or jumping to conclusions. Finally, note that distinguishing between completely automatic or totally controlled processes is not possible. In fact, most consumer cognitive processing tasks—such as judging which sweater looks best, deciding where to go out to eat, or choosing between two brands of jeans—involve complex interactions of both automatic and controlled processes.

In sum, a great deal of cognitive processing can occur even though consumers respond rapidly, with little apparent effort and little awareness that anything has happened. In fact, most cognitive processes are so familiar and well learned that they occur automatically, without any conscious awareness. The very automaticity of these processes (and the corresponding lack of control by consumers) allows the marketer some degree of influence over consumers' cognitive processes.

[a]John G. Lynch, Jr. and Thomas K. Srull (1982), "Memory and Attention Factors in Consumer Choice: Concepts and Research Methods," *Journal of Consumer Research* (September), pp. 18–37.
[b]Roy Lachman, Janet L. Lachman and Earl C. Butterfield (1979), *Cognitive Psychology and Information Processing: An Introduction*, Hillsdale, N.J.: Lawrence Erlbaum, p. 207.
[c]John Jonides and David E. Irwin (1981), "Capturing Attention," *Cognition* (March), pp. 145–150; William James (1890), *The Principles of Psychology*, New York: Henry Holt.
[d]D. LaBerge (1975), "Acquisition of Automatic Processing in Perceptual and Associative Learning," in *Attention and Performance*, Vol. V, P. Rabbitt and S. Dornic (eds.), London: Academic Press.
[e]George Mandler (1975), *Mind and Emotion*, New York: John Wiley & Sons.
[f]William Schneider and Richard M. Shiffrin (1977), "Controlled and Automatic Human Information Processing: I. Detection, Search, and Attention," *Psychological Review* (January), pp. 1–66; and Richard M. Shiffrin and William Schneider (1977), "Controlled and Automatic Human Information Processing: II. Perceptual Learning, Automatic Attending, and a General Theory," *Psychological Review* (March), pp. 127–190.

comprehension processes. Third, consumers have limited cognitive capacity, and thus, can consider relatively few meanings or beliefs at a time. Finally, many (perhaps most) attention and comprehension processes occur automatically, with little or no conscious awareness (see Highlight 6–1). Some attention and comprehension processes, however, are under the consumer's control. Figure 6–2 summarizes several of the key differences between automatic and controlled cognitive processes.

Exposure to Information

Although not a part of cognition in a strict sense, **exposure** to information is critically important for understanding consumers' interpretation processes. Consumers are exposed to information in the environment, including marketing strategies, primarily through their own *behaviors*. We can distinguish between two types of exposure to marketing information: *purposive or intentional* and *accidental or random* exposure.

FIGURE 6–2　　**Characteristics of Automatic versus Controlled Cognitive Processes**

Characteristic	Automatic Processes	Controlled Processes
• Amount of cognitive capacity required	Little or none	Some part needed
• Degree of conscious control over process	Little or none	High degree of control
• Monitoring of process	None; process runs to end once begun	Process is monitored and controlled
• Speed of process	Usually very fast	Usually slow
• Flexibility: ability to change or modify process	Fixed; no changes	Flexible; easily changed or modified
• Sequence of subprocesses	Preset sequence	Flexible sequence
• Effects of prolonged practice or repetition	No changes	Becomes more automatic
• Ability to describe processing operations	Difficult or impossible to describe	Certain aspects can probably be described

Intentional Exposure to Information

Consumers are exposed to some marketing information due to their own intentional, goal-directed behavior. Consumers may seek marketing information to use in solving a purchasing problem. Before buying a camera, for instance, a consumer might read product evaluations of 35mm cameras in *Consumer Reports* or photography magazines. Or a consumer might ask a friend or a salesperson for advice about which brand of earphones to buy for her Walkman radio.

Intentional exposures to information are usually called **search** by marketing researchers. Most investigations of consumer search for information have found that levels of intentional exposure are rather low.[2] Often only a few stores are visited, and relatively few salespersons and external sources of information are consulted.[3] This limited search may be surprising, until you realize that most consumers already have stored in their memories substantial knowledge, meanings, and beliefs concerning product classes, forms, brands, and models. If they feel confident in their existing knowledge, or if the decision is not very involving (important), consumers may have little motivation to engage in extensive search behaviors. (We will discuss search behavior again in Chapter 8, in the context of consumer decision making.)

Accidental Exposure to Information

In the consumer-oriented environments of most industrialized countries, marketing information is everywhere. In the United States, for instance, advertisements for products and services are found in magazines and newspapers, on radio and TV, on bus placards and bus-stop shelters—and they are increasing. Between 1967 and 1982, the total number of ads doubled; and by 1997 that number is expected to double again.[4] Billboards and signs promoting products, services, and retail stores are found along most highways. Stores contain a great deal of marketing information, including signs, point-of-purchase displays, and advertisements, in addition to information on packages. Consumers also receive product information from friends and relatives, from salespersons, and occasionally even from strangers.

---

[2]Joseph W. Newman (1977), "Consumer External Search: Amount and Determinants," in *Consumer and Industrial Buying Behavior,* A.G. Woodside, J.N. Sheth and P.D. Bennett (eds.), New York: Elsevier-North Holland Publishing, pp. 79–94.

[3]Richard W. Olshavsky and Donald H. Granbois (1979), "Consumer Decision Making—Fact or Fiction?" *Journal of Consumer Research* (June), pp. 63–70.

[4]Leo Bogart (1984), "Executives Fear Ad Overload Will Lower Effectiveness," *Marketing News* (May 25), pp. 4–5.

Alan Carey/The Image Works

Transit advertising increases accidental exposure.

Typically, consumers' exposure to these types of marketing information is not the result of intentional search behavior. Instead, most exposures are random or semirandom events that occur as consumers move through their environments and "accidentally" come into contact with marketing information. For instance, when consumers watch television, they seldom intentionally seek information about products or services; yet they accidentally expose themselves to many commercials during a 30-minute program. And since consumers probably aren't very involved with most of the products promoted in these ads, their attention and comprehension processes during exposure are not extensive.

Selective Exposure to Information

As the amount of marketing information in the environment increases, consumers become more adept at avoiding exposure altogether (some consumers intentionally avoid reading product test reports). Or they do not maintain accidental exposure to marketing information (some people automatically throw away all junk mail unopened). Such behaviors result in **selective exposure** to marketing information. Consider the problem marketers are having with consumers' exposure to TV commercials. Current technology enables consumers to control what ads they see on TV more easily than ever before. In the "old days," consumers could always go to

HIGHLIGHT 6–2   **Creating Zap-Proof Commercials**

Good news, television viewers. Advertising agencies say that fast, fast, FAST relief is on the way. No longer will you have to reach for your remote-control device at the first sign of a program break to zap the commercials off your screen. More and more ads are being turned into million-dollar epics to keep you glued to your screen. Have you noticed?

For instance, Wrangler sportswear produced commercials featuring a young couple straight out of movies like *Raiders of the Lost Ark* and *Romancing the Stone* who bounce from one escapist cliche to another. For example, the adventurers pluck a huge emerald from a stone idol's forehead, then flee for their lives as the statue crumbles and spews tons of rubble after them. They escape by swinging on vines across a deep chasm. A voice solemnly intones: "Out here, people need a Wrangler style . . . because no matter what they're doing, they want to look their best. Anytime, anywhere."

This ad and similarly epic commercials for Apple computers, Pepsi-Cola, and Data General are attempts to capture viewers' attention. "If people aren't intrigued by your commercial in the first couple of seconds," says Len Sugarman, ad executive at Foot, Cone & Belding, "you might as well give up and go home." As zapping, zipping, and just plain turning away from boring ads have become more widespread, advertisers are trying to create ads that people would rather watch than zap.

But this attention-gathering power doesn't come cheap. The Wrangler ads cost about $1 million to produce, and this doesn't include the approximately $100,000 cost to show a 30-second ad on network prime time. Pepsi-Cola spent about $2 million on the ads featuring pop singer Michael Jackson. Later they signed singer Lionel Richie to star in three blockbuster ads for the soft drink for an estimated $3 million. Apple spent about $500,000 on its *1984* ad that introduced the Macintosh computer, yet the ad aired only once—on the 1984 Super Bowl game.

Edward Bauman, chairman of Blue Bell, parent company of Wrangler, acknowledges some trepidation over the cost. "You know, it's difficult for me to tell whether those things sell products or not," he says, "but they do cost a lot of money and we're putting significantly more [money] into producing them and showing them than in the past."

Some experts think "extravaganza advertising" is a terrible waste of money. In the case of the Wrangler ads, consultant Miner Raymond suggests, "People see a guy in a beat-up fedora and think about seeing *Raiders of the Lost Ark* again. It [the Wrangler ads] may sell a lot of videocassettes."

Source: Felix Kessler (1985), "In Search of Zap-Proof Commercials," Fortune *(January 21), pp. 68-70.*

the kitchen for a snack during a commercial break; but now the situation is different. Thanks to remote controls for TV sets, viewers can turn off the sound or "dial hop" from one station to another during a commercial break. Consumers who have videocassette recorders (VCRs) can run fast-forward past commercials on taped programs. In advertising circles, these practices are known as **zapping** and **zipping,** respectively. In homes with remote controls, the zapping (tune-out) factor was estimated as being as high as 40 percent during the average commercial.[5] As remote controls become even more popular, the situation will get worse. Advertisers, who are paying media rates based on a full audience (currently $100,000 or more for 30 seconds of prime time on a major network), are worried that they are not getting their money's worth. One of their strategies to combat zapping is to develop commercials that are so interesting and exciting they won't be zapped.

Marketing Implications

Because of the crucial importance of exposure, marketers should develop specific strategies to enhance the probability that consumers will be exposed to their information and products. There are three ways to do this: facilitate intentional exposure, maximize accidental exposure, and maintain exposure.

Facilitate Intentional Exposure

In cases where many exposures to marketing information are the result of intentional search, marketers should make appropriate marketing information available when and where the consumer needs it. For instance, to increase sales, IBM trains its retail salespeople to answer consumers' technical questions on the spot so that consumers don't have to wait while the salesperson looks up the answer. Consumers' intentional search for information should be made as easy as possible. This requires that marketers anticipate consumers' needs for information and devise strategies to meet them. A lumber company, for example, might distribute brochures to their suburban customers describing how to use their products to construct decks and fences.

Maximize Accidental Exposure

Marketers obviously should try to place their information in environmental settings where the chances of accidental exposure to the appropriate target groups of consumers are maximized. For instance, a billboard for an up-scale clothing store should be placed on a highway connecting a city to an upper-class suburb. Certain types of retail outlets such as convenience stores, ice cream shops, and fast-food restaurants, should be placed in locations where accidental exposure is high. High-traffic locations such as

---

[5]Felix Kessler (1985), "In Search of Zap-Proof Commercials," *Fortune* (January 21), pp. 68–70.

HIGHLIGHT 6–3   **Measuring Consumers' Exposure to Television Programs**

Media buyers purchase time (on radio and TV programs) and space (in magazines and newspapers) in which to place advertisements. To buy time on the most appropriate television programs, advertisers need to know a great deal about consumers' TV viewing behavior. Marketers need to know (a) how many people are watching (because this determines the price of the time slot) and (b) what types of people are watching (in order to select a TV audience that closely matches their target market).

Currently, A.C. Nielsen Company provides the only nationwide measures of U.S. television audiences. On the basis of Nielsen's measurements, corporations doled out $9 billion (!) in 1984 to buy time for TV advertisements. Nielsen earned an estimated $100 million for its services.

For the past 35 years, Nielsen has measured consumers' exposure to television programing using a combination of two techniques. A meter attached to the TV sets in about 1,700 homes automatically records which channel the set is tuned to. But it doesn't indicate whether anyone is watching. So Nielsen has a separate group of 2,600 households fill out a weekly diary that records what each family member viewed during 15-minute segments of the day. Even though this procedure involves obvious problems (try to remember what shows you watched yesterday!), the method seemed adequate until cable became popular. Currently, the average home has access to 10 channels, and some can tune in 80. With

remote controls (making channel changes easier) and VCRs, the diary keeper is hard pressed to keep track of every channel change. The problems with the Nielsen diary procedure have become more obvious.

Now a British company, AGB Research, is trying to break Nielsen's monopoly with a measurement system that it claims is more refined and less expensive. AGB's system, called the PeopleMeter, assigns a number to each member of the household. Viewers are expected to push their number on a set of buttons on the meter when they begin watching a program and again when they finish. Thus, the PeopleMeter system records not only what program the set is tuned to, but also who is present in the room and therefore exposed to the advertisements. (Of course, the PeopleMeter can't tell if anyone is paying attention!) AGB claims viewers are more likely to press numbers than to fill out diaries, but the system still requires the viewer's participation.

Nielsen is quietly testing its own people meter. So is Arbitron, a third major competitor. With the huge monies at stake in TV advertising, the company that establishes an accurate system of measuring TV exposure can expect to do very well.

Source: Jaclyn Fierman (1985), "Television Ratings: The British Are Coming," Fortune (April 1), p. 109.

malls, busy intersections, and downtown locations are prime spots. Interestingly, one of the highest-grossing McDonald's in the world is located in the middle of nowhere in Nevada. But it is along the main highway between Los Angeles and Las Vegas, where thousands of travelers are accidentally exposed to it every day. Many of them stop to consume a Big Mac.

Most media strategies are intended to maximize accidental exposures to firms' advertisements. Media planners must carefully select a mix of media (magazines, billboards, radio and TV programming) that will maximize the chances that the target segment will be exposed to their company's ads. Solving this very complex problem is crucial to the success of the company's communication strategy, because the ads cannot have any impact if no one sees them.

A company's distribution strategy plays the key role in creating accidental exposures to their products. Distribution is to products such as beer, cigarettes, chewing gum, and potato chips, as location is to fast-food restaurants—it's nearly everything. Obviously, if the product is not on the grocery store shelves, at the checkout counter, or in the vending machine, the consumer cannot be exposed at the point of purchase, and sales will suffer. For instance, compare the success of Amstel Light beer to that of Kronenbourg. Both beers were first imported in 1980. Amstel Light was distributed by the importer of Heineken, a beer that, over the years, had achieved wide distribution in all 50 states. Using that distribution network, it was relatively easy to move Amstel Light into the same outlets that sell Heineken. Sales rose from 250,000 cases in 1980 to 1.5 million cases in 1985. In contrast, Kronenbourg had more difficulty obtaining adequate distribution and had much smaller sales increases over the same period (from 300,000 to only 700,000 cases).[6]

Maximum exposure at the retail level is not desirable for all products, though. For instance, Burberry all-weather coats and accessories (with the distinctive plaid lining) or Bang & Olafson stereo equipment are sold only in a few exclusive, high-quality stores. Exposure is controlled by using a highly selective distribution strategy. In sum, one of the most important functions of a company's distribution strategy is to create the *appropriate level of exposure* to the product.

Maintain Exposure

Other marketing strategies are intended to maintain exposure, once initiated. Between programs, Showtime cable channel presented short segments featuring leotard-clad young women doing aerobics, while the cameras zoomed in for close-ups. These features had nothing to do with exercise. They were designed to keep viewers tuned to Showtime, and they did.[7]

---

[6]Kelly Walker (1985), "Not Funny," *Forbes* (June 17), p. 166.

[7]"Four More Years: The Marketing Implications," *Marketing News* (January 4, 1985), pp. 1, 50, and 52.

Attention Processes

Once consumers are exposed to marketing information, whether accidentally or through intentional behaviors, interpretation processes (attention
and comprehension) are engaged. In this section, we discuss attention
processes, levels of attention, and factors affecting attention, and we describe several marketing implications of influencing consumers' attention.

What Is Attention?

What does it mean for a consumer to attend to a marketing stimulus such
as a newspaper ad, a display in a store, or a clerk's sales pitch? First,
attention implies **selectivity.** Attending to certain information involves *selecting* it from a large set of information and ignoring other information.
Consider the cognitive processes of shoppers in a crowded, noisy department store. They must selectively attend to conversations with salespersons, attend to certain products and brands, read labels and signs, and
so on. At the same time, they must ignore other stimuli in the environment. Attention also connotes **awareness** and **consciousness.** To attend to
a stimulus usually means being conscious of it. Attention also suggests
intensity and **arousal.** Consumers must be somewhat alert and aroused to
attend to something; and their level of alertness influences how intensively
they process the information.[8] If you have ever tried to study when you
were very tired, you know about the importance of arousal. If your level of
arousal is very low, you might drift off to sleep while trying to read a text
chapter (not this one, we hope!). When arousal is low, attention (and comprehension) suffer.

Levels of Attention

According to current theories of attention, all information to which consumers are exposed is analyzed for meaning by their cognitive system, but
not to the same degree.[9] Attention processes vary along a continuum from
an automatic, **preconscious level** to a conscious level called **focal attention.**
This view of levels of attention is summarized in Figure 6–3. As attention
processes shift from preconscious toward focal levels, consumers gradually

---

[8]Roy Lachman, Janet L. Lachman and Earl C. Butterfield (1979), *Cognitive Psychology and
Information Processing: An Introduction,* Hillsdale, N.J.: Lawrence Erlbaum.
[9]Ibid.

FIGURE 6–3   **Levels of Attention**

Preconscious Attention	Focal Attention
• Uses activated knowledge from long-term memory	• Uses activated knowledge from long-term memory
• No conscious awareness	• Conscious awareness
• Automatic processes	• Controlled processes
• Uses little or no cognitive capacity	• Uses some cognitive capacity
• More likely for familiar, frequently encountered concepts, with well-learned memory representations	• More likely for novel, unusual, infrequently encountered concepts, without well-learned memory representations
• More likely for concepts of low to moderate importance or involvement	• More likely for concepts of high importance or involvement

become more conscious of paying attention to (intentionally selecting) a stimulus, and more effort and cognitive capacity is needed. At focal levels, attention processes are controlled, in that consumers "decide" which stimuli they will attend to and process for comprehension. As the cognitive processes reach focal levels of attention, they shade off into comprehension processes and meaning analyses become more controlled. In sum, attention processes vary in terms of automaticity, degree of conscious awareness, and amount of processing capacity needed.[10]

Factors Influencing Attention Processes

Because most aspects of the environment are familiar, consumers are likely to possess substantial relevant knowledge, meanings, and beliefs. This knowledge tends to be automatically activated upon exposure and affects initial attention processes in an unconscious manner. That is, the salient meanings in the activated schemas or scripts automatically direct consumers' attention toward the corresponding stimuli.

---

[10]Daniel Kahneman (1973), *Attention and Effort*, Englewood Cliffs, N.J.: Prentice-Hall.

Selective Attention

How are marketing stimuli "selected" for attention (and comprehension) processes? Consumers' attention is greatly influenced by the activated needs, goals, and values that reflect their enduring involvement with the stimulus and their situational involvement due to the environmental context. Marketing stimuli that are linked to important, involving consequences and values at the time of exposure tend to receive attention and are likely to be processed further via comprehension processes. Thus, a consumer who is very involved with cars in general, or Corvettes in particular, will tend to notice and attend to ads for those cars.

As you learned in Chapter 5, consumers' salient consequences, values, and goals are highly contingent on situational or contextual factors (situational involvement). A magazine called *Rx Being Well*, which is distributed to some 150,000 physicians' offices around the country, bases its marketing strategy on consumers' situational involvement. *Rx Being Well* is promoted to advertisers of health-care products as an ideal medium to "reach consumers when they are most receptive. People in waiting rooms aren't just waiting. They're thinking about their health . . . You'll be reaching consumers right before they go to drug stores or supermarkets with pharmacies where they'll see, remember, and buy your product."[11]

Environmental Prominence

Of course, the stimuli created by marketing strategies also affect attention processes. Every marketing stimulus in the environment is *not* equally likely to activate its meaning representations, receive high levels of attention, or be comprehended. Some stimuli are simply more prominent in the environment than others—they stand out and are more likely to receive attention. Loud sounds (radio and TV commercials are often louder than the surrounding program material) and odors (bakeries often exhaust the scent of baking onto the sidewalk or into the mall) are prominent environmental stimuli that activate consumers' cognitive representations and receive attention.

Marketing Implications

Many marketing strategies are designed not only to attract consumers' attention, but to influence their comprehension processes, as well. We will examine strategies focused on consumers' involvement with the product and strategies based on environmental prominence.

---

[11]Adapted from an advertisement in *Advertising Age* (November 4, 1985), p. 69.

Involvement

Marketers have little direct control over the cognitive factors that influence consumers' attention. The usual strategy is to carefully research (or try to guess) consumers' key consequences, values, and goals and *design marketing stimuli to activate those meanings* and thus attract consumers' attention (and subsequent comprehension) processes.

Consider, for instance, that many marketers of antiperspirants emphasize "stops odor" and "stops wetness"—both rational, simplistic, functional consequences of the product. However, the marketers of Sure deodorant identified the more abstract psychosocial consequences (higher-level ends) of this product category—social confidence and avoidance of embarrassment. They capitalized on these more involving meanings with their ad campaign, "Raise your hand if you're Sure," that showed coatless consumers in social situations raising their arms and not being embarrassed by damp underarms. As another example, the marketers of Vaseline Intensive Care lotion identified the key consequences that defined many consumers' involvement with the hand-lotion product category. While brands such as Touch of Sweden were being promoted for their greaseless formulas, Vaseline identified *skin restoration* as the key functional consequence and promoted the implied psychosocial consequence of "looking younger." Marketers conveyed these meanings through ads that showed dried up leaves before and after being rejuvenated with Intensive Care lotion.[12]

Factors Affecting Prominence

Marketers take advantage of the many factors affecting the prominence of marketing information by designing bright, colorful, or unusual packages; by developing novel advertising executions; or by setting unique prices (say, having a sale on small items, all priced at 88 cents). Because they must attract the attention of consumers hurrying by the newsstand, magazine covers often feature photos known to have high attention value—such as those of celebrities, babies, or dogs, or those that use that old standby, sex (attractive, seductively clothed models).

Visual Prominence. Vivid pictorial images can attract consumers' attention and help focus it on the product. Nike, for instance, places powerful graphic portrayals of athletes (wearing Nike shoes, of course) on large billboards. Window displays in retail stores attract the attention (and subsequent interest) of consumers who happen to pass by. Tiffany's (the famous New York jeweler) once used a window display showing

---

[12]Both examples were taken from "Intuition, Microstudies, Humanized Research Can Identify Emotions that Motivate Consumers," *Marketing News* (March 19, 1982), p. 11.

construction of a giant doll, four times larger than the figures who were working on it. The doll had nothing to do with jewelry; it was intended to attract the attention of shoppers during the Christmas season.[13] Many stores use creative lighting to emphasize selected merchandise and thus attract and focus consumers' attention on the products. Mirrors are used in clothing shops and hair salons to focus consumers' attention on their appearance.

Novelty. Novel, unusual stimuli often can stimulate focal levels of attention. An unfamiliar stimulus that doesn't "fit" with the consumers' activated knowledge, meanings, and beliefs may be "selected" for additional attention and comprehension processing (to figure out what it is). For instance, a British ad agency created a dramatic stimulus to attract attention to the staying qualities of an adhesive called Araldite. The product was used to attach a car to a billboard placed along a major road into London. The headline read, "It also sticks handles to teapots."[14] Not only did this ad attract consumers' attention, it also won awards for creativity. Marketers must be careful in using novel and unusual stimuli over long periods, though, because over time the prominence effect due to novelty wears off and fails to attract extra attention. For instance, placing a black-and-white ad in a magazine where all the other ads are in color will capture consumers' attention only as long as few other black-and-white ads are used.

Competition for Prominence. The strategy of trying to capture consumers' attention with prominent stimuli sometimes backfires. When many marketers are trying very hard to gain their attention, consumers may tune most of the stimuli out, giving little attention to any of them. Consider the "miracle-mile strips" of fast-food restaurants, gas stations, and discount stores—each with a large sign—that line highways in many American cities. Individually, each sign is large, bright, colorful, and vivid. Together, the signs are cluttered, and none is particularly prominent in the environment. Consumers find it easy to ignore individual signs, and their attention (and comprehension) levels are likely to be low. Unfortunately, the typical marketing strategy is to make even larger and more garish signs in hope of becoming a slightly more prominent stimulus in the environment. The clutter gets worse, consumers' attention decreases further, and communities become outraged and pass ordinances limiting signs.

---

[13]"Four More Years."

[14]Brian Davis (1985), "FCO's Run of Bad Luck," *Advertising Age* (June 10), p. 58.

Don Smetzer: Click/Chicago
Sign clutter in Las Vegas.

Comprehension Processes

In the most general sense, comprehension refers to the cognitive processes involved in **understanding** and **knowing,** key activities of human cognition. Through comprehension processes, consumers cognitively represent salient concepts, objects, and events in their environments as **meanings** or **knowledge.** We use the term **comprehension** to emphasize the *interpretive, sense-making* aspects of these representation processes. In this section, we discuss how comprehension works, ways in which it varies, factors influencing comprehension, and implications for marketing strategy.

How Does Comprehension Work?

As you have seen, attention to certain environmental stimuli activates relevant knowledge from long-term memory. The activated knowledge schema or script, as a network of meanings, acts somewhat like a framework or template that guides or directs comprehension processes. In this way, existing knowledge influences the meanings that are constructed to represent the new information. As shown in Figure 6–1, the knowledge,

HIGHLIGHT 6–4   **In League with the Devil?**

"Thank you for calling Procter & Gamble concerning the malicious and completely false stories about our company's trademark," begins the recording. This toll-free message was just one of the

The bedeviled logo

mors false. The rumors died down, but resurfaced again in late 1984 and early 1985.

In April 1985 Procter & Gamble finally decided that the 103-year-old logo had become more of a headache than it was worth. Frustrated by an inexplicable resurgence of the rumors on the East coast, P&G announced that it would start removing the trademark from all its packages within a year. The trademark will be retained as a symbol on corporate stationery and on buildings. The change is not likely to cause a comprehension problem for consumers. Although P&G was quite attached to its long-time symbol, marketing research showed that most consumers never noticed it (low attention).

ways in which P&G tried to quash a persistent rumor alleging that its man-in-the-moon logo is satanic, and that the company is somehow involved in devil worship. According to P&G, the stars in the symbol represent the original 13 colonies, and the quarter-moon with the human face was simply a popular image of the late 1800s.

The giant (P&G's 1984 sales were $12.9 billion!) Cincinnati-based manufacturer of dozens of products from Jif peanut butter to Crest toothpaste to Tide detergent had been bedeviled (pun intended) by this rumor since 1982. The rumors created a wave of 15,000 telephone calls from uneasy consumers in July of that year. Initially P&G took a get-tough stance by filing lawsuits against persons distributing the information and by enlisting prominent clergy to declare the ru-

This unusual example illustrates the power of consumers' knowledge, meanings, and beliefs. Even though only a few consumers seemed to believe this bizarre rumor, they created enough controversy to affect a giant company.

Source: Adapted from "The Man in the Moon Disappears," Time (May 6, 1985), p.63; Joe Kay (1985), "Procter & Gamble Drops Logo to Dispel Rumors of Satanism," State College, Pa.: Centre Daily Times (April 25), p. B-3.

meanings, and beliefs produced by comprehension processes may be stored in long-term memory where they may modify the knowledge structures from which they were generated. In addition, these new meanings could be used in integration processes, such as attitude formation or decision making.

How Does Comprehension Vary?

Consumers' comprehension processes vary in three important ways. First, comprehension processes differ in the extent to which they are *automatic* versus controlled. Second, they vary in *depth*, which produces meanings at different levels of abstraction. Third, comprehension processes vary in *elaboration*, which produces different numbers of meanings.

Automatic versus Controlled Processes

Like attention, much comprehension is automatic (refer back to Highlight 6–1). Perhaps the simplest example of automatic comprehension is the recognition response that occurs when a consumer is exposed to a familiar stimulus. For instance, when most consumers see a can of Coca-Cola or a McDonald's restaurant, they immediately recognize (comprehend) the stimulus as "a Coke" or "McDonald's." That is, simple exposure to the stimulus automatically activates its meaning representation from memory—usually its name, and perhaps other associated meanings. Cognitive capacity or conscious, controlled comprehension processes are not required.

Comprehension of less familiar stimuli, however, may require conscious control and more cognitive effort. When exposed to new, unfamiliar information (for which well-established knowledge structures are not available in memory), consumers must consciously try to interpret the meaning of the information—or choose to ignore it. Such controlled comprehension involve reasoning and thinking processes, using activated knowledge structures that may be only partially relevant. This may require substantial cognitive effort. As noted earlier, naturally-occuring comprehension involves a combination of both automatic and controlled processes.

Level or Depth of Comprehension

The meanings that are formed to represent an object or event in the environment are determined by the types of comprehension processes that occur during interpretation. Comprehension processes vary in **level** or **depth,** which produces meanings at different levels of abstraction.[15] **Shallow comprehension processes** produce meanings at a *concrete, sensory level,* which represent the physical, tangible characteristics of the stimulus. Shallow processing of product or brand information produces attribute or functional-consequence meanings. In contrast, **deep comprehension processes** produce more *abstract, semantic meanings* that represent intangible, symbolic aspects of the stimulus. Deep processing of product or brand information produces meanings at the psychosocial-consequence and value levels.

---

[15]The term *depth* is being used as a metaphor, of course. Depth does not connote any physical dimension of brain storage.

Figure 6–4 summarizes the major characteristics of deep and shallow comprehension processes.

Level of comprehension processing has many implications for marketing. For instance, marketers introducing a new product attribute must consider how consumers comprehend that characteristic. Consider the unusual strategy that Searle, a large pharmaceutical company, used to promote NutraSweet, their brand name for aspartame, an artificial sweetener used in many beverages and foods. Although selling NutraSweet is business-to-business marketing (the primary market is soft-drink manufacturers), Searle spent about $50 million from 1983 to 1986 on an advertising campaign directed at *consumers.* As part of their strategy to convert soft-drink manufacturers from saccharin to NutraSweet, Searle had to develop

FIGURE 6–4   **Level or Depth of Comprehension**

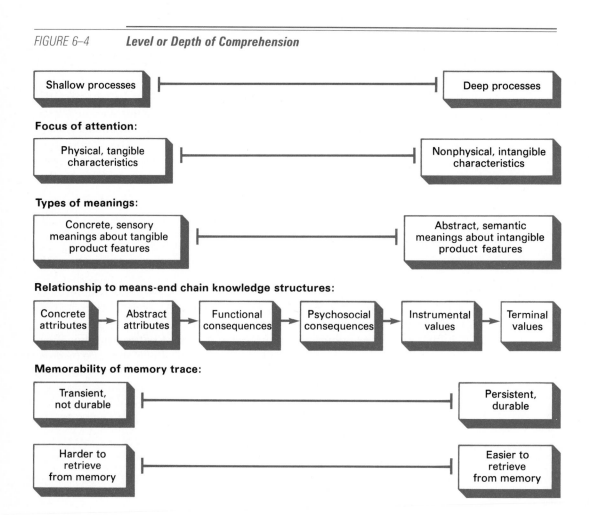

consumer awareness and comprehension of (and preferences for!) Nutra-Sweet. The company developed ads with the tagline, "100% NutraSweet—Why some things taste better than others."[16] Consumers who comprehended this information at a sensory, shallow level probably understood little of its meaning. But consumers who engaged in deeper levels of comprehension could have formed a variety of more abstract meanings about NutraSweet, including *benefits* such as "tastes better than saccharin" or "tastes as good as sugar" (both meanings were intended by Searle)—or even *values* such as "NutraSweet is healthful." The strategy worked. Many consumers comprehended the deeper meanings of NutraSweet and most soft-drink manufacturers converted to 100 percent NutraSweet fairly quickly.

Elaboration Processes

Comprehension processes also vary in **level of elaboration.** *Elaboration* refers to the knowledge, meanings, and beliefs produced by comprehension processes and the complexity of their interconnections. Elaboration is a function of the *amount of comprehension processing* that takes place during interpretation.[17] Less elaborate comprehension involves minimal cognitive capacity, low effort (little control), and little time, and produces few meaning representations. Highly elaborate comprehension processing requires more cognitive capacity and additional effort (controlled thinking), and produces more meaning concepts that tend to be interconnected in complex networks of meanings. Figure 6–5 summarizes the differences between more and less elaborate comprehension processes.

Effects of Depth and Elaboration on Memory

Both depth and elaboration of comprehension processing affect consumers' memories for certain events in their lives. The *persistence* or *durability* of consumers' knowledge, meanings, and beliefs in memory is affected by the depth and elaboration of the comprehension processes that created the knowledge. Specifically, deeper comprehension processes create more abstract, more self-relevant meanings that are *remembered better* than the sensory-level meanings created by shallow processes.[18] Elaborate

---

[16]Kevin Higgins (1985), "Conversion of Diet Soft Drinks to 100% NutraSweet Is Latest Coup in Searle's Long-Range Marketing Strategy," *Marketing News* (February 15), p. 10.

[17]John R. Anderson and Lynne M. Reder (1979), "An Elaboration Processing Explanation of Depth of Processing," in *Levels of Processing in Human Memory,* Larry S. Cermak and Fergus I. M. Craik (eds.), Hillsdale, N.J.: Lawrence Erlbaum.

[18]Fergus I.M. Craik and Robert S. Lockhart (1972), "Levels of Processing: A Framework for Memory Research," *Journal of Verbal Learning and Verbal Behavior,* pp. 671–689.

comprehension processes produce more meanings that tend to be richly interconnected in memory. Memorability is enhanced, because the activation of one of the interrelated meanings has a greater chance of spreading to and activating the desired memory representation.

Marketing Implications

These ideas have important implications for marketing strategies. For instance, marketers should create messages that "fit" consumers' established knowledge structures, to make it easier for them to interpret the information and form the desired meanings. Typically, marketers want consumers to be able to remember certain key meanings produced by their marketing strategies. For example, advertisers hope consumers will remember the brand name and the main attributes or benefits conveyed in their ads when a purchase decision is made. Retailers want consumers to remember their location and the dates of their special sales. Marketers want consumers to remember the coupons they received in the mail. And so on. According to the notions of depth and elaboration of processing, marketing strategies should be designed to encourage deeper, more elaborate comprehension processes to enhance memorability.

FIGURE 6–5   **Elaboration Processes in Comprehension**

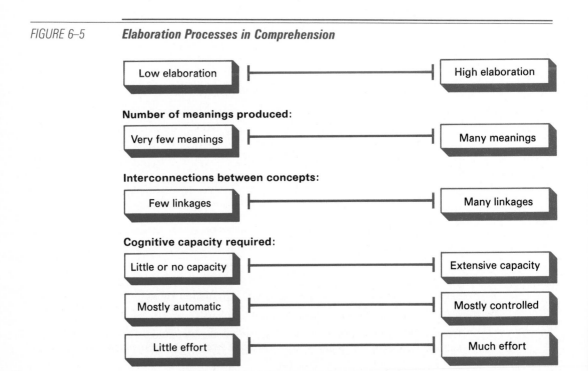

What Factors Affect Comprehension Processes?

Besides the actual information inherent in marketing strategies, two other factors affect the depth and elaboration of comprehension processing. First, the *knowledge, meanings, and beliefs* activated from memory (in schemas and scripts) determine consumers' **ability to comprehend information.**[19] Simply stated, the meanings that are activated from memory largely determine the meanings that can be produced by comprehension processes. Second, *the degree of felt involvement* in these activated knowledge structures determines consumers' **motivation to engage in comprehension processes.**[20] Higher levels of involvement lead to deeper and more elaborate comprehension processing, which produces more abstract, better interconnected meanings. Note that consumers' content and level of involvement and activated knowledge, meanings, and beliefs are not completely independent, but in fact, tend to be related. As consumers' involvement with a product or brand increases, their knowledge about it also increases and becomes more complex, and vice versa.

Effects of Existing Knowledge

The content of the activated knowledge structures has a major effect on consumers' *ability to comprehend* marketing information. You have seen that activated knowledge can vary in amount, level of abstraction, and the types and number of linkages between items. These characteristics are highly influenced by the consumers' past experiences with the product or brand.

Consumer Expertise. The knowledge that consumers have acquired through their past experiences is often discussed in terms of **expertise** or **product familiarity.**[21] "Expert" consumers who are well informed about a product category (or product form or brand) tend to possess substantial amounts of knowledge at multiple levels of abstraction. Moreover, experts' knowledge tends to be organized into richly interrelated network struc-

---

[19]Jerry C. Olson (1980), "Encoding Processes: Levels of Processing and Existing Knowledge Structures," in *Advances in Consumer Research*, Vol. 7, Jerry C. Olson (ed.), Ann Arbor, Mich.: Association for Consumer Research, pp. 154–160.

[20]Robert E. Burnkrant and Alan G. Sawyer (1983), "Effects of Involvement and Message Content on Information-Processing Intensity," in *Information Processing Research in Advertising*, Richard J. Harris (ed.), Hillsdale, N.J.: Lawrence Erlbaum, pp. 43–64; Andrew A. Mitchell (1981), "The Dimensions of Advertising Involvement," in *Advances in Consumer Research*, Vol. 8, Kent Monroe (ed.), Ann Arbor, Mich.: Association for Consumer Research.

[21]Eric J. Johnson and J. Edward Russo (1984), "Product Familiarity and Learning New Information," *Journal of Consumer Research* (June), pp. 542–550.

tures.[22] When activated, those knowledge structures enable expert consumers to comprehend new product information at deeper, more abstract, and more elaborate levels than novices are capable of.[23] Because novices have little prior experience with the product (or brand), they tend to have minimal, relatively shallow meanings and beliefs that are not well organized into knowledge networks. Thus, they are able to comprehend the same product information at only relatively shallow and nonelaborate levels of meaning. Differences in stored knowledge structures explain why more experienced people seem to get more out of a book, a movie, a football game, or even an advertisement than less knowledgeable people do.

To develop marketing strategies that consumers can comprehend, marketers need to determine the types and levels of knowledge, meanings, and beliefs of their target consumers. For example, the cable channel Home Box Office (HBO) created a commercial showing dad sitting in his easy chair surrounded by smiling kids, with the TV screen pulsating with light.[24] The strong meanings of family, home, comfort, togetherness, and shared pleasure were effectively communicated to the target audience of families with children, one of HBO's prime segments.

Effects of Involvement

Consumers' level of felt involvement affects their *motivation* to engage in comprehension processes. More highly involved consumers have means-end chains that represent certain products or brands as *personally relevant* for achieving important consequences, values, and goals central to their self-image. The felt involvement experienced when such personally relevant knowledge structures are activated, motivates consumers to process the information in a more conscious, intensive, and controlled manner.[25] That is, they tend to form more elaborations about the incoming information. And they tend to comprehend products and brands at deeper, more abstract levels of meaning. They are more likely to consider the product in terms of psychosocial consequences and values that are more closely related to self.

---

[22]Andrew A. Mitchell and Peter Dacin (1986), "The Measurement of Declarative Knowledge," in *Advances in Consumer Research,* Vol. 13, Richard Lutz (ed.), Ann Arbor, Mich.: Association for Consumer Research.

[23]Larry J. Marks and Jerry C. Olson (1981), "Toward a Cognitive Structure Conceptualization of Product Familiarity," in *Advances in Consumer Research,* Vol. 8, Kent B. Monroe (ed.), Ann Arbor, Mich.: Association for Consumer Research, pp. 145–150.

[24]"Four More Years."

[25]Richard E. Petty, John T. Cacioppo and David Schumann (1983), "Central and Peripheral Routes to Advertising Effectiveness: The Moderating Role of Involvement," *Journal of Consumer Research* (September), pp. 135–146.

The following example illustrates how levels of involvement and amount of existing knowledge affect consumers' comprehension processes.

Assume that two consumers, Susan and Seth, are accidentally exposed to a print ad for a new Volvo 760 automobile. Susan is highly involved with the product form of imported sedans, as she has decided to buy a car of this type within the next few weeks. In fact, Susan finds herself actively thinking about this category much of the time. Seth, on the other hand, isn't much interested in cars. Last year he bought a used Toyota to drive back and forth to work, but he doesn't give his car much thought. How are these consumers likely to react to this ad?

When Susan and Seth see this ad, their knowledge, meanings, and beliefs for Volvo and competing brands in this product form are activated. But Susan's product knowledge is quite different from Seth's. Compared to Seth, Susan has more knowledge, and it is better organized. Given her forthcoming purchase, Susan's inter-pretation-processing goal is to learn about the potential relevance of the Volvo for her needs. She is motivated to examine the ad closely (focal attention) and to comprehend the relevance of the Volvo for her needs (deep, elaborate comprehension). Susan's extensive comprehension processes are controlled by her already extensive knowledge about the important attributes and consequences of this product form.

In contrast, Seth has no specific processing goals regarding this ad, because he doesn't really care about the product form or the ad. Therefore, he doesn't pay much attention. Seth is not likely to read the ad copy, as he has no motivation to do so; nor does he have well-developed knowledge, meanings, or beliefs to use in comprehending the ad message. His comprehension processes are shallow and simple (not deep or elaborate). In fact, his comprehension may be only a simple recognition that this is an ad for Volvo.

In contrast, consumers who activate low-involvement knowledge structures when exposed to product information tend to find the information uninteresting and irrelevant. Therefore, they are not likely to exert much effort in interpreting the information. Because of their low motivation to comprehend, they will produce a minimal amount of elaboration and relatively shallow meanings. At very low levels of involvement, comprehension processes may produce only a few, simple, sensory-level meanings. Such comprehension processing is likely to be automatic, with low levels of conscious awareness.

Inference Processes during Comprehension

Deeper and more elaborate comprehension processes necessarily involve drawing **inferences.** Forming inferences involves *constructing meanings*

Durrett Wagner/The Bookworks Inc.

What inferences might consumers draw about Mother's Used Cars?

about concepts and relationships that *are not explicit* in the environmental information. Inferences are strongly influenced by previously learned relationships between meaning concepts. If this knowledge is activated from memory, it may be used as the basis for forming **inferential elaborations.**[26] For instance, a common consumer inference is based on the perceived relationship between the price and the quality of a product. Many consumers believe (or act as if they believe) that more expensive brands are higher in quality than cheaper brands. Being exposed to the price of a product may activate this knowledge, and this knowledge may lead consumers to draw an inference (create a meaning) about the quality of the product.[27]

---

[26]Jerry C. Olson (1978), "Inferential Belief Formation in the Cue Utilization Process," in *Advances in Consumer Research,* Vol 5, H. Keith Hunt (ed.), Ann Arbor, Mich.: Association for Consumer Research, pp. 706–713.

[27]Jerry C. Olson (1977), "Price as an Informational Cue: Effects on Product Evaluations," in *Consumer and Industrial Buying Behavior,* A.G. Woodside, J.N. Sheth and P.D. Bennett (eds.), New York: Elsevier North-Holland, Publishing, pp. 267–286.

Constructing Means-End Chains

You have seen that different levels of comprehension processing produce meanings ranging from shallow representations of a product's physical attributes to more abstract semantic meanings (the consequences of product use), to very abstract, symbolic meanings (the values and goals the product helps to achieve). Through inferential elaboration processes, these meanings may be combined into causal propositions, which in turn, may be linked together to form a means-end chain of product knowledge.

For example, Kellogg tried an advertising strategy for All-Bran that seems to be based on consumer inferences. Print ads were headlined, "At last, some news about cancer you can live with." The ads repeated the National Cancer Institute's recommendation for increasing levels of fiber in the diet and then stated that "no cereal has more fiber" than All-Bran.[28] Apparently Kellogg hoped that consumers would make the inference that the product attribute (high fiber) leads to the consequence (reduced risk of cancer). Most consumers would then form the obvious inference that "reduced risk of cancer" helps to achieve the universal values of "long life," "health," and "happiness." The motivational influence of such a high-involvement knowledge structure is obvious.

Inferential Cues

Consumers often use *tangible* product attributes as cues in making inferences about *abstract* attributes, consequences and values. Simple inferences or elaborations are influenced largely by these **inferential cues,** and in highly familiar situations, may be made automatically without much conscious awareness. For instance, some consumers draw inferences about the cleaning power of a powdered laundry detergent from the color of the granules: blue and white are known to connote cleanliness. Or consumers could form inferences about product quality from physical characteristics (color, shape, or material) of the package. Some products thus are packaged in gold or silver foil, which implies quality to many consumers. Hershey, for example, sells a premium-priced candy bar, Golden Almond, wrapped in gold foil. Marketers of perfumes and colognes know that tangible attributes of the bottle (especially its shape, material, and color) affect consumers' inferences about other attributes and consequences of the product. Even the brand name of a product can serve as a cue to consumers for drawing inferences (see Highlight 6–6).

---

[28]Janet Neiman (1984), "All-Bran Ads May Inspire Health Trend," *Advertising Age* (October 29), p. 6.

HIGHLIGHT 6–6   **What's in a Name?**

Marketers try to create marketing strategies that enable consumers to comprehend the appropriate meanings for their products. A key aspect of the marketing strategy for a new product is the brand name. Consumers can form inferences about important meanings just from the brand name—and those meanings, of course, should be consistent with the intended brand image. For instance, Ford selected a nonword, Merkur, for its new imported car. Although the word really doesn't mean anything, it is German-sounding and connotes a high-tech image, just the meanings Ford wanted consumers to infer.

A primary function of a brand name is to differentiate the item from the competition. That is, the name should be different from other names and should help create a distinctive image (a unique network of meanings). The dominant image for most fragrances has been romance, so many of the brand names are quite similar—Cie, Ciara, Cerissa, Chimere, Cachet, and Chanel. Marketers of some fragrances have tried to create more distinctive images by using different types of names like Votre, Charlie, Scoundrel, and Babe.

The brand name should describe or connote the key meaning of the product, if possible. Consider how clearly names such as Pudding Pops

frozen snacks, Liquid Plumber drain cleaner, Head and Shoulders shampoo, Easy-Off oven cleaner, and Seduction cologne convey the product's basic function or key benefit.

Finally, a brand name should be memorable and easy to pronounce. Many believe that short names have an advantage here. For instance, the name Acura was selected for Honda's new luxury car, because it was thought to connote precision (as in accuracy), which was Honda's intended meaning. *Acura* also meets other important criteria for a coined word. Because it ends with an "a," it is read as a noun and is obviously the name of something. Also, the word begins and ends with the same letter, making it more memorable. Finally, *Acura* contains three clearly voiced syllables in only five letters, making it easy to pronounce.

In sum, the key consideration in selecting a brand name, whether short or long, is that it conveys a set of distinctive meanings that are consistent with the image intended by the marketing strategy.

Source: Daniel Doeden (1981), "How to Select a Brand Name," Marketing Communications *(November), pp. 56–61; Jeffrey A. Trachtenberg (1985), "Name That Brand,"* Forbes *(April 8), pp. 128, 130.*

Other Influences on Comprehension Processes

Many other factors interact with consumers' existing knowledge and levels of involvement to affect their comprehension processes. These factors fall into two categories: consumer characteristics and environmental characteristics. *Consumer characteristics* include cognitive processing abilities, mood and emotional factors, and current goals. *Environmental factors* that influence consumers' comprehension processes include information format, opportunity to process, contextual influences, and other miscellaneous factors. The effects of these characteristics on comprehension processes are summarized in the appendix to this chapter.

Discussion

Marketing strategies involve changing aspects of consumers' environment. To be successful, marketers must devise strategies that consumers will attend to and comprehend accurately. When marketing information is compatible with consumers' knowledge structures, the probability of attention and correct comprehension increases.

Marketers who are concerned about the effectiveness of their strategies can conduct research to determine whether consumers are comprehending the desired meanings. For instance, most consumer-goods companies routinely check consumers' comprehension of their advertisements. (This procedure, called copy testing, is discussed in Chapter 18.) Consumers' comprehension of other important components of marketing strategy (price, product features, distribution factors) are less commonly measured. Thus, some marketing strategies fail to influence consumer behavior as intended, often because consumers comprehended the information differently than the marketer intended. In the appendix to this chapter, we briefly discuss methods of measuring consumers' comprehension.

Implications for Marketing Strategies

In this chapter we discussed exposure, attention, and comprehension processes by which consumers acquire knowledge about marketing information in their environments. Designing and implementing successful marketing strategies—whether price, product, promotion, or distribution strategies—requires that marketers consider each of these processes. Basically, the marketer must address three questions:

1. How can I maximize exposure of the marketing information to my target segment of consumers?
2. How can I capture the attention of my target segment of consumers?
3. At what depth and amount of elaboration do I want the target segment of consumers to comprehend my information?

In the concluding section of this chapter, we examine the relevance of these exposure, attention, and comprehension issues for several marketing problems.

Product Labeling

Consumers are exposed to an immense amount of information on product labels—tags, stickers, and panels printed on the package. The effectiveness of label information depends on whether consumers pay attention to it and whether they understand it. For instance, research typically finds that most consumers pay relatively little attention to the nutrition information provided on the packages of many processed food products, even though they claim to be interested.[29] Of course, some consumer segments do attend to label information on nutrition. Consumers with special health problems or those with children tend to be more involved with nutrition and therefore are more motivated to attend to and comprehend nutritional information.[30]

Information Labels

Many types of information are presented on product labels. Refrigerators and air conditioners have stickers showing their energy-efficiency ratings; new cars have labels with the EPA estimated highway mileage; gasoline pumps have octane-rating labels. Ingredient labels identify the specific composition of processed foods and drug products. Despite the huge amount of information on product labels, however, much of this information does not seem to have a major effect on consumers' behaviors.[31] Research suggests that although most consumers are aware of the label information, they do not pay much attention to it until they become sufficiently involved with the product or the type of information. Thus, consumers are not likely to be concerned about the energy-efficiency ratings on an air conditioner unless they are about to buy one. And, if these situationally involved consumers lack relevant knowledge structures, they *still* may not be able to accurately comprehend the information.[32]

Warning Labels

Some product labels contain warnings to alert and inform consumers of potential dangers and risks. Warning labels are found on such products as

---

[29]Jacob Jacoby, Robert W. Chestnut and William Silberman (1977), "Consumer Use and Comprehension of Nutrition Information," *Journal of Consumer Research* (September), pp. 119–128.

[30]Joyce A. Vermeersch and Helene Swenerton (1980), "Interpretations of Nutrition Claims in Food Advertisements by Low-Income Consumers," *Journal of Nutrition Education* (January–March), pp. 19–25.

[31]For example, see Dennis L. NcNeill and William L. Wilkie (1979), "Public Policy and Consumer Information: Impact of the New Energy Labels," *Journal of Consumer Research* (June), pp. 1–11.

[32]For example, see Jacoby, Chestnut and Silberman "Consumer Use and Comprehension of Nutrition Information."

HIGHLIGHT 6–7   ***Icelanders to Be Told that Smoking Kills***

REYKJAVIK, Iceland, June 25 (Reuters)—Full-color warnings stating bluntly that smoking kills will appear starting next week on cigarette packages sold in Iceland, despite loud protests from international tabacco companies.

Unlike the cautiously worded message previously printed on the bottom of packs—"Cigarette smoking may be detrimental to health"—the new warnings, compulsory from next Monday, are unambiguous.

The warnings, to appear on the front of the packs, say "Every year hundreds of Icelanders die from smoking" and "Smoking increases the danger of heart attacks" and "Smoking endangers the health of mother and child."

Packs will also carry drawings of the human organs that are damaged by cigarette smoke.

"International tobacco companies are horrified by the new labels," the Health Ministry Director General Pall Sigurdsson, said.

Cigarette producers have had to bear the cost of the new labels, which they say interfere with the packs' design, and some have threatened to halt deliveries to Iceland altogether.

What are the marketing implications of this proposed action?

How effective do you think this policy will be in reducing smoking behavior?

Historical Pictures Service, Inc./Chicago

Source: The New York Times, *June 26, 1985;* *Courtesy Reuters Ltd.*

---

cigarettes, lawn mowers, antacids, and soft drinks sweetened with saccharin. Again, most research seems to indicate that warning messages have relatively little effect on the broad population, although persons for whom the danger or risk is especially salient (higher in involvement) are more likely to pay attention and comprehend the warning. Over prolonged periods of exposure, however, consumers seem to get used to warnings and tend not to attend to them anymore. Because warnings seem to wear out over time, it has been suggested that warning labels be rotated on a regular basis, to keep the message novel (see Highlight 6–7).[33]

Pricing Strategies

Although price may seem like a simple marketing stimulus, consumers may comprehend a variety of different meanings for a particular price ($4.95), a price change (an increase of 2 cents per gallon in the cost of gasoline), or a specific pricing strategy (a $750 rebate on all Chevrolet cars). As is true of all meanings, price meanings are highly sensitive to context. For instance, a $10 meal might seem unreasonably expensive in a fast-food restaurant, but in a trendy sidewalk cafe, it would be comprehended as a bargain. Consumers are likely to draw inferences about the *reasons* for some price strategies that might affect their behavior. If consumers interpret a rebate program as necessary to sell a poor-quality product that nobody would buy at full price, they will be much less likely to buy the product, for instance. (Consumers' reactions to pricing strategies are discussed in Chapter 19.)

Distribution Strategies

The type of store where a product is sold and the network of store meanings and images often provide powerful contextual cues that influence consumers' meanings for products. Thus, for some consumers, the same brand of jeans purchased in Saks or Macy's may have a more positive set of meanings than the jeans would if they were bought in K mart or Target. Consumers' store-image meanings can affect their comprehension of brand meanings. (Consumers reactions to distribution strategies are discussed in Chapter 20.)

Advertising Strategies

More research has focused on consumers' comprehension of meanings conveyed through advertising—especially TV and print—than on the other elements of marketing strategy, probably because of the huge sums of money involved in these types of promotions. Advertisers have tried many strategies—including humor, slice of life, and emotional appeals—

---

[33]Raymond E. Schucker, Raymond C. Stokes, Michael L. Stewart and Douglas P. Henderson (1983), "The Impact of the Saccharin Warning Label on Sales of Diet Soft Drinks in Supermarkets," *Journal of Public Policy and Marketing,* pp. 46–57.

In 1984, J.C. Penney was at a critical juncture in its strategy to change its image from a basic discount store to a full-scale department store. The image-change strategy had several components, including a $1 billion store-modernization program and a $22 million advertising campaign to tell consumers about the new Penney's. These strategy elements involved changes in consumers' environment. Now Penney's had to get consumers to attend to and correctly comprehend these changes.

A major aspect of the Penney's strategy involved changes in the merchandise they sold. The store had begun to carry several up-scale, high-quality product lines, including well-known brands such as Halston and Santa Cruz for women and Lee Wright and Stafford for men. A major influence on a retailer's image is the brands that it sells; in return, the brand image is also influenced by the store image.

Another aspect of Penney's marketing strategy concerned advertising appeals. Penney's ads are intended to evoke emotional responses, as well as create beliefs about the fashions. For instance, one ad shows a lawyer's day in court before he goes off to coach a children's football team. Another shows an old curmudgeon of a college professor who spiffs up with new tweeds from Penney's. Comprehension of these ads was intended to create a mood or set of feelings that Penney's hoped would also create positive meanings for the store.

Source: Adapted from Pat Sloan (1984), "Penney's Pitch: Change for the Better," Advertising Age (September 17), pp. 6 and 90.

many of which we will discuss in Chapter 18. For now, we consider another aspect of consumers' comprehension processes that marketers should consider when deciding on an advertising strategy: What level and amount of attention and comprehension do we want consumers to engage in during exposure to this ad?

To be successful, certain advertising strategies require that consumers comprehend the ads at a deep and elaborate level. Such intensive comprehension processing would be most advantageous for ads that promote highly involving products. Consider the typical print ad strategies followed by Saab, Porsche, or Mercedes-Benz. Most of these ads contain a great deal of information describing technical and functional aspects of the cars. To fully comprehend this information, consumers must have fairly sophisticated knowledge, meanings, and beliefs about automobiles plus a sufficient level of involvement to engage in deep, elaborate comprehension processes.

With other advertising strategies, however, marketers may not want consumers to process ads at a deep, elaborate level. Sometimes, a minimal, sensory level of processing is desired. Consider the typical advertising for cologne, soft drinks, or cigarettes. Often these ads contain virtually no written information beyond a brief slogan such as "Come to Marlboro Country" or "Coke is it!" If consumers were to try to process these ads at a deep and elaborate level, they would become aware that these slogans have relatively little semantic meaning. Comprehension of such ads does not produce rational means-end chains of associated attributes or suggest higher-ordered consequences. In fact, many of these ads seldom mention product attributes. Instead, marketers hope that consumers will engage in relatively shallow, nonelaborate comprehension processes. Many of these ads are just "reminders" to activate the brand name and keep its top-of-

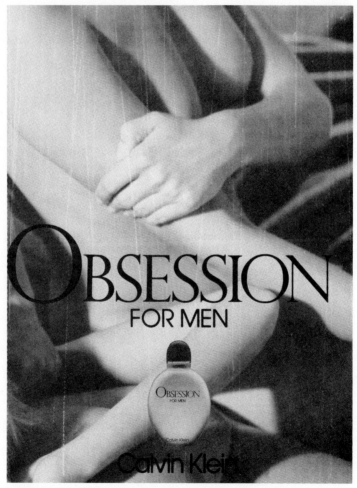

Courtesy Calvin Klein

What meanings do you think consumers might form about Obsession for Men?

mind awareness at a high level. The outcome might be brand-name recognition and perhaps one or two vague, but positive, meanings.

In other cases, marketers such as Calvin Klein have created intentionally ambiguous ads. When comprehended, the symbolic meanings of these ads may vary widely from consumer to consumer. Such strategies may be effective as long as consumers' interpretations are generally favorable.

Miscomprehension of Marketing Information

Given the complex set of internal and external factors that influence consumers' comprehension processes, you might expect that a substantial amount of marketing information is miscomprehended—that consumers form inaccurate, confused, or inappropriate meanings. In fact, most (perhaps all) marketing information is probably miscomprehended by at least some consumers. The type of miscomprehension can vary from confusion over similar brand names (see Highlight 6–9) to completely misinterpreting a product claim.

The results of a recent study suggested that people miscomprehend an average of about 30 percent of many different types of information, including ads, news reports, etc.[34] Although some researchers feel the estimate is too high (due to problems in the research methodology),[35] it is clear that consumers do misinterpret some of the information in their environments. Unethical marketers may try to create intentionally confusing or misleading information that will be miscomprehended by consumers; but most professional marketers work hard to create marketing information that is understood correctly. Given the many influences on consumers' attention and comprehension processes, however, it is not possible to create marketing information that all consumers will always comprehend accurately and identically.

Public-Policy Implications

The concepts we have presented regarding consumer attention to and comprehension of marketing information also have implications for public pol-

---

[34]Jacob Jacoby and Wayne D. Hoyer (1982), "Viewer Miscomprehension of Televised Communication: Selected Findings," *Journal of Marketing* (Fall), pp. 12–26.

[35]Gary T. Ford and Richard Yalch (1982), "Viewer Miscomprehension of Televised Communication—A Comment," *Journal of Marketing* (Fall), pp. 27–31; Richard W. Mizerski (1982), "Viewer Miscomprehension Findings Are Measurement Bound," *Journal of Marketing* (Fall), pp. 32–34.

HIGHLIGHT 6–9   **Confusing Brand Names**

Marketers guard their brand names jealously. Establishing a brand name in consumers' minds (making it familiar and meaningful) usually requires a large financial investment. When another manufacturer uses the same brand name or a similar one, companies feel that their hard work and creative marketing strategy is being "stolen." Lawsuits often result.

For example, Coors beer company of Golden, Colorado, filed a trademark infringement suit against Robert Corr, owner of a small Chicago company, Corr's Natural Beverages, which manufactures an eight-flavor line of "natural sodas."

The two companies reached an out-of-court settlement in which Corr's Natural Beverages agreed to change the name of their product from Corr's to Robert Corr. Corr, who claimed to be happy with the agreement said, "It is probably better for us not to be associated in consumers' minds with a beer company."

Photo courtesy R. J. Corr Naturals, Inc.

Source: Scott Hume (1984), "Of Corr's There's a Happy Ending," Advertising Age (June 11), p. 12.

icy. Over the past 20 years, government policymakers, especially at the Federal Trade Commission and the Food and Drug Administration, have become quite active in developing strategies for providing relevant information to consumers and requiring marketers to disclose certain information.[36] If these programs are to be effective, public-policy strategists must also determine how to maximize exposure, capture attention, and generate an appropriate level of comprehension.[37]

---

[36]James R. Bettman (1975), "Issues in Designing Consumer Information Environments," *Journal of Consumer Research* (December), pp. 169–177.

[37]Michael B. Mazis and Richard Staelin (1982), "Using Information-Processing Principles in Public Policymaking," *Journal of Public Policy & Marketing*, Vol. 1, pp. 3–14.

Back to the Case

Now, what types of attention and comprehension processes do you think the GE *Star Wars*–type ad generated? First, consider how the ad is likely to be interpreted by the target segment of consumers (16- to 25-year-olds). The sci-fi theme seems likely to attract the attention of these consumers, if they are exposed to it. Media placement is critical for achieving adequate exposure. But will the target segment form the meanings GE wants them to? What meanings could be formed? Does GE want consumers to think that GE is "modern and up-to-date," or that GE "makes good stereo products?" Another critical question is whether these meanings will be activated at the time of a decision. They must be, if the ad is to affect consumers' choice of a new stereo.

Summary

In this chapter, we discussed three processes by which consumers acquire knowledge about marketing information in their environment—exposure, attention, and comprehension. Attention and comprehension processes form meaningful representations of the environment. The knowledge, meanings, and beliefs produced by these information acquisition processes are stored in memory. Later they may be activated and used in subsequent information-processing operations.

For familiar informational stimuli, attention and comprehension processes are likely to be automatic. That is, as a consumer becomes more experienced with certain types of information, attention and comprehension processes require less cognitive capacity and conscious control and become highly automatic.

Four factors affect interpretation processes—the marketing information itself, aspects of the environment, consumers' activated knowledge structures, and the level of consumers' involvement. The latter two factors influence, respectively, consumers' ability and motivation to process the information.

In sum, the success of marketing strategies requires that consumers are exposed to, attend to, and comprehend the information in marketing strategies. Interpretation processes have many implications for developing effective marketing strategies.

Additional Reading

Gabriel Biehal and Dipankar Chakravarti (1982), "Information-Presentation Format and Learning Goals as Determinants of Consumers' Memory Retrieval and Choice Processes," *Journal of Consumer Research* (March), pp. 431–441.

Noel Capon and Richard J. Lutz (1979), "A Model and Methodology for the Development of Consumer Information Programs," *Journal of Marketing* (January), pp. 58–67.

Walter A. Henry (1980), "The Effect of Information-Processing Ability on Processing Accuracy," *Journal of Consumer Research* (June), pp. 42–48.

Marilyn Jackson-Beeck and John P. Robinson (1981), "Television Nonviewers: An Endangered Species?" *Journal of Consumer Research* (March), pp. 356–359.

Werner Kroeber-Riel (1979), "Activation Research: Psychobiological Approaches in Consumer Research," *Journal of Consumer Research* (March), pp. 240–250.

Michael B. Mazis, Richard Staelin, Howard Beales and Steven Salop (1981), "A Framework for Evaluating Consumer Information Regulation," *Journal of Marketing* (Winter), pp. 11–21.

Charles M. Schaninger and Donald Sciglimpaglia (1981), "The Influence of Cognitive Personality Traits and Demographics on Consumer Information Acquisition," *Journal of Consumer Research* (September), pp. 208–216.

Lynette S. Unger and Jerome B. Kernan (1983), "On the Meaning of Leisure: An Investigation of Some Determinants of the Subjective Experience," *Journal of Consumer Research* (March), pp. 381–392.

Peter Wright (1979), "Concrete Action Plans in TV Messages to Increase Reading of Drug Warnings," *Journal of Consumer Research* (December), pp. 256–269.

Valarie A. Zeithaml (1984), "Issues in Conceptualizing and Measuring Consumer Response to Price," in *Advances in Consumer Research*, Vol. 11, Thomas C. Kinnear (ed.), Ann Arbor, Mich.: Association for Consumer Research, pp. 612–616.

Appendix: Influencing and Measuring Consumers' Comprehension Processes

Consumer Characteristics that Influence Comprehension Processes

Cognitive Processing Abilities

Consumers' **cognitive skills and abilities** affect their comprehension processes. Consumers vary widely in their intelligence and creativity[38] and in their self-confidence about their ability to accurately process information.[39] These factors can affect the depth and elaboration of marketing information.

Mood and Emotional Factors

Consumers' moods and emotions during comprehension processes affect their interpretations of marketing information. Activation of an **emotion** or **mood** tends to spread to other memory representations with which it is connected.[40] Thus, when in a good mood, consumers are more likely to attend to positive, upbeat information and to comprehend positive meanings. Conversely, consumers in a negative mood are more likely to attend to negative information and to form negative knowledge and beliefs. Therefore, marketers try to create emotions or moods that are consistent with the overall meanings they want consumers to acquire. For example, life insurance salespeople attempt to create a serious, somber mood conducive for getting consumers to think about the financial consequences of dying. In contrast, the typical marketing strategies for products such as soft drinks, long-distance phone services, vacation spots, and sportswear attempt to generate a positive, upbeat mood, because the desired meanings of these products are highly related to having fun, enjoyment, and happy social situations.

---

[38]Elizabeth C. Hirschman (1980), "Innovativeness, Novelty Seeking, and Consumer Creativity," *Journal of Consumer Research* (December), pp. 283–295.

[39]James M. Munch and John L. Swasy (1981), "An Examination of Information Processing Traits: General Social Confidence and Information Processing Confidence," in *Advances in Consumer Research*, Vol. 8, Kent B. Monroe (ed.), Ann Arbor, Mich.: Association for Consumer Research, pp. 349–354; Peter Wright (1975), "Factors Affecting Cognitive Resistance to Advertising," *Journal of Consumer Research* (June), pp. 1–9.

[40]Gordon H. Bower (1981), "Mood and Memory," *American Psychologist* (February), pp. 129–148.

Current Goals

Motivation to interpret information is influenced by the consumers' current **goals.**[41] For example, a consumer who is considering buying a new stereo system has a greater motivation to attend to and comprehend the information in a brochure describing a new Sony compact disk player. The additional effort exerted in comprehension tends to produce more abstract and more elaborate product meanings.

Environmental Characteristics that Influence Comprehension Processes

Information Format

One of the most studied aspects of the marketing environment is the impact of information format on consumer information processing.[42] **Format** refers to the content and organization of the information in the environment. The format of marketing information has been found to have a substantial impact on consumers' behaviors.[43]

Opportunity to Process

Attention and comprehension processes are highly influenced by the environment's impact on consumers' opportunity to process the information. One of the most important differences between print (magazines and newspapers) and broadcast (radio and TV) media is the opportunity they give consumers to process information. In print, consumers control the length of time they are exposed—they can spend as much time as they wish reading an advertisement. They have control over their focus of attention and the rate of comprehension processing.

In contrast, consumers have no control over exposure time to broadcast media. The rate of information transmission is determined by the marketer, who can develop faster- or slower-paced ads. Consumers' focus of attention is thus driven by the stimulus: cues in the ad will activate rele-

---

[41]Meryl P. Gardner, Andrew A. Mitchell and J. Edward Russo (1978), "Chronometric Analysis: An Introduction and An Application to Low Involvement Perception of Advertisements," in *Advances in Consumer Research,* Vol. 7, H. Keith Hunt (ed.), Ann Arbor, Mich.: Association for Consumer Research.

[42]James R. Bettman and Pradeep Kakkar (1977), "Effects of Information Presentation Format on Consumer Information Acquisition Strategies," *Journal of Consumer Research* (March), pp. 233–240.

[43]Valarie A. Zeithaml (1982), "Consumer Response to In-Store Price Information Environments," *Journal of Consumer Research* (March), pp. 357–369.

vant knowledge structures as the ad proceeds. If too much information is presented too fast, or if inappropriate knowledge structures are activated, the consumer simply won't be able to comprehend the information.

Contextual Influences

Besides the direct effects discussed above, the environment in the exposure situation also provides an overall **context,** which influences the types of meanings produced by comprehension processes.

Contextual cues in the environment affect attention and comprehension processes by activating context-specific memory representations that can spread through the memory network to related concepts. These activated meanings can influence comprehension processes and the encoded meanings of the marketing stimuli. Sometimes, contextual cues activate an overall meaning or theme that influences more specific comprehension processing. For instance, the anchor stores in a mall (the major stores placed at the ends) provide an overall context—a kind of blanket image— for the entire mall and the other stores in it. Malls anchored by Sears and Penney's have a completely different context (and a different image, flavor, or feeling) than those with anchor stores such as Nieman-Marcus, Saks, or I. Magnin.

As another example, consider the broad context provided by the general state of the economy. Price reductions and rebates are interpreted by consumers within the context of their immediate economic circumstances. Such marketing strategies are likely to be seen as more attractive in the context of hard times. As a final example, a TV program provides a context that can influence the way consumers respond to ads that are embedded in it. Strange juxtapositions (such as placing a humorous, frivolous commercial within a serious news program) might produce inappropriate meanings. Consumers' attention to and comprehension of a particular ad is also influenced by the context provided by the other ads in a *pod* (the cluster of ads shown during a TV commercial break).[44]

Miscellaneous Factors

Many environmental characteristics are not controllable by marketers, yet they have powerful effects on consumer information processing and overt behavior. For instance, the amount of crowding or noise in a store can distract consumers from attending to and comprehending product infor-

---

[44]Peter H. Webb (1979), "Consumer Initial Processing in a Difficult Media Environment," *Journal of Consumer Research* (December), pp. 225–236.

FIGURE 6–6   **Approaches to Measuring Comprehension**

Cognitive responses	Example: "List all the thoughts you had while watching (reading, listening to) this ad (sales presentation, etc.)."
	Consumers describe their thoughts verbally or in writing. These descriptions are interpreted as indications of consumers' comprehension processes, or of the meanings resulting from comprehension.
Recall	Example: "Tell me everything you can remember about the ad (brochure, sales presentation)."
	The concepts recalled are considered to reflect the meanings that were created during comprehension processing.
Belief rating	Example: "How strongly do you believe that . . . ?"
	The strength of belief is assumed to indicate the creation of specific propositional meanings.

mation in store displays. As another example, the weather affects consumers' involvement/motivation and opportunity to process information. Although rain, wind, and cold may not stop letter carriers, these factors can have significant effects on consumers' shopping behavior. Daily changes in the weather activate certain knowledge from memory that affects attention and comprehension processing. The ever-present street vendors in New York City know very well that umbrellas sell best when it is raining. The weather also affects the salience of certain products: it is quite difficult to sell snow skis in summer and water skis in winter.

Measuring Comprehension Processes

Although comprehension processes and outcomes are critically important for understanding consumers' responses to marketing strategies, relatively little research has attempted to directly measure consumer comprehension processes or the meanings they produce. Most research on comprehension has focused on attitude change and persuasion (discussed in Chapter 7) rather than on the more general process of meaning formation as we have presented it here.[45]

---

[45]William J. McGuire (1976), "Some Internal Psychological Factors Influencing Consumer Choice," *Journal of Consumer Research* (March), pp. 302–319.

Broadly speaking, three approaches have been used to measure consumers' comprehension processes and the resulting meanings—cognitive responses, recall, and belief ratings. These procedures are briefly described in Figure 6–6. Note that each of these verbal-report procedures is best suited for measuring deeper, more elaborate levels of comprehension and for determining semantic, language-based meanings. Shallow, sensory-level, nonelaborate comprehension processes are often so automatic that consumers have little to report. In addition, nonverbal meanings—such as visual, tactile (touch), or olfactory (smell) representations—are not well represented by these verbal report procedures. As yet, marketers do not have good methods for measuring these "other" important meanings.

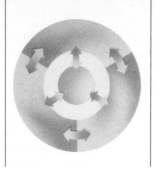

Chapter Seven

Attitudes and Intentions

Coca-Cola Learns about Consumer Attitudes

In 1985, Coca-Cola made one of the boldest marketing decisions in history by changing the 99-year-old formula of the world's favorite soft drink and introducing a slightly sweeter, smoother new Coke. Coke executives thought they had studied and considered every aspect of the change. They spent about $4 million on taste tests and other marketing research that convinced them many consumers liked Coke's new formulation better than the old one and preferred it to Pepsi. However, they overlooked the intensity of consumers' attitudes toward Coke. As one loyal Coke drinker who keeps a multicase supply of Coke stashed in the basement of her Chicago home said, "I love Coke. We all do—my husband, my kids."

Thus, Coke executives were unprepared for the emotional reaction they received from loyal Coke drinkers who were furious about the change in "their" Coke. According to Roberto Goizueta, chairman and CEO of Coca-Cola, "We knew some people were going to be unhappy, but we could never have predicted the depth of their unhappiness." Clearly, a large number of American soft-drink consumers had very positive attitudes toward Coca-Cola, and very negative attitudes toward removing it from the marketplace.

So after only six weeks, chastened Coke officials announced that the old Coke would be back, now dubbed "Classic Coke." They had to placate the consumers who were demanding their old "friend."

Source: Adapted from John S. DeMott (1985), "Fiddling with the Real Thing," Time (May 6), pp. 54–56.

Attitudes have been called the most important concept in the study of consumer behavior. Each year marketing managers spend millions of dollars researching consumers' attitudes toward products and brands, and many more millions trying to influence those attitudes through advertisements, sales efforts, and other types of persuasion. In this chapter, we consider attitudes as a particular type of meaning created by consumers' cognitive systems, and we examine the information integration processes by which consumers form such meanings. We also discuss the relationships between consumers' attitudes and their intentions and the integration processes by which intentions are formed. Finally, we consider the relationship between intentions and actual behaviors, especially purchase behaviors. Throughout, we identify the implications of these concepts for marketing strategies.

What Is an Attitude?

Over the 100 or so years that they have been studying attitudes, psychologists have developed at least 100 definitions and more than 500 different measures of attitudes.[1] Although the dominant approach to attitudes has changed over the years (see Highlight 7–1), most definitions of attitude have one thing in common: they refer to the person's affective reaction to, or *overall evaluation* of, an object or concept.[2]

Evaluative Meaning

As we discussed in earlier chapters, consumers' interpretation processes create meanings (mental representations) that are used to "get along" in the world. An **attitude** is a special type of broad, *abstract meaning*—an overall or summary *evaluation*. In forming attitudes, the consumer's cognitive system seems to be answering questions such as: What does this concept have to do with me? Is this a good or bad thing for me? Do I like or dislike this object? In sum, *an attitude is a person's overall evaluation of a concept.*

Obviously, it is useful for people to know whether objects are good or bad for them. We assume, therefore, that consumers have attitudes for

---

[1]Martin Fishbein and Icek Ajzen (1975), *Belief, Attitude, Intention and Behavior: An Introduction to Theory and Research,* Reading, Mass.: Addison-Wesley, p. 2.

[2]Martin Fishbein (1975), "Attitude, Attitude Change, and Behavior: A Theoretical Overview," in *Attitude Research Bridges the Atlantic,* Philip Levine (ed.), Chicago: American Marketing Association, pp. 3–16.

HIGHLIGHT 7–1   **A Brief History of the Study of Attitude**

Attitude has been called "the most distinctive and indispensable concept in contemporary Americal social psychology." And it is one of the most important concepts marketers use to understand consumers. Over the years, researchers have tried a variety of approaches to studying attitude in an attempt to provide a more complete understanding of behavior.

One of the earliest definitions of attitude was introduced by Thurstone in 1931. He viewed attitude as a fairly simple concept—the amount of *affect* a person has for or against an object. A few years later, Allport proposed a much broader definition: "Attitude is a mental and neural state of *readiness to respond,* organized through experience, and exerting a directive and/or dynamic influence on behavior."

Triandis and others combined three response types (thoughts, feelings, and actions) into the *tripartite model of attitude.* In this scheme, attitude was seen as comprising three related components—*cognition* (knowledge about the object), *affect* (positive or negative evaluations of the object), and *conation* (intentions or actual behavior toward the object). Later, Fishbein, like Thurstone, argued that it is most useful to consider attitude as a simple, unidimensional concept—the amount of affect a person feels for an object.

Today, most researchers agree that the simple concept of attitude proposed by Thurstone and Fishbein is the most useful. That is, attitude represents a person's favorable or unfavorable feelings toward the object in question. Beliefs (cognition) and intentions to behave (conation) are seen as related to attitude, but are separate concepts, not part of attitude itself. This is the perspective we take in this book.

Source: Adapted from Martin Fishbein (1980), "An Overview of the Attitude Construct," in A Look Back, A Look Ahead, *G. B. Hafer (ed.), Chicago: American Marketing Association, pp. 1–19; and Richard J. Lutz (1981), "The Role of Attitude Theory in Marketing," in* Perspectives in Consumer Behavior, *3d ed., H. H. Kassarjian and T. S. Robertson (eds.), Glenview, Ill.: Scott, Foresman, pp. 234–235.*

most concepts that are uniquely represented in their memories. As **evaluative meanings,** attitudes are also stored in memory and may be activated for use in cognitive processes.

Attitudes toward What?

Consumers' attitudes are always *toward* some concept. Marketers often distinguish between two broad types of concepts—objects (in the environment) and behaviors. That is, consumers can have *attitudes toward various objects* (A_o) in their environment—including products, brands, models, stores, people, and aspects of marketing strategy, as well as imaginary concepts or ideas. Consumers also have *attitudes toward their own behaviors or actions* (A_{act})—either their past actions or future behaviors. Figure 7–1 lists several attitude concepts commonly measured in consumer research.

Measuring Attitudes

Attitudes can be measured simply and directly by asking consumers to evaluate the concept of interest. For instance, marketing researchers might ask consumers to indicate their attitudes toward McDonald's french fries on three evaluative scales:

McDonald's french fries

Extremely unfavorable	-3	-2	-1	0	$+1$	$+2$	$+3$	Extremely favorable
Dislike very much	-3	-2	-1	0	$+1$	$+2$	$+3$	Like very much
Very bad	-3	-2	-1	0	$+1$	$+2$	$+3$	Very good

FIGURE 7–1   **Types of Consumer Attitude Concepts**

Attitude Concept	**Examples: Attitudes toward . . .**
Product object (A_o)	
Class	Automobiles, coffee, pens
Form	Sports cars, decaffeinated coffee, felt-tip pen
Brands	Corvette, Sanka coffee, Bic felt-tip pen
Models	Corvette with automatic transmission, Sanka instant coffee, blue Bic pen
Other objects (A_o)	
Company	General Motors, Pillsbury, Procter & Gamble, IBM
Advertisement	Television commercial for Burger King, newspaper ad for a grocery store, Marlboro advertisement in *Playboy* magazine
Store	Bloomingdale's, Sears, K mart, the Exxon gas station downtown
People	Best friend, mother, Bill Cosby, salesperson at the camera store
Marketing strategies	General Motors' rebate program, Coca-Cola's reintroduction of the old flavor as Classic Coke
Ideas	Fair price for gasoline, foreign-made electronic components
Behaviors (A_{act})	
Specific actions, behaviors	Buying a Corvette, cup of Sanka, Bic pen, going to K mart this afternoon, talking with a friend about compact discs

Ralph Shaffer has to be tough. Over the last few years, he has rejected new product ideas for a 6-foot-wide inflatable Frisbee, a toy pig with "I love you" on its pull-out tongue, and a Waldo the Wiggle Dog that didn't wiggle enough. Shaffer is the top creative mind at Those Characters from Cleveland, an American Greetings Corporation subsidiary, and birthplace of such huge toy hits as Strawberry Shortcake and the Care Bears. His job is to invent characters that children like so much they will drag their parents into the stores to buy.

At the end of 1985, Shaffer was betting on the "Popple," a plush toy that folds into its own pouch, enabling kids to make its arms, legs, and fluffy tail appear and disappear at will. To catch kids' attention and begin to develop positive beliefs and attitudes about the Popple, American Greetings will spend about $10 million promoting the furry creatures. Included in the budget is a half-hour TV special and a Sunday morning cartoon series starring the toys. Popples are aimed squarely at the 11 million girls in the United States between the ages of 4 and 10.

Shaffer says he looks for a toy with "play value." If kids have a positive attitude toward the toy, parents may buy it. How does he know? Well, he takes prototype toys home to see whether his own children like them. American Greetings also does more formal marketing research to determine kids' reactions to their toy prototypes. But "a kid's got to be able to do something with a toy other than have Mom buy it and put it on a shelf." Why? Because, as Ralph Shaffer says, "If the kid falls in love with it, she'll tell other kids." In the world of kids' toys, word of mouth can spread positive attitudes fast.

Source: Pamela Sherrid (1985), "The Making of a Popple," Forbes *(December 16), pp. 174-176.*

Consumers' overall attitudes toward McDonald's french fries (A_o) are indicated by the average of their ratings across the three evaluative scales. Note that attitudes can vary from *negative* (ratings of -3, -2, or -1) through *neutral* (a rating of 0) to *positive* (ratings of $+1$, $+2$, or $+3$). Also note that attitudes are not necessarily intense or extreme. On the contrary, many consumers have essentially neutral evaluations (neither favorable nor unfavorable) toward relatively unimportant, noninvolving concepts. A neutral evaluation is still an attitude, however, although probably a weakly held one.

Levels of Abstraction and Specificity

The objects about which consumers have attitudes vary in **level of abstraction.** Figure 7–2, for example, shows several fast-food restaurant concepts that vary in level of abstraction. Consumers' attitudes toward these different concepts are likely to vary, even though all concepts are in the same product domain. For instance, Rich has a moderately positive attitude toward fast-food restaurants in general, but he has a highly favorable attitude toward one product form (hamburger restaurants). However, his attitude toward McDonald's, a specific brand of hamburger restaurant, is only slightly favorable. (He likes Wendy's better.) Finally, his attitude toward a particular "model"—the McDonald's on the corner of Grant and Main—is unfavorable. (He's had several unpleasant meals there.)

FIGURE 7-2   **Variations in Levels of Abstraction and Specificity of Attitude Objects**

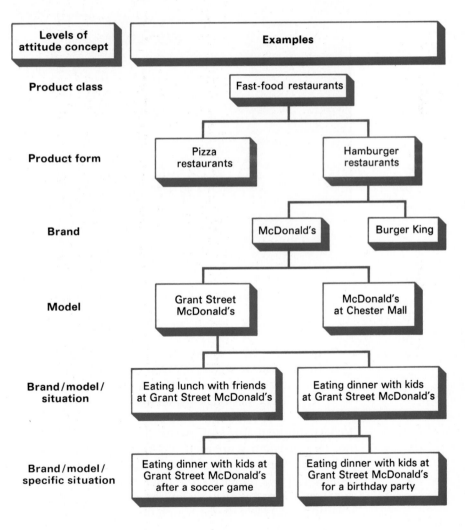

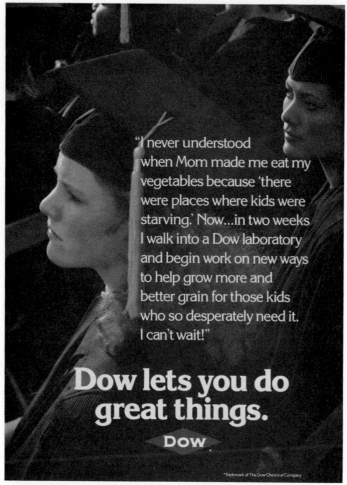

"I never understood when Mom made me eat my vegetables because 'there were places where kids were starving.' Now...in two weeks I walk into a Dow laboratory and begin work on new ways to help grow more and better grain for those kids who so desperately need it. I can't wait!"

Dow lets you do great things.

DOW

*Trademark of The Dow Chemical Company

Courtesy The Dow Chemical Company

This ad attempts to influence consumers' attitudes toward a company.

Figure 7–2 also shows that attitude concepts vary in their **level of specificity.** That is, some concepts are quite specific to particular behavioral and situational contexts (Rich might eat dinner with his children at the Grant Street McDonald's after a soccer game), whereas other concepts are more general (eating at McDonald's restaurants). Consumers are likely to have different attitudes toward these concepts, and the attitudes might not be consistent with each other. Our friend Rich has an unfavorable attitude toward eating lunch with his friends at the Grant Street McDonald's. (He'd rather go to a full-service restaurant.) However, he has a somewhat favorable attitude toward eating dinner there with his kids. (It's easy and fast.) Note that although the same McDonald's "object" is present in each of these concepts, Rich's attitudes are *toward the object/situation combinations,* which are quite different concepts than the object alone.[3]

For some purposes, marketers may be concerned with consumers' attitudes toward a *general concept:* "How do you feel about IRAs—Individual Retirement Accounts?" In other cases, the focus is on more *specific attitude concepts:* "How favorable are you toward an IRA at Mellon Bank that has a certificate of deposit drawing 9.3 percent interest?" In sum, because consumers are likely to have different attitudes toward different attitude concepts, *marketers must precisely identify the attitude concept at the level of abstraction and specificity that is most relevant to the marketing problem of interest.*

The Basis for Attitudes toward Objects

In this section, we discuss the basis for consumers' *attitudes toward objects—A_o.* (Attitudes toward *behaviors, A_{act},* are discussed later in the chapter.) Obviously, people are not born with evaluations of the objects described in Figure 7–1. Rather, most attitudes are *learned* by *interpreting* and *integrating information* about such objects.[4] According to our model of cognitive processing, as consumers attend to and comprehend information in their environments, they form *propositions* or *beliefs* that link the meanings of these objects. For example, after seeing an ad that claims the picture quality of Sylvania TVs is superior to that of Sony, a consumer might form the belief, "Sylvania has excellent picture quality." Then, through the learning processes of accretion and tuning, separate beliefs may be combined to form belief structures such as means-end chains, schemas, and scripts.

Salient Beliefs

Through their varied experiences, consumers acquire many beliefs about products, brands, and other objects in their environments. As an example, Figure 7–3 presents some of the beliefs one consumer has about Crest toothpaste. Figure 7–3 also shows these beliefs as an associative network of meaning nodes stored in long-term memory. Because of the limited

[3]Kenneth E. Miller and James L. Ginter (1979), "An Investigation of Situational Variation in Brand Choice Behavior and Attitude," *Journal of Marketing Research* (February), pp. 111–123.

[4]An alternative perspective holds that attitudes may be acquired directly, perhaps through classical conditioning processes, without forming any beliefs about the object. (See Andrew A. Mitchell and Jerry C. Olson (1981), "Are Product Attribute Beliefs the Only Mediator of Advertising Effects on Brand Attitude?" *Journal of Marketing Research* (August), pp. 318–332.) This possibility is discussed later in this text.

Courtesy 3M
This ad attempts to create salient beliefs about Thinsulate.

capacity of active memory, only a few beliefs can be activated and consciously considered at once. These activated beliefs (highlighted in the network) are called **salient beliefs.** Note that the subset of salient beliefs about an object (those that are activated at a particular time and in a specific context) cause or create a person's attitude toward that object.[5]

[5]See Fishbein and Ajzen, *Belief, Attitude, Intention and Behavior;* Mitchell and Olson, "Are Product Attribute Beliefs the Only Mediator of Advertising Effects on Brand Attitude?" pp. 318–332.

FIGURE 7–3   **Relationship between Salient Beliefs about an Object and Attitude toward the Object**

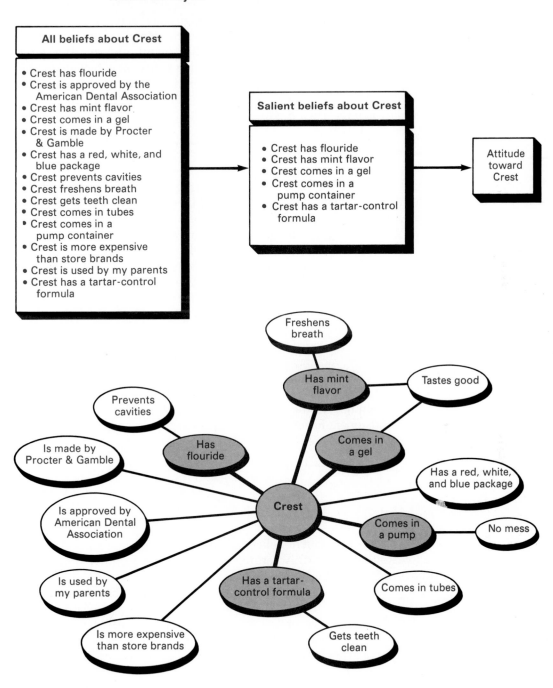

All beliefs about Crest

- Crest has flouride
- Crest is approved by the American Dental Association
- Crest has mint flavor
- Crest comes in a gel
- Crest is made by Procter & Gamble
- Crest has a red, white, and blue package
- Crest prevents cavities
- Crest freshens breath
- Crest gets teeth clean
- Crest comes in tubes
- Crest comes in a pump container
- Crest is more expensive than store brands
- Crest is used by my parents
- Crest has a tartar-control formula

Salient beliefs about Crest

- Crest has flouride
- Crest has mint flavor
- Crest comes in a gel
- Crest comes in a pump container
- Crest has a tartar-control formula

Attitude toward Crest

Freshens breath

Has mint flavor

Tastes good

Prevents cavities

Has flouride

Comes in a gel

Is made by Procter & Gamble

Has a red, white, and blue package

Is approved by American Dental Association

Crest

Comes in a pump

No mess

Is used by my parents

Has a tartar-control formula

Comes in tubes

Is more expensive than store brands

Gets teeth clean

Salient Beliefs about What?

In principle, consumers can have salient beliefs about any type and level of meaning associated with a product. For instance, consumers with complete means-end chains of product knowledge could activate beliefs about the product's attributes, its functional consequences, or the values achieved through using it. In addition, beliefs about other types of product-related meanings could be activated. Such beliefs may include tactile, olfactory, and visual images as well as emotions and moods associated with the product. If activated, any of these beliefs could influence a consumer's attitude toward a product.

Factors Affecting Belief Salience

The key to understanding consumers' attitudes is to identify the underlying set of salient beliefs. Many factors influence which beliefs about an object will be activated in a situation and thus become a salient determinant of A_o. They include the object itself, prominent stimuli in the immediate environment (point-of-purchase displays, advertisements, package information), recent events, consumers' moods and emotional states, and the means-end chains that are dominant in the situation.

Marketers may find that for some products, consumers' salient beliefs vary over time or situations. That is, different sets of salient beliefs about a product are likely to be activated in different situations or at different times. For instance, consumers who have just returned from the dentist are more likely to activate beliefs about tooth decay and cavities when thinking about which brand of toothpaste to buy. Variations in the set of salient beliefs over time and situations may lead to changes in consumer attitudes depending on the situation, context, time, consumer's mood, and so forth. Consumers have more stable attitudes toward objects that have a stable set of salient beliefs.

Multiattribute Models of Attitude

How do consumers' salient beliefs about a product create an overall attitude toward that product? According to our model of cognitive processing, attitudes are formed by an **information integration process.** In information integration, the salient beliefs about the object are combined to form an overall evaluation or attitude. The beliefs to be integrated may be activated from long-term memory or acquired by interpreting information in the immediate environment.

A great deal of marketing research has focused on developing models for predicting the attitudes produced by this integration process.[6] These are called **multiattribute models,** because they focus on consumers' beliefs about several product or brand attributes. Of these, Martin Fishbein's model has been most influential in marketing.[7]

Fishbein's Multiattribute Attitude Model

The key proposition in Fishbein's theory is that the evaluations of salient beliefs cause overall attitude.[8] Simply stated, people tend to like objects they associate with "good" characteristics and dislike objects they believe to have "bad" ones. In Fishbein's multiattribute model, overall attitude toward an object is a function of two factors: the *strengths* of the salient beliefs associated with the object and the *evaluations* of those beliefs.[9] Formally, the model proposes that:

$$A_o = \sum_{i=1}^{n} b_i e_i$$

where:

A_o = attitude toward the object.
b_i = the strength of the belief that the object has attribute *i*.
e_i = the evaluation of attribute *i*.
n = the number of salient beliefs about the object.

Components of the Multiattribute Attitude Model

The two major elements of Fishbein's multiattribute model are the *strengths* and *evaluations* of the salient beliefs. Figure 7–4 illustrates how these com-

---

[6]See William L. Wilkie and Edgar A. Pessemier (1973), "Issues in Marketing's Use of Multiattribute Attitude Models," *Journal of Marketing Research* (November), pp. 428–441. However, relatively little work has investigated the integration process itself—see Joel B. Cohen, Paul W. Miniard and Peter R. Dickson (1980), "Information Integration: An Information Processing Perspective," in *Advances in Consumer Research*, vol. 11, Thomas C. Kinnear (ed.), Ann Arbor, Mich.: Association for Consumer Research, pp. 161–170.

[7]Another influential model, particularly in the early days of marketing research on attitudes, was developed by Milton J. Rosenberg (1956), "Cognitive Structure and Attitudinal Affect," *Journal of Abnormal and Social Psychology* (November), pp. 367–372. Although different terminology is used, Rosenberg's model is quite similar to Fishbein's.

[8]Fishbein and Ajzen, *Belief, Attitude, Intention and Behavior.*

[9]Martin Fishbein (1967), "A Behavior Theory Approach to the Relations between Beliefs about an Object and the Attitude toward the Object," in *Readings in Attitude Theory and Measurement*, M. Fishbein (ed.), New York: John Wiley & Sons, pp. 398–400.

ponents are combined to form attitudes toward two brands of soft drinks. This consumer has salient beliefs about three attributes and consequences for each brand. These beliefs vary in content, strength, and evaluation. The Fishbein model predicts that this consumer has a more favorable attitude toward 7UP than toward Diet Pepsi.[10]

Strength of Beliefs

Belief strength (b_i) is the perceived probability of association between an object and its relevant attributes or consequences. Belief strength is measured by having consumers rate this probability of association for each of their salient beliefs, as shown here.

"How likely is it that 7UP has no caffeine?"

| Extremely unlikely | 1 2 3 4 5 6 7 8 9 10 | Extremely likely |

"How likely is it that 7UP is made from all natural ingredients?"

| Extremely unlikely | 1 2 3 4 5 6 7 8 9 10 | Extremely likely |

Consumers who are quite certain that 7UP has no caffeine would probably indicate a very strong belief strength, perhaps 9 or 10. Consumers who have only a moderately strong belief that 7UP is made from only natural ingredients might rate their belief strength as 5 or 6.

The strength of consumers' product or brand beliefs are affected by past experiences with the object. Beliefs about product attributes or consequences tend to be stronger when based on actual use of the product. Beliefs that were formed indirectly from mass advertising or conversations with a salesperson tend to be weaker.[11] For instance, consumers are more likely to form a strong belief that "7UP tastes good" if they actually drink a 7UP and experience its taste directly, than if they read a product claim in an advertisement. Because they are stronger (and more likely to be activated), beliefs based on direct experience tend to have a greater impact on

---

[10]Note that the actual A_o scores computed by the multiattribute model are useful only for relative purposes, such as comparing consumers' attitudes toward different brands. Taken separately, each A_o score has little absolute meaning.

[11]See Philip A. Dover and Jerry C. Olson (1977), "Dynamic Changes in an Expectancy-Value Attitude Model as a Function of Multiple Exposures to Product Information," in *Contemporary Marketing Thought*, B. A. Greenberg and D. N. Dellenger (eds.), Chicago: American Marketing Association, pp. 455–459; or Robert E. Smith and William R. Swinyard (1982), "Information Response Models: An Integrated Approach," *Journal of Marketing* (Winter), pp. 81–93.

FIGURE 7–4   **An Example of the Multiattribute Attitude Model**

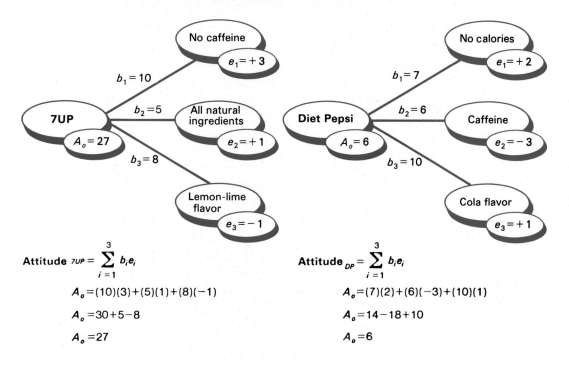

$$\text{Attitude } _{7UP} = \sum_{i=1}^{3} b_i e_i$$

$$A_o = (10)(3) + (5)(1) + (8)(-1)$$

$$A_o = 30 + 5 - 8$$

$$A_o = 27$$

$$\text{Attitude } _{DP} = \sum_{i=1}^{3} b_i e_i$$

$$A_o = (7)(2) + (6)(-3) + (10)(1)$$

$$A_o = 14 - 18 + 10$$

$$A_o = 6$$

A_o.[12] Marketers, therefore, try to give their potential customers use experience with their product. They may distribute free samples; sell small, less-expensive trial sizes; offer cents-off coupons; or have a no-obligation trial policy.

Number of Salient Beliefs

Fishbein argued that the typical number of salient beliefs about an attitude object is not likely to exceed seven to nine.[13] Given consumers' limited capacities for interpreting and integrating information, we might expect even fewer salient beliefs for many objects. In fact, when consumers have little knowledge about low-involvement products, their attitudes might be based on very few salient beliefs, perhaps only one or two. In contrast,

[12]Russell H. Fazio and Mark P. Zanna (1978), "Attitudinal Qualities Relating to the Strength of the Attitude-Behavior Relationship," *Journal of Experimental Social Psychology*, vol. 14, pp. 398–408.

[13]Fishbein and Ajzen, *Belief, Attitude, Intention and Behavior.*

their attitudes toward products or brands that are highly self-relevant are likely to be based on a greater number of salient beliefs.

Evaluations of Beliefs

Each salient belief has an **evaluative aspect** (e_i) that reflects how favorably the consumer perceives that attribute or consequence. Marketers measure the e_i component by having consumers indicate their evaluation of (favorability toward) each salient belief, as shown below.

"7UP has no caffeine."

Very bad -3 -2 -1 0 $+1$ $+2$ $+3$ Very good

"7UP has all natural ingredients."

Very bad -3 -2 -1 -0 $+1$ $+2$ $+3$ Very good

As shown in Figure 7–4, the evaluative aspects of the salient beliefs influence the overall A_o in proportion to the strength of each belief (b_i). Thus, strong beliefs about positive attributes have greater effects on A_o than do weak beliefs about equally positive attributes. Likewise, negative e_is reduce the favorability of A_o in proportion to their b_i "weights."

Where Do Attribute Evaluations Come From? The evaluation of each salient attribute of a product is like a "miniattitude."[14] The e_i of each attribute is determined by the evaluations of the salient beliefs about functional consequences of the attribute. In turn, consumers may have beliefs about the psychosocial consequences and values that are satisfied by those functional consequences. As we discussed in Chapter 5, these beliefs may be linked together to form means-end chains of product knowledge.

Figure 7–5 presents means-end chains for three salient beliefs about the attributes of 7UP. Note that the evaluation of each level of product meaning in a means-end chain is ultimately derived from the evaluation of the end level in that chain. As shown in Figure 7–5, the evaluation of the end state "flows down" the means-end chain to determine the evaluations of the less abstract consequences and attributes.[15] For instance, a person who positively evaluates the end, "relaxation," would tend to positively

---

[14]Richard J. Lutz (1981), "The Role of Attitude Theory in Marketing," in *Perspectives in Consumer Behavior*, H. H. Kassarjian and T. S. Robertson (eds.), Glenview, Ill.: Scott, Foresman, pp. 233–250.

[15]An early discussion of this idea was provided by James M. Carmen (1978), "Values and Consumption Patterns: A Closed Loop," in *Advances in Consumer Research*, vol. 5, H. Keith (ed.), Ann Arbor, Mich.: Association for Consumer Research, pp. 403–407.

evaluate the consequence, "I'm not jittery." In turn, the product attribute, "no caffeine," which is perceived to lead to not being jittery and relaxation, would have a positive evaluation.

Consumers' evaluations of a salient belief are not necessarily fixed over time, constant across different situations, or the same for different consumers. For instance, consumers may change their minds about how good or bad an attribute is as they learn more about its higher-order consequences. Situational factors can also change e_is. In a different situation, some consumers may want to be stimulated (when getting up in the morning or working late at night to finish a project). If so, the now-negative evaluation of the end "relaxation" would flow down the means-end chain and create a *negative* evaluation of the "no caffeine" attribute—which in turn, would contribute to a less positive overall attitude toward 7UP (for that situation). In this situation, the consumer might have a more positive attitude toward Diet Pepsi, which does contain caffeine. This is yet another example of how the environment affects consumers' cognitions.

Information Integration Processes

The Fishbein multiattribute attitude model provides an account of the **information integration process** by which various meanings (the evaluations and strengths of salient beliefs) are combined to form an overall evaluation

---

FIGURE 7–5   ***The Means-End Chain Basis for Attribute Evaluations***

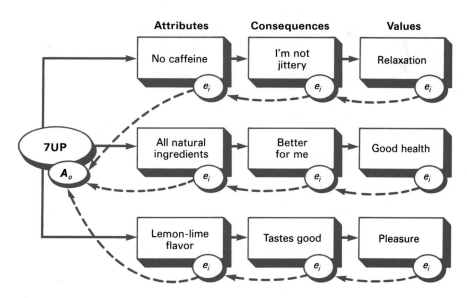

or attitude.[16] However, Fishbein does not claim that consumers actually add up the products of belief strength and evaluation when forming attitudes toward objects.[17] Rather, this and similar models attempt to *predict the attitude outcome* of the integration process; they are not meant to describe the actual cognitive operations by which knowledge is integrated. In this book, we consider the Fishbein multiattribute model to be a useful tool for *investigating* attitude formation and *predicting* attitudes.

Marketing Applications of Multiattribute Models

Marketers have been using multiattribute models to explore consumer behavior since the late 1960s. In part, they are popular because the models have an intuitive appeal to researchers and managers and are relatively easy to use in research.[18] We will discuss a few of the many applications of these models below.

Diagnosis of Marketing Strategies

Although multiattribute models such as Fishbein's were developed to predict attitudes, marketers often use them to diagnose marketing strategies. To do so, marketers break down a multiattribute model into the component beliefs that underlie consumers' attitudes. Sometimes these data can suggest a new marketing strategy. By comparing consumers' beliefs about competing brands, a marketer can learn a great deal about the bases for brand preferences. For instance, the simple example in Figure 7–4 provides fairly detailed reasons why one consumer likes 7UP better than Diet Pepsi. This type of data could be used to evaluate current marketing strategies: Has our advertising campaign created the appropriate beliefs about our brand? Marketers also could segment consumers according to their beliefs about the attributes or consequences of brands and develop strategies based on these perceptions. As you will see below, knowledge of the sa-

---

[16]Fishbein and Ajzen, *Belief, Attitude, Intention and Behavior.*

[17]In fact, other combining procedures have been proposed. For instance, the overall evaluation could be the *average* of the individual e_is of the salient beliefs. Although the specific form of information integration has generated considerable interest among some consumer researchers, the research results are not conclusive. Therefore, we will not discuss this controversy here.

[18]Richard J. Lutz and James R. Bettman (1977), "Multiattribute Models in Marketing: A Bicentennial Review," in *Consumer and Industrial Buying Behavior,* A.G. Woodside, J.N. Sheth and P.D. Bennett (eds.), New York: Elsevier-North Holland Publishing, pp. 137–150.

lient beliefs underlying attitudes can suggest alternative persuasion strategies to change these attitudes.

Environmental Stimuli

As we discussed earlier, prominent aspects of the environment tend to activate certain sets of salient beliefs which then affect A_o.[19] For instance, some U.S. wine companies such as Ste. Chapelle (Idaho) and Oak Knoll (Oregon) have placed special gold and silver labels on their bottles, touting the awards their wines won in taste competitions.[20] These companies hope that the beliefs activated by these prominent labels will enhance consumers' attitudes toward the products.

Situational Contexts

The situational context can have a major effect on consumers' attitudes toward some products and brands.[21] Highlight 7–3 illustrates how usage situations activate key beliefs about the most relevant product attributes and consequences. People are likely to think about good things (activate favorable beliefs) when they are in a good mood. Negative beliefs are more likely to be salient when a person is in a bad mood.[22] Many TV ads such as those for Kodak film try to create positive, warm moods that activate positive beliefs and lead to the formation of a positive brand attitude.

Tracking Consumers' Attitudes

Because many marketing strategies are intended to affect consumers' general attitudes toward products and brands, marketers may use changes in A_o to measure the success of those strategies. For instance, many companies conduct large-scale attitude surveys, called **tracking studies,** on a regular basis. The trends in A_o over time can be useful in monitoring consumers' feelings about a brand and the competitive brands in the market.

One company that failed to track consumers' increasingly unfavorable attitudes was Howard Johnson's, one of the original restaurant chains in

---

[19]Meryl P. Gardner (1983), "Advertising Effects on Attributes Recalled and Criteria Used for Brand Evaluations," *Journal of Consumer Research* (December), pp. 310–318.

[20]Richard Paul Hinkle (1985), "Medals from Wine Competitions Win Sales," *Advertising Age* (January 31), p. 31.

[21]See Jerry C. Olson (1980), "Ideas on Integrating Attitude Theory with Information Processing Theory," in *Attitude Research Enters the 80s,* R. Olshavsky (ed.), Chicago: American Marketing Association, pp. 1–13.

[22]Meryl Paula Gardner (1985), "Mood States and Consumer Behavior: A Critical Review," *Journal of Consumer Research* (December), pp. 281–300.

HIGHLIGHT 7–3   **Situational Influences on Belief Salience**

Situations	Salient Attributes and Consequences of Snack Food			
	Economical	Convenient	Nutritious	Good Taste
For everyday desserts	42	7	3	30
For watching TV in evening	32	9	5	40
For kids' lunch	38	4	4	42
For children's party	11	33	95	1

The relative salience or importance of beliefs about certain product attributes and consequences is often greatly affected by the situation in which the object is used. Situations vary in terms of many factors, including time of day, consumer mood, environmental setting, the weather, and hundreds of other variables. These different characteristics affect which beliefs are activated from memory to affect attitudes toward products and brands that might be used in those situations.

The table above shows how the salient beliefs about a sweet snack product are contingent on the situations in which the product will be used. The numbers were produced by a research technique called *conjoint analysis*. They reflect the relative importance of the attributes and consequences to the consumers in each situation.

Note that in the first three situations consumers have similar salient beliefs about economy and taste while beliefs about convenience and nutrition are not important at all. The fourth situation—a children's party—is quite different, however. In this context, the consequences of convenience and nutrition are most salient. These differences in salient beliefs are likely to lead to different attitudes toward snack brands in these different situations.

Source: Adapted from John B. Palmer and Russ H. Crupnick (1986), "New Dimensions Added to Conjoint Analysis," Marketing News (January 3), p. 62.

the United States. During the highway building boom in the 1950s and 60s, HoJo's was known as a clean place with nice washrooms, predictable but wholesome food, and ice cream the kids would like. Consumers' attitudes were positive, and Howard Johnson's prospered. But over the next 20 years, HoJo's did not monitor customers' attitudes; nor did it respond effectively to the strategies of competitors who were passing them by. For instance, Howard Johnson's used informal gauges of consumer attitudes, such as comment cards left on restaurant tables. Competitors such as Marriott, Denny's, and McDonald's ran sophisticated market tests that told them what customers liked and didn't like. Finally, after a long decline, Marriott bought out the once-powerful chain of Howard Johnson's restaurants in 1985.[23]

Attitude-Change Strategies

The multiattribute model is a useful guide for devising strategies to change consumers' attitudes. Basically, a marketer has three ways of changing consumers' attitudes: (*a*) add a new salient belief about the attitude object—ideally, one with a positive e_i; (*b*) increase the strength of an existing positive belief; or (*c*) increase the evaluation of a strongly held belief.[24]

Adding a new salient belief to the existing beliefs that consumers have about a product or brand is probably the most common attitude-change strategy. This strategy usually requires an actual change in the product. In 1984, for example, Crest toothpaste quickly introduced a tartar-control formula to counteract their rapidly declining sales. Crest's market share had dropped from 36 to 30 percent over a short six-month period. Procter & Gamble hoped the benefits provided by this new attribute would be positively evaluated by consumers, who would then have more favorable attitudes toward Crest.

Marketers can also try to change attitudes by *changing the strength of already salient beliefs.* They can attempt to *increase* the strength of beliefs about *positive* attributes and consequences; or they can *decrease* the strength of beliefs about *negative* attributes and consequences. Consider the $10 million promotion campaign developed in 1985 by the Beef Industry Council to develop more favorable attitudes toward beef.[25] Beef consumption had fallen steadily from a high of 94 pounds per capita in 1976 to about 75 pounds in 1985. At the same time, consumption of chicken rose from 43 to 70 pounds per capita. Consumers' attitudes also changed dramatically as the percentage of people who said they were "meat lovers" dropped from 22 percent in 1983 to only 10 percent in 1985. To weaken consumers' negative beliefs that beef is fattening and has high levels of cholesterol, TV and print ads claimed that three ounces of trimmed sirloin has about the same calories and cholesterol as a three-ounce chicken breast. To strengthen consumers' beliefs that beef is healthful, charts displayed at many super-

---

[23]This example is adapted from John Merwin (1985), "The Sad Case of the Dwindling Orange Roofs," *Forbes* (December 30), pp. 75–79.

[24]Richard J. Lutz (1975), "Changing Brand Attitudes through Modification of Cognitive Structure," *Journal of Consumer Research* (March), pp. 49–59.

[25]This example is adapted from Edward C. Baig (1985), "Trying to Make Beef Appetizing Again," *Fortune* (November 25), p. 64.

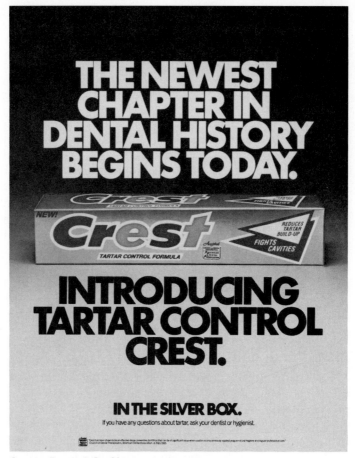

Courtesy Procter & Gamble

Adding a new attribute to an existing product.

market meat counters showed that the calorie and cholesterol levels for a cut of beef compared favorably with the dietary standards recommended by the American Heart Association.

Finally, marketers can try to change consumers' attitudes by *changing the evaluative aspect of an existing, strongly held belief* about a salient attribute or consequence. This requires constructing a new means-end chain by linking a more positive, higher-ordered consequence to that attribute or consequence. Consider how cereal manufacturers such as Kellogg's have tried to enhance consumer's attitudes by linking the food attribute, fiber, to cancer prevention. Sometimes natural changes in consumers' values can affect their product or brand attitudes. After a period of negative attitudes

HIGHLIGHT 7–4   **Changing Consumers' Brand Attitudes through Packaging**

A growing number of manufacturers are turning to packaging innovations in an attempt to improve consumers' attitudes toward old brands. A new and unusual packaging feature is like a new product attribute; sometimes it can create the perception of a strong new product.

Real breakthroughs are rare, especially in mature markets like personal-care products, and many consumers have become indifferent to the "new and improved" approach tried by many marketers. For instance, Gillette had difficulty convincing consumers that its For Oily Hair Only shampoo was really different from other hair cleaners on the market. But they have had no difficulties with Brush Plus, a new packaging device that dispenses shaving cream through a brush.

Clever packages do more than increase consumers' attitudes toward an old product. The Brush Plus refill cartridge costs about a third more than Gillette's Foamy shaving cream in a can, although it yields about the same number of shaves. Consumers will often pay a premium if they perceive the packaging innovation to provide important benefits.

When improved packaging is combined with a better product, consumer attitudes become even more positive. This happened with Liquid Tide, a more powerful version of Procter & Gamble's famous powdered detergent. Six months after its introduction, Liquid Tide had captured 10 percent of the $2 billion heavy-duty detergent market. Consumers liked its drip-proof spout and bottle cap, which doubles as a measuring cup, as much as its improved cleaning ability.

In all of these examples, the new package is perceived as a product attribute, and consumers may form beliefs about its functional and psychosocial consequences. If these beliefs are positive, consumers' attitudes toward the product should become more positive.

Source: Adapted from Amy Dunkin (1985), "Want to Wake Up a Tired Old Package? Repackage It," Business Week (July 15), pp. 130 and 134.

toward wearing natural furs, some American women have developed more favorable attitudes over the past few years. These women no longer feel embarrassed or guilty about wearing furs (once negative ends). In fact, many are buying furs for themselves rather than waiting to receive one as a gift. With these changes in mind, Fred the Furrier, an East Coast fur retailer, promotes the practicality of furs in his ads and enhances the fun and fantasy of buying a fur by building elaborate stores featuring a dramatic entrance of huge columns, marble floors, and an atrium.[26]

---

[26]Pat Winters (1985), "Furry Dreamcoats: Fur Vaults Crack Suburbs," *Advertising Age* (January 21), p. 62e.

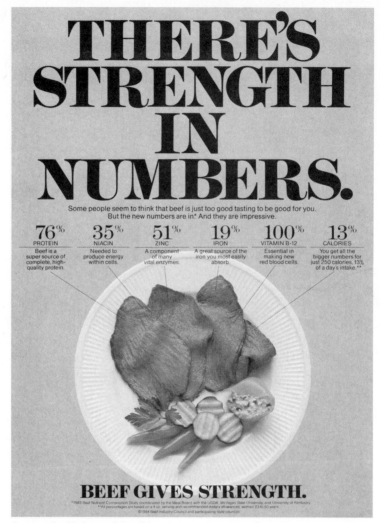

Courtesy Beef Industry Council

An attempt to influence consumers' beliefs and attitudes.

Attitudes and Behavior

Consumers' attitudes have been studied intensively, but marketers tend to be more concerned about consumers' overt *behavior*, especially their purchase behavior. Thus, it is not surprising that a great deal of research has tried to establish the relationship between attitudes and behavior. Based on the idea of consistency, attitudes toward an object (A_o) are usually expected to be related to behaviors toward the object. For instance, Fishbein claims that "most market researchers believe, and operate under the assumption, that the more favorable a person's attitude toward a given product (or brand), the more likely the person is to buy or use that product (or brand)."[27]

Thus, a marketing researcher might measure the attitudes of consumers toward Pizza Hut and use this to predict whether each person will purchase a pizza at Pizza Hut within the next month. This approach probably seems reasonable. But you may be surprised to learn that consumers' *attitudes toward objects* often are *not good predictors* of their *specific behaviors* regarding those objects. In fact, with a few notable exceptions, most research has found rather weak relationships between A_o and specific behaviors.[28]

Why Isn't A_o Strongly Related to Specific Behaviors?

One of the problems with relating A_o to specific behaviors is illustrated in Figure 7–6. This figure presents the relationships between the beliefs, attitude, and behaviors of a consumer named Judy concerning a particular object—Pizza Hut. First, note that Judy has a *single overall attitude* toward Pizza Hut (in her case, a favorable A_o), which is based on her salient beliefs about Pizza Hut. Second, note that Judy *can engage in a variety of different behaviors* regarding Pizza Hut. For instance, she might go to Pizza Hut on Friday night and order a pizza, ignore a Pizza Hut ad on television, use a Pizza Hut coupon for a free soft drink, or recommend Pizza Hut to her boss. However, none of these specific behaviors is necessarily consistent with or strongly related to her overall A_o, although some of them might be.

Does this mean that consumers' attitudes are not related to their behaviors? No, indeed. As shown in Figure 7–6, *Judy's overall attitude (A_o) is related to the overall pattern of her behaviors* (all of her behaviors regarding Pizza Hut taken together). However, *her overall attitude has no direct relationship with any single behavior*.

Although this proposition may seem strange, there are many examples of its validity. Consider that many consumers probably have positive attitudes toward Porsche cars, Rolex watches, and vacation homes, but most do not buy these products. Because favorable attitudes toward these

---

[27]Martin Fishbein (1980), "An Overview of the Attitude Construct," in *A Look Back, A Look Ahead,"* G. B. Hafer (ed.), Chicago: American Marketing Association, p. 3.

[28]See Icek Ajzen and Martin Fishbein (1977), "Attitude-Behavior Relations: A Theoretical Analysis and Review of Empirical Research," *Psychological Bulletin* (September), pp. 888–918; Alan W. Wicker (1969), "Attitudes versus Action: The Relationship of Verbal and Overt Behavioral Responses to Attitude Objects," *Journal of Social Issues,* vol. 25, pp. 41–78, among others.

FIGURE 7–6   **Relationships between Beliefs, Attitude, and Behaviors Regarding a Specific Object**

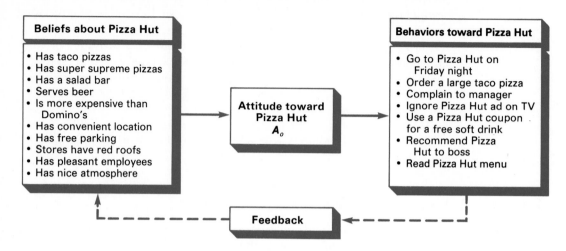

Source: Adapted from Martin Fishbein (1980), "An Overview of the Attitude Construct," in A Look Back, A Look Ahead, *G. B. Hafer (ed.), Chicago: American Marketing Association, pp. 1–19.*

products can be expressed in many different behaviors, it is difficult to predict which behavior will be performed. One consumer may read ads and test reports about Porsches. Another consumer may go to showrooms to look at Porsches. A third consumer may just daydream about Porsches. In sum, having a generally favorable or unfavorable attitude toward a product does not predispose a consumer to perform every possible specific behavior regarding that product. Marketers need a model that identifies the attitudinal factors that affect specific behaviors; such a model is available in Fishbein's theory of reasoned action.

Fishbein's Theory of Reasoned Action

Fishbein recognized that people's *attitudes* toward an object may *not* be strongly or systematically related to their specific *behaviors.*[29] Rather, the

---

[29]See Fishbein, "An Overview of the Attitude Construct"; and Fishbein and Ajzen, *Belief, Attitude, Intention and Behavior.*

immediate determinant of whether or not consumers will engage in a behavior is their *intention* to engage in that behavior. Fishbein modified and extended his multiattribute attitude model to relate consumers' beliefs and attitudes to their behavioral intentions.[30] The entire model is presented in Figure 7–7.

The model is called a **theory of reasoned action,** because it assumes that consumers consciously consider the consequences of the alternative behaviors under consideration and choose the one that leads to the most desirable consequences.[31] The outcome of this choice process is an **intention** to engage in the selected behavior.[32] This **behavioral intention** is the single best predictor of their actual behavior. In sum, the theory of reasoned action proposes that any reasonably complex, voluntary behavior (such as buying a pair of shoes) is determined by the person's *intention* to perform that behavior.[33]

Formally, the theory of reasoned action can be presented as follows:

$$B \sim BI = A_{act}\,(w_1) + SN\,(w_2)$$

where:

B = a specific behavior.

BI = consumer's intention to engage in that behavior,

A_{act} = consumer's attitude toward engaging in that behavior.

SN = subjective norm regarding whether other people want the consumer to engage in that behavior.

w_1 and w_2 = weights that reflect the relative influence of the A_{act} and SN components on BI.

According to the theory of reasoned action, people tend to perform behaviors that are evaluated favorably and that are popular with other people. They tend to refrain from behaviors that are regarded unfavorably and that are unpopular with others.

---

[30]Fishbein and Ajzen, *Belief, Attitude, Intention and Behavior.*

[31]Icek Ajzen and Martin Fishbein (1980), *Understanding Attitudes and Predicting Social Behavior,* Englewood Cliffs, N.J.: Prentice-Hall.

[32]Note that this notion is consistent with our means-end chain conceptualization of consumers' product knowledge.

[33]Note that we are concerned with large-scale, "macro" behaviors, not extremely simple muscle movements (e.g., individual finger movements while typing) or actions that are usually involuntary (e.g., swallowing or natural eye blinks). Marketers tend to be interested in "larger" behaviors or actions such as going to the store, buying a quart of milk, or reading an advertisement.

FIGURE 7-7 **Fishbein's Theory of Reasoned Action**

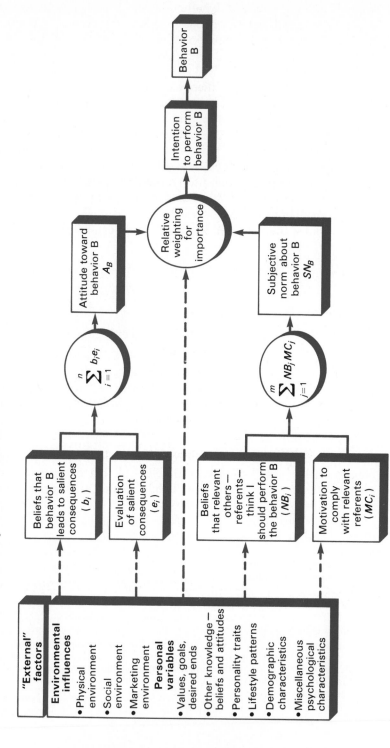

Source: Adapted from Martin Fishbein (1980), "An Overview of the Attitude Construct," in A Look Back, A Look Ahead, G. B. Hafer (ed.), Chicago: American Marketing Association, p. 8.

Components of the Theory of Reasoned Action

In this section, we describe and discuss each component of the theory of reasoned action, beginning with behavior.[34] Note that all the components of the model are defined in terms of a specific behavior, *B*.

What Is a Behavior?

A **behavior** is a complex action/event combination that varies in terms of four factors: the particular *action* involved; the *target* ("object") at which the action is directed; the *time* at which the action is performed; and the *context* or situational/environmental circumstances in which it occurs.[35] Figure 7–8 illustrates these characteristics for several behaviors that vary in terms of the specificity with which the action, target, time, and context are defined. These elements are important since all the components of the theory of reasoned action are defined and measured in terms of the same specific behavior.

Behavioral Intentions

Basically, an **intention** is a proposition that connects self with an action: "I intend to go shopping this Saturday." Behavioral intentions are created through a choice/decision process in which beliefs about two types of behavioral consequences—A_{act} and *SN*—are considered and integrated to evaluate and select from among alternative behaviors. Behavioral intentions vary in strength, which can be measured by having consumers rate the probability that they will perform the behavior of interest, as shown below:

"All things considered, how likely are you to use newspaper coupons when buying groceries this week or next?"

Extremely unlikely	1	2	3	4	5	6	7	Extremely likely

Attitude toward Act

As shown in Figure 7–7, the strengths and evaluations of a consumer's salient beliefs about the *functional consequences* of an action are combined

---

[34]For a detailed exposition, see Terence A. Shimp and Alican Kavas (1984), "The Theory of Reasoned Action Applied to Coupon Usage," *Journal of Consumer Research* (December), pp. 795–809.

[35]Icek Ajzen and Martin Fishbein (1977), "Attitude-Behavior Relations: A Theoretical Analysis and Review of Empirical Research." *Psychological Bulletin* (September), pp. 888–918.

FIGURE 7–8   **The Major Components of Behavior**

Components of Behavior

Behavior Example	Action	Target	Time	Context
Buy Crest	Buy	Crest	?	?
Take plane trip within three months	Fly	? (Unspecified; any airline)	Within 3 months	? (Unspecified; any reason)
Go to Ford dealer this Friday night	Go (drive old car)	Ford dealer	This Friday night	? (Unspecified; to look, buy, meet someone?)
Buy case of Pepsi at grocery store this Saturday	Purchase	Case of Pepsi	Saturday	During shopping trip to grocery store

Increasing Specificity

$(\sum_{i=1}^{m} b_i e_i)$ to form an *attitude toward the behavior action* (A_{act}). A_{act} reflects the consumer's overall evaluation of performing the behavior. Marketers measure the strengths and evaluations of the salient beliefs about the consequences of a behavior in the same way that they measure beliefs about product attributes.

Note that A_{act} is quite different from A_o. Although both attitudes are based on an underlying set of salient beliefs, the beliefs are about different concepts. For instance, consider the following salient beliefs about "Chevrolet" (an object) and "buying a Chevrolet in the next three years" (a specific action involving the object).[36]

Chevrolet (A_o)

Moderately priced (+)
Ordinary (−)
Well built (+)
Dependable (+)
Easily serviced (+)

Buying a Chevrolet in the next 3 years (A_{act})

Gives me a mode of transportation (+)
Will put me in financial difficulty (−)
Will lead to high upkeep costs (−)
Will cost more now than later (−)
Will lead to high insurance rates (−)

Note that these salient beliefs have quite different evaluations. Thus, we should not be surprised to find that some consumers like Chevrolet in general (A_o), but have negative attitudes toward buying a Chevrolet within the next three years (A_{act}).

[36]These beliefs are from a small-scale study reported in Fishbein, "Overview of the Attitude Construct."

HIGHLIGHT 7–5 **Increasing A$_{act}$ and Behavioral Intentions (BI)**

Marketers of credit cards have a difficult marketing task. First, they have to get consumers to accept the cards; then they have to get consumers to *carry* and *use* the cards. Over the years, marketers have tried such inducements as free flight insurance when air travel is charged on an American Express card, and discounts on merchandise that most consumers probably wouldn't buy anyway. Neither of these promotions was evaluated very highly, and card usage was not affected very much.

Credit-card marketers are finally getting serious. Now they are giving away cold, hard cash. If you use their card to charge lodging expenses, you can get a 10 percent cash refund. That's what The Bank of New York (TBNY) is offering holders of its Visa and MasterCard credit cards. Just book (in advance) at least $150 worth of hotel expenses and send in a claim with a copy of the credit card receipt.

Will this marketing strategy work? Well, note that TBNY's strategy adds a belief about a new consequence (getting money back) to the behavior they want consumers to perform more often—using the TBNY credit card. Of course, nearly everyone has a positive evaluation of receiving "free" money. Therefore, we would expect most consumer's attitudes toward using the TBNY card to become more favorable. This in turn, should increase their intentions to use the card.

Some believe that more credit-card issuers will be forced to offer cash rebates to consumers for using their card. According to the *Nilson Report*, a credit-card newsletter, the average card holder now carries about 7.5 pieces of plastic. Issuers can't make money on cards that aren't used—thus, they need strategies to make A$_{act}$ and *BI* more positive.

Source: Adapted from Mary Kuntz (1985), "Credit Cards as Good as Gold," Forbes *(November 4), pp. 234–236.*

Implications for Marketers. Marketing strategies may have a differential impact on A$_o$ and A$_{act}$. For instance, one study found that information about the store where a new product was sold affected consumers' attitudes toward purchasing the product (A$_{act}$); but it did not influence their attitudes toward the product itself (A$_o$).[37] Marketers, therefore, must be careful to specify whether the attitude of interest concerns the object in general or some action regarding the object (such as buying it). Only attitudes toward behaviors are likely to be strongly related to specific behavioral intentions.

---

[37]Barbara Loken (1983), "Effects of Uniquely Purchase Information on Attitudes Toward Objects and Attitudes Toward Behaviors," in *Advances in Consumer Research*, Vol. 10, R. P. Bagozzi and A. M. Tybout (eds.), Ann Arbor, Mich.: Association for Consumer Research, pp. 88–93.

In addition, marketers must carefully identify the level of specificity most appropriate for the marketing problem. Attitudes at one level of specificity are not always consistently related to attitudes at other levels. For instance, Rick and Linda very much like to go shopping (a general behavior); yet they dislike shopping on Saturdays when the malls are crowded (a more specific behavior).

Subjective Norm

The *subjective or social norm (SN)* component reflects consumers' perceptions of what other people want the consumer to do. Consumers' salient *normative beliefs (NB_j)* regarding "doing what other people want me to do" and their *motivation to comply* with the expectations of these other people *(MC_j)* are combined ($\sum\limits_{j=1}^{m} NB_jMC_j$) to form *SN*. Along with A_{act}, *SN* affects consumers' behavioral intentions *(BI)*.

Measuring the strength of normative beliefs is similar to the belief-strength measures discussed earlier.

"Members of my family are in favor of my using coupons."

Extremely unlikely	1	2	3	4	5	6	7	Extremely likely

Motivation to comply is measured by asking consumers whether they want to conform to other peoples' desires.

"Generally, how much do you want to do what your family wants you to?"

Not at all	−3	−2	−1	0	+1	+2	+3	Very much

Relative Influences of A_{act} *and* SN

The theory of reasoned action proposes that A_{act} and *SN* combine to affect behavioral intentions *(BI)*, and that their relative influence varies from situation to situation.[38] During the information integration process that creates *BI*, A_{act} and *SN* may be weighted differently (see Figure 7–7). Some behaviors will be primarily affected by the *SN* factor. For instance, intentions to wear a certain style of clothing to a party or to work are likely to

---

[38]Some researchers have argued that the strong distinction between A_{act} and *SN* may not be justified (see articles by Miniard and Cohen 1979, 1981 and Ryan 1982 listed in the Additional Reading section at the end of the chapter). Alternatively, the underlying salient beliefs for both A_{act} and *SN* could be considered as one set of activated beliefs that are combined to form a single, global A_{act} (one version of such a model was proposed by Miniard and Cohen 1983; see Additional Reading). For simplicity, however, we will follow the separate approach advocated by the theory of reasoned action.

be influenced more strongly by the normative beliefs underlying SN than beliefs about the general consequences of wearing those clothes (A_{act}). For other behaviors, normative influences are minimal, and consumers' intentions are largely determined by A_{act}. For instance, consumers' intentions to purchase Contac cold remedy are more likely to be affected by their salient beliefs about the functional consequences of using Contac and the resulting attitude toward buying it, rather than by what other people expect them to do.

Situational Influences on Intentions

The situational context in which behavior takes place can have powerful influences on consumers' behavioral intentions. In a particular situation, physical and social aspects of the environment activate salient product-related and social normative beliefs, which are combined to create the A_{act} and SN components. These elements, in turn, are differentially weighted in the integration process to form behavioral intentions, which in turn, affect behavior. If the situation changes—even if only in a subtle way—a different set of beliefs may be activated which, in turn, may create different A_{act} and SN components and a different BI.

Consider a consumer named Brian, a 26-year-old assistant brand manager for General Foods. Last week, Brian had to decide whether to buy imported or domestic beer in two different situations. In the first situation, Brian was planning to drink a few beers at home over the weekend while watching sports on TV. In the other context, he was having a beer after work in a plush bar with a group of his co-workers. The different sets of product-related and social beliefs that were activated in the two situations created different A_{act} and SN components. In the at-home situation, Brian's product beliefs and A_{act} had the dominant effect on his intentions. (He bought an inexpensive domestic beer.) In the bar situation, his normative beliefs and SN had the greater impact on his intentions. (He bought an expensive imported beer.)

Implications for Marketing

It is important to determine whether the A_{act} or SN component has the major influence on behavioral intentions (and thus on behavior). Different marketing strategies are required to influence behavioral intentions (and ultimately behavior) when A_{act} or SN factors are dominant. If the primary reason for a behavior (shopping, searching for information, buying a particular brand) is normative (you think others want you to), marketers need to emphasize that the relevant normative influences (friends, family, co-workers) are in favor of the behavior. Often this is done by portraying social influence situations in advertising. On the other hand, if intentions are largely influenced by A_{act} factors, the marketing strategy should attempt to create a set of salient beliefs about the positive consequences of the behavior, perhaps by demonstrating those outcomes in an advertisement.

In sum, the theory of reasoned action identifies the cognitive factors that underlie a consumer's intention to perform a specific behavior. Although intentions determine most large-scale voluntary behaviors, *measures of consumers' intentions* are not always perfect indicators of the actual intentions that determine the behavior. In the following section, we discuss the problems of using intention measures to predict behaviors.

Measured Intentions and Actual Behaviors

Predicting consumers' future behaviors, especially their purchase behaviors (sales, to marketers), is a critically important aspect of forecasting and marketing planning. According to the theory of reasoned action, predicting consumers' purchase behaviors is a relatively simple matter of measuring their intentions to buy *just before they make a purchase.* In almost all cases, however, this would be quite impractical. When planning strategies, marketers need predictions of consumers' purchase and use behaviors weeks, months, or sometimes years in advance.

Unfortunately, predictions of specific behaviors based on intentions measured before the behavior may not be very accurate. For instance, one survey found that only about 60 percent of people who intended to buy a car did so within a year.[39] And of those who claimed they did not intend to buy a car, 17 percent bought one anyway. Similar examples could be cited for other product categories (many with even worse accuracy). This does not mean that the theory of reasoned action is wrong in identifying intentions as an immediate influence on behavior. Rather, failures to predict the behavior of interest often lie with *how* intentions are measured.

Reasons for Inaccurate Measures of Intentions

Figure 7–9 lists several factors that can weaken the relationship between measured behavioral intentions and the observed behaviors of interest. These factors include intervening time, measuring different levels of specificity, unforeseen environmental events or situational contexts, degree of consumer's voluntary control, instability of consumer's intentions, and exposure to new information. In situations where few of these factors operate, measured intentions should predict behavior quite well.

---

[39]Cited in Kenneth A. Longman (1968), "Promises, Promises," in *Attitude Research on the Rocks,* L. Adler and L. Crespi (eds.), Chicago: American Marketing Association, pp. 28–37.

FIGURE 7–9   **Factors that Reduce or Weaken the Relationship between Measured Behavioral Intentions and Observed Behavior**

Factor	Examples
Intervening time	As the time between measurement of intentions and observation of behavior increases, more factors can occur that act to modify or change the original intention, so that it no longer corresponds to the observed behavior.
Different levels of specificity	The measured intention should be specified at the same level as the observed behavior, otherwise the relationship between them will be weakened. For instance, we measured Judy's intentions to wear jeans to class (in general). But we observed her behavior on a day when she made a class presentation and didn't think jeans were appropriate in that specific situation.
Unforeseen environmental events	Sam fully intended to buy Frito's chips this afternoon, but the store is sold out. Sam could not carry out the original intention and had to form a new intention on the spot to buy Ripple chips.
Unforeseen situational context	Sometimes the situational context the consumer had in mind when the intentions were measured was different from the situation at the time of behavior. In general, Peter has a negative intention to buy Andre champagne. However, when he prepared a holiday punch calling for eight bottles of champagne, Peter had a positive intention to buy the inexpensive Andre brand.
Degree of voluntary control	Some behaviors are not under complete volitional control. Thus, intentions may not predict the observed behavior very accurately. For instance, Becky intended to go shopping on Saturday when she hoped to be recovered from a bout with the flu, but she was still sick and couldn't go.
Stability of intentions	Some intentions are quite stable. They are based on well-developed structure of salient beliefs for A_{act} and SN. Other intentions are not stable, as they are founded on only a few, weakly held beliefs that may be easily changed.
New information	Consumers may receive new information about the salient consequences of their behavior, which leads to changes in their beliefs and attitudes toward the act and/or in the subjective norm. These changes in turn, change the intention. The original intention is no longer relevant to the behavior and does not predict the eventual behavior accurately.

HIGHLIGHT 7–6   **Watch Out for Overestimation of Purchase Intentions**

In some cases, simplistic "intent to purchase" questions can overestimate consumers' "true" intentions, often by a great margin. For instance, many consumers, when asked in a 25-minute phone survey on stereo equipment whether they intend to buy a new compact disc player, will answer yes without considering the costs, procedures, effort, and timing inherent in such a decision. Yet each of these factors might reduce consumers' "true" intentions to buy. Marketers, therefore, need to measure intentions very carefully.

In one recent survey on compact disc players, a series of "filter" questions were designed to force consumers to consider the factors that probably would influence their actual behavioral intentions. A series of increasingly specific intention questions were asked that dealt with timing and price factors. Consumers were asked questions designed to indicate how firm their intentions were, whether they had done any shopping yet, whether they had discussed the purchase with any knowledgeable people, whether they had actually listened to a compact disc player, and so on.

The answers to these questions were quite different from the "standard" intention measure. About 25 percent of respondents had expressed a general intention to buy a compact disc player at $199. However, only 9 percent expressed a firm commitment to buy. Finally, the proportion of consumers who had already begun seeking information in preparation for purchase was a mere 2 percent. In this case, the "standard" intention measure would have forecast sales about 10 times higher than the prediction of 2 percent based on the more realistic intention measure. Because marketers make plans and develop strategies based on sales forecasts derived from measured intentions, they must be very careful in predicting future purchase behavior.

Interestingly, the 2 percent intention figure was not a low forecast. In fact, it showed that twice as many consumers seriously intended to buy a compact disc player as were currently buying the product.

Source: Adapted from Arthur Shapiro and Jim Schwartz (1986), "Research Must Be as Sophisticated as the Products It Studies," Marketing News *(January 3), p. 2.*

To accurately predict behaviors, measures of consumers' intentions should be defined at the same level of abstraction and specificity as the action, target, and time components of the behavior. Situation context also should be specified, when it is important. In sum, marketers should recognize that if they measure intentions at a different level (usually more general) than the level of the actual behavior of interest, the intention's predictive accuracy is likely to be weakened.

In a broad sense, *time* is the major factor that reduces the predictive accuracy of measured intentions. Intentions, like other cognitive factors, can and do change over time. The longer the intervening time period, the more unanticipated circumstances (such as exposure to the marketing strategies of competitive companies) can occur and change consumers' original purchase intentions. Thus, marketers must expect lower levels of predictive accuracy when intentions are measured long before the behavior occurs. Unanticipated events can also occur during very short time periods. An appliance manufacturer once asked consumers entering an appliance store what brand they intended to buy. Of those who specified a brand, only 20 percent came back out with it![40] Apparently, events occurred in the store to change these consumers' beliefs, attitudes, intentions, and behavior.

Despite their less-than-perfect accuracy, measures of purchase intentions are often the best way to predict future purchase behavior. For instance, every three months, United Air Lines conducts a passenger survey measuring intentions to travel by air during the following three months. Obviously, many events in the ensuing time period can change consumers' beliefs, A_{act} and SN about taking a personal or business trip by airplane. To the extent that these unanticipated factors occur, the measured intention will give less accurate predictions of future airline travel.

Can Any Behavior Be Predicted from Intentions?

Certain behaviors cannot be accurately predicted from beliefs, attitudes, and intentions.[41] Obvious examples include nonvoluntary behaviors such as sneezing or getting sick. It is also difficult to predict purchase behaviors when the alternatives (brands) are very similar and the person has positive attitudes toward several of them. Finally, behaviors about which consumers have little knowledge and low levels of involvement are virtually impossible to predict, because consumers have very few beliefs in memory on which to base attitudes and intentions. In such cases, consumers' measured intentions were probably *created* to answer the marketing researcher's question—such intentions are likely to be unstable and poor predictors of eventual, actual behavior. In sum, before relying on measures of attitude and intentions to predict future behavior, marketers need to determine whether consumers can reasonably be expected to have well-formed beliefs, attitudes, and intentions toward those behaviors.

---

[40]Cited in Kenneth A. Longman (1968), "Promises, Promises," in *Attitude Research on the Rocks*, L. Adler and L. Crespi (eds.), Chicago: American Marketing Association, pp. 28–37.

[41]For an interesting discussion of this issue, see Gordon R. Foxall (1985), "Consumers' Intentions and Behavior: A Note on Research and a Challenge to Researchers," *Journal of the Market Research Society*, Vol. 26, pp. 231–241.

Back to the Case

Measuring consumers' attitudes toward an *object* such as Coca-Cola, or toward an *action* such as buying Coke, requires great care. Predicting consumers' purchase behaviors from measures of their cognitions—beliefs, attitudes, and intentions—is also a tricky business. (Figure 7–10 presents several guidelines for measuring attitudes, intentions, and behaviors.) Although Coca-Cola spent millions of dollars for marketing research on certain aspects of consumers' cognitions, such as taste perceptions, they failed to understand other cognitions, such as beliefs, attitudes, and intentions. In fact, in early 1986, almost eight months after the formula change, Classic Coke still was outselling the "new" Coke by five and six times in most markets. Apparently, many consumers still had strong favorable attitudes and intentions toward buying and drinking the "old" Classic Coke, while relatively few consumers had developed positive attitudes and intentions regarding the "new" Coke.

FIGURE 7–10   **General Implications of Attitudes and Intentions for Marketers**

The relationships we have discussed between beliefs, A_o, A_{act}, behavioral intentions (BI), and actual behavior (B) have several general implications for marketing practice.

1. *To measure consumers' A_o or A_{act}*, a direct measure of general evaluation of the appropriate attitude concept is best. Be sure to precisely define the attitude concept at the level of specificity of interest.

2. *To understand the basis for consumers' attitudes,* whether A_o or A_{act}, examine the strengths and evaluations of the salient beliefs that are activated when consumers think about the attitude concept. Again, be sure to define the attitude concept at the appropriate level of specificity.

3. *To merely predict consumers' behaviors,* measure their intentions to behave. Be sure to define the intention so that it closely corresponds to the level of specificity of the behavior of interest.

4. *To understand the basis for consumers' intentions,* examine the salient beliefs underlying A_{act} and SN, and examine how A_{act} and SN are combined to form an intention.

5. *To understand the basis for the intention/behavior relationship,* examine the potential of intervening events to change consumers' beliefs about the personal and social consequences of the behavior.

Summary

We began this chapter by defining attitude as a consumers' overall evaluation of an object. We discussed how attitude objects varied in levels of abstraction and specificity. We then discussed consumers' attitudes toward objects, A_o, and described Fishbein's multiattribute model of how salient beliefs create A_o. We also discussed Fishbein's theory of reasoned action that identifies consumers' attitudes toward performing behaviors (A_{act}) and social influences (SN) as the basis for behavioral intentions (BI). Finally, we considered the problems of using measures of behavioral intentions to predict actual behaviors. Throughout, we identified implications for marketers. In this chapter, we identified consumers' activated knowledge, in the form of beliefs, as the basic factor underlying their attitudes, subjective norms, and intentions—and ultimately, their behaviors. Moreover, we showed that these activated salient beliefs, and the resulting attitudes and intentions, are sensitive to situational factors in the environment, including marketing strategies. This provides another example of how cognition, environment, and behavior interact in a continuous, reciprocal process to create new behaviors, new cognitions (beliefs, attitudes, and intentions), and new environments.

Additional Reading

Joel B. Cohen (1980), "Applying Expectancy-Value Models to Liking, Preference, and Choice," in *A Look Ahead, A Look Behind*, G. B. Hafer (ed.), Chicago: American Marketing Association, pp. 20–29.

Joseph A. Cote, James McCullough and Michael Reilly (1985), "Effects of Unexpected Situations on Behavior-Intention Differences: A Garbology Analysis," *Journal of Consumer Research* (September), pp. 188–194.

Gary M. Erickson, Johny K. Johansson and Paul Chao (1984), "Image Variables in Multi-Attribute Product Evaluations: Country-of-Origin Effects," *Journal of Consumer Research* (September), pp. 694–699.

Barbara Loken (1984), "Attitude Processing Strategies," *Journal of Experimental Social Psychology* Vol. 20, pp. 272–296.

Richard J. Lutz (1977), "An Experimental Investigation of Causal Relations among Cognitions, Affect, and Behavioral Intention," *Journal of Consumer Research* (March), pp. 197–208.

Paul W. Miniard and Joel B. Cohen (1979), "Isolating Attitudinal and Normative Influences in Behavioral Intentions Models," *Journal of Marketing Research* (February), pp. 102–110.

Paul W. Miniard and Joel B. Cohen (1981), "An Examination of the Fishbein-Ajzen Behavioral Intentions Model's Concepts and Measures," *Journal of Experimental Social Psychology* Vol. 17, pp. 309–339.

Paul W. Miniard and Joel B. Cohen (1983), "Modeling Personal and Normative Influences on Behavior," *Journal of Consumer Research* (September), pp. 169–180.

David J. Reibstein, Christopher H. Lovelock and Recardo de P. Dobson (1980), "The Direction of Causality between Perceptions, Affect, and Behavior: An Application to Travel Behavior," *Journal of Consumer Research* (March), pp. 370–376.

Deborah L. Roedder, Brian Sternthal and Bobby J. Calder (1983), "Attitude-Behavior Consistency in Children's Responses to Television Advertising," *Journal of Marketing Research* (November), pp. 337–349.

Michael J. Ryan (1982), "Behavioral Intention Formation: The Interdependency of Attitudinal and Social Influence Variables," *Journal of Consumer Research* (December) pp. 263–278.

Mita Sujan (1985), "Consumer Knowledge: Effects on Evaluation Strategies Mediating Consumer Judgments," *Journal of Consumer Research* (June), pp. 31–46.

William D. Wells (1985), "Attitudes and Behavior: Lessons from the Needham Life Style Study," *Journal of Advertising Research* (February), pp. 40–44.

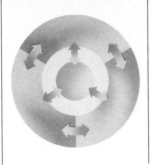

Chapter Eight

Integration Processes: Consumer Decision Making

Buying a Set of Dishes

In mid-September, Barbara decided to host a dinner party for 10 people on October 17. She immediately called and invited all the guests. But now she had a problem: She didn't have enough dishes to serve 10 people. Actually Barbara had two sets of dishes—Wedgewood stoneware and Lenox china—but several pieces of the stoneware had broken over the years, and she only had seven place settings of the china. Barbara decided she had to buy some new dishes. Given her budget restrictions, Barbara decided to replace the missing pieces of stoneware, as she thought the stoneware would be less expensive than the china.

That Friday, Barbara called several department stores, only to discover that none of them had her pattern in stock. In fact, they said it would take from two to six months to get the dishes, and that Wedgewood would probably discontinue the pattern soon. Barbara decided to order the stoneware and borrow dishes for the party. First, though, she would check with her husband.

Barbara's husband was not very enthusiastic. He felt that replacing the stoneware might be more expensive than buying a complete set of new dishes, especially with the sales at the department stores; and he noted that a six-month wait was also a high cost. Besides, their old stoneware was chipped and scratched. But Barbara argued that at the sale prices, it might be better to replace the missing stoneware or to add three place settings to the china. Barbara developed a complex plan to take all of these factors into consideration. She decided that if finishing her set of china cost $200 or less than the stoneware replacements, she would buy three place settings of china. If a new set of stoneware cost $100 or less than replacing the missing stoneware, she would buy the new set of stoneware dishes. But if these two alternative actions were more expensive, she would order the replacement pieces for her Wedgewood stoneware.

When she called stores to check sale prices, Barbara learned that the sales offered 25 percent off all dishes in stock. She also learned that one store was selling a service for eight of Chinese porcelain for $100. At that price, she could buy two sets (a service for 16) for less than any of her other options would cost. She decided to buy the Chinese porcelain, if she liked it.

On Saturday morning, Barbara's mother-in-law happened to call, and Barbara reviewed the situation with her. She said to forget the Chinese porcelain because it is too fragile—either bone china or stoneware is much stronger. She also told Barbara about a factory outlet that had a large inventory and very low prices, but she forgot the name. (Barbara's sister-in-law knew, but was out of town for a few days.) Barbara decided to go back to her previous plan, but to check out the factory outlet, too.

Barbara began to visit department stores. She learned from one salesperson that porcelain and bone china are equally strong and both are stronger than stoneware. She also discovered that ordering the replacement Wedgewood would cost several hundred dollars and could take up to 12 months. Barbara saw an Imari stoneware pattern she liked that was on sale and within her budget. She decided to check with the factory outlet to see whether they had the Imari pattern, because she might be able to save a lot of money buying at the outlet. If the price was low enough, it might be worth the hour and a half round-trip drive.

Barbara found the number of the outlet and called it. She learned that they did not have the Imari pattern in stock, and an order would take two months. However, they did have a large number of other patterns. Although they could not quote prices over the phone, Barbara was told that many people drive a considerable distance to shop there. Now, Barbara was in a quandary. She could probably save considerable money by going to the outlet, but it was a long drive and she couldn't go until the weekend. But by then the department store might be sold out of the Imari pattern she liked. And there was a chance that she wouldn't find anything she liked at the outlet. However, the outlet did have a large inventory, so she probably would find an acceptable pattern. Barbara decided to check out the Chinese porcelain and buy it if she liked it. Otherwise, she would drive to the outlet on the weekend and buy something.

On Wednesday, Barbara went to the department store to examine the Chinese porcelain. Although it was pretty, it only came in a delicate flower pattern, which she did not like. She decided to drive to the outlet right away. If they didn't have anything she liked, she could go back to the department store and buy the Imari pattern.

Barbara drove 45 minutes to the outlet. They had a huge inventory at much lower prices than the department store. However, none of the stoneware had the Oriental pattern she wanted. So she telephoned the department store to see whether they still had the Imari pattern. They did, but they didn't have 10 place settings left. Perhaps this disappointment led Barbara to ask once again if the outlet had the Imari pattern. She was surprised to find that they did have the pattern in stock, and even better, it was on sale for 25 percent off the already low price. Unfortunately, the dishes were at the warehouse and couldn't be picked up for 7 to 10 days. Barbara was pleased to find a complete set of the dishes she liked best at an acceptable price. Her only worry was that the dinner party was exactly 10 days away. She decided to order the Imari dishes and take the chance that they would be there on time. (They were . . . and the dinner party was a great success.)

Source: Adapted from Barbara Hayes-Roth (1982), "Opportunism in Consumer Behavior," in Advances in Consumer Research, *Vol. 9, Andrew A. Mitchell (ed.), Ann Arbor, Mich.: Association for Consumer Research, pp. 132–135.*

This chapter is concerned with consumer decision making. **Decisions** involve choices "between two or more alternative actions [or behaviors]."[1] A decision always involves a choice between different *behaviors.* For instance, after examining the products in a vending machine, Joe chose a Snickers candy bar instead of a package of Reese's Pieces. His decision was really between the alternative actions of *buying Snickers* versus *buying Reese's Pieces.* Jill is trying to decide whether to see a particular movie. Her decision is really between the set of behaviors involved in *attending the movie,* versus the behaviors involved in *staying home* (or going bowling, or whatever behavioral alternatives she was considering). Thus, even though marketers often refer to consumers' choices between objects (products, brands, or stores), the actual choices are between alternative *behaviors.*

Figure 8–1 lists several types of behavior that frequently involve consumer choices. Marketers are particularly interested in consumers' choices of alternative purchase behaviors, especially their purchases of different brands. Given the marketing orientation of this text, we emphasize consumers' purchase choices (e.g., which brand of jeans should I buy?). It must be recognized, however, that consumers make many decisions about other, nonpurchase behaviors. Sometimes these nonpurchase choices can influence consumers' brand purchase decisions (going for a walk or watching TV may expose consumers to marketing stimuli), and these behaviors may be the targets of marketing strategies—"Come down to our store this afternoon for free coffee and doughnuts." Our analyses of purchase decision making can be generalized to these nonpurchase choices.

All aspects of cognition are involved in consumers' choice decisions—including the knowledge, meanings, and beliefs activated from

---

[1]Flemming Hansen (1976), "Psychological Theories of Consumer Choice," *Journal of Consumer Research* (December), pp. 117–142.

FIGURE 8–1   **Consumers' Choices of Alternative Actions**

- Purchase actions
    Should I buy a car or a pickup truck? (product classes)
    Should I buy a station wagon or a sports sedan? (product forms)
    Should I buy a Ford Taurus or an Audi 5000? (brands)
    Should I buy a Taurus with or without air conditioning? (models)
    Should I buy one or two cans of peaches? (number of units)

- Consumption actions
    Should I ride my bike today or walk to class?
    Should I eat these chips or not?

- Disposal actions
    Should I keep my old stereo for another year, or junk it and get a new system?
    Should I sell my old car myself, or trade it in on the new car?

- Media actions
    Should I watch TV or read a magazine?
    Should I watch "60 Minutes" or "Walt Disney"?

- Shopping actions
    Should I go to Macy's or Gimbels?
    Should I pay by credit card, check, or cash?
    Should I go shopping this afternoon, or wait until Saturday?
    Should I buy now, or wait until the sale next month?

- Miscellaneous actions
    Should I take the job at General Foods or Exxon?
    Should I vote for the Democrat or the Republican candidate for governor?

memory, and the attention and comprehension processes involved in interpreting new information.[2] (Refer back to our model of the cognitive processes in consumer decision making in Figure 3–2). In this chapter, we are especially interested in the *integration processes* by which knowledge, meanings, and beliefs are combined to *evaluate* two or more alternative

---

[2]It is important to recognize that consumer decision making is actually *a seamless, continuous flow of cognitive processes and behavioral actions.* Researchers "divide" this flow into separate stages and subprocesses for our convenience in trying to research and understand the entire process, and for helping to develop market strategies.

The year 1985 was a tumultuous time for marketers of "up-scale cars," loosely defined as autos costing $15,000 or more. The well-heeled American consumer could choose from among 41 brands and models produced by 15 manufacturers, many of them European, with sticker prices of from $15,000 to $60,000. In addition, buyers could consider several somewhat lower-priced cars with all the essential up-scale attributes and amenities.

The target market of about one million customers (in 1985) consisted primarily of maturing baby boomers in their 30s and 40s and at or nearing their peak income-earning years. By 1990, this market is expected to expand about 25 percent to about $25 billion a year in sales. The auto manufacturer who hopes to survive in this market must understand how these consumers make their decisions to buy these expensive cars. Consider the following examples.

- Five years after starting his own computer business, Rusty Gordon, 32, felt he needed a reward. So he bought himself a $21,000 BMW 325e, after comparing it with the $27,000 Maserati Biturbo. As Gordon explained, "The BMW had wider distribution, and the technology seemed more refined. It was just the right blend for me. It was luxurious and dressy enough that I could take customers out in it, but it wasn't ostentatious. And it was sporty enough so I could zip around."

- Reynold Stein, 32, a Miami Beach family practitioner, bought his first Volvo because of its reputation for safety. Stein still thinks Volvos are extra-safe cars, but his new Volvo station wagon is also fun. "It's so souped up—I mean, that car is so powerful. It's got the intercooler turbo," he says. "I remember the other day we were going to the zoo with the kids. These fast cars were coming by, and I wanted to get on the highway. So I said to my wife, 'I'm going to floor it.' And that car hit 80 in a second—it just passed everyone. I said: 'What a station wagon!'" Stein is so turned on by the wagon that he sold his former fun car, a BMW 320i. "For one thing, it doesn't even light a candle to the Volvo. So I traded it in for a Jeep Renegade."

- Edith Holden, 29, a Connecticut marketing executive, bought a Saab 900S. "Saabs aren't flashy cars like BMW or Mercedes-Benz, where everybody knows the price tag." But like others who buy the $16,000 Saab, Holden is no ascetic. "While others buy jewels or furs with their extra money, I bought a Saab because its performance is as much a pleasure to me as the voluptuousness of a mink coat might be to another woman," she says. "It's a sporty, jocky, sleek, fun-loving, exciting car. It's not a 'girl' car. It's tough and sturdy."

Source: Adapted from Anne B. Fisher (1985), "Courting the Well-Heeled Car Shopper," Fortune (August 5), pp. 51–56.

behaviors and *select* one.[3] The outcome of these integration processes is a **choice,** which is represented cognitively as a **behavioral intention (*BI*).** A behavioral intention is a *plan* (sometimes called a **decision plan**) to engage in some behavior or set of behaviors.

As we discussed in Chapter 7, all voluntary behaviors are based on the intentions produced when consumers consciously choose from among alternative courses of action. However, a conscious decision-making process does not necessarily occur each time such behaviors are performed.[4] Some voluntary behaviors are based on intentions that were produced by a past decision-making process and are stored in memory. When activated, these previously formed intentions automatically influence behavior; additional decision-making processes may not be necessary. Finally, some behaviors are not completely voluntary and are affected largely by environmental factors. For instance, product displays and aisle placements dictate how consumers move through stores.

In this chapter, we view consumer decision making as a problem-solving process. We begin with a general discussion of this perspective. Next, we identify and describe the key elements in a problem-solving approach. Then, we discuss the problem-solving processes involved in purchase decisions. We identify three levels of problem-solving effort and describe several influences on problem solving activities. We conclude by identifying several implications of consumer problem solving for marketing strategy.

Decision Making as Problem Solving

Figure 8–2 presents a generic model of problem solving and identifies five basic stages or processes in consumer decision making. The first stage involves *problem recognition.* In the opening case, Barbara's plan to host a dinner party made her aware of her problem—she needed a set of dishes for 10 people. The next stage of the problem-solving process involves *searching for alternataive solutions.* (In the case, Barbara called and visited stores, talked to salespeople, and discussed the purchase with her mother-in-law.)

[3]Joel B. Cohen, Paul W. Miniard and Peter R. Dickson (1980), "Information Integration: An Information Processing Perspective," in *Advances in Consumer Research*, Vol. 7, Jerry C. Olson (ed.), Ann Arbor, Mich.: Association for Consumer Research, pp. 161–170; Jerry C. Olson (1978), "Theories of Information Encoding and Storage: Implications for Consumer Behavior," in *The Effect of Information on Consumer and Market Behavior*, Andrew A. Mitchell (ed.), Chicago: American Marketing Association, pp. 49–60.

[4]Richard W. Olshavsky and Donald H. Granbois (1979), "Consumer Decision Making— Fact or Fiction?" *Journal of Consumer Research* (September), pp. 93–100.

At the next stage, *alternatives are evaluated* and the most desirable action is *chosen.* (Barbara evaluated dishes as she found them through her search. In the end, she decided—formed a behavioral intention—to buy the Imari pattern at the factory outlet.) In the next stage, *purchase,* the *choice/intention is carried out.* (Barbara ordered the dishes and then returned a few days later to pay for them and pick them up.) Finally, the purchased product is *used,* and the consumer may *reevaluate* the wisdom of the decision. (Apparently Barbara was quite satisfied with the dishes and with her problem-solving process.)

This basic model identifies several important activities involved in problem solving—activating the initial motivation to engage in problem solving, searching for information relevant to the problem, evaluating alternative actions, and choosing an action. However, for several reasons, the generic model often cannot account for actual problem-solving processes such as those in the opening case.

FIGURE 8–2   **A Generic Model of Consumer Problem Solving**

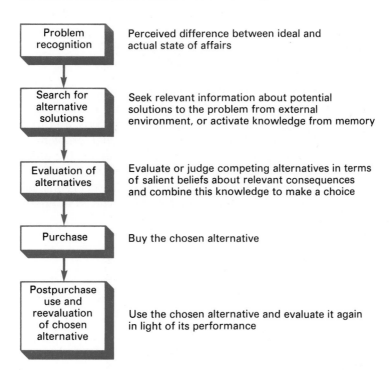

Source: There are many sources for this general model: See James Engel and Roger D. Blackwell (1982), Consumer Behavior, *4th ed., Hinsdale, Ill. Dryden Press.*

One reason is that *actual consumer problem-solving seldom proceeds in the linear sequence* portrayed in the generic model. For instance, Barbara evaluated alternative dishes as soon as she found them; she did not wait until all alternatives had been found.

Second, as shown in our wheel of consumer analysis (Figure 2–3), *actual problem-solving processes involve multiple, reciprocal interactions among consumers' cognitive processes, their behaviors, and aspects of the physical and social environment.*[5] Reciprocal interactions occurred throughout Barbara's problem-solving process. For instance, her cognitions (beliefs) changed as a function of the environmental factors her behaviors lead her to: first her mother-in-law said Chinese porcelain is fragile, but later a salesperson said it is quite strong. These important interactions are not easily handled by the generic model.

Third, *most problem-solving processes actually involve multiple problems and multiple decisions.* Consider the number of separate decisions Barbara made during the two weeks of her problem-solving process: Should I go to the department store? Should I drive to the factory outlet? When should I go? Should I get the Chinese porcelain? Actual problem-solving processes usually produce several choices (multiple behavioral intentions). Each intention and behavior is a step in an overall **decision plan** (go to the grocery store, find Campbell's soup section, pick up two cans of tomato soup). Decision plans, in turn, produce *a sequence of purposive actions* that consumers perform to achieve desired consequences, values, and goals. The generic model implies that consumer decision making involves one overall decision, which is seldom the case.

Our cognitive processing model of consumer decision making is more flexible. It can account for the nonlinear flow, for the reciprocal interactions among behaviors, environments, and cognitions, and for the multiple decisions that are involved in actual consumer problem-solving episodes. Moreover, it can incorporate the key problem-solving processes of problem recognition, search for information, and evaluation of alternatives. Before using this model to analyze actual consumer decisions, however, we must discuss the special concepts or elements involved in problem solving.

Elements of Problem Solving

In this section, we describe the basic elements of problem solving: problem representation, end goals, goal hierarchies, product knowledge, and

---

[5]A similar notion is presented by Girish N. Punj and David W. Stewart (1983), "An Interaction Framework of Consumer Decision Making," *Journal of Consumer Research* (September), pp. 181–196.

choice alternatives and criteria. We also discuss how they are integrated into our cognitive model of consumer decision making.

Problem Representation

When faced with a choice, consumers form a cognitive representation of the decision. This **problem representation** includes (*a*) the *end goal,* (*b*) a set of *subgoals* associated with the problem, (*c*) the *relevant product knowledge* that is activated from memory and derived from the immediate decision environment, and (*d*) a set of *choice rules* or simple *heuristics* by which consumers search for, evaluate, and integrate this knowledge to reach a choice. Consumers' initial problem representations are not necessarily clear or well developed. Neither are they fixed. In fact, the elements of a problem representation often change during the decision-making process, as was true in the opening case. Marketers sometimes try to influence how consumers represent or frame a purchase choice.[6] For instance, consumers might be portrayed in advertisements as structuring and then trying to solve a purchase problem in a particular way. Salespeople may try to influence how consumers represent a choice problem.

End Goals

The overall objectives, needs, or values that consumers want to achieve or satisfy are called **end goals.** These goals are activated at the problem recognition stage and provide the focus for the entire problem-solving process. Therefore, to understand consumer problem solving in various decision-making situations, marketers must determine consumers' major end goals.

Consumers' end goals vary in a number of different ways, including *level of abstraction.* Some end goals represent more concrete, tangible consequences; other end goals are more abstract. For instance, a purchase decision to replace a bulb for a flashlight probably involves a concrete end goal of obtaining a bulb that lights up—a simple functional consequence. More abstract end goals might involve desired psychosocial consequences of a product—some consumers want a wine that indicates their good taste to their guests. Finally, end goals such as instrumental and terminal values are even more abstract and general—consumers might choose a car that makes them happy or enhances their self-esteem. End goals also vary in

---

[6]Peter Wright and Peter D. Rip (1980), "Product Class Advertising Effects on First-Time Buyers' Decision Strategies," *Journal of Consumer Research* (September), pp. 176–188.

Courtesy Southwest Airlines

This ad portrays a positive end goal.

evaluative direction. Some consumer decisions are oriented toward positive, desirable end goals. Other decisions are focused on negative end goals that represent aversive consequences the consumer wishes to avoid.

The particular end goals consumers are striving to achieve have a powerful effect on the problem-solving process. Figure 8–3 presents five very abstract end goals that lead to quite different problem-solving

FIGURE 8–3   **Types of Purchase End Goals and Related Problem-Solving Processes**

Dominant End Goal	Basic Purchase Motivation	Examples
• Optimize satisfaction	Seek maximum positive consequences	Buy dinner at the best restaurant in town
• Prevention	Avoid potential unpleasant consequences	Buy rust-proofing for a new car
• Resolve conflict	Seek satisfactory balance of positive and negative consequences	Buy a moderately expensive car of very good quality
• Escape	Reduce or escape from current aversive circumstances	Buy a shampoo to get rid of dandruff
• Maintenance (Satisfice)	Maintain satisfaction of basic need with minimal effort	Buy bread at the nearest convenience store

Source: Adapted from Geraldine Fennell (1975), "Motivation Research Revisited," Journal of Advertising Research *(June), pp. 23–28; and J. Paul Peter and Lawrence X. Tarpey, Sr. (1975), "A Comparative Analysis of Three Consumer Decision Strategies,"* Journal of Consumer Research *(June), pp. 29–37.*

processes.[7] For instance, consumers who have an *optimizing* end goal are likely to expend substantial effort searching for the best possible alternative. In contrast, consumers with a *satisficing/maintenance* end goal are likely to engage in minimal search behavior. In yet other decisions, consumers may have conflicting end goals that must be resolved in the problem-solving process.

In general, marketers have relatively little direct influence over consumers' very abstract end goals, such as basic values. However, marketers do try to influence less abstract end goals, such as desired functional or psychosocial consequences, through promotional strategies. Perhaps the major implication for marketers is to identify the dominant goals in consumers' problem representations and design product and promotion strategies to be consistent with and appeal to those goals.

---

[7]Geraldine Fennell (1975), "Motivation Research Revisited," *Journal of Advertising Research* (June), pp. 23–28.

Goal Hierarchies

Some end goals (e.g., being happy) are so general and abstract that they cannot be directly acted on by consumers. For instance, most consumers cannot specify the decision plan of specific actions that will yield the best brand of calculator or avoid a "lemon" of a car. When consumers must solve problems involving abstract end goals, they basically work backwards by breaking down the general goal into several more specific, less abstract subgoals. This process continues until a level of subgoal is reached for which consumers can construct a decision plan. The end goal and its subgoals are a **goal hierarchy.** Forming a goal hierarchy is analogous to decomposing a complex problem into a series of simpler subproblems, each of which can be dealt with separately. Thus, the consumer can solve the overall problem by solving the simpler subproblems, in order.

Figure 8–4 presents part of the goal hierarchy for Pat, who has an optimization end goal of buying the best brand of personal cassette player for under $100. Pat has broken down this abstract end goal into simpler and more actionable subgoals, which in turn, are further reduced to even less abstract subgoals. Eventually, Pat's goal hierarchy reaches a level of subgoal that he knows how to achieve—that is, he knows which behaviors to perform to solve that subproblem. Note how this well-defined set of subgoals identifies Pat's *decision plan.* When Pat performs the behaviors at the base level in his goal hierarchy, he sequentially achieves each subgoal. By continuing this process, Pat eventually will achieve his abstract end goal.

Goal hierarchies (and the eventual decision paths) vary in *complexity,* or the number of subgoals. Goal hierarchies for unfamiliar decisions such as buying your first computer, software, or more involving decisions such as buying a business suit, are relatively complex; thus, the decision plans are also complex and involve many behaviors. In contrast, goal hierarchies for problems such as running out of mouthwash are usually quite simple, and so are the decision plans: go to the Thrift Drugstore, find the mouthwash section, and buy Scope.

Moreover, as is true of end goals, goal hierarchies vary in how *well-developed or clear* they are to the consumer at the beginning of the problem-solving process. For many decisions, consumers may only have a vague sense of a goal hierarchy by which they might achieve their end goal. In some cases, the goal hierarchy may have to be constructed during the problem-solving process, essentially through trial and error.

Finally, goal hierarchies are *not fixed,* once formed. In fact, goal hierarchies frequently change as the problem-solving process progresses. For instance, serendipitous events (as when Pat saw a promotion of $175 cassette players on sale for $119) may create a new problem representation, including a new end goal (Pat now wants the best player under $125).

FIGURE 8–4   **A Partial Goal Hierarchy for a Consumer Purchase Decision**

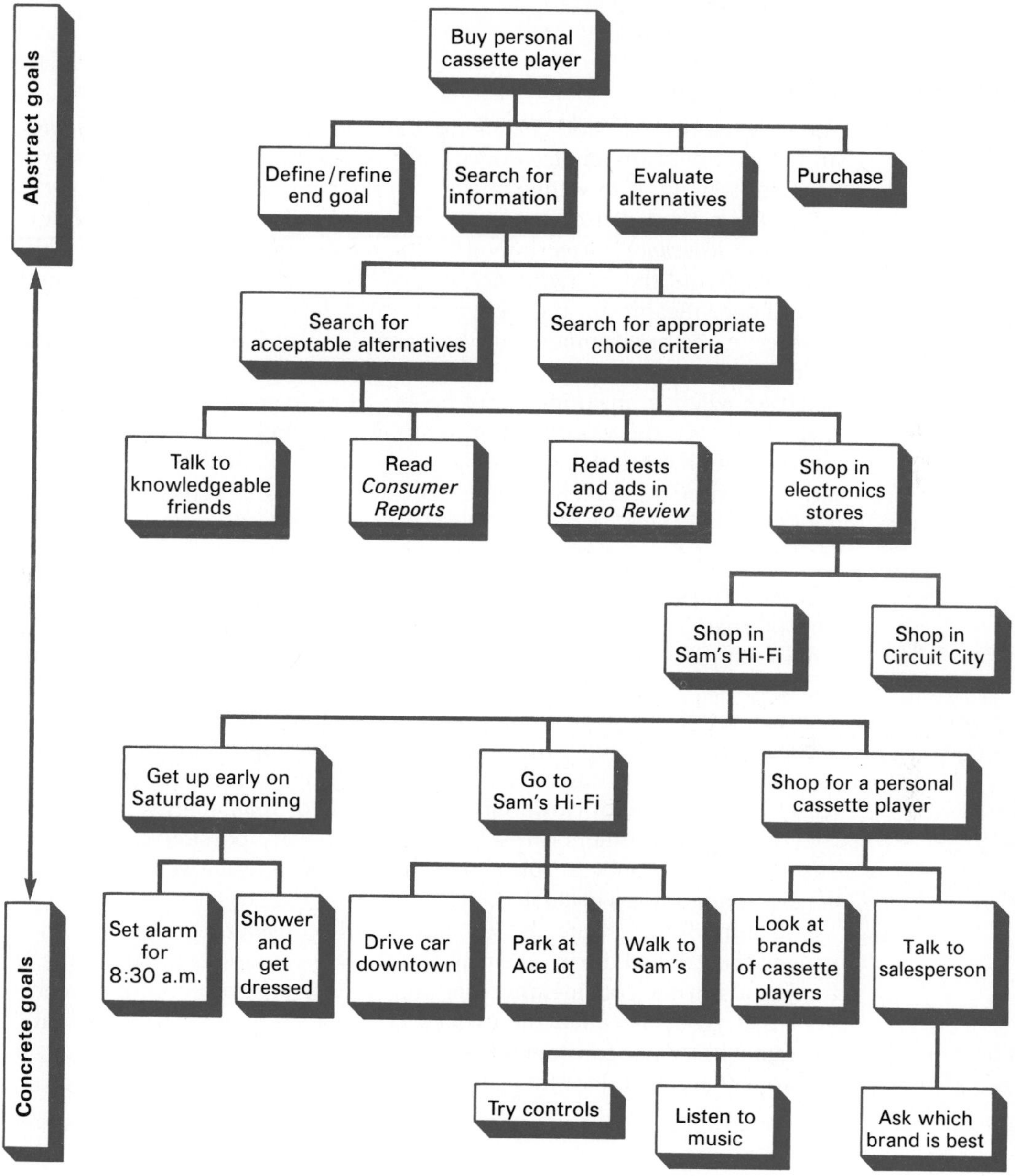

Sometimes these changes produce a different goal hierarchy and a different problem-solving process.

Relevant Knowledge

Along with end goals and goal hierarchies, consumers' *knowledge, meanings,* and *beliefs* about the choice domain are important elements of consumer problem solving. Knowledge relevant to the subgoal currently being considered is activated from long-term memory and used to solve that subproblem.[8] *Relevance* is determined by the means-end linkages between the knowledge and the currently active goal. Consumers may also form new knowledge, meanings, and beliefs by interpreting information they encounter in the environment. In the opening case, Barbara learned about porcelain, factory outlets for dishes, and price ranges for dishes. The activated knowledge, meanings, and beliefs from memory and the environment influence the various interpretation and integration processes that occur throughout decision making. Two types of knowledge are particularly important in problem solving—choice alternatives and choice criteria.

Choice Alternatives

The alternative actions that consumers consider for each subgoal/subproblem in the problem-solving process are called choice alternatives. For purchase decisions, the **choice alternatives** are the different product classes, product forms, brands, or models the consumer considers buying. For other types of decisions, the choice alternatives might be different stores to visit, times of the day or week to go shopping, or methods of payment (cash, check, or credit card). Given their limited time, energy, and cognitive capacity, consumers can seldom consider every possible choice alternative. Usually, only a subset of all possible alternatives—called the **consideration set**—is evaluated.

Figure 8–5 illustrates how a manageable consideration set of brands may be constructed during the problem-solving process. Note that some of the brands in the consideration set may be activated directly from memory—this group is called the **evoked set.**[9] For highly familiar decisions, consumers may not consider any brands beyond those in the evoked set. If consumers are confident they already know the important choice alterna-

---

[8]Gabriel Biehal and Dipankar Chakravarti (1983), "Information Accessibility as a Moderator of Consumer Choice," *Journal of Consumer Research* (June), pp. 1–14.

[9]John Howard and Jagdish N. Sheth (1969), *The Theory of Buyer Behavior,* New York: John Wiley & Sons.

tives, they are not likely to search for additional ones. Some of the choice alternatives in the consideration set may be found through *intentional search activities* such as reading *Consumer Reports,* talking to knowledgeable friends, or finding brands while shopping. Finally, consumers may learn of still other choice alternatives through *accidental exposures* to information in the environment, such as overhearing a conversation about a new brand, new store, or sale. In the opening case, Barbara learned about the factory outlet from her mother-in-law, essentially by accident. However the choice alternatives are generated, they form a **consideration set** of possible purchase options to be evaluated in the decision-making process.

To be successful, a brand must be included in the consideration sets of at least some consumers. Marketers, therefore, develop strategies to increase the likelihood that a brand will be activated from consumers' memories and included in their evoked sets of choice alternatives. The activation potential of a brand, sometimes called its *top-of-mind awareness,* is influenced by many factors. One is the amount of past purchase and use experience consumers have had with the brand. Consumers are much more likely to think of (activate) brands that they have used before. Thus, popular brands with higher market shares have a distinct advantage. Because they are used by more consumers, these brands are more likely to be activated in evoked sets and included in more consumers' consideration sets. This increases the brand's probability of purchase, which in turn increases its activation potential, and so on. In contrast, unfamiliar and

---

FIGURE 8–5   ***Forming a Consideration Set of Brand Choice Alternatives***

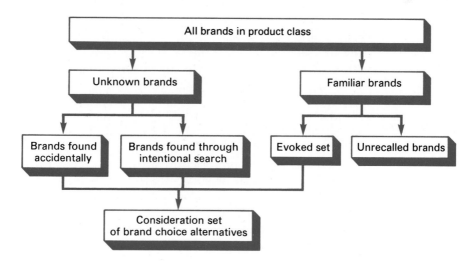

low-market-share brands are at a disadvantage, as they are much less likely to be included in consumers' evoked sets. Such brands are less likely to be considered as choice alternatives.

One marketing strategy to increase the activation potential of a brand is the repetitive and costly advertising campaigns devised by marketers of cigarettes, beer, soft drinks, and toothpaste (among others). The heavy expenditures may be worth it, because brands with high top-of-mind awareness are more likely to be included in the evoked set of choice alternatives that "come to mind" during problem-solving processes.

Finally, a company's *distribution strategy* can have a critical influence on whether a brand is in the consideration sets. Consider food products, where an estimated 65 percent of decisions are made in the store. A key marketing strategy for such products is making sure the product is on the shelf. This enhances the likelihood that consumers will encounter the brand at the time of the decision, which increases its chances of being in consumers' consideration sets.

Choice Criteria

As we described in Chapter 7, consumers' evaluations of the choice alternatives in the consideration set are based on their beliefs about the *consequences of buying* those products or brands. The specific consequences that are used to evaluate and choose among choice alternatives are called **choice criteria.** Virtually any type of product-related consequence can be a choice criterion in a brand-choice decision, including salient beliefs about functional consequences (product performance), psychosocial consequences (emotions, moods, and feelings), or value consequences (a sense of achievement or self-esteem). Consumers probably have beliefs stored in memory about certain relevant consequences of at least some of the choice alternatives in the consideration set. If additional knowledge is desired, consumers may form the subgoal of obtaining information about those choice alternatives. Achieving this subgoal may require intentional search behaviors such as visiting stores, reading *Consumer Reports,* and talking with knowledgeable friends. In the opening case, Barbara engaged in a substantial amount of intentional search to identify possible choice alternatives, as well as to form beliefs about appropriate choice criteria.

Marketers are very interested in determining which aspects of consumers' product knowledge are used as choice criteria in a problem-solving process. The probability that product knowledge is activated and used in the evaluation process is highly influenced by the *relevance* of that knowledge to the goal or subgoal currently being considered. Product consequences that are more closely related to the current goal (through means-end chains) are more likely to be activated and used as choice criteria. For instance, if the dominant end goal is self-esteem, then beliefs about product consequences that are perceived as helping to achieve self-esteem are most likely to be used as choice criteria. Differences in the purchase context may activate different end goals; these, in turn, could activate entirely different means-end chains of product knowledge. For instance, buying a sweater for yourself versus buying one as a gift may activate different end goals (being perceived as stylish versus being perceived as generous). These end goals in turn, may activate different choice criteria (fashionable design versus looks like it cost a lot).

As we discussed in earlier chapters, marketers may place prominent stimuli in the immediate decision environment to activate certain choice criteria from consumers' memories. For instance, special price tags activate beliefs about price consequences (saving money). Prominent package labels on foods, such as "sugar-free" or "low sodium," enhance the likelihood that the consequences associated with those attributes are used as choice criteria. Finally, salespeople often emphasize certain product benefits in their sales pitches, which increases the likelihood that beliefs about those consequences are used as choice criteria.

We must note that not every activated belief about product or brand consequences is necessarily used as a choice criterion in integration processes. Only **discriminant consequences**—consequences that are perceived to differ across choice alternatives—can be used as choice criteria.[10] Beliefs about common or very similar consequences of the choice alternatives cannot be used as choice criteria, because they do not discriminate between alternative actions. To present an obvious example, if all the soft drinks in a vending machine contain caffeine, the consequences of caffeine (stimulation—"I get a lift") cannot be used as a choice criterion for deciding which brand to buy. Note, however, that even though caffeine content is not a discriminant product attribute *in this situation*, it might be if a different set of choice alternatives (brands that vary in caffeine content) is being considered.[11]

Consumers' choice criteria also vary in *evaluative direction*. Some choice criteria are perceived as positive, desirable consequences. Other choice criteria, such as price, may be thought about in negative terms, as unpleasant consequences to be avoided (see Highlight 8–2). Choice alternatives that are perceived to have negative consequences tend to be rejected, unless they also have several positive consequences. For example, many consumers have acquired a negative choice criterion for soft drink—caffeine content. The popularity of this choice criterion has been influ-

---

[10]Mark I. Alpert (1980), Unresolved Issues in Identification of Determinant Attributes," in *Advances in Consumer Research*, Vol. 7, Jerry C. Olson (ed.), Ann Arbor, Mich.: Association for Consumer Research, pp. 83–88.

[11]John U. Farley, Jerrold Katz and Donald R. Lehmann (1978), "Impact of Different Comparison Sets on Evaluation of a New Subcompact Car Brand," *Journal of Consumer Research* (September), pp. 138–142.

Shopping by mail from catalogs is perceived by many consumers as a risky undertaking. Direct-mail marketers, therefore, try to reduce this risk by giving consumers various guarantees. A common strategy is to offer consumers their "money back with no questions asked." Thus, no financial loss can be incurred (other than postage expenses).

The Performance Bicycle Shop, a mail-order company selling high quality bicycle components, has a somewhat unusual price strategy to give consumers confidence that they are getting the "best deal," a powerful desired consequence for many consumers. Note that this pricing stratgy has the added advantage of building shopping loyalty toward the catalog company.

Performance Price Protection Guarantee

We at Performance work hard to provide you with the best values in the cycling market combined with excellent service and the best guarantee you can get on the cycling products you purchase—The "Performance 100% Guarantee."

Occasionally, another company may offer a special sale price on an item which is lower than our current catalog price. The Performance Price Protection Guarantee allows you to buy now from one source the cycling products you want, with the assurance that you received the best value.

This is how the Performance Price Protection Guarantee works: If there is a current nationally advertised special price on the same item you want and you are shopping by telephone, just tell the operator when you are ordering the price and the source where the special is printed. If ordering by mail, send a copy of the ad with your order. This becomes your new Performance Price. That is all there is to it, no more inconvenience of filling out multiple orders or paying multiple shipping charges. And of course, rather than having a limited or no guarantee on these items, you will have bought with the confidence of the "Performance 100% Guarantee"—if any item does not meet your expectations, just send it back for a complete refund, exchange or credit—your choice. You cannot get a better guarantee on the cycling products you buy. Combined with the Performance Price Protection Guarantee, you can shop in complete confidence that you're getting the best value for your money.

Courtesy Performance Bicycle Shop

enced by basic changes in societal values about health and by 7UP's no-caffeine marketing strategy launched in 1982—"Never had it, never will." Other soft-drink manufacturers quickly responded to consumers' increasing use of this negative choice criterion by introducing their own brands of caffeine-free soft drinks.[12]

---

[12]Scott Hume (1985), "Seven-Up Stands Up to Cola's Challenge," *Advertising Age* (May 20), pp. 4 and 92.

Integration Processes

The integration processes involved in problem solving must perform two tasks: the choice alternatives must be *evaluated* in terms of the choice criteria, and then one of the alternative actions must be *chosen*.[13] Two types of integration procedures have been proposed to account for these evaluation and choice processes: *formal integration strategies* and simpler procedures called *heuristics.*

Formal Integration Strategies

Figure 8–6 presents several formal models of the integration processes involved in evaluating and choosing among choice alternatives.[14] The key distinction is between compensatory and noncompensatory strategies.

Compensatory integration procedures combine the salient beliefs about the consequences of the choice alternatives to form an overall evaluation or attitude (A_{act}) toward each behavioral alternative. The multi-attribute attitude model ($A_{act} = \Sigma\ b_i e_i$) is a compensatory model, because a negative consequence (expensive) can be compensated for or balanced by a positive consequence (high quality). It is important to recognize that consumers do not necessarily consider large numbers of beliefs in their evaluation processes. In fact, given the limited capacity of consumers' active memory, the number of choice criteria that is considered at one time may be quite restricted, perhaps to as few as one or two criteria.[15]

Although the multiattribute attitude model accounts for how the choice alternatives are evaluated, it does not specify how the consumer chooses which behavior to perform. Typically, marketers assume that consumers select the alternative with the most positive A_{act}. Other *choice rules* are possible, however. For instance, consumers might choose the first alternative they find with a positive A_{act}.

Several types of **noncompensatory integration strategies** are also described in Figure 8–6. They are noncompensatory because the salient beliefs about the positive and negative consequences of the choice alternatives do not balance or compensate for each other. For example, applying the *conjunctive* choice rule requires that an alternative be rejected if any *one* of its consequences does not surpass a minimum threshold level

---

[13]Peter Wright (1975), "Consumer Choice Strategies: Simplifying versus Optimizing," *Journal of Marketing Research* (February), pp. 60–67.

[14]James R. Bettman (1979), *An Information Processing Theory of Consumer Choice*, Reading, Mass.: Addison-Wesley, provides a thorough discussion of these rules.

[15]Ibid.; Herbert Simon (1974), "How Big Is a Chunk?" *Science* (February), pp. 484–488.

FIGURE 8–6   **Formal Models of Consumer Integration Processes**

┌─────────────────────────────┐
│ **Compensatory processes** │
└─────────────────────────────┘

Multiattribute model   A perceived weakness or negative
                              evaluation on one criterion is
                              compensated for by a positive evaluation
                              on another criterion. Separate
                              evaluations for each choice alternative
                              are combined (added or averaged) to form
                              overall evaluation of each one. Then
                              highest-rated alternative is chosen.

┌─────────────────────────────┐
│ **Noncompensatory processes** │
└─────────────────────────────┘

Conjunctive   Consumer establishes a minimum acceptable
                              level for each choice criterion. Accept
                              an alternative only if every criterion
                              equals or exceeds the minimum cutoff
                              level.

Disjunctive   Consumer establishes acceptable standards
                              for each criterion. A product is
                              acceptable if it exceeds the minimum level
                              on at least one criterion.

Lexicographic   Consumer ranks choice criteria from most
                              to least important. Choose the best
                              alternative on the most important criterion.
                              If tie occurs, select best alternative on
                              second most important criterion, and so
                              on.

Elimination by   Consumer establishes minimum cutoffs for
aspects   each choice criterion. Select one
                              criterion and eliminate all alternatives
                              that do not exceed the cutoff level.
                              Continue eliminating alternatives until
                              one alternative remains. Choose it.

┌─────────────────────────────┐
│ **Combination processes**   │   Mix of compensatory and noncompensatory
└─────────────────────────────┘   processes, combined or "constructed" on
                                         the spot to adapt to environmental
                                         factors.

Source: Adapted from James R. Bettman (1979), An Information Processing Theory of
Consumer Choice, *Reading, Mass.: Addison-Wesley.*

of acceptability. Thus, Edie might reject a particular model of Reebok aerobic shoe if it had one negative consequence (too expensive), even though it had several other positive consequences (comfortable, stylish colors). As another example, applying a *lexicographic* integration strategy might require a consideration of only one choice criterion. Tina might evaluate a pair of dress shoes favorably and buy them because they were superior to the other alternatives on the most important consequence (the color exactly matched her outfit), even though other consequences were somewhat unfavorable (not durable and slightly uncomfortable).

Consumers do not seem to follow any single rule or strategy in evaluating and choosing from among alternatives.[16] For one thing, they probably do not have sufficient cognitive capacity to simultaneously integrate several beliefs about many alternatives.[17] Compensatory integration processes are especially likely to exceed the capacity limitations of consumers' active memories.[18] Moreover, many purchase decisions do not involve a single choice to which a single integration rule could be applied. Instead, consumers make multiple choices in most purchase decisions (choices of information sources to examine, stores to visit, product forms or brands to buy, methods of payment). Each choice is a separate subproblem that requires separate integration processes.

Rather than a single integration strategy, consumers are likely to use a combination of strategies in many problem-solving processes.[19] A noncompensatory strategy might be used to reduce the choice alternatives to a manageable number by rejecting those that lack one or two key criteria (a conjunctive strategy). For example, Bill might reject all restaurants that do not have a salad bar. The remaining brands in his consideration set

---

[16]James R. Bettman and C. Whan Park (1980), "Effects of Prior Knowledge and Experience and Phase of the Choice Process on Consumer Decision Processes: A Protocol Analysis," *Journal of Consumer Research* (December), pp. 234–248; Joel B. Cohen, Paul W. Miniard and Peter R. Dickson (1980), "Information Integration: An Information Processing Perspective," in *Advances in Consumer Research*, Vol. 7, Jerry C. Olson (ed.), Ann Arbor, Mich.: Association for Consumer Research, pp. 161–170; Wayne D. Hoyer (1984), "An Examination of Consumer Decision Making for a Common Repeat Purchase Product," *Journal of Consumer Research* (December), pp. 822–829.

[17]Bettman, *Information Processing Theory*; Denis A. Lussier and Richard W. Olshavsky (1979), "Task Complexity and Contingent Processing in Brand Choice," *Journal of Consumer Research* (September), pp. 154–165.

[18]Merrie Brucks and Andrew A. Mitchell (1981), "Knowledge Structures, Production Systems and Decision Strategies," in *Advances in Consumer Research*, Vol. 8, Kent B. Monroe (ed.), Ann Arbor, Mich.: Association for Consumer Research.

[19]Bettman and Park, "Effects of Prior Knowledge;" Wayne D. Hoyer (1984), "An Examination of Consumer Decision Making for a Common Repeat Purchase Product," *Journal of Consumer Research* (December), pp. 822–829.

(perhaps only two or three restaurants) could be evaluated on several choice criteria (price level, variety, atmosphere) using a more strenuous compensatory strategy.[20]

Another issue is: Do consumers have complete integration rules *stored in memory* ready to be activated and applied to the relevant product beliefs? Current research suggests instead that most integration processes are *constructed* at the time they are needed, to fit the current situation.[21] This suggests that rather than following fixed strategies, consumers' integration processes are relatively simple, very flexible, and easily adapted to varying decision situations.[22] These simple integration "rules" are called *heuristics*.

Heuristics

Basically, **heuristics** are simple "if . . . , then . . . " propositions that connect an event with an action. Because they are applied to only a few bits and pieces of knowledge at a time, heuristics are highly adaptive to specific environmental situations[23] and do not exceed cognitive capacity limits.[24] Heuristics may be stored in memory like mini decision plans or scripts that are applied fairly automatically to information encountered in the environment. Or they may be constructed on the spot in response to the immediate environment.[25] Consider Jim's general heuristic for clothing purchases—"If clothes are on sale at 30 percent off or more, look them over carefully and consider buying. Otherwise, don't even bother browsing." Note how this heuristic greatly simplifies Jim's problem-solving process— he has to attend to, comprehend, evaluate, and integrate information about only those clothes which are discounted at least 30 percent.

---

[20]Lussier and Olshavsky, "Task Complexity and Contingent Processing"; John W. Payne (1976), "Task Complexity and Contingent Processing in Decision Making: An Information Search and Protocol Analysis," *Organizational Behavior and Human Performance* (August), pp. 366–387.

[21]James R. Bettman and Michel A. Zins (1977), "Constructive Processes in Consumer Choice," *Journal of Consumer Research* (September), pp. 75–85; Bettman and Park (1980), "Effects of Prior Knowledge."

[22]Hoyer, "Examination of Consumer Decision Making."

[23]Payne, "Task Complexity and Contingent Processing."

[24]David Grether and Louis Wilde (1984), "An Analysis of Conjunctive Choice: Theory and Experiments," *Journal of Consumer Research* (March), pp. 373–385.

[25]Hoyer, "Examination of Consumer Decision Making."

FIGURE 8–7   **Examples of Consumer Heuristics**

Search heuristics

Examples

Store selection — Always go to Sam's Hi-Fi when buying stereo equipment.

Sources of information — Read the test reports in *Consumer Reports* to find the alternatives worth searching for.

Source credibility — Don't believe product tests in magazines that accept advertisements from the tested products.

Evaluation heuristics

Examples

Key criteria — Compare processed foods on sodium content.

Negative criteria — If a salient consequence is negative (high sodium content), give this choice criterion extra weight in the integration process.

Significant difference — If alternatives are similar on a salient consequence (all low sodium), ignore that choice criterion.

Choice heuristics

Examples

For familiar, frequently purchased products:

Works best — Choose the product that you think works best—that provides the best level of performance on the most relevant functional consequences.

Affect referral — Choose the alternative you like the best over all (select the alternative with the most favorable attitude).

Bought last — If the alternative you used last was satisfactory, choose it again.

Important person — Choose the alternative that some "important" person (spouse, child, friend) likes.

Price-based rule — Buy the least-expensive alternative, or buy the most expensive, depending on your beliefs about the relationship of price to product quality.

Promotion rule — Choose an alternative for which you have a coupon or can get at a price reduction (seasonal sale, promotional rebate, special price reduction).

For new, unfamiliar products:

Wait and see — Don't buy any software until someone you know has used it for at least a month and recommends it. Don't buy a new car (computer, etc.) until the second model year.

Expert consultant — Find an expert or more knowledgeable person. Have them evaluate the alternatives in terms of your goals. Buy the alternative the expert selects.

Source: Parts were adapted from Wayne D. Hoyer (1984), "An Examination of Consumer Decision Making for a Common Repeat Purchase Product," Journal of Consumer Research *(December), pp. 822–829.*

Figure 8–7 presents examples of three types of heuristics that are particularly important in consumers' problem-solving processes. **Search heuristics** are simple procedures for *seeking information* relevant to a goal. For example, some consumers have a simple search rule for buying any durable product such as a radio or a kitchen appliance—read the product tests in *Consumers' Reports.* **Evaluation heuristics** are procedures for *evaluating and weighting beliefs* in terms of the current goal being addressed in the problem-solving process. For instance, some consumers may have a heuristic that identifies the most important choice criteria for food—low calories and the resulting consequence of losing weight. **Choice heuristics** are simple procedures for *comparing evaluations* of alternative actions in order to choose one. For example, a simple heuristic is to select the alternative you bought last time, if it was satisfactory.

Decision Plans

By applying search, evaluation, and choice heuristics, consumers identify the choice alternatives in a consideration set, evaluate them, and choose among them. When this problem-solving process is applied to the various subgoals in a goal hierarchy, a sequence of behavioral intentions is produced, one for each of the subgoals. This sequence of intentions constitutes a **decision plan.**

Decision plans vary in specificity and complexity. Some behavioral intentions concern *specific* actions in highly defined situations: "This afternoon Jim intends to buy a blue cotton sweater at The Limited to go with his new slacks." Other intentions are quite *general:* "Paula intends to buy a new car sometime soon." A behavioral intention could be *a simple plan to perform a single behavior:* "Andy intends to buy a large-size tube of Aim toothpaste on his next shopping trip." Or an intention could be *a more complex plan to engage in a sequence of behaviors:* "Val intends to go to Bloomingdale's and Macy's, browse through their sportswear departments, and look for a tan, lightweight jacket."

Having a decision plan increases the likelihood that these behaviors will be performed. But, as we discussed in Chapter 7, behavioral intentions are not perfect predictors of behavior. For instance, a purchase intention may be blocked or modified if environmental circumstances make it difficult for the decision plan to be carried out: Andy found the store was sold out of large-sized tubes of Aim, so he decided to buy two medium-sized tubes. Sometimes unanticipated events identify additional choice alternatives or change beliefs about choice criteria, which in turn, could

If something new and exciting turns you on, you'll find it at Sears Electronic Showplace!

You take your leisure life as seriously as your work. So you want your entertaining sights and sounds to be state-of-the-art. Come to Sears and discover the Electronic Showplace. Surprise! It's all here. Component TV that's stereo ready.

The latest in VCR's and compact stereos. Even the new digital audio disc players. Come in and browse to you heart's content. Any questions? Ask away. Sears has the answers to your quest for entertainment!

Available in most Sears retail stores. Simulated reception for all TV's. ©Sears Roebuck and Co. 1984

There's more for your life at **SEARS**

Courtesy Sears, Roebuck & Co.

An attempt to create a search heuristic—shop at Sears

produce a different intention/plan: While reading the newspaper, Val learned that Saks was having a 25-percent-off sale on lightweight jackets, so she decided to shop there instead of at Bloomingdale's. In sum, decision plans are not always carried out. Sometimes the problem-solving process "recycles," and a new decision plan is developed.

Problem-Solving Processes in Purchase Decisions

In this section, we examine how consumers solve problems in making purchase decisions. We identify three levels of decision-making effort: extensive, limited, and habitual. We discuss how these levels differ in the amount of conscious cognitive processing, the amount of search, and the degree of evaluation processes. Next, we examine how problem-solving processes change over time. We also discuss the implications of these three levels for marketing strategy.

Levels in Consumer Problem Solving

The amount of cognitive and behavioral effort consumers put into their problem-solving processes is highly variable. Problem-solving activity varies from virtually none (a decision plan is activated from memory and carried out automatically) to very extensive. For convenience, marketers have divided this continuum into three levels of problem-solving activity: extensive, limited, and routine or habitual.[26] Figure 8–8 identifies these three levels and summarizes the major ways in which they differ.

A few of consumers' choice problems require **extensive decision making.** A key aspect is the substantial amount of effortful search behavior required to identify choice alternatives and the appropriate choice criteria with which to evaluate them. In addition, extensive decision making involves multiple choices and substantial cognitive and behavioral effort. It is also likely to take rather long periods of time—such as Barbara's decision to buy new dishes in the opening case or purchasing your first stereo system.

Many consumers' choice problems require **limited decision making.** The amount of problem-solving effort in limited decision making ranges from low to moderately high. Compared to extensive decision making, limited decision making involves low to moderate amounts of search for information. Fewer choice alternatives are considered, and less integration processing is required. In sum, choices involving limited decision making are carried out fairly quickly, with moderate levels of cognitive and behavioral effort.

For still other problems, consumers' choice behavior is habitual or routine. **Routinized choice behavior**—such as buying another Pepsi from the vending machine down the hall or purchasing a package of gum at the

---

[26]This terminology is borrowed from John Howard (1979), *Consumer Behavior: Applications of Theory,* New York: McGraw-Hill.

checkout counter—occurs relatively automatically with little or no apparent cognitive processing. Compared to the other levels, routinized choice behavior requires very little cognitive capacity or conscious control. Basically, a previously learned decision plan is activated from memory and is carried out relatively automatically to produce the behavior.

Changes in Problem Solving with Experience

The amount of effort consumers exert in problem solving changes over time as they learn more about a product and gain experience in making decisions. With repeated decisions, consumers acquire more product and brand knowledge, which becomes organized into means-end structures and becomes more clearly related to their self-concepts. In addition, consumers learn new productions and heuristics, which become organized into scripts or decision plans stored in memory. When activated, these

FIGURE 8–8   *Levels of Problem-Solving Effort*

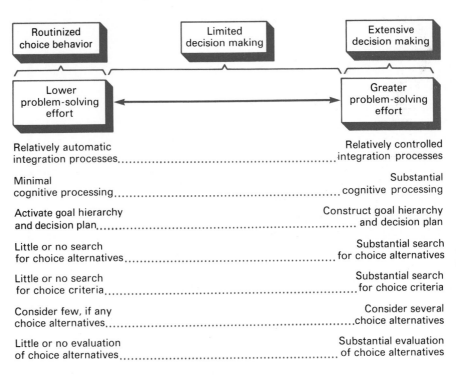

HIGHLIGHT 8–3   **Routinized In-Store Choices**

In a recent study, 120 consumers were observed shopping and buying laundry detergent in three chain grocery stores. An observer stationed in the detergent aisle coded shoppers' activities as they moved down the aisle and picked out the detergent they wanted. The results show that, for most consumers, laundry detergent choice behavior has become quite routinized.

Typically, consumers examined very few packages of detergent. In fact, 72 percent of the consumers looked at only one package, and only 11 percent looked at more than two. An even lower number of packages were physically picked up—83 percent of the consumers picked up only one package, and only 4 percent picked up more than two. Obviously, most of these consumers were not engaged in much in-store problem-solving activity for this product. In fact, hardly any across-brand or within-brand comparisons were made; the vast majority of consumers made none. Fi-

nally, consumers took an average of 13 seconds from the time they entered the aisle to make their detergent choice. Given that the laundry detergent section spans an entire aisle and that several seconds were required to walk to the appropriate area, it is quite obvious that the typical consumer is making an extremely quick choice that involves only minimal cognitive and behavioral effort.

The majority of consumers in this study were engaged in routinized choice behavior. They were merely carrying out a simple decision plan: for example, find the large size of Tide and buy it. Are most other grocery store products purchased in such an automatic way?

Source: Wayne D. Hoyer (1984), "An Examination of Consumption Decision Making for a Common Repeat Purchase Product," Journal of Consumer Research (December), pp. 822–829.

heuristics and decision scripts automatically affect purchase-related behaviors. Running down to the convenience store for a loaf of bread or stopping to tank up the car at a favorite gas station are well-developed decision scripts that require little cognitive effort. In summary, consumers develop *increasingly routinized, automatic problem-solving processes* as they gain experience making various purchase decisions.

The degree to which problem-solving processes become automatic depends on the knowledge consumers have acquired about the purchase decision and their level of involvement with the product. Consumers are more likely to develop automatic choice processes for less-involving, frequently purchased products such as food and personal-care products. In contrast, decision processes for refrigerators, automobiles, and minicomputers are not likely to achieve this degree of routinization. For one thing, consumers may consider their stored knowledge about the latter products to be somewhat obsolete. These purchases are infrequent, and market offerings may change dramatically between purchase decisions. Moreover, consumers' involvement with such products tends to be higher, which motivates some degree of problem-solving effort. Thus, consumers are likely to engage in at least some search and limited problem-solving effort to update their knowledge. In the next section, we consider several factors that affect these wide variations in consumers' problem-solving activity.

Influences on Consumers' Problem-Solving Activities

The level of consumers' problem-solving effort in making brand purchase decisions is influenced by cognitive and environmental factors. Perhaps the prime cognitive influence is the knowledge, meanings, and beliefs activated during the problem-solving process. We discuss three aspects of this activated knowledge that have direct effects on problem solving: (*a*) consumers' *goal hierarchies*; (*b*) their *knowledge* about choice alternatives and choice criteria, as well as heuristics for using this knowledge; and (*c*) their level of felt *involvement*. The latter is a function of consumers' enduring involvement with the choice alternatives and their situation involvement with problem-solving process. Following the discussion of these cognitive influences, we examine several environmental influences on consumer problem solving.

Effects of Goal Hierarchies on Problem Solving

Consumers' goal hierarchies for a problem have a powerful influence on problem-solving processes. For instance, consumers who can construct a complete goal hierarchy (based on their past experiences) are better able to identify a decision path or script involving appropriate actions that will satisfy the various subgoals in the hierarchy and eventually enable them to reach the end goal. If this goal hierarchy is sufficiently well defined, it may be stored in memory. Then, when it is activated, the decision plan may be carried out automatically. Even if a complete decision plan is not stored in memory, a general goal hierarchy provides a useful structure for developing an effective decision plan, without a great deal of problem-solving effort.

In contrast, when consumers' goal hierarchies are not well devel-

HIGHLIGHT 8–4   **Browsing as Entertainment and Search**

Sometimes consumers browse as a vague search plan. But frequently, browsing consumers have no specific decision plan in mind. They are "shopping" for other reasons—recreation, stimulation from store environments, social contact, escape from home or work, or even exercise. In other words, some consumers get satisfaction from shopping/browsing, apart from solving a purchase problem. Browsing, thus, can be both a form of leisure behavior and a problem-solving strategy.

One reason for browsing without a specific decision plan in mind is that the consumer is involved with a particular product class or form and likes to associate with it. Consumers who are very interested in music may enjoy browsing in record shops. Some consumers are involved with a particular store or set of stores in a mall or a shopping area in town. Perhaps the atmosphere of these stores is exciting and stimulating, and this provides part of the attraction. Of course, browsing can and usually does serve multiple goals, needs, and values for different consumers.

Retail stores need to pay attention to browsers, because they can have a major impact on the success of the store. The retailer may have a serious problem if browsers crowd the store and keep serious customers away. Discouraging browsers is relatively easy—just have a salesperson follow the browser around the store asking if he can be helped. Some clothing stores seem to do this effectively. But driving browsers away can be risky. Many browsers become buyers at a later time. If a particular store creates a negative reaction, the browser may make a purchase in a different store.

Some retailers seem to have trouble dealing with browsers. Consider auto dealers. Many people feel uncomfortable going into auto showrooms to browse, partly because of the aggressive salespeople who descend upon them. One strategy has been to set up regional auto shows in the shopping mall, where consumers feel more comfortable browsing without having to deal with an enthusiastic salesperson.

Another retailing strategy is to develop a store environment that stimulates impulse buying. In-store promotions, displays, and special signs can help convert a browser to a buyer.

Finally, browsers seem likely to relay information to other consumers. Thus, browsers are doubly important. Not only might they buy something themselves, but they are more likely to spread word-of-mouth information to less well-informed consumers.

Source: Adapted from Peter H. Bloch and Marsha L. Richins (1983), "Shopping without Purchase: An Investigation of Consumer Browsing Behavior," in Advances in Consumer Research, Vol. 10, *R.P. Bagozzi and A.M. Tybout (eds.), Ann Arbor, Mich.: Association for Consumer Research, pp. 389–393.*

oped, the effective decision path is not evident. In such cases, problem solving is likely to proceed haltingly, by trial and error. This is often the case for first-time buyers of relatively involving products (stereos, sports equipment, cars, houses). In such instances, consumers must identify a series of subgoals that seem related to the end goal and develop decision plans to achieve each subgoal. A consumer who is trying to buy a compact disc player may go to the electronics section of a department store to search for information about this product. If that action is not effective, the consumer must back up and develop another subgoal and a new decision plan: "I didn't find anything in that store. I'll call Peter and ask him what stores would be good." In these types of decisions, marketers are likely to find confused or frustrated consumers, who use general "strategies" such as wandering around various stores in a mall, hoping to accidentally run into something that will satisfy their end goal (see Highlight 8–4). In sum, goal hierarchies are often *constructed* via trial and error, especially for unfamiliar decisions. Over multiple purchase decisions, consumers tend to learn an appropriate goal hierarchy and an accompanying decision plan.

Effects of Involvement and Knowledge on Problem Solving

Consumers' problem-solving processes are greatly affected by the *amount of product knowledge* they have acquired through their past experiences, and by their *level of involvement* with the product (enduring involvement) and the choice process (situational involvement). The activated knowledge about goal hierarchies, choice alternatives and choice criteria, and heuristics affects consumers' *ability* to engage in integration processes. Consumers' involvement with the product or decision affects their *motivation* to engage in a problem-solving process.[27] Figure 8–9 shows how product knowledge and involvement affect specific elements of consumers' problem representations and the overall problem solving process.

Low Involvement/Low Knowledge

Many (perhaps most) consumer purchase decisions involve products that are not very personally relevant—consider bread, ketchup, toothpaste, socks, or pens.[28] Problem representations for buying such products are probably relatively simple. Because these products have little personal importance and are physically simple besides, most consumers have relatively little product knowledge. Moreover, the end goals being sought are not strongly related to psychosocial consequences or values. Instead, the

---

[27]Bettman and Park (1980), "Effects of Prior Knowledge."

[28]Harold H. Kassarjian (1978), "Presidential Address, 1977: Anthropomorphism and Parsimony," in *Advances in Consumer Research,* Vol. 5, H. Keith Hunt (ed.), Ann Arbor, Mich.: Association for Consumer Research, pp. xiii–xiv.

FIGURE 8–9 *Effects of Involvement and Product Knowledge on Consumers' Problem-Solving Processes*

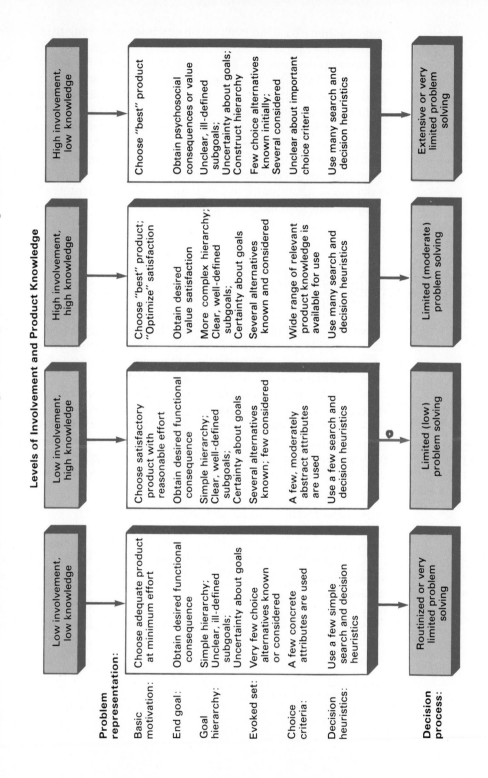

Levels of Involvement and Product Knowledge

Problem representation:	Low involvement, low knowledge	Low involvement, high knowledge	High involvement, high knowledge	High involvement, low knowledge
Basic motivation:	Choose adequate product at minimum effort	Choose satisfactory product with reasonable effort	Choose "best" product; "Optimize" satisfaction	Choose "best" product
End goal:	Obtain desired functional consequence	Obtain desired functional consequence	Obtain desired value satisfaction	Obtain psychosocial consequences or value
Goal hierarchy:	Simple hierarchy; Unclear, ill-defined subgoals; Uncertainty about goals	Simple hierarchy; Clear, well-defined subgoals; Certainty about goals	More complex hierarchy; Clear, well-defined subgoals; Certainty about goals	Unclear, ill-defined subgoals; Uncertainty about goals; Construct hierarchy
Evoked set:	Very few choice alternatives known or considered	Several alternatives known; few considered	Several alternatives known and considered	Few choice alternatives known initially; Several considered
Choice criteria:	A few concrete attributes are used	A few, moderately abstract attributes are used	Wide range of relevant product knowledge is available for use	Unclear about important choice criteria
Decision heuristics:	Use a few simple search and decision heuristics	Use a few search and decision heuristics	Use many search and decision heuristics	Use many search and decision heuristics
Decision process:	Routinized or very limited problem solving	Limited (low) problem solving	Limited (moderate) problem solving	Extensive or very limited problem solving

most salient end goals tend to be functional consequences of product performance.

How are decisions about such products made? Intentional search is not likely. The first few purchases may involve a very limited amount of problem-solving effort, perhaps using trial purchases of some brands as an efficient way to search for an acceptable choice. But as consumers repeatedly make purchases over time, they quickly form simple goal hierarchies and a simple decision plan (always buy the brand on sale, or always buy Cheerios). This decision plan is activated whenever the decision problem occurs (run out of Cheerios) and automatically generates the purchase behavior. Once a decision plan is formed, there is virtually no problem-solving effort. Search for new information is very low or nonexistent, and little or no evaluation of choice alternatives (brands) takes place. In sum, the automatic problem-solving process is characterized as habitual or *routinized choice behavior.*

> *Example.* Consider how Mary and Sam buy toothpaste. Because she does not think brands of toothpaste have important differences, Mary has acquired a very simple problem representation containing a simple decision heuristic that she habitually applies to her evoked set of brands to reach a choice: "Choose whichever of Crest, Aim, or Gleem is cheapest." Sam, on the other hand, doesn't even make a brand choice. He merely applies a *brand loyalty heuristic* to make this unimportant decision: "always buy Crest."

Low Involvement/High Knowledge

Less common decision problems sometimes occur in which consumers have substantial amounts of product knowledge, but have a rather low level of involvement with the product and/or the decision. This could occur for products that were once highly self-relevant, but now are not. Much of the extensive product knowledge acquired while involvement was high still may be available in memory, although it will tend to gradually fade over time. In a decision situation, parts of this knowledge might be activated and used to create goal hierarchies, to evaluate and to compare choice alternatives, and to generate decision plans. However, due to a lack of motivation, problem-solving processes are likely to be *quite limited,* although probably not entirely routinized.

> *Example.* Jerry was once highly involved with sports cars. He has owned five such cars, including three Porsches, but now he is more interested in other things. Although he no longer feels personal involvement with this product form or with specific brands, Jerry still retains a great deal of relevant product knowledge about sports cars. When he is considering purchase of any car, aspects of this knowl-

edge are likely to be activated from memory and used in evaluation and choice processes. Thus, Jerry's decision-making processes are likely to be limited, involving somewhat more search and integration processing than does routinized choice behavior, but still a relatively low amount.

High Involvement/High Knowledge

Some consumers may be highly involved in a product and also have a lot of product knowledge due to their substantial purchase and use experience (such as an expert skier choosing his sixth pair of skis). Parts of this knowledge will be activated from memory during problem solving. This extensive product knowledge probably includes an evoked set of choice alternatives as well as well-developed means-end chains of product knowledge. In addition, such consumers have a clear sense of their end goals and the goal hierarchies appropriate to achieve them. They probably also possess useful search, evaluation, and integration heuristics for achieving those subgoals.

Even though these expert consumers are highly motivated, their problem-solving processes are not likely to be extensive. With their depth of knowledge, expert consumers may require only a moderate level of cognitive effort to represent the problem and reach a satisfactory decision. In sum, these consumers engage in *a moderate, but still limited level of decision making.*

> *Example.* Consider Keith, a wine connoisseur, who is choosing a bottle of wine to serve at a dinner party. Keith is personally involved with wine. He has acquired extensive knowledge about wine in general, various forms of wine, and different brands of wine. His end goals and goal hierarchies are well developed and specific to particular consumption situations. He has different evoked sets of alternative wines for various situations, and he knows the appropriate criteria to use in choosing from among these alternatives. He knows many heuristics that help him move quickly and simply from one subgoal to another. As Keith shops in the wine store, he is able to process substantial amounts of information rather easily and quickly (sometimes automatically). Keith's effort in the problem-solving process is limited, not extensive.

High Involvement/Low Knowledge

Some consumers have a *high level of involvement* with the product class/form/brand model or with making a good decision, but have *little relevant knowledge* in memory. For example, consumers may just be learning about a product that they have taken an interest in. Because the product class or

Peter LeGrand: Click/Chicago

Purchasing high-involvement, low-knowledge products often involves extensive problem solving.

form is perceived to be personally relevant, consumers probably have an optimizing end goal (buy the best) and are motivated to try to achieve it. However, because they lack experience, these consumers probably do not have an appropriate goal hierarchy for the decision. Moreover, they probably lack knowledge of potential choice alternatives and relevant choice criteria. In sum, such consumers lack the ability to make a good decision, even though they are motivated to do so.

Two very different levels of problem-solving effort can occur in this situation: quite limited or extensive. Basically, consumers' confidence in their ability to interpret new information about the problem will determine which level of problem solving occurs. Consumers who fear they will not understand new information will avoid search and extensive problem solving. Instead, they will use a simple heuristic to produce a choice (see Figure 8–7). One common heuristic is to rely on a **decision consultant**—a knowledgeable friend, family member, or trusted salesperson. One study found that many consumers make life insurance decisions in this way.[29]

[29]Roger A. Formisano, Richard W. Olshavsky and Shelley Tapp (1982), "Choice Strategy in a Difficult Task Environment," *Journal of Consumer Research* (March), pp. 474–479.

HIGHLIGHT 8–5   **The Ultimate Decision Consultant**

One way to dramatically simplify a difficult decision-making process is to rely on the advice of a **decision consultant**, a person whose help may range from giving general advice about alternatives or choice criteria to actually making the choice for you. Consumers frequently use knowledgeable friends as unpaid purchase consultants, and marketing representatives (salespeople) are also used at times.

In trendy Boca Raton Florida, Judy and Steve Chefan offer what may be the ultimate decision consulting service. Consumers with a spare million or so, who need a place to call home, can call on Steve, who is president of Stevenson Building and Design Inc. Stevenson simplifies the very complex decision process of buying and furnishing a luxury house by supplying million-dollar-plus houses, completely decorated right down to the towels in the bathrooms. No agonizing over the proper arrangement for the modular sofa or where to put the Ming vase. Steve and Judy take care of everything, including color coordinating the bathroom tissue.

Chefan started Stevenson Building and Design after selling his chain of clothing stores in 1979. "I felt I could merchandise houses like I did clothing," he says. "You buy a home the same way you would buy a dress or an automobile—to reflect your taste." So, why not hire someone to help you portray that taste?

Plenty of people seem to agree, as Stevenson's revenues jumped from $3.2 to $20 million in four years. "We've identified a market that wasn't being served," Chefan explains. "There's a fallacy in our society that a woman isn't fulfilled until she decorates her own home." According to Stevenson, after she decorates one or two, she realizes the job isn't all it's cracked up to be, and she is more than happy to turn it over to someone else. In fact, most of Stevenson's customers are buying their second or third homes.

Source: Donna Fenn (1984), "Made-To-Order Houses," INC. (April), p. 27.

Even though most consumers had low levels of knowledge about life insurance (40 percent claimed to have little or no knowledge), they engaged in little search for alternatives. Fully 75 percent investigated only one policy, and 66 percent read no material relevant to the insurance decision. Instead, they relied on the advice of others; 71 percent said they chose the policy recommended by the insurance agent. It would seem that the key decision for most consumers was whether or not to trust the salesperson's advice.

In contrast, consumers who are confident of their ability to understand new information are more likely to engage in extensive decision making. They perceive a payoff from their search behavior that nonconfident consumers do not. Extensive problem-solving processes involve high-effort search behaviors—including store visits, reading product information in ads and brochures, seeking out friends and salespersons—to identify potential choice alternatives and the relevant choice criteria with which to evaluate them. Extensive decision making may also involve difficult interpretation processes. Because relevant knowledge is not well developed, consumers must consciously construct the meanings of much of the information they find and judge its personal relevance.

Finally, the integration processes are also likely to require substantial effort. The lack of clear end goals and decision heuristics, along with an initially vague goal hierarchy, makes formulating a decision plan difficult and awkward. The problem-solving process in such cases is likely to be long and complex, with many interruptions and restarts. However, because high involvement/low knowledge conditions are relatively rare, consumers probably do not engage in such *extensive problem-solving processes* very often.

> *Example.* Consider Sally Peters, who has decided to buy a complete set of ski equipment. After skiing three times at the end of last season using rented equipment, Sally "fell in love" with the sport (skiing has become personally relevant). At this time, however, she knows very little about skis, boots, poles or bindings. She doesn't know much about product forms, competing brands, price ranges, or what key attributes and consequences she should be looking for in her equipment. She doesn't even know what stores to shop in. Sally is likely to engage in a fairly extensive search for information—including reading books and magazine articles, talking with knowledgeable friends, visiting stores and talking with salespersons, trying on boots, etc. Gradually, she will acquire relevant product knowledge and develop a problem representation. She will identify important end goals and construct a goal hierarchy that she will use as a framework to integrate her knowledge and make a series of purchase decisions. Sally's decision-making process is likely to be quite extensive—relatively long, difficult, effortful, and probably somewhat frustrating.

Environmental Effects on Problem Solving

Thus far in the text, we have identified a number of environmental influences on cognitive processes, such as prominent stimuli in the environment. Below, we discuss how environmental factors can affect consumer decision making by interrupting the ongoing flow of the problem-solving process.

Interrupts

Once problem solving has begun, it may be interrupted at any time. Four types of interrupting events, or **interrupts,** have been identified.[30] First, interrupts can occur when *unexpected information* (inconsistent with established knowledge structures) is encountered in the environment. For instance, carrying out a decision plan or script may be interrupted when you unexpectedly find that aspects of the physical or social environment have changed—a store has been remodeled and departments have been moved around, a rejected brand now has a new attribute, or your friends now favor a different night spot. These environmental interrupts may cause the consumer to take conscious control of the problem-solving process, identify a new end goal, develop a new goal hierarchy, and construct a different decision plan.

Second, *prominent environmental stimuli* can interrupt a problem-solving process. Many marketing strategies are intended to interrupt consumers' ongoing problem solving. For instance, a large in-store display for Oreo cookies, "as advertised" shelf tags, or the announcement of a sales promotion ("Attention, K mart shoppers. In aisle 3B we are offering . . .") may interrupt an ongoing problem-solving process as well as activate new knowledge or goals from memory.

Third, *physiological "events"* such as feeling hungry, sleepy, or thirsty can interrupt an ongoing problem-solving process. For instance, feeling tired during a shopping trip might activate new goals and start a different problem-solving process (find a comfortable place to sit down and have a soda pop or cup of coffee).

Fourth, *conflicts* that arise during the course of purchase decision making can interrupt the problem-solving process.[31] *Goal conflict* occurs when consumers recognize the presence of incompatible goals.[32] Goal conflict may be noted while constructing a goal hierarchy or later as consumers discover that alternatives cannot be found to satisfy incompatible goals. For instance, Susan may experience an *approach-approach conflict* in choosing between a new camera and a new stereo receiver, because each product leads to a desirable goal (creativity and relaxation, respectively), but neither product provides both goals. *Avoidance-avoidance conflicts* occur when consumers choose between two alternatives with different negative consequences. For instance, Sam is trying to decide whether to buy a new suit. He doesn't want to be embarrassed by his old suit, but he doesn't want to spend money on a new one, either. Finally, *approach-avoidance con-*

---

[30]This section was adapted from Bettman, *Information Processing Theory.*

[31]Flemming Hansen (1976), "Psychological Theories of Consumer Choice," *Journal of Consumer Research* (December), pp. 117–142.

[32]Bettman, *Information Processing Theory.*

flicts occur when consumers consider both the positive and negative consequences of a purchase or action. For instance, Paul is trying to decide about a new personal cassette player that is on sale for a very low price (positive outcome), but he is afraid that the quality may be low (negative outcome).

Effects of Interrupts. The effects of interrupts on consumers' problem-solving processes depend on how consumers interpret (comprehend) the interrupting event. In general, consumers tend to resume an interrupted problem-solving task, especially if it is important or involving.[33] Thus, a consumer might attend to and comprehend an interrupting event, discount it if it seems unimportant or irrelevant, and continue with the original problem-solving process.

In other cases, however, an interrupting event can change the problem-solving process. For instance, an interrupt might activate new end goals that require changes in the original goal hierarchy. Interrupt events (such as learning about a new product attribute) might activate other knowledge structures that may suggest new decision paths. Or a heuristic might be activated by the interrupt (a friend recommends a brand, and you decide to take her advice). Finally, an especially strong interrupt, such as losing your job, might block the current problem-solving process (choosing a new car), and the process might not resume again. In sum, the effects of interrupts depend on their meanings to the consumer. For instance, is your hunger severe enough to stop shopping for a new suit, or can you skip lunch today? Does this new brand of styling mousse seem worth trying, or should you ignore it? Do you care that your friend thinks these shoes are ridiculous?

Implications for Marketing Strategy

To develop effective marketing strategies, marketers need to know what type of problem-solving processes their customers use to make purchase decisions. As you have seen, these processes vary widely. Marketers who target consumer segments with different problem-solving processes may have to develop multiple strategies to influence the different decision outcomes. In the following section, we consider several general implications for marketing strategies for routinized choice behavior and limited and extensive decision making.

---

[33]George A. Miller, Eugene Galanter and Karl H. Pribram (1960), *Plans and the Structure of Behavior,* New York: Henry Holt.

Routinized Choice Behavior

Much consumer choice behavior is routinized. Consumers often feel that they know all they need to about a product domain, and they are not motivated to search for new information. Their choice behavior is based on a learned decision plan. In such cases, the appropriate strategy depends on the strength of the brand's position in the market.

Marketers of *established brands with substantial market shares* must maintain their brand in the evoked sets (the choice alternatives activated at the beginning of the problem-solving process) of a significant segment of consumers. Because consumers in this situation engage in little or no search, marketers have minimal opportunities to interject their brand into consumers' consideration sets during problem solving. In general, the more automatic the choice process becomes, the more difficult it is for marketers to interrupt and influence the process.

Marketers of *new brands or brands with a low market share* must somehow interrupt consumers' automatic problem-solving processes. They may develop strategies of producing prominent environmental stimuli such as large or unusual store displays, create strong package graphics that stand out on the shelf, give away free samples, and run sales promotions (buy one, get one free). Such strategies are intended to catch consumers' attention and interrupt their routine choice behavior. The goal is to jolt consumers into a more conscious and controlled level of limited decision making that might include the new brand.

Finally, marketers of leading products such as Doritos snack chips, Snickers candy bars, Budweiser beer, and IBM computers may *want* consumers to follow a routine choice process. Because these brands already have a high market share, they are in the evoked sets of most buyers. It is important for these marketers to avoid marketing-related environmental interrupts such as stockouts, which could jolt consumers into a limited decision-making process and lead them to try a competitor's brand. One critical aspect of the overall marketing strategy for such brands is an efficient distribution system to keep the brands fully stocked and available (in a prominent shelf/display position) whenever consumers are in a choice situation. Frito-Lay, the manufacturer of Fritos, Ruffles potato chips, and many other snack products, developed a superb distribution system partly for this reason. Highlight 8–6 gives several examples of how marketers of industrial products attempt to make their buyers' decision-making processes more routine.

Limited Decision Making

The majority of consumer decisions involve limited effort. Because most consumers already have a lot of information about the product from previous experiences, the basic marketing strategy here is to make additional "pieces" of information available to consumers when and where they need

The basic purpose of marketing is to create and keep customers. The key to keeping customers, of course, is to keep them satisfied. One way industrial-goods companies are keeping their corporate customers satisfied is by routinizing their decision making processes.

Companies as diverse as Inland Steel, Eastman Kodak, and First Boston bank are placing computer terminals connected to the main corporate computer system on their customer's desks, free of charge. The network is called a *channel system,* because it enables customers to simplify the channel of distribution by ordering supplies instantly and directly from the supplying company. Buyers can thus better manage their expensive inventories. Basically, these systems solve many customers' problems. Although the systems are vastly expensive and very tricky to implement successfully, many companies are making the investment, because such systems "destroy your customers' interest in competitors' products."

Back in 1974, American Hospital Supply (AHS) installed one of the pioneer systems in the stockrooms of large hospitals. Instead of having to order from salespeople making regular rounds, purchasing agents and stock clerks could use the terminals to order routine supplies easily and quickly (and directly from AHS). As with most channel systems, customers tend to buy more from the supplier of the system and less from competitors. By making its customers' decision-making process more routine, the marketing company makes it easier than ever to buy from them.

Kodak developed a system called Technet that is targeted at the owners of minilabs (storefront film developers) and that takes routinization to an extreme. Based on an IBM PC, the system does everything but feed the night watchdog. It automatically monitors print quality, offers advice on pricing, and keeps track of sales and complaints. The system also detects when paper and chemicals are running low and automatically reorders from Kodak. To get Technet, the lab must agree to use Kodak paper and chemicals exclusively and to let Kodak monitor its adherence to quality guidelines.

These channel systems and other computerized strategies may be only the early steps toward a time when many (perhaps most) marketing transactions are conducted electronically.

Source: Adapted from Peter Petre (1985), "How to Keep Customers Happy Captives," Fortune (September 2), pp. 42–46.

it. Advertisements to increase top-of-mind awareness may help get a brand into the evoked set of choice alternatives at the *beginning* of the decision process. This is important, because most consumers are not likely to search extensively for other alternatives. Moreover, it is critical that the brand is perceived to have the few key choice criteria used in the evaluation process. Advertisements that capture the attention of the consumer and communicate favorable beliefs about the attributes and consequences of the brand may be able to create that knowledge. Finally, because consum-

Courtesy General Motors Corporation

A simple ad to increase top-of-mind awareness.

ers are giving some conscious thought to the decision, successful interrupts are not as difficult as they are with routinized problem solving.
Highlight 8–7 describes a store environment set up to stimulate impulsive,
limited decision making.

Extensive Decision Making

Compared to more common routinized choices and limited decision making, relatively few consumer decisions involve extensive problem solving.
However, when consumers do engage in extensive decision making, marketers must recognize and satisfy their special needs for information. In

A deep-discount California retailer called Pic 'N' Save has been ringing up some very impressive financial results. Aftertax profits have averaged 15 percent of sales since 1980—more than twice the average profit margin of other successful retailers such as Toys-"Я"-Us.

Why the success? The oddball, ever-changing nature of Pic 'N' Save merchandise seems to be the source of much of the chain's appeal. The company's buyers scour the world for goods—from screwdrivers and wine to T-shirts and Hula-Hoops—that manufacturers are willing to sell at fire sale prices, either because they made too many or they are going out of business. Pic 'N' Save then resells the products in its stores for 40 to 70 percent below suggested retail prices. For instance, two weeks before the 1984 Olympics, Pic 'N' Save bought up $16 million worth of Olympic-logo travel bags, figurines, toys, and miscellaneous items from a panicked manufacturer. They sold nearly all of it at a profit.

What factors motivate customers to shop at Pic 'N' Save? The low prices are obviously a big factor, but what other effects do the merchandise and the store environment have on customers? Because most products in Pic 'N' Save sell for less than $10, purchases tend to be made on impulse, with a limited problem-solving process. Perhaps consumers feel that they must decide quickly, because the item won't be here next shopping trip. Moreover, the items sold in Pic 'N' Save come from all over the world and are often unique in the selling area. Therefore, comparable items may not be available in other stores, making a complex search and comparison process unlikely. In fact, the typical choice facing the consumer is "either buy this thing now or don't."

In sum, the unusual in-store environment of Pic 'N' Save contibutes to impulsive, limited decision making on the part of its many customers. Consumers seem to like the bargains they find; the company estimates that more than three fourths of its customers drop by at least once a month to browse—and to buy.

Source: Adapted from John Paul Newport, Jr. (1985), "Profits in Castoffs," Fortune *(September 30), pp. 75–76.*

many extensive decision-making situations where their knowledge is low, consumers need information about everything—including which end goals are important, how to organize goal hierarchies, which choice alternatives are relevant, what choice criteria are appropriate, and so on. Marketers should strive to make the necessary information available, in a format and at a level of abstraction that consumers can understand and use in the problem-solving process.

Because consumers intentionally seek product information during extensive decision making, interrupting their problem-solving processes is relatively easy. Informational displays at the point of purchase—for instance, displays of mattresses that are cut apart to show construction details—or presentations by salespersons can be effective sources of

HIGHLIGHT 8–8   **Inducing Trial with Free Samples**

In 1985, a very interesting and expensive free sampling strategy was tried in, of all places, the computer software market. Xanaro Technologies, a Toronto company, borrowed a sampling concept from packaged-goods marketers. They bound two demonstration discs for their Ability integrated software into the November issue of *PC World,* accompanied by 16 consecutive pages of advertising support. (*PC World* had a subscription base of 350,000 and newstand sales of about 50,000.)

Xanaro's target was to sell 30,000 packages of Ability, which retails at $495. Purchasing, duplicating, and packaging the 800,000 floppy discs that were bound into the magazine cost Xanaro more than $1.5 million, while the 16 ad pages in *PC World* cost $800,000, and ads in other publications cost another $200,000. Altogether, the company spent about $10 million on the launch.

According to Xanaro President Robert Hryniak, "What we're doing is preselling Ability. We're going directly to 400,000 computer software users and saying, 'Here it is. Use it. You be the judge.'" He adds, "I happen to believe that advertising alone doesn't work for software. It needs touch and feel."

What do you think? It turns out that Xanaro's bold marketing strategy did not pay off. By late 1985, the company was on the verge of bankruptcy, owing several million dollars to creditors. Despite the lack of success of Xanaro's strategy, however, computer software manufacturers are likely to borrow other strategies from package-goods marketing.

Source: Adapted from Scott Hume and Cleveland Horton (1985), "Samples Key Sale-Ability," Advertising Age *(September 2), p. 56.*

information. Complex sales materials such as brochures and product specifications may be effective, along with high-information advertisements. Consumers in extensive problem-solving situations will attend to relevant information, and they are motivated enough to comprehend it. Marketers may take advantage of the information receptivity of consumers by offering free samples, coupons, or easy trial (take it home and try it for a couple of days) to help consumers gain knowledge about their brand. Highlight 8–8 illustrates one costly strategy designed to get people to try a new product.

Back to the Case

In this chapter, we examined a number of concepts that can help us understand Barbara's problem-solving process. Her decision to buy dishes involved fairly extensive problem-solving activities, including a substantial amount of search behavior and quite a bit of cognitive activity in evaluating alternative courses of action. As you review the case, note that her choice alternatives and choice criteria were greatly influenced by the information she came across in the environment, as she had relatively little knowledge about dishes stored in memory. Her goal hierarchy and decision plan were constructed through trial and error during the problem-solving process. This case clearly shows the importance of the continuous, reciprocal interactions among cognition, behavior, environment, and marketing strategy. Many limited decision-making processes are also like this, although perhaps less complex. In contrast, habitual choice behavior involves little or no problem solving. Because the decisions were made in the past and stored in memory, purchase behaviors are generated automatically when the decision plan is activated. Thus, environmental factors have less chance to interrupt and influence the purchase process.

Summary

In this chapter, we examined consumers' decision-making processes. Consumers make many types of choices, but our primary focus was on choices of products and brands. We conceptualized decision making as a problem-solving process in which the consumers' cognitive representation of the problem is a key to understanding the process. Problem representation involves end goals, a goal hierarchy, activated product knowledge, and choice rules and heuristics. Consumers use simple decision rules called heuristics for finding, evaluating, and integrating beliefs about alternatives in solving each subgoal in a goal hierarchy. The entire set of decisions (behavioral intentions) is the decision plan. Working through a problem may involve having to solve several interrelated subproblems, each with its own set of subgoals.

We also saw that consumers' purchase decisions vary widely in complexity (number of separate decisions and goal hierarchies involved). Some purchase decisions require very extensive problem-solving effort, while other choices are made virtually automatically in a highly routinized manner. A great many purchases involve limited decision making, that fall somewhere between these two extremes. We described how the amount of consumers' product knowledge and their level of involvement affect the problem-solving process. And we discussed how various aspects of the decision environment affect the problem-solving process.

Additional Reading

James R. Bettman (1979), "Memory Factors in Consumer Choice: A Review," *Journal of Marketing* (Spring), pp. 37–53.

Lawrence A. Crosby and James R. Taylor (1981), "Effects of Consumer Information and Education in Cognition and Choice," *Journal of Consumer Research* (June), pp. 43–56.

Michael D. Johnson (1984), "Consumer Choice Strategies for Comparing Noncomparable Alternatives," *Journal of Consumer Research* (December), pp. 741–753.

John G. Lynch, Jr. and Thomas K. Srull (1982), "Memory and Attentional Factors in Consumer Choice: Concepts and Research Methods," *Journal of Consumer Research* (June), pp. 18–37.

Richard W. Olshavsky and Donald H. Granbois (1980), "Rejoinder," *Journal of Consumer Research* (December), pp. 333–334.

C. Whan Park and Richard J. Lutz (1982), "Decision Plans and Consumer Choice Dynamics," *Journal of Marketing Research* (February), pp. 108–115.

Michael Ursic (1980), "'Consumer Decision Making—Fact or Fiction?' Comment," *Journal of Consumer Research* (December), pp. 331–333.

Peter Wright and Barton Weitz (1977), "Time Horizon Effects on Product Evaluation Strategies," *Journal of Marketing Research* (November), pp. 429–443.

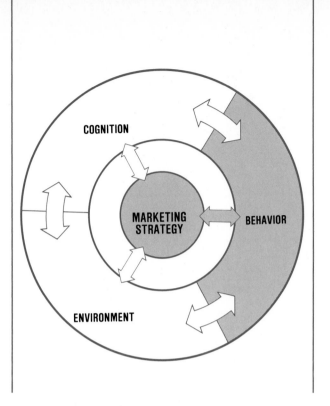

Section Three

Behavior Theory and Marketing Strategy

Chapter Nine
Applied Behavior Analysis

Dryads of the Mind

The dryad was a tree nymph. Every tree had its protecting spirit which was born with the tree, lived in or near it in intimate association, watching over its growth, and died when the tree fell. The dryad was thus a personification of the life of the tree. . . . .

In the physical world today there is less room for supernatural influences than there used to be. There are fewer homes for dryads. But in the world of the mind, some of them still seem to lurk in the woods and thickets. Of course, they are not called dryads. Those who speak with scholarly care call them hypothetical constructs. Sometimes they are called traits. More often they are not regarded as members of any class. Those who accept them as real and important do not inquire too closely as to what stuff they may be made of. But they are cherished because they seem to explain why different people behave in different ways. To those who enjoy mystery, the fogs of vagueness that surround them do more to augment than to diminish respect for them. Mystery, these people believe, is what one ought to expect when one is dealing with ultimate essences.

The history of these dryads is a long one. Originally they were thought to dwell not just in the brain but throughout the whole body. There were four humors—blood, phlegm, yellow bile, and black bile—that were held responsible for the behavioral manifestations of cheerfulness, impassivity, irritability, and melancholy, respectively. A person's behavior in a particular instance, as well as his or her general temperament, were attributed to the relative abundance or potency of these four humors in the body. There was, of course, nothing dryadic about these four substances. They were, with one possible exception, tangible, observable substances. Dryads enter the picture in the hypothetical influence of these substances on behavior and temperament.

Later on, as the mind took up residence principally in the brain, the dryads reappeared in the guise of mental faculties: attention, perception, memory, reasoning, imagination, willpower, and the like. These faculties were regarded as general powers of the mind, gifts of a favored inheritance, or fruits of a disciplined education. Phrenologists made a pseudoprofession out of attempts to discover relationships between the shape of a person's skull and the degree of over- or underdevelopment of the various mental faculties.

The humors of our ancestors have been replaced to some extent by hormones, which are much more numerous and more limited and specific in their relation to bodily processes and behavior. But we no longer have much faith in the ancient humors, in skull contours, or in mental faculties as determiners of behavior. Those particular dryads are pretty well gone, so far as most of us are concerned. But others have appeared to take their place—and they have gained acceptance in some of the best circles of behavioral science. To question them is to invite an argument, but I believe they need to be questioned. When they are used simply to *describe* behavior, they are soundly meaningful, and I have no quarrel with them. But when they are used to *explain* the behavior, they take on all of the questionable characteristics of the dryads of long ago.

Source: Excerpted from Robert L. Ebel (1974), "And Still the Dryads Linger," American Psychologist *(July), pp. 485–492.*

In the previous section, an in-depth analysis of consumer cognitive processes and structures was presented. The major focus of that section was an attempt to understand the internal psychology or mental aspects of consumer behavior. In this section the focus changes. Our concern here is with attempting to understand overt consumer behavior; i.e., behavior that can be directly observed and measured. We will focus on what consumers *do* rather than on what they think, and we will delineate some processes by which this behavior can be changed to achieve marketing objectives.

In this chapter we first compare *cognitive* and *behavior* approaches in terms of some differences in philosophical positions and assumptions, research approaches and practices, and views of marketing. We do this so that you can appreciate the differences between the approaches and can understand why there are so few attempts to integrate them. We maintain that both cognitive and behavior approaches have value for the study of consumer behavior and for achieving marketing management objectives. We view attempts to keep the perspectives totally separated as counter-productive and as a detriment to consumer behavior inquiry. While cognitive and behavior perspectives may not be fully reconcilable, useful information and procedures can be gleaned from each.

After we review the differences in perspectives, some examples of applied behavior analysis are discussed. These examples demonstrate the value of the approach in marketing settings. The chapter concludes with a discussion of some common misconceptions about behavior approaches.

In Chapter 10, respondent (classical) and operant (instrumental) conditioning are explained and illustrated with a variety of marketing examples. We then turn to vicarious learning and its value for marketing (Chapter 11). These two chapters provide an overview of the major technology employed in applied behavior analysis. In Chapter 12, the last chapter of this section, we develop a model of overt consumer behavior and a management model for systematically influencing these behaviors.

Cognitive versus Behavior Views

Cognitive approaches dominate the field of consumer behavior and much of the thinking in marketing. Although behavior approaches have been an important part of psychology for many years, they are relatively new to consumer research and often are not well understood or appreciated. For this reason, we think it is important to give a detailed account of the differences between the two approaches.

There are, of course, many types of cognitive theories and assumptions and a variety of behavior positions. For example, some cognitive approaches attempt to apply cognitive theories in explaining overt behavior. Others are concerned only with explaining the mind and mental processes. Some behaviorists view cognitive events as covert behavior to be analyzed in the same way as overt behavior. Other behaviorists see cognitive events as little more than words that may be useful for communication purposes but useless as scientific explanations. It is unlikely that any discussion of differences between cognitive and behavior perspectives would be accepted by all advocates of either position, but we will attempt to offer representative accounts of them.

The **behavior approach** is based on a current view called "applied behavior analysis." The **cognitive view** is based on current research on topics such as information processing and cognitive science. You will soon see why the two perspectives have been antagonists: they involve much different views of the world, with conflicting philosophies, assumptions, approaches to research, and beliefs about what counts as scientifically important. Most important for our purposes, these approaches often have different implications for designing marketing strategies and consumer research.

FIGURE 9–1   **A Comparison of Philosophical Positions and Assumptions**

Philosophical Positions	Behavior Approaches	Cognitive Approaches
• View of concepts	Observational, physical	Theoretical, mental
• Explanations sought	Functional	Structural
• Type of inferences	Primarily inductive	Primarily deductive
Major Assumptions		
• Role of the environment	Predominant controlling variable	One influence among many others
• Role of cognitive factors	Merely mediators	Predominant controlling variables
• View of freedom	All behavior is controlled by environmental factors	Humans are autonomous, independent centers of action

Philosophical Positions and Assumptions

In Figure 9–1 we provide an overview of some of the major differences in philosophical positions and assumptions between the two approaches. While both the behavior and cognitive approaches have their roots in a philosophy called logical positivism, each has selected different routes to seeking knowledge about humans. The behavior view typically prefers observing behavior that can be measured somewhat directly, as is done in classical physics. The cognitive view allows for theoretical or mental variables that are measured indirectly through such means as verbal reports. The behavior view usually seeks explanations for functional relationships between behavior and the environment; cognitive approaches often focus on the structure of conscious experience. Finally, the behavior approach often attempts to draw inductive inferences, while the cognitive approach is primarily based on deduction.

We believe that both approaches have value, but that neither one alone can provide a complete set of guidelines for developing marketing strategy. Neither approach has escaped severe criticism in the literature on the philosophy of science, and the history of science demonstrates clearly that there are many useful approaches to seeking knowledge.[1] Thus, we feel marketing and consumer researchers would be well advised to use whatever means are available to gain knowledge and not attempt to force

---

[1]See Paul F. Anderson (1983), "Marketing, Scientific Progress, and Scientific Method," *Journal of Marketing* (Fall), pp. 18–31; J. Paul Peter and Jerry C. Olson (1983), "Is Science Marketing?" *Journal of Marketing* (Fall), pp. 111–125.

themselves into one or the other mold. In fact, attempts to follow only one set of values have resulted in the schism between the behavior and cognitive views.

Causes of Behavior

A critical difference between the two perspectives concerns the cause or causes of behavior. Many behaviorists argue that the *environment* controls behavior, while many cognitivists insist that *individuals* control their own behavior through the mental processes involved in cognitive processing and decision making. This demonstrates why the two perspectives are not fully reconcilable. For many behaviorists, even if cognitive events are viewed as affecting behavior, the environment still causes the cognitive events. Thus, the environment is the cause and controller of behavior. However, many cognitivists believe that consumers are independent decision makers who consciously choose their behavior.

The assumption that much consumer behavior is controlled by the environment is one that many people refuse to accept. All of us like to view ourselves as decision makers who control the environment rather than seeing the environment as controlling us. Yet consider the following example. Most every adult in our society purchases and uses deodorant. In fact, it is socially unacceptable *not* to use it. The social environment conditions this behavior, for its performance is rewarded with social acceptance, and lack of performance is often punished with social sanctions. Are we really free to choose whether or not to use deodorant, given the consequences? Isn't this "choice" determined by the environmental contingencies? In any event, you can see that to the degree that the environment influences behavior, marketing stimuli are a very important part of the environment.

Research Approaches and Stages

Figure 9–2 presents a comparison of typical approaches and stages in the research process from the two points of view. Behavior approaches often take the *prediction and control of behavior* to be the fundamental goal of research; cognitive approaches are often concerned with *explanation* and *theory testing.* Typically, behavior approaches suggest that data be collected through observation; cognitive research often employs verbal reports obtained through questionnaires.

A major difference between the two is in the starting point for conducting research. Applied behavior analysis often starts with a "behavior problem," such as littering, and then attempts to change this behavior. Cognitive research often starts with a theory and attempts to design research to test it. For example, the dominant approach to consumer research

FIGURE 9–2   **A Comparison of Research Approaches and Stages**

A. Research Approaches

Research Dimensions	Behavior Approaches	Cognitive Approaches
a. Research objectives	Change behavior	Test theory
b. Object of study	Overt behavior; functional relationships	Mind: mental structures and processes
c. Basic data	Observation	Verbal reports
d. Criteria for successful research	Socially significant amount of behavior change	Logical relationships and statistical significance
e. Typical research setting	Natural	Laboratory

B. Research Stages

Behavior Approaches	Cognitive Approaches
1. Identify behavior problem	Find/develop cognitive theory
2. Measure current frequency of behavior problem and environmental conditions	Determine hypotheses
3. Design intervention	Develop measures/manipulations
4. Determine intervention setting/ subjects	Sample subjects
5. Implement intervention	Collect data
6. Remeasure target behavior	Analyze data
7. Determine amount of behavior change	Draw inference about internal psychology

involves attempts to test cognitive theories in a marketing context. While there are some similarities at a number of research stages, the criteria by which research is judged is quite different. Behavior research is usually considered successful if a sufficient amount of behavior is changed; cognitive research is generally considered successful if a logical, statistically significant relationship is supported.[2]

Both research approaches can provide valuable information for designing marketing strategies. For example, cognitive research employing verbal reports could be very useful for investigating differences in consumer perceptions of Gates versus Saranac ski gloves. Behavior research could be very useful for investigating the impact of various sales promotion tools, such as a $20 factory rebate on Head skis.

---

[2]For a discussion of problems with this approach, see Alan G. Sawyer and J. Paul Peter (1983), "The Significance of Statistical Significance Tests in Marketing Research," *Journal of Marketing Research* (May), pp. 122–133.

Don Smetzer: Click/Chicago

Do you think rebates change consumer behavior?

Views of Marketing

Figure 9–3 offers a comparison of how users of each approach tend to view the field of marketing. From a behavior perspective, marketing can be viewed as a *technology* that seeks solutions to practical problems. From a cognitive perspective, marketing is often viewed as a *science* that seeks explanations. Behavior approaches offer basic principles of behavior as a

---

FIGURE 9–3   **A Comparison of Views of Marketing**

Marketing Issues	Behavior Approaches	Cognitive Approaches
Status of the field	Technology	Science
Role of marketing	Modify and control consumer behavior to achieve organizational objectives	Satisfy needs of consumers at a profit
Guide to marketing planning	Behavior principles	Marketing concept
Role of marketing/consumer research	Investigate strategies for predicting and controlling consumer behavior	Describe internal psychology
View of marketing effectiveness	Recognizes the effectiveness of marketing in changing behavior	Often overlooks the effectiveness of marketing

guide to marketing planning and strategy. Cognitive approaches often depend on the marketing concept as a guide to strategy development.

Using the marketing concept, those supporting the cognitive approach might offer the following view: Because the marketing concept suggests that marketing action should be based on an attempt to satisfy needs at a profit, two cognitive assumptions underlie it. First, it is assumed that consumers have something called "needs," which they attempt to satisfy through purchase and consumption. Second, it is assumed that consumers are somewhat autonomous and rational, and are decision makers whose preferences and purchases are largely personally controlled. This view also recognizes that marketing strategies attempt to change consumer cognitions, such as beliefs and attitudes, but usually denies that marketing can *create* consumer needs and wants or even modify them very much. Similarly, the question of whether marketing is very effective at changing consumer behavior is seldom addressed by cognitivists.

In contrast, many behaviorists would tend to offer a different account of marketing activity. Marketing may be seen as an attempt to achieve organizational objectives by predicting and influencing consumer behavior. These objectives typically involve increases in profits and/or market share, both of which are usually achieved by increasing sales. Two primary methods of increasing sales are: (1) influencing current buyers to buy more of the product, and (2) maintaining current buyers and influencing non-buyers to become buyers. Both of these involve changing consumer purchase behavior. Many behaviorists would argue that marketing strategies are often effective at changing and maintaining consumer behavior—and that a variety of current marketing tactics are quite consistent with behavioral principles. Some behaviorists might even suggest that marketing executives typically pay little attention to consumer needs in developing new products,[3] and that discussions of topics such as pricing, advertising, and personal selling in marketing texts are far more concerned with tactics for making profitable sales than with satisfying consumer needs.

In summary, the two approaches, when applied to marketing and consumer behavior, differ considerably. Which approach is "true" or "right" is not an important question. What is important is which approach or combination of approaches is most *useful* in various stages of solving marketing problems and developing marketing strategies.

We believe that a combination of both approaches is superior to either one taken separately. For example, if consideration of consumer needs is helpful in the development of successful new products, and if operant

---

[3]See L. Lawton and A. Parasuraman (1980), "The Impact of the Marketing Concept on New Product Planning," *Journal of Marketing* (Winter), pp. 19–25.

Many marketing practitioners are very effective at using a combination of cognitive and behavioral approaches. For example, LIFETIME Cable Network conducted cognitive research on why viewers were not watching its programs. A finding of this research was that one in five viewers erroneously thought LIFETIME was a religious network.

The network set three behavioral objectives: (1) to get more people to "sample" LIFETIME's new programming; (2) to get those who may look at LIFETIME now to watch a wider variety of programs; and (3) to get people to *keep* watching.

The strategy used to accomplish these objectives featured a "Chance of a Lifetime" game. The game required viewers to match symbols from a game card with symbols shown on the air. The game cards were sent to viewers with their cable bills, or could be obtained in *TV Guide* or through requests during on-air promotion. The game was easy to understand and play, lasted long enough to keep people watching, and spread winning symbols over the entire programming day. The $400,000 worth of prizes included stereo systems, personal computers, romantic getaway weekends for two, and many other prizes with universal appeal. There was a game each week for eight weeks, and 200 prizes per week were awarded. A "second chance" drawing offered the grand prize of a $25,000 tour of Europe.

This strategy greatly increased viewer interest and cable system support. For example, on a single day, nearly 1,100 subscribers sent in entries. Tens of thousands of entries for the "second chance" contest were received before the main contest even finished. Thus, by analyzing cognitions to identify the problem, and by devising a unique behavioral intervention to solve the problem, a successful marketing strategy was developed.

Source: Based on "Behind the Lifetime Sweeps" (1985), Promotion Hotline, *Ogilvy & Mather Promotions (May), pp. 1–2.*

conditioning is helpful in increasing market share for the product, there is no reason to ignore one or the other approach.

We will now provide some examples of applied behavior analysis research. All of these examples come from the psychological literature but deal with behavior of concern to marketing, primarily social marketing.

Examples of Applied Behavior Analysis Research

As we noted previously, applied behavior analysis research starts with identifying a behavior problem and focuses on methods to change the behavior. While much of this type of research is reasonably straightforward and easy to understand and evaluate, there are a few research terms that may be unfamiliar to students of marketing and consumer behavior. We will explain some of these so that they can be used in describing the examples that follow.

First, the frequency of the problem behavior prior to an intervention strategy is called the **baseline.** Thus, the baseline is the rate of performance of the problem behavior and is used to evaluate the effect of the intervention. For example, suppose the problem behavior is smoking. The baseline would be the current rate of smoking prior to any attempts to decrease this behavior.

Multiple-baseline designs are commonly used in applied behavior analysis. These designs demonstrate the effect of an intervention across several different behaviors, individuals, or situations at different times. For example, suppose the intervention for decreasing smoking was to have the subjects snap rubber bands on their wrists every time they started to smoke. Several different situations might be studied, including the subjects at home, in the office, and at a cocktail party. This would be a multiple-baseline study across situations. If the behavior decreased in all situations, this would indicate that the intervention and not some other factor in the environment caused the change.

Finally, a very commonly employed research approach is the **reversal design.** In this approach, the problem behavior of a subject or group of subjects is first assessed to determine baseline performance. After a stable rate of behavior is determined, the intervention is introduced until behavior changes. A reversal phase follows, in which the intervention is withdrawn and then reintroduced. A functional relationship is inferred if the behavior changes in each of the intervention phases but returns to baseline (or close to baseline) when the intervention is removed. For example, suppose the rubber band intervention was used at randomly selected hours during the day to attempt to decrease smoking behavior. If smoking decreased during the intervention hours but returned to baseline at other times of day, this would be strong evidence for the effectiveness of the intervention.

With an understanding of these few terms, we can now investigate several examples of applied behavior analysis research. We have selected six examples of behaviors involved in social marketing. These include three studies that attempted to *decrease* behaviors and three that attempted to *increase* behaviors. The studies to decrease behavior deal with reducing smoking, littering, and jaywalking. The studies to increase behavior deal with regular dental care, seat-belt usage, and car pooling. A review of these studies should point out the usefulness of this approach for other types of marketing problems and show how this approach differs from cognitive research; namely, it focuses on overt behavior and investigates methods to change it.

---

1. Applied—In this type of research, the behavior, stimulus, and/or organism under study is chosen because of its importance to society rather than its importance to theory.

2. Behavioral—It is concerned with how it is possible to get individuals to *do* certain things effectively rather than to *say* certain things (unless, of course, a verbal response is the behavior of interest).

3. Analytic—It requires a believable demonstration of the events responsible for the occurrence or nonoccurrence of that behavior, i.e., a demonstration of experimental control.

4. Technological—It requires that the techniques making up a particular behavioral application are completely identified and described so that the research could be replicated.

5. Conceptual—Research procedures should be linked to basic principles of behavior to foster the development of a discipline rather than a collection of tricks.

6. Effective—The research should produce effects great enough to be of practical, social value.

7. Generality—The research should be concerned with examining the maintenance of behavioral change over time, across different settings or stimulus conditions, across related behaviors, and across individuals.

Source: Based on Steven C. Hayes, Arnold Rincover and Jay V. Solnick (1980), "The Technical Drift of Applied Behavior Analysis," Journal of Applied Behavior Analysis *(Summer), pp. 275–285.*

Decreasing Cigarette Smoking

Much marketing activity is concerned with increasing smoking—but there is considerable evidence that smoking is unhealthy. One particular social problem is that of passive smoking, that is, nonsmokers inhale the smoke of nearby cigarette users. Passive smoking has been shown to be particularly troublesome for children: research has shown increases in the incidence of admissions to hospitals for bronchitis and pneumonia of infants exposed to cigarette smoke.

Jason and Liotta investigated the effects of several interventions designed to decrease smoking in target areas of a cafeteria.[4] Each day of the week during lunchtime, observers recorded the number of individuals who smoked one or more cigarettes and the number of minutes any smok-

---

[4]Leonard A. Jason and Richard F. Liotta (1982), "Reduction of Cigarette Smoking in a University Cafeteria," *Journal of Applied Behavior Analysis* (Winter), pp. 573–577.

ing occurred within the target area. Two different types of interventions were employed. First, signs were put on the walls and on each table with the following words: "No-Smoking Section for Health and Comfort of Patrons." A second intervention included the signs plus a verbal request by a student to any smoker in the area, "I'm concerned about keeping this section for nonsmokers. Would you either stop smoking in this area or move to the smoking area?" If the smoker did not comply, a second request was made.

FIGURE 9–4   **Minutes Smoking and Number of Smokers Observed in the Cafeteria's No-Smoking Section across Experimental Conditions**

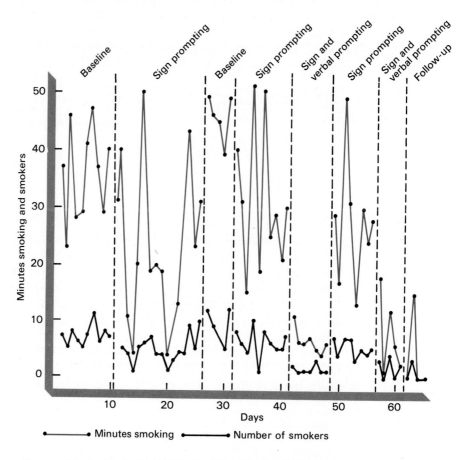

Source: Leonard A. Jason and Richard F. Liotta (1982), "Reduction of Cigarette Smoking in a University Cafeteria," Journal of Applied Behavior Analysis (Winter), pp. 573–577.

Figure 9–4 presents the overall reversal design and the results of the study. During the two baseline phases, cigarette smoke was present for an average of 39 out of the observed 50 minutes. An average of 7.7 individuals were observed smoking in the target area per day. During the sign phases, the average number of smokers was 5.3 per session, and cigarette smoke was observed for an average of 26 minutes. The most effective condition was the sign plus prompting by the student, in which an average of 1.6 smokers were observed smoking for an average of 6.2 minutes. Most of the smokers (81 percent) at least partially complied with the request. A follow-up study three months later found low incidence of smoking in the no-smoking area.

This study demonstrated that, for smoking, signs alone were not effective at reducing the frequency of this behavior in a no-smoking area, although verbal prompts were quite effective. In other studies, however, signs have been found to be effective in getting people to use special trash receptacles, buy returnable bottles, turn off lights, and not steal certain items in a store. Verbal prompts have previously been found to be effective in influencing newspaper recycling, bus ridership, and seat-belt usage.

Decreasing Littering

In recent years there has been a growing concern in this country with the quality of the physical environment. In addition to air and water pollution, there has also been a concern with littering in public places. Not only is litter an eyesore, but considerable expense is involved in cleaning it up. Many studies have found that giving people a reward for not littering is an effective antilittering tactic. This approach is based on the principles of operant conditioning (a topic discussed in detail in Chapter 10). However, this approach may entail considerable cost and involves logistical problems in distributing the rewards to people who do not litter.

Another approach is to simply provide the appropriate stimuli to attempt to control littering behavior. This approach was taken by O'Neill, Blanck, and Joyner. They attempted to reduce litter in a football stadium by altering the refuse containers.[5] This study compared a conventional litter receptacle (a 55-gallon drum) and a specially designed 55-gallon drum with a wooden lid designed to look like the hats worn by many of the football fans. The "hat" had the word "PUSH" painted on a door affixed to the front of it, and when the door was pushed, the word "THANKS!" was exposed.

---

[5]George W. O'Neill, Linda S. Blanck and Marcia A. Joyner (1980), "The Use of Stimulus Control over Littering in a Natural Setting," *Journal of Applied Behavior Analysis* (Summer), pp. 379–381.

Mark Antman/The Image Works

Charles Gatewood/The Image Works

Other strategies for decreasing litter.

Data were gathered during four home games by collecting, counting, and weighing the litter deposited in the two types of containers. The containers were in different locations for each of the four games to control for any effects due to position. Figure 9–5 presents the results of that study. In all but two cases (trays and hot dog wrappers in game 4) more items were deposited in the experimental receptacle than in the standard drum. In the majority of cases, almost twice as many items and twice the total weight of items were deposited in the experimental container.

This study provides an example of a stimulus (the hat) that may focus attention on proper behavior (litter disposal). In addition, it seems likely that seeing someone deposit litter in the receptacle may encourage others to do so. This is called "modeling" (a topic discussed in detail in Chapter 11). The total cost of the hat was under $10, but of course, comparisons with other methods would be required to see whether this is a cost-effective method of litter reduction.

FIGURE 9–5   **Number of Specific Items and Weight of Litter Deposited in the Containers**

Game	Candy Bar Wrappers		Concession Stand Trays		Hot Dog Wrappers		Cups		Weight	
	E	C	E	C	E	C	E	C	E	C
1	14	4	6	1	11	4	44	12	2.3	0.9
2	6	5	2	1	5	3	34	26	1.3	0.6
3	5	4	3	1	11	0	31	9	0.7	0.8
4	8	2	1	1	0	2	29	11	0.9	0.3
Total:	33	15	12	4	27	9	138	58	5.2	2.6

Note: E = Experimental trash container, C = Conventional trash container. Weight expressed in kg.

Source: George W. O'Neill, Linda S. Blanck and Marcia A. Joyner (1980), "The Use of Stimulus Control over Littering in a Natural Setting," Journal of Applied Behavior Analysis *(Summer), pp. 379–381.*

Decreasing Jaywalking

Jaywalking may not seem like a very important, socially significant behavior. In one recent year, however, more than 8,000 pedestrians were killed in traffic accidents. Thus, designing environments that encourage safe street-crossing behavior is very significant, indeed.

Jason and Liotta investigated the effects of the timing of "Walk" and "Don't Walk" signs on jaywalking.[6] The site of the study was a busy intersection on the north side of Chicago. From 1977 to 1980, there were 152 traffic accidents at the target intersection; 39 people were injured, 10 of whom were pedestrians. Pedestrians who wished to cross both streets and were traveling in a clockwise direction had to wait an average of 36 seconds (range 35 to 37 seconds), while pedestrians traveling in a counterclockwise direction had to wait an average of only 11 seconds (range 10 to 12 seconds). It was predicted that the majority of jaywalking violations would occur for pedestrians traveling clockwise, because longer waits were required.

Figure 9–6 presents the results of observation of pedestrians for 10 minutes per day for each of five days. Of the 142 pedestrians observed traveling clockwise, 100 jaywalked; of the 161 pedestrians observed traveling counterclockwise, only 4 jaywalked. A follow-up questionnaire given

---

[6]Leonard A. Jason and Richard Liotta (1982), "Pedestrian Jaywalking under Facilitating and Nonfacilitating Conditions," *Journal of Applied Behavior Analysis* (Fall), pp. 469–473.

to a subsample of pedestrians asked whether there was any difference in the amount of time they had to wait at the intersection if the signs were obeyed and they were walking one way or the other. All subjects except one said there was no difference in waiting time; the single exception incorrectly stated that walking clockwise is quicker at the intersection.

While this study did not directly intervene to reduce jaywalking, the results were given to the Commissioner of Traffic for the City of Chicago in an attempt to influence light-timing sequences to facilitate compliance with stipulated rules and to increase safety. The study does demonstrate, however, that behavior is affected by an environmental factor in a natural

---

FIGURE 9–6   *Average Percentage of Violations for Pedestrians Traveling in a Clockwise (Long-Delay) or Counterclockwise (Short-Delay) Direction*

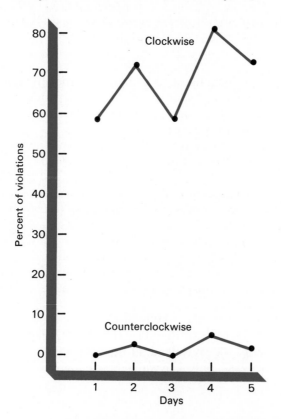

Source: Leonard A. Jason and Richard Liotta (1982), "Pedestrian Jaywalking under Facilitating and Nonfacilitating Conditions," Journal of Applied Behavior Analysis *(Fall), pp. 469–473.*

setting—and that apparently, people are not consciously aware of the factor's impact.

Increasing Dental Care

Dental care is extremely important. It is estimated that at least 50 percent of the population suffer from some form of periodontal disease. Mass screening programs have been popular, but have had little impact on actual health-related behaviors such as getting consumers to make regular visits to the dentist. This is particularly true for the poor. It is not uncommon for health screening to result in less than 50 percent compliance with recommendations to seek care.

A study was conducted by Reiss and Bailey to investigate the impact of four interventions designed to increase follow-up dental care among the poor.[7] Families who had participated in the Medicaid Screening Program were randomly assigned to five different conditions. The first condition was the control: after a single screening examination, parents of children with dental problems were given the name of a dentist to contact. This was the standard method employed by dental clinics performing the screening. A multiple-contact procedure was employed with the second group, in which parents received a postcard and two telephone reminders. A problem-solve procedure was used for the third group; a social worker aide conducted a brief session to help the parents make a dental appointment. An incentive procedure was employed for the fourth group; parents received a coupon worth $5 in cash or a selected gift item that was redeemable from the Health Department on the child's first visit to the dentist. The final group received both the problem-solve and incentive procedures.

Figure 9–7 presents the percentage of families who brought their child for an initial dental visit and the percentage who completed all of the recommended care. Quite clearly, all four procedures increased dental visits significantly above the procedure normally used. Of course, an important issue is the cost of implementing these procedures. The cost efficiency of the treatments can be determined by dividing the total cost by the number of families making an initial dental visit and completing care. For the five groups, the cost efficiency is as follows: control, $.50 per initial visit and $1.12 per completed care; problem-solve, $2.08 per initial visit and $2.56 per completed care; incentive, $4.69 per initial visit and $7.57 per completed care; incentive plus problem-solve, $6.48 per initial visit and $9.29 per completed care.

---

[7]Maxin L. Reiss and Jon S. Bailey (1982), "Visiting the Dentist: A Behavioral Community Analysis of Participation in a Dental Health Screening and Referral Program," *Journal of Applied Behavior Analysis* (Fall), pp. 353–362.

FIGURE 9–7 **Percentage of Families Making Initial Dental Visit and Completing Care across Five Treatments**

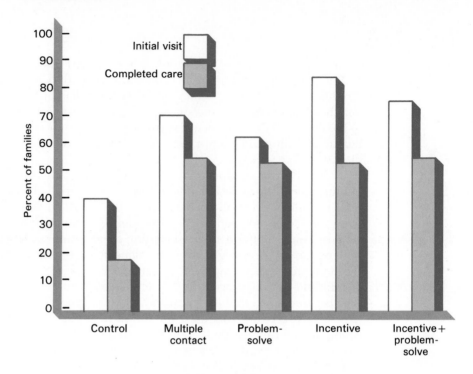

Source: Maxin L. Reiss and Jon S. Bailey (1982), "Visiting the Dentist: A Behavioral Community Analysis of Participation in a Dental Health Screening and Referral Program," Journal of Applied Behavior Analysis (Fall), pp. 353–362.

The decision as to which procedure to use is important and involves a trade-off between using the most effective procedure and the very high costs of public health programs. Viewed in this way, the multiple contact treatment is perhaps the "best buy," although it is difficult to trade off the dental care of children who would only be helped by their parents if an incentive program were available.

Increasing Seat-Belt Usage

Vehicle seat belts have proven lifesaving and injury-reduction potential. The Highway Safety Research Center has estimated that accident victims wearing a shoulder and lap harness are 56.5 percent less likely to sustain

Mark Antman/The Image Works

Alan Carey/The Image Works

Other strategies for increasing seat-belt usage.

a moderate injury and 56.8 percent less likely to incur a severe injury than are those who do not wear seat belts. However, a 1982 survey by the U.S. Department of Transportation, which included observations of more than 150,000 drivers over several years, found that only about 10 to 15 percent of drivers use seat belts.

Geller, Paterson, and Talbott designed a study to investigate interventions to increase seat-belt usage.[8] Two parking lots at a university were chosen for the two conditions. In the first lot, drivers were stopped, and if they were wearing a seat belt, they were given a flier promoting seat-belt use and describing a game in which certain combinations of symbols on the flier could earn prizes. Fliers given to drivers not wearing seat belts did not contain contest symbols but had a slip of paper with a message to wear seat belts and receive a chance to win a valuable prize. Thus, the

---

[8]E. Scott Geller, Lisa Paterson and Elizabeth Talbott (1982), "A Behavioral Analysis of Incentive Prompts for Motivating Seat Belt Use," *Journal of Applied Behavior Analysis* (Fall), pp. 403–415.

chance to win a prize was contingent upon seat-belt usage. In the other lot, all drivers, regardless of seat-belt usage, were given a flier prompting them to wear seat belts but including a chance to win a prize. (This was the noncontingent condition.)

Figure 9–8 presents the results of this study. Only when the chance to win a prize was contingent upon seat-belt usage did drivers dramatically increase wearing them. Prompting and noncontingent rewards were not sufficient to motivate seat-belt usage.

A contingent reward program could be readily adapted for large-

FIGURE 9–8   **Daily Percentages of Drivers Wearing a Seat Belt as a Function of Experimental Phase (Baseline, Treatment, and Withdrawal) and Treatment Condition (Contingent Rewards versus Noncontingent Rewards)**

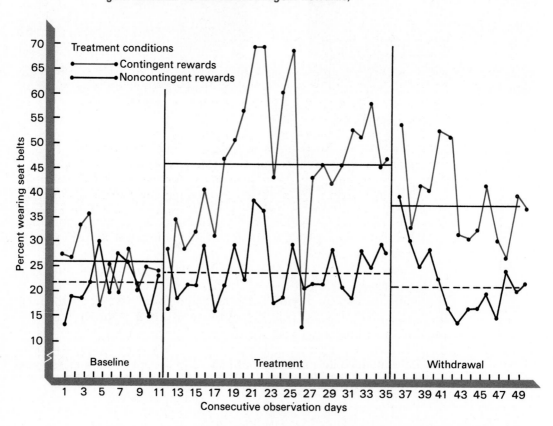

Source: E. Scott Geller, Lisa Paterson and Elizabeth Talbott (1982), "A Behavioral Analysis of Incentive Prompts for Motivating Seat Belt Use," Journal of Applied Behavior Analysis (Fall), pp. 403–415.

scale, community application by offering rewards at various places such as parking lot entrances at apartment complexes, airports, and shopping centers as well as other places in which drivers conduct transactions from their cars, such as banks and fast-food restaurants. Given the estimate that the nonuse of seat belts nationwide costs $10 billion in personal and societal losses, a 20 percent increase in seat-belt usage, such as was obtained in this study, could be very significant.

Increasing the Use of Car Pools

The use of personal automobiles provides convenient transportation, but is not without significant social costs. For example, in one recent year, over 75 billion gallons of gasoline were consumed by personal automobiles, which represented 30 percent of the nation's total petroleum supply for

George W. Gardner

An incentive to increase car-pooling.

that year. In addition, there are significant costs in air-pollution damage to property, materials, health, and vegetation. One way to reduce these costs is to increase car pooling.

Jacobs et al. conducted a study to investigate methods of increasing car pooling among university students.[9] After baseline observation of car pooling in four parking lots for five days, the next four days of baseline were used to set up the intervention. Drivers entering three of the lots were given a flier that listed the benefits of car pools, were told that parking spaces would be reserved for car poolers in Lots A and B beginning the following Monday, and were asked that each car occupant fill out a form for a program that matched them with other potential car poolers who lived within one half mile of them. Results of the matching program were mailed to each participant the following week with information on how to form a car pool. In addition to receiving reserved parking, each member of the car pool received a 25-cent coupon redeemable for merchandise at local stores for every day they used the car pool. Storekeepers were reimbursed for the coupons each week. After 19 days of this intervention, car poolers were given one day's notice that the bonus coupons would no longer be distributed in Lot A, but that reserved parking would still be available in that lot.

Figure 9–9 presents the results of this study. In Lot A, car pooling increased from an average of 11 percent during baseline to 21 percent during treatment conditions. The removal of the coupons from this lot in the final 10 days of the study appeared to have no effect on participation. In experimental Lot B, however, car pooling only increased from 11 percent to 14 percent. In the two control lots, car pooling decreased 1.2 percent and .5 percent. While a cost-benefit analysis demonstrated that the program was very cost effective for the university and resulted in substantial savings for the students, the failure to achieve a higher rate of car pooling in Lot B suggests that other contingencies should be considered. However, the fact that 83 percent of the coupons were redeemed suggests that they may be a useful reinforcer for developing car-pooling behavior.

Misconceptions about Applied Behavior Analysis

The previous examples demonstrate typical applied behavior analysis research. Because increasing or decreasing the specific behaviors described

---

[9]Harvey E. Jacobs, David Fairbanks, Cheryl E. Poche and Jon S. Bailey (1982), "Multiple Incentives in Encouraging Car Pool Formation on a University Campus," *Journal of Applied Behavior Analysis* (Spring), pp. 141–149.

FIGURE 9–9

The Percentage of Car Pools as a Function of Total Cars Entering Each Lot across Experimental Days

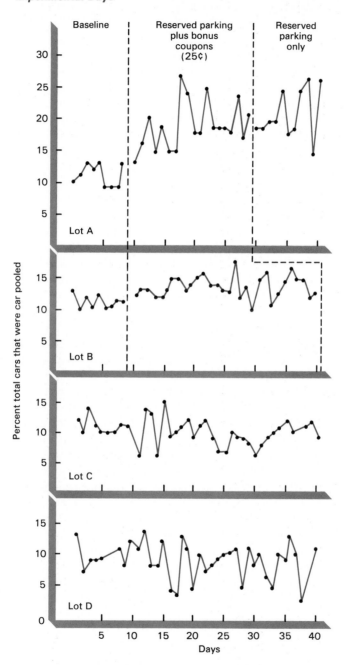

Source: Harvey E. Jacobs, David Fairbanks, Cheryl E. Poche and Jon S. Bailey (1982), "Multiple Incentives in Encouraging Car Pool Formation on a University Campus," Journal of Applied Behavior Analysis (Spring), pp. 141–149.

is considered socially desirable given current value systems, these examples may not have generated strong concern over the use of this approach. Also, to this point in the text, we have intentionally not referred to the approach as "behavior modification," as this term frequently generates strong feelings and negative reactions. However, these reactions frequently occur because of misconceptions about the nature of behavior modification or applied behavior analysis. Because we believe it is very important to clarify these issues, we will now investigate three major questions concerning the nature of the approach in general and its application in marketing. (1) Aren't behavior approaches manipulative and unethical? (2) Don't behavior approaches deny that people can think? (3) Why have consumer researchers ignored behavior approaches?

Aren't Behavior Approaches Manipulative and Unethical?

There is no question that behavior approaches involve changing behavior. They have been criticized as manipulative and unethical because they attempt to change behavior in a systematic way—and they have been found to be very effective in many cases.

The fact that these approaches attempt to change behavior does not make them different from the majority of day-to-day activities in which we all engage. For example, professors attempt to get students to study, and students attempt to get professors to give them good grades; employers attempt to get employees to work hard, and employees attempt to get employers to pay them more money; parents attempt to get their children to behave well, and children attempt to get parents to give them treats; the government attempts to get people to pay taxes and obey laws, while people attempt to get the government to provide municipal services. In fact, very few human interactions are not concerned with one or more individuals attempting to change the behavior of one or more other individuals. Thus, behavior approaches should not be singled out for criticism as manipulative and unethical solely because they involve systematic and effective methods for doing what most of us are attempting to do anyway.

There is an important ethical question involved in attempts by marketing managers to get consumers to change or maintain behavior. However, this issue is much larger than questioning the use of behavior technology, for consumer behavior maintenance and change (e.g., brand loyalty and brand switching) are the bases of a competitive, capitalistic system. Firms that survive and prosper in this system are those that are most effective at modifying consumer behavior to purchase and repurchase their products and brands.

It is also true that taking a cognitive approach to marketing and consumer behavior does not avoid questions of manipulation. Cognitive variables are studied in terms of marketing and consumer behavior because they are believed to influence overt behavior. In some cases, cognitive variables are changed in order to change behavior. For example, beliefs and attitudes (and other cognitive variables) are often studied to investigate how they are formed and how they can be changed to increase purchase of a particular brand.

In other cases, cognitive variables are studied to develop more efficient marketing strategies to change behavior *without* changing the cognitive variable. For example, needs and benefits sought by consumers are often studied for the purpose of segmenting markets. In these cases, the knowledge gained is used to develop products and marketing strategies that reach a particular market segment seeking certain benefits or need satisfactions. However, this is of little value unless the firm develops a marketing strategy that effectively changes a sufficient number of these consumers' behaviors so that they actually purchase and repurchase the product.

Similarly, cognitive processes are studied in order to develop more effective advertising and marketing strategies for reaching the consumer—not as an end in itself, but to increase the probability of purchase and other overt consumer behaviors. Thus, whether attempts are made to change cognitive variables as an intermediate step (such as increasing awareness or knowledge of a product) or cognitive variables are examined in order to develop other types of marketing strategies (such as market segmentation), the role of cognitive approaches in marketing is still ultimately concerned with efficiently changing or maintaining overt consumer behavior.

In summary, a major concern of human activity in general and of marketing in particular is to change or maintain overt behavior. Society allows this to occur, and in many cases encourages it. Strategy development in marketing is clearly concerned with influencing overt consumer behavior, regardless of whether behavior or cognitive approaches are used. Thus, to argue that behavior approaches are unethical and manipulative—but that societal, marketing, and cognitive approaches to marketing are not—is an emotional reaction unsupported by logic.

Don't Behavior Approaches Deny that People Can Think?

It is commonly believed that behaviorists view people as machines who are incapable of cognitive activity. While many behaviorists believe that behavior is controlled by the environment, few (if any) argue that there is nothing going on in people's minds. The major questions deal with the ability to analyze cognitive variables "scientifically," what causes cognitive processes, and the importance of thinking versus doing.

As we have noted, some behavior approaches emphasize the importance of observation, much as is done in classical physics. Historically, behaviorists have been skeptical of the scientific value of cognitive events, because they cannot be observed directly and are generally only inferred from overt behavior. Because they must be inferred, cognitive events are usually not considered to be explanations of behavior. Even nonbehaviorists have argued that the cognitive approach leads to considerable difficulties in measurement that are not encountered in the behavior approach.[10] Part of the argument against cognitive approaches, then, is that the variables cannot be observed and measured easily.

Many behaviorists today do include self-report measures of cognitive events in their research and find them useful as supplemental, supporting information. However, these behaviorists do not view cognitive information as a substitute for studying overt behavior. In marketing, it has been argued that it would be quite useful to investigate *what* behaviors consumers perform before we develop cognitive theories designed to explain *why* the behaviors are performed.[11]

Also as we noted previously, some behaviorists argue that even if cognitive processes do mediate behavior, these processes are developed through interactions with the environment. Interactions with the environment teach the individual which behaviors are rewarded and which are punished, and this becomes part of the individual's conditioning history. While cognitivists might argue that these interactions are stored in memory, behaviorists would say that the person is changed through the interaction.

Most behaviorists believe that what people *do* is much more important than what they *think*. They believe that what goes on inside peoples' heads is of little consequence, because rewards or punishment occur in society only for what people actually do. In this sense, it is unimportant whether consumers need a product, want a product, like a product, plan to purchase a product, or think they would be satisfied with a product, until some overt behavior is performed, such as telling someone else about the product or actually buying it. What goes on in the private world inside one's head makes no difference to society until some overt public behavior is performed. For example, we may like a particular presidential candidate, but only by working for and voting for the candidate do we have any impact. Simply liking the candidate makes no difference in the outcome of the election.

---

[10]See Donald W. Fiske (1979), "Two Worlds of Psychological Phenomena," *American Psychologist* (September), pp. 733–739.

[11]J. Paul Peter (1981), "Construct Validity: A Review of Basic Issues and Marketing Practices," *Journal of Marketing Research* (May), pp. 133–145.

Creating positive feelings about a product through respondent conditioning.

ITALIAN DESIGN ON WHEELS: ABOUT $72,300

ITALIAN DESIGN ON HEELS: ABOUT $60

Nickels

"CINEMA," THE NEW SOFT SHOE IN SOFT KID.
AT FINE STORES EVERYWHERE. NICKELS, A DIVISION OF INTERSHOE, INC., 1370 AVENUE OF THE AMERICAS, N.Y., N.Y. 10019.

Courtesy Nickels, a division of Intershoe, Inc.

Modeling an enjoyable product-use experience.

**Make home your favorite health club—
with exercise equipment from Sears.**

Now you can work out in convenience and
comfort and never set foot in a health club.
With exercise equipment from Sears you can
easily turn part of a room into a workout area.
Sears has some of the latest equipment.

Like the DXC 5000* and the DP Gympac,* as
well as Nautilus, AMF and many other name
brands. There's also a large selection of active-
wear. So when you want to look your best,
Sears has what it takes for fitness.

*Available in most Sears retail stores.   © Sears, Roebuck and Co., 1984

There's more for your life at **SEARS**

Courtesy Sears, Roebuck & Co.

A strategy designed to change credit card usage behavior.

WHAT PEOPLE CARRIED BEFORE THEY CARRIED THE CITIBANK PREFERRED VISA CARD.

The bulging wallet. Universal symbol of success and power.

The Citibank Preferred Visa Card deflates that myth.

We offer you a credit line from $5,000 to $50,000. That's more than enough to start taking some credit cards out of your wallet.

You'll also get four times the acceptance of the American Express Gold Card. That's another card you can leave at home.

But most importantly, only the Citibank Preferred Visa lets you tap into the worldwide financial resources of Citicorp. That means opportunities to invest in CDs, high interest savings plans,*—even the chance to buy gold bullion.

And everything you buy with your card earns you bonuses. You can use them to get guaranteed savings on anything from reproductions of antiques to original works of contemporary art.

To get all this power behind you, just fill out the attached application and send it in. But you'll need an income of at least $25,000 to qualify. If you'd like more information, call us toll-free at 800-952-2152.

Then start emptying your wallet to make room for the Citibank Preferred Visa. Even though it's just one card, you'll be carrying a lot more weight.

A CITICORP COMPANY

THE CARD TO END ALL CARDS

Courtesy Citibank

An ad showing product consumption.

Pen Pal.

Now from Cutex, the amazing Nailcolor Pen. The quickest, easiest, maybe even prettiest way to polish.

In 18 hot new shades, it zips on rich shiny color that stays for days. And no spills, no blobs, no slow drying, no sloppy touch-ups.

The Cutex Nailcolor Pen. Take it with you everywhere. More than a pen, it's a pal.

NEW!

CUTEX
PERFECT COLOR

Courtesy Chesebrough-Pond's, Inc.

In summary, behaviorists do not argue that people are machines who are incapable of thought or feeling. However, thoughts and feelings are viewed as less operational, as being caused by the environment, and as less important for scientific study than behavior. We believe, however, that the major limitation of behavior approaches historically has been the attempt to exclude cognitive variables from study and to ignore their usefulness; and a major limitation of marketing and consumer research has been to ignore overt behavior.

Why Have Consumer Researchers Ignored Behavior Approaches?

There seem to be three reasons why behavior approaches have been ignored in consumer research. First, **consumer behavior** as a field of study developed in the early 1960s. At that time, behavior approaches were declining in popularity in psychology while cognitive approaches were becoming more popular. Because consumer researchers have always borrowed concepts and methods from psychology and applied them to marketing problems, the strong cognitive emphasis in marketing may be, in part, a historical accident. Since behavior approaches involve a different world view and different research methods than cognitive approaches, it may have been convenient for consumer analysts to ignore them. However, behavior approaches are still one of the three major schools of modern psychology and cannot be ignored.

Second, issues of manipulation and ethical concerns may have led researchers to adopt cognitive approaches, which superficially overcome these problems. Similarly, the popularity of the marketing concept and need satisfaction may have constrained research by focusing too narrowly on cognitive variables.

Third, in most academic fields, basic researchers are considered to have higher status than applied researchers. Many consumer researchers may view their work as basic research and may not want to be concerned with application in marketing. One way to appear to be a basic researcher is to avoid studying overt behavior—and to ignore the question of whether the research is useful for specific purposes.

Back to the Case

In marketing and consumer behavior, we commonly use cognitive terms such as needs, attitudes, and satisfaction. Ebel has no argument with using these terms as long as they are considered to be partial descriptions of behavior. He also believes they should be precisely defined and focused on relationships between observable phenomena in order to be useful. However, if these terms are used in consumer research as though they provided causal explanations of behavior, Ebel would consider them to be dryads of the mind.

Ebel also argues that too often the use of cognitive terms involves circular reasoning: the only evidence we have of the existence of these terms is the behavior they are supposed to explain. For example, the only evidence we have that people are highly motivated is that they work hard to achieve a goal. To say that they work hard because they are highly motivated is completely circular.

This case demonstrates how differently Ebel views the nature of commonly used cognitive terms. Whether or not you agree with his position is not important. What is important is that you now see the behavior and cognitive approaches are fundamentally different and cannot be completely integrated, at least at a conceptual level. This is not a problem in developing marketing strategies, however. In fact, it is an advantage, because by examining marketing problems from different perspectives, new insights may well be gained and better strategies can be developed.

Summary

This chapter introduced the topic of applied behavior analysis by comparing it with the cognitive approaches that currently dominate marketing and consumer/behavior research. Although behavior approaches involve a different world view that requires different methods of research and analysis than those used with the cognitive approach, it is very consistent with the goals and practice of marketing management. Several examples of applied behavior analysis research were reviewed to demonstrate approaches to changing behavior in what are commonly viewed as social marketing settings. The chapter concluded with a discussion of several misconceptions concerning behavior approaches. Marketing strategies that include analyses of cognitions, behaviors, and the environment are superior to strategies that ignore any of these three components.

Additional Reading

E. S. Geller, R. A. Winett and P. B. Everett (1980), *Preserving the Environment: New Strategies for Behavior Change,* New York: Pergamon Press.
D. S. Glenwick and L. A. Jason (1980), *Behavioral Community Psychology: Progress and Prospect,* New York: Praeger Publishers.
James G. Holland (1980), "Behaviorism: Part of the Problem or Part of the Solution?" *Journal of Applied Behavior Analysis* (Spring), pp. 163–174.
Joseph Wolpe (1978), "Cognition and Causation in Human Behavior and Its Therapy," *American Psychologist* (May), pp. 437–446.

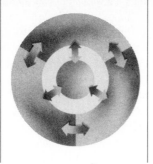

Chapter Ten

Respondent and Operant Conditioning

American Family Publishers

It's late December, and for the last few weeks you've been subjected to a media blitz of Ed McMahon telling you about the American Family Publishers Sweepstakes. You've seen friendly, trustworthy Ed introducing a past winner of $1 million. You've seen the letter on TV. Finally, it arrives, your "LAST CHANCE! Million Dollar Document" warning you, "Don't Throw Away! This is the letter you just saw on TV!"

The little blue envelope on the front is labeled, "Open This Envelope First!" Inside you find instructions on how to double your prize by removing the gold seal and placing it on the entry blank.

You now open the big envelope. On the large, official-looking document, you find your name printed throughout the text at least 20 times in various sizes of type. The first set of large print catches your eye: there's your name before "...SHALL BE PAID A FULL ONE MILLION DOLLARS." In contrasting color in the upper margin is the constant reminder, "LAST CHANCE!" A little farther down, there's your name again with nine—count 'em—*nine* Personal Prize Claim Numbers. Unfolding the document further, you find Ed McMahon with a "Last Chance Letter" telling you that he may have the pleasure of congratulating you on the "Tonight Show" for winning One Million Dollars. On the back of this document are photos of Ed and six or seven previous cash winners and the rest of the letter; on one of the figures it tells you "No Purchase Necessary to Enter or Win" (which is required by law).

The next piece of paper has a color picture of Ed, more instructions, and photos of a Mercedes, a mink coat, a cabin cruiser, and a beautiful home. "Become a Multimillionaire and Treat Yourself to the Things You Want Most!" you're told.

After extensive reading you finally figure out what to paste where to enter the contest. You also have a big page of colorful, perforated, sticky stamps that can be pasted on the entry blank to purchase any of a variety of magazines. Another full-color sheet from Ed tells you, "You can take it from me—THERE ARE NO LOWER PRICES AVAILABLE ANYWHERE TO THE GENERAL PUBLIC. American Family values are GUARANTEED UNBEATABLE!" There is also a list of selected magazines that offer Free Bonus Gifts, such as watches and desk clocks. You decide a Money-Manager Calculator would be useful—so you order *Newsweek,* which will keep you better informed for school. Besides the good price, you don't have to pay now, because you'll be billed in the future. Also, there's a money-back guarantee if you don't like the subscription— and, as it says, "You risk nothing!" So, you get the calculator, *Newsweek* at a great price, and maybe . . . just maybe . . . BIG, BIG BUCKS!!!

This chapter is concerned with two related processes. The first is called **respondent** or **classical conditioning,** and the second is **instrumental** or **operant conditioning.** Many current marketing strategies and tactics are very consistent with conditioning principles, yet only recently has published research on the subject become available in the consumer behavior literature. This is perhaps because the majority of consumer researchers are cognitively oriented and have not found the area of conditioning to be of much value for investigating cognitive processes. Traditionally, conditioning processes have been primarily concerned with the influence of environmental factors on behavior. But researchers now find that cognitive approaches provide additional insights into these effects. For example, abundant psychological research demonstrates the effectiveness of conditioning processes in changing behavior. Cognitive approaches that attempt to describe the internal mechanisms involved in conditioning processes

FIGURE 10–1   **The Process of Respondent Conditioning**

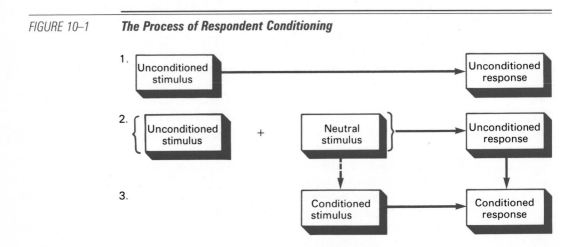

not only add insight but also help to develop more effective conditioning strategies.

The chapter has two major sections. In the first, the process of respondent conditioning is explained and illustrated. In the second section, operant conditioning is explained, some successful applications are described, and examples from marketing practice are given. We treat these two conditioning processes as conceptually distinct, although they overlap in a number of areas.

Respondent Conditioning

Respondents are a class of behaviors that are under the control of the stimuli that precede them.[1] Generally, these behaviors are assumed to be governed by the autonomic nervous system and thus not usually susceptible to conscious control. Pavlov's classical conditioning experiments provide the basic paradigm for this approach.

In general, **respondent conditioning** can be defined as a process through which a previously neutral stimulus, by being paired with an unconditioned stimulus, comes to *elicit* a response very similar to the response originally elicited by the unconditioned stimulus. This process is depicted in Figure 10–1. Four features of this process should be noted. First, respondent conditioning can be accomplished not only with unconditioned stimuli but also with previously conditioned stimuli. For example, most of us are previously conditioned to the sound of a doorbell ringing and will look up almost automatically upon hearing it. This previously conditioned stimulus is used in the beginning of Avon TV commercials to attract consumers' attention to the ad itself as well as to Avon's services.

Second, respondent behaviors are controlled by stimuli that occur *before* the behavior. For example, in Pavlov's experiment, the meat powder and bell were presented before salivation occurred. (See Highlight 10–1.)

Third, respondent behaviors are assumed to be *glandular* responses, which are controlled by the "smooth muscles." Thus, they are assumed to be involuntary and not consciously controlled.

Last, and perhaps most important for marketing and consumer behavior, behaviors called "emotions" appear to follow the principles of respondent conditioning. For example, when a new product for which

---

[1]Much of the material in this chapter is based on Walter R. Nord and J. Paul Peter (1980), "A Behavior Modification Perspective on Marketing," *Journal of Marketing* (Spring), pp. 36–47, and J. Paul Peter and Walter R. Nord (1982), "A Clarification and Extension of Operant Conditioning Principles in Marketing," *Journal of Marketing* (Summer), pp. 102–107.

HIGHLIGHT 10–1   **Coca-Cola Turns to Pavlov . . .**

Do television commercials make people behave like Pavlov's dogs? Coca-Cola Company says the answer is yes. In recent years, the Atlanta soft-drink company has been refining an ad-testing procedure based on the behavioral principles developed by the Russian physiologist. So far, Coke says, its new testing system has worked remarkably well.

In his classic experiment, Ivan Pavlov discovered he could get dogs to salivate at the ring of a bell by gradually substituting the sound for a spray of meat powder. Coca-Cola says that, just as Pavlov's dogs began to associate a new meaning with the bell, advertising is supposed to provide some new image or meaning for a product.

Although the specifics of Coke's test are a secret, the company says it attempts to evaluate how well a commercial "conditions" a viewer to accept a positive image that can be transferred to the product. During the past three years, Coca-Cola says, ads that scored well in its tests almost always resulted in higher sales of a soft drink.

"We nominate Pavlov as the father of modern advertising," says Joel S. Dubow, communications research manager at Coke. "Pavlov took a neutral object and, by associating it with a meaningful object, made it a symbol of something else; he imbued it with imagery, he gave it added value. That," says Dubow, "is what we try to do in modern advertising."

Source: The Wall Street Journal, *January 19, 1984, p. 31.*

people have neutral feelings is repeatedly advertised during exciting sports events (such as the Super Bowl), it is possible for the product to eventually generate excitement on its own solely through the repeated pairing with the exciting events. Similarly, an unknown political candidate may come to elicit patriotic feelings in voters simply by having patriotic music constantly played in the background of his/her political commercials. A number of firms currently use stimuli in commercials and ads that are designed to generate emotions. These firms include Hallmark, AT&T, and Procter & Gamble, maker of Luvs disposable diapers.

Because it can account for many of the responses that environmental stimuli elicit from individuals, respondent conditioning has important implications for marketing and consumer behavior. Through it, a particular stimulus can come to evoke positive, negative, or neutral feelings. Consequently, respondent conditioning can influence an individual to work to obtain, to avoid, or be indifferent to a wide variety of products and services.

Consider product-related stimuli. External stimuli that elicit positive emotions can be paired with the product so that the product itself elicits a positive effect. Behavior may then be triggered that brings the potential consumer into closer contact with the product. "Closer contact" refers to a

Courtesy American Airlines

An ad designed to generate emotion.

general relationship between a person's behavior and a given stimulus (e.g., a product). For example, if a product elicits positive affect, an individual exposed to it is more apt to behave positively toward it than if negative emotions are elicited. **Attending behavior** is also apt to be a function of respondently conditioned affect. Stimuli that elicit stronger emotional responses (either positive or negative) are, at least over a considerable range, apt to receive more attention from an individual than stimuli that are affectively neutral. To the degree that attending behavior is necessary for product purchase or other product-related behavior, respondent conditioning influences whether consumers come into contact with products.

Similarly, stimuli may produce certain general emotional responses, such as relaxation, excitement, nostalgia, or some other emotion that is likely to increase the probability of a desired behavior (such as product purchase). Radio and TV ads often use famous broadcasters whose voices have been paired for years with exciting sports events. These voices may elicit excitement as a result of this frequent pairing. Repeated pairings of the voices with the advertised product can result, via higher-order respondent conditioning, in feelings of excitement associated with the product. For example, Don Meredith and Frank Gifford of "Monday Night Football" were featured in a series of ads for Planter's peanuts.

Music, sexy voices and bodies, and other stimuli are used in similar ways. For example, magazine ads for Calvin Klein's Obsession perfume featured a naked woman being kissed by three men. Such stimuli may influence behavior without this "higher order conditioning" simply by drawing attention to the ad. Of course, the attention-generating properties of the stimulus itself are apt to have developed through previous conditioning that occurs "naturally" in society.

The use of telephones ringing or sirens in the background of radio and TV ads, and the presence of famous celebrities are common examples of how stimuli that are irrelevant to the content of an ad or the function of the product, are used to increase attention paid to the ad itself. For example, John McEnroe was featured in a series of commercials for Bic razors. In this context, one of the major resources that organizations use to market their product is made available through previous respondent conditioning of members of society.

Stimuli at or near the point of purchase also serve the goals of marketers through the stimuli's ability to elicit respondent behaviors. Christmas music in a toy department is a good example. Although no data are available to support the point, we suspect that carols are useful in eliciting the emotions labeled the "Christmas spirit." Once these feelings have been elicited, we suspect (and retailers seem to share our expectations) that people are more apt to purchase a gift for a loved one. In other words, Christmas carols are useful in generating emotions that are compatible with purchasing gifts.

There are several generalizations concerning respondent conditioning as a marketing tool. First, the concept of respondent conditioning directs attention to the presentation of stimuli which, due to previous conditioning, elicit certain feelings in the potential consumer. Sometimes (as with Christmas music) these stimuli trigger emotions that are apt to increase the probability of certain desired behaviors (or reduce the probability of undesired responses). Second, in many cases, marketers may find it useful to actually condition responses to stimuli. When promoting political candidates, for example, it may be desirable to pair the candidate with

HIGHLIGHT 10–2   **Some Marketing Tactics Consistent with Respondent Conditioning Principles**

A.   Conditioning Responses to New Stimuli

Unconditioned or Previously Conditioned Stimulus	Conditioned Stimulus	Examples
Exciting event	A product or theme song	New product advertised during the Super Bowl
Patriotic events or music	A product or person	Patriotic music as background in political commercial

B.   Use of Familiar Stimuli to Elicit Responses

Conditioned Stimulus	Conditioned Response(s)	Examples
Popular music	Relaxation, excitement, "good will"	Christmas music in retail stores
Familiar voices	Excitement, attention	Famous sportscaster or movie star narrating a commercial
Sexy voices, bodies	Excitement, attention, arousal	Diet Pepsi commercials and many others
Familiar cues	Excitement, attention, anxiety	Sirens sounding, telephones or doorbells ringing in commercials
Familiar social cues	Feelings of friendship and love	Television ads depicting calls from family or close friend

the American flag repeatedly to condition the feelings elicited by the flag to the candidate. Then, the candidate alone may stimulate the same feelings in voters as the flag does. In fact, research on respondent conditioning, as well as advertising research, supports the idea that repetition increases the strength of the association between stimuli.

Consumer Research on Respondent Conditioning

There are several studies in the marketing/consumer behavior literature demonstrating respondent conditioning effects. The best known of these was conducted by Gorn; it was the first demonstration of these effects in a

Richard Younker: Click/Chicago

Conditioning patriotic feelings to a political candidate.

marketing context.[2] This study investigated the effects on consumer choices of the music used in advertising. The first study identified one musical selection that was liked and one that was disliked by consumers. It also identified two colors of pens that had neutral evaluations (light blue and beige). This created four conditions: (1) liked music, light blue pen; (2) liked music, beige pen; (3) disliked music, light blue pen; (4) disliked music, beige pen. After looking at an ad for one of the pens while hearing a tape of one of the types of music, subjects were allowed to select and keep one of the pens.

If respondent conditioning were taking place, then subjects should select the advertised pen when it was paired with the liked music. Similarly, they should select the other pen when the advertised pen was paired with the disliked music. Figure 10–2 shows the results of this experiment. Clearly, the vast majority of subjects appear to have been influenced by the pairing of the unconditioned stimulus (liked and disliked music) with the neutral stimulus (light blue and beige pens) resulting in predicted choice behaviors (pen selection).

A second experiment by Gorn compared pen selections after advertisements that contained either product information or music. Subjects

---

[2]Gerald J. Gorn (1982), "The Effects of Music in Advertising on Choice Behavior: A Classical Conditioning Approach," *Journal of Marketing* (Winter), pp. 94–101.

FIGURE 10–2   **Liked versus Disliked Music and Pen Choices**

	Pen Choice	
	Advertised Pen	**Nonadvertised Pen**
Liked Music	79%	21%
Disliked Music	30%	70%

Source: Adapted from Gerald J. Gorn (1982), "The Effects of Music in Advertising on Choice Behavior: A Classical Conditioning Approach," Journal of Marketing *(Winter), pp. 94–101.*

were either in a decision-making or a non-decision-making situation. It was hypothesized that product information would influence pen choice in the decision-making situation, but that music would influence pen choice in the non-decision-making situation. Figure 10–3 presents the results of this experiment. Clearly, the majority of subjects appear to be respondently conditioned in the non-decision-making situation but less so in the decision-making situation. These differences might be explained in terms of involvement—the non-decision-making task may be less involving for

FIGURE 10–3   **Information versus Music and Pen Choices**

	Decision-Making Situation	**Non-Decision-Making**
Advertised with Information	71%	29%
Advertised with Music	37%	63%

Source: Adapted from Gerald J. Gorn (1982), "The Effects of Music in Advertising on Choice Behavior: A Classical Conditioning Approach," Journal of Marketing *(Winter), pp. 94–101.*

HIGHLIGHT 10–3   **Can Automobile Purchases Be Respondently Conditioned?**

Research by the Young & Rubicam advertising agency found that awareness of Mercury automobiles was low among the target audience of people aged 24 to 44. The research also found an almost fervent loyalty of this audience to music from the 1960s.

A series of ads known as the "Big Chill" campaign was developed. The first TV spot from this campaign was called "Reunion," and was aired in 1984. The story line of this commercial was a college reunion set to the song "Ain't No Mountain High Enough."

Research conducted after the ad was aired showed that the target audience was reading a variety of positive things into the commercial. The audience recalled all kinds of wonderful moments from their college days, and attributed those moments to Mercury. Mercury's market share climbed from 4.3 percent in 1983 to 5.1 percent in 1985.

Apparently, by featuring the Mercury cars and brand name with well-liked music and scenes from a college reunion, awareness of Mercury increased and feelings of nostalgia were produced. More important, positive affect was associated with the brand, and purchase behavior was elicited. This example can certainly be interpreted as a successful application of respondent conditioning.

Source: Based on "Emotions Sell More than Perfume; It Sells Cars, Too," Marketing News *(November 1985), p. 4.*

subjects. In fact, some researchers have suggested that respondent conditioning may be most useful in low-involvement situations:

> Consumer involvement is low when the products have only minor quality differences from one another . . . . This is especially the case in saturated markets with mature products. It is exactly in these markets that product differentiation by means of emotional conditioning is the preferred strategy of influencing consumers.[3]

Because a variety of markets meet these conditions, respondent conditioning should be a useful strategy for low-involvement purchases. However, respondent conditioning principles can also be used in high-involvement situations such as the purchase of a car (see Highlight 10–3).

Another study of respondent conditioning investigated the effects of a credit card on the amount of money consumers reported they would be

---

[3]Werner Kroeber-Riel (1984), "Emotional Product Differentiation by Classical Conditioning," in *Advances in Consumer Research*, Vol. 11, Thomas C. Kinnear (ed.), Provo, Utah: Association for Consumer Research, pp. 538–543.

George W. Gardner

Credit-card stimuli influences consumer behavior.

willing to spend on specific items.[4] These items included dresses, tents, sweaters, lamps, electric typewriters, and chess sets. In a simulated buying task, consumers consistently reported they would spend more in the "credit-card present" condition. This research suggests that credit cards and related stimuli may become associated with spending, partly through respondent conditioning.[5]

---

[4]Richard A. Feinberg (1982), "Classical Conditioning of Credit Cards: Credit Cards May Facilitate Spending," in *Proceedings of the American Psychological Association, Division of Consumer Psychology*, Michael B. Mazis (ed.), Washington, D.C.: American Psychology Association, pp. 28–30.

[5]For additional discussion and empirical research on respondent (classical) conditioning, see Francis K. McSweeney and Calvin Bierley (1984), "Recent Developments in Classical Conditioning," *Journal of Consumer Research* (September), pp. 619–631; Chris T. Allen and Thomas J. Madden (1985), "A Closer Look at Classical Conditioning," *Journal of Consumer Research* (December), pp. 301–315; Calvin Bierley, Francis McSweeney and Renee Vannieuwkerk (1985), "Classical Conditioning of Preferences for Stimuli," *Journal of Consumer Research* (December), pp. 316–323; M. Carole Macklin (1985), "Classical Conditioning Effects in Product/Character Pairings Presented to Children," in *Advances for Consumer Research*, Vol. 13, Richard J. Lutz (ed.), Provo, Utah: Association for Consumer Research, pp. 198–203.

In summary, respondent conditioning may account for a wide variety of consumer responses. It is commonly used in advertising and in-store promotion, although it may be used by marketing practitioners only on an intuitive basis. More research in this area may be useful not only for marketing practitioners but also for understanding how consumers process information. In fact, Preston has attempted to integrate this approach with consumer cognitive processing in order to better describe the advertising communication process.[6]

Operant Conditioning

Operant conditioning differs from respondent conditioning in at least two important ways. First, whereas respondent conditioning is concerned with involuntary responses, **operant conditioning** deals with behaviors that are usually assumed to be under the conscious control of the individual. By "conscious control," behaviorists mean under the control of the skeletal nervous system that governs the "striped" muscles; they are not stating that behaviors are under the control of cognitions. Second, while respondent behaviors are *elicited* by stimuli that occur *prior* to the response, operant behaviors are *emitted* because of consequences that occur *after* the behavior.

In any given situation, at any given time, there is a certain probability that an individual will emit a particular behavior. If all of the possible behaviors are arranged in descending order of probability of occurrence, the result is a **response hierarchy.** Operant conditioning has occurred when the probability that an individual will emit a behavior is altered by changing the events or consequences that follow that behavior.

Some events or consequences increase the frequency with which a given behavior is likely to be repeated. For example, a cash rebate given at the time of purchase may increase the probability that a shopper will purchase in the same store in the future. In this case, because the cash rebate has the effect of *increasing* the probability of the preceding behavior, it is **positive reinforcement.** In other cases, the frequency of a given behavior can be increased by removing an aversive stimulus. This is called **negative reinforcement.** Although there are relatively few examples of negative reinforcement in marketing, one illustration is the situation in which a consumer purchases a product primarily to avoid the high-pressure tactics of an overzealous salesperson.

---

[6]See Ivan L. Preston (1982), "The Association Model of the Advertising Communication Process," *Journal of Advertising* (2), pp. 3–15; also see Larry G. Gresham and Terence A. Shimp (1985), "Attitude Toward the Advertisement and Brand Attitudes: A Classical Conditioning Perspective," *Journal of Advertising* (1), pp. 10–17.

FIGURE 10–4   **Operant Conditioning Methods**

Operation Performed after Behavior	Name	Effect
• Present positive consequences	Positive reinforcement	Increases the probability of behavior
• Remove aversive consequences	Negative reinforcement	Increases the probability of behavior
• Neutral consequences	Extinction	Decreases the probability of behavior
• Presents aversive consequences	Punishment	Decreases the probability of behavior

Sometimes operant techniques are used to decrease the probability of a response. If the environment is arranged so that a particular response results in neutral consequences, over a period of time that response will diminish in frequency. This process is referred to as **extinction.** For example, if you raise your hand to answer questions in class and are never called on, it is likely that eventually you will quit raising your hand. If the response is followed by a noxious or aversive event, the frequency of the response is likely to decrease even more. The term **punishment** is usually used to describe the latter process. As an example, if you raise your hand in class, are called on, and the instructor chews you out for giving a poor answer, it is likely that you will not raise your hand in class again for some time. Punishment is often confused with negative reinforcement, but they are distinctly different concepts. Figure 10–4 presents a summary of the four methods of operant conditioning.[7]

There are a number of other important ideas about operant conditioning. We discuss three—reinforcement schedules, shaping, and discriminative stimuli—which have major implications for designing marketing strategies to influence consumers' behavior.

Reinforcement Schedules

A number of different reinforcement schedules can be employed. For example, it is possible to arrange conditions where a positive reinforcer is administered after every desired behavior or every second desired behav-

---

[7]There are also a number of other possibilities, such as punishment by the removal of a positive consequence. For complete descriptions of these processes, see Arthur W. Staats (1975), *Social Behaviorism,* Chicago: Dorsey Press.

ior, etc. When every occurrence of the behavior is reinforced, a **continuous schedule** is being employed. When every second, third, tenth, etc., response is reinforced, a **fixed-ratio schedule** is being used. Several years ago, McDonald's ran a promotion in which a free Big Mac was given after the consumer had purchased a Big Mac on four previous occasions. This was a fixed-ratio schedule of reinforcement.

Similarly, it is possible to have a reinforcer follow a desired consequence *on an average* of one half, one third, one fourth, etc. of the time the behavior occurs, but not necessarily every second time or third time, etc. This is called a **variable ratio schedule.** The various state lotteries are examples of prizes being awarded on variable ratio schedules.

David S. Strickler: Click/Chicago

Behavior reinforced on a variable ratio schedule.

The ratio schedules are of particular interest, because they produce high rates of behavior that are reasonably resistant to extinction. Gambling devices are good examples. Slot machines are very effective in producing high rates of response, even under conditions that often result in substantial financial losses. This property of the ratio schedule is particularly important for marketers, because it suggests that a great deal of desired behavior can be developed and maintained with relatively small, infrequent rewards. Deslauriers and Everett found that by giving a free token for riding a bus on a variable ratio schedule, the same amount of bus riding could be obtained as when rewards were given on a continuous schedule.[8] Thus, for approximately one third the cost of the continuous schedule, the same amount of behavior was sustained.[9]

Numerous other examples of the use of the variable ratio schedule can be found in marketing practices. In addition to state lotteries, common examples include sweepstakes, contests, and door prizes, in which individuals must behave in a certain way to be eligible for a prize.

Shaping

Another operant-conditioning concept that has important implications for marketing and consumer behavior is **shaping**. Shaping is important because—given consumers' existing response hierarchies—the probability that they will make a particular desired response may be very small. In general, **shaping** involves a process of arranging conditions that change the probabilities of certain behaviors *not as ends in themselves, but to increase the probabilities of other behaviors*. Usually, shaping involves the positive reinforcement of successive approximations of the desired behavior or of behaviors that must be performed before the desired response can be emitted.

Many firms employ marketing activities that are roughly analogous to shaping. For example, loss leaders and other special deals are used to reward individuals for coming to a store. Once customers are in the store, the probability that they will make other desired responses (such as purchasing full-priced items) is much greater than when they are not in the

---

[8]B.C. Deslauriers and P.B. Everett (1977), "The Effects of Intermittent and Continuous Token Reinforcement on Bus Ridership," *Journal of Applied Psychology* (August), pp. 369–375.

[9]There are a number of other possible reinforcement schedules. However, we will limit our attention to continuous and ratio schedules. Also, we will not deal with the consequences that the different schedules have on the pattern, rate, and maintenance of behavior. For a detailed treatment of these effects, see W. K. Honig (1966), *Operant Behavior: Areas of Research and Application*, New York: Appleton-Century-Crofts.

Courtesy Steve Feldman & Associates

A shaping strategy.

store. Shopping centers or auto dealers who hold carnivals in their parking lots may be viewed as attempting to shape behavior, because consumers are more likely to come in and purchase when they are already in the parking lot than when they are at home. Similarly, free trial periods may be employed to make it more likely that the user will have contact with the product so that he/she can experience the product's reinforcing properties. Real estate companies that offer free trips to look over resort property are employing a shaping tactic, as are casinos that offer free trips to gamblers. In both cases, moving people to the place of purchase or place of gambling increases the probability of these behaviors being performed.

Shaping is not confined to a one-step process, but can be used to influence several stages in a purchase sequence. For example, suppose a car dealer wants to shape an automobile purchase. Free coffee and dough-nuts are offered to anyone who comes to the dealership. Five dollars cash is offered to any licensed driver who will test drive a car. A $500 rebate is offered to anyone who purchases a car. This example demonstrates not only how operant principles can be used in a multistep process, but also how they can be used in a high-involvement purchase situation.

Discriminative Stimuli

It is important to distinguish between the reinforcement and discriminative functions played by stimuli in the operant model. In our treatment of respondent conditioning, we noted that a stimulus can act as a reinforcer or can function to trigger certain emotions or other behaviors. So far in this section, the focus has been on the reinforcing function. However, the mere presence or absence of certain stimuli can serve to change the probabilities of behavior. These are called **discriminative stimuli.**

Many marketing stimuli are discriminative. Store signs ("50 percent off sale") and store logos (K mart's big red "K") or distinctive brandmarks (the Levi tag, the Izod crocodile) are good examples. Previous experiences have perhaps taught the customer that purchase behavior will be rewarded when the distinctive symbol is present and not rewarded when the symbol is absent. For example, sales of apparel with the Izod-Lacoste crocodile attached increased from $15 million per year in the late 1960s to over $450 million per year in the '80s.

Consumer Research on Operant Conditioning

While there is considerable research employing operant conditioning procedures in consumer-related contexts, most of it is not reported in the traditional literature on marketing or consumer behavior. However, one exception investigated the effects of positive reinforcement on jewelry store customers.[10] In this study, jewelry store charge-account customers were divided into three groups. One group received a telephone call thanking them for being customers; a second group received a telephone call thanking them and informing them of a special sale; the third group was a control group and received no telephone calls. This study reported a 27 percent increase in sales during the test month over the same month of the previous year. This figure was considered impressive because year-to-date sales were down 25 percent. Seventy percent of the increase came from the "thank-you only" group; the remaining 30 percent of the increase

---

[10]J. Ronald Carey, Stephen H. Clicque, Barbara A. Leighton and Frank Milton (1976), "A Test of Positive Reinforcement of Customers," *Journal of Marketing* (October), pp. 98–100.

HIGHLIGHT 10–4   **Some Marketing Tactics Consistent with Operant Conditioning Principles**

A. Continuous Reinforcement

Desired Behavior	Reward Given Following Behavior:
Product purchase	Trading stamps, cash bonus or rebate, prizes, coupons

B. Partial Reinforcement

Product purchase	Prize for every second, or third, etc. purchase
	Prize to some fraction of people who purchase

C. Shaping

Approximation of Response	Consequence Following Approximation	Final Response Desired
Opening a charge account	Prizes, etc. for opening account	Expenditure of funds
Trip to point-of-purchase	Loss leaders, entertainment, or event at the shopping center	Purchase of products
Entry into store	Door prize	Purchase of products
Product trial	Free product and/or some bonus for using	Purchase of product

D. Discriminative Stimuli

Desired Behavior	Reward Signal	Examples
Entry into store	Store signs	50% off sale
	Store logos	K mart's big red "K", McDonald's golden arches
Brand purchase	Distinctive brandmarks	Levi tag, Izod crocodile

came from the "thank-you and sale-notification" group. Purchases made by customers in the control group were unchanged. The authors suggested that positive reinforcement resulted in sustained increases in purchases for every month but one in the remainder of the year.

As we have noted, extensive treatment of operant conditioning in marketing and social marketing contexts exists outside of the traditional marketing and consumer-behavior literature. Most of this research deals with changing such behaviors as energy conservation, smoking, littering, charitable contributions, and other socially relevant actions. Examples of this research were reviewed in the preceding chapter.

One interesting example of the use of this technology by a profit-

FIGURE 10–5   **Effects of Punishment on Directory Assistance Calls**

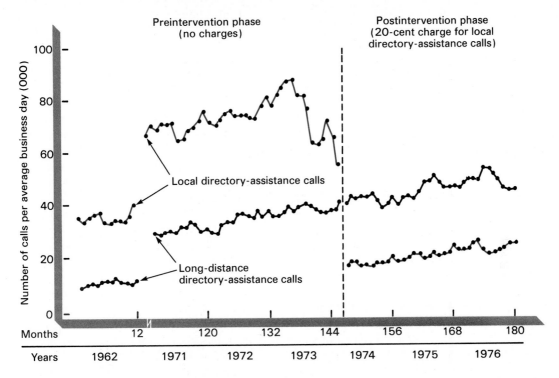

Source: A. J. McSweeney (1978), "Effects of Response Cost on the Behavior of a Million Persons: Charging for Directory Assistance in Cincinnati," Journal of Applied Behavioral Analysis *(Spring), pp. 47–51.*

oriented firm concerns the use of punishment by charging phone customers for local directory assistance.[11] Directory assistance is an expensive, labor-intensive service. This study reported the effects of charging 20 cents per local directory-assistance call for more than three calls in a given period. Long-distance directory-assistance calls were not charged. The results of this study are reported in Figure 10–5.

As the figure shows, local directory-assistance calls dropped dramatically through the use of a response-cost punishment. The fact that long-distance directory assistance did not change supports the conclusion that

---

[11]A. J. McSweeny (1978), "Effects of Response Cost on the Behavior of a Million Persons: Charging for Directory Assistance in Cincinnati," *Journal of Applied Behavioral Analysis* (Spring), pp. 47–51.

the response cost and not some other factor led to the change in phone customers' behavior. Other types of punishment include voiding car warranties if owners do not perform required maintenance.

Back to the Case

This case demonstrates a variety of the topics discussed in the chapter. The end behavior sought is, of course, actually ordering one or more magazines. Note how effectively this behavior is developed. The frequent TV commercials, a variety of previously conditioned slogans ("Last Chance!"), other stimuli such as the person's own name in print, and a well-known TV personality all may stimulate attentive behaviors and excitement. Note that it probably takes about 10 to 15 minutes to go through the material just to enter the contest correctly. This is a tremendous amount of time for a consumer to spend with promotional stimuli for what is commonly an unsought good. Note also that the major prizes (over 20,000 of them) are given on a very powerful schedule of reinforcement—a variable ratio schedule. The individual gifts for subscribing to particular magazines are given on a continuous schedule.

Of particular importance are the behaviors required to actually enter the contest and be eligible for doubling any prize won. These behaviors amount to licking and sticking various coupons in particular places on the entry blank. This is the same kind of behavior that is required to order magazines. Thus, the consumer is moved from attentively reading and studying the information to entering the contest. Clearly, the probability of ordering one or more magazines at this point is dramatically increased. This is no doubt an effective marketing strategy and is employed by a number of other companies.

Although these contests clearly state that "no purchase is necessary," we suspect many consumers believe their chances of winning are enhanced if they do order a magazine. If so, this belief increases the probability of the end behavior sought, magazine purchase.

Summary

This chapter has provided an overview of respondent and operant conditioning processes and has illustrated their use in marketing practice. While research in consumer behavior is in its infancy in these areas, the study of these processes in conjunction with cognitive approaches can increase the effectiveness of marketing strategies as well as our understanding of consumer behavior.

Additional Reading

H. H. Kassarjian (1978), "Presidential Address, 1977: Anthropomorphism and Parsimony," in *Advances in Consumer Research*, H. K. Hunt (ed.), Vol. 5, Chicago: Association for Consumer Research, pp. xiii–xiv.

Alan E. Kazdin (1984), *Behavior Modification in Applied Settings*, 3rd ed., Homewood, Ill.: Dorsey Press.

R. J. Markin and C. L. Narayana (1976), "Behavior Control: Are Consumers Beyond Freedom and Dignity?" in *Advances in Consumer Research*, B. B. Anderson, (ed.), Vol. 3, Chicago: Association for Consumer Research, pp. 222–228.

M. L. Ray (1973), "Psychological Theories and Interpretations of Learning," in *Consumer Behavior: Theoretical Sources*, S. Ward and T. S. Robertson (eds.), Englewood Cliffs, N.J.: Prentice-Hall, pp. 45–117.

Michael L. Rothschild and William C. Gaidis (1981), "Behavioral Learning Theory: Its Relevance to Marketing and Promotions," *Journal of Marketing* (Spring), pp. 70–78.

B. F. Skinner (1953), *Science and Human Behavior*, New York: Macmillan.

_____(1969), *Contingencies of Reinforcement: A Theoretical Analysis*, New York: Appleton-Century-Crofts.

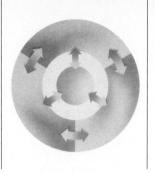

Chapter Eleven

Vicarious Learning: Modeling Effects on Consumer Behavior

Budweiser Light Beer

In 1983, Budweiser began a series of TV commercials depicting professional athletes overcoming obstacles in their careers. One of these shows a summer camp for a professional football team. The cocky veterans are lined up and prepared to teach the rookies a lesson in big-league football. The seasoned, knowledgeable coach looks on. The rookies, names on their helmets, prepare to block the veterans. The audience hears the thoughts of one not-too-sure rookie lamenting, "I wasn't drafted till the seventh round. They don't even know my name."

The action starts. The rookie lands face down after the first encounter with a veteran linebacker. The coach watches closely, eyebrow raised. On the second attempt, the rookie is a bit more successful, and on the third, blocks the veteran out of the play. They push each other, and the veteran looks at the name tag on the rookie's helmet and says, "Kroeder, huh?" The commercial ends with the players drinking Bud Light together. Kroeder is accepted; he's made the team. The theme song in the background beckons, "Bring out your best! You've got to reach deep inside . . . ."

This chapter is concerned with vicarious learning or modeling influences on consumer behavior. While vicarious learning has been used successfully in psychological work for many years, surprisingly, it has been almost ignored in published consumer and marketing research. None-theless, there are a variety of examples of its use in marketing strategy. In fact, we discuss several real-world marketing examples and suggest that vicarious learning offers a useful approach to develop marketing strategy and consumer education programs. We use the terms **vicarious learning, modeling, observational learning,** and **imitative learning** interchangeably in this chapter, although other writers sometimes draw distinctions between these terms.

Vicarious learning is a deceptively simple idea. Basically, it refers to attempts to change consumers' behavior by having them observe the actions of other people. In this part of the chapter, we will focus on overt modeling. **Overt modeling** requires that consumers actually observe the model in person; examples include a salesperson demonstrating a product *(live modeling)* or means such as TV commercials or in-store video tapes *(symbolic modeling).*

The modeling process is depicted in Figure 11–1. As an example, many commercials for cosmetics and grooming aids show the model using the product and then being complimented or sought after by a member of the opposite sex. Clairol commercials frequently show a woman with dull, drab hair (and an equivalent social life) being admired and dated by a handsome well-dressed man after using Clairol products. Thus, the modeled behavior (use of the product) is shown to have reinforcing consequences (attention from man).

FIGURE 11–1   **The Modeling Process**

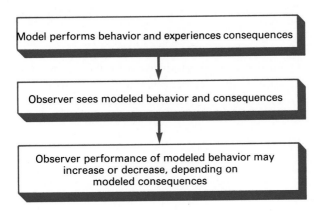

Uses of Modeling

There are three major uses of modeling in marketing. First, modeling can be used to help observers *acquire one or more new response patterns* that did not previously exist in their behavioral repertoires. Second, modeling can be used *to decrease or inhibit undesired behaviors.* Third, there is *response facilitation,* whereby the behavior of others "serves merely as discriminative stimuli for the observer in *facilitating the occurrence of previously learned responses.*"[1]

Developing New Responses

Modeling can be used to develop new responses that were not previously in the consumer's behavioral repertoire. Consider, for example, the video-cassette machines used in a variety of department and other stores to demonstrate use of a product. Sears has long used this method to demonstrate the appropriate and safe use of its chain saws. The appropriate use of Berkeley fishing equipment and Olt duck calls are also demonstrated in this way. New behaviors also are frequently modeled in TV commercials. For example, insurance is traditionally purchased from an agent either at the agent's office or in the consumer's home. Traditionally it is not sold in retail stores. A modeling strategy was used by Sears when it began in-store sale of Allstate insurance. Basically, the TV commercial shows a family coming to the Sears store and dropping off its old insurance policy for comparisons with Allstate rates. After a pleasant shopping trip, the family returns and is told that Allstate can give them a better deal, thus modeling the positive consequences of the new behavior. Similarly, Arm & Hammer baking soda ads showed new uses of the product as a carpet and refrigerator freshener and portrayed the models being complimented on the freshness of their homes.

These examples offer several generalizations about the use of modeling to develop new consumer behaviors.[2] First, modeling can be used to develop behaviors that enable potential consumers to use products appropriately. Demonstrating ways to use a product may make purchase more probable, particularly if the model(s) appear to experience positive consequences from using the product. Moreover, repurchase, or influencing one's friends, may become more probable if the consumer has learned to

---

[1]Albert Bandura (1969), *Principles of Behavior Modification*, New York: Holt, Rinehart Winston, p. 120. This is a classic reference in the psychological literature.

[2]This discussion of the three major types of modeling influences is based on Walter R. Nord and J. Paul Peter (1980), "A Behavior Modification Perspective on Marketing," *Journal of Marketing* (Spring), pp. 40–41.

Alan Carey/The Image Works

Overt modeling—demonstrating new behaviors.

use the product appropriately by watching someone else. This type of modeling is commonly used by those selling industrial and consumer products that are technically complex.

Second, models may be very helpful in developing the desired purchasing behaviors. Suppose, for example, a firm has a product that is technically superior to those of the firm's competitors. It may be important to teach potential consumers to ask questions about such technical advantages at the point of purchase. Advertisements could show individuals doing just this or behaving in other ways that appear to give the product a differential advantage.

Third, particularly at early stages in the purchase process, it is often necessary to find ways to increase the degree to which potential customers attend to information in ads and other messages about a product. This can be facilitated by applying findings from recent research on factors that influence the attention observers pay to models. For example, **attending behavior** is influenced by such factors as: incentive conditions, the characteristics of the observers, the characteristics of the model, and the characteristics of the modeling cues themselves. These are discussed in more detail later in the chapter.

Advertising practitioners seem to be sensitive to these factors. Many ads reflect their creators' accurate awareness of salient characteristics of the target audience, of the models in the ad, and of the behaviors exhibited by the model. Many ads show the models receiving positive social or other reinforcement from the purchase or use of the product. Finally, modeling can also be beneficial for consumers, because it can help them to develop effective behaviors in the marketplace and to avoid costly errors resulting from poor product purchases or inappropriate uses of the product.

Inhibiting Undesired Responses

Modeling can also be used to decrease the probability of undesired behaviors. Because of the ethical and practical problems involved in using punishment to affect consumer behavior, we have given little attention to ways of reducing the frequency of "undesired" responses. Such problems are far less prevalent when aversive consequences are administered to models rather than to actual consumers, however. Thus, vicarious learning may be one of the few approaches that can be used to reduce the frequency of unwanted elements in the behavioral repertoire of a potential or present consumer.

It is well known from the modeling literature that, under appropriate conditions, observers who see a model experience aversive outcomes following a particular act will reduce their tendency to exhibit that behavior. Similarly, vicarious learning can employ extinction to reduce the frequency of behavior.

Consider the following examples. Hefty bags are frequently advertised on TV using a modeling approach. Various family members are shown taking out the trash in "bargain bags." Of course, the bargain bag breaks and garbage is spewed all over the driveway. This is a very annoying experience! The frustrated family member is then told about Hefty bags, uses them successfully, and is socially reinforced for doing so. Head and Shoulders shampoo commercials show people initially being found attractive by members of the opposite sex but then being rejected when the models scratch their heads, indicating they may have dandruff. Following the use of the advertised product, the model is shown being happily greeted by an attractive member of the opposite sex.

Courtesy Oxford Industries Inc.

Modeling the types of people who use and enjoy a brand of sportswear.

A common use of this type of modeling is in public service advertising. Many behaviors considered socially undesirable can be modeled and shown to have aversive consequences. These behaviors include littering, smoking, drunken driving, overeating, wasting energy, and polluting. One commercial, for example, showed a drunken driver being caught, taken to court, and given a considerable fine and jail sentence for his behavior.

Response Facilitation

In addition to developing new behaviors and inhibiting undesired ones, modeling can be used to facilitate the occurrence of desired behaviors that

HIGHLIGHT 11–1   **Some Applications of Modeling Principles in Marketing**

Modeling Employed	Desired Response
Instructor, expert, salesperson using product (in ads or at point of purchase)	Use of product in correct, technically competent way
Models in ads asking questions at point of purchase	Ask questions at point of purchase that highlight product advantages
Models in ads receiving positive reinforcement for product purchase or use	Try product; increase product purchase and use
Models in ads receive no reinforcement or receive punishment for performing undesired behaviors	Extinction or decrease of undesired behaviors
Individual or group (similar to target) using product in novel, enjoyable way	Use of product in new ways

Source: Walter R. Nord and J. Paul Peter (1980), "A Behavior Modification Perspective on Marketing," Journal of Marketing *(Spring), p. 43.*

are currently in the consumer's repertoire. Modeling has been used extensively in advertising not only to illustrate the uses of a product but also to show what "types" of people use it and in what settings. Because many of these uses involve behaviors already in the observer's response hierarchy, the model's function is merely to *facilitate these responses* by depicting positive consequences for using the product appropriately. For example, Nyquil ads show adult cold sufferers using the product before going to bed and then sleeping comfortably. This technique also appears frequently in advertising for high-status products. Such ads do not demonstrate any new behaviors, but show the positive consequences of using the product. A series of Lowenbrau ads stressing the use of this beer for very special occasions is a good example.

It is also possible to influence emotional behavior through a vicarious learning approach. Bandura noted that many emotional behaviors can be acquired through observations of others, as well as through direct respondent conditioning:

Vicarious emotional conditioning results from observing others experience positive or negative emotional effects in conjunction with particular stimulus events. Both direct and vicarious conditioning processes are governed by the same basic principles of associative learning, but they differ in the force of the emotional arousal. In the direct prototype, the learner himself is the recipient of pain- or pleasure-producing stimulation, whereas in vicarious forms somebody else experiences the reinforcing stimulation and his affective expressions, in turn, serve as the arousal stimuli for the observer.[3]

To the degree that positive emotions toward a product are desired, vicarious emotional conditioning may also be useful for the design of effective advertisements.

Covert and Verbal Modeling

Up to this point, we have been discussing the most commonly studied and used type of vicarious learning, overt modeling. Two other types of modeling should be mentioned: covert and verbal modeling.

Covert Modeling

In **covert modeling,** no actual behaviors or consequences are shown or demonstrated. Rather, subjects are told to imagine observing a model behaving in various situations and receiving particular consequences.[4] For example, covert modeling could be used in radio commercials as follows. The commercial could tell listeners to *imagine* that Joe Smith, a burly construction worker, just got off work. It's July, it's hot and humid, and Joe has just worked 12 hours pouring concrete. He's driving home; he's tired and thirsty. His mouth is parched and his throat is dry. Imagine how good that first, cold frosty mug of Oscar's root beer is going to taste!

Covert modeling has received less research attention than has overt modeling, but a review of the literature suggests the following generalizations:

1. Covert modeling can be as effective as overt modeling in modifying behavior.
2. The parameters that affect overt modeling should have similar effects on covert modeling.

---

[3]Bandura, *Principles of Behavior Modification*, p. 167.

[4]See Joseph R. Cautela (1976), "The Present Status of Covert Modeling," *Journal of Behavior Therapy and Experimental Psychiatry* (December), pp. 323–326.

3. Covert modeling can be tested and shown to be effective.

4. Covert modeling can be made more effective if alternative consequences of the model's behavior are described.[5]

While we are aware of no consumer or marketing research on covert modeling, we believe it is a potentially useful marketing tool and should be investigated.

Verbal Modeling

In **verbal modeling,** behaviors are not demonstrated, and people are not asked to imagine a model performing a behavior. Instead, people are *told* how others similar to themselves behaved in a particular situation. This procedure thus sets a social norm that may influence behavior. One study, for example, investigated the effects of verbal modeling on contributions to charity.[6] People were contacted door-to-door for donations to the United Way Drive. One condition in the experiment manipulated the percentage of households the solicitor said had already contributed to the drive: "More than (three fourths/one fourth) of the households that I've contacted in this area have contributed so far." People who were told that three fourths of their neighbors had contributed usually donated more. Verbal modeling also outperformed several other strategies, such as the amount people were told others had given, social responsibility arguments, and arguments for helping less-fortunate people. It was concluded that verbal modeling was an effective means of eliciting behavior.

Again, as with covert modeling, little is known about verbal modeling in other consumer behavior contexts. However, the procedure is quite convenient to administer, because actual models need not be present.

Verbal modeling is easily employed in personal selling situations. For example, salespeople sometimes inform potential buyers that people like themselves have purchased a particular product, brand, or model. This may be an effective tactic, but it would be unethical for the salesperson to lie or to use the tactic to induce customers to buy only the most expensive products.

---

[5]Cautela, "Present Status."

[6]Viola Catt and Peter L. Benson (1977), "Effect of Verbal Modeling on Contributions to Charity," *Journal of Applied Psychology* (February), pp. 81–85.

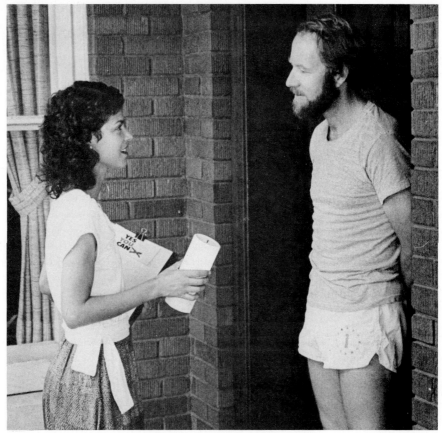

S.A. De Jesus

A United Way door-to-door campaign—this solicitor could be using verbal modeling.

Figure 11–2 offers a summary of overt, covert, and verbal modeling and suggests appropriate media in which these types of modeling could be used. Investigations of the effectiveness of these procedures using different media and approaches could add considerable insight into effective modeling processes and development of marketing strategies.

Why Does Modeling Work?

In this section, we investigate two related issues. First, we discuss some of the factors that affect how well a particular modeling attempt works. Sec-

FIGURE 11–2   **A Comparison of Three Types of Modeling**

Type	Description	Example	Useful Media
Overt modeling (live and symbolic)	Consumer observes modeled behavior and consequences	Allstate Insurance commercials demonstrating new method of purchasing insurance	Television, personal selling, in-store video machines
Covert modeling	Consumer is told to image a model (or self) performing behavior and consequences	Airline or travel agency commercial during cold, northern winter inviting consumers to "Imagine you're on the warm, sunny beaches of Florida."	Radio, personal selling, possibly print advertising
Verbal modeling	Consumer is given a description of how others similar to themselves (or aspirational groups) behave in purchase/use situation	United Way solicitor reporting on gift-giving behavior of neighbors	Personal selling, radio, direct mail, possibly other print advertising

ond, we examine several explanations of why modeling is effective. The fact that there is no consensus on the cognitive processes that mediate modeling influences suggests the need for further inquiry into this area.

Factors Influencing Modeling Effectiveness

There is no question that watching a model perform a behavior often increases the likelihood that the observer will also perform the behavior. It is well established in the psychological literature that in many situations, modeling is effective in changing behavior. However, certain factors have been found to increase the likelihood that vicarious learning will occur. These factors can be divided into three groups: (1) model and modeled behavior characteristics, (2) observer characteristics, and (3) characteristics of modeled consequences.

Model and Modeled Behavior Characteristics

Several personal characteristics of observed models influence the probability that an observer will imitate the modeled behavior.[7] Models who are found to be attractive may be sought out, while less attractive models may be ignored. Models who are perceived to be credible and successful exert greater influence than those who are not. In addition, high-status and competent models are more influential in determining modeling success.

Observers are also influenced by the manner in which the modeled behavior is performed. If the sequence of the modeled behavior is detailed very carefully and vividly, modeling effects tend to increase. The rate of learning also depends on the salience and complexity of the modeled behaviors. Interestingly, models who display a bit of apprehension and difficulty and yet complete the task are more effective than models displaying no struggle or difficulty. A reason for this has been suggested by Manz and Sims:

> It appears that an observer can identify more with a model who struggles and overcomes the difficulties of a threatening task than a model who apparently has no problem. A model who is seen as possessing substantially greater abilities may not be considered a reasonable reference point for the observer. However, experts who display little difficulty in completing a task (e.g., professional athletes) may serve as ideals to be emulated in nonthreatening situations.[8]

Another factor that influences the effectiveness of models is the perceived similarity of the model to the observer. This finding supports the common practice of using models similar to persons in the target market in commercials and of attempts to increase similarities between customers and salespersons when hiring and assigning sales personnel. Many advertisers take advantage of these characteristics in developing commercials.

---

[7]See Charles C. Manz and Henry P. Sims (1981), "Vicarious Learning: The Influence of Modeling on Organizational Behavior," *Academy of Management Review* (January), pp. 105–113. For discussions of model characteristics in advertising, see Michael J. Baker and Gilbert A. Churchill, Jr. (1977), "The Impact of Physically Attractive Models on Advertising Evaluations," *Journal of Marketing Research* (November), pp. 538–555; "Models Clothing Speaks to Ad Market: Study," *Marketing News* (November 22, 1985), p. 16; Lynn R. Kahle and Pamela M. Homer (1985), "Physical Attractiveness of the Celebrity Endorser: A Social Adaptation Perspective," *Journal of Consumer Research* (March), pp. 954–961.

[8]Manz and Sims, "Vicarious Learning," p. 107.

They can't stay away from Mr J®

©Fashion Fair Cosmetics 1985

and why would any woman want to? This sexy fragrance is sophisticated, spirited, and very special to be near. It was made for a man who settles for nothing but the best whether it's a suit, a scent, or a siren. That's why we call it Mr J.

Another fine product from EBONY. Mr J Atomizer and Splash Cologne, and After Shave available at the Fashion Fair counter at fine stores every where or write: Fashion Fair Cosmetics, 820 South Michigan Avenue, Chicago, IL 60605

Courtesy Fashion Fair Cosmetics

Modeling social reinforcement for product use.

Characteristics of Observers

Any number of individual difference variables in observers could be expected to mediate successful modeling. For example, individual differences in cognitive processing as well as in physical ability to perform a modeled behavior may affect the process. In covert modeling, people apparently differ in their ability to imagine modeled behavior. Bandura suggests than in many cases, observers who are dependent, lack confidence and self-esteem, and who have been frequently rewarded for imitative behavior are especially prone to adopt the behavior of successful models.[9]

---

[9]Albert Bandura (1977), *Social Learning Theory,* Englewood Cliffs, N.J.: Prentice-Hall, p. 89. This book discusses a number of other variables affecting the modeling process.

HIGHLIGHT 11–2   *Diffusion of Innovations: A Modeling Process?*

Modeling plays a prime role in spreading new ideas, products, and social practices within a society, or from one society to another. Successful diffusion of innovation follows a common pattern: new products and behaviors are introduced by prominent examples, the product/behavior is adopted at a rapidly accelerating rate, and adoption then either stabilizes or declines, depending upon the product/behavior's functional role. The general pattern of diffusion is similar, but the mode of transmission, the speed and extent of adoption, and the life span of innovations varies for different products and forms of behavior.

Modeling affects adoption of innovations in several different ways. It instructs people in new styles of behavior through social, pictorial, or verbal displays. Some observers are initially reluctant to buy new products or embark on new undertakings that involve risks until they see the advantages gained by earlier adopters. Modeled benefits accelerate diffusion by weakening the restraints of more cautious, later adopters. As acceptance spreads, the new gains further social support. Models not only exemplify and legitimate innovations, they also serve as advocates for products by encouraging others to adopt them.

Source: Adapted from Albert Bandura (1977), Social Learning Theory, *Englewood Cliffs, N.J.: Prentice-Hall, pp. 50–51.*

However, perceptive and confident people readily emulate idealized models who demonstrate highly useful behaviors.

Perhaps most important is the value the observer places on the consequences of the modeled behavior. For example, if consumers value the social approval obtained by a model in a Grecian Formula (hair coloring) commercial, they are more likely to purchase and use the product.

Characteristics of Modeled Consequences

Just as operant conditioning places importance on the consequences of behavior, so does vicarious learning. Of course, in vicarious learning, the observer does not experience the consequences directly. Thus, a major advantage of vicarious learning for consumers is that they can learn effective purchase and use behavior while avoiding negative consequences.

Research has demonstrated that positively reinforcing a model's behavior is a key factor in facilitating vicarious learning. In terms of consumer behavior, much fruitful research could be done on identifying appropriate reinforcers for various types of products. Currently, however, little is known about what types of positive consequences would be most effective to model. Similarly, for modeling applications that seek to decrease undesired behaviors, the most effective types of negative consequences to model in commercials are unknown. While it has been demonstrated that modeling is useful in deterring smoking,[10] reducing drinking,[11] reducing uncooperative behavior of children,[12] and reducing energy consumption,[13] many other areas of consumer behavior are unexplored.

Theories of Modeling

As we noted earlier, there is no question in the psychological literature that modeling is an effective procedure. However, as with many phenomena, there is considerable disagreement about why modeling works. It has been analyzed from an *operant conditioning* perspective that viewed modeling as a discriminative stimulus which changes the probability of the modeled behavior. Operant conditioning approaches did not attempt to describe the cognitive functioning required for successful modeling, however.

Expectancy theory has also been suggested as appropriate for describing modeling effects.[14] This theory suggests that models influence observer behavior by influencing expectations. These expectations are of two types: self-efficacy and outcome expectations. **Self-efficacy expectations** deal with the observers' convictions that they can successfully perform the behavior that produces the outcome. In other words, after seeing a model perform the behavior, observers' confidence in their own ability increases. **Outcome expectations** refer to observers' assessment of whether they will receive the same consequences the model receives. In other words, modeling provides information that helps observers form expectations about the outcomes of performing the modeled behavior.

---

[10]Richard I. Evans, Richard M. Rozelle, Scott E. Maxwell, Betty E. Raines, Charles A. Dill and Tanya J. Guthrie (1981), "Social Modeling Films to Deter Smoking in Adolescents: Results of a Three-Year Field Investigation," *Journal of Applied Psychology* (August), pp. 399–414.

[11]Denise A. DeRicco and John E. Niemann (1980), "*In Vivo* Effects of Peer Modeling on Drinking Rate," *Journal of Applied Behavioral Analysis* (Spring), pp. 149–152; Barry D. Caudill and Thomas R. Lipscomb (1980), "Modeling Influences on Alcoholics' Rates of Alcohol Consumption," *Journal of Applied Behavioral Analysis* (Summer), pp. 355–365.

[12]Trevor F. Stokes and Suzanne H. Kennedy (1980), "Reducing Child Uncooperative Behavior During Dental Treatment through Modeling and Reinforcement," *Journal of Applied Behavioral Analysis* (Spring), pp. 41–49.

[13]Richard A. Winnett, Joseph W. Hatcher, T. Richard Fort, Ingrid N. Lechliter, Susan Q. Love, Anne W. Riley and James F. Fishback (1982), "The Effects of Videotape Modeling and Daily Feedback on Residential Electricity Conservation, Home Temperature and Humidity, Perceived Comfort and Clothing Worn: Winter and Summer," *Journal of Applied Behavioral Analysis* (Fall), pp. 381–402.

[14]See Manz and Sims, "Vicarious Learning," p. 106.

FIGURE 11–3   **Social Learning Description of Modeling Process**

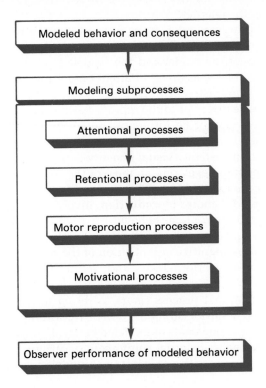

A third way of describing modeling effects is a cognitive processing approach called **category accessibility.**[15] This suggests that the process of viewing a model's behavior involves the activation of an interpretive schema. Once the schema is activated, the information in it becomes more accessible for subsequent use. If the schema incorporates (or is closely related to) information that helps specify behavior, that information becomes more accessible as well, thus making it more likely to influence overt behavior. Modeled consequences are considered less important with this approach than with others.

The most-detailed and best-documented account of modeling is provided by Albert Bandura in his **social learning** theory.[16] This approach recognizes four subprocesses that intervene in modeling. These four,

---

[15]William J. Froming and William Chambers (1983), "Modeling: An Analysis in Terms of Category Accessibility," *Journal of Experimental Social Psychology* (September), pp. 403–421.

[16]Bandura, *Social Learning Theory,* pp. 24–29.

shown in Figure 11–3, include attentional, retentional, motor reproduction, and motivational subprocesses. We briefly describe each of these before concluding the chapter.

Attentional processes refer to the ways in which observers attend to and extract information about the major features of the modeled behavior. The characteristics of the model and the modeled behavior, as described earlier, affect this process, as do other attention-getting tactics such as the use of novelty and contrast.

Retention processes refer to the representation of observed models in memory. Observers cannot be influenced much by modeled behavior if they do not remember it. Retention processes include both visual and verbal representation systems. Visual imagery is particularly important in early periods of human development; most of the cognitive processes that regulate behavior are thought to be verbal.

The third process, **motor reproduction,** involves converting symbolic representations into appropriate behavior. A modeled behavior is reproduced by organizing responses in accordance with the modeled pattern. This process requires cognitive organization of the response, initiating the response, monitoring performance, and refinement on the basis of feedback.

Finally, **motivational process** refers to the factors by which consequences of modeled behaviors are judged to be rewarding or unrewarding. If consumers value the outcomes of modeled behavior, they are more likely to perform the behavior. External reinforcers, vicarious reinforcers, and self-reinforcers can increase the probability of modeled responses.

Back to the Case

This commercial contains only 15 words, none of which gives any information about product attributes. However, it is a very powerful ad, and one most viewers can identify with—not because they are football players, but because they can feel the joy of being accepted by a group and the feeling of accomplishment in achieving a difficult objective. The emotions generated by the commercial are quite positive, and pairing them with the product may generate positive feelings. Thus, this commercial can be interpreted as vicarious emotional conditioning as well as an attempt to respondently condition positive emotions toward the product. The facts that the model is in a high-status profession and had to struggle to be accepted are consistent with the research findings discussed in the chapter, which suggest that these factors increase the effectiveness of modeling.

Summary

This chapter provided an overview of vicarious learning or modeling processes that can be used to develop new responses, inhibit undesired responses, and facilitate previously learned responses. Several factors that increase the effectiveness of modeling were also discussed, as were some theories of how modeling works. While a consensus has not been reached on *why* it works, it is well established that modeling is an effective procedure. Modeling is currently employed in marketing, yet there is little research on the topic in the traditional marketing or consumer-behavior literature. This area represents an excellent opportunity for increasing the effectiveness of current marketing strategies and for integrating cognition, behavior, and the environment.

Additional Reading

Albert Bandura (1971), *Psychological Modeling: Conflicting Theories,* Chicago: Aldine Publishing.

R.J. Markin and C.L. Narayana (1976), "Behavioral Control: Are Consumers Beyond Freedom and Dignity?" in *Advances in Consumer Research,* Vol. 3, B.B. Anderson (ed.), Chicago: Association for Consumer Research, pp. 222–228.

Chapter Twelve

Analyzing Consumer Behavior

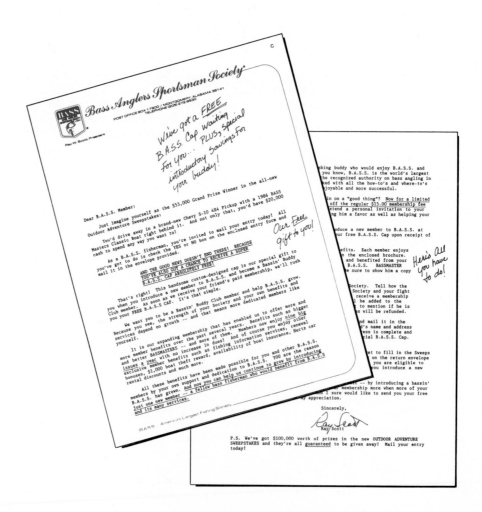

C

Bass Anglers Sportsman Society

POST OFFICE BOX 17900 / MONTGOMERY, ALABAMA 36141
TELEPHONE (205) 272-9530

Ray W. Scott, President

*We've got a FREE
B.A.S.S. Cap waiting
For you... PLUS, special
introductory savings for
your buddy!*

Dear B.A.S.S. Member:

   Just imagine yourself as the $53,000 Grand Prize Winner in the all-new
Outdoor Adventure Sweepstakes:

   You'd drive away in a brand-new Chevy S-10 4X4 Pickup with a 1986 BASS
Masters Classic Boat right behind it. And not only that, you'd have $20,000
cash to spend any way you want to!

   As a B.A.S.S. fisherman, you're invited to mail your entry today! All
you've got to do is check the YES or NO box on the enclosed entry form and
mail it in the envelope provided.

                *Our Free
                gift to you!*

          AND THE GOOD NEWS DOESN'T END THERE! BECAUSE
          YOU'VE ALSO GOT A CHANCE TO RECEIVE A SUPER
          B.A.S.S. CAP ABSOLUTELY FREE!

   That's right! This handsome custom-designed cap is our special gift to
you when you introduce a new member to B.A.S.S. and become a Bassin' Buddy
Club member. As soon as we receive your friend's paid membership, we'll rush
you your FREE B.A.S.S CAP. It's that simple.

   We want you to be a Bassin' Buddy Club member and help B.A.S.S. grow.
Because you see, the strength of your Society and your own benefits and
services depend on growth -- and that means more dedicated members like
yourself.

   It is our expanding membership that has enabled us to offer more and
more member benefits over the past several years. Benefits such as bigger
and better BASSMASTERS -- and more of them. Members now enjoy nine big
issues a year with no increase in dues! And of course you enjoy other
exclusive member benefits such as fishing information services, renewal
bonuses, $1,000 boat theft reward, availability of boat insurance, Hertz car
rental discounts and much more.

   All these benefits have been made possible for you and other B.A.S.S.
members by your own support and dedication to B.A.S.S. YOU are the reason
B.A.S.S. has grown. And now you can help us continue to grow by introducing
just one new member -- a fellow bass fisherman who would benefit from B.A.S.S
and its many services.

B.A.S.S. – America's Largest Fishing Society

I'm sure you have a bass fishing buddy who would enjoy B.A.S.S. and BASSMASTER as much as you do. As you know, B.A.S.S. is the world's largest fishing society and BASSMASTER is the recognized authority on bass angling in the fishing world today. It's packed with all the how-to's and where-to's aimed at making your fishing more enjoyable and more successful.

So why not let a fishing buddy in on a "good thing"? Now for a limited time only, your friend can save $3.00 off the regular $15.00 membership fee and join B.A.S.S. for just $12.00. Extend a personal invitation to your buddy to join B.A.S.S. You'll be doing him a favor as well as helping your Society!

Here's all you have to do to introduce a new member to B.A.S.S. at special introductory rates and receive your free B.A.S.S. Cap upon receipt of his paid membership.

1. Tell a friend about B.A.S.S. benefits. Each member enjoys all the membership benefits listed in the enclosed brochure. Tell your friend how you have enjoyed and benefited from your membership and your association with B.A.S.S. BASSMASTER Magazine is one outstanding feature. Be sure to show him a copy of your magazine.

Here's all you have to do!

2. Explain the Bass Anglers Sportsman Society. Tell how the Society began. Mention the goals of the Society and your fight against water pollution. Explain he will receive a membership packet immediately and that his name will be added to the BASSMASTER subscription list. Don't forget to mention if he is not completely satisfied, his membership dues will be refunded.

3. Fill in the enclosed application form and mail it in the return envelope provided. Fill in your friend's name and address on the back and be sure your own name and address is complete and correct so that we can send you your FREE Official B.A.S.S. Cap.

And while you're looking at the form, don't forget to fill in the Sweeps information on the card and check the appropriate box on the return envelope so we can enter your name in the contest. Remember, you are eligible to enter the new OUTDOOR ADVENTURE SWEEPSTAKES whether you introduce a new member or not.

But, I hope you will help us -- and yourself -- by introducing a bassin' buddy to your Society. You'll enjoy your membership more when more of your friends wear a B.A.S.S. patch! And I sure would like to send you your free B.A.S.S. Cap as a token of my appreciation.

Sincerely,

Ray Scott

P.S. We've got $100,000 worth of prizes in the new OUTDOOR ADVENTURE SWEEPSTAKES and they're all guaranteed to be given away! Mail your entry today!

At this point in the text, you should have a good understanding of the major aspects of applied behavior analysis. It is now time to tie this perspective more directly to consumer behavior and marketing strategy development. This chapter does so by explaining two related models. First, a model of the behaviors involved in a common purchase situation is presented, and alternative marketing strategies used to change these behaviors are discussed. Second, we develop a consumer behavior management model that integrates many of the ideas discussed in this section with traditional marketing approaches.

A Sequential Model of Consumer Behavior

Traditional views of the purchase or adoption process in marketing treat it as a series or chain of cognitive events followed by a single behavior, usually called *adoption* or *purchase*. Consider the models, in Figure 12–1, of the adoption process as it is commonly treated in marketing. These models are consistent with the view that *cognitive variables* (awareness, comprehension, interest, evaluation, conviction, etc.) are the main concern of

FIGURE 12–1   **Traditional Models of the Adoption/Purchase Process**

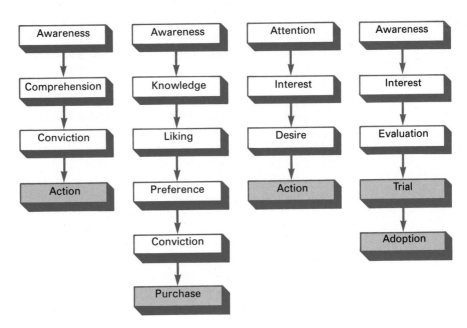

marketing and the primary controllers of behavior. According to this view, the marketing task is to change these cognitive variables and move consumers through each stage until a purchase is made.

However, adoption or purchase can also be analyzed as a *sequence of behaviors.* From this perspective, marketing managers usually want to increase the frequency of these behaviors, and they design strategies and tactics for doing so. While strategies and tactics to change cognitive processes such as attention or attitude may be useful intermediate steps, they must ultimately change behavior to be profitable for marketers.

In Figure 12–2 we offer a model of a behavior sequence that occurs in the purchase of many consumer goods. Before discussing each of these stages, several qualifications should be noted. First, while we suggest that this is a logical sequence, many other combinations of behavior are also commonly performed by consumers. For example, an unplanned (impulse) purchase of Twix cookie bars could start at the store contact stage. We do not claim that every purchase follows the sequence shown in Figure 12–2 or that every purchase requires that all of these behaviors be performed. However, the model is useful for categorizing a variety of marketing strategies in terms of the behaviors they are designed to influence.

Second, the model in Figure 12–2 is intended to illustrate only one type of behavior sequence for retail purchases; similar models could be developed for other types of purchases—such as mail-order, phone, or catalog-showroom exchanges. Further, the sequences involved with other behaviors of interest to consumer analysis, such as voting, physician care, banking, or consumer education, could also be modeled in much the same way. In fact, we believe that any attempt to influence behavior should include an analysis of the behavior sequence that is necessary or desired. Unfortunately, many marketing managers do not consider exactly what behaviors are involved in the actions they are attempting to get consumers to perform.

Third, the time it takes for a consumer to perform these behaviors depends on a variety of factors. Different products, consumers, and situations may affect not only the total time to complete the process but also the time lags between stages. For example, an avid water-skier purchasing a Mastercraft powerboat likely will spend more time per stage, and more time will elapse between stages, than will be true for a consumer purchasing a Timex quartz watch.

Fourth, members of the channel of distribution usually vary in the emphasis they place on encouraging particular behaviors. Retailers may be more concerned with increasing store contact than with purchase of a particular brand; manufacturers are less concerned with the particular store patronized, but attempt to increase brand purchase; credit-card companies may be less concerned with particular store or product contacts so long as their credit card is accepted and used. However, while emphasis may vary, all three of these behaviors are common for a retail exchange, and all three organizations can benefit from the others' efforts.

Finally, the seven categories of the consumer behavior chain in Figure 12–2 deserve comment. While we believe that these are logical and useful categories of behavior, other labels or breakdowns could also be useful. For instance, this behavior chain could be carefully broken down into individual actions of each muscle in the consumer's body, and research could be conducted at that level. However, given the lack of knowledge concerning

---

FIGURE 12–2   **A Common Behavior Sequence for Retail Consumer-Goods Purchase**

Consumption Stage	Type of Behavior	Examples of Behaviors
Prepurchase	1. Information contact	Read/observe newspaper, magazine, billboard ads Listen to radio commercials Listen to/watch TV commercials Listen to salespersons, friends
	2. Funds access	Withdraw cash from bank or cash machine Write a check Obtain a credit card, loan, or other line of credit
Purchase	3. Store contact	Locate outlet Travel to outlet Enter outlet
	4. Product contact	Locate product in store Obtain product Take product to checkout counter
	5. Transaction	Exchange funds for product Take product to use location
Postpurchase	6. Consumption	Consume/use product Dispose of packaging/used product Repurchase
	7. Communication	Tell others of product experience Fill out warranty cards Provide other information to the firm

overt consumer behavior, the levels in Figure 12–2 are a useful starting point. With these qualifications, we now turn to a discussion of each type of behavior and some marketing strategies currently employed to increase the probability of one or more of them.

Information Contact

A common early stage in the purchase sequence occurs when consumers come into contact with information about the product or brand. This stage includes behaviors such as reading or observing newspaper, magazine, and billboard ads, listening to radio commercials, watching TV commercials, as well as talking to salespeople and friends. At this point, the practical problem for marketers is to increase the probability that consumers will observe and attend to the information, and that this will increase the probability of other behaviors.

Not only do marketers seek to provide consumers with information, but consumers also search for information about products, brands, stores, and prices.[1] Marketing managers for brands with low market shares usually want to increase overall search behavior, because it may increase the probability of switching to the firm's brand. High market-share brands may try to discourage external search behaviors, because the behavior may result in a shift to another brand. For example, Heinz currently has a major share of the market for ketchup and does not want most consumers to search for information concerning different brands. Ads showing Heinz as the thicker, richer ketchup while depicting other brands as thin and unsavory may discourage loyal consumers from searching for an alternative. They may also help attract non-Heinz purchasers by demonstrating the negative consequences of using another brand. The extent of a consumer's search depends on many factors, such as those listed in Figure 12–3.

From a public-policy standpoint, information search is encouraged to develop more knowledgeable consumers.[2] However, there are differences in the effort required by consumers to obtain information from different

---

[1] For example, see John A. Carlson and Robert J. Gieseke (1983), "Price Search in a Product Market," *Journal of Consumer Research* (March), pp. 357–365; Geoffrey C. Kiel and Roger A. Layton (1981), "Dimensions of Consumer Information Seeking Behavior," *Journal of Marketing Research* (May), pp. 233–239; Calvin P. Duncan and Richard W. Olshavsky (1982), "External Search: The Role of Consumer Beliefs," *Journal of Marketing Research* (February), pp. 32–43.

[2] For a complete discussion of these issues, see Howard Beales, Michael B. Mazis, Steven Salop and Richard Staelin (1981), "Consumer Search and Public Policy," *Journal of Consumer Research* (June), pp. 11–22.

FIGURE 12–3   **Determinants of the Extent of Consumers' Information Search**

Market environment
  Number of alternatives
  Complexity of alternatives
  Marketing mix of alternatives
  Stability of alternatives on the market (new alternatives)
  Information available

Situational variables
  Time pressure
  Social pressure (family, peer, boss)
  Financial pressure
  Organizational procedures
  Physical and mental condition
  Ease of access to information sources

Potential payoff/product importance
  Price
  Social visibility
  Perceived risk
  Differences among alternatives
  Number of crucial attributes
  Status of decision-making activity (in the family, organization, society)

Knowledge and experience
  Stored knowledge
  Rate of use of product
  Previous information
  Previous choices (number and identity)
  Satisfaction

Individual differences
  Training
  Approach to problem solving (compulsiveness, open-mindedness, preplanning,
    innovativeness)
  Approach to search (enjoyment of shopping, sources of information, etc.)
  Involvement
  Demographics (age, income, education, marital status, household size, social class,
    occupation)
  Personality/lifestyle variables (self-confidence, etc.)

Conflict and conflict-resolution strategies

*Source: William L. Moore and Donald R. Lehmann (1980), "Individual Differences in
Search Behavior for a Nondurable,"* Journal of Consumer Research *(December), pp.
296–307.*

sources—and in the believability of the information. For example, Figure 12–4 illustrates five common sources of information and rates them on these two dimensions. This model predicts that internal sources (stored experiences) and personal sources (friends and relatives) are commonly used, because they are easiest to access and most believable. Marketing sources (advertising) would also be commonly used because they are readily available. However, marketing sources are not as believable, because advertisers have something to gain from the transaction. Finally, public sources (*Consumer Reports* and other impartial studies) and experiential sources (personally examining or testing the product) are less likely to be used, at least in this early stage, because more effort is required to obtain information from these sources. Information search could also be broken down into a sequence of basic behaviors. However, the main marketing task is to increase the probability that the target market comes into contact with product, brand, or store information and pays attention to it.

Currently, numerous marketing strategies are directed at bringing about these attentive behaviors. All are remarkably consistent with behavior approaches. For example, the topics of media scheduling, message content and layout, color and humor in advertising, and repetition all involve presenting stimuli to increase the probability that potential consumers will attend to relevant cues. In addition, *fear appeals* are used to bring about attentive behaviors and to vicariously stimulate emotions by exposing the observers to possible aversive consequences of certain conditions (inadequate insurance, faulty tires and batteries, the absence of smoke alarms, not flossing regularly). Strategies such as contests and prizes bring about attentive behavior and promise rewards for engaging in certain actions that bring the consumer into closer contact with the product or point of purchase. Finally, ads that show models receiving positive reinforcement in the form of social approval and satisfaction for purchasing a product provide stimuli that can move the consumer closer to purchase by stimulating the "buying mood."

FIGURE 12–4   **A Comparison of Information Sources**

Source	Effort Required	Believability
Internal (stored experiences in memory)	Low	High
Personal (friends, relatives)	Low	High
Marketing (advertising)	Low	Low
Public (*Consumer Reports,* other studies)	High	High
Experiential (examining or testing product)	High	High

HIGHLIGHT 12–1: **Encouraging Information Contact for Magazine Subscriptions**

Including subscription cards in magazines is a useful marketing tactic, because the cards are available while the magazine is being read and enjoyed. These cards make it convenient for readers of the magazine (the likely target market for future issues) to renew a subscription or start a new one.

Traditionally, magazine marketers bound subscription cards to the magazines. One drawback to the "bind-in" cards is that readers often simply ignore them. Because the cards are bound to the issue, readers leaf through the entire magazine without giving the card (or the idea of starting or renewing a subscription) any consideration.

An alternative method of including subscription cards in magazines is to place them between the pages, unbound. These are called "blow-in" cards. When magazines are being read or carried, blow-in cards frequently fall out. Consumers usually pick up the cards and examine them for at least a moment. In other words, the probability of information contact is increased when blow-in rather than bind-in cards are used. It is not surprising, then, that blow-in cards are more effective than bind-in cards at generating subscription renewals.

Funds Access

Current views of marketing emphasize **exchange** as the key concept for understanding the field. However, relatively little attention has been given *to what consumers exchange* in the marketing process. While there are time and effort costs involved, **money** is the primary medium of consumer exchanges. The consumer must access this medium in one form or another before an exchange can take place. The primary marketing issues at this stage are (1) the methods used by consumers to pay for particular purchases, and (2) the marketing strategies to increase the probability that the consumers are able to access funds for purchase.

There are, of course, a variety of ways by which consumers can pay for a product offering. These include cash in pocket; bank withdrawal of cash; writing a check; using credit cards such as Visa, MasterCard, and American Express; opening a store charge account; using debit cards; and drawing on other lines of credit, such as bank loans and GMAC financing. Another issue concerns the *effort* exerted by the consumer to obtain the actual funds that are spent or used to repay loans. It seems likely that funds obtained from tax refunds, stock sales and dividends, gambling winnings, awards, or regular paychecks may be valued differently by the consumer and spent in different ways. Some retailers encourage the pur-

Michael Hayman: Click/Chicago

Charles Gatewood/The Image Works   Alan Carey/The Image Works

Funds access can occur in a number of ways.

chase of big-ticket items by offering interest-free loans for a few months while consumers are waiting for their tax refunds.

There are a variety of other strategies to increase the ability and probability that consumers can access funds for purchases. For example, Sears offers a small gift to anyone who fills out a Sears credit-card application. The probability of purchasing at Sears is increased when a consumer has a credit card, because cash may not always be available. Further, a Sears credit card gives the holder check-cashing authorization at Sears stores—which gives the consumer another method of obtaining funds. Other strategies include locating cash machines in malls, instituting liberal credit terms and check-cashing policies, and accepting of a variety of credit cards. During a recent period when interest rates were high, a variety of "creative financing" alternatives were developed to facilitate purchases. Deferred payment plans and layaway plans that allow the consumer additional time to raise the required funds help stores avoid lost sales. Gift certificates are also used to presell merchandise and to provide some consumers with another source of funds that is restricted for particular purchases.

All of these strategies have a common goal—to increase the probability of an exchange by increasing the probability of accessing funds. The consumer is similar to the rat in the Skinner box. If the rat cannot reach the bar, it cannot obtain its food; if the potential customer cannot reach financial resources, products cannot be purchased.

Other strategies can be employed to increase certain types of purchases. For example, a store could offer a small discount for using cash to avoid the costs of paying credit-card fees. An analysis of the conditions surrounding particular purchases may lead to other successful tactics. For example, many major home appliances are purchased only when both husband and wife are present, and a necessary condition is that they can obtain funds. One tactic for an appliance store might be to offer a small gift to any couple who will come to the store with their checkbook or approved credit card. Thus, the appropriate contingencies are prearranged for an appliance sale. Any number of other tactics (such as offering rebates) could also be used in conjunction with this tactic to further increase the probability of purchase.

Store Contact

Although catalog and telephone-order purchases are important, most consumer-goods purchases are still made in retail stores. Thus, a major task of retailers is to get consumers into the store where purchase can take place. **Store contact** includes (1) locating the outlet, (2) traveling to the outlet, and (3) entering the outlet.

One factor that affects the probability of store contact involves the

HIGHLIGHT 12–2: **The American Express Platinum Card**

There is no question that credit cards make funds contacts more convenient for consumers. However, snob appeal and prestige are the major selling points for premium credit cards, such as the American Express Platinum Card that costs $250 per year. This card is offered once a year—by invitation only—to American Express customers whose charges totaled at least $10,000 in the previous year. Platinum Card holders receive special treatment, including year-end itemized billing and membership in a network of exclusive clubs.

American Express created the premium category with its Gold Card in 1966. It wasn't until 1982 that Visa and MasterCard followed with premium cards of their own. In 1984, American Express Gold Card holders charged $13 billion, compared with $4.1 billion for Visa's Premier Card and $3.4 billion for the gold MasterCard.

Since the standard card market is close to saturation with 125 million cards in circulation, growth is expected primarily in the premium market. The premium market is also more profitable, since fees tend to be higher and premium card holders use them 50 percent more often and charge, on average, 150 percent more than standard card customers.

The Platinum Card was an American Express effort to stay on top. The company expected that about 10,000 consumers would be interested in purchasing the card, yet in the first year, 60,000 consumers purchased it. Apparently, American Express and other premium-card companies have made funds access not only convenient, but also a way for consumers to derive social benefits from accessing their funds.

Source: Adapted from Christine Dugas (1985), "Plastic Prestige: Credit Cards that Make You Somebody," Business Week *(November 11), p. 62.*

nature of the consumers in their roles as shoppers. Some consumers may enjoy the process of shopping and spend many hours looking in stores. To others, shopping may be drudgery. Some shoppers may be primarily price oriented and favor particular low-price outlets. Others may seek a high level of service or unique products and stores in which to express their individuality. These differences are important dimensions when designing market segmentation strategies for stores.

Many strategies in current use are designed to increase the probability of store contact. For example, consider the methods used to increase the probability that shoppers will be able to locate a particular outlet. Selecting convenient locations in high-traffic areas with ample parking has been very successful for many retailers, such as 7-Eleven convenience stores and Denny's restaurants. A major advantage for retailers locating in shopping malls is the increase in consumers' ability to find the outlet as well as the additional shopping traffic created by the presence of the other stores. Yellow Pages, newspaper, and other ads frequently include maps

Cynthia Rymer: Click/Chicago

Locating in malls . . .

David S. Strickler: Click/Chicago

The presence of the Easter Bunny . . .

Don Smetzer: Click/Chicago

Ample parking . . .

George W. Gardner

And extended store hours . . .

Strategies that facilitate store contacts.

and information numbers to aid shoppers in locating an outlet. Outdoor signs and logos (such as Holiday Inn's distinctive sign) are well-known discriminative stimuli. One recreational vehicle dealer close to Columbus, Ohio, used an interesting modeling approach to aid potential customers in locating the dealership. The dealer's TV ads consisted of the actual scenery, landmarks, and road signs people would see when traveling to the dealership. Every turn was shown, as were directional signs on the highway, to help potential customers find the outlet.

Other tactics are used to get potential customers to the vicinity of stores or malls. For example, carnivals in mall parking lots, free style shows or other mall entertainment, and visits by celebrities such as Santa

Claus, the Easter Bunny, and Sesame Street and soap-opera characters are used to shape behavior. Further, mall directories and information booths help shoppers find particular stores.

Finally, some tactics are used to get the potential customer physically into the store. Frequently advertised sales, sale signs in store windows, door prizes, loss leaders, sounds (such as popular music), and smells (such as fresh popcorn) are commonly employed for these purposes. A variety of other in-store issues are discussed later in the text, particularly in Chapter 20.

Product Contact

While a major concern of retailers is increasing and maintaining *selective store patronage,* manufacturers are primarily concerned with *selective demand*—purchase of their particular brands and models. Many of the methods employed to accomplish this end involve **push strategies** such as trade discounts and incentives to enhance the selling effort of retailers. For example, offering retailers a free case of Tide liquid detergent for every 10 cases purchased can be a powerful incentive for retailers to feature liquid Tide in newspaper ads, put it in prominent displays, and even sell it at a lower price while maintaining or increasing profit margins. However, many approaches also involve **pull strategies,** such as cents-off coupons to encourage the consumer to purchase the manufacturer's brand. In any event, once potential buyers are in the store, three behaviors are usually necessary for a purchase to take place. They must (1) locate the product or brand in the store, (2) physically obtain the product or brand, and (3) take the product or brand to the point of exchange (e.g., checkout counter).

Once consumers are in the store, it is important that products can be located. Store directories, end-of-aisle and other displays, in-store signs, information booths, and helpful store personnel all help consumers move into visual contact with products. While consumers are in the store, their visual contact with the many other available products increases the probability of purchase.

One interesting tactic employed by a major chain involves a variation of "blue-light specials." Blue-light specials were pioneered by K mart. They offer shoppers in the store the opportunity to purchase products at special prices when a blue light is flashing at a particular location. Usually, the sale item is a low-priced item that is sold at its normal location. A variation of this tactic involves moving the sale merchandise and blue light to a location in the store where high-priced or high-margin items are located. This brings the blue-light shoppers into the vicinity of such products and into visual contact with them—which, of course, increases the probability of making these more profitable sales. This has been reported to be a very successful tactic.

Reprinted by permission of Hershey Foods Corporation. HERSHEY's is a registered trademark of Hershey Foods Corporation.

Cents-off coupons encourage product contact.

Physically coming into contact with a product provides an extremely important source of stimuli and possible consequences that influence whether or not a purchase will occur. Attractive, eye-catching packaging and other aspects of product appearance influence the stimuli attended to by the consumer. Trying the product in the store can also affect purchase probabilities. The behavior of sales personnel can also be a major factor affecting the contingencies at the point of purchase. Sales personnel can positively reinforce certain behaviors, extinguish or punish others, influence the stimuli attended to, and model appropriate product usage. Even negative reinforcement can be employed. For example, consider salespeople who are overly aggressive and use high-pressure tactics. One way for consumers to remove the aversive treatment is to purchase the product—and some consumers do this rather than walk away. Thus, the consumer is negatively reinforced to purchase; and the probability of this response would probably be increased in similar situations in the future. Note also that the *salesperson* is positively reinforced by making the sale using a high-pressure approach. We would predict that the salesperson's use of an aggressive selling approach will also increase.

Salespeople can also change the contingencies for purchasing versus not purchasing. For example, one of our associates told us of his experience in selling furniture to ambivalent customers who state their intention to "go home and think it over." Once the potential buyer leaves the store, the probability of a sale is reduced. Our associate, however, changed the contingencies for leaving. Potential buyers who wanted to think it over were told, "If you buy now, the price is $150. If you go home and come back later, the price will be the original $175." While we are not advocating this specific practice, we do want to stress that salespeople can modify the behavior of potential buyers.

There are also a number of tactics for getting potential buyers to the checkout or payment location. For example, checkout counters are commonly placed next to the exit and parking vouchers are usually validated at this location. Also, salespeople frequently escort the buyer to the checkout where they may help arrange financing.

Transaction

In a macro sense, *facilitating exchanges* is viewed as the primary objective of marketing. In a micro sense, this involves **transactions** in which consumers' funds are exchanged for products and services. Many marketing strategies involve removing obstacles to transactions. The credit methods discussed earlier are examples. So is the use of express checkout lanes and electronic scanners to decrease the time consumers must wait in line. (Some consumers will leave stores without making a purchase if checkout lines are too long.) Credit-card companies offer prompt purchase approvals to decrease the chances that a sale will be missed because of a long wait. American Express, for example, spends $300 to $400 million annually to ensure prompt service for its 15 million customers. From its Phoenix computer center, the company approves 250,000 credit-card transactions a day from all over the world in an average of five seconds or less.[3]

---

[3]"American Express Plays Its Trump Card," *Business Week* (October 24, 1983), p. 62.

Because the behavior of checkout personnel has long been recognized as an important influence on purchase, these personnel are often trained to be friendly and efficient. McDonald's personnel frequently offer *prompts* in an attempt to increase the total amount of purchase. Regardless of the food order, prompts for additional food are offered: "Would you like some fresh, hot French fries with that?" or "How about some McDonald's cookies today?" Because these are very low-cost tactics, few incremental sales are required to make them quite profitable.

The positive reinforcers involved are critical elements in obtaining transactions. Tactics such as rebates, friendly treatment and compliments by store personnel, and contest tickets may increase the probability of purchase and repurchase. The reinforcing properties of the product or service itself are also important. These may involve both functional and psychosocial benefits.

Consumption

While consumption or use would seem to be very simple behaviors to delineate, they are not, because of the vast differences in the nature of various products and services. For example, compare typical behaviors involved in the purchase of nondurables such as a burger and fries versus a durable such as an automobile. The burger and fries are likely to be consumed rather quickly and the packaging disposed of properly. Certain strategies can increase the probability that consumption will be rather quick—such as seats in a restaurant that are comfortable for only short periods of time. As a result, customers do not take up space that could be used for new customers. Prompts are often used to encourage proper disposal of packaging, such as "Thank You" signs on refuse containers.

On the other hand, an automobile purchase usually involves several years of consumption or use. In addition, periodic service is required, and additional complementary products such as gas must be purchased. Finally, an automobile may be disposed of in several ways (selling it outright, junking it, or trading it in on another model). At present, little is known about the process by which consumers dispose of durable goods.

Regardless of the type of product, however, a primary marketing concern is increasing the probability of repurchase. For nondurable package goods, commonly employed tactics include the use of in- or on-package coupons to encourage the consumer to repurchase the same brand. (Many consumers frequently use coupons and take pride in the money they save.) In addition, proof-of-purchase seals have often been used to encourage the consumer to purchase the same brand repeatedly, thereby obtaining enough seals to receive "free" gifts. Gold Medal flour has long used this tactic; and Pampers diapers ran a promotion in which a coupon for a free box of diapers was sent to buyers who mailed in three proof-of-purchase

George W. Gardner

A positive consumption experience increases the probability of repurchase.

seals. For durable goods, proper instructions on the care and use of the product may be useful, for they help the consumer receive full product benefits. In addition, high-quality service and maintenance provided by the seller can help to develop long-term client relationships.

Communication

A final set of behaviors that marketers attempt to increase involves **communication.** There are two basic audiences with whom marketers want consumers to communicate. They want consumers to (1) provide the company with marketing information and (2) tell other potential consumers about the product and encourage them to purchase it.

From Consumers to Marketers

Marketers typically want at least three types of information from consumers. First, they want *information about the consumer* to investigate the quality of their marketing strategy and the success of market segmentation. Warranty cards are commonly used for this purpose. These cards commonly ask about consumer demographics, what magazines consumers read, where they obtained information about the product, where they purchased it, and what competing brands they own or have tried. Free gifts are sometimes offered to encourage consumers to return warranty cards—as well as subtle threats that the warranty will be canceled if the card is not filled out and returned promptly.

A second type of information sought from consumers is the *names of other potential buyers* of the product. Some firms and organizations offer awards if the names of several potential buyers are given and a larger award if any of the prospects actually makes a purchase. Finally, marketers also seek consumer information about *defective products.* Money-back or other guarantees that require the consumer to contact the store or company provide this information and also reduce the risk of loss to the consumer. For example, General Mills offers "a prompt adjustment of equal value" if the consumer is dissatisfied with Cheerios.

From Consumers to Consumers

Marketers also want consumers to tell their friends and others about the product. A product that is effective and performs well may encourage this behavior. However, other tactics also can encourage it. Tupperware parties have long been used to take advantage of the fact that consumers respond favorably to information from their friends and to create an environment in which purchase is heavily encouraged. This approach has been so successful that, over the first 25 years of its existence, Tupperware doubled its sales and earnings every 5 years. Recent declines in sales may be the result of market saturation from such a successful approach, for it is estimated that the average family of four owns 28 pieces of Tupperware![4]

Newly opened bars and lounges frequently offer customers free drinks to encourage them not only to return but to tell others about the place and to bring their friends. Word-of-mouth communication is the primary way such establishments become popular. Health clubs, such as Elaine Powers and Vic Tanny, often run promotions in which members who bring in new customers get special rates for themselves as well as for their friends. One cable TV company ran a promotion in which any subscriber who got a friend to purchase the service received $10. Such tactics not only increase communication but also other behaviors in the purchase sequence.

---

[4]See Gwen Kinkead (1984), "Tupperware's Party Times Are Over," *Fortune* (February 20), pp. 113–120.

A Consumer Behavior Management Model

The preceding part of this chapter outlined a common behavior sequence for retail purchases. A number of examples of current marketing strategies were categorized according to the factors in this model. In this last part of the chapter, we describe a model by which managers can analyze consumer behavior and develop marketing programs to increase the probability of behaviors that are necessary to achieve organizational objectives. This general approach could also be used to develop strategies for decreasing undesired behaviors. We will not emphasize such strategies, however, because of the ethical and practical problems of using punishment or extinction in many marketing management situations.

Two tasks must be performed to use this model. First, given appropriate marketing objectives, the manager must develop a sequential model of the behaviors that are necessary or desired of the consumer. To develop this sequence, we will use our seven-stage model (refer back to Figure 12–2), but other models would have to be developed for other types of purchase/consumption situations.

Second, after the behaviors are delineated, their frequency must be measured to determine baseline data. This step is necessary to identify problem behaviors and to provide a benchmark for comparing the success of the implemented strategy. There are many ways to measure various consumer behaviors; some examples are provided in Figure 12–5. These measurement methods are commonly employed in current marketing research, although they are not always used sequentially to assess every behavior stage.

One approach that does allow a number of stages in a purchase sequence to be monitored is the **scanner cable** method available from research companies such as Information Resources Inc. (IRI) and Adtel Marketing Services. Because this approach is very consistent with the requirements of a consumer behavior management model, we will briefly describe how IRI's BehaviorScan system works.

BehaviorScan is used by many leading marketing companies, including Procter & Gamble, General Foods, General Mills, Quaker Oats, R. J. Reynolds, and Ralston Purina. The system is designed to predict which products will be successful and which ads will work best to sell them. A number of consumer behaviors can be tracked and measured in the process. IRI has constructed consumer panels of 2,500 members in several demographically representative cities such as Marion, Indiana; Eau Claire, Wisconsin; and Midland, Texas. Here's how BehaviorScan works:

> When Nancy Wiegand, the wife of a repairman for the Coca-Cola bottler in Marion, Indiana, flicks on her TV set, that interesting fact is recorded by a microcomputer on the back of the set, which tracks the Wiegands' every viewing whim. When she shops for her family

of five at Owen's County Market on Thursdays, her purchases are scrupulously recorded by the scanners IRI has bought and installed at Owen's. For enlisting in the program, the market gets high-tech labor-saving equipment costing $20,000 per lane that can be used for all its customers. [In return], IRI gets a readout on Mrs. Wiegand's purchases.

Once IRI has a fix on the buying patterns of Mrs. Wiegand and the other 2,499 Marion participants, the company can test, say, a commercial for a new product and see how the audience responds at

FIGURE 12–5   **Examples of Methods Used to Measure Consumption Behaviors**

Types of Behavior	Measurement
1. Information contact	Day-after recall scores Scanner-cable data
2. Funds access	Loan applications Checkbook entries Credit-card debits Scanner-cable data
3. Store contact	"Laboratory" store studies Physical count of shoppers Videotapes of shopping behavior Scanner-cable data
4. Product contact	Inventory analysis Physical count of items removed from display or other locations Consumer diaries or other verbal reports Scanner-cable data
5. Transaction	Monitor cash register tapes Credit-card receipts Consumer purchase diaries Scanner-cable data
6. Consumption	In-home inventory and use research After-purchase telephone surveys Consumer diaries Repurchase rate research Scanner-cable data
7. Communication	Diffusion research Sociometric net research Warranty card information Consumer complaint/compliment responses

the store. New technology allows advertisers to cut into any program carried by cable and replace their commercial with a different ad, though IRI is permitted to change only those advertising slots their client has purchased. All this happens with the flick of a few switches at IRI's Marion studio.

For her cooperation, Mrs. Wiegand receives a $20 annual prize—a blender, for example—which she selects from a catalog. To remind her to present her coded identification card when shopping in the seven Marion-area markets covered by IRI's scanner network, each use of her card enters her name in a pool from which IRI draws 300 winners a month. Prizes range from $15 to a one-week trip for two to Mexico.[5]

A number of behaviors in the purchase sequence can be efficiently monitored using scanner cable methods. For example, information contact can be monitored and partially controlled by switching various commercials. It may also be possible to record consumer eye movements during commercials to investigate the quality of attentive behaviors. Funds access information could be monitored on the cash register tape by recording the method of payment. (Given that the majority of grocery purchases may soon be paid for with credit cards, even more information about consumer methods of payment for a larger variety of purchases may be available.) Because every purchase in the store is recorded, store contact, product contact, and transaction information is also available, along with the dates of these behaviors. Thus, it is possible to analyze the time between various behaviors, such as information contact and purchase. Also, an analysis of the time between purchase of a particular product and repurchase could offer information about consumption time. Self-report questionnaires could also be used to investigate cognitive variables (such as product knowledge and attitudes) as well as other behaviors (such as communication).

Overall, our discussion is intended to demonstrate that consumer behaviors can be measured quite well using current technology. However, as with any element of marketing strategy, the costs and benefits of extended research on consumer behaviors must be carefully analyzed. P&G spent $1.3 million on BehaviorScan in a recent year. While there are substantial benefits, many firms have to use less costly methods. Even simpler, less expensive methods—such as analysis of advertising expenditures and shipping orders in various markets—may provide useful information about consumer behavior.

---

[5]Fern Schumer (1983), "The New Magicians of Market Research," *Fortune* (July 25), p. 72; also see Joseph Poindexter (1983), "Shaping the Consumer," *Psychology Today* (May), pp. 65–68.

Courtesy Information Resounds Inc.

Consumers use a BehaviorScan coded ID card when shopping in the markets covered by the scanner network.

Given that a sequence of consumer behaviors can be developed and that they can be measured quite well with current and developing technologies, Figure 12–6 offers a model for managing such behaviors. This model, based on ideas in applied behavior analysis, is concerned with the development and maintenance of consumer behavior. It is fully consistent with the objectives of marketing management and common marketing strategies. The model offers a more systematic and efficient approach than many of those used in current marketing practice, however. We now discuss each stage in the Consumer Behavior Management (CBM) model shown in Figure 12–6.

Identify Problem Behavior

Each behavior in the purchase/consumption sequence is dependent upon many factors. In some cases—such as the promotion of a clearly superior product—information contact may be sufficient to drive the entire behavior chain and result in the successful performance of all of the required behaviors. Even a simple comment about a product by a trusted friend may result in the performance of all of the required behaviors. In many cases, however, initial consumer behaviors are performed with sufficient frequency and quality to lead to other behaviors—but the other behaviors do not occur. For example, consumers may go to retail stores where the product is carried and may even come into visual contact with the product, but not purchase it. In other cases, information contact may not occur, and thus, no additional behaviors are performed.

FIGURE 12–6   **A Consumer Behavior Management Model**

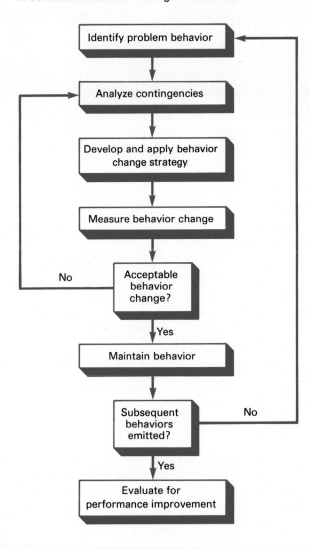

The **problem or target behavior** is the earliest behavior in the sequence that is not being performed—or is not being performed appropriately or frequently enough to lead to the next behavior. Any behavior in the sequence could be a problem behavior. The problem behavior is identified by examining the differences in behavior frequencies from one stage to the next. For example, consumer research indicated the following:

1. Information contact—90 percent of the target market has been exposed to two commercials per week in their homes for the past month. Unaided recall scores are 40 percent; 30 percent indicate they like the features of our product.

2. Funds access—87 percent of the target market purchases a competitive brand at the same price as ours; 67 percent pays with credit cards.

3. Store contact—96 percent of the target market shops at least once per week in stores where our brand is carried; 40 percent comes into the physical vicinity of our product once per week.

4. Product contact—30 percent of the target market comes into visual contact with our product; 14 percent picks up the product and inspect it; 2 percent takes our product with them.

5. Transaction—slightly less than 2 percent pays for our product; a few replace it on the shelf.

6. Consumption—most purchasers use the product within two weeks of purchase.

7. Communication—no indication of significant communication with other consumers; 60 percent of warranty cards are returned in three weeks.

What is the problem behavior in this example? It appears that consumers' information contact, accessing funds, and store contact are all exceptionally good. Even some phases of product contact are good; but few consumers actually take the product with them. Thus, we might conclude that the problem behavior is product contact. Potential ways to deal with the problem behavior are discussed below.

Analyze Contingencies

Once the problem behavior is identified, the contingencies or relationships among the behavior and the environment must be analyzed. Among the major contingencies are the efforts of competition and their success in maintaining or changing consumer behavior. Many successful firms attempt to interfere with new-product test marketing (or other marketing efforts) of their competitors to avoid losing market share and to confound competitors' research results. Other contingencies that require analysis are the nature of the target market and the marketing-mix elements, particularly those elements most closely related to the problem behavior. Figure 12–7 suggests the major marketing-mix elements associated with particular problem behaviors. While each element requires analysis, Figure 12–7 suggests useful starting points for consideration.

Analyzing contingencies is, of course, an extremely important step in the process, because it represents a search for the reasons why particular behaviors are not being performed. While some behavior modifiers may focus only on behavior-environment interactions, the assessment of cognitive variables may also contribute valuable information. For example, many new products fail because consumers do not perceive a difference in the new product. Thus, research on consumer perceptions and attitudes can be very useful for investigating the problem and analyzing contingencies.

Returning to the example in which product contact is the problem behavior, analysis of the contingencies might begin with a comparison of our product and package with those of successful competitors. We could interview consumers to investigate their perceptions of and attitudes toward our product. We might directly investigate other contingencies, such as competitive differences in packaging, labeling, instructions for use, colors, and price markings.

Develop and Apply Behavior Change Strategy

Once the problem behavior is delineated and the contingencies surrounding it have been analyzed, a **behavior change strategy** is developed and applied. Such strategies might include any number of the processes we

---

FIGURE 12–7   **Primary Relationships between Consumer Behaviors and Marketing-Mix Elements**

Consumer Behaviors	Product	Price	Promotion	Place
			Elements	
1. Information contact			X	
2. Funds access		X		
3. Store contact				X
4. Product contact	X			X
5. Transaction	X	X	X	X
6. Consumption	X			
7. Communication	X	X	X	X

discussed earlier, such as positive reinforcement, negative reinforcement, shaping, respondent conditioning, or modeling, among others. Positive reinforcement is generally recommended for increasing behavior, because it is both effective and flexible. Of course, as with any approach to marketing strategy, the costs and benefits of various procedures must be carefully assessed.

Returning to our example, suppose the analysis reveals an important difference between our product and those of successful competitors. Their packaging gives detailed assembly and use instructions, whereas our package instructions are rather sketchy. We might decide to improve the instructions, and also to add pictures of models appropriately assembling and using the product. We could also include a toll-free number consumers can call for additional information or help.

Measure Behavior Change

After implementation of the strategy, the problem behavior must be remeasured to determine whether the problem has been solved. If the behavior has not changed sufficiently, we must go back and reanalyze the contingencies and develop a new intervention strategy.

How much behavior has to change for the strategy to be successful depends on the marketing objectives, the particular behavior, and the situation. For example, if after implementing the strategy, only 3 percent (instead of 2 percent) of those who inspect the product actually purchase it, this probably would not be considered a successful strategy—and in fact, may not even cover the cost of the toll-free number.

If the majority of those who inspect the product now purchase it, however, we might conclude that we have successfully solved the behavior problem. In some cases, a very small amount of behavior change may be sufficient for a strategy to be successful. For example, Procter & Gamble increased market share for Crest toothpaste from 35 percent to 41 percent by updating the formula, adding a gel version, and sharply increasing advertising and promotion. While a change in toothpaste market share of 6 percent may not sound impressive, it translates into additional sales of $42 million!

Maintain Behavior

Up to this point, our main focus has been on developing behavior. If the new strategy is successful in developing a sufficient amount of behavior, we must consider methods of maintaining that behavior. Because much consumer behavior is habitual, maintaining behavior is usually much easier and less expensive than developing it. In fact, one of the major reasons new-product introductions are so expensive is the promotional cost of developing the behavior. Once the behavior is developed, these costs usually can be decreased and behavior can be maintained much more cheaply. As an example, in the most successful cigarette introduction in history, Brown & Williamson gave away free cartons of cigarettes and spent an estimated $150 million to develop use of Barclay cigarettes. Once they obtained about a 2 percent market share—and each share point is worth about $125 million to the manufacturer—carton giveaways were eliminated and promotional spending was decreased. Still, much of the market share was maintained.

Often when positive reinforcers are used, their frequency and amount can be decreased without a loss in behavior performance. If continuous schedules of reinforcement were initially employed, it may be possible to switch to ratio schedules and still maintain behavior. Discount coupons of lower value may also be effective; requiring multiunit purchases to receive the same discount may maintain certain behaviors. In fact, encouraging multiunit purchases may not only help develop brand loyalty but also increase usage, because additional units would be readily available in home inventory.

Different organizations may be primarily concerned with maintaining different behaviors in the purchase-consumption chain. Credit-card companies want to maintain card usage or loyalty across a variety of purchase situations; retailers want to maintain store contact or store loyalty; manufacturers want to maintain product contact or brand loyalty. From a behavior viewpoint, these actions are controlled by contingencies in the environment, and loyalty is no more than the degree to which the behaviors are repeated.

Many scholars are critical of viewing loyalty as repeat behavior. They argue that past behavior does not always predict future behavior. While we agree that past behavior is not a perfect predictor, it is still a very good predictor and can be measured more directly than many other variables.

In addition to changing and then maintaining the behavior that was formerly a problem, we must also investigate whether the remaining behaviors are now being performed appropriately and frequently enough to achieve our objectives. If not, we identify the new problem behavior that is blocking the behavior chain—the next one in the sequence that is not being performed appropriately. We then repeat the stages in the consumer behavior management model. This process continues until all of the behaviors are being performed appropriately.

Evaluate for Performance Improvement

Regardless of how successful a particular marketing strategy is, there is always room for improvement. In general, marketing strategies must be

HIGHLIGHT 12–3   ***A Tactic to Encourage Repeat Purchase and Use and Trial of a Similar Product***

Courtesy Swift & Company, an Esmark Company

Traditionally, soup is made by either starting from scratch or by just adding water or milk to a can of condensed soup or dry ingredients. Soup Starter requires different behaviors, in that the consumer adds water, meat, and any additional vegetables desired to a package of dry ingredients. Thus, to develop a long-run change in the method of soup preparation, it may be important to get the consumer to try the product more than once. This coupon encourages multiple purchases of the product to receive a "free" package of another product, Stew Starter, which requires similarly new methods of stew preparation. Overall, then, the tactic may accomplish several objectives and increase the probability of several consumer behaviors. These include increasing sales of Soup Starter, encouraging repeat purchase, loading up the consumer with the product to encourage use, encouraging use of this method for making stew, and—hopefully—developing loyalty to this method of preparation as well as brand loyalty to Soup Starter and Stew Starter.

monitored for more efficient methods of maintaining behavior as well as of increasing it. For example, in 1983, General Motors had a record $74.6 billion in sales and record profits of $3.7 billion. However, GM was in the process of reorganizing its divisions to be more independent in hopes of developing an even more effective company.

Any consumer behavior may decrease in frequency because of changes in the environment (such as more powerful or more frequent reinforcement by a competitor). Thus, while the model in Figure 12–6 provides a systematic way to approach marketing strategy development that focuses directly on consumer behavior, it does not replace situational analyses such as careful monitoring and responding to competitive strategies. Of course, this is part of analyzing contingencies in an ongoing marketing program.

Back to the Case

This letter contains a number of interesting features that are consistent with the contents of this chapter. Of prime importance is the strategy used to get current members to introduce their friends to the organization. The three-point sequence offers members a potentially effective selling approach to increase the probability of purchase. The "free" B.A.S.S. cap is offered as a reward for a successful sale. The reduced price to friends is also a useful selling point; and the chance to win a large prize such as a truck or boat may encourage members to perform selling behaviors.

 This is clearly the communication stage of the sequential model of consumer behaviors, in which attempts are made to get consumers to communicate with their friends about the product or service. While we don't know how effective this approach is, B.A.S.S. is "America's Largest Fishing Society"!

Summary

This chapter developed two models that integrated consumer behavior with marketing strategy development. The first model (Figure 12–2) outlined the purchase process as a sequence of behaviors that included information contact, funds access, store contact, product contact, transaction, consumption, and communication. The second model (Figure 12–6) was concerned with a systematic approach to managing consumer behavior and increasing those behaviors required for successful marketing strategies. The steps in this model include identifying the problem behavior, analyzing contingencies, developing intervention strategies, measuring behavior change, maintaining behavior, and evaluating the program for performance improvement. While the chapter emphasized relationships between behavior and the environment, a number of attempts were made to demonstrate that additional analyses of cognitive variables could improve the effectiveness of the behavior approach.

Additional Reading

Barbara Buell (1985), "Big Brother Gets a Job in Market Research," *Business Week* (April 8), pp. 96–97.

Gordon R. Foxall (1983), *Consumer Choice,* New York: St. Martin's Press.

Gillian Garcia (1980), "Credit Cards: An Interdisciplinary Survey," *Journal of Consumer Research* (March), pp. 327–337.

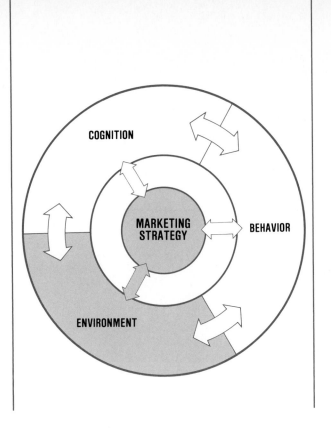

Section Four

Environmental Theory and Marketing Strategy

Chapter Thirteen

Environmental Influences on Consumer Behavior

Caesars Boardwalk Regency

A glimpse of the majestic marble lobby with its Roman statues will lure gamblers off Atlantic City's boardwalk and funnel them through carefully placed lights and open spaces into the casino.

There, they'll end up betting more and enjoying it—even if they lose their shirts.

At least that's what interior designer Bob DiLeonardo said would happen when he redesigned Caesars Boardwalk Regency, a 509-room hotel-casino that, with its then-current art deco decor, was only three years old in 1983.

DiLeonardo, who owns the 21-employee DiLeonardo's Interiors Inc. in Cranston, R.I., said his mission at Caesars was "to create an environment that relaxes the morality of people." Achieving this is so complex, however, that he enlisted the aid of an "environmental psychologist"—a relatively new breed of psychologist who studies the impact of the environment on behavior. (They're the ones who put uncomfortable seats in fast-food joints to cut down on lingering.)

The fancy consultant helped DiLeonardo feel less anxious about the size of the Caesars contract, which, at $7 million, was more than three times his company's annual gross.

And, with work about to begin on Caesars lobby, he felt free to reveal some of his secrets. Lobby windows, for instance, would be replaced by sheets of creamy Italian marble so that "people won't be able to relate to time. Once they step inside, they'll be in an adult Disneyland."

He would use materials that "enhance" noise for the casino because "noise creates excitement." Lighting for the blackjack tables would extend far enough to envelop the player, but not far enough to include spectators, who "may interrupt [the player's] sense of security."

The eight restaurants would be done in "vestment colors"—gold, plum, deep reds—to suggest a kinship between gambling and royalty. Restaurants would have thick rugs and mohair wall coverings, meant to impart a "sensuality" and warmth so patrons would "have another brandy," DiLeonardo said.

But the high rollers who get complimentary suites would taste the flip side of environmental psychology. DiLeonardo said their suites would be done in bold, contrasting colors with lighting so bright and with noise enhanced to such high levels that the occupants would practically run to the roulette wheels.

Source: Adapted from Stephen P. Morin (1983), "Interior Designer Sets Out to Make Casino that Relaxes Your Morality," The Wall Street Journal (January 10), p. 21.

In Sections Two and Three of this text, we discussed cognitive and behavior approaches in detail. While there are many differences between the two approaches, both recognize that environmental forces must be considered in the development of theories of consumer behavior and are critical in the development of marketing strategies. Environmental psychology is one of the fastest-growing areas in social science. There is also interest in the effects of situational influences, as attested to by several reviews in the marketing literature.[1] One might assume, then, that the impact of the environment and situations on consumer behavior would be well understood—or at least that well-accepted definitions of these variables would be available.

Unfortunately, this is not the case. In both psychology and marketing there is little consensus of how environments and situations should be conceptualized. A major barrier to development in this area is the question of whether environments and situations should be defined and studied as *objective* or *subjective* phenomena. Is the appropriate unit of analysis the environment or situation "as it is" or "as it is perceived to be"? If the answer is the former, we must ask the important *philosophical* question: How can an environment be known independent of the researcher's perceptions? If the answer is the latter, we must ask the *practical* question:

---

[1]See James H. Leigh and Claude R. Martin (1981), "A Review of Situational Influence Paradigms and Research," in *Review of Marketing 1981*, Ben M. Enis and Kenneth J. Reering (eds.), Chicago: American Marketing Association, pp. 57–74; Pradeep Kakkar and Richard J. Lutz (1981), "Situational Influences on Consumer Behavior," in *Perspectives in Consumer Behavior*, Harold H. Kassarjian and Thomas S. Robertson (eds.), 3d ed., Glenview, Ill.: Scott, Foresman, pp. 204–215; Joseph A. Cote, Jr. (1985), "Situational Variables in Consumer Research: A Review," Working Paper, Washington State University.

I suppose you're just going to lie there blaming all your problems on the environment?

Source: APA Monitor (March 1983), p. 4.

What does an analysis of the environment contribute over and above the study of perception and other cognitive variables?

In this chapter, we provide an overview of environmental influences on consumer behavior. Our intention is to provide a framework for the analysis in subsequent chapters and to point out a number of influences on consumer behavior that may have to be considered in the development of marketing strategies. We discuss three related types of influences: the social, the physical, and the marketing environments. However, first we clarify our position on basic definitional issues in environmental analysis.

Basic Definitional Issues in Environmental Analysis

As we noted, a major problem in studying environmental and situational influences on consumer behavior is offering acceptable definitions for these terms. We believe that no single definition can incorporate the many meanings of these terms. However, if the terms are properly qualified, much confusion and disagreement can be avoided. There are at least three different levels of environmental analysis that need to be delineated: the *complete* environment, the *perceived* environment, and the *consensual* environment.[2]

1. The Complete Environment. This refers to the total complex of sensory stimuli available to the consumer. This conception of the environment can be broken down in infinite detail but can never be fully described. It is useful to recognize this conception of the environment, but our ability to study it is limited. In addition, it is quite clear that consumers screen out many environmental stimuli.

2. The Perceived Environment. This is the environment as it is interpreted by a particular consumer. To the degree that the consumer is aware of environmental stimuli, it is the perceived environment that the consumer reacts to, responds to, and acts upon. Because of differences in backgrounds and values, the perceived environment may vary from consumer to consumer. Research on consumers' perceptions of environmental factors typically investigates self reports by consumers, because the perceived environment is subjectively determined.

3. The Consensual Environment. This is the interpretation of the environment as agreed upon by a group with similar backgrounds and values. This conceptualization recognizes that environmental factors can only be perceived and interpreted through sense impressions and previous learning. Thus, knowledge of the environment is never really objective. As explained by Newman and Newman:

> We all assume that there is an objective reality, a world of colors, sounds, shapes, and textures that we can experience. Our knowledge of reality can be indirect or direct. Indirect knowledge might come through reading or hearing someone describe something. Direct knowledge seems to come when the stimulus actually impinges on our receptors. Yet the stimulus itself and the sensations we experi-

---

[2]Adapted for the purposes of this text from Jack Block and Jeanne H. Block (1981), "Studying Situational Dimensions: A Grand Perspective and Some Limited Empiricism," in *Toward a Psychology of Situations: An Interactional Perspective,* David Magnusson (ed.), Hillsdale, N.J.: Lawrence Erlbaum, pp. 85–102. Interest in situational influences in consumer research was pioneered by Professor Russell W. Belk. For example, see Russell W. Belk (1975), "Situational Variables and Consumer Behavior," *Journal of Consumer Research* (December), pp. 157–167.

ence are not the same thing. There is always some gap between objective reality and the sensory experiences associated with that reality. In some ways, our knowledge of reality from sensation is as indirect as the knowledge that comes from a written or spoken description. We watch a car move along the street. We sense color, shape, movement, and sound, yet those sensations are not the car itself.[3]

In our text, we consider the *consensual* environment unless otherwise noted. We consider a *situation* to be simply the environment at a particular moment. It may be a **consensual situation** (how people with similar backgrounds describe it) or it may be a **perceived situation** (how a particular consumer describes it).

From a marketing strategy point of view, the idea that the environment cannot be known objectively emphasizes the importance of subjectively determined meanings and perceptions on consumer behavior. It is unimportant whether a *marketing manager* perceives a product to be better than those of competitors or can produce test results that demonstrate the product's superior characteristics; the test is whether *consumers* perceive a difference and are willing to pay for it.

For example, some models of Chevrolets and Cadillacs come off the same assembly lines with the same basic bodies, chassis, engines, and transmissions. The major difference between the cars is the brand name placed on them (and the price!) However, some consumers clearly perceive a significant difference between the cars and are willing to pay considerably more for a Cadillac. It is the *perception* of value and social status that is controlling behavior here, rather than major physical differences in products.

Major Types of Environmental Influence

As we noted previously, environmental influences can be placed into three categories: social, physical, and marketing. Figure 13–1 shows these three environments and the relationships between them and consumer cognitions and behaviors. While we are treating these as separate environments for purposes of discussion, they are closely related and overlap in some cases. For example, the marketing environment includes both physical

---

[3]Philip R. Newman and Barbara M. Newman (1983), *Principles of Psychology*, Homewood, Ill.: Dorsey Press, p. 132.

objects (such as products and stores) and social interactions (such as conversations with salespeople).

The Social Environment

Broadly defined, the **social environment** includes all human activities and interactions. A consumer may either be actively involved in a social situation (discussing stereos with a friend) or passively involved (watching a friend negotiate a car price) and can learn from and be influenced by both.

Much of a consumer's knowledge in general as well as specific opinions about products, services, stores, prices, and even advertising are strongly affected by the opinions of other people, such as family members and peer groups. Many consumers purchase the same products and frequent the same stores as their parents without ever having made a conscious decision to do so. Traditional brands such as Kleenex tissue, Campbell soups, and Heinz ketchup may be so familiar to these consumers from childhood on that the performance of these brands may define product quality to them. In other words, good-tasting soup may be perceived as soup that tastes like Campbell's.

Unlike environmental influences in general, social influences have a well-accepted typology in consumer research. This typology includes culture, subculture, social class, reference group, and family influences. Because these influences are the major topics of Chapters 14 and 15, we briefly introduce them here.

Figure 13–2 presents a model of social influences on consumer behavior. These influences are listed in order of the type and degree of influence

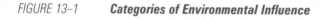

FIGURE 13–1   **Categories of Environmental Influence**

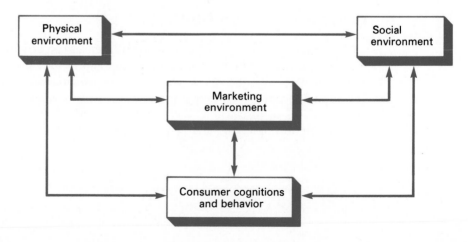

they are likely to have on a specific purchase. For example, culture is more likely to affect broad product class decisions (a bicycle versus a car for transportation), while reference groups and family influences may affect these as well as specific brand and model decisions (a pair of Adidas Boston versus a pair of Brooks Chariot running shoes).

Culture and Subculture

Culture is one of the most basic influences on an individual's cognitions and behaviors, because all facets of life are carried out against a background of shared values and artifacts of the society in which the person lives. Cultural values are transmitted through family, religious organizations, and educational institutions. While marketing does affect cultural values, the major task of marketing management in this context is to *monitor* changes in these values in both domestic and international markets. Changes in cultural values often result in marketing opportunities. For example, the increased emphasis in our culture on physical fitness generated entirely new industries concerned with running shoes and apparel, as well as exercise clubs such as the Healthy Attitude or Chicago Health and Racquetball Club.

Within a given culture, *subcultures* arise from geographic, religious, nationality, and ethnic differences, among others. While many of these traditional subcultural influences may be decreasing because of mass com-

---

FIGURE 13–2   **Social Influences on Consumer Behavior**

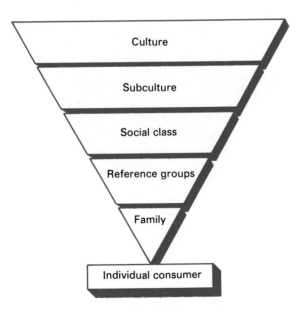

munication and mass transportation in our country, subcultures based on age may be increasing in influence. (Cultural and subcultural influences are discussed further in Chapter 14.)

Social Class

Society is stratified on the basis of factors such as wealth, skill, and power. The resulting social classes are of interest to consumer analysts because of differences in attitudes and values across classes and the potential of this variable for market segmentation. (This topic is also discussed further in Chapter 14.)

Don Smetzer: Click/Chicago

A primary reference group.

HIGHLIGHT 13–2   **Communication and the Social Environment**

One of the most important aspects of the social environment is face-to-face communication. However, face-to-face communication is much more than simply the words people speak. Below is a list of some other factors that influence cognitions and behaviors during a conversation. These can be very powerful and dramatically affect the meaning of spoken words and listeners' reactions to them.

1. **Paralanguage.** The way people use their voices and the timbre of the voice can change the meaning of a spoken message. Rising or falling inflections, and rapid or slow speech patterns can create different meanings. For example, "Pizza Hut has great pizza" can be either an endorsement or a sarcastic slur, depending on how the words are spoken.

2. **Body language.** The way people use their bodies in communicating to others can affect the perceptions of and attention paid to a spoken message. For example, sitting up straight and looking a customer right in the eyes while saying "I really think this is the right insurance policy for you," may affect perceptions of the sincerity of the spoken words.

3. **Facial expressions.** The 80 muscles in the face can create over 7,000 expressions. A pout, glare, or smile can change a listener's reactions to a spoken message.

4. **Clothes.** The clothes people wear can affect reactions to spoken words. For example, we are likely to react differently when the person speaking to us is wearing a flannel shirt and blue jeans versus a police officer's uniform.

5. **Touch.** Touching someone while speaking can affect cognitions and behaviors. For example, whether or not a coach puts his/her hand on a player's shoulder while giving instructions may have different influences on the player's actions.

6. **Proxemics.** The distance between people while talking can affect social interactions. For example, moving very close to people while speaking loudly may intimidate listeners.

Reference Groups and Family

Groups that directly influence an individual are called reference groups. *Primary reference groups* include family and close friends; *secondary reference groups* include fraternal organizations and professional associations.

Consumers usually have several reference groups for various subjects or purchases. The nature of the product and the stage in the purchase process influence which of these groups a consumer is likely to consult. Reference group influence is generally thought to be stronger for products that are "public" or socially conspicuous, that is, products that other people see the individual using, such as clothes or automobiles.

As we have noted, the family is generally recognized as an important reference group. In addition, various family members may play different roles in the purchase-consumption process. The actual purchaser of a product may not be the final user or the person who made the purchase decision. For example, father may have made the decision to buy a new Lawnboy, mother may have selected the purchase location and made the purchase, and junior may end up cutting the grass. For this reason, researchers argue that the household, rather than the individual, is often the relevant unit of analysis for consumer research. (Issues concerning reference group and family influences are considered in Chapter 15.)

The Physical Environment

The **physical environment** can be defined as the collection of nonhuman elements that comprises the field in which consumer behavior occurs.[4] At a basic level, the physical environment can be divided into spatial and nonspatial elements. Spatial elements include countries, cities, buildings, stores, furniture, and the interior design of rooms, among other things. Nonspatial elements include factors such as temperature, humidity, illumination, noise level, and time.

Environmental psychology is the study of the impact of these variables on cognitions and behavior. It is closely related to four other fields: ecological psychology, eco-cultural psychology, behavioral geography, and cross-cultural psychology.[5]

Research in these areas has demonstrated quite clearly that a number of elements in the physical environment—such as in-store signs, colors, displays, and music—are quite important in designing retail stores. (We discuss these further in Chapter 20.) However, many other elements in the physical environment also affect behavior. We briefly discuss three of these: time, weather, and lighting.

Time

A variety of basic conceptual and empirical research has examined the effects of time on consumer behavior.[6] Marketing practitioners are also

---

[4]Adapted from William D. Crano and Lawrence A. Messe (1982), *Social Psychology: Principles and Themes of Interpersonal Behavior,* Homewood, Ill.: Dorsey Press, p. 15.

[5]See James A. Russell and Lawrence M. Ward (1982), "Environmental Psychology," in *Annual Review of Psychology,* Vol. 33, Mark R. Rosenzweig and Lyman W. Porter (eds.), Palo Alto, Calif.: Annual Reviews, pp. 651–688.

[6]For example, see Robert J. Graham (1981), "The Role of Perception of Time in Consumer Research," *Journal of Consumer Research* (March), pp. 335–342; Laurence P. Feldman and Jacob Hornik (1981), "The Use of Time: An Integrated Conceptual Model," *Journal of Consumer Research* (March), pp. 407–419; Jacob Hornik (1982), "Situational Effects on the Con-

Courtesy Mars Inc.

Marketing strategies may vary by the time of the year.

interested in this topic, because sales of some products may be influenced by time factors. For example, the Daylight Saving Time Coalition petitioned Congress to increase the period of daylight savings time by seven weeks per year. Advocates of this change include the management of 7-Eleven convenience stores, who believe that more women would stop at

sumption of Time," *Journal of Marketing* (Fall), pp. 44–55; Jacob Hornik (1984), "Subjective versus Objective Time Measures: A Note on the Perception of Time in Consumer Behavior," *Journal of Consumer Research* (June), pp. 615–618.

its stores on the way home from work if it were still light outside. The company estimates that this extra daylight would increase sales by $30 million.

Another advocate of this change is the Barbeque Industry Association. Reasoning that people would cook out more if it were light during the dinner hour, this association estimates an increase in sales of charcoal briquettes of 15 percent ($56 million) and increases in sales of starter fluid of 13 percent ($15 million). It is also estimated that golfers would play 4 million more rounds and buy an additional $7 million worth of clubs and balls, and tennis buffs could get in 9.8 million more hours of outdoor play and spend another $7 million on equipment. Thus, what might seem to be a very small change in time, could well have considerable impact on consumer behavior.[7]

Weather

Many firms have recognized that weather influences consumer behavior. Obviously, ear muffs, gloves, and heavy coats are winter products, and suntan lotion, air conditioners, and bathing suits are summer products. Yet some firms are increasing the attention they pay to the weather, not just for a season, but on a *daily* basis. For example, Campbell Soup Company has based its spot radio advertising on weather reports. Whenever a storm is forecast, Campbell's ads urge listeners to stock up on soup before the weather worsens; after the storm hits, the ad copy changes to tell people to relax indoors and warm themselves with soup. While research on the relationships between weather and consumer behavior is in its early stages, it seems likely that weather is often an important influence on cognitions (such as moods) and on purchase behavior.[8]

Lighting

There is considerable research evidence that lighting affects behavior. In general, it has been found that people work better in brighter rooms, but workers find direct overhead lighting unpleasant. In business meetings, people who intend to make themselves heard sit under or near lights, whereas those who intend to be quiet often sit in darker areas. Intimate candlelight may draw people together; bright floodlights can cause people

---

[7]See Fern Schumer Chapman (1984), "Business's Push for More Daylight Time," *Fortune* (November 12), pp. 149–162.

[8]See Debra A. Michals (1985), "Pitching Products by the Barometer," *Business Week* (July 8), p. 45; Ronald Alsop (1985), "Companies Look to Weather to Find Best Climate for Ads," *The Wall Street Journal* (January 19), p. 27; Fred Ward (1985), "Weather, Behavior Correlated in New Market Test," *Marketing News* (June 7), p. 9.

to hurry past a location. Overall, lighting may affect the way people work and interact with others, their overall comfort, and even their mental and physical health.[9]

While it seems likely that lighting could affect consumers' moods, anxiety levels, willingness to shop, and purchase behavior, little research is available on this topic. However, one discussion of lighting in retail stores and malls suggested that specialized lighting systems increased sales dramatically. Pillowtex Corporation used tiny spotlights attached to glass shelves, rather than overhead lighting, for illumination in its Dallas World Trade Center showroom. The corporation attributes one third of its $3 million-plus annual sales to this lighting approach.[10]

The Marketing Environment

The **marketing environment** includes all stimuli and situations that affect consumer cognitions and behaviors, either directly or indirectly. It includes elements from the social environment (customer/salesperson interactions) as well as the physical environment (products, stores, ads). We discuss four issues concerning this definition of the marketing environment: the role of marketing, the boundaries of marketing, indirect marketing influences, and direct marketing influences.

The Role of Marketing

The above definition of the marketing environment recognizes that marketing stimuli are a large and powerful part of the social and physical environment. For example, a major difference between social classes involves the amount and nature of possessions (marketed products) and the value placed on them, as well as the services (such as education) received by members of various classes. Much of the activity of members of society is involved with the production, marketing, and purchase and use of goods and services. Further, much of the physical environment of most cities is devoted to products and services, to places to market and store them, and to billboards and signs promoting them. In sum, we believe that marketing is not only a very important part of the fabric of society, but also plays a significant role in shaping its values, activities, and landscape.

---

[9]See Jeff Meer (1985), "The Light Touch," *Psychology Today* (September), pp. 60–67.

[10]See Mark Harris (1984), "Evaluate Lighting Systems as a Marketing Device, Not Overhead," *Marketing News* (October 26), p. 1.

The Boundaries of Marketing

Identifying the boundaries of the marketing environment is important. Which situations and environments are the concern of marketing and consumer analysis and which are not? There is no simple answer to this question. In general, if the nature of marketing is held to be business exchanges between organizations and consumers, then the marketing environment includes all situations in which consumer cognitions and behaviors are affected by marketing stimuli. There are four closely related, overlapping environments of concern from this perspective: the information, shopping, purchasing, and consumption environments.

The Information Environment. This environment includes information that is available to consumers via their senses as well as information that con-

George W. Gardner
Window shopping.

sumers share with others. Thus, it includes situations in which the consumer engages in the two behaviors of information contact and communication, as well as the relevant cognitive processes that occur. For example, two people discussing the weather are not a part of the marketing information environment. Yet if the conversation shifts to a discussion of the relative merits of various personal computers, then it would be part of the marketing information environment.

The Shopping Environment. This environment includes not only the physical environment of malls and retail stores, but also situations in which the consumer engages in such activities as telephone and catalog shopping. Thus, it includes situations in which the consumer engages in the two behaviors of store contact and product contact, as well as the relevant cognitive processes that occur. For example, visiting a mall to window-shop would be part of the shopping environment.

The Purchasing Environment. This environment includes the stimuli and situations involved in an actual exchange of money for products and services. Thus, it includes situations in which the consumer engages in the two behaviors of funds access and transaction, as well as the relevant cognitive processes that occur. In some cases, the purchasing and shopping environments differ in terms of location within the store, time, and cognitions and behaviors. In other cases, these two environments may be totally separate. For example, a consumer may shop for a stereo at a store (the shopping environment) and later call from home to purchase the stereo and have it delivered (the purchasing environment).

The Consumption Environment. This environment concerns the stimuli and situations involving the actual use and disposal of products. Thus, it includes situations in which the consumer engages in consumption-related behaviors and the relevant cognitive processes that occur. For example, the use of a Kenmore washer over a number of years and its disposal at a garage sale would be part of the consumption environment.

Figure 13–3 offers some examples of the four marketing environments and relevant consumer behaviors. Similar analyses could be offered if the focus shifts to a broader, societal view of marketing and consumer behavior. Until consensus is reached on the definition of marketing, however, firm boundaries on what constitutes all elements of the marketing environment cannot be specified.

Indirect Marketing Influences

From an environmental perspective, marketing activity involves managing the environment to achieve organizational objectives. This is frequently done by changing elements in the marketing mix to directly affect consumer cognitions and behaviors. Yet many marketing processes and activities affect consumer cognitions and behaviors only indirectly. Consider the marketing strategies listed in Figure 13–4 for managing the environment. While many of these strategies directly affect the consumer, some of them have an indirect impact. Mergers, acquisitions, legal actions, and coalitions are strategies directed not at the consumer, but at other constituencies. However, these activities are likely to have a long-run impact on the consumer (such as affecting the number of products available in the marketplace).

Direct Marketing Influences

As we noted, the **marketing mix**—product, promotion, price, and place (channels of distribution)—are the major aspects of marketing strategies. Although these topics (along with the critical topic of market segmentation) are analyzed in detail in the next section of our text, we briefly describe them here. We do so because *the marketing mix represents the major environmental stimuli marketing managers use to affect consumer cognitions and behaviors.*

FIGURE 13–3   **Marketing Environments and Consumer Behaviors**

Environment	Behavior	Examples
Information	Information contact	Reading a billboard while driving
	Communication	Discussing running shoes with a friend at a track meet
		Watching a TV commercial at home
Shopping	Store contact	Window-shopping in a mall
	Product contact	Browsing through an L. L. Bean catalog in a restaurant
		Comparing brands of shirts in-store
Purchasing	Funds access	Obtaining a Visa card at a bank
	Transaction	Going to a checkout counter at Sears
		Calling in an order to L. L. Bean from home
Consumption	Use and repurchase	Eating a taco at Taco Bell
		Recycling aluminum cans at a weigh station
		Disposing of a hot-dog wrapper at a hockey game

FIGURE 13–4   **Some Marketing Strategies for Managing the Environment**

Environmental Management Strategy	Definition	Examples
	Independent Strategies	
Competitive aggression	Company exploits a distinctive competence or improves internal efficiency of resources for competitive advantage	Product differentiation Aggressive pricing Comparative advertising
Competitive pacification	Independent action to improve relations with competitors	Helping competitors find raw material Advertising campaigns that promote entire industry Price umbrellas
Public relations	Establishing and maintaining favorable images in the minds of those making up the environment	Corporate advertising campaigns
Voluntary action	Voluntary management of and commitment to various interest groups, causes, and social problems	McGraw-Hill's efforts to prevent sexist stereotypes 3M's energy conservation program
Dependence development	Creating or modifying relationships such that external groups become dependent on the focal organization	Raising switching costs for suppliers Production of critical defense-related commodities Providing vital information to regulators
Legal action	Company engages in private legal battle with competitor on antitrust, deceptive advertising, or other grounds	Private antitrust suits brought against competitors
Political action	Efforts to influence elected representatives to create a more favorable business environment or limit competition	Corporate constituency programs Issue advertising Direct lobbying
Smoothing	Attempting to resolve irregular demand	Telephone company's lower weekend rates Inexpensive airline fares at off-peak times
Demarketing	Attempts to discourage customers in general or a certain class of customers in particular, on either a temporary or a permanent basis	Shorter hours of operation by gasoline service stations

FIGURE 13–4   (concluded)

Environmental Management Strategy	Definition	Examples
Cooperative Strategies		
Implicit cooperation	Patterned, predictable, and coordinated behaviors	Price leadership
Contracting	Negotiation of an agreement between the organization and another group to exchange goods, services, information, patents, etc.	Contractual vertical and horizontal marketing systems
Co-optation	Process of absorbing new elements into the leadership or policymaking structure of an organization as a means of averting threats to its stability or existence	Consumer representatives, women, and bankers on boards of directors
Coalition	Two or more groups coalesce and act jointly with respect to some set of issues for some period of time	Industry association Political initiatives of the Business Roundtable and the U.S. Chamber of Commerce
Strategic Maneuvering		
Domain selection	Entering industries or markets with limited competition or regulation coupled with ample suppliers and customers; entering high-growth markets	IBM's entry into the personal computer market Miller Brewing Company's entry into the light beer market
Diversification	Investing in different types of businesses, manufacturing different types of products, vertical integration, or geographic expansion to reduce dependence on single product, service, market, or technology	Marriott's investment in different forms of restaurants General Electric's wide product mix
Merger and acquisition	Combining two or more firms into a single enterprise; gaining possession of an ongoing enterprise	Merger between Pan American and National Airlines Phillip Morris's acquisition of Miller Beer

Source: Carl P. Zeithaml and Valarie A. Zeithaml (1984), "Environmental Management: Revising the Marketing Perspective," Journal of Marketing (Spring), pp. 50–51.

HIGHLIGHT 13–3: **Direct Marketing Influences on Consumer Cognitions and Behaviors**

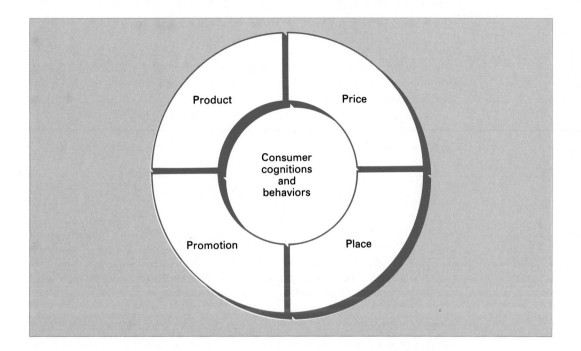

Product. From an environmental perspective, a basic task of marketing management is to place products and services in the consumer's environment so that the products may be purchased, used, and repurchased. Services present special marketing problems, because they are intangible and thus cannot be stored or placed in the environment in the same way that products can. Basic product stimuli include such things as the product itself, packaging, labels, brand marks, and other identification. Even for simple, convenience products, the number of marketing stimuli available for sensory input and analysis is quite large. Consider, for example, some of the stimuli available in examining a simple bar of soap. There are color, size, shape, hardness, smell, feel, weight, and possibly an imprinted brand mark. In the packaging of the soap bar, there are color, brand name, size, net weight, price, ingredients, packaging material, and other promotional and manufacturer information. Thus, even for simple products, there are a variety of stimuli placed in the consumer's environment. (Product strategies are discussed further in Chapter 17 of our text.)

Promotion. Promotion consists of advertising, personal selling, sales promotion, and publicity. From an environmental perspective, promotion consists of placing appropriate information about products and services, their prices, and places where they can be purchased, in the consumer's environment. Promotion is also used to create images of products and services. Overall, the purpose of promotion is to *change* consumer cognitions and behaviors (if consumers are not performing the desired behaviors, such as purchase) and to *maintain* cognitions and behaviors (if the appropriate behaviors are being performed frequently enough to achieve marketing objectives). Promotion is thus a powerful tool for affecting consumer cognitions and behaviors and for achieving marketing objectives. (Promotion strategies are discussed in more detail in Chapter 18.)

Price. Price is the most intangible element of the marketing mix. Marketers can only place *information* about this variable (like a price tag) in the environment, because price is an abstract concept. It is usually perceptions of price that are important, rather than actual dollar amounts. Price perceptions may vary in terms of the individual consumer's financial position and the value the consumer places on money versus various products and services. For example, the oversupply of IBM PCs in 1984 signaled a decrease in price and an opportunity to purchase for consumers who had perceived the previous price to be too high or who simply could not afford one. Price is a very important variable for positioning products, because consumer perceptions of product and service quality (and other dimensions) are often influenced by price. (Pricing strategies are discussed in greater depth in Chapter 19.)

Place. It is often argued in the marketing literature that channels of distribution should be designed from the bottom up. In other words, the appropriate intermediaries for delivering products and services can only be determined by a comprehensive analysis of consumer behavior. This is certainly the view we take in this text. The location and design of retail stores and in-store stimuli are key aspects of successful marketing strategies.

From an environmental perspective, such "place" decisions primarily concern providing products and services when and where they are most likely to favorably affect consumer cognitions and behaviors. For example, the ability to carefully analyze traffic patterns and place restaurants in locations that capitalize on heavy traffic has been one of the keys to the success of McDonald's restaurants. In other words, the restaurants are placed in the physical environment in a way that maximizes the number of consumers who come into visual contact with them. (Channel strategies are discussed further in Chapter 20 of our text.)

Back to the Case

As we noted in this chapter, environmental psychology is a rather new area of study that can hardly supply reliable data to support the promises of DiLeonardo. However, this does not mean that the environmental manipulations described would not affect gambling behavior. Gambling is often a strong habit, which is reinforced on a powerful variable ratio schedule. Also, consider the environment of a gambling casino. The social environment consists of friends, other gamblers, dealers, pit bosses, bartenders, and attractive waiters and waitresses—all of whom generally encourage increased gambling. Free drinks are supplied to gamblers, which could well impair betting decisions as well as perceptions of time. Free food may be given to keep gamblers from leaving a casino to eat.

It should also be noted that a casino's interior is a closed physical environment that offers the potential for considerable behavior control. The lack of windows and clocks, the attractive colors and lighting, exciting noises, celebrities, and happy winners, plus the convenient placement of various gambling devices, tables, and bars encourage consumers to stay in the environment and gamble.

Overall, then, while it is not clear what differential advantage Caesars has for attracting gamblers compared to other casinos, it is a safe bet that Caesars' environment will affect gambling behavior.

Summary

This chapter presented an overview of environmental influences on consumer behavior. Three basic types of environmental influences were delineated: social, physical, and marketing. The social environment includes the effects on consumer behavior of culture, subculture, social class, reference group, and family. The physical environment includes the effects of both spatial and nonspatial factors. The marketing environment includes all stimuli that affect consumer cognitions and behaviors either directly or indirectly. The marketing environments most relevant for consumer research include the information, shopping, purchasing, and consumption environments. A basic premise of the chapter was that marketing strategies must not only be adapted to changing environmental conditions, but also play an important role in creating the environment.

Additional Reading

David C. Funder and Daniel J. Ozer (1983), "Behavior as a Function of the Situation," *Journal of Personality and Social Psychology* (January), pp. 107–112.

Amos Rapoport (1982), *The Meaning of the Built Environment*, Beverly Hills, Calif.: Sage Publications.

Barbara Tversky and Kathleen Hemenway (1983), "Categories of Environmental Scenes," *Cognitive Psychology* (January), pp. 121–149.

Allan W. Wicker (1979), *An Introduction to Ecological Psychology*, Monterey, Calif.: Brooks/Cole Publishing.

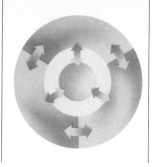

Chapter Fourteen

Macro Social Influences: Culture, Subculture, and Social Class

Wheels for the Baby Boom

Scene: A handsome couple in their mid-30s and prosperous looking, drives along a rocky coast in a wire-wheeled white Cadillac convertible. A message reads: "The Cadillac of convertibles is back."

Scene: The smartly dressed, youngish career woman steps away from her father and husband to stand beside her new Buick Regal. She informs those watching: "Now I make my own decisions . . . I must admit, the guys help a bit. I let them pick the color."

Scene: Lee Iacocca, probably the most recognized businessman in America and possibly the most trusted, walks through a Chrysler auto plant. He's talking about Chrysler's new mini vans—the T-115 Plymouth Voyager and the Dodge Caravan— saying they're built right and priced right and designed with versatility and backed by five year/50,000-mile protection.

The above situations may seem familiar. They should. You've likely seen them many times in magazines or newspapers, or on television. They're just a few examples of the new wave of automotive advertising. Today's automotive ads, and the products they promote, reflect a heightened awareness of the new demographics of the American population.

While major car companies want to sell cars to all age groups, at the top of the list is the baby-boom generation. "[The baby boomers] are really the key to our marketing—both in developing products and in selling the products we have," says an AMC spokesperson. A Chrysler marketing vice president says, "We will have a large segment of new car buyers, bigger than ever before. . . . They want quality and durability. That's the price of admission." An executive in charge of advance design for

General Motors adds, "It's a critical, large group of people that we're going to have to address over the next decade."

As a group, the baby boomers are affluent, well-educated, demanding, and skeptical—and more than any other group, they buy foreign cars. In fact, one third of the baby boomers own a foreign car, compared to 22 percent of the rest of the adult population.

Another of Detroit's target groups is "the mature market," as Madison Avenue refers to older folks. Many of these Americans are at the peak of their earning power. Members of the mature market like to "buy American," often the same make they bought last time. They are conservative and brand loyal. They want good reasons to switch from one make to another.

Baby boomers and the mature market are both hard groups to sell. However, the size and income of these groups suggests it is well worth making the effort.

Source: Excerpted from William Dunn (1984), "Wheels for the Baby Boom: Detroit Discovers Demographics," American Demographics *(May), pp. 27–29.*

Society develops a variety of rules, customs, and objects to influence the cognitions and behaviors of its members. Collectively, these may be referred to as **macro social influences,** in that they are concerned with broad, pervasive phenomena that affect the entire society, or at least large groups within it. Typically, these rules, customs, and objects are designed to enhance the survival of the society or group and the quality of life of its members.

In this chapter we discuss three related types of macro social influences: culture, subculture, and social class. While there is relatively little recent research on these topics in the literature on consumer behavior, the topics are important for two basic reasons. First, in some cases, macro social influences have direct implications for the design of marketing strategies. For example, differences in cognitions and behaviors across various cultures can have a significant influence on the success of international marketing strategies. Second, macro social influences have value for understanding consumer behavior in that they represent the social background that shapes the values, attitudes, and behaviors of various consumer groups. In the cognitive section of our text, these values were represented in the means-end chain as the "ends" that influence consumer decision-making processes. In the behavior section of our text, the analysis of macro social influences was useful in determining appropriate reinforcers for influencing behavior.

Figure 14–1 presents a view of the process by which individuals learn macro social values and behaviors. Four points should be noted. First, we have delineated three types of macro social influences (culture, subculture, and social class), but their definitions and the distinctions between them are not always clear in the literature. In fact, the meaning of these terms is often quite vague. Some authors, for example, treat social class as a type of subcultural influence; others treat it as an entirely separate entity. Similarly, there are seldom clear boundaries delineating cultural from subcultural influences. However, we will offer what we think are useful definitions and distinctions—in spite of a lack of consensus on these issues.

Second, we believe that macro social influences often work in a hierarchical fashion, as shown in Figure 14–1. Different subcultures may respond to cultural values in different ways, just as different social classes may respond to subcultural values in different ways. Consider the commonly discussed American cultural value of achievement. In a rural sub-

FIGURE 14–1   ***Learning Macro Social Values and Behaviors***

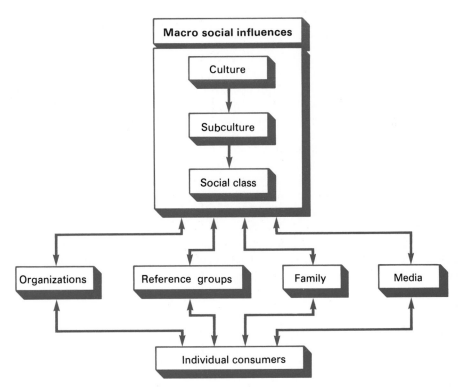

culture, this value may be operationalized by going to an agricultural college, earning a degree, and becoming an excellent farmer. In an urban or suburban subculture, the same achievement value may be operationalized by going to a law school, earning a degree, and becoming a successful lawyer. Similarly, depending on the social class of the individual, decisions may differ greatly in terms of what type of college or university is selected, e.g., a local college or an internationally famous university. Thus, while many individuals may share the same cultural values, their methods of responding to them may differ greatly depending on their subculture and social class, as well as a variety of other influences.

Third, macro social influences are *learned* values and behaviors that are acquired through interaction with the environment. As shown in Figure 14–1, individuals learn these values and behaviors by their contact with organizations, reference groups, family, and the media. Organizations include schools, churches, and work environments, among others. In fact, a primary societal role of teachers and clergy is to transmit cultural or subcultural values to children. Reference groups and families also play a critical role in this process; we will discuss them in the next chapter. A frequently overlooked method by which values are learned is through what collectively could be called "the media." Media influences include both advertising and the content of TV shows, literature, music, and films. We believe the media have a very strong impact on behaviors, values, meanings, and expectations of what life in a particular society should be like.

A final point concerning Figure 14–1 is that consumers learn macro social values and behaviors both directly and vicariously. A primary task of schools, churches, and parents is to teach macro social values and behaviors directly to young children; but we know that even children learn many values and behaviors by observing others and the consequences of their behaviors. In fact, much consumer behavior is likely to be learned vicariously.

Cultural Influences

No single definition of the term *culture* is fully accepted; and in fact, probably several hundred definitions are available in the anthropological and sociological literature.[1] However, for our purposes, we define **culture** as a

---

[1]For example, Sturdivant reports that an earlier study found over 164 definitions of culture. See Frederick D. Sturdivant (1973), "Subculture Theory: Poverty, Minorities, and Marketing," in *Consumer Behavior: Theoretical Sources,* Scott Ward and Thomas S. Robertson (eds.), Englewood Cliffs, N.J.: Prentice-Hall, pp. 469–520.

complex of learned values and behaviors that are shared by a society and are designed to increase the probability of the society's survival. Culture can also be defined to include *material elements,* man-made objects such as products that are created, marketed, purchased, and used by members of society.

Culture is a very broad concept that can include the analysis of any aspect of society. Various types of cultural research have focused on such things as language and communication, religious beliefs and educational methods, values and attitudes, legal and political processes and organizations, economic and technological development, social organizations and institutions, and methods of survival and life enhancement. While all of these could be examined for their effects on consumer cognitions and behaviors, our interest in culture is primarily concerned with how it affects marketing exchanges with consumers in both international and domestic markets.

Cultural Influences in International Markets

There is little question that cultural differences provide difficult challenges for international marketers. Even something that seems simple, such as translating a brand or model name into another language, can cause problems. When Coca-Cola was first introduced into China in the 1920s, the translated meaning of this brand name was "bite the wax tadpole"! The symbols were later changed to mean "happiness in the mouth." The Chevrolet Nova was introduced in Puerto Rico without changing the model name. Unfortunately, Nova when spoken in Spanish is *no va,* which means "it doesn't go." Similarly, the American Motors Matador brand had problems in Puerto Rico because matador means "killer." Ford Motor Company changed the name of the Comet to Caliente when it introduced this car in Mexico. The low sales levels were understood when it was discovered that *caliente* is slang for streetwalker. Sunbeam Corporation introduced its mist-producing hair curling iron in the German market under the name Mist-Stick, which translated meant "manure wand."[2]

The above examples illustrate how a simple difference in language and meanings across cultures can strongly affect the success of a marketing strategy. However, while differences in cultures can often be isolated, there is no full agreement on how these differences should be treated. There are at least three overall approaches, which we discuss below. First, a firm can *adapt its marketing strategy* to the characteristics of each culture. Second, a

---

[2]For further discussion of these and many other examples, see David A. Ricks (1983), *Big Business Blunders: Mistakes in Multinational Marketing,* Homewood, Ill.: Dow Jones-Irwin.

HIGHLIGHT 14–1   **A Comparison of Cultural Differences between the United States and East Asian Countries**

United States	East Asian Countries
• Wealth is more important than equity	Equity is more important than wealth
• Consumption is highly valued	Saving and conserving resources are highly valued
• Individual is the most important part of society	Group is the most important part of society
• Little respect is shown for age and traditional values	Great respect is shown for age and traditional values
• Emphasis on individual motivation	Emphasis on group motivation
• Nuclear families	Cohesive and strong extended families—family ties are important
• Protestant work ethic has declined	Highly disciplined and motivated work force and societies
• Distrust of government	Public service is a moral responsibility
• Personal conflicts common—many lawyers	Avoidance of personal conflicts—few lawyers
• Fluid society; no close social ties	Network of intricate social ties
• Informality is important	Strong sense of protocol and rank
• Education is an investment in individual success	Education is an investment in the prestige of the family

Source: Martin C. Schnitzer, Marilyn L. Liebrenz and Konrad W. Kubin (1985), International Business, *Cincinnati: South-Western Publishing, p. 150.*

firm can *standardize its marketing strategy* across a variety of cultures. The argument over which of these is the preferred strategy has been raging for more than 20 years in the literature on marketing and consumer behavior. Third, a firm can *use a marketing strategy to change the culture.*

Adapting Strategy to Culture

The traditional view of international marketing is that each local culture should be carefully researched for possible differences from the domestic market. Differences in consumer needs, wants, preferences, attitudes, values, as well as shopping, purchasing, and consumption behaviors should be carefully examined. The marketing strategy should then be tailored to appeal to the specific values and behaviors of the culture.

This approach advocates modifying the product, the promotion mix, or any other aspect of marketing strategy to appeal to local cultures. Black & Decker, for example, has to modify its hand tools because electrical outlets and voltages vary in different parts of the world. Philip Morris had to alter its promotions for Marlboro cigarettes in Britain, because the government believed that British children are so impressed with American cowboys, they might be moved to take up smoking. Gillette International avoided advertising razors to European women, because the majority of them do not shave. Nestlé modifies its Nescafé coffee and the promotion for it in the adjoining countries of France and Switzerland to accommodate different tastes and preferences in each nation.[3] Overall, adaptation is considered the tried-and-true method of treating cultural differences in international marketing.

Standardizing Strategy across Cultures

This approach is often called **global marketing.** It argues for marketing the same product in essentially the same way everywhere in the world. It is not a new idea—Coca-Cola has used this basic approach for over 40 years. Coca-Cola calls the approach "one sight, one sound, one sell." Other companies such as Eastman Kodak, Gillette, and Timex have marketed standard products in essentially the same way for several decades.

One of the major advocates of the standardized approach is Professor Theodore Levitt of Harvard Business School. Levitt argues that because of cheap air travel and new telecommunications technology, consumers the world over are thinking and shopping increasingly alike. Tastes, preferences, and motivations of people in different cultures are becoming more homogeneous.[4] Thus, a common brand name, packaging, and communications can be used successfully for many products. For example, given the international popularity of the "Dallas" TV show, actress Victoria Principal sells Jhirmack shampoo all over the world. Similarly, Victor Kiam sells his Remington shavers using the same pitch in 15 different languages. Sales of Remington shavers have gone up 60 percent in Britain and 140 percent in Australia using this approach. Playtex markets its WoW bra in 12 countries using the same advertising appeal.

One advantage of the standardized approach is that it is often less expensive in terms of advertising costs. Executives at Coca-Cola, for in-

[3]See Anne B. Fisher (1984), "The Ad Biz Gloms onto 'Global'," *Fortune* (November 12), pp. 77–80. The examples in this section are taken from this article. Also see Bill Saporito (1984), "Black & Decker's Gamble on 'Globalization'," *Fortune* (May 14), pp. 40–48.

[4]For example, see "Levitt: Global Companies to Replace Dying Multinationals," *Marketing News* (March 15, 1985), p. 15; Theodore Levitt (1983), *The Marketing Imagination*, New York: The Free Press, chapter 2; Theodore Levitt (1983), "The Globalization of Markets," *Harvard Business Review* (May–June), pp. 92–102.

HIGHLIGHT 14–2   **Coca-Cola: A Successful Global Marketing Strategy**

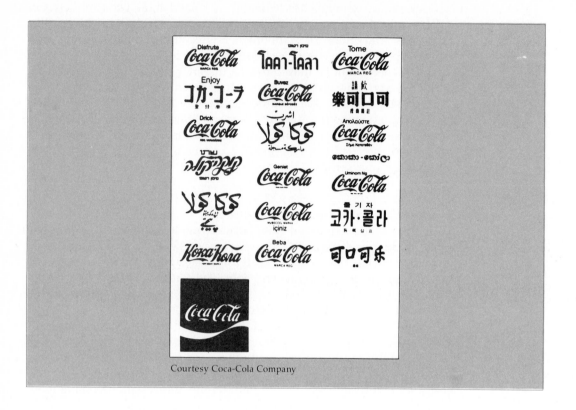

Courtesy Coca-Cola Company

stance, estimate that they save more than $8 million a year in the cost of thinking up new imagery. Texas Instruments runs the same ads throughout Europe rather than having individual ad campaigns for each country, and estimates its savings at $30,000 per commercial. Playtex produced

Courtesy of International Playtex, Inc.

Frames from TV commercials for WoW bras: The WoW logo is used in English-speaking countries; Armagique is the French version; and Alas is Spanish.

standardized ads for 12 countries for $250,000, whereas the average cost of producing a single Playtex ad for the United States is $100,000.[5]

There is no question that, for some products, a global (standardized) marketing approach works well. However, we believe that two issues cloud the debate between advocates of adapting versus standardizing international marketing approaches. First is the question of the nature of the product and how "standardized" the global approach is. For example, advocates of standardizing recognized that Black & Decker had to modify its products to suit local electrical outlets and voltages; yet they would argue that the meaning and use of such products is becoming similar across cultures. Thus, the same type of promotion campaign could work well in different cultures.

Second, and perhaps more important, is the question of whether advocates of the standardizing approach are focusing on a long-term trend toward similarity across cultures or are suggesting that cultures are nearly identical today. Unlike the detractors of this approach, we believe that global marketing advocates are focusing on a long-term trend toward global homogeneity. We also believe advocates are suggesting that this is a trend marketers should be aware of and adapt to when appropriate. Thus, in essence, both sides are arguing for marketers to adapt to cultural trends; and there would seem to be little disagreement between the two positions at this level.

Change the Culture

The first approach we discussed argues for adapting marketing strategy to local cultures. The second approach argues that differences in various cultures are decreasing and in some cases can be ignored. The third strategy suggests that in some cases there are important cultural factors at work in a market, and that marketing strategies can be developed to successfully change these factors to achieve organizational objectives.

One thing we want to make clear is that cultural values and behaviors are usually difficult to change. In fact, most changes in cultures have historically been slow. However, this should not obscure the fact that cultures *do* change and that marketing strategies can play an important role in this change. Marketing does not simply adapt to changing cultural values and behaviors of consumers, but is an active part of the change process.

For example, consider the changes in Communist China reported in a recent *Fortune* article:

> China fever is easy to catch. Upbeat music from the American movie *Flashdance* greets arriving executives at Peking Airport. The new

---

[5]Christine Dugas and Marilyn A. Harris (1985), "Playtex Kicks Off a One-Ad-Fits-All Campaign," *Business Week* (December 16), pp. 48–49.

Great Wall Hotel, a U.S. joint venture, resembles the Hyatt Regency in Dallas. American-style blue jeans and brightly colored ski parkas are beginning to replace baggy pants and Mao jackets. Offices and factories no longer shut down for two hours at midday so that everyone can take a nap, and Chinese negotiators, long famous for haggling endlessly over every detail of a deal, now are saying things like "time is money."[6]

Apparently, this culture is changing. It is moving from a strict Communist society to one that accepts, if not encourages, the development of capitalism. While it may be argued that Western capitalists who invest in China are simply adapting to a cultural change, it seems likely that they are at least in part responsible for the change. By actively seeking exchanges in the huge Chinese market, and by making capital, products, and marketing skills available to it, marketers are playing an important part in bringing this cultural change about. Similarly, Japan, Taiwan, and Singapore did not become dynamic industrialized countries independent of Western marketing organizations that sought exchanges with them.

Our discussion is intended to make two points. First, marketing is not a phenomenon that is separate from cultures or societies, but is an integral part of them that both changes and is changed by them. Second, to achieve organizational objectives, one long-run strategy may be to attempt to change cultural values and behaviors. For example, several years ago, a manufacturer of baby formula marketed vigorously to change mothers in some Third World countries from breast feeding to using the company's product. The campaign was very successful in convincing mothers that breast feeding was not as healthful for their children as the company's formula, and it dramatically changed their feeding practices. Unfortunately, because of poor sanitation and improper formula preparation, infant mortalities increased. Thus, the preference for and practice of breast feeding had to be reinstilled in those countries, which was done successfully. This company clearly changed cultural preferences and behaviors— and then changed them back—in a relatively short time.

Cultural Influences in the Domestic Market

In the domestic market, cultural influences are just as important as they are in international markets; but they may be more difficult to see, because they are part of our daily lives. For example, in Chapter 12 we presented a

---

[6]Louis Kraar (1985), "China after Marx: Open for Business?" *Fortune* (February 18), pp. 28–33.

FIGURE 14–2   **What Is this Figure, Really?**

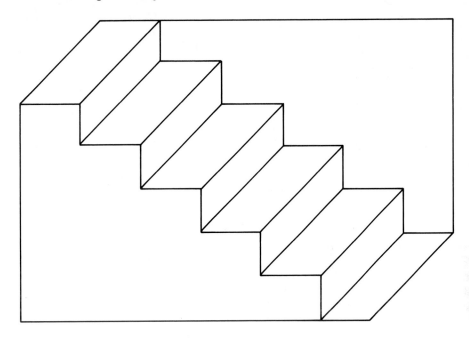

model of a behavior sequence for a retail goods purchase (Figure 12–2). We suspect that most of you could readily identify with and understand the behaviors listed. This is because all of the behaviors are common for most members of our culture. Yet it is unlikely that many of you have previously delineated each of these behaviors or considered them a cultural phenomenon, because they are such a common part of our day-to-day lives.

Similarly, you may not have considered the degree to which cognitions are culturally based. For example, what do you see when you look at Figure 14–2? Most of us consider it to be a drawing of a staircase with the upper surface of the stairs visible. However, when viewed by members of a number of African tribes whose culture does not include the custom of depicting three-dimensional objects by two-dimensional drawings, the figure was seen only as an array of lines. Thus, even what we "see" and our interpretation of objects are influenced by our culture.[7]

As is the case in international markets, it is usually easier to adapt to cultural values than to try to change them. Many lists of values have been

---

[7]See A. F. Chalmers (1976), *What Is This Thing Called Science?* St. Lucia, Queensland, Australia: University of Queensland Press, pp. 22–23.

developed which are designed to characterize the core values of Americans. Figure 14–3 presents a summary of 10 such values and their relevance for consumer behavior and marketing strategy.[8]

A variety of examples of marketing and promotion strategies seem to be fully consistent with one or more of the values in Figure 14–3. For example, McDonald's restaurants ran a series of ads focusing on the "You deserve a break today" theme; and Miller's beer ran a series of ads with the "It's Miller time" theme. What values are these ads directed at? It seems clear that achievement, success, and activity are all being considered, as well as the idea that these products are rewards for a job well done.

As further examples of how marketing is directed at specific values, Xerox ran a series of ads depicting hard-working individuals spending time at home with the family on special occasions. This freedom was made possible by the installation of a new Xerox information processing system at the office. The system was so efficient and practical that work could be finished much more quickly. Michelob beer ads typically model "the good life" and material comforts. Highly visible brand names and symbols on automobiles and clothing enable consumers to differentiate themselves and assert their individuality. At the same time, the brands must be acceptable to consumers' social groups to exhibit external conformity. Avis's classic commercials for rental-car service that argue, "We're number two, so we try harder" may appeal to humanitarian values. Finally, the multi-billion-dollar cosmetic industry prospers and grows primarily to serve the cultural value of youthfulness.

While many American marketers design strategies that are consistent with established cultural values, we note that marketing also plays a role in the development and acceptance of those values. For example, many factors may have contributed to the fact that people eat out more often; but certainly the availability and marketing of fast-food restaurants strongly influenced this change. Similarly, the dramatic change in values and behaviors connected with the use of birth control were strongly influenced by the availability and marketing of improved birth control methods. We can see, then, that marketing strategies and tasks are part of a culture and not independent of it.

Subcultural Influences

Subcultures are segments within a culture that share distinguishing values and patterns of behavior that differ from those of the overall culture.

---

[8]For a discussion of some major cultural changes, see John Naisbitt (1984), *Megatrends: Ten New Directions Transforming Our Lives,* New York: Warner Books.

FIGURE 14–3   **Summary of American Core Values**

Value	General Features	Relevance to Consumer Behavior and Marketing Management
1. Achievement and success	Hard work is good; success flows from hard work	Acts as a justification for acquisition of goods ("You deserve it")
2. Activity	Keeping busy is healthy and natural	Stimulates interest in products that are time-savers and enhance leisure-time activities
3. Efficiency and practicality	Admiration of things that solve problems (e.g., save time and effort)	Stimulates purchase of products that function well and save time
4. Progress	People can improve themselves; tomorrow should be better	Stimulates desire for new products that fulfill unsatisfied needs, acceptance of products that claim to be "new" or "improved"
5. Material comfort	"The good life"	Fosters acceptance of convenience and luxury products that make life more enjoyable
6. Individualism	Being one's self (e.g., self-reliance, self-interest, and self-esteem)	Stimulates acceptance of customized or unique products that enable a person to "express his or her own personality"
7. Freedom	Freedom of choice	Fosters interest in wide product lines and differentiated products
8. External conformity	Uniformity of observable behavior; desire to be accepted	Stimulates interest in products that are used or owned by others in the same social group
9. Humanitarianism	Caring for others, particularly the underdog	Stimulates patronage of firms that compete with market leaders
10. Youthfulness	A state of mind that stresses being young at heart or appearing young	Stimulates acceptance of products that provide the illusion of maintaining or fostering youth

Source: Leon G. Schiffman and Leslie Lazar Kanuck (1983), Consumer Behavior, *2d ed., Englewood Cliffs, N.J.: Prentice-Hall, p. 420.*

FIGURE 14–4   **Geographic Difference in Most Popular Vehicle**

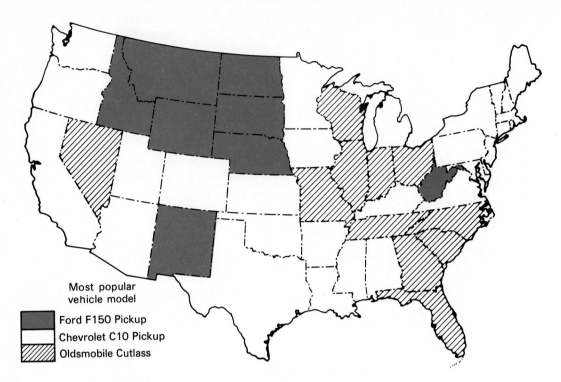

Source: Eugene Carlson, "Personality of Area's Drivers Offers Key to Auto's Success,"
The Wall Street Journal, *December 13, 1983, p. 33. Reprinted by permission of* The
Wall Street Journal," © *Dow Jones & Company, Inc., 1983. All rights reserved.*

Many types of distinctions have been used to classify subcultures. For
example, socioeconomic group (upper class, lower class), ethnic/racial
group (black, Hispanic), geographic area (South, Midwest), age (adolescents, the elderly), community type (rural, urban), institutional affiliation
(educational, corporate), religious organization (Catholic, Muslim), political entities (conservatives, radicals), and a number of others.[9] Because a
detailed treatment of each of these subcultures is beyond the scope of this
text, we have selected just three for further consideration: geographic area,

---

[9]See Sturdivant, "Subculture Theory," pp. 476–477.

age group, and ethnic group. In addition, we will analyze socioeconomic groups in our discussion of social class.

Geographic Areas

People in different parts of the country often exhibit different patterns of behavior and share different values and lifestyles. These differences may be affected by such things as topography, climate, natural resources, economic and population structure, and the distribution of various nationality groups within the region.

Consumption behavior also varies across different parts of the country.[10] For example, the map in Figure 14–4 indicates the most popular vehicles in different states. The Ford pickup is the favorite in a number of northwestern states, while the Chevy pickup dominates a number of southern states. The Oldsmobile Cutlass is a clear favorite in a number of Great Lakes and south Atlantic states.

There are many ways of dividing the United States for geographic subculture analysis. In one creative approach, Joel Garreau divided the North American continent into nine geographic areas that he labeled the "nine nations" of North America.[11] Garreau argued that a variety of economic, social, cultural, political, topographical, and nature resource factors combine to form these nine areas. U.S. marketers concentrate on the eight areas shown in Figure 14–5.

Figure 14–6 presents a capsule summary of the nature of these nine areas. For some products and services, this framework may be useful in developing specific marketing strategies to appeal to consumers in each area. For example, preferences for and consumption of various beverages varies dramatically in different geographic areas of the United States, and analysis of these profiles may help to determine which beverages can be marketed most effectively.[12]

Age Groups

Age groups can also be analyzed as subcultures, in that they often have distinctive values and behaviors. Many different age groups can be iden-

---

[10]See Thomas Moore (1985), "Different Folks, Different Strokes," *Fortune* (September 16), pp. 65–72.

[11]Joel Garreau (1981), *The Nine Nations of North America*, Boston: Houghton Mifflin Co.

[12]For a more detailed discussion, see Del I. Hawkins, Don Roupe, and Kenneth A. Coney (1981), "The Influence of Geographic Subcultures in the United States," in *Advances in Consumer Research*, Vol. 8, Kent B. Monroe (ed.), Ann Arbor, Mich.: Association for Consumer Research, pp. 713–717.

FIGURE 14–5   **The Eight Nations of the United States**

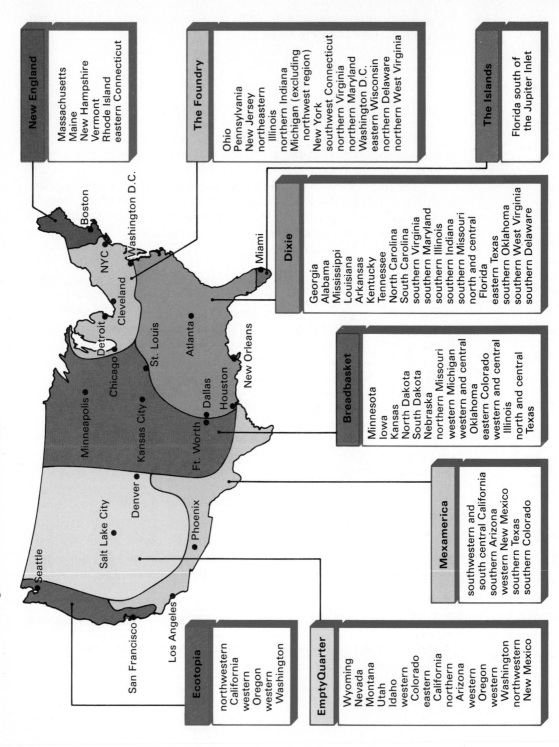

Source: Adapted from Nine Nations of North America by Joel Garreau. Copyright ©1981 by Joel Garreau. Adapted and reprinted by permission of Houghton Mifflin Company.

FIGURE 14–6   **Capsule Summary of the Nine Nations**

Nation	Description
The Foundry Capital: Detroit	Industrialized, urban, losing population, jobs; heavy unionism; old technology; work oriented. On the decline but will bounce back because of water resources; Emulators, Inner Directeds, I-Am-Me's.
Mexamerica Capital: Los Angeles	Heavy Hispanic culture; mix of well and poorly educated; hardworking, entrepreneurial spirit, growth-oriented. Becoming most influential nation, Emulators, Achievers, Societally conscious.
The Islands Capital: Miami	Caribbean and Latin American influence, heavy illegal drug trade, young and old live here; has little in common with rest of Florida and Dixie; diverse population.
Quebec Capital: Quebec City	French-speaking Canada; steeped in history, tradition, ethnic pride; very homogeneous culture; plentiful resources; diversified economy; fiercely independent.
Dixie Capital: Atlanta	Trying to catch up; smalltown way of life; undergoing rapid social and economic change; economy minded. Need-Driven, Belongers.
New England Capital: Boston	Poorest nation but "high-tech" influx bringing it back; politically diverse, cautious, brand loyal. Inner Directed, Societally conscious, Achievers.
The Empty Quarter Capital: Denver	Wide-open spaces, energy rich, mineral rich; largest area, smallest population; frontier ethic; major economic growth foreseen; hardworking, conservative, blue-collar; Inner Directed.
Ecotopia Capital: San Francisco	"High-tech," interest-rate-based economy; quality of life important; mottos: Leave me alone, Small is beautiful; young, educated, affluent; Inner Directed, Experientials.
Breadbasket Capital: Kansas City	Agricultural economy; mainstream America; stable, at-peace-with-itself population; conservative; Conformist Belongers.

Source: Adapted from Nine Nations of North America *by Joel Garreau. Copyright © 1981 by Joel Garreau. Adapted and reprinted by permission of Houghton Mifflin Company.*

HIGHLIGHT 14–3 **Teenage Spending**

Boys Aged 16 to 19		Girls Aged 16 to 19	
Income		Income	
Allowance	$21.80	Allowance	$22.05
Earnings	31.65	Earnings	32.55
Total	$53.45	Total	$54.60
Expenditures		Expenditures	
Movies, dating, entertainment	$8.90	Clothing	$13.30
Gasoline and auto	8.50	Cosmetics and fragrances	10.25
Clothing	8.15	Gasoline and auto	4.40
Food and snacks	6.60	Movies and entertainment	4.30
Personal grooming	3.45	Food and snacks	3.90
Hobbies	2.00	Beauty parlor and hair products	2.40
Coin-operated video games	1.90	Jewelry	2.10
Books, paperbacks	.95	Records	1.45
Magazines	.95	Books, paperbacks	1.10
Records	.90	School supplies	.85
School supplies	.80	Magazines	.70
Cigarettes	.20	Coin-operated video games	.30
Total	$43.30	Cigarettes	.25
Savings	$10.15	Total	$45.30
		Savings	$9.30

The weekly incomes of teenage boys and girls are about the same, but they spend their money differently.

Source: Rand Youth Poll (1983), Teenage Economic Power, as reported in Doris L. Walsh (1985), "Targeting Teens," American Demographics (February), p. 25.

tified and analyzed, but we will discuss three: teens, baby boomers, and the mature market.

The Teen Market

The American teenage population has been gaining affluence, although it has been shrinking in size.[13] There are about 26 million persons in the

---

[13]This discussion is based on Doris L. Walsh (1985), "Targeting Teens," American Demographics (February), pp. 20–25.

United Stages aged 13 to 19. This number is expected to decrease to about 23 million in the early 1990s and then increase to about 27 million by the year 2000.

This group is important not only because it has a major influence on household purchases, but also because of its own discretionary purchasing power. The annual Rand Youth Poll estimated that teenagers spent over $45 billion in 1983 and put more than $9 billion into savings. Fully 16 percent of teens own a car, 66 percent own a record player, 34 percent a television, 86 percent a camera, 21 percent a telephone, 12 percent a home computer, and 14 percent own stocks and bonds.

Courtesy Golden Grain Macaroni Co.

A food ad in *Seventeen* magazine directed to teenagers.

Several studies have found that teenagers do a large portion of the grocery shopping for the family. Estimates are that from 49 to 61 percent of teenage girls and 26 to 33 percent of teenage boys frequently do the grocery shopping for the family. In addition, about 60 percent of teens help make up the supermarket shopping list, and 40 percent select some of the brands to be purchased. It is no wonder that brand-name food marketers advertise in magazines such as *Seventeen* to reach this market.

Brand loyalty has also been found to form early among teenage shoppers. In a survey of women ages 20 to 34, at least 30 percent said they made a brand decision as a teenager and continued to use the brand to the present. Sixty-four percent said they looked for specific brands when they were teenagers. Thus, a final reason this market is so important for many products and services is the potential to develop brand loyalty that may last a lifetime!

Baby Boomers

Baby boomers are often defined as those persons born between 1946 and 1962. There are about 68 million people in this group—about a third of the U.S. population. This group is currently in its early 20s to late 30s and entering its prime earning and spending years. The baby-boomer market will be the largest and most affluent in history, and will have a major economic impact for the next 45 years (see Figure 14–7).[14] In fact, in 1982 dollars, by 1995 the 35 to 44 age group will have $870 billion to spend, well over twice as much as the same age group did in 1980. Within the next decade or so, baby boomers will account for about half of all discretionary spending.[15]

The baby-boomer subculture is characterized as having a blend of "me-generation" and old-fashioned family values, and as strongly influencing the values of other groups. A study by Cadwell Davis Partners ad agency found that most people who aren't baby boomers feel as if they are. Baby boomers place high emphasis on health and exercise and have reduced their consumption of cigarettes, coffee, and strong alcoholic beverages. Forty-six percent of this market has completed college, and two thirds of baby-boomer wives work, compared with about half the wives in the rest of the population. In terms of products, this group places major emphasis on quality and is far less concerned with bargain hunting than were their parents.

---

[14]This discussion is based on Geoffrey Calvin (1984), "What the Baby-Boomers Will Buy Next," *Fortune* (October 15), pp. 28–34.

[15]William Dunn (1984), "Wheels for the Baby Boom: Detroit Discovers Demographics," *American Demographics* (May), pp. 27–29.

Baby boomers will clearly have a strong impact on markets for housing, cars, food, clothing and cosmetics, and financial services. In addition, although they are having fewer children per household, the sheer size of the group will lead to an increase in births into the 1990s—a "baby-boom echo." Given the large incomes and small family sizes of this group, spending per child will likely be the largest in history. Markets for children's products will expand accordingly. Toy sales, for example, are ex-

Courtesy Campbell Soup Co.

Yuppies—young, urban professionals—are the prestige market of the baby-boom generation. This ad in a food service trade magazine was keyed to a specific opportunity market.

FIGURE 14–7   **Aging of the Baby Boomers**

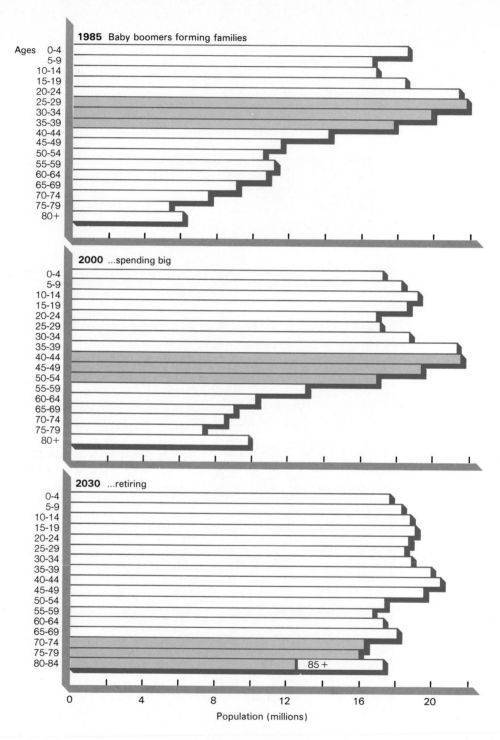

Source: Adapted from Geoffrey Calvin (1984), "What the Baby Boomers Will Buy Next," Fortune (October 15), p. 31.

pected to increase more than twice as fast as the population of children for whom they are intended. Other markets, such as child care services and computer software for tots, may double in the next few years.

The baby-boomer market is, then, the most lucrative and challenging marketers have ever seen. It is no wonder many firms are designing new products and redesigning and repositioning old ones for this market. Wheaties used to appeal to kids as "the breakfast of champions"; now it is promoted to adults with slogans as "what the big boys eat." Commercials for Snickers candy bars show adults rather than children eating this candy for a snack. Crest and other brands have introduced toothpaste formulas to fight plaque, a distinctively adult problem. Levi Strauss has redesigned its jeans to give a little extra room in the seat to accommodate "booming boomer bodies." Even Clearasil, traditionally an antiacne medication for teenagers, has developed Clearasil Adult Care to appeal to the growing number of baby-boomer adults with skin problems.

The Mature Market

Many marketers have traditionally ignored the **mature market,** because it was assumed to have low purchasing power. While some marketers have catered to the 55 to 64 age group, those over 65 have often been ignored. However, there is now a growing recognition of the size and changing economic character of this market.[16]

A breakdown of several age groups in the mature market is shown in Figure 14–8. In total, the mature market will grow from about 51 million in 1985 to 56 million persons in 1995, representing about one fifth of the U.S. population.

In addition to its sheer size, the economic character of this market deserves careful consideration. While many of the members of this group no longer work, they often have considerable discretionary income. Unlike younger groups, members of mature markets are usually free of most of the financial burdens associated with child rearing, mortgages, and furnishing a household. Given these differences, *per capita discretionary income* is higher for the mature group than for any other age group. In 1980, for example, for those aged 55 to 59, per capita discretionary income was $3,500; for those aged 60 to 64 per capita discretionary income was $3,700; for those aged 65 and over, it was the highest of all—$4,100. These figures compare quite favorably with the approximately $2,000 in discretionary income available to people aged 30 to 39.

It is also important to recognize how the mature market is changing.

---

[16]This discussion is based on William Lazer (1985), "Inside the Mature Market," *American Demographics* (March), pp. 23–25.

In 1985, only 9 percent of the elderly had a college degree and only some 44 percent had graduated from high school. By 1995, the share of older people with college educations will rise to more than 12 percent, and at least one fourth will have had some college. Thus, the mature market is becoming more educated and likely will have greater incomes. The increase in income will also come about because many of those in tomorrow's mature market will benefit from much improved pension and retirement plans.

Finally, because many people in the mature market subculture are retired, they have more time to enjoy entertainment and leisure activities. Although this market has historically spent more money on food at home than away from home, restaurants now cater to them with senior citizen discounts, early bird dinners, and menus designed for the tastes and re-

---

FIGURE 14–8   **The Mature Markets: 1985 and 1995**

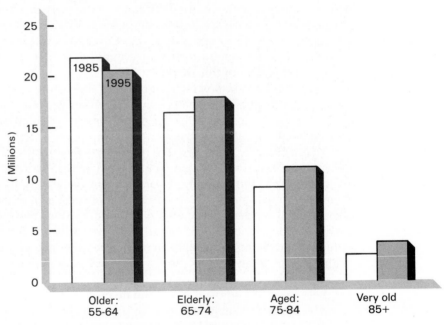

Though the "older" population (aged 55 to 64) will shrink slightly in the next decade, it will remain the largest segment of the mature market.

Source: Bureau of the Census (1984), "Projections of the Population of the United States by Age, Sex, and Race, 1983 to 2080," Current Population Reports, *Series P-25, No. 952, as reported in William Lazer (1985), "Inside the Mature Market,"* American Demographics *(March), p. 24.*

There's no better time
to have the
time of your life.

≈AARP≈   The **Prudential** 🅿
We want to help.

Courtesy AARP and Prudential Life Insurance Co.

Tasteful ads appeal to the mature market.

quirements of older people. The elderly represent a significant market for skin care products, vitamins and minerals, health and beauty aids, and medications that ease pain and promote the performance of everyday activities. In addition, they are a significant market for condominiums in the Sun Belt states, time-share arrangements, travel and vacations, cultural activities, and luxury items given as gifts to their children and grandchil-

HIGHLIGHT 14–4   **Problems with Ads for Older Folks**

Creating ads that please older people continues to be a thorny issue for marketers, as evidenced by the fuss over the three old women in the Wendy's "Where's the Beef?" commercials. Ads that aren't carefully planned may not pass muster at some of the magazines targeted at people over 50. *Modern Maturity,* for example, appeals to some advertisers because it has a circulation of more than 9 million. But it won't accept what it deems to be downbeat ads or promotions for products such as diapers for incontinent adults. It also censors words like "pain" and "suffer" from headlines.

Even a seemingly tasteful ad for Eastern Air Lines' special travel discounts for older people drew frowns from some of the magazine's staff. It showed a couple literally jumping for joy. "We ran it but thought it was silly and undignified," says Treesa Drury, advertising standards manager. Now, Eastern ads show tourist-style snapshots of an attractive gray-haired couple simply posing in front of the Manhattan skyline and the Golden Gate Bridge.

Source: Ronald Alsop (1984), "Firms Try New Way to Tap Growing Over-50 Population," The Wall Street Journal (August 23), p.37.

dren. Overall, then, the mature market subculture represents an excellent marketing opportunity that will become even better in the future.[17]

Ethnic Groups

One in five Americans today is black, Hispanic, Asian, or a member of some other minority group. In most major cities, the minority share of the population is much higher than this and is steadily rising. In New York, Chicago, Los Angeles, and Detroit, over half the population belongs to one of these minority groups. By the year 2000, nearly 70 percent of the residents of Chicago will be minorities.[18] At present, the two major minority groups targeted by marketers are the black and Hispanic subcultures.

---

[17]For a complete work on this market, see Charles D. Schewe (1985), *The Elderly Market: Selected Readings,* Chicago: American Marketing Association. Also see Eleanor Johnson Tracy (1985), "The Gold in the Gray," *Fortune* (October 14), pp. 137–138.

[18]John D. Kasarda (1984), "Hispanics and City Change," *American Demographics* (November), pp. 24–29.

FIGURE 14–9 **Demographic and Socioeconomic Characteristics of Blacks, Hispanics, and Whites**

Characteristic	Black Subculture	Hispanic Subculture	Whites
Demographic			
Median age	25.2	23.0	31.2
Mean family size	3.7	3.4	3.2
Percent urban	81.1%	87.6%	73.3%
Percent households with female head	47.2%	28.2%	11.9%
Socioeconomic			
Median income	$12,618	$14,711	$20,840
Percent with 4 + years in college	8.4%	7.7%	17.2%
Percent white-collar job	37.8%	21.6%	54.3%

Source: Statistical Abstract of the United States, Washington, D.C.: U.S. Government Printing Office (1983).

The Black Subculture

As with any subculture, it would be erroneous to believe that all blacks share the same values and behavior patterns, or that these values and behaviors are necessarily different from those of white Americans. However, the majority of this group shares a common background of income and educational deprivation, the results of which can be seen in Figure 14–9.

Overall, the black subculture is the largest American minority group, with 28 million persons and purchasing power of $168 billion. Although not true in the past, today it is common to see black models featured in ads, especially for products targeted to this group. This is particularly true for food, clothing, and health and beauty aids. In the latter category, blacks spend over $750 million per year. As a result, a number of major companies such as Revlon and Max Factor have designed specific products for this market.[19]

As we have noted, there are many differences in black consumption patterns and purchasing behavior, as is true of any subculture. Figure

---

[19]See Nejdet Delener (1985), "Cosmetics & HBA's for Black Consumers: A Growing, Profitable—But Ignored—Market," Marketing News (March 15), p. 32.

14–10 presents the results of one study that identified five different lifestyles for black women. Clearly, these differences could have important implications for designing marketing strategies for different groups within the black subculture.

The Hispanic Subculture

The Hispanic subculture comprises a number of different Spanish-speaking nationalities such as Mexican, Puerto Rican, and Cuban. While each of these could be analyzed as a separate subculture, they are usually grouped together for marketing purposes, because they share a common language. This group, sometimes called the Latin subculture, is estimated to have over $70 billion in purchasing power. As we showed earlier in Figure 14–9, Hispanics share several demographic similarities with the black subculture. Income and education levels more closely resemble those of the black subculture than they do the white group, for instance.

The Hispanic subculture is the most rapidly growing minority group, due to high immigration and birth rates. Figure 14–11 shows how some marketers are actively pursuing this rapidly growing market.

FIGURE 14–10   **Lifestyle Differences among Black Females, Ages 18 to 49**

Segment	Size	Age	Income	Basic Lifestyle Attitude
Conservative traditionalist	32%	Older	Higher	Views drugs and liquor as steps along the path to degeneration
Fashion conscious	31	Younger	Lower	Liberated in ideas about sex, liquor, and drugs, likes to try new hairstyles and would rather dress for fashion than comfort
Independent	16	Middle	Significantly higher	Outgoing and on the way up, financially secure and independent, prefer living in suburbs to city
Girl next door	12	Younger	Significantly lower	Described as the girl next door, she has strong moral values and likes trying new hairstyles as much as she likes to bake, which she often does
Conservative thinker	9	Older	Significantly lower	They shop for sales, disapprove of installment purchases and believe that men should rule the household while women take care of it

Source: "New Survey Reveals Five Lifestyle Segments of Age 18–49 Black Women," Marketing News *(August 21, 1981), p. 6.*

However, just as is true in international marketing to various cultures, marketing to domestic subcultures requires a careful analysis of values and behaviors. For example, a telephone company tried to target to the Hispanic market by employing Puerto Rican actors. In the ad, the wife said to her husband, "Run downstairs and phone Mary. Tell her we'll be a little late." However, the commercial ignored Hispanic values and behaviors. For one thing, Hispanic wives seldom order their husbands around; and for another, few Hispanics would feel it necessary to phone if they will be late, because being late is expected. Similarly, Coors ads featuring the slogan "Taste the high country" were not effective with Mexican Americans, who could not identify with mountain life. The Spanish-language Coors ads were modified to suggest that the mountains were a good source of beer, but that one did not need to live in the mountains to enjoy it. The

FIGURE 14–11   **Marketing Efforts Directed at Hispanic Consumers**

Durrett Wagner/The Bookworks, Inc.

These billboards were erected in the Hispanic section of El Paso, Texas; three of them have the same slogans that were used on English-language billboards throughout the country.

new slogan in its English translation became "Take the beer from the high country and bring it to your high country—wherever it may be."[20]

Social Class Influences

One of the leading experts in social class research, Richard Coleman, has made the following observations:

> There are no two ways about it: social class is a difficult idea. Sociologists, in whose discipline the concept emerged, are not of one mind about its value and validity. Consumer researchers, to whose field its use has spread, display confusion about when and how to apply it. The American public is noticeably uncomfortable with the realities about life that it reflects. All who try to measure it have trouble. Studying it rigorously and imaginatively can be monstrously expensive. Yet, all these difficulties notwithstanding, the proposition still holds: social class is worth troubling over for the insights it offers on the marketplace behavior of the nation's consumers.[21]

We agree with Coleman's observations concerning both the problems with social class and the value of the concept. For the purposes of our text, **social class** refers to a national status hierarchy by which groups and individuals are classified on the basis of esteem and prestige. According to Coleman, identification with each class is influenced most heavily by educational credentials and occupation (including income as a measure of work success); but it is also affected by social skills, status aspirations, community participation, family history, cultural level, recreational habits, physical appearance, and social acceptance by a particular class. Thus, social class is a composite of many personal and social attributes rather than a single characteristic such as income or education.

Figure 14–12 presents a social class hierarchy and a thumbnail sketch of the types of persons who make up these groups. There are three points to note. First, this approach views social classes as consisting of three major groups—Upper Americans, Middle Americans, and Lower Americans—each of which shares distinct values and behavior patterns to some

---

[20]Ricks, *Big Business Blunders,* p. 70. Also see Edward C. Baig (1985), "Buenos Dias, Consumers," *Fortune* (December 23), pp. 79–80.

[21]Richard P. Coleman (1983), "The Continuing Significance of Social Class to Marketing," *Journal of Consumer Research* (December), pp. 265–280. Much of the discussion in this part of the chapter is based on Coleman's view of social class, as described in this excellent article.

An appeal to the cultural value of achievement.

Changing a product form to appeal to changing values and lifestyles.

Courtesy Del Monte Corporation

A product targeted to upscale social classes.

Dessert.

Dessert, in its truest sense, is no longer considered an indulgence that can only follow a meal. Not when you can indulge in the spell of Godiva® Chocolate at the merest quirk of temptation. You need only dream of the intriguing shapes and delectable fillings. Then dessert will be at your beck and call. Godiva Chocolates are available in three, two, one and one-half pound assortments, packaged in scintillating golden ballotins.

GODIVA®
Chocolatier
BRUXELLES · NEW YORK
PARIS · COLOGNE

Godiva Chocolatier, 701 Fifth Avenue, New York, New York 10022.

Courtesy Godiva Chocolatier

In families, purchasers of products are not always the users.

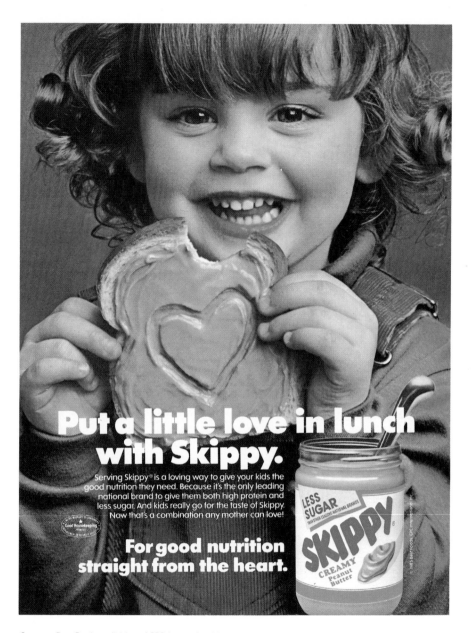

Courtesy Best Foods, a division of CPC International Inc.

degree. Second, in each of these three major groups there are two or three subgroups with values and behaviors that can be further differentiated. While there are a number of similarities in values and behaviors within groups in a given class, there are still vast differences in family situations and income totals among subgroups.

Third, there are families in each group that could be further classified as relatively overprivileged, average, or underprivileged. Overprivileged families in each social class are those with incomes usually 25 percent to 30 percent above the median for the class, who therefore have money left over to seek forms of a "better life" preferred by the class. However, because these families continue to share values, behaviors, and associations with other members of the class, they typically do not become part of a higher social class. The average families are those in the middle income range and can afford the kind of house, car, apparel, food, furniture, and appliances expected by their peers. Finally, the underprivileged families have incomes that fall at least 15 percent below the class midpoint and

---

FIGURE 14–12   ***A Social Class Hierarchy***

Upper Americans

Upper-Upper (0.3% of population), "old family names"; inherited wealth and aristocratic backgrounds

Lower-Upper (1.2% of population), "accepted new money"; the newer social elite drawn from professional and corporate leadership

Upper-Middle (12.5% of population), "collegiate credentials expected"; college-educated managers and professionals who enjoy private clubs, causes, and the arts

Middle Americans

Middle-Class (32% of population), "white-collar associations"; average-pay white-collar workers and their blue-collar friends who live on "the better side of town" and "do the proper things"

Working-Class (38% of population), "blue-collar lifestyle"; average-pay blue-collar workers who lead a working-class life regardless of income or school background

Lower Americans

Lower but not the Lowest (9% of population), "definitely below the mainstream"; working and not on welfare, living standard is just above poverty

Real Lower-Lower (7% of population), "the welfare world"; on welfare; visibly poverty-stricken; "dirtiest jobs" when occasionally working; "bums"; "common criminals"

Source: Adapted from Richard P. Coleman (1983), "The Continuing Significance of Social Class to Marketing," Journal of Consumer Research *(December), p. 267.*

therefore must scrimp and sacrifice in purchasing to make proper appearances.

Social class and relative standing within a class are important sources of consumers' values and behaviors. Most of the people an individual interacts with on a day-to-day basis are likely to be members of that person's social class. Family, peer groups, and friends at work, school, and in the neighborhood are all likely to be of the same social class. These people teach the individual appropriate values for the class as well as behaviors that are acceptable to it. This process can occur either through direct instruction ("You don't have a chance anymore unless you go to college") or vicariously (an individual sees neighborhood friends going to college, graduating, and purchasing expensive new cars).

At a conceptual level, then, detailed breakdowns of social classes are very useful for investigating the process by which consumers develop different values and behavior patterns. For example, the upper-upper class may well be socially secure and not find it necessary or desirable to purchase the most expensive brands to impress other people. The lower-upper class, on the other hand, often engages heavily in such conspicuous consumption.

From a marketing strategy perspective, which typically focuses on mass-marketed consumer goods, it is not clear that such fine distinctions are always necessary. For example, for most mass-marketed products, differences in the three upper American groups are likely to be relatively unimportant, although for luxury goods and services the differences may be critical. Given the small size of the top two groups, Coleman argues that for mass-marketing purposes, it may be well to treat upper Americans as a single group.

Because of the large size and clear differences in the middle class and working class, Coleman argues that maintaining a distinction between them is very important. The two lower classes can likely be combined for consumer analysis, however. Following Coleman's recommendations results in four major social class groups for consumer analysis. Figure 14–13 presents a capsule description of and marketing implications for these four groups.

Social Class versus Income

The social class concept aids in the understanding of consumer values and behavior; it is also useful for market segmentation and prediction of consumer behavior. However, there has long been a controversy as to whether social class or income is the better variable for use in consumer analysis. Advocates of each position muster a number of arguments for the superiority of their variable and point out a variety of methodological and conceptual problems with the other one.

FIGURE 14–13   **Social Class Groups for Consumer Analysis**

Upper Americans (14 percent of population). This group consists of the upper-upper, lower-upper, and upper-middle classes. They have common goals and are differentiated mainly by income. This group has many different lifestyles, which might be labeled postpreppy, conventional, intellectual, and political, among others. The class remains the segment of our society in which quality merchandise is most prized, special attention is paid to prestige brands, and the self-image ideal is "spending with good taste." Self-expression is more prized than in previous generations, and neighborhood remains important. Depending on income and priorities, theater, books, investment in art, European travel, household help, club memberships for tennis, golf, and swimming, and prestige schooling for children remain high consumption priorities.

Middle-Class (32 percent of population). These consumers definitely want to "do the right thing" and buy "what's popular." They have always been concerned with fashion and following recommendations of "experts" in print media. Increased earnings result in better living, which means a "nicer neighborhood on the better side of town with good schools." It also means spending more on "worthwhile experiences" for children, including winter ski trips, college educations, and shopping for better brands of clothes at more expensive stores. Appearance of home is important, because guests may visit and pass judgment. This group emulates upper Americans, which distinguishes it from the working class. It also enjoys trips to Las Vegas and physical activity. Deferred gratification may still be an ideal, but it is not so often practiced.

Working-Class (38 percent of population). Working-class Americans are "family folk" depending heavily on relatives for economic and emotional support, e.g., tips on job opportunities, advice on purchases, help in times of trouble. The emphasis on family ties is only one sign of how much more limited and different working-class horizons are socially, psychologically, and geographically compared to those of the middle class. In almost every respect, a parochial view characterizes this blue-collar world. This group has changed little in values and behaviors in spite of rising incomes in some cases. For them, "keeping up with the times" focuses on the mechanical and recreational, and thus, ease of labor and leisure is what they continue to pursue.

Lower Americans (16 percent of population). The men and women of lower America are no exception to the rule that diversities and uniformities in values and consumption goals are to be found at each social level. Some members of this world, as has been publicized, are prone to every form of instant gratification known to humankind when the money is available. But others are dedicated to resisting worldly temptations as they struggle toward what some believe will be a "heavenly reward" for their earthly sacrifices.

Source: Excerpted from Richard P. Coleman (1983), "The Continuing Significance of Social Class to Marketing," Journal of Consumer Research *(December), pp. 265–280.*

Recently, consumer researchers have recognized that each variable has its advantages and disadvantages; and the choice between using social class, income, or a combination of the two depends on the product and the situation. For example, Shaninger offers the following tentative generalizations from his study of the issue:

1. Social class is superior to income for areas of consumer behavior that do not involve high dollar expenditures, but do reflect underlying lifestyle, values, or homemaker role differences not captured by income (e.g., using imported or domestic wines). Social class is superior for both method and place of purchase of highly visible, symbolic, and expensive objects such as living room furniture.

2. Income is generally superior for major kitchen and laundry appliances, and products which require substantial expenditures but are not status symbols within the class.

3. The combination of social class and income is generally superior for product classes that are highly visible, serve as symbols of social class or status within class, and require either moderate or substantial expenditure (e.g., clothing, automobiles, television sets).[22]

Thus, we believe that whether social class, income, a combination of these, or other variables is most useful in a particular situation is part of the analysis of the relationships between the product and the consumer. In other words, consumer cognitions, behaviors, and the environment must be analyzed to develop appropriate marketing strategies.

Back to the Case

This case offers a quick overview of how the automobile industry is responding to baby boomers and the mature market. We have seen that within these large groups there are a number of subgroups with specialized needs, lifestyles, and behaviors that must be considered.

In some cases, however, a product can be developed that has unique appeal to a variety of these groups. For example, Pontiac's Fiero is a sporty, high performance, two seater that resembles a Porsche, but costs less than $10,000. The Fiero is intended to appeal to trendy baby boomers, of course, but also to older persons who "think young." Its relatively low price and good looks also make it attractive to first-time car buyers, singles, and those needing a low-priced second car. Within two months of its introduc-

---

[22]Adapted from Charles M. Schaninger (1981), "Social Class versus Income Revisited: An Empirical Investigation," *Journal of Marketing Research* (May), pp. 192–208.

tion, the company sold 30,000 Fieros, fully one third of the scheduled production for the year. Various attributes of the car obviously appealed to a variety of subgroups, resulting in a very successful new-product introduction.

Summary

This chapter provided an overview of three macro social influences—culture, subculture, and social class. We discussed cultural influences in both international and domestic markets and subcultural influences in terms of geographic area, age, and ethnic groups. Social class influences were discussed in terms of both their role in understanding consumer behavior and as a strategic tool. Overall, macro social influences teach individuals appropriate ways of thinking, feeling, and behaving relative to their physical, social, and marketing environments.

Additional Reading

Russell W. Belk (1984), "Cultural and Historical Differences in Concepts of Self and Their Effects on Attitudes toward Having and Giving," in *Advances in Consumer Research,* Vol. 11, Thomas C. Kinnear (ed.), Provo, Utah: Association for Consumer Research, pp. 753–760.

S. T. Cavusgil and John R. Nevin (1983), *International Marketing: An Annotated Bibliography,* Chicago: American Marketing Association.

Warren A. French and Richard Fox (1985), "Segmenting the Senior Citizen Market," *Journal of Consumer Marketing* (Winter), pp. 61–74.

Paul Fussell (1983), *Class,* New York: Ballantine Books.

J. Michael Munson and W. Austin Spivey (1981), "Product and Brand User Stereotypes among Social Classes," in *Advances in Consumer Research,* Vol. 8, Kent B. Monroe (ed.), Ann Arbor, Mich.: Association for Consumer Research, pp. 696–701.

Francesco M. Nicosia and Robert N. Mayer (1976), "Toward a Sociology of Consumption," *Journal of Consumer Research* (September), pp. 65–75.

Terence A. Shimp and J. Thomas Yokum (1981), "Extensions of the Basic Social Class Model Employed in Consumer Research," in *Advances in Consumer Research,* Vol. 8, Kent B. Monroe (ed.), Ann Arbor, Mich.: Association for Consumer Research, pp. 702–707.

David Terpstrat (1985), *The Cultural Environment of International Business,* 2d ed., Cincinnati: South-Western Publishing.

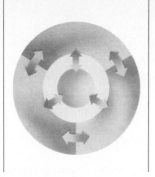

Chapter Fifteen

Micro Social Influences: Reference Groups and Family

A Day in the Life of an Up-scale Baby

Lauren Frank, 18 months old, of Needham, Massachusetts, wakes at 8 A.M. in her Lewis of London beechwood crib ($650) lined with brightly colored bumpers and quilt ($50), designed to match the two wall hangings (about $25 each) and the wallpaper border ($34) in her nursery. Surrounded by her "babies"—an assortment of stuffed animals and dolls—Lauren burbles and plays until her mother, Ellen, 28, lifts her out of the crib, and Lauren walks into the kitchen.

Once there, Lauren sits in her Italian Chicco high chair ($125), designed by a pediatrician, and waits for breakfast. Much of the cereal ends up on the carpeted floor because Lauren has decided it's high time she fed herself. While her mother cleans up, Lauren plays with her toys. Her current favorite is the eight-key Cookie Monster piano ($17), but she has been practicing animal sounds with the help of a Mattel See 'N Say ($12). Frequent tumbles down her Care Bears slide ($30) help to prevent boredom.

With the breakfast dishes done, Ellen announces it is time to get dressed. Lauren heads for the nursery and opens her double closet filled with chic, coordinated outfits by Petit Bateau ($30 each), OshKosh overalls and skirts ($18 to $20), and a few party dresses ($30 to $60). Lauren's shoe collection includes a pair of pink moccasins ($19), ballet slippers ($14), a pair of patent leather party shoes ($22), Stride Rite "sturdy shoes" ($25), Sporto waterproof boots ($22), and Nike sneakers ($19).

Today nothing much is planned, so Lauren wears her casual clothes—a pair of overalls and a jersey. A babysitter ($2 an hour) will be coming to spend the afternoon while Ellen teaches two dance classes, as she does twice a week. But first there is an errand to run. Ellen carries the Aprica stroller ($119, on sale) to the car, straps Lauren into her car seat ($55), puts the stroller in the trunk, and off they go.

They're back in time for a quick lunch before the babysitter arrives. After dance class, Ellen prepares an early dinner for Lauren, who needs her rest because tomorrow morning she and her father, David, 28, a printing company executive, are going to their first "Dad and me" exercise class. They've been on a waiting list for three months. The 45-minute class costs $56 and will meet once a week for eight weeks.

It's 7:15 P.M., David carries Lauren, much against her will, off to her bath. A Gerry portable bathtub ($10) is already snapped into place in the larger tub. A waterproof, floatable Sesame Street book ($5) relieves some of the trauma. From the tub, Lauren runs to her room and takes her pajamas from the second drawer of her Lewis of London beechwood dressing table/bureau ($530). After David has wrestled her into the pajamas and placed her in the crib, Ellen comes to kiss her goodnight.

Source: Excerpted from Andrea Dunham (1985), "Goo-Goo Chic: A Day in the Life of an Up-scale Baby," Business Week *(April 22), p. 62.*

As we noted in Chapter 14, macro social influences are broad, pervasive influences on society as a whole, or on large groups within it. In this chapter, we turn our attention to the analysis of micro social influences. Our analysis is concerned with the interactions between small groups and individuals, and the impact of these interactions on consumers' cognitions and behaviors.

Two related types of micro social influences, reference groups and families, are discussed. These topics have both conceptual and managerial importance. Conceptually, they represent a very influential part of a consumer's environment; and they dramatically affect how consumers perceive various elements in the environment, including products, stores, advertising, and prices. In addition, it is through interactions with these groups and individuals that consumers develop a self-image and learn appropriate behaviors in various situations. Managerially, they are important because analysis of these factors can often lead to better marketing strategies. For example, as we saw in Chapter 14, many teenagers are heavily involved in selecting family grocery products and brands. Thus, ads designed for teenagers and placed in media used by them may be more effective than traditional promotions targeted only to parents.

Reference Groups

In general, **reference groups** are people who influence an individual's cognitions and behaviors. Many types of reference groups (or reference individuals) have been delineated, including formal and informal, primary and secondary, and membership, aspirational, and dissociative groups. These are shown in Figure 15–1. Three points should be noted.

First, several of the distinctions can be combined to better describe specific groups. For example, families and peers can be referred to as primary informal groups. Second, while distinctions between all of these groups are useful, consumer behavior research has focused on two types of primary informal groups, peers and family. Third, issues of major importance to marketing concerning reference-group influence include: (1) What types of influence do reference groups exert on individuals? (2) How does reference group influence vary across products and brands? and (3) How can the concept of reference groups be used in developing marketing strategies?

Types of Reference Group Influence

It is quite likely that most of us are members of a number of different primary informal groups. For example, we may interact with several different groups of friends from work, school, or our neighborhood, as well as with people such as doctors and dentists who influence specific aspects of our lives. The process by which influence occurs and the types of influence are likely to vary depending on such things as the size of the group and the roles and status of its various members. In general, consumer researchers have identified three basic types of influences: informational, utilitarian, and value expressive.[1] These influences are discussed below.

Informational Influences

In one sense, all interpersonal influence is "informational." That is, people can only be influenced by others through information that is transmitted about themselves, about other persons, or about aspects of the physical environment, such as products or stores. This information may be given directly (through various types of verbal or other communication) or indirectly (through observational processes). For example, a friend may tell you that she has purchased a Cross pen, likes it very much, and suggest that you should buy one. This would be direct communication. Alternatively, you may see your friend smiling while using her new Cross pen, infer that she must really like it, and consider purchasing one yourself. This would be indirect communication.

---

[1] C. Whan Park and V. Parker Lessig (1977), "Students and Housewives: Differences in Susceptibility to Reference Group Influences," *Journal of Consumer Research* (September), pp. 102–110.

FIGURE 15–1   **Distinctions between Types of Reference Groups**

Type of Reference Group	Distinctions
Formal versus informal	Formal groups have a clearly specified structure and mission; informal groups do not.
Primary versus secondary	Primary groups involve face-to-face interactions; secondary groups do not.
Membership versus aspirational or dissociative	Membership groups are those in which the individual is a member; aspirational groups are those an individual wants to join; dissociative groups are those an individual wants to avoid.

Park and Lessig suggest that reference group information will influence consumers if the information is perceived as enhancing knowledge of the environment or the ability to cope with some aspect of it.[2] In other words, consumers will accept **informational reference group influence** if they believe it will help them in some way, such as getting along with group members or solving a purchasing problem. As we saw in our discussion of modeling, highly credible sources of information (such as opinion leaders or experts) are more likely to exert informational influence.

Finally, we note that informational influence can occur in three different situations. First, an individual may *seek out information* from others about particular issues. For example, you may tell a friend that you've been having a problem finding a decent pen and ask what brand he or she recommends. Second, a reference group member may simply *volunteer information* that may influence the listener. Third, the information may be transmitted through *observation,* as in the above example where the person was smiling while using her new pen.

Utilitarian Influence

Utilitarian reference group influence is reflected in compliance with the perceived expectations of others in order to achieve rewards or avoid punishments. It is very similar to normative social influence, as we discussed earlier concerning the extended Fishbein model. Basically, an individual

---

[2]Ibid.

HIGHLIGHT 15–1   **Some Common Verbal Tactics Used by Reference Groups**

Below are several types of verbal influence tactics that can change an individual's cognitions and behaviors. For each of the examples, consider how your cognitions and behaviors might change if the statement were made to you by a close friend or someone you admired or respected. Also, consider whether your cognitions about the person, and your behaviors when with that person, might change if he/she made the statement to you. What would your verbal response be?

Tools	Definitions	Examples
Reporting	Talking about preferences and behaviors	"All of us drink Budweiser"
Recommendations	Suggesting appropriate behaviors	"You should get a Schwinn High Sierra."
Invitations	Asking for participation in events	"Do you want to go to the Lionel Richie concert with us?"
Requests	Asking for behavior performance	"Would you run down to the corner and get me a newspaper?"
Prompts	Suggesting desired behaviors	"It sure would be nice if someone would buy us a pizza!"
Commands	Telling someone what to do	"Get me some Kleenex, and be quick about it!"
Promises	Offering a reward for performing a behavior	"If you'll go to Penney's with me, I'll take you to lunch later."
Coercion	Threatening to punish for inappropriate behavior	"If you don't shut up, I'm going to stuff a sock in your mouth!"
Criticism	Saying something negative about a behavior	"Quit hassling the salesclerk. You're acting like a jerk."
Compliments	Saying something positive about a behavior	"You really know how to shop. I bet you got every bargain in the store!"
Teasing	Good-natured bantering about behavior or appearance	"Man, that shirt makes you look like Bozo the clown!"

will comply with the desires of a group (or another person) if (1) the individual perceives that the group can present rewards and punishments, (2) the individual believes the behavior will be visible or known to the group, and (3) the individual is motivated to receive rewards or avoid punishment from the group.

Suppose, for example, your best friends at school are all planning to go to Florida over spring break to party hard and escape the pressure of school for a week or so. You really like these people and want to maintain them as friends. Let's say you have two papers to write over spring break and are really a bit short on cash. However, your friends have invited you, have encouraged you by offering you a ride, and have even teased you about being a nerd if you don't go with them. To the degree that you change your plans in order to maintain your relationship with the group, you would understand the power of utilitarian reference group influence! Similarly, many product and brand purchases may be influenced by a desire to identify with particular groups or individuals.

Value-Expressive Influences

Value-expressive reference group influence relates to an individual's use of groups to enhance or support his/her self-concept. An individual may seek positive referents and avoid negative referents for this purpose. Value-expressive influence may result in a person accepting the group's position and behaving like the group in order to bolster his or her ego through association—or simply because the person is attached to and likes the group members.

In some cases, value-expressive influences can result in difficult marketing problems. For example, consider a problem that has faced the mar-

David S. Stricker: Click/Chicago

Primary reference groups often have strong value-expressive influences on their members.

keters of Harley-Davidson motorcycles for many years. This brand is purchased and used primarily by one market segment that might be characterized as the "macho biker." This group is epitomized by gangs such as the Hell's Angels, some of whom have the Harley-Davidson logo tattooed on their arms or chests. It seems clear that membership in these gangs and ownership of this brand has an important value-expressive function for these consumers. However, while Harley-Davidson apparently serves this group very well, it is a relatively small part of the total motorcycle market. Thus, the problem: efforts to attract the mass motorcycle market have been somewhat unsuccessful, and such efforts risk alienation of current, highly brand-loyal consumers. Yet, potential for growth is severely limited by ignoring the mass market.

Reference Group Influence on Products and Brands

It is unlikely that reference groups influence all product and brand purchases to the same degree. However, for certain products and brands, reference group influence is both more likely to occur and more likely to be strong. What determines the extent of reference group influence? This varies by individual and purchase situation, and the nature of the product or brand under consideration.

Based on earlier work, Bearden and Etzel have proposed that reference group influence on product and brand decisions varies on at least two dimensions.[3] The first dimension concerns the degree to which the product or brand is a necessity or a luxury. A **necessity** is owned by virtually everyone (e.g., clothes). A **luxury** is owned only by consumers in particular groups (e.g., a sailboat).

The second dimension on which reference group influence on products and brands may vary is the degree to which the object in question is a public or a private good. A **public good** is one that other people are aware an individual owns and uses; one for which they can identify the brand with little or no difficulty (e.g., a car). A **private good** is one that is used at home or in private so that other people (outside the immediate family) would be unaware of its possession or use (e.g., a hair dryer).

By combining these two dimensions, Bearden and Etzel produced the matrix shown in Figure 15–2. This figure suggests that reference group influence will vary depending on whether the products and brands are

---

[3]William O. Bearden and Michael J. Etzel (1982), "Reference Group Influences on Product and Brand Purchase Decisions," *Journal of Consumer Research* (September), pp. 183–194. The discussion in this section is based heavily on this excellent work.

FIGURE 15–2   **Combining Public-Private and Luxury-Necessity Dimensions with Product and Brand Purchase Decisions**

Public

Brand \ Product	**Weak reference group influence (−)**	**Strong reference group influence (+)**
Strong reference group influence (+)	***Public necessities*** Influence: Weak product and strong brand Examples: Wrist-watch, automobile, man's suit	***Public luxuries*** Influence: Strong product and brand Examples: Golf clubs, snow skis, sailboat
Weak reference group influence (−)	***Private necessities*** Influence: Weak product and brand Examples: Mattress, floor lamp, refrigerator	***Private luxuries*** Influence: Strong product and weak brand Examples: TV game, trash compactor, icemaker

Necessity (left side)   *Luxury* (right side)

Private

Source: William O. Bearden and Michael J. Etzel (1982), "Reference Group Influences on Product and Brand Purchase Decisions," Journal of Consumer Research (September), p. 185.

public necessities, private necessities, public luxuries, or private luxuries. Consider wristwatches, which are labeled public necessities. Usually, everyone can see whether or not a person is wearing a wristwatch, and thus the *brand* may be susceptible to reference-group influence. However, because the product class is owned and used by most people, there is likely to be little reference group influence on whether one should purchase a watch.[4]

---

[4]For further discussion and an alternative approach to studying reference group influences, see Peter H. Reingen, Brian L. Foster, Jacqueline Johnson Brown and Stephen B. Seidman (1984), "Brand Congruence in Interpersonal Relations: A Social Network Analysis," *Journal of Consumer Research* (December), pp. 771–783.

Reference Groups and Marketing Strategy

We have seen that reference groups are an important influence on consumers. Not only do members of primary informal groups affect consumer knowledge, attitudes, and values, but they also affect the purchase of specific products and brands—and even the selection of stores in which purchases are made. From a marketing strategy perspective, there are some

For the playing fields that come after the game.

Courtesy PUMA USA, Inc.

Some reference groups have a strong influence on clothing-brand choices.

cases in which the analysis of primary informal group influences can be used. For example, in industrial marketing, a careful analysis of the group dynamics of various purchasing departments may be useful for determining appropriate marketing approaches. Similarly, peer-group influence is a major asset of firms that sell in-home to groups, as in the case of Tupperware parties. In such instances, individuals may conform to the norms of the group by purchasing some items.

Salespeople frequently offer cues about the similarity of a particular customer to previous purchasers of the product; e.g., "There was a couple in here last week very similar to you. They bought the JVC speakers." They also offer cues about the similarity of the customer to themselves, e.g., "Oh, your two children go to East High School? My kids go there, too. We bought them an IBM PCjr to help them with their science projects."

Finally, soliciting experts to aid in the direct sale of products can be a successful strategy for some firms. For example, a consumer's dentist is likely to be a highly influential reference individual, particularly for products related to dental care. Thus, if a manufacturer of, say, the Water Pik, offered gifts to dentists for encouraging patients to use the product, this could well be an effective tactic. The company could keep track of a dentist's sales by having consumers list their dentist on the warranty card for the product.

For most mass-marketed products, a detailed analysis of the interactions of specific primary informal groups is impractical. However, as Bearden and Etzel note, both primary informal and aspirational groups are commonly portrayed in advertising:

> Reference group concepts have been used by advertisers in their efforts to persuade consumers to purchase products and brands. Portraying products being consumed in socially pleasant situations, the use of prominent/attractive people endorsing products, and the use of obvious group members as spokespersons in advertising are all evidence that marketers and advertisers make substantial use of potential reference group influence on consumer behavior in the development of their communications. Alluding to reference groups in persuasive attempts to market products and brands demonstrates the belief that reference groups expose people to behavior and lifestyles, influence self-concept development, contribute to the formation of values and attitudes, and generate pressure for conformity to group norms.[5]

There are many examples of the use of reference group concepts in advertising. Pepsi has featured popular recording stars such as Lionel

---

[5]Bearden and Etzel, "Reference Group Influences," p. 184.

Richie and Michael Jackson, and popular athletes such as Joe Montana and Dan Marino, whom many young people may well aspire to emulate. Converse, Puma, Nike, and other running shoe companies for many years spent a large portion of their promotion budget in shoe giveaways to successful athletes, as well as to hiring these athletes to recommend their brands. The very popular series of Miller Lite advertisements featuring well-known retired athletes likely appeals to baby boomers who followed the careers of these personalities and may consider some of them heroes to be emulated.

Family

The major focus of consumer and marketing research is on the individual as the unit of analysis. The concern has been with describing and trying to understand how individuals make purchases and how marketing strategies can be developed to more effectively influence this process.

The area of family research is an exception: it views the *family* as the unit of analysis. **Family research** attempts to describe and understand how family members interact and influence one another in terms of individual, family, or household purchases. One of the important lessons learned from this research is that different persons may perform different tasks in the purchase process. For example, the family member who purchases Jif peanut butter for lunchtime sandwiches may not be the same one who prepares the sandwiches or eats them. In fact, the purchaser may have been indifferent to the various brands and purchased Jif only because one or more other family members expressed a preference for it.

The simple example above illustrates two points: first, family decision making and purchasing processes are very complex and difficult to study; and second, family influences are often an important factor in developing marketing strategies. With the individual as the unit of analysis, it is no small task to try to understand consumer behavior. However, with the *family* as the unit of analysis, the cognitions, behaviors, and environments of several persons require consideration—as do the interactions among them. From the perspective taken in our text, each family member becomes part of the environment for the other family members and both influences and is influenced by them.

This reciprocal process is illustrated in Figure 15–3 for a family with one child. Not only would we need to analyze the cognitions, behaviors, and environments of the three individuals, but also the three possible interaction patterns between each of the family members. We would also have to study all of this across time, plus the influences of other persons and events. Even if we studied and observed the entire purchase/

consumption process and developed an excellent description of it for a single product, this would not necessarily tell us anything about (1) purchase and consumption of other products and brands by this family, (2) purchase and consumption of the same product by other families, or (3) purchase and consumption of other products and brands by other families. Thus, it would require a series of studies using different families and products before even tentative generalizations could be offered.

Also, consider the effects of family size on the analysis. For example, in a five-member family, there are five sets of cognitions, behaviors, and environments to analyze plus 15 possible interaction patterns among family members! Clearly, a complete analysis of even a single purchase by a family could be a very difficult task.

Nonetheless, our Jif peanut butter example shows that, in spite of the complexity and difficulty involved, knowledge of family influences is often very important for developing successful marketing strategies. There are at least three major reasons for analyzing families from a marketing strategy perspective. First, once it is recognized that the same individual may not perform all of the purchase/consumption tasks for even a single product, it becomes clear that the development of a successful marketing mix in some cases depends on answers to questions such as:

1. Is the product likely to be purchased for individual or joint family use?
2. Is the product likely to be purchased with individual or family funds?

FIGURE 15–3   **Reciprocal Influence of Family Members**

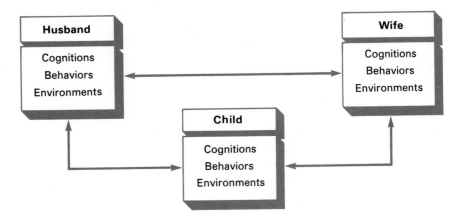

3. Is the product so expensive that its purchase involves an important trade-off in purchasing other products for the family?

4. Are family members likely to disagree about the value of the product? If so, what can be done to enhance product value for the family?

The refrigerator that's programmed to serve the needs of your family.

Who ever heard of a smart refrigerator? We did. In fact, we built one. A refrigerator with a brain that protects your food. A refrigerator that's been designed to tell you when things are right and when things are wrong. You see, at Whirlpool we know how much a refrigerator means to a family. That's why we build them the way we do.

Computer controls that help protect your food.

Our Serva-Door® refrigerator is a computerized marvel. And it does something that most refrigerators can't do. Its Systems Sentinel® II computer control system will independently maintain separate yet accurate temperatures in the refrigerator and the freezer at the same time.

A monitor that gives you a warm warning.

Sometimes the refrigerator door is open for an extended period of time, like after school, or grocery day. When that happens a computerized monitor in the door will automatically tell you that the temperature is getting a bit warm inside. Then all you have to do is program it for maximum cooling. And you can do it with just a touch of your finger.

Convenience everywhere you look.

Of course, computers are just part of the story. We know how important convenience is. That's why we offer so many extra convenience features. Like textured-steel doors that help hide messy fingerprints. Adjustable glass shelves. Plus crispers and meat-keepers that have their own climate controls.

A promise of quality that we stand behind.

Every Whirlpool appliance is backed by our promise of good, honest quality. It's a promise we've kept for 75 years, and we support it with programs like our toll-free, 24-hour Cool-Line® service* to help you with problems or questions. It's just one more way we can make your world a little easier.

*Call 800-253-1301. In Alaska and Hawaii, 800-253-1121. In Michigan, 800-632-2243.

Making your world a little easier.

Courtesy Whirlpool Corp.

Product modifications to accommodate different family members.

5. Is the product likely to be used by more than one family member; if so, are product modifications necessary to accommodate different persons?

6. Which family members will influence the purchase and what media and messages should be used to appeal to each?

7. Are particular stores preferred by various family members or by various families in the target market?

Answers to questions such as these may dramatically change the appropriate marketing mix. For example, if a car is being purchased by a family for teenagers to drive to school, the type of product, method of financing, price, and appropriate promotion message and media may vary dramatically from those involved with the family's purchase of a car for primary use.

A second reason family analysis is important for marketing strategy development is the long-term influence of family purchasing patterns on children's behavior. Parents teach children both directly and through ob-

Alan Carey/The Image Works

Children influence the purchase of many products.

HIGHLIGHT 15–2   **Common Terms Used in Family Research**

Term	Meaning
Household	All persons who occupy a housing unit: people living alone, a group of unrelated people, or a family.
Family	A group of two or more persons related by blood, marriage, or adoption, and residing together.
Nuclear family	A group of two or more persons related to one another by blood, marriage, or adoption, and of the same or adjoining generations.
Conjugal family	A marriage or a relationship between a husband and wife as the basis for a family structure.
Extended family	Family structures that extend beyond the nuclear family to include aunts, uncles, etc.
Family of procreation	The family one establishes through marriage.
Family of orientation	The family one is born into.

Source: Based on Michael P. Heffring (1980), "Measuring Family Decision Making: Problems and Prospects," in Advances in Consumer Research, Vol. 7, Jerry C. Olson (ed.), Ann Arbor, Mich.: *Association for Consumer Research, pp. 492–498.*

servation how, when, where, why, and what to purchase. We suspect that for many types of staple and other goods, offspring may well purchase brands they used when growing up. In fact, many consumers have perhaps never considered purchasing brands of some products other than the brand their parents purchased for them as children. For example, traditional brands of canned soup, toothpaste, ketchup, laundry detergent, and many other products may often be purchased and used throughout an individual's adult life without serious consideration of other brands. This is a marketer's dream— consumers who are highly brand loyal for many decades!

A third reason family analysis is important for marketing strategy development is the dramatic influence of children on budget allocation and purchase/consumption behavior of the family. The birth of a child creates a demand for a wide variety of products a couple never needed or considered purchasing previously. In addition, children influence the purchase of many products both directly (e.g., presweetened cereal) and indirectly (e.g., a four-door Ford station wagon rather than a Mazda RX-7). Thus, in a child-oriented culture such as ours, children can dramatically affect family expenditures. In fact, it has been estimated that a child born in 1985 will cost its parents $300,000 to raise to age 17!

Sociologists have long been concerned with studying families, and their work has been the foundation for research on the consumer behavior of families. As such, much of the work is not designed specifically for application by marketing managers. However, it is useful for understanding the dynamics of family purchase/consumption behavior and, in some cases, has direct implications for designing marketing strategies. We will discuss three issues in family research: (1) demographic changes in families, (2) family life cycle, and (3) family influence and decision making.

Demographic Changes in Families

Traditionally, families are often thought of as two parents with a couple of children, all of whom live together. The male spouse is employed and provides the only source of income for the family. The female spouse is the homemaker, who takes care of the house and purchases the majority of mass-marketed consumer goods for the family. While there are still many families who can be described this way, there have also been some dramatic changes in family structures:

> Only 19 percent of American families consist of married couples with children in which only the husband is employed, down from 30 percent in 1970. According to the Census Bureau's *Current Population Survey*, there were fewer married couples with children in 1980 than there were in 1970, even though the total number of households rose 26 percent during the decade . . . . American households have changed radically in recent years, but the family lives on. It just looks different than it used to, with a later age at first marriage, fewer children, and more divorces than in the past. Nevertheless, over 90 percent of all Americans marry, and, among families with children, two [children] is still the most popular number.[6]

Of the many changes in family structure that have occurred, four are particularly dramatic, although strongly interrelated: (1) changes in household composition, (2) changes in female employment, (3) changes in marriage and divorce, and (4) changes in childbirth and rearing.

---

[6]Bryant Robey (1983), "Five Myths," *American Demographics* (December), p. 2.

FIGURE 15–4   **Changes in Household Composition**

	1981	Projection 1990	Percent Change 1981–1990
All households (millions)	82,368	95,076	15.4%
Percent	100.0%	100.0%	
Married-couple households	59.8%	55.1%	6.2%
With children under 18	30.2	25.8	− 1.9
No children under 18	29.6	29.3	14.2
Other, woman as householder	26.5%	29.0%	26.0%
With children under 18	6.8	7.9	33.0
No children under 18	19.7	21.1	23.6
Woman living alone	14.2	15.4	25.0
Other	5.5	5.7	19.6
Other, man as householder	13.6%	15.9%	35.4%
With children under 18	0.8	0.9	32.7
No children under 18	12.8	15.0	35.5
Man living alone	8.8	10.3	34.4
Other	4.0	4.7	35.6

Households composed of married couples with children will decline in this decade, while less traditional household types will rapidly increase.

Source: U.S. Bureau of the Census, 1980 Current Population Survey, *as reported in Paul C. Glick (1984), "How American Families Are Changing,"* American Demographics *(January), p. 23.*

Changes in Household Composition

Figure 15–4 illustrates some dramatic changes in households from the traditional structure described above and projects these trends into the future. While many households still consist of married couples with children, the size of this group is projected to continue to decline. In its place, the trend toward single parent households will continue. Interestingly, while unmarried-couple households are commonly discussed, they represent the rarest household type. However, unmarried-couple households have increased dramatically in the past decade, and it is estimated that they will account for 3 percent of all households and 5 percent of all two-person households by 1990.[7]

---

[7]Paul C. Glick (1984), "How American Families Are Changing," *American Demographics* (January), pp. 20–25.

Changes in Female Employment

Contrary to the homemaker role in our traditional description of the family, today over half of all women are in the labor force—52 percent, to be exact. In fact, over two thirds of women in their 20s, 30s, and early 40s are employed outside the home. Of the women who do work, 45 percent are

Courtesy Campbell Soup Co.

Increases in female employment create opportunities for new products.

employed full-time the year around, compared to 65 percent of men who work full-time the year around. Of women with preschool children, fully 50 percent are working, up from 30 percent in 1970.[8]

For married couples, when both spouses work outside the home, disposable income can increase dramatically. This enables the family to afford more products and higher quality goods. In addition, it has been speculated that one result of a wife's employment would be an increase in the use of convenience foods and time-saving durables, such as microwave ovens. However, while a variety of studies have investigated this idea, the majority have found no support for it.[9]

Changes in Marriage and Divorce

About 95 percent of the U.S. population aged 45 and older had married at least once by 1980. Younger Americans are less apt to marry, however. In 1970, 45 percent of the men and 64 percent of the women in their early 20s had already married. However, in 1980, only 31 percent of the men and 50 percent of the women in this age group had married. Thus, it appears that younger people are postponing marriage, remaining single for life, or cohabitating without marriage to a greater extent than in the past.

Divorce rates for younger Americans are at higher levels than in previous generations. As shown in Figure 15–5, divorce rates vary dramatically with level of education. The likelihood of first marriages ending in divorce is much greater for those who attended college but did not graduate than for those who did graduate but did not go to graduate school.[10]

Changes in Childbirths and Rearing

As baby boomers now have or are beginning their own families, the number of births has increased to near the record levels of the late 1950s, a kind of "baby-boom echo." However, the number of births is up because there are more potential parents, not because individual families are having

---

[8]Robey, "Five Myths," p. 4.

[9]For a review of these studies and discussion of the issue, see Michael D. Reilly (1982), "Working Wives and Convenience Consumption," *Journal of Consumer Research* (March), pp. 407–418. Also see Charles M. Schaninger and Chris T. Allen (1981), "Wife's Occupational Status as a Consumer Behavior Construct," *Journal of Consumer Research* (September), pp. 189–196; Charles B. Weinberg and Russell S. Winer (1983), "Working Wives and Major Family Expenditures: Replication and Extension," *Journal of Consumer Research* (September), pp. 259–263.

[10]Glick, "How American Families Are Changing," p. 24.

FIGURE 15–5   ***Young Adults and Divorce***

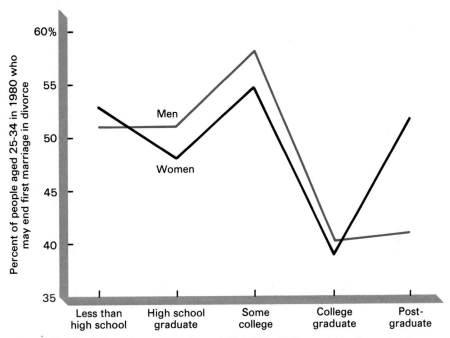

About half of the first marriages of people aged 25 to 34 in 1980 may end in divorce, but the chances of divorce vary by education

Source: U.S. Bureau of Census, 1980 Current Population Survey, *as reported in Paul C. Glick (1984), "How American Families Are Changing,"* American Demographics *(January), p. 24.*

more children. In fact, the average number of children born to a woman of childbearing age is only about half of what it was during the 1950s.[11]

The data in Figure 15–6 suggest that a large percentage of children are raised by only one parent or by stepfamilies, and this trend is projected to continue. By 1990, about 31 percent of children will be raised in this "nontraditional" manner; and 59 percent of the children born in the early 1980s may expect to live with only one parent for at least a year before reaching age 18.[12]

---

[11]Robey, "Five Myths."

[12]Glick, "How American Families Are Changing," p. 25.

Marketing Implications

It appears that marketers can expect families to continue to be smaller, more affluent, and less permanent, and can also expect changes in child-rearing patterns. These changes suggest that

> Many households, particularly those with two earners, will place a premium on time. Improved customer service, immediate availability, trouble-free operation of products, and dependable maintenance and repair services will be valued. We will see a new willingness to pay the price for services that assure product performance and limit inconvenience. In general . . . marketers should upgrade their

---

FIGURE 15–6   **How Children Live**

	1981	Projection 1990	Percent Change 1981–1990
All children under 18 (millions)	62,918	58,735	6.6%
Percent	100.0%	100.0%	
Living with 2 parents	76.4%	69.4%	17.9%
Living with 1 parent	20.0	26.5	23.5
Living with mother	18.1	24.0	23.3
Divorced	7.8	11.3	35.7
Married	5.6	6.3	5.8
Separated	4.9	6.1	16.8
Widowed	1.8	1.7	13.7
Never married	2.9	4.5	47.5
Living with father	1.9	2.5	25.4
Divorced	1.0	1.5	47.7
Married	0.5	0.5	2.0
Separated	0.4	0.5	28.0
Widowed	0.3	0.2	27.1
Never married	0.2	0.3	49.1
All other	3.6	4.1	7.0

The number of children under 18 who live with both parents will decline over the decade, while the number of children living with one parent or in stepfamilies will increase dramatically.

Source: U.S. Bureau of the Census, 1980 Current Population Survey, *as reported in Paul C. Glick (1984), "How American Families Are Changing,"* American Demographics *(January), p. 25.*

Courtesy Caravelle Fashions

A luxury product for children.

focus and concentrate on higher-quality, higher-priced goods and services.[13]

Fewer children per household and greater per-household affluence suggest that today's children will enjoy the highest level of material goods

---

[13]William Lazer (1984), "How Rising Affluence Will Reshape Markets," *American Demographics* (February), p. 21.

in history. Even in cases of divorce, the parent who does not receive custody is likely to purchase expensive gifts for the child as a way of making up for his or her absence. Thus, the types of products purchased for children are likely to parallel those used by their parents, i.e., a large number of high-quality, high-priced products. Retail chains that specialize in children's products, such as Toys-"Я"-Us, have become very successful by serving this market.

Family Life Cycle

Family life cycle is a sociological concept that describes changes in families across time. Many different family life cycles have been proposed, with the number of suggested stages in the cycle varying from 4 to 10.[14] Traditionally, differences in stages are based on major life events, such as the birth, growth, and departure of children from the family. The best-known family life-cycle concept used in marketing and consumer research is presented in Figure 15–7. It includes nine stages and suggests that the family's buying and behavior patterns change dramatically across stages. To the degree this approach is valid, it has clear implications for segmenting families into various markets.

However, because of changes in family demographics, such as those described earlier, several attempts have been made to modernize the traditional family life-cycle concept. Given the changes in household composition, female employment, divorces, and childbirths, the traditional family life cycle ignores a large percentage of families in today's society.

One attempt at modernizing the family life-cycle approach was developed by Murphy and Staples.[15] Their model, shown in Figure 15–8, makes provision for divorced persons and childless couples at various stages. To the degree that these groups represent viable market segments for particular products, these additions appear to be useful. However, research on clothing expenditures across family life cycles found little difference in the predictive ability of the two approaches.[16]

---

[14]For a review of a number of these, see Patrick E. Murphy and William A. Staples (1979), "A Modernized Family Life Cycle," *Journal of Consumer Research* (June), pp. 12–22.

[15]Ibid. For other approaches and discussion, see Frederick W. Derrick and Alane K. Lehfeld (1980), "The Family Life Cycle: An Alternative Approach," *Journal of Consumer Research* (September), pp. 214–217; Mary C. Gilly and Ben M. Enis (1982), "Recycling the Family Life Cycle: A Proposal for Redefinition," in *Advances in Consumer Research*, Vol. 8, Andrew Mitchell (ed.), Ann Arbor, Mich.: Association for Consumer Research, pp. 271–276.

[16]See Janet Wagner and Sherman Hanna (1983), "The Effectiveness of Family Life Cycle Variables in Consumer Expenditure Research," *Journal of Consumer Research* (December), pp. 281–291.

FIGURE 15–7   **A Traditional Family Life Cycle**

Stage in Life Cycle	Buying or Behavior Pattern
1. Bachelor stage: Young, single people not living at home	Few financial burdens. Fashion opinion leaders. Recreation oriented. Buy basic kitchen equipment, basic furniture, cars, equipment for the mating game, vacations.
2. Newly married couples: Young, no children	Better off financially than they will be in near future. Highest purchase rate and highest average purchase of durables. Buy cars, refrigerators, stoves, sensible and durable furniture, vacations.
3. Full nest I: Youngest child under six	Home purchasing at peak. Liquid assets low. Dissatisfied with financial position and amount of money saved. Interested in new products. Buy washers, dryers, TV, baby food, chest rubs and cough medicines, vitamins, dolls, wagons, sleds, skates.
4. Full nest II: Youngest child six or over	Financial position better. Some wives work. Less influenced by advertising. Buy larger-sized packages, multiple-unit deals. Buy many foods, cleaning materials, bicycles, music lessons, pianos.
5. Full nest III: Older couples with dependent children	Financial position still better. More wives work. Some children get jobs. Hard to influence with advertising. High average purchase of durables. Buy new, more tasteful furniture, auto travel, nonnecessary appliances, boats, dental services, magazines.
6. Empty Nest I: Older couples, no children living with them, head in labor force	Home ownership at peak. Most satisfied with financial position and money saved. Interested in travel, recreation, self-education. Make gifts and contributions. Not interested in new products. Buy vacations, luxuries, home improvements.
7. Empty nest II: Older married couples, no children living at home, head retired	Drastic cut in income. Keep home. Buy medical-care products that improve health, sleep, and digestion.
8. Solitary survivor, in labor force	Income still good, but likely to sell home.
9. Solitary survivor, retired	Same medical and product needs as other retired group. Drastic cut in income. Special need for attention, affection, and security.

Source: William D. Wells and George Gubar (1966), "Life Cycle Concept in Marketing Research," Journal of Marketing Research *(November), pp. 355–363, as reported in Gilly and Enis, "Recycling . . ."*

FIGURE 15–8 *A Modernized Family Life Cycle*

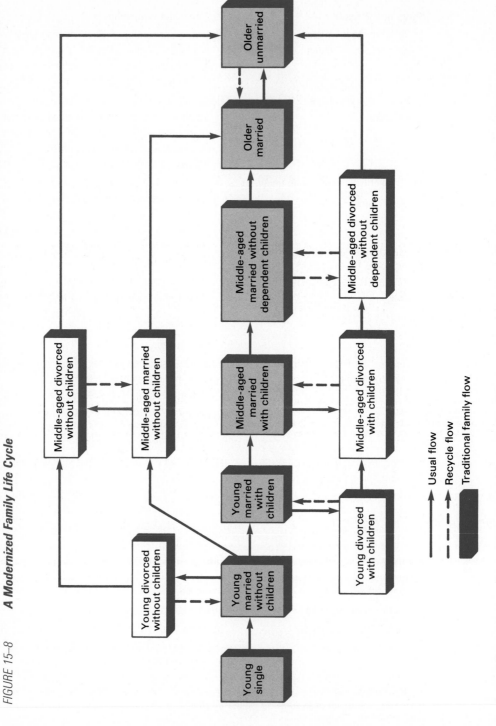

Source: Patrick E. Murphy and William A. Staples (1979), "A Modernized Family Life Cycle," Journal of Consumer Research (June), pp. 12–22.

Family Influence and Decision Making

Among the areas explored in research on family decision making are the following: (1) differences in product class and their relationship to family decision making, (2) the structure of husband/wife roles, and (3) the determinants of joint decision making.[17] At this time, relatively few generalizations for consumer analysis can be offered about family decision making. In fact, several years ago in a review of the subject, the major conclusions were:

1. Husband-wife involvement varies widely by product class.
2. Husband-wife involvement within any product class varies by specific decisions and decision stages.
3. Husband-wife involvement for any consumer decision is likely to vary considerably among families.[18]

We find little reason to believe that more specific conclusions could be offered today. In addition, we suspect that little more could be said if the involvement of children were included in the above statements. For example, consider Figure 15–9. For each of the stages in the model, consider which members of your family would be involved in the purchase of the following items: (1) a new car, (2) a microwave oven, (3) a pair of jeans for you, (4) a dinner at a fast-food restaurant. We suspect there will often be considerable variance both in the persons involved at each stage and in the extent to which they are involved. Now, compare your responses with those of several of your classmates. Again, we suspect you will find considerable differences across families.

This exercise should not lead you to believe that family influences are unimportant in consumer analysis, however. As we have said, families are important in determining an individual's cognitions and behaviors, and families are often a useful unit of analysis. Yet, there is considerable evidence that family influence and decision making is contextual—strongly influenced by the individuals involved, the product, and the situation.

We also suspect, for several reasons, that serious conflict among family members concerning purchase and consumption decisions is not very common. First, although families may influence the purchases an individual makes, many purchases are still made by the individual, for that individual, and with his or her own money. To the degree that the purchase

---

[17]Daniel Seymour and Greg Lessne (1984), "Spousal Conflict Arousal: Scale Development," *Journal of Consumer Research* (December), pp. 810–821.

[18]Harry L. Davis (1976), "Decision Making within the Household," *Journal of Consumer Research* (March), pp. 241–260.

does not interfere with family values and/or place a burden on family resources, there is likely to be little conflict. There are exceptions, but food, clothing, textbooks, and personal care items are not likely to involve much family conflict.

There is also little conflict over many products purchased for joint use by family members. For example, given all the grocery items purchased by a family in a typical week, how many involve serious disagreements among family members? This does not mean that various family members do not influence purchases or request particular items. For the majority of the purchases, though, the particular product or brand is not likely to offend other family members; or if it does, the subject typically is not worth arguing about.

Finally, making joint purchases can be a source of entertainment for the family. Even in cases where there are huge disagreements as to the attributes sought in a particular product (such as a home computer), collecting and comparing information with that obtained by other family members and finding the most suitable alternative can be fun. Thus, we suspect that serious conflicts are not common, and the family that has

FIGURE 15–9 **Examining Influence of Family Members in the Purchase/Consumption Process**

	Parents		Children		
	Mother	Father			
Information contact					
Funds access					
Store contact					
Product contact					
Transaction					
Consumption					
Communication					

Which family members would be involved in each stage of purchase for the following items?

1. New car
2. Microwave oven
3. Jeans for you
4. Dinner at a fast-food restaurant

HIGHLIGHT 15–3   **Women Left Behind when Men Shop for Clothes**

A Response Analysis November 1983 survey suggests that husbands like to leave their wives at home when [the men] go clothes shopping.

Our research consisted of interviews in clothing stores along the East Coast among 300 men who had either purchased a suit in the past year or intended to do so in the next three months. Fifty-eight percent of this sample were married.

We found that 60 percent of the men were alone when shopping for a suit. Among those accompanied by someone else, half were with their wives, one third with a female friend or relative, and the remainder with a male friend or relative.

Men taking spouses, friends, and relatives with them said these companions were not influential in determining the respondent's choice of store, but that they did have a say in the actual purchase decision. Over half the respondents reported that this influence was at least moderate and two fifths said it was quite strong.

Source: The Sampler from Response Analysis *(November 1984), p. 4.*

serious conflicts over every purchase is not likely to remain a family very long!

There are clearly times when most families will have a disagreement about the appropriate purchase, and members will attempt to influence the purchase decision. In these cases, a variety of strategies are commonly used.

One study proposed and investigated six types of influence strategies that could be used in attempts to persuade other family members.[19] These strategies, shown in Figure 15–10, summarize much of the literature dealing with family persuasion. Depending on the product, the family members involved, and the situation, any one of these strategies may be effective.

Of course, several influence strategies could be mixed at the same time. In a study of furniture and major-appliance purchases, Spiro classified six different groups in terms of the mix of influence strategies reported. A description of these groups and the percentage of the sample for each group are reported in Figure 15–11. While this study did not include children's' influence on the purchase, it presents an interesting way to consider persuasion methods used by family members in decision making.

---

[19]Rosann L. Spiro (1983), "Persuasion in Family Decision Making," *Journal of Consumer Research* (March), pp. 393–402.

In summary, there are few generalizations to offer about which products and which stages in the purchase/consumption process will be influenced by particular family members. This should not be surprising considering the major changes taking place in family structures, the com-

---

FIGURE 15–10   ***Six Common Types of Family Influence Strategies***

Expert influence is reflected in a spouse's enumeration of specific information concerning the various alternatives. For example, one spouse can try to convince the other that she/he is more knowledgeable concerning the products under consideration by presenting detailed information about various aspects of these products.

Legitimate influence deals with one spouse's attempts to draw upon the other's feelings of shared values concerning their role expectations. Therefore, the spouse's influence is based on the shared belief that she/he should make the decision because she/he is the "wife/husband." For example, the husband can argue that since he is the "man of the house," he should make a particular decision.

Bargaining involves attempts by one spouse to turn the joint decision into an autonomous one in return for some favor granted to the other spouse. For example, in return for autonomy in a particular decision, one spouse may agree to give the other autonomy in another decision when she/he had previously refused to do so. "If you do this, I'll do that" may be the most common type of bargaining attempt.

Reward/referent influence is based on a combination of the reward and referent power/influence typologies. Reward influence is the influence based on an individual's ability to reward another—i.e., one spouse may be able to reward the other by doing something that the other would enjoy. Referent influence is the influence based on the identification or feeling of oneness (or desire for such an identity) of one person with another. Referent influence in marriage stems from the desire of spouses to be like their concepts of the "ideal" husband or wife.

Emotional influence attempts are influence techniques that involve displaying some emotion-laden reaction. For example, one spouse may get angry at the other. These attempts are often nonverbal techniques. For example, one spouse may cry or pout, and another may use the "silent treatment."

Impression management encompasses premeditated persuasive attempts to enhance one's influence differential in a dyadic relationship. For example, one spouse may claim that the other's preferred brand was "out of stock" when, in fact, it wasn't. The objective is to convince the spouse to attribute the influence attempt to external pressures beyond the influencer's control.

Source: Rosann L. Spiro (1983), "Persuasion in Family Decision Making," Journal of Consumer Research *(March), p. 394.*

plexities of studying families in depth, and the differences in individual family-member experiences. Thus, with products for which strong family influence and joint decision making is expected, firms may need to rely on marketing research tailored to the specific problem.

FIGURE 15–11   **Family Influence Strategy Mixes**

Noninfluencers. This group, which characterizes 22 percent of the individuals in the sample, is substantially lowest in reported use of all the influence types. When the people in this group do attempt to influence their spouses, they are most likely to use the expertise type of influence.

Light Influencers. This was the largest subgroup in the sample (35.9 percent). The mean scores on all the influence types are substantially higher than the scores for Noninfluencers, but relatively low compared to all the other groups. Their relative use of the various influence strategies is very similar to (although higher than) the Noninfluencers, with the exception of their use of impression management. Light Influencer individuals are more likely to use some impression management as well as "expert" influence.

Subtle Influencers. This mix characterizes 18.8 percent of the sample. Relative to their use of other strategies, these people rely heavily on the reward/referent strategy and secondly on the expert strategy. Apparently, they attempt to put their partners in a favorable "mood" (e.g., by being very nice, "buttering up") before a decision is made.

Emotional Influencers. This category represents one of the two smallest groups (6.6 percent of the sample), yet its profile is quite distinctive. This profile displays the widest variations in the extent to which the different types of influence are used. These people report a high use of emotional influence and almost as high a use of reward/referent influence, a low use of legitimate and impression management, and a moderate use of both expert and bargaining strategies.

Combination Influencers. This mix (9.9 percent of the sample) is generally characterized by moderate use of all the influence strategies. In fact, there is less than one half a scale-point difference between the strategy used least—legitimate—and the strategy used most frequently—expert.

Heavy Influencers. The final group (6.6 percent of the sample) uses each of the six types of influence much more than does any of the other groups. The people in this group use bargaining, reward/referent influence, and the emotional strategy more than they use expert and legitimate influence and impression management, but all of the mean scale scores are high, indicating their heavy use of all the influence strategies.

Source: Rosann L. Spiro (1983), "Persuasion in Family Decision Making," Journal of Consumer Research *(March), p. 397.*

Back to the Case

This case illustrates several of the points made in the chapter. First, it illustrates the affluence of a growing number of families and their willingness to spend freely on their children, purchasing high-quality, high-priced products. Second, it is not surprising that the parents are both in their late 20s and have only one child, illustrating trends toward later marriages and smaller families. Third, as is now common, Ellen works, but only part-time. Fourth, the birth of Lauren led to the purchase of a variety of products and services that the Franks would never have considered otherwise.

Finally, while not noted in the case, a child such as Lauren will cost her parents more than $21,000 for goods and services by the time she enters kindergarten. Many of these products and services, such as disposable diapers and organized day care, barely existed when her parents were growing up. Within the next few years, parents will spend $20 billion on children each year—$11 billion on clothes alone. It is no wonder that many firms are developing new products and services for this market!

Summary

This chapter investigated two types of influence in the social environment: reference groups and family. Three types of reference group influence were discussed: informational, utilitarian, and value-expressive. The role of reference groups in product and brand purchases was explained, and several ideas were offered about how reference groups can be used in marketing strategy. Three major family issues were discussed: demographic changes in families, family life cycles, and family influence and decision making. Overall, while reference groups and families provide very powerful environmental influences on consumers' cognitions and behaviors, they also provide very challenging areas from which to derive generalizations for marketing analysis.

Additional Reading

Russell Belk, Robert Mayer and Amy Driscoll (1984), "Children's Recognition of Consumption Symbolism in Children's Products," *Journal of Consumer Research* (March), pp. 386–397.

Harry L. Davis and Benny P. Rigaux (1974), "Perceptions of Marital Roles in Decision Making," *Journal of Consumer Research* (June), pp. 51–63.

Gerald J. Gorn and Renee Florsheim (1985), "The Effects of Commercials for Adult Products on Children," *Journal of Consumer Research* (March), pp. 962–967.

Sunil Gupta, Michael R. Hagerty and John G. Myers (1983), "New Directions in Family Decision Making Research," in *Advances in Consumer Research*, Vol. 10, Richard P. Bagozzi and Alice M. Tybout (eds.), Ann Arbor, Mich. Association for Consumer Research, pp. 445–450.

Lakshman Krishnamurthi (1983), "The Salience of Relevant Others and Its Effects on Individual and Joint Preferences: An Experimental Investigation," *Journal of Consumer Research* (June), pp. 62–72.

Marilyn Lavin (1985), "Husband-Wife Decision Making: A Theory-Based, Process Model," in *1985 AMA Educator Proceedings,* Robert F. Lusch, et al. (eds.), Chicago: American Marketing Association, pp. 21–25.

George P. Moschis (1985), "The Role of Family Communication in Consumer Socialization of Children and Adolescents," *Journal of Consumer Research* (March), pp. 898–913.

Dennis L. Rosen and Donald H. Granbois (1983), "Determinants of Role Structure in Family Financial Management," *Journal of Consumer Research* (September), pp. 253–258.

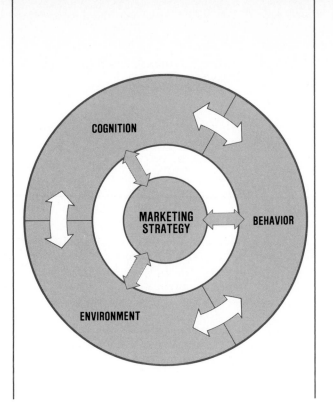

Section Five

Marketing

Strategy

Development

Chapter Sixteen

Market Segmentation Analysis

Campbell Soup Company

Ever since R. Gordon McGovern took the helm at Campbell Soup Company in 1980, the old-line food processor, known best for its soups and its Pepperidge Farm, Swanson, Franco-American, and Godiva products, has been undergoing a rapid and remarkable transformation. McGovern has been working feverishly to shift the company's emphasis from production to marketing.

McGovern started by reorganizing Campbell's four divisions into about 50 business groups and making group managers responsible for the marketing, manufacturing, and profit and loss of their units. He believes this structure fosters entrepreneurship and brings "the managers much closer to the market."

"There's a tremendous feeling of urgency because an overseas company could come in here with innovative packaging and technology and just take us to the cleaners on basic lines we've taken for granted for years," McGovern said, pointing to the success of Japanese companies selling *ramen* noodles in the dry-soup category. "They've made a penetration at the low end of the American food market, just as they did with cheap cars, and they are going to smash into a lot of other things," he worries.

To keep that from happening to Campbell, the push is on to target the consumer and improve quality. "I think we've had some serious problems in losing touch with our markets," said McGovern. He raised industry—and company—eyebrows when he publicly labeled the Swanson TV-dinner line "junk food." McGovern insisted: "It was great in 1950, but in today's world it didn't go into the microwave; it didn't represent variety or a good eating experience to my palate." Campbell set up Project Fix to improve the quality of its old standbys, and the Swanson line was bolstered by the high-priced Le Menu entrées.

McGovern's goal for Campbell is "to be positioned with consumers as somebody who is looking after their well-being." The company set up a health and fitness business unit, and it bought a small maker of fitness and sports medicine products. Campbell is also emphasizing segments such as frozen foods, fish (it acquired Mrs. Paul's Kitchens Inc. in 1982), juices (Pepperidge Farm apple juice was introduced in 1983), and produce (Campbell now sells fresh mushrooms).

Much of the new strategy hinged on targeting the consumer. "My 83-year-old mother doesn't eat like my son," McGovern observed. "And my daughters eat differently than their parents, and we eat differently from the people around the corner." So Campbell targeted particular products and ads to specific groups, and even began to do regional marketing. For instance, it sold its spicy Ranchero Beans only in the South and Southwest.

Source: Excerpted from "Campbell Soup: Cooking up a Separate Dish for Each Consumer Group" (1983), Business Week *(November 21), pp. 102–103.*

Market segmentation is one of the most important concepts in the consumer behavior and marketing literature. In fact, a primary reason for studying consumer behavior is to identify bases for effective segmentation, and a large portion of consumer research is concerned with segmentation. From a marketing strategy point of view, selection of the appropriate target market is paramount to developing successful marketing programs.

The logic of market segmentation is quite simple: it is based on the idea that a single product usually will not appeal to *all* consumers. Consumers' purchase goals, product knowledge, involvement, and purchase behavior vary; and successful marketers often adapt their marketing strategies to appeal to specific consumer groups. Even a simple product such as chewing gum comes in multiple flavors and package sizes, and varies in sugar content, calories, consistency (e.g., liquid centers), and colors to appeal to different consumers. While a single product will seldom appeal to all consumers, it can almost always serve more than one consumer. Thus, there are usually *groups of consumers* who can be served well by a single item. If a particular group can be served *profitably* by a firm, then it comprises a viable market segment. A marketer should then develop a marketing mix to serve that group.

In this chapter, we consider market segmentation. We define **market segmentation** as the process of dividing a market into groups of similar consumers and selecting the most appropriate group(s) for the firm to serve. We can break down the process of market segmentation into five tasks, as shown in Figure 16–1. In the remainder of this chapter, we discuss each of the market segmentation tasks shown in the figure. While we

FIGURE 16–1   **Tasks Involved in Market Segmentation**

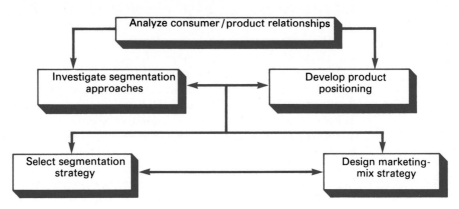

recognize that these tasks are strongly interrelated and their order may vary (depending on the firm and the situation), market segmentation analysis can seldom (if ever) be ignored. Even if the final decision is to "mass market" and not to segment at all, this decision should only be reached *after* a market segmentation analysis has been conducted. Thus, market segmentation analysis is critical for sound marketing strategy development.

Analyze Consumer/Product Relationships

The first task involved in segmenting markets is analyzing consumer/product relationships. In other words, relevant consumer cognitions, behaviors, and environments for a particular product are studied and identified. This task involves consideration of such questions as:

1. What does this product mean to consumers and how involved are they in purchasing it?
2. What behaviors are involved in the purchase/consumption process for this product?
3. What environmental factors are involved in the purchase/consumption process for this product?

Research and analysis of such questions is designed not only to provide a better understanding of consumer/product relationships in general, but also to identify some basic differences among various consumer groups. For many products, there is a prestige market that seeks the highest-quality (and often the highest-priced) product available. Often, particular products for consumers in this market have very important meanings, such as expression of good taste, expertise, and status. Brands such as Rolex watches, Mercedes automobiles, Hartmann luggage, and Gucci handbags are targeted to these consumers. The marketing strategies for these products generally involve selling in exclusive stores at high prices and promoting the products in prestige media. These strategies differ from those used in mass marketing to reflect differences in consumer cognitions (meaning of the product), behaviors (shopping activities), and environments (place of information and store contact). Thus, the initial analysis of consumer/product relationships has important implications for all of the tasks involved in market segmentation and strategy development.

Investigate Segmentation Approaches

There are many approaches to segmenting markets for particular products, and a major task is to investigate their relative usefulness. Three important questions involved in this process are considered here:

1. Should the segmentation be a priori (before a segmentation study is conducted) or post hoc (after a segmentation study is conducted)?
2. How are the relevant segmentation bases and descriptors determined?
3. What are some useful bases and descriptors for segmenting markets?

A Priori versus Post Hoc Segmentation

There are two general patterns for segmenting markets.[1] In an **a priori segmentation approach,** the marketing manager has decided on the appropriate bases for segmentation in advance of doing any research on the market. For example, a manager may decide that a market should be divided on the basis of whether consumers are nonusers, light users, or

---

[1]Yoram Wind (1978), "Issues and Advances in Segmentation Research," *Journal of Marketing Research* (August), pp. 317–337; Paul E. Green (1977), "A New Approach to Market Segmentation," *Business Horizons* (February), pp. 61–73.

HIGHLIGHT 16–1 **Designing Segmentation Research: A Priori and Post Hoc Models**

A priori segmentation models have as the dependent variable (the basis for segmentation) either product-specific variables (product usage, loyalty) or general customer characteristics (demographic factors). The typical research design for an a priori segmentation model involves seven stages.

1. Selection of the (a priori) basis for segmentation.

2. Selection of a set of segment descriptors (including hypotheses on the possible link between these descriptors and the basis for segmentation).

3. Sample design—mostly stratified and occasionally a quota sample according to the various classes of the dependent variable.

4. Data collection.

5. Formation of the segments based on a sorting of respondents into categories.

6. Establishment of the (conditional) profile of the segments using some appropriate analytical procedure.

7. Translation of the findings about the segments' estimated size and profile into specific marketing strategies, including the selection of target markets and the design or modification of specific marketing strategy.

Post hoc segmentation models differ from a priori models only with respect to the way the basis for segmentation is selected; i.e., in this approach the number and type of segments are not known in advance and are determined from the clustering of respondents on their similarities on some selected set of variables. Most commonly the variables used in post hoc models are needs, attitudes, lifestyle and other psychographic characteristics, or benefits sought.

Source: Adapted from Yoram Wind (1978), "Issues and Advances in Segmentation Research," Journal of Marketing Research *(August), p. 321–322.*

heavy users of a particular product. Segmentation research is then conducted to determine the size of each of these groups, and appropriate descriptors are selected to provide demographic or psychographic profiles.

In **post hoc segmentation,** people are grouped into segments on the basis of research findings. For example, people interviewed about their attitudes or the benefits sought in a particular product class are grouped according to their responses. The size of each of these groups and their demographic or psychographic profiles are then determined.

Both the a priori and post hoc approaches are valuable. The question of which to use depends in part on how much is known about consumers' cognitions, behaviors, and environments for particular products. If (through research in the previous stage or previous experience) a marketing manager has successfully isolated a number of key market dimensions, then an a priori approach may provide more useful information. For entirely new products, a post hoc approach may be useful for determining key market dimensions. However, even when using a post hoc approach, some consideration must be given to the variables to be included in the research design. Thus, some consideration must be given to the relevant segmentation dimensions prior to research, regardless of which approach is used.

Relevant Segmentation Dimensions

Unfortunately, there is no simple way to determine the relevant dimensions for segmenting markets. In most cases, however, at least some initial dimensions can be determined from previous research, purchase trends, and managerial judgment. For example, suppose we wish to segment the market for all-terrain vehicles. Several dimensions come to mind for initial consideration: sex (male); age (18 to 35); lifestyle (outdoorsman); and income level (perhaps $15,000 to $25,000). At a minimum, these variables should be included in subsequent segmentation research. One market-oriented approach to segmentation is on the basis of what benefits potential consumers are seeking. This approach will be considered in some detail in the following section.

Bases for Segmentation

A number of bases for segmenting consumer markets are presented in Figure 16–2. This is by no means a complete list of possible segmentation variables, but represents some useful categories. Two commonly discussed approaches for segmenting markets are benefit segmentation and psychographic segmentation. A third promising approach is called person-situation segmentation. These three approaches will be discussed in some detail below.

Benefit Segmentation
The belief underlying this segmentation approach is that the *benefits* people are seeking in consuming a given product are the basic reasons for the existence of true market segments.[2] This approach thus attempts to mea-

---

[2]Russell I. Haley (1968), "Benefit Segmentation: A Decision-Oriented Research Tool," *Journal of Marketing* (July), pp. 30–35; also see Russell I. Haley (1971), "Beyond Benefit Segmentation," *Journal of Advertising Research* (August), pp. 3–8; Russell I. Haley (1983), "Benefit Segmentation—20 Years Later," *Journal of Consumer Marketing* (2), pp. 5–13.

Courtesy L'eggs Products, Inc.

Courtesy Marks Ltd.

There are many bases for segmenting markets.

FIGURE 16–2   ***Useful Segmentation Bases for Consumer Markets***

Segmentation Bases/Descriptors	Illustrative Categories
Geographic	
Region	Pacific; Mountain; West North Central; West South Central; East North Central; East South Central; South Atlantic; Middle Atlantic; New England
Size of city, county, or standard metropolitan statistical area (SMSA)	Under 5,000; 5,000–19,999; 20,000–49,999; 50,000–99,999; 100,000–249,999; 250,000–499,999; 500,000–999,999; 1,000,000–3,999,999; 4,000,000 or over.
Population density	Urban; suburban; rural
Climate	Warm; cold
Demographic	
Age	Under 6; 6–12; 13–19; 20–29; 30–39; 40–49; 50–59; 60 +
Sex	Male, female
Family size	1–2; 3–4; 5 + persons

FIGURE 16–2   (concluded)

Segmentation Bases/Descriptors	Illustrative Categories
Family life cycle	Young, single; young, married, no children; young, married, youngest child under 6; young, married, youngest child 6 or over; older, married, with children; older, married, no children under 18; older, single; other
Income	Under $5,000; $5,000–$7,999; $8,000–$9,999; $10,000–$14,999; $15,000–$24,999; $25,000–$34,999; $35,000 or over
Occupation	Professional and technical; managers, officials, and proprietors; clerical, sales; craftsmen, foremen; operatives; farmers; retired; students; housewives; unemployed
Education	Grade school or less; some high school; graduated from high school; some college; graduated from college; some graduate work; graduate degree
Religion	Catholic; Protestant; Jewish; other
Race	White; black; Oriental; other
Nationality	American; British; French; German; Italian; Japanese
Psychosocial	
Social class	Upper Americans, middle-class, working-class, Lower Americans
Life style	Traditionalist; sophisticate; swinger
Personality	Compliant; aggressive; detached
Cognitive and Behavioral	
Attitudes	Positive; neutral; negative
Benefits sought	Convenience; economy; prestige
Readiness stage	Unaware; aware; informed; interested; desirous; intention to purchase
Perceived risk	High; moderate; low
Innovativeness	Innovator; Early Adopter; Early Majority; Late Majority; Laggard; Nonadopter
Involvement	Low; high
Loyalty status	None; some; total
Usage rate	None; light; medium; heavy
User status	Nonuser; exuser; potential user; current user
User situation	Home; work; commuting; vacation

FIGURE 16–3   **Toothpaste Market Benefit Segments**

	The Sensory Segment	The Sociable Segment	The Worrier Segment	The Independent Segment
Principal benefit sought	Flavor, product appearance	Brightness of teeth	Decay prevention	Price
Demographic strengths	Children	Teens, young people	Large families	Men
Special behavioral characteristics	Users of spear-mint-flavored toothpaste	Smokers	Heavy users	Heavy users
Brands disproportionately favored	Colgate	Macleans, Ultra Brite	Crest	Cheapest brand
Lifestyle characteristics	Hedonistic	Active	Conservative	Value oriented

Source: Adapted from Russell I. Haley (1968), "Benefit Segmentation: A Decision-Oriented Research Tool," Journal of Marketing (July), pp. 30–35.

sure consumer value systems and consumers' perceptions of various brands in a product class. The classic example of a benefit segmentation, provided by Russell Haley, concerned the toothpaste market. Haley identified four basic segments—Sensory, Sociable, Worrier, and Independent—as presented in Figure 16–3. Haley argued that this segmentation could be very useful for selecting advertising copy, media, commercial length, packaging, and new-product design. For example, colorful packages might be appropriate for the Sensory segment, perhaps aqua packages (to indicate fluoride) for the Worrier group, and gleaming white packages for the Sociable segment because of their interest in white teeth.[3]

Calantone and Sawyer also used a benefit segmentation approach to segment the market for bank services.[4] A summary of the groups they identified is provided in Figure 16–4. Their research was concerned with whether benefit segments remained stable across time. They found some stability in segments, but there were some differences in attribute importance, size, and demographics at different times. Thus, they argue for

---

[3]Haley, "Benefit Segmentation . . ."

[4]Robert J. Calantone and Alan G. Sawyer (1978), "The Stability of Benefit Segments," *Journal of Marketing Research* (August), pp. 395–404.

FIGURE 16–4 **Bank Services Benefit Segments**

	Front-Runners	Loan Seekers	Representative Subgroup	Value Seekers	One-stop Bankers
Principal benefits sought	Large; bank for all; good advertising	Good reputation; loans easily available; low loan interest	No differences (about average on all benefits sought)	High savings interest; quick service; low loan interest; plenty of parking	Wide variety of services; convenient hours; quick service; encourages financial responsibility; convenient branch
Demographic characteristics	Young; rent home	More transient; more blue-collar		Tend to save more	Older
Lifestyle characteristics	High ability to manage money	Liberal about use of credit; positive about bank loans		Conservative overall lifestyle; conservative about use of credit; low propensity toward risk taking	Conservative about use of credit; positive toward checking account
Percentage of sample market	2.3%	14.8%	34.3%	25.9%	22.7%

Source: Roger J. Calantone and Alan G. Sawyer (1978), "The Stability of Benefit Segments," Journal of Marketing Research, (August), p. 400.

ongoing benefit-segmentation research to keep track of any changes in a market that might affect marketing strategy.[5]

Psychographic Segmentation

Psychographic segmentation divides markets on differences in consumer lifestyles. Generally, psychographic segmentation follows a post hoc model. That is, consumers are first asked a variety of questions about their lifestyles and then are grouped on the basis of the similarity of their responses. Lifestyles are measured by asking consumers about their activities (such as work, hobbies, vacations), interests (such as family, job,

---

[5]Also see James R. Merrill and William A. Weeks (1983), "Predicting and Identifying Benefit Segments in the Elderly Market," in *AMA Educator's Proceedings,* Patrick Murphy et al. (eds.), Chicago: American Marketing Association, pp. 399–403.

community) and opinions (about such things as social issues, politics, business). The **activity, interest,** and **opinion (AIO)** questions in some studies are of a very general nature. In others, at least some of the questions are related to specific products.

Psychographic segmentation studies often include hundreds of questions and provide a tremendous amount of information about consumers. Thus, psychographic segmentation is based on the idea that "the more you know and understand about consumers, the more effectively you can communicate and market to them."[6]

To date, no consensus has been reached concerning how many different lifestyle segments there are in the United States—or in other countries. Psychographic studies frequently reach different conclusions about the number and nature of lifestyle categories. For this reason, the validity of psychographic segmentation is sometimes questioned.[7]

A well-known psychographic segmentation was developed at SRI International in California. It is called **VALS**™, which stands for **Values and Lifestyles.** This approach divides consumers into four major groups. *Need-driven consumers* purchase primarily to satisfy basic, subsistence level needs. *Outer-directed consumers* are influenced by a desire to impress other people. *Inner-directed consumers* are motivated by a desire for self-awareness. *Combined outer- and inner-directed consumers* integrate social and self orientations. These groups are then further refined into the nine psychographic segments that are profiled in Figure 16–5.

Research has found differences in purchase behavior consistent with these lifestyles. For example, Achievers tend to buy luxury cars; Belongers tend to buy family-sized cars; the Societally Conscious tend to buy economy cars; Emulators and Experientials tend to buy muscle cars: Inner-directed consumers are far more likely to buy foreign cars than are Belongers.[8]

Person/Situation Segmentation

Markets can often be divided on the basis of the usage situation in conjunction with individual differences of consumers. For example, clothing

---

[6]Joseph T. Plummer (1974), "The Concept and Application of Life Style Segmentation," *Journal of Marketing* (January), p. 33.

[7]See W. D. Wells (1975), "Psychographics: A Critical Review," *Journal of Marketing Research* (May), pp. 196–213; John L. Lastovicka (1982), "On the Validation of Lifestyle Traits: A Review and Illustration," *Journal of Marketing Research* (February), pp. 126–38.

[8]Arnold Mitchell (1983), *The Nine American Lifestyles: Who We Are & Where We're Going*, New York: Macmillan, p. 165. Also see James Atlas (1984), "Beyond Demographics," *The Atlantic Monthly* (October), pp. 49–58.

FIGURE 16–5   **VALS™ Nine American Lifestyles**

Need-Driven Consumers

Survivors (4 percent of the U.S. adult population) These consumers are elderly and intensely poor. They are often widowed and living only on Social Security income. Some have been born into poverty and never escape it; others have slipped to this lifestyle because of bad luck, lack of enterprise, or the onslaughts of old age. Entertainment consists of watching television; basic staples are purchased with an emphasis on low price.

Sustainers (7 percent of the U.S. adult population) These consumers are angry, distrustful, anxious, combative, and live on the edge of poverty. Unlike Survivors, Sustainers have not given up hope; they try for a better life. They are careful shoppers and cautious buyers for their large families.

Outer-Directed Consumers

Belongers (38 percent of the U.S. adult population) These consumers typify what is generally regarded as middle-class America. Traditional, conservative, and old-fashioned, these consumers prefer the status quo or the ways of the past and do not like change. These consumers want to fit in rather than stand out, and they follow the rules of society. They value their home and family and seek security.

Emulators (10 percent of the U.S. adult population) These consumers are intensely striving people, seeking to be like those they consider richer and more successful. They are more influenced by others than any other lifestyle group and are ambitious, competitive, and ostentatious. Many have attended technical school; few have college degrees. Emulators are in a turbulent transition stage; most of them will not make it to Achiever status. They are conspicuous consumers.

Achievers (20 percent of the U.S. adult population) These consumers are the driving and driven people who have built "the system" and are now at the helm. They are effective corporate executives, skilled professionals such as doctors, lawyers, and scientists, adroit politicians, money-oriented athletes and entertainers, and successful artists. They live comfortable, affluent lives and in so doing they have set the standard for much of the nation. They are major consumers of luxury and top-of-the-line products.

Inner-Directed Consumers

I-Am-Me (3 percent of the U.S. adult population) These consumers are young and in a transition period from an outer-directed to an inner-directed way of life. Many have come from Achiever parents and the transition to new values is full of turmoil and confusion of personal identity. Most are students in their 20s and have very energetic, active lives. Clothes and other purchases may be made to differentiate these consumers from their parents and Establishment values.

Experientials (5 percent of the U.S. adult population) Many of these consumers passed through the I-Am-Me stage a few years earlier. They tend to be artistic, liberal, and to seek vivid, direct experiences with other persons, things, and events. They are highly educated, very energetic, and engage in social activities ranging from outdoor sports to wine tasting. Most are in their late 20s and prefer natural products.

FIGURE 16–5   *(concluded)*

Societally Conscious (11 percent of the U.S. adult population) These consumers are well educated, prosperous, politically liberal, and deeply concerned with social issues. They are approaching 40 years of age and are the leaders of movements for improving consumer rights, reducing environmental pollution, and protecting wildlife. Many ride a bike or drive an economy car, insulate their home or install solar heating, and eat only foods grown without pesticides and prepared without additives.

Combined Outer-and Inner-Directed Group

Integrateds (2 percent of the U.S. adult population) These consumers are psychologically mature and find both outer-direction and inner-direction good, powerful, and useful. They have an unusual ability to weigh consequences and to solve difficult problems. They tend to be open, self-assured, self-expressive, keenly aware of nuance, and command respect and admiration. They tend to be middle-aged or older.

Source: Adapted from Arnold Mitchell (1983), The Nine American Lifestyles: Who We Are & Where We're Going, *New York: Macmillan Publishing Company; and The Values and Lifestyles Program, SRI International, Menlo Park, Calif.*

and footwear markets are divided not only on the basis of the consumer's sex and size, but also on usage situation dimensions such as weather conditions, physical activities, and social events.[9] As another example, expensive china is designed for special occasions; Corelle dinnerware is designed for everyday family use. Dickson argues, "In practice the product whose unique selling propositions (quality, features, image, packaging, or merchandising) is not targeted for particular people in particular usage situations is probably the exception rather than the rule."[10] Thus, Dickson suggests the approach to segmentation outlined in Figure 16–6. This approach not only combines the person and the situation, but also other important segmentation bases: benefits sought, product and attribute perceptions, and marketplace behavior.

Operationally, Dickson suggests that this segmentation approach involves the following steps:

Step 1: Use observational studies, focus group discussions, and secondary data to discover whether different usage situations exist and

---

[9]Russell W. Belk (1979), "A Free Response Approach to Developing Product Specific Consumption Situation Taxonomies," in *Analytic Approaches to Product and Marketing Planning,* Allan D. Shocker (ed.), Cambridge, Mass.: Marketing Science Institute.

[10]Peter R. Dickson (1982), "Person-Situation: Segmentation's Missing Link," *Journal of Marketing* (Fall), p. 57.

HIGHLIGHT 16–2   **Typical Items Used in Psychographic Segmentation Research**

1. I often watch newspaper advertisements for announcements of department store sales.

2. I like to watch or listen to baseball or football games.

3. I often try new stores before my friends and neighbors do.

4. I like to work on community projects.

5. My children are the most important thing in my life.

6. I will probably have more money to spend next year than I have now.

7. I often seek the advice of my friends regarding which store to buy from.

8. I think I have more self-confidence than most people.

9. I enjoy going to symphony concerts.

10. It is good to have charge accounts.

(These items are scored on a "agree strongly" to "disagree strongly" scale.)

Source: Alvin C. Burns and Mary Carolyn Harrison (1979), "A Test of the Reliability of Psychographics," Journal of Marketing Research (February), p. 34.

---

whether they are determinant, in the sense that they appear to affect the importance of various product characteristics.

Step 2: If step 1 produces promising results, undertake a benefit, product perception, and reported market behavior segmentation survey of consumers. Measure benefits and perceptions by usage-situation as well as by individual difference characteristics. Assess situation usage frequency by recall estimates or usage-situation diaries.

Step 3: Construct a person/situation segmentation matrix. The rows are the major usage situations and the columns are groups of users identified by a single characteristics or combination of characteristics.

Step 4: Rank the cells in the matrix in terms of their submarket sales volume. The situation/person combination that results in the greatest consumption of the generic product would be ranked first.

Step 5: State the major benefits sought, important product dimensions, and unique market behavior for each nonempty cell of the matrix. (Some person types will never consume the product in certain usage situations.)

Step 6: Position your competitors' offerings within the matrix. The person/situation segments they currently serve can be determined by the product feature they promote and other marketing strategies.

Step 7: Position your offering within the matrix on the same criteria.

Courtesy Speed Queen, a Raytheon Company

A product designed for a person/situation segment: Apartment dwellers.

Step 8: Assess how well your current offering and marketing strategy meet the needs of the submarkets compared to the competition's offering.

Step 9: Identify market opportunities based on submarket size, needs, and competitive advantage.[11]

---

[11] Ibid., p. 61.

FIGURE 16–6   ***Person Situation Benefit Segmentation***

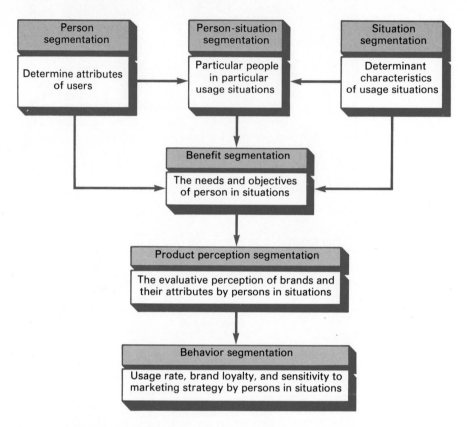

Source: Adopted from Peter R. Dickson (1982), "Person-Situation: Segmentation's Missing Link," Journal of Marketing *(Fall)*, pp. 55–64.

This approach has the advantage of incorporating all four of the major factors discussed in our text—cognition, behavior, environment, and marketing strategy. It thus offers a more comprehensive analysis than many other approaches.

Develop Product Positioning

By this time, the firm should have a good idea of the basic segments of the market that potentially could be satisfied with its product. The next step involves positioning the product relative to competing products in the minds of consumers.[12] A classic example of positioning is the 7UP "Uncola" campaign. Prior to this campaign, 7UP had difficulty in convincing consumers that the product could be enjoyed as a soft drink and not just as a mixer. Consumers believed that colas were soft drinks, but they apparently did not think of 7UP in this way. However, by promoting 7UP as the Uncola, the company positioned it both as a soft drink that could be consumed in the same situations as colas and as an alternative to colas. This positioning was very successful.[13]

The key objective of positioning strategy is to form a particular brand image in consumers' minds. This is accomplished by developing a coherent strategy that may involve all of the marketing mix elements. There are at least five approaches to positioning strategy, including positioning by attribute, by use or application, by product user, by product class, and by competitor.[14] We discuss these approaches below.

Positioning by Attribute

Probably the most frequently used positioning strategy is associating a product with an attribute, a product feature, or a customer benefit. Consider imported automobiles. Datsun and Toyota have emphasized economy and reliability. Volkswagen has used a "value for the money" association. Volvo has stressed safety and durability, showing commercials of crash tests and citing statistics on the average long life of their cars. Fiat, in contrast, has made a distinct effort to position itself as a European car with European craftsmanship. BMW has emphasized handling and engineering efficiency, using the tag line, "the ultimate driving machine" and showing BMW performance capabilities at a race track.

A new product can also be positioned with respect to an attribute that competitors have ignored. Paper towels had emphasized absorbency until Viva stressed durability, using demonstrations supporting the claim that Viva "keeps on working." Bounty paper towels are positioned as being "microwave safe" with dyes that do not come off in microwave ovens.

Sometimes a product can be positioned in terms of two or more attributes simultaneously. In the toothpaste market, Crest became a dominant brand with positioning as a cavity fighter, a claim supported by a

---

[12]It should be noted that the concept of "positioning" is somewhat ambiguous in the marketing literature and is used in a number of different ways. See John P. Maggard, "Positioning Revisited," *Journal of Marketing* (January 1976), pp. 63–73.

[13]See Jack Trout and Al Ries (1982), "The Positioning Era Cometh," in *Readings in Marketing Strategy*, Jean-Claude Larreche and Edward L. Strong (eds.), Palo Alto, Calif.: The Scientific Press, pp. 141–151. Also see Al Ries and Jack Trout (1981), *Positioning: The Battle for Your Mind*, New York: McGraw-Hill.

[14]David A. Aaker and J. Gary Shansby (1982), "Positioning Your Product," *Business Horizons* (May–June), pp. 36–62. The discussion that follows is based on this work.

Courtesy Volvo

Positioning by safety attributes.

medical-group endorsement. However, Aim achieved a 10 percent market share by positioning in terms of two attributes, good taste and cavity prevention. More recently, Aqua-fresh was introduced by Beecham as a gel paste that offers both cavity-fighting and breath-freshening benefits.

The price/quality attribute dimension is commonly used for positioning products as well as stores. In many product categories, some brands offer more in terms of service, features, or performance—and a higher price is one signal to the customer of this higher quality. For example, Curtis-Mathes TVs are positioned as high-priced, high-quality products. Conversely, other brands emphasize low price and good quality. The Yugo automobile, for example, is so positioned.

In general merchandise stores, Neiman-Marcus, Bloomingdale's, and Saks Fifth Avenue are near the top of the price/quality scale. Below them are Macy's, Robinson's, Bullock's, Rich's, Filene's, Dayton's, Hudson's, and so on. Stores such as Sears, Montgomery Ward, and J. C. Penney are positioned below these but above discount stores like K mart or Shopko. Interestingly, Sears, Penneys, and K mart have all attempted to upgrade their positions to avoid competing directly with successful discount and warehouse stores such as Wal Mart.

Positioning by Use or Application

Another positioning strategy is to associate the product with use or application. Campbell's soup for many years was positioned for use at lunch time and advertised extensively over noontime radio. Now, many Campbell's soups are positioned for use in sauces and dips, or as an ingredient in main dishes. AT&T has positioned long-distance calling by particular uses. For example, the "reach out and touch someone" campaign positions long-distance calls as a method of communicating with loved ones.

Products can, of course, have multiple positioning strategies, although increasing the number involves difficulties and risks. Often a positioning-by-use strategy represents a second or third position designed to expand the market. Thus, Gatorade, introduced as a summer beverage for athletes who need to replace body fluids, attempted to develop a winter positioning strategy as the beverage to drink when the doctor recommends drinking plenty of fluids. Similarly, Quaker Oats attempted to position a breakfast food as a natural whole-grain ingredient for recipes. Arm & Hammer baking soda has successfully positioned their product as an odor-destroying agent in refrigerators.

Positioning by Product User

Another positioning approach is to associate a product with a user or a class of users. Revlon's Charlie cosmetic line has been positioned by asso-

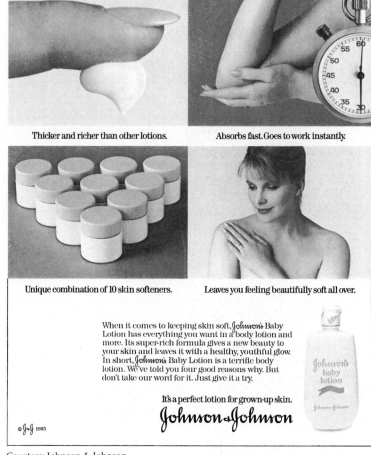

Courtesy Johnson & Johnson

Positioning by product user.

ciating it with a specific lifestyle profile. Johnson & Johnson increased its market share from 3 to 14 percent when they repositioned their shampoo from a product used for babies to one used by people who wash their hair frequently and therefore need a mild shampoo.

In 1970, Miller High Life was the "champagne of bottled beers," was purchased by the upper class, and had an image of being a woman's beer. Phillip Morris repositioned it as a beer for the heavy beer-drinking, blue-

HIGHLIGHT 16–3 **An Operational Approach to Product Positioning**

1. *Identify the Competitors.* This step involves defining the relevant market for the firm's offering. For example, Diet Coke might define its competition as (*a*) other diet cola drinks, (*b*) other cola drinks, (*c*) other soft drinks, (*d*) other nonalcoholic beverages, (*e*) other beverages. Usually, there will be a primary group of competitors (other diet colas) and a secondary group (other colas and soft drinks). Research identifying consumer product-use situations is useful here.

2. *Determine How Competitors Are Perceived and Evaluated.* This step involves identifying product attributes and associations made by consumers so that competitive brand images can be defined.

3. *Determine the Competitor's Position.* This step involves determining how competitors (including the firm's own entry) are positioned with respect to the relevant product associations. Multidimensional scaling and other multivariate approaches are useful at this stage.

4. *Analyze the Customers.* This step involves developing a thorough knowledge of the behavior of various market segments, including the role of the product class in the customer's lifestyle, and consumer motivations, habits, and behavior patterns.

5. *Select the Position.* While there is no cookbook solution for selecting an optimal position, key decision criteria include (*a*) the nature of the market segments, (*b*) economic criteria, especially market potential and penetration probability, (*c*) a consistent image across time, and (*d*) not positioning the product to be better than it is.

6. *Monitoring the Position.* A positioning strategy should be monitored across time to evaluate it and to generate diagnostic information about future positioning strategies. This involves ongoing research and may include one or more techniques such as multidimensional scaling.

Source: Condensed from David A. Aaker and Gary Shandy (1982), "Positioning Your Product," Business Horizons *(May–June), pp. 56–62.*

collar working man. Miller's Lite beer, introduced in 1975, used convincing beer-drinking personalities to position it as a beer for the heavy beer drinker who dislikes that "filled-up feeling." In contrast, earlier efforts to introduce low-calorie beers positioned with respect to the low-calorie attribute were dismal failures. Miller's positioning strategies are in part why it moved up to the number two brewing company in the United States.

Positioning by Product Class

Some critical positioning decisions involve product-class associations. For example, Maxim freeze dried was positioned with respect to regular and instant coffee. Some margarines are positioned with respect to butter. A maker of dried milk introduced an instant breakfast drink positioned as a breakfast substitute and a virtually identical product positioned as a meal substitute for those on diets. The soap Caress, made by Lever Brothers, was positioned as a bath-oil product rather than a soap. The 7UP example we discussed earlier is also an example of positioning by product class.

Positioning by Competitors

In most positioning strategies, an explicit or implicit frame of reference is the competition. Often, the major purpose of this type of positioning is to convince consumers that a brand is better than the market leader (or other well-accepted brand) on important attributes. Positioning with respect to a competitor is commonly done in advertisements in which a competitor is named and compared. For example, Burger King ads argued that McDonald's burgers had less beef and did not taste as good as Burger Kings' because McDonald's product was not flame broiled. Both Pepsi and Coke have run comparative ads claiming that their brand tastes better than the other one.

A classic example of this type of positioning was the Avis "We're number two, so we try harder" ad campaign. The strategy was to position Avis with Hertz as a major car-rental agency and away from National, which at the time was at least as large as Avis. This strategy was quite successful.

Select Segmentation Strategy

Having completed the analysis in the previous stages, the appropriate segmentation strategy can now be considered. There are four basic alternatives. *First,* the firm may decide not to enter the market. Analysis to this stage may reveal that there is no viable market niche for the product, brand, or model. *Second,* the firm may decide not to segment but to be a mass marketer. This may be the appropriate strategy in at least three situations:

1. When the market is so small that marketing to a portion of it is not profitable.
2. When heavy users make up such a large proportion of the sales volume that they are the only relevant target.

3. When the brand is dominant in the market and targeting to a few segments would not benefit sales and profits.[15]

Third, the firm may decide to market to only one segment. *Fourth,* the firm may decide to market to more than one segment and design a separate marketing mix for each. In any case, marketers must have some criteria on which to base its segmentation strategy decisions. Three important criteria are that a viable segment must be measurable, meaningful, and marketable:

1. *Measurable.* For a segment to be selected, marketers must be able to measure its size and characteristics. For example, one of the difficulties with segmenting on the basis of social class is that the concept and its divisions are not clearly defined and measured. Alternatively, income is much easier to measure.

2. *Meaningful.* A meaningful segment is one that is large enough to have sufficient sales and growth potentials to offer long-run profits.

3. *Marketable.* A marketable segment is one that can be reached and served profitably.

Segments that meet these criteria are viable markets for the product. The marketer must now give further attention to the marketing mix.

Design Marketing-Mix Strategy

The firm is now in a position to complete its marketing strategy by finalizing the marketing mix for each segment. Selecting the target market and designing the marketing mix go hand in hand, and thus many marketing-mix decisions should have already been carefully considered. For example, if the target market selected is price sensitive, some consideration has already been given to price levels. Product positioning also has many implications for selecting appropriate promotions and channels. Thus, many marketing mix decisions are made *in conjunction with* (rather than after) target-market selection. In the remaining chapters of this section, consumer behavior and marketing mix strategies will be discussed in more detail.

---

[15]Shirley Young, Leland Ott and Barbara Feigin (1978), "Some Practical Considerations in Market Segmentation," *Journal of Marketing Research* (August 1978), p. 405.

Back to the Case

The Campbell soup case illustrates the importance and value of market segmentation and product positioning. As a production-oriented company, Campbell was mired in traditions of understated advertising and dependence on its soup products to represent a "good value for the money" lunchtime meal for the traditional homemaker. Advertising expenditures were frequently cut at the end of a fiscal quarter to boost earnings. This, of course, hurt Campbell's sales and gave it a terrible reputation with the media.

How did the new marketing orientation work for Campbell? According to *Business Week*, for the 1982–83 fiscal years, average tonnage rose 6.5 percent—exceeding the firm's 5 percent goal and a big improvement over the previous two years, which showed an average decline of 2 percent. "Our share of market is holding and in some cases building," McGovern said. Their Mrs. Paul's division, for example, reversed a market-share decline, going from 24 to 27 percent in one year. For the fiscal year ended August 1, 1983, Prego division ran up sales of around $100 million, even though it was not in national distribution for the full year. In late 1983, it became the number two bottled Italian-style sauce behind Ragu, grabbing a 22 percent market share.

Advertising strategy was also rethought and ad spending increased. Ad expenditures for fiscal 1983 rose 39 percent over the previous year, to $144 million. Fiscal 1984's budget was $175 million. Some of the ad messages focused on the nutritional benefits of the products. "Soup is good food," is an example. Others focused on using soup in recipes as well as positioning it as an excellent hot food to warm up with during the cold winter months.

Summary

The purpose of this chapter was to provide an overview of market segmentation analysis. Market segmentation was defined as the process of dividing a market into groups of similar consumers and selecting the most appropriate group(s) for the firm to serve. Market segmentation was analyzed in terms of five interrelated tasks: (1) analyze consumer/product relationships; (2) investigate segmentation approaches; (3) develop product positioning; (4) select segmentation strategy; and (5) design marketing mix strategy. Market segmentation analysis is a major cornerstone of sound marketing strategy development and is one of the major bridges between the literature dealing with marketing strategy and with consumer behavior.

Additional Reading

Thomas V. Bonoma and Benson R. Shapiro (1983), *Segmenting the Industrial Market,* Lexington, Mass.: Lexington Books.

Alfred S. Boote (1981), "Market Segmentation by Personal Values and Salient Product Attributes," *Journal of Advertising Research* (February), pp. 29–35.

Stephen C. Cosmas (1982), "Life Styles and Consumption Patterns," *Journal of Consumer Research* (March), pp. 453–55.

George S. Day, Allan D. Shocker and Rajendra K. Srivastava (1979), "Customer-Oriented Approaches to Identifying Product Markets," *Journal of Marketing* (Fall), pp. 8–19.

Terry Elrod and Russell S. Winer (1982), "An Empirical Evaluation of Aggregation Approaches for Developing Market Segments," *Journal of Marketing* (Fall), pp. 65–74.

Ronald Frank, William Massy, and Yoram Wind (1972), *Market Segmentation,* Englewood Cliffs, N.J.: Prentice-Hall.

Richard M. Johnson (1971), "Market Segmentation: A Strategic Management Tool," *Journal of Marketing Research* (February), pp. 13– 18.

John W. Keon (1983), "Product Positioning: TRINODAL Mapping of Brand Images, Ad Images, and Consumer Preferences," *Journal of Marketing Research* (November), pp. 380–392.

William R. Swinyard (1977), "Market Segmentation in Retail Service Industries: A Multiattribute Approach," *Journal of Retailing* (Spring), pp. 27–34.

Yoram Wind and Richard Cardozo (1974), "Industrial Market Segmentation," *Industrial Marketing Management* (March), pp. 153– 166.

Frederick W. Winter (1979), "A Cost-Benefit Approach to Market Segmentation," *Journal of Marketing* (Fall), pp. 103–111.

Sonia Yuspeh and Gene Fein (1982), "Can Segments Be Born Again?" *Journal of Advertising Research* (June–July), pp. 13–22.

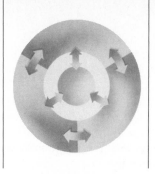

Chapter Seventeen

Product Strategy and Consumer Behavior

Admiral Home Appliances

It has been a long time since product innovation played much of a role in the refrigerator business. The first frost-free units were introduced in 1954, automatic ice makers in 1956. But in the years since, the "only thing else that's changed much is the colors," says John Green, president of Admiral Home Appliances, a division of Magic Chef, Inc. "The industry has pretty much operated on the theory that all consumers want is a reliable and economic box to keep their food fresh."

Green is trying to change that. Operating under what he calls his Marketing Manifesto, Admiral has embarked on an ambitious plan to introduce at least one new product each year. Begun with a refrigerator called the Entertainer (featuring a built-in wine rack and microwave storage trays), the strategy seems to be meeting with success. In fact, it has increased Admiral's fourth-place share of the refrigerator and freezer market by 50 percent and has turned annual losses into profits.

Admiral's gains in an industry dominated by much larger and richer companies has also given a boost to Magic Chef, which bought the then-floundering Admiral business from Rockwell International in 1979. At the time, Admiral was posting annual deficits of close to $40 million a year, and some appliance experts believed Magic Chef was making a mistake. "They practically bet the whole company on Admiral," said Eugene Mondry, president of Highland Appliance, a Detroit retail chain.

Admiral brought out an even more expensive model in 1983. It was priced at $1,299 and could make ice cream, soup, and chilled drinks. "The idea was to turn a refrigerator partly into a food processor," said Green. Sales of the model, called the A la Mode, exceeded $22 million in the first 12 months, sharply higher than even Admiral's ambitious forecast. Almost all of the sales represented new business.

Combined with a new blast freezer that, among other things, can make ice cubes in 45 minutes, Admiral's new products have given it an estimated 15 percent of the more than $4.5 billion-a-year refrigerator and freezer market, up from about 10 percent in 1980.

To some extent, Green attributes Admiral's recent success to the chance to stick to a long-term marketing plan. "At Rockwell, the Admiral division had virtually a new management and a new operating team every year. A lot of those plans probably would have worked just as well as ours, but they never had a chance. We haven't altered our strategy once in the last five years."

Source: Excerpted from John Koten (1984), "Innovative, Upscale Iceboxes Mark a Sales Coup for Admiral," The Wall Street Journal (April 19), p. 29.

The product area is considered by many experts to be the most important element of the marketing mix. For example, Booz, Allen & Hamilton, a business consulting company, noted a number of years ago, "If it is accepted that products are the medium of business conduct, then business strategy is fundamentally product planning."

Of course, a key element in product planning is the matching of products with consumer markets. While products may be the medium of business conduct from the producer's viewpoint, the exchange of consumer assets for products is the acid test that determines whether products will succeed or fail.

In this chapter, we focus on product strategy and some consumers' product-related cognitions, behaviors, and environmental factors. Figure 17–1 provides the framework for this chapter and lists the topics to be discussed. Although many of the topics previously discussed in our text concern consumer/product relationships, the topics in this chapter have special relevance for product strategy. We begin by investigating product strategy and then examine consumers' product-related environmental factors, cognitions, and behaviors.

FIGURE 17–1   *The Wheel of Consumer Analysis: Product Strategy Issues*

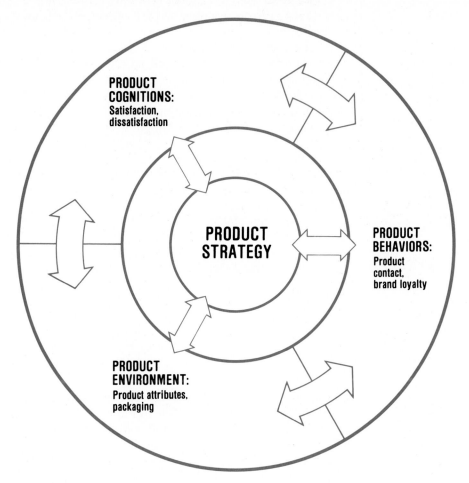

Product Strategy

Product strategies are designed to influence consumers in both the short and the long run. In the short run, new-product strategies are designed to influence consumers to try the product; in the long run, product strategies are designed to develop brand loyalty and obtain large market shares.

A critical aspect of designing product strategies involves analyzing consumer/product relationships. This means that consumers' product-related cognitions, behaviors, and environments should be carefully considered in introducing new products and should be monitored throughout a product's life cycle. In this section, we first examine some personal characteristics of consumers that affect product adoptions. Then, we examine some characteristics of products that influence the adoption process.

Characteristics of Consumers

In analyzing consumer/product relationships, it is important to recognize that consumers vary in their willingness to try new products. Different types of consumers may adopt a new product at different times in the product's life cycle. Figure 17–2 presents the classic adoption curve and five categories of adopters. The adoption curve represents the cumulative percentage of purchasers of a product across time.

Traditionally, the five adopter groups are characterized as follows: **Innovators** are venturesome and willing to take risks; **Early Adopters** are respectable and often influence the Early Majority; the **Early Majority** avoid risks and are deliberate in their purchases; the **Late Majority** are skeptical and cautious about new ideas; **Laggards** are very traditional and set in their ways.

Designers of product strategies find Innovators particularly important because they may influence Early Adopters, who in turn, may influence the Early Majority to purchase. Thus, a new product's chances of

FIGURE 17–2   **The Adoption Curve**

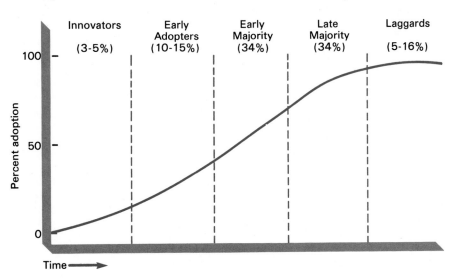

success are increased once Innovators purchase the product and tell others about it. Also, Early Adopters and others can learn vicariously about the product by seeing Innovators using it.

A major focus of consumer research has been to identify the characteristics of Innovators and their differences from other consumers. A review of this research found that Innovators tend to be more highly educated and younger, and to have greater social mobility, more favorable attitudes toward risk (more venturesome), greater social participation, and higher opinion leadership than other consumers.[1]

Innovators also tend to be heavy users of other products within a product class. For example, Dickerson and Gentry found that adopters of home computers had greater experience with other technical products—such as programmable pocket calculators and video television games—than did nonadopters.[2] Innovators may have better developed knowledge structures for particular product categories. This may enable them to understand and evaluate new products more rapidly and thus adopt earlier than other consumers.[3]

Finally, it should be noted that the five adopter categories and the percentages in Figure 17–2 are somewhat arbitrary. These categories were developed in research in rural sociology that dealt with major farming innovations. Their validity has not been fully supported in consumer research, particularly for low-involvement products.[4]

However, the idea that different types of consumers purchase products in different stages of the product's life cycle does have important implications for product strategy. Namely, product strategy (and other elements of marketing strategy) must change across time to appeal to different types of consumers. Figure 17–3 suggests some changes in strategy that may be required to appeal to various consumers at different stages in the product life cycle.

Characteristics of Products

In analyzing consumer/product relationships, it is also important to consider the product characteristics listed in Figure 17–4. A number of these characteristics have been found to influence the success of new products and brands.[5] There is no absolute demarcation; but some of the dimensions

---

[1]Hubert Gatignon and Thomas S. Robertson (1985), "A Propositional Inventory for New Diffusion Research," *Journal of Consumer Research* (March), pp. 849–867.

[2]Mary Dee Dickerson and James W. Gentry (1983), "Characteristics of Adopters and Non-Adopters of Home Computers," *Journal of Consumer Research* (September), pp. 225–235.

[3]Elizabeth C. Hirschman (1980), "Innovativeness, Novelty Seeking, and Consumer Creativity," *Journal of Consumer Research* (December), pp. 283–295.

[4]Gatignon and Robertson, "A Propositional Inventory," p. 861.

[5]See Everett M. Rogers (1983), *Diffusion of Innovations,* New York: Free Press.

are more directly involved with facilitating trial, while others both facilitate trial and encourage brand loyalty. We will discuss each of these characteristics below.

Compatibility

Compatibility refers to the degree to which a product is consistent with consumers' current cognitions and behaviors. Other things being equal, a

---

FIGURE 17–3 **Elements of Marketing Strategy in Product Life Cycle**

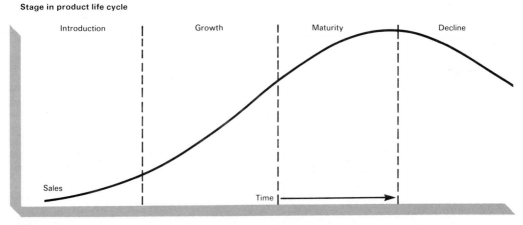

Stage in product life cycle

Marketing strategy elements	Introduction	Growth	Maturity	Decline
Objective:	To get trial.	Establish strong brand position with distributors and users.	Maintain and strengthen customer loyalty.	Seek remaining profit.
Product:	Few models, high quality.	Modular, flexible, more models for segments emerging.	Tighten lines not serving good markets; product improvement and differentiation.	Reduce line to major profit producers.
Price:	Good value, trade discounts.	Long price line from low to premium.	Attention to broadening market; promotional pricing to extend brand coverage.	Maintain profit levels without regard to share of market.
Distribution:	Exclusive or selective.	Intensive and extensive; quick service to dealers; high dealer inventory.	Intensive and extensive; quick service to dealers; low dealer inventory.	Phase out marginal dealers.
Promotion:	Create awareness, get early trial; fairly heavy advertising and free samples.	Create strong brand awareness and preference; maximum use of mass media.	Maintain and strengthen customer-dealer relations; continue mass media, sales promotion.	Rapid phaseout; sustain enough to sell profitable volume only.
Marketing research:	Discover weaknesses; identify emerging segments.	Market position, market gaps; product gaps.	Attention to product improvement; search for broader market and new promotion themes.	Determine point of product elimination.

Source: Adapted from Chester R. Wasson, Dynamic Competitive Strategy and Product Life Cycles *(Austin, Tex.: Austin Press, 1978).*

product that does not require an important change in consumer values and beliefs or purchase and use behaviors is more likely to be tried by consumers. For example, Chewels chewing gum—the gum with a liquid center—required little change on the part of consumers to try the product.

Trialability

Trialability refers to the degree to which a product can be tried on a limited basis or divided into small quantities for an inexpensive trial. Other things being equal, a product that facilitates a nonpurchase trial or a limited-purchase trial is more likely to influence the consumer to try the product. Test driving a car, trying on a sweater, tasting bite-sized pieces of a new frozen pizza, accepting a free trial of a new encyclopedia, or buying a sample-size bottle of a new shampoo are ways that consumers can try products on a limited basis and reduce risk..

Observability

Observability refers to the degree to which products or their effects can be sensed by other consumers. New products that are public and frequently discussed are more likely to be adopted rapidly. For example, many clothing styles become popular after consumers see movie and recording stars wearing them. Satellite disks are highly observable, and this feature likely influences their purchase.

Speed

Speed refers to how fast the benefits of the product are experienced by the consumer. Because many consumers are oriented toward immediate rather than delayed gratification, products that can deliver benefits sooner rather

---

FIGURE 17–4   ***Some Important Questions in Analyzing Consumer/Product Relationships***

1. ***Compatability***—How well does this product fit consumers' current cognitions and behaviors?
2. ***Trialability***—Can consumers try the product on a limited basis with little risk?
3. ***Observability***—Do consumers frequently see or otherwise sense this product?
4. ***Speed***—How soon do consumers experience the benefits of the product?
5. ***Simplicity***—How easy is it for consumers to understand and use the product?
6. ***Relative advantage***—What makes this product better than competitive offerings?
7. ***Product symbolism***—What does this product mean to consumers?
8. ***Marketing strategy***—What is the role of other marketing mix elements in creating a functional or image-related relative advantage?

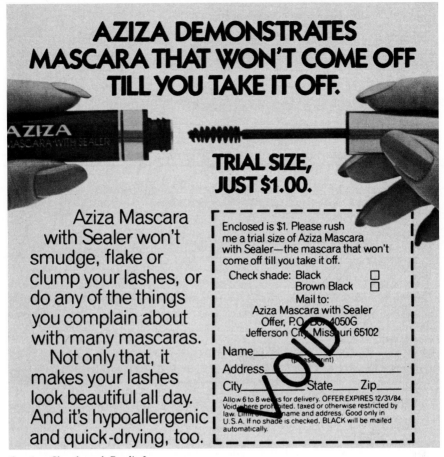

Courtesy Chesebrough-Pond's, Inc.

A marketing strategy to increase trialability.

than later have a higher probability of at least being tried. For example, weight-loss programs that promise results within the first week are more likely to attract consumers than are those that promise results in six months.

Simplicity

Simplicity refers to the degree to which a product is easy for a consumer to understand and use. Other things being equal, a product that does not require complicated assembly and extensive training for the consumer to use it has a higher chance of trial. For example, many computer products are promoted as being "user friendly" to encourage purchase.

HIGHLIGHT 17–1 **Nine Types of New Products**

1. A product performing an entirely *new function,* such as television, which for the first time permitted the transmission of audiovisual signals.
2. A product that offers *improved performance of an existing function,* such as a wristwatch whose balance wheel has been replaced by a tuning fork.
3. A product that is a *new application of an existing product.* For example, the aerosol bomb, which was first developed for insecticides, was later applied to paints.
4. A product that offers *additional functions.* The hands-free telephone, for example, does what the earlier telephone did, plus more.
5. An existing product offered to a *new market.* This may be done, for example, by repositioning or by taking a regional brand into other regions.

6. A product that through *lower cost,* is able to reach more buyers. Hand calculators are an example.
7. An upgraded product defined as an *existing product integrated into another existing product.* The clock radio is an example.
8. *A downgraded product.* For example, a manufacturer switches from buying a component to producing a cheaper component in house and marketing it.
9. *A restyled product.* Annual auto and clothing changes are examples.

Source: Saul Sands and Kenneth M. Warwick, "Successful Business Innovation" (1977), California Management Review *(Winter), p. 7. Also see C. Merle Crawford (1986),* New Products Management *(Homewood, Ill.: Richard D. Irwin, p. 35.*

Relative Advantage

Relative advantage refers to the degree to which an item has a *sustainable, competitive differential advantage* over other product classes, product forms, and brands. There is no question that relative advantage is a most important product characteristic not only for obtaining trial, but also for continued purchase and the development of brand loyalty.

In some cases, a relative advantage may be obtained through technological developments. For example, at the product-class level, RCA introduced the video disc player, which showed programs on any TV set. The disc player cost half as much as cassette machines, and the discs were cheaper than video cassettes. However, video cassettes had a relative advantage over the disc player: they could record programs, and the disc players could not. RCA thought that recording ability was not an important factor to consumers—and lost more than $500 million finding out otherwise.

At the brand level, however, it is often difficult to maintain a technological relative advantage. This is because new or improved technology is quickly copied by competitors. For example, Sony pioneered the Betamax system of videotape recorders, and in 1975 had the entire video recorder market. By 1982, however, Sony held only 14 percent of the market and was fighting for survival. Competitors simply copied the technology and—by saving money on R&D—could sell at a lower price.

Relative advantage is a most important element of successful product strategies. However, such an advantage can seldom be sustained through technology or modifications of product attributes alone. We believe that one of the most important sources of a sustainable relative advantage is product symbolism.

Product Symbolism

Product symbolism refers to what the product or brand means to the consumer and what the consumer experiences in purchasing and using it. Consumer researchers recognize that some products possess symbolic features, and that consumption of them may depend more on their social and psychological meaning than on their functional utility.[6] For example, the blue-jean market is dominated by major brands such as Levi's, Wrangler's, and Lee's, and it is difficult to determine clear differences in these jeans except in pocket design and brand labeling. If these brand names meant nothing to consumers and were purchased only on the basis of product attributes such as materials and styles, it would be difficult to explain differences in market shares, given the similarity among brands. Similarly, it would be difficult to describe how a brand such as Guess? jeans obtained $200 million in sales in its first three years. It seems clear that jeans brand names have meanings and symbolize different values for consumers. For example, teenagers make up a large portion of the market for Guess? jeans. These consumers may be seeking to present an identity different from that of wearers of traditional brands, such as their parents.

It is also likely that appropriate images can be far more important than technological superiority. For example, the IBM personal computer is not the fastest, most technologically advanced PC on the market. In fact, many users even criticize its keyboard layout. IBM was not the first in the

---

[6]Michael R. Solomon (1983), "The Role of Products as Social Stimuli: A Symbolic Interactionism Perspective," *Journal of Consumer Research* (December), pp. 319–329. Also see Morris B. Holbrook and Elizabeth C. Hirschman (1982), "The Experiential Aspects of Consumption: Consumer Fantasies, Feeling, and Fun," *Journal of Consumer Research* (September), pp. 132–140; Morris B. Holbrook, Robert B. Chestnut, Terence A. Oliva and Eric A. Greenleaf (1984), "Play as a Consumption Experience: The Roles of Emotions, Performance, and Personality in the Enjoyment of Games," *Journal of Consumer Research* (September), pp. 728–739.

PC market and had little experience in consumer goods marketing. However, IBM dominates the PC market—perhaps because of its superior company image as a computer manufacturer; that is, IBM *means* computers to many people.

Marketing Strategy

To this point, we have suggested that a variety of product characteristics partially account for the success or failure of products and brands. Though not strictly a product characteristic, the quality of the **marketing strategy** employed also has an important bearing on whether or not a product is successful and profitable.

We have also argued that at the brand level, the image or symbolism a brand carries is often the only relative advantage that a firm has to offer. This frequently happens because in many product classes, the brands offered are relatively homogeneous in their functional utility to the consumer.

In many cases, a favorable image is created through the other elements of the marketing mix. *Promotion* is commonly used to create a favorable image for the brand by pairing it with positively evaluated stimuli, such as attractive models. In addition, promotion informs consumers as to what attributes they should be looking for in the product class and emphasizes the superiority of the brand in terms of those attributes. It is well known that few consumers can tell the difference in the taste of various brands of beer—and that in fact, many consumers do not initially like the taste of beer. Thus, many commercials try to teach consumers that a particular brand tastes great, or at least as good as more expensive beers. We suspect that brand image is a key determinant of beer brand choice, although many consumers would likely disavow image and insist that taste is the most important consideration.

Price can also create brand images as well as provide a functional relative advantage. In terms of brand images, high prices can connote high quality for some products; and it is often stated that consumers perceive a relationship between price and quality. Price can also be used to position a brand as a good value for the money; e.g., Suave hair-care products are as good as the expensive brands but much cheaper. As a functional relative advantage, through vast economies of scale and large market shares, a firm can sometimes sustain a price advantage that no competitor can meet. Campbell's soups have long enjoyed such an advantage. In the airlines industry, People Express has had a price-oriented differential advantage.

Finally, a variety of *distribution* tactics can be used to gain a relative advantage. Good site locations and a large number of outlets are important advantages in the fast-food market and in the markets for other products and services. Also, a variety of in-store stimuli, such as displays, can offer products at least a temporary relative advantage.

HIGHLIGHT 17–2 **Characteristics of Classes of Consumer Goods and Some Marketing Considerations**

Characteristics and Marketing Considerations	Type of Product		
	Convenience	**Shopping**	**Specialty**
Characteristics:			
1. Time and effort devoted by consumer to shopping	Very little	Considerable	Cannot generalize; may go to nearby store and exert minimum effort or may have to go to distant store and spend much time
2. Time spent planning the purchase	Very little	Considerable	Considerable
3. How soon want is satisfied after it arises	Immediately	Relatively long time	Relatively long time
4. Are price and quality compared?	No	Yes	No
5. Price	Low	High	High
6. Frequency of purchase	Usually frequent	Infrequent	Infrequent
7. Importance	Unimportant	Often very important	Cannot generalize
Marketing considerations:			
1. Length of channel	Long	Short	Short to very short
2. Importance of retailer	Any single store is relatively unimportant	Important	Very important
3. Number of outlets	As many as possible	Few	Few; often only one in a market
4. Stock turnover	High	Lower	Lower
5. Gross margin	Low	High	High
6. Responsibility for advertising	Manufacturer's	Retailer's	Joint responsibility
7. Importance of point-of-purchase display	Very important	Less important	Less important
8. Advertising used	Manufacturer's	Retailer's	Both
9. Brand or store name important	Brand name	Store name	Both
10. Importance of package	Very important	Less important	Less important

Source: William J. Stanton (1984), Fundamentals of Marketing, *New York: Mc-Graw-Hill, p. 138.*

The Product Environment

The **product environment** refers to product-related stimuli that are attended to and comprehended by consumers. In general, the majority of these stimuli are received through the sense of sight, although there are many exceptions. For example, the way a stereo sounds or how a silk shirt feels also influence consumer cognitions and behaviors. In this section, we will focus on two types of environmental stimuli: product attributes and packaging.

Product Attributes

Products and product attributes are major stimuli that affect consumer cognitions and behaviors. These attributes may be evaluated by consumers in terms of their own values, beliefs, and past experiences. Marketing and other information also influence whether purchase and use of the product is likely to be rewarding or not. For example, the product attributes of a new shirt might include color, material, sleeve length, type and number of buttons, and type of collar. By investigating these attributes and by trying the shirt on, a consumer might conclude, "This shirt is well made and I look good in it"; "This shirt is for nerds"; or "This shirt is well made but just isn't for me."

It is unlikely that many consumers would purchase a shirt based on these product attributes alone, however. The price of the shirt would likely be important; the store selling the shirt (and the store's image) might be considered. In addition, the packaging, brand name, and brand identification would likely be factors. In fact, for many purchases, the image of the brand created through the nonproduct variables of price, promotion, and channels of distribution, may be the most critical determinant of purchase.

Packaging

Packaging is an element of the product environment for which marketers spend over $50 billion annually. Traditionally, four packaging objectives are considered. First, packaging should *protect* the product as it moves through the channel to the consumer. Second, packaging should be *economical* and not add undue cost to the product. Third, packaging should allow *convenient* storage and use of the product by the consumer. Fourth, packaging can be used effectively to *promote* the product to the consumer.

In some cases, packaging has been used as the key to obtaining a relative advantage. For example, in 1983, Brik Pak Inc. sold $50 million worth of aseptic "paper bottles" to a variety of consumer-goods companies.

HIGHLIGHT 17–3 **Characteristics of a Good Brand Name**

- Short and simple
- Easy to spell and read
- Easy to recognize and remember
- Pleasing when read or heard—and easy to pronounce
- Pronounceable in only one way
- Pronounceable in all languages (for goods to be exported)
- Always timely (does not go out of date)
- Adaptable to packaging or labeling needs
- Legally available for use (not used by another firm)
- Not offensive, obscene, or negative
- Suggestive of product benefits
- Adaptable to any advertising medium (especially billboards and television)

Source: E. Jerome McCarthy and William D. Perreault, Jr. (1984), Basic Marketing, *8th ed., Home-wood, Ill.: Richard D. Irwin, p. 312.*

The advantage of these packages is that they are 50 percent cheaper than cans and 70 percent cheaper than bottles, do not require refrigerated shipment and storage, and are more convenient for the consumer. The sales volume of Hi-C fruit drinks increased 20 percent by using this form of packaging. As another example of a packaging advantage, Chesebrough-Pond's increased nail-polish sales by 22 percent with its Aziza Polishing Pen, which was perceived as easier to use than the traditional brush in a bottle. D-Con Company emphasized the advantages of its pen dispenser for insecticide rather than the insecticide formula when it introduced Exact.[7] In these examples, mature products were differentiated on the basis of packaging alone.

Package Colors

In addition to the nature of the package itself, it has been argued that package colors have an important impact on consumers' cognitions and behaviors. This impact is more than just attracting attention by using eye-

---

[7]Amy Dunkin (1985), "Want to Wake Up a Tired Old Product? Repackage It," *Business Week* (July 15), pp. 130–134.

Courtesy Procter & Gamble Company

Packaging can give a product a relative advantage.

catching colors (like Tide's day-glow orange). Rather, it has been argued that package colors connote meaning to consumers and can be used strategically.[8]

For instance, the color of the Ritz cracker box was changed to a deeper red trimmed with a thin gold band. This change was made to appeal to

[8]These examples are taken from Ronald Alsop (1984), "Color Grows More Important in Catching Consumers' Eyes," *The Wall Street Journal* (November 29), p. 37.

young, affluent consumers. Microsoft Corporation changed its software packages from green to red and royal blue, because consultants argued that green was not eye-catching and connoted frozen vegetables and gum to consumers rather than high-tech software. Swanson dropped the turquoise triangle from its frozen dinners, because that color was thought to give the product a dated, 1950s look. Canada Dry changed the color of its cans and bottles of sugar-free ginger ale from red to green and white when consultants argued that red sent a misleading cola message to consumers. Canada Dry sales were reported to increase 25 percent after this color change.

It has also been reported that consumer perceptions of products may change with a change in package color. For example, when designers at Berni Corporation changed the background hue on Barrelhead sugar-free root beer cans from blue to beige, consumers reported that the product tasted more like old-fashioned root beer—even though the beverage itself remained exactly the same. Similarly, consumers ascribed a sweeter taste to orange drinks when a darker shade of orange was used on the can or bottle.

Brand Identification and Label Information

The brand identification and label information on the package (as well as on the product) provide additional stimuli for consideration by the con-

Arnold Crane: Click/Chicago

Label information can influence purchase behavior.

sumer. Brand identification in many cases simplifies purchase for the consumer and makes the loyalty development process possible. As we noted previously, brand names such as Gloria Vanderbilt, Cadillac, or Florsheim may well be discriminative stimuli for consumers.

Label information includes use instructions, contents, lists of ingredients or raw materials, warnings for use and care of the product, and the like. For some products, this information can strongly influence purchase. For example, consumers often carefully examine label information on over-the-counter drugs such as cough medicines. Health-conscious consumers often consult package information to determine the nutritional value, sugar content, and calories in a serving of products such as cereal.

Product Cognitions

Much of our discussion of cognition in Section Two of this text focused on products and how consumers interpret and integrate information about them. One area of cognitive research that deserves special consideration in product strategy concerns *satisfaction* and *dissatisfaction*.

Satisfaction

Consumer satisfaction is a critical concept in marketing thought and consumer research. It is generally argued that if consumers are satisfied with a product or brand, they will be more likely to continue to purchase and use it and to tell others of their favorable experiences with it. If they are dissatisfied, they will be more likely to switch brands and complain to manufacturers, retailers, and other consumers about the product.

Given its importance to marketing, then, considerable consumer research has been conducted on satisfaction.[9] While there are a variety of approaches, the most heavily researched is called the *disconfirmation paradigm*, advocated by Oliver.[10] This approach views satisfaction with prod-

---

[9]In fact, there are a number of reviews of the literature on consumer satisfaction. See, for example, Stephen A. LaTour and Nancy C. Peat (1979), "Conceptual and Methodological Issues in Consumer Satisfaction Research," in *Advances in Consumer Research,* Vol. 6, William L. Wilke (ed.), Ann Arbor, Mich.: Association for Consumer Research, pp. 431–437; Denise T. Smart (1982), "Consumer Satisfaction Research: A Review," in *Consumer Behavior: Classical and Contemporary Dimensions,* James U. McNeal and Stephen W. McDaniel (eds.), Boston: Little, Brown, pp. 286–306.

[10]For example, see Richard L. Oliver (1980), "A Cognitive Model of the Antecedents and Consequences of Satisfaction Decisions," *Journal of Marketing Research* (November), pp. 460–469.

ucts and brands as a result of two other cognitive variables, prepurchase expectations and disconfirmation. **Prepurchase expectations** are beliefs about anticipated performance of the product; **disconfirmation** refers to the difference between prepurchase expectations and perceptions of post-purchase. Prepurchase expectations are confirmed when the product performs as expected and are disconfirmed when it does not. There are two types of disconfirmation: **negative disconfirmation** occurs when product performance is less than expected, and **positive disconfirmation** occurs when product performance is better than expected. *Satisfaction* occurs when performance is at least as good as expected; dissatisfaction occurs when performance is worse than expected.

Based on these ideas, Oliver defines satisfaction as follows:

> Satisfaction may best be understood as an evaluation of the surprise inherent in a product acquisition and/or consumption experience. In essence, it is the summary psychological state resulting when the emotion surrounding disconfirmed expectations is coupled with the consumer's prior feelings about the consumption experience. Moreover, the surprise or excitement of this evaluation is thought to be of finite duration, so that satisfaction soon decays into (but nevertheless greatly affects) one's overall attitude toward purchasing products, particularly with regard to specific retail environments.[11]

One advantage of Oliver's approach is that it integrates the concept of satisfaction with consumers' attitudes and purchase intentions. As shown in Figure 17–5, prepurchase intentions are a function of prepurchase attitudes, which in turn, are a function of prepurchase expectations. After the product is purchased and experienced, it is hypothesized that prepurchase expectations, if positively disconfirmed or confirmed, will lead to satisfaction; if they are negatively disconfirmed, this will lead to dissatisfaction. Postpurchase attitudes and intentions are then influenced by the degree of satisfaction/dissatisfaction as well as the prepurchase levels of these cognitions.

Most research on consumer satisfaction using this approach has supported the model.[12] One exception is the work by Churchill and Surprenant, which found support for the model with a nondurable good but not

---

[11]Richard L. Oliver (1981), "Measurement and Evaluation of Satisfaction Processes in Retail Settings," *Journal of Retailing* (Fall), p. 27.

[12]For example, see P. A. LaBarbera and D. Mazursky (1983), "A Longitudinal Assessment of Consumer Satisfaction/ Dissatisfaction: The Dynamic Aspect of the Cognitive Process," *Journal of Marketing Research* (November), pp. 393–404.

FIGURE 17–5   **Cognitive Antecedents and Consequences of Satisfaction**

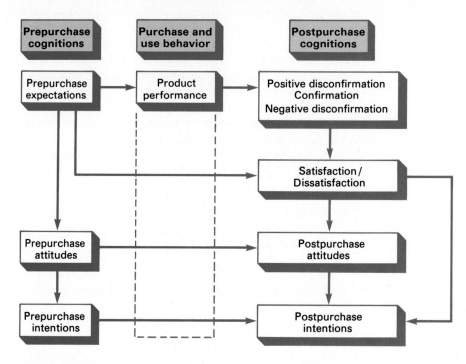

Source: Adapted from Richard L. Oliver (1980), "A Cognitive Model of the Antecedents and Consequences of Satisfaction Decisions," Journal of Marketing Research
(November), p. 462.

with a durable good.[13] Bearden and Teel found support for the model and
also extended it to the study of dissatisfaction and complaining behavior.[14]

Dissatisfaction

As we have noted, **dissatisfaction** occurs when prepurchase expectations
are negatively disconfirmed, i.e., the product performs worse than expected. Consumers who are dissatisfied with products are not likely to

[13]Gilbert A. Churchill, Jr. and Carol Suprenant (1982), "An Investigation into the Determinants of Customer Satisfaction," *Journal of Marketing Research* (November), pp. 491–504.

[14]William O. Bearden and Jesse E. Teel (1983), "Selected Determinants of Consumer Satisfaction and Complaint Reports," *Journal of Marketing Research* (February), pp. 21–28.

BUSINESS REPLY CARD

FIRST CLASS   PERMIT NO 773   COLUMBUS, OHIO

POSTAGE WILL BE PAID BY ADDRESSEE

NO POSTAGE
NECESSARY
IF MAILED IN THE
UNITED STATES

Mr. Todd Barnum, President
Max & Erma's Restaurants, Inc.
1561 Leonard Ave.
P.O. Box 03325
Columbus, Ohio 43203

Dear Customer,
    We are most happy to have you with us, and we hope you are pleased with our facilities, service and food. Our desire is to provide you with the type of restaurant you are looking for, always emphasizing quality and good service. In order to help us to live up to this goal, may we ask you to take a moment to fill out this postage-free card and either leave it with our cashier or drop it in the mail. Your comments are most valuable and appreciated . . . Thank you, Todd Barnum

I visited Max & Erma's Detroit location on _____ 19 ___ at _____ am/pm.

Waiter's/Waitress' Name _____

I am in the following age bracket: _____ under 21 _____ 21-35 _____ 35 or older

Were there children in your party _____ yes _____ no

Was your food service: _____ Excellent _____ Good _____ Fair _____ Poor

Was your bar service: _____ Excellent _____ Good _____ Fair _____ Poor

Was your food portion: _____ Too Small _____ Adequate _____ Too Large

Was the quality of your food: _____ Excellent _____ Good _____ Fair _____ Poor

Was the quality of the drink: _____ Excellent _____ Good _____ Fair _____ Poor

How far did you travel _____ less than 3 miles _____ 3 to 5 miles _____ more.

What could we do to make your experience better?

_____
_____
_____
_____

What is your favorite radio station? _____

Name _____ Phone _____

Address _____

Courtesy Max & Erma's Restaurants, Inc.

Marketers sometimes conduct surveys to gauge consumer satisfaction.

HIGHLIGHT 17–4 **Handling Consumer Complaints at P&G**

Since they first instituted an 800 number in 1974, Procter & Gamble has been a leader in "consumer services" (their term for the system that allows customers easy access to the company). By 1979, P&G had printed the 800 number on every consumer product they sold in the United States.

In 1983, P&G received 670,000 mail and telephone contacts about its products, and this amount increases nearly every year. P&G employs 75 people in the consumer service department, 30 to answer calls, and the rest to answer letters and analyze the data. As of mid-1984, the system was not computerized; data were tabulated by hand.

According to Gibson Carey, P&G manager for general advertising, the calls fall into three broad categories—requests for information, complaints, and testimonials (praise). P&G uses these data to spot problems and correct them early. Because most consumers call with the package in their hand, and because each package has a code printed on it that identifies the plant, the manu-

facturing date, and sometimes even the shift and line that made it, P&G can trace a problem to the source and correct it. Based on calls received about various products, P&G has:

- Included instructions for baking at high altitudes on Duncan Hines brownies packages.
- Added a recipe for making a wedding cake to its white cake mix package.
- Told users what to do if Downy liquid fabric softener accidentally freezes. (Numerous customers had that problem during a cold spell.)

Carey notes that "we don't look at [consumer service] as a source for new product ideas." Instead, P&G considers the 800-number system as "a distant, early warning signal" of product problems. Without it, "we wouldn't find out about them for weeks or months."

Source: "Customers: P&G's Pipeline to Product Problems," Business Week *(June 11, 1984), p. 167.*

---

purchase them again and may well complain to manufacturers, retailers, and other consumers. Several generalizations have been offered about consumer dissatisfaction and complaint behavior:

1. Those who complain when dissatisfied tend to be members of more up-scale socioeconomic groups than are those who do not complain.

2. Personality characteristics, including dogmatism, locus of control, and self-confidence, are only weakly related to complaint behavior, if at all.

3. The severity of dissatisfaction or problems caused by the dissatisfaction are positively related to complaint behavior.

4. The greater the blame for the dissatisfaction placed on someone other than the one dissatisfied, the greater the likelihood of a complaint.

5. The more positive the perception of retailer responsiveness to consumer complaints, the greater the likelihood of a complaint.[15]

Product Behaviors

From a strategic viewpoint, a major objective of marketing is to increase the probability and frequency of consumers coming into contact with products, purchasing and using them, and repurchasing them. We will discuss this objective in terms of two classes of consumer behavior—product contact and brand loyalty.

Product Contact

When we introduced the idea of product contact in this text, we discussed it in terms of a common retail purchase sequence. We argued that in the context of a retail store purchase, product contact involved behaviors such as locating the product in the store, examining it, and taking it to the checkout counter. In addition, a number of marketing tactics designed to increase product contacts were mentioned.

Product contacts can occur in other ways besides visits to retail stores, of course. For example, many students may become familiar with personal computers from courses taken while in school. We suspect that when the time comes to purchase a personal computer, the product contact at school may strongly influence the brand purchased. Computer firms seem well aware of this possibility, for they frequently donate their products to universities or offer them at reduced costs.

Consumers may come in contact with products and experience them in a variety of other ways, also. They may receive a free sample in the mail or on their doorstep, or be given a sample in a store; they may borrow a product from a friend and use it; they may receive a product as a gift; or they may simply see someone else using the product and experience it vicariously.

---

[15]Marsha L. Richens (1983), "Negative Word-of-Mouth by Dissatisfied Consumers: A Pilot Study," *Journal of Marketing* (Winter), p. 69.

Brand Loyalty

From a marketing strategy viewpoint, brand loyalty is a very important concept. Particularly in today's low-growth and highly competitive marketplace, retaining brand-loyal customers is critical for survival; and it is often a more efficient strategy than attracting new customers. Indeed, it is estimated that it costs the average company six times more to attract a new customer than it does to hold a current one.[16]

Unfortunately, little research has been reported on brand loyalty in recent years. Much research was conducted on this topic in the 1950s and 1960s, but a comprehensive review of the literature by Jacoby and Chestnut found few generalizations to offer.[17] In fact, few conclusions could be drawn in spite of the fact that over 300 articles had been published on the topic.

A major problem that has plagued the study of brand loyalty is the question of whether it is better to conceptualize this variable as a cognitive or a behavior phenomenon. As a *cognitive phenomenon*, brand loyalty is often thought of as an internal commitment to purchase and repurchase a particular brand. As a *behavior phenomenon*, brand loyalty is simply repeat purchase behavior.

Consistent with the theme of our book, we believe that both cognitive and behavior approaches to studying brand loyalty have value. We define **brand loyalty** as repeat purchase intentions and behaviors. While the major focus of our discussion is on brand loyalty as a behavior, we want to emphasize that cognitive processes strongly influence the development and maintenance of this behavior.

In some cases, brand loyalty may be the result of extensive cognitive activity and decision making. A consumer may seriously compare and evaluate many brands of automobiles, conclude that a Honda Accord is the perfect car, and purchase a new one every few years. In other cases, brand-loyal behavior may occur without the consumer ever comparing alternative brands. A consumer may drink Ovaltine as a child, and purchase and use the product throughout life without ever considering other brands. Yet even in this case, cognitive activity must occur. Decisions have to be made about where and when to purchase the product; some knowledge of the product and its availability must be activated from memory; intentions to purchase it and satisfaction influence the purchase behaviors.

As shown in Figure 17–6, brand loyalty can be viewed on a continuum from undivided brand loyalty to brand indifference. The market for a

---

[16]See Larry J. Rosenberg and John A. Czepiel (1983), "A Marketing Approach to Customer Retention," *Journal of Consumer Marketing* (2), pp. 45–51.

[17]Jacob Jacoby and Robert W. Chestnut (1978), *Brand Loyalty: Measurement and Management*, New York: John Wiley & Sons.

particular brand could be analyzed in terms of the number of consumers in each category, and strategies could be developed to enhance the brand loyalty of particular groups.

Undivided brand loyalty is, of course, an ideal. In some cases, consumers may purchase only a single brand and forego purchase if it is not available. *Brand loyalty with an occasional switch* is likely to be more common, though. Consumers may switch occasionally for a variety of reasons: their usual brand may be out of stock; a new brand may come on the market and is tried once; a competitive brand is offered at a special low price; or a different brand is purchased for a special occasion.

Brand-loyalty switches are a competitive goal in low-growth or declining markets. Competitors in the blue-jean market or the distilled-spirits industry must obtain brand switches for long-run growth, as an example. However, switching loyalty from one to another of the brands of the same firm can be advantageous. For example, Procter & Gamble sells both Pampers and Luvs disposable diapers. A switch from Pampers to Luvs might be advantageous to P&G in that Luvs are more expensive and may have a higher profit margin.

Divided brand loyalty refers to consistent purchase of two or more brands. For example, the shampoo market has a low level of brand loyalty. One reason for this might be that households purchase a variety of shampoos for different family members or for different purposes. Johnson's Baby Shampoo may be used for the youngsters and heavy shampoo users. Other household members may have dandruff problems and use Head and Shoulders. Thus, this household would have loyalty divided between the two brands.

Brand indifference refers to purchases with no apparent repurchase pattern. This is the opposite extreme from undivided brand loyalty. While we suspect total brand indifference is not common, some consumers of some products may exhibit this pattern. For example, a consumer may make weekly purchases of whatever bread is on sale, regardless of the brand.

In many ways these loyalty categories are somewhat arbitrary. The point is that there are various degrees of brand loyalty. The degree of

---

FIGURE 17–6   **Examples of Purchase Pattern Categories and Brand Purchase Sequences**

Purchase Pattern Category	Brand Purchase Sequence
Undivided brand loyalty	A A A A A A A A A A
Brand loyalty/Occasional switch	A A A B A A C A A D
Brand loyalty/switch	A A A A A B B B B B
Divided brand loyalty	A A B A B B A A B B
Brand indifference	A B C D E F G H I J

Sue Markson

Purchase of generics indicates brand indifference.

brand loyalty can be viewed as a continuum, and various quantitative indexes can be developed to categorize individuals or households in terms of particular products.[18]

Developing a high degree of brand loyalty among consumers is an important goal of marketing strategy. Yet the **rate of usage** by various consumers cannot be ignored. For example, the 18-to-24-year-old age group uses almost twice as much shampoo as the average user, and families of three or more people make up 78 percent of the heavy users of

---

[18]For example, see John W. Keon and Judy Bayer (1984), "Analyzing Scanner Panel Households to Determine the Demographic Characteristics of Brand Loyal and Variety Seeking Households Using a New Brand Switching Measure," in *AMA Educators' Proceedings*, Russell W. Belk et al. (eds.), Chicago: American Marketing Association, pp. 416–420.

shampoo. Clearly, obtaining brand loyalty among these consumers is preferable to attracting consumers who purchase and use shampoo less frequently, other things being equal.

The relationship between brand loyalty and usage rate is shown in Figure 17–7. For simplicity, we have divided the dimensions into four categories of consumers rather than consider each dimension as a continuum.

Figure 17–7 shows that achieving brand-loyal consumers is most valuable when the consumers are also heavy users. This figure could also be used as a strategic tool by plotting consumers of both the firm's brands and competitive brands on the basis of brand loyalty and usage rates. Depending on the location of consumers and whether they are loyal to the firm's brand or a competitive one, several strategies might be useful:

1. If the only profitable segment is the brand-loyal heavy user, focus on switching consumer loyalty to the firm's brands. For example, comparative advertising such as that used by Avis in the car-rental industry or by Burger King in the fast-food industry may have been appropriate strategies for switching heavy users.

2. If there is a sufficient number of brand-loyal light users, focus on increasing their usage of the firm's brand. For example, the baking soda market might have been characterized as being composed of

---

FIGURE 17–7   **Brand Loyalty and Usage Rate**

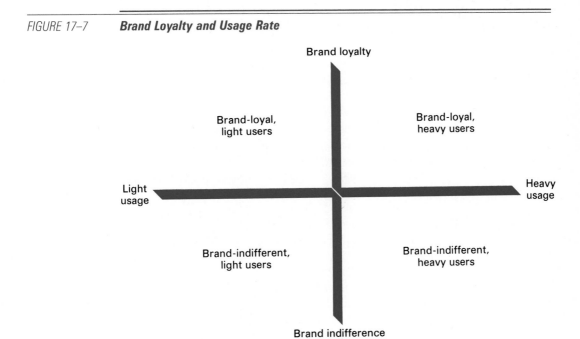

brand-loyal light users of Arm & Hammer baking soda. This brand then demonstrated new uses of the product, such as for freshening refrigerators. It is reported that half the refrigerators in America now contain a box of baking soda.

3. If there is a sufficient number of brand-indifferent heavy users, attempt to make the firm's brand name a salient attribute and/or develop a new relative advantage. For example, no firm in the hot-dog market has more than a 10 percent market share. Firms such as Oscar Mayer stress the brand name in advertising in an attempt to increase the importance of brand name to the consumer. In addition, Oscar Mayer successfully developed the market for hot dogs with cheese in them to increase sales.

4. If there is a sufficient number of brand-indifferent light users, attempt to make the firm's brand name a salient attribute and increase usage of the firm's brand among consumers, perhaps by finding a sustainable relative advantage. For example, a portion of the market for People Express flights are brand-indifferent consumers who are attracted by lower prices.

As we noted, it is also important to plot consumers of competitive brands to develop appropriate strategies. For example, if a single competitor dominates the brand-loyal heavy-user market and has too much market power to be overcome, then strategies may have to be focused on other markets.

Back to the Case

Admiral was clearly successful in introducing its new up-scale refrigerators, which included several product-design modifications. Admiral designed the Entertainer model based on consumer surveys that showed a trend toward increased entertaining at home. Although it introduced the premium-priced refrigerator during a recession, and at a time when most other manufacturers were pushing economical, stripped-down models, the new refrigerator almost instantly became the company's best-selling unit, with deliveries equaling $10 million in the first year. The success of the A la Mode model has already been noted.

However, one must question whether the addition of product attributes such as a built-in wine rack and microwave storage trays is a sufficient reason for the success of this product. We suspect that the higher price of these models may have been important in generating a favorable quality image. That is, a mature product generally considered a dull necessity may have been converted into a status symbol by the higher price. In other words, perhaps the relative advantage was created partly through product symbolism, as well as a few relatively inexpensive product modifications.

The fact that many of the purchases were made by consumers who enjoyed entertaining at home suggests that these purchasers may have an "audience" of guests (a reference group) to whom they can show the new appliance. The product-design modifications offer an entree for showing off the product and a justification for the high price paid. In addition, during a recession, many consumers may have foregone purchasing a new home and stayed in an apartment or remodeled their current home. It is possible that remodeling and adding high-quality appliances may have been substituted for new home purchases. In essence, then, the purchase and display of an expensive refrigerator with convenience-oriented design features and psychosocial consequences may have been a way for consumers to tell themselves and others that they are doing well, even if they aren't buying a new home.

The new premium refrigerators did enhance the overall quality image of the company's entire product line—with both consumers and retailers. In fact, the number of outlets selling Admiral refrigerators rose 33 percent, to more than 6,000. Thus, while consumer demand may have pulled the refrigerators to the retail level, the increase in the number of outlets also helped to increase product contacts.

Overall, then, whether it was the result of product-design modifications or changes in other marketing-mix variables (price and distribution), the success of Admiral's long-term marketing strategy is noteworthy.

Summary

This chapter investigated product strategy and some consumer product-related environmental factors, cognitions, and behaviors. Initially, product strategy was discussed in terms of characteristics of consumers and of products that affect product adoption. In terms of the product environment, product attributes and packaging were discussed. The product cognitions discussion focused on satisfaction and dissatisfaction; the discussion of product behaviors examined product contact and brand loyalty. The relationships between brand loyalty and usage rates of brands and some potential strategies incorporating these variables were also presented.

Additional Reading

Peter H. Bloch and Marsha L. Richens (1983), "A Theoretical Model for the Study of Product Importance Perceptions," *Journal of Marketing* (Summer), pp. 69–81.

C. Merle Crawford (1986), *New Products Management,* Homewood, Ill.: Richard D. Irwin.

Philip Kotler (1984), *Marketing Management: Analysis, Planning, and Control,* 5th ed., Englewood Cliffs, N.J.: Prentice-Hall, Chapters 10 and 11.

Christopher H. Lovelock (1983), "Classifying Services to Gain Strategic Marketing Insights," *Journal of Marketing* (Summer), pp. 9–20.

Jack Reddy and Abe Berger (1982), "Three Essentials of Product Quality," *Harvard Business Review* (July–August), pp. 153–159.

John E. Swan and David R. Rink (1982), "Fitting Market Strategy to Varying Product Life Cycles," *Business Horizons* (January–February), pp. 72–76.

Kenneth P. Uhl and Gregory D. Upah (1983), "The Marketing of Services: Why and How Is It Different?" *Research in Marketing,* Vol. 6, pp. 231–257.

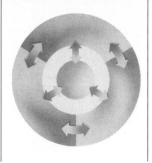

Chapter Eighteen

Promotion Strategy and Consumer Behavior

Three Winning Promotion Strategies

Each year the Promotion Marketing Association of America honors the most effective consumer promotions in the country with Reggie Awards, in the form of small golden cash registers. In 1984, McDonald's won the Super Reggie Award for its successful sales promotion strategy called "When the USA Wins, You Win." That year, McDonald's was a major sponsor of the Los Angeles Olympic Games. To capitalize on their investment, the restaurant chain developed a sales promotion game with the objectives of increasing store contacts by 8 percent and sales by 5 percent. Customers were given a game card with a rub-off spot that revealed the name of an Olympic event. If a U.S. athlete won a gold medal in that event, the card bearer received a free sandwich. French fries and soft drinks were given for silver and bronze medals. As recognized by the Reggie award, McDonald's promotion was quite successful. Store contacts increased by 11.2 percent, and sales at the average franchise increased $10,000. As an extra benefit, the promotion also encouraged TV viewership of the Olympic games, thus increasing the impact of McDonald's heavy advertising investment.

General Foods won a Gold Reggie for their sales promotion intended to wean consumers away from their dependency on coffee coupons. During the month of December for the past several years, GF has offered a free holiday ornament attached to Maxwell House Instant coffee containers. In 1984, three different ornaments were used to encourage multiple purchases, and each was dated to encourage collectability. On a national basis, the promotion increased brand market share by 3.8 percent, and GF rated the program 40 percent more effective than typical consumer promotions.

Beatrice/Hunt-Wesson also won a Gold Reggie. Although the company had a winning product in its Orville Redenbacher popcorn, they wanted a promotion strategy to further increase consumer awareness, trial, and consumption. With the help of a promotion consulting company, they conceived the "Watch My Bow Tie" contest that offered a trip for five to Hollywood to dine with Orville Redenbacher himself. They distributed freestanding newspaper inserts that contained two coupons for the product plus details on the contest. To enter, consumers had to watch Redenbacher's TV ads to determine the color of his bow tie. The promotion strategy was supported with TV and print ads and in-store displays depicting Orville without tie, as well as price reductions on the product. Not only did the three-month promotion increase advertising awareness and impact, but it helped boost brand sales 38 percent over the previous year.

Source: "McDonald's Olympic Promotion Gets the Gold," Marketing News (June 7, 1985), pp. 12–13.

Marketers use promotions such as these to *communicate* information about their products and *persuade* consumers to buy them. As is true of all marketing strategies, **promotions** are environmental stimuli created by marketers specifically to influence consumers' cognitions and behaviors. The major promotional methods include advertising, sales promotions, personal selling, and publicity. The combination of these strategies is the **promotion mix.** From the point of view of marketing management, the importance of promotion strategies cannot be overstated. Most successful products and brands require promotions such as those described in the opening case to create a **sustainable differential advantage** over their competitors.

Perhaps because they are so highly visible, promotion strategies are often the target of marketing critics. Some critics claim that promotion is an expense that adds nothing to the value of the product, but increases its cost to the consumer. Supporters, on the other hand, argue that marketing promotions inform consumers about product attributes and consequences, prices, and places where products are available. This information may save consumers both time and money by reducing the costs of search. Moreover, advocates of promotion point out that some promotion strategies save consumers money directly. One study found that manufacturers' coupons, a prime sales promotion strategy, saved American consumers an estimated $502 million in 1978, yet increased prices a mere 0.25 percent.[1]

In this chapter we discuss how various promotion strategies and the environment affect selected aspects of consumers' cognitions and behaviors. We begin by discussing the four basic promotion methods. Then we discuss the communication process. After providing an overview of how

---

[1]Kevin Higgins (1984), "Couponing's Growth Is Easy to Understand: It Works," *Marketing News* (September 28), p. 12.

Creating a successful product position: skin rejuvenation.

Courtesy Chesebrough-Pond's, Inc.

Adding a new attribute to an existing product can be a successful marketing strategy.

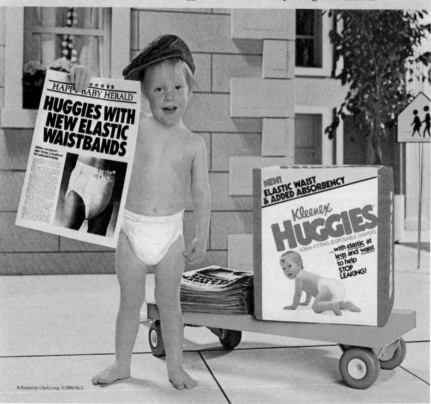

"Extra! Extra! Huggies® hug with new elastic waistbands!"

Read all about it!
Kleenex® Huggies® diapers have new elastic waistbands—soft, cuddly elastic at the waist. So now Huggies hug gently all over.

Plus there's more thick, fluffy padding. To help stop leaking better than ever. And to help keep babies extra happy.
Huggies with new elas-

tic waistbands. Now available in medium and large sizes. Good news for the whole town.
Now Huggies diapers help stop leaking better than ever.

HAPPY BABY HERALD

HUGGIES WITH NEW ELASTIC WAISTBANDS

NEW!
ELASTIC WAIST & ADDED ABSORBENCY

Kleenex
HUGGIES
FORM-FITTING DISPOSABLE DIAPERS
...with elastic at legs and waist to help STOP LEAKING!

® Kimberly-Clark Corp. © 1986 K-C'C

Reproduced with permission of Kimberly-Clark Corporation

Using a sales promotion strategy to encourage purchase.

Offering a guarantee to reduce the risk of product purchase.

TASTE GUARANTEE
You'll love the taste, or you'll get your money back.

New Instant Sanka® has a delicious fresh-brewed taste because it's perked with our patented fresh-brewing process.

Ground Sanka® is made from a fine blend of select coffee beans to give you irresistible aroma and great coffee taste.

Sanka® Brand Decaffeinated Coffee. Deliciously smooth and satisfying. And of course, still 97% caffein free. We're so sure you'll love it, we can guarantee it.

We guarantee that you will love the smooth and satisfying taste of Sanka®. If you don't agree, just send the unused portion of the package and a cash register tape with the purchase price dated after 10/1/85 for a full refund including postage. This offer is good only on New Instant Sanka® with fresh-brewed taste and Ground Sanka® with the Freshlock™ packet. Send to General Foods, Post Office Box 4597 (for Instant) or 4598 (for Ground), Kankakee, Illinois 60902. Offer expires 3/31/86. Limit one (Instant and Ground) per family.

SANKA and FRESH LOCK are registered trademarks of General Foods Corporation

FIGURE 18–1   **The Wheel of Consumer Analysis: Promotion Strategy Issues**

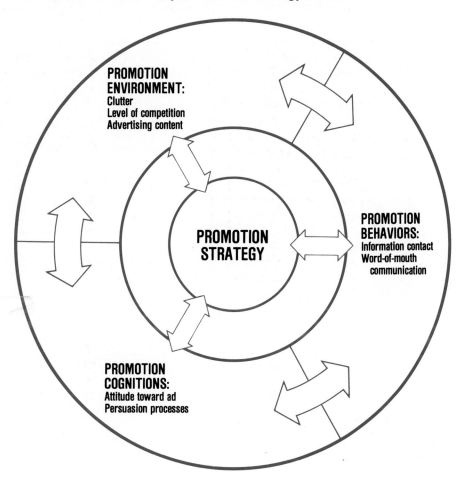

marketing managers develop promotion strategies, we discuss selected aspects of the promotion environment, promotion cognitions, and promotion behaviors; the specific topics are shown in Figure 18–1.

Major Promotion Methods

In this section, we identify and briefly discuss the major promotion methods used by marketers—advertising, sales promotions, personal selling, and publicity. Each plays a role in helping marketers achieve their promotion objectives. Perhaps the most prevalent promotion strategy is advertising.

Advertising

Advertising is any paid, nonpersonal presentation of information about a product, brand, company, or store. It usually has an identified sponsor. Much advertising is intended to influence consumers' cognitions—especially their images, beliefs, and attitudes toward products, brands, and behaviors. In fact, advertising has been characterized as *image management*—creating and maintaining images and meanings in consumers' minds.[2] Advertisements may be conveyed via a variety of media—TV, radio, print (magazines, newspapers), billboards, signs, and miscellaneous media such as hot-air balloons or T-shirt decals. Although the typical consumer is exposed to literally hundreds of ads daily, the vast majority of these messages receive low levels of attention and comprehension. Thus, it is a major challenge for marketers to develop ad messages and select media that expose consumers, capture their attention, and generate appropriate comprehension processes.

In the mid-1980s, Nike Corporation made a big splash with a series of billboard ads featuring strong visual images of athletes—Carl Lewis long jumping or Michael Jordan leaping for the basket—and little else. The outdoor ads contained only the Nike "swoosh" logo in the corner; and, of course, the athletes were wearing Nike shoes and clothes. At first, consumers probably had to look twice to comprehend what product was being advertised. But once the association was made, it was easily activated when consumers encountered other ads in the series. In markets where the ads were run, Nike sales increased an average of 30 percent.[3]

Sales Promotions

Sales promotions are direct inducements to the consumer to make a purchase.[4] Although TV advertising may be more glamorous, more money is spent on sales promotion techniques and methods. In 1984, about 64 percent of promotion budgets was spent on sales promotions, compared to 36 percent on advertising.[5] The $12 billion spent on TV advertising in 1983

---

[2]Thomas J. Reynolds and Jonathan Gutman (1984), "Advertising Is Image Management," *Journal of Advertising Research* (February–March), pp. 27–37.

[3]Kevin Higgins (1985), "Billboards Put Nike Back in the Running," *Marketing News* (June 7), p. 7.

[4]For example, see Katherine E. Jocz, ed. (1984), *Research on Sales Promotion: Collected Papers,* Cambridge, Mass.: Marketing Science Institute; James Cross, Steven W. Hartley and Richard Rexeisen (1985), "Sales Promotion: A Review of Theoretical and Managerial Issues," in *Marketing Communications—Theory and Research,* Michael J. Houston and Richard J. Lutz (eds.), Chicago: American Marketing Association, pp. 60–64.

[5]Curt Schleier (1985), "Marketing Image Plots Turnaround," *Advertising Age* (August 15), pp. 15–16.

If you have visited summer vacation spots such as Martha's Vineyard, Hampton Beach, San Diego, Virginia Beach, or Santa Monica, you may have noticed a new wrinkle in your favorite resort's tourist business: cute, brightly painted trolleys rolling along the main boulevard. Over the past few years, more than 35 resort towns have allowed trolley owner/operators onto their streets.

The fares tourists pay to ride the trolleys don't pay the costs. Fortunately, though, trolleys are also a splendid vehicle for advertising. In fact, advertising accounts for about 70 percent of the revenues for the typical trolley. In Santa Monica, for instance, trolley operators charge about $500 for a small interior ad that runs six months and $2,500 to $5,000 for an exterior ad. Most trolleys can take 11 of the large exterior poster ads. These advertising fees add from $60,000 to $110,000 per year to the revenues produced by each trolley, depending on the length of the season.

Are these moving billboards effective? David Shumway, president of American Trolley Lines, says, "Heads always turn. Trolleys receive much more attention than ordinary billboards." Yes, but what makes trolleys truly effective as a promotion medium is their practice of jiggering routes to include stops at their large advertisers' premises. Using trolleys as an advertising medium literally "delivers an audience."

Source: Ellen Paris (1985), "Follow the Moving Sign," Forbes *(September 9), p. 116.*

equaled the total spent on just one type of sales promotion: premiums and incentives.[6]

The wide variety of sales promotions makes defining them difficult. Many of these can be classified as either sales promotion or some other marketing or promotion tool, depending on their use. For example, Highlight 18–2 lists a number of sales promotion methods that might be considered advertising, price reductions, or sales training in certain circumstances. According to Parker Lindberg, president of the Promotion Marketing Association of America, the key aspect of sales promotions is to "move the product today, not tomorrow. A sales promotion gets people to pick the product up at retail and try it by offering something concrete—a premium, cents off, or whatever."[7] In sum, most sales promotions are oriented at changing consumers' short-run purchase behaviors.

Consider a back-to-school promotion Dow offered on its Ziploc sandwich bags.[8] The promotion included a 15-cent coupon plus a mail-in offer

---

[6]Robert J. Kopp (1985), "Premiums Provide Great Impact, But Little Glamour," *Marketing News* (June 7), pp. 12 and 14.

[7]"McDonald's Olympic Promotion Gets the Gold," *Marketing News* (June 7, 1984), pp. 12–13.

[8]Ibid.

HIGHLIGHT 18–2　　**Some Types of Sales Promotion**

- Specialty ads (imprinted novelties, gadgets, calendars, matchbooks, souvenirs, etc.) and business gifts.
- Temporary price reductions via coupons; cents-off deals; extended, interest-free or low-interest credit; refunds; rebates; price-off deals; combination offers; bonus packs; multiple packs; one-cent sales; other methods.
- Promotions designed to get trials, such as coupons, cents-off deals, refunds, rebates, price-off deals, bonus packs, samples, sample sizes, trial offers, trial sizes, free trials, special guarantees, combination offers, multiple packs, premiums, self-liquidating premiums, label savings promotions, in-packs, on-packs, near-packs, reusable containers, continuity premiums, free-in-the-mail premiums, and souvenirs.
- Contests and sweepstakes.
- Business, industrial, trade, and technical papers; journals; publications; and magazines.
- Directories and buyers guides.
- Trading stamps, redemption coupons, divided coupons, and continuity premiums.
- When held for a firm's salespeople, middlemen, or customers: meetings, sessions, seminars, symposiums, conferences, conventions, showrooms, classes, fashion shows, demonstrations, taste tests, and exhibits.
- When held for a number of competing vendors: trade shows, world fairs, state fairs, county fairs, fairs, shows, conventions, exhibitions, conferences, seminars, meetings, trade marts, and showrooms.
- Displays, point-of-purchase materials, inflatables, show windows, and in-store signs and banners.
- Push money, spiffs, demonstrators, trade deals, cooperative advertising, dealer-listing promotions, count and recount, bounce-backs, buybacks, extended credit, consignment, free

- goods, dealer loaders, store resets, inventory checking, and premiums directed at the trade, middlemen, and dealers.
- Publicity directed at the firm's salespeople, middlemen, and customers.
- Catalogs, booklets, brochures, bulletins, reprints, tear sheets, broadsides, postcards, price lists, flyers/handouts, package inserts, manuals, folders, stuffers, pamphlets, books, house organs, house magazines, newsletters, histories, instruction sheets, instruction books, annual reports, and any printed material that describes the product or gives product information for the purpose of selling, training, installing, using, and/or servicing.
- Direct mail and some of the items listed above, when used for direct mail.
- Packaging, labels, and labeling.
- Trademarks, brands, logos, marks, symbols, slogans, nicknames, signs, insignia, letterheads, business cards, tags, nameplates, labels, decals, binders, covers, shipping labels, shipping tapes, bindings, and other forms of company or corporate identification.
- Sponsorships, special events, and charity-linked sales promotions.
- Testimonials, endorsements, company spokespeople, and advertising spokespeople.
- Audio and visual aides, including picture albums, slides, movies, cassettes, tapes, records, flip charts, easels, personal computers, blackboards, models, sample cases, exhibits, and sample cards (paint, wallpaper, material, lipstick, nail polish), either as props for the salesperson or for sales training.
- Joint promotions (horizontal co-op) and tie-ins with other manufacturers, sellers, or vendors, including licensing of trademarks, logos, etc., for use on various products or reproductions.
- Skywriting, skytyping, aerial signs, hot-air bal-

balloons, blimps, inflatables, and sign towing.
- Entertainment (such as golf outings) and meals; may be handled through the salesperson's expense account.
- Hospitality suites and receptions.
- Announcements, thank-you notes, and birthday cards.

- Plant tours or visitor tours, visitors center, open house, and familiarization tours.

Source: Ernest F. Cooke (1985), "Defining Sales Promotion Difficult, Important," Marketing News, *(November 8), p. 38.*

for free bread with two proofs of purchase. A premium was also included in the package—a set of stickers of the beasties from the movie *Gremlins*. As Ziploc was the number two brand with a 28 percent share, this promotion was intended to get consumers to stock up on the brand, thereby preempting purchases of competitive brands. Sales volume increased 42 percent, and Ziploc became the top brand in the category for the first time.

Personal Selling

Personal selling involves direct interactions between a salesperson and a potential buyer. Personal selling can be a powerful promotion method. Because two-way communication is possible, situation involvement tends to be fairly high, and salespeople can adapt their sales presentations to effectively influence consumers. Over the years, personal selling in retailing has decreased as self-service merchandising has become more popular. However, certain products still are heavily promoted through personal selling—life insurance, automobiles, and houses are examples. As the costs of direct, face-to-face selling increases (between $100 and $200 per sales call in 1985), personal selling by telephone—called **telemarketing**—has become increasingly popular.[9] Highlight 18–3 shows how conventional selling differs from telephone selling.

Both Avon and Mary Kay Cosmetics, among the largest U.S. marketers of skin-care products, were built on personal selling. In their earlier days, neither company spent much on advertising or customer sales pro-

---

[9]Mary Ann Falzone (1985), "Survey Highlights Lower Costs, Higher Productivity of Telemarketing," *Telemarketing Insider's Report* (Special Report), pp. 1–2.

HIGHLIGHT 18–3: **Conventional Personal Selling versus Telemarketing**

Conventional Salesperson	Telemarketing Salesperson
• Often travels	• Never travels
• Independent	• Part of a "team"
• Improvises	• Follows a "script"
• Less structured	• Highly structured
• Works 8-12 hours per day	• Works 4-6 hours per day
• Completes 2 to 10 sales calls per day	• Completes 20 to 50 sales calls per day
• One-hour sales calls	• 60- to 120-second sales calls
• Mixes business and fun	• All business
• Loosely supervised	• Closely supervised

Source: Stewart W. Cross (1985), "Can You Turn a Salesperson into a TSR?" Telemarketing Insider's Report *(April), p. 2.*

motions. Mary Kay, for instance, spent a minuscule $1 million on advertising in 1980 (out of $167 million in sales). Instead, most of the Mary Kay promotion budget was spent on sales incentives directed at their salespeople. In addition to symbolic prizes such as medals, ribbons, and commemorative certificates, Mary Kay gives jewelry, calculators, briefcases, and furs as rewards to their salespeople. Top sellers receive the use of pink Cadillacs or Buick Regals. Mary Kay also spends heavily on motivational and training programs for their sales personnel, which in 1980, numbered some 150,000 women (Mary Kay has virtually no salesmen).[10]

Publicity

Publicity is any unpaid form of communication about the marketers' company, products, or brands. For instance, an article in *PC World* comparing various brands of word-processing software provides useful product information to consumers, at no cost to the marketers of the software. Similarly, descriptions of new products or brands; brand comparisons in trade journals, newspapers, or news magazines; or discussions on radio and TV talk shows provide product information to consumers.

---

[10]David Einhorn (1982), "Dynamo of Direct Sales," *Marketing Communications* (February), pp. 12–14.

HIGHLIGHT 18–4 **The Impact of Publicity**

A syndicated columnist wrote an article about Canfield's Diet Chocolate Fudge Soda that appeared in newspapers around the country. The article reported that the dieting columnist used this two-calorie, salt-free soda as a substitute for chocolate cake or chocolate cookies to help lose weight. The soda, produced in Chicago, was normally distributed only in Illinois, Indiana, Michigan, Wisconsin, and Iowa.

A few weeks after the article appeared, the columnist reported the striking effects of his initial story. For one thing, Canfield had gone into 24-hour production of the Diet Chocolate Fudge Soda. It was producing 1,200 cans a minute, and still could not meet the demand. Canfield said it was trying to get the soda delivered to cities around the country that were clamoring for it. The company also reported that in the first nine days after the column appeared, 1.5 million cans of the diet soda were sold—more than was sold in the entire previous year! In addition, Canfield reported that when company executives visited 35 grocery stores, they found that 33 of them were completely sold out of the product. Apparently, in this case at least, publicity was a very effective promotion device for creating demand.

Publicity can be either positive or negative, of course. Nike received a bonanza of free publicity in the form of favorable news stories about their billboard campaign. In one case, a TV news segment in Los Angeles concluded with the reporter urging viewers to "give a honk for Nike, which has raised the billboard from visual blight to at least camp art."[11] Tylenol, on the other hand, *twice* received a great deal of unfavorable publicity when people were poisoned by Tylenol capsules that had been tampered with.

Sometimes, publicity can be more effective than advertising, for consumers may not screen out the messages so readily. In addition, publicity communications may be considered more credible, because they are not being presented by the marketing organization. Publicity is difficult to manage, however. Marketers sometimes stage "media events" in hopes of garnering free publicity. Procter & Gamble, for example, held a glitzy news conference at a New York City disco to introduce new Liquid Tide—complete with a 20-foot-high inflatable replica of the product![12] They hoped that the media would report the event and perhaps show a picture of the

---

[11]Kevin Higgins (1985), "Billboards Put Nike Back in the Running," *Marketing News* (June 7), p. 7.

[12]Bill Saporito (1985), "Procter & Gamble's Comeback Plan," *Fortune* (February 4), pp. 30–37.

Jeff Jacobson/Archive Pictures Inc.

Procter & Gamble's promotion for Liquid Tide included 20-foot-high inflatable replica of the product.

product. P&G had little control over what type of publicity (if any) would result, however.

In sum, marketers can choose from among many different promotion strategies. They often combine several different promotions into an overall strategy called the **promotion mix.** Figure 18–2 summarizes advantages and disadvantages of each type of promotion strategy.

A General Communication Model

The various promotion methods described above are the most direct ways that marketers communicate with consumers. Developing a successful promotion strategy, then, is largely a communication problem. Figure 18–3

FIGURE 18–2   ***Some Advantages and Disadvantages of Major Promotion Methods***

Advertising

Advantages

Can reach many consumers simultaneously

Relatively low cost per exposure

Excellent for creating brand images

High degree of flexibility and variety of media to choose from; can accomplish many different types of promotion objectives

Disadvantages

Many consumers reached are not potential buyers (waste of promotion dollars)

High visibility makes advertising a major target of marketing critics

Advertisement exposure time is usually brief

Advertisements are often quickly and easily screened out by consumers

Personal Selling

Advantages

Can be the most persuasive promotion tool; salespeople can directly influence purchase behaviors

Allows two-way communication

Often necessary for technically complex products

Allows direct one-on-one targeting of promotional effort

Disadvantages

High cost per contact

Sales training and motivation can be expensive and difficult

Personal selling often has a poor image, making salesforce recruitment difficult

Poorly done sales presentations can hurt sales as well as company, product, and brand images

Sales Promotion

Advantages

Excellent approach for short-term price reductions for stimulating demand

A large variety of sales promotion tools to choose from

Can be effective for changing a variety of consumer behaviors

Can be easily tied in with other promotion tools

Disadvantages

May influence primarily brand-loyal customers to stock up at lower price but attract few new customers

May have only short-term impact

Overuse of price-related sales promotion tools may hurt brand image and profits

Effective sales promotions are easily copied by competitors

Publicity

Advantages

As "free advertising," publicity can be positive and stimulate demand at no cost

Disadvantages

Company cannot completely control the content of publicity messages

FIGURE 18–2   *(concluded)*

Publicity

Advantages   **Disadvantages**

May be perceived by consumers as more   Publicity is not always available
credible, because it is not paid for by
the seller   Limited repetition of publicity messages;
                                                  seldom a long-term promotion tool for
Consumers may pay more attention to   brands
these messages, because they are not
quickly screened out as are many   Publicity can be negative and hurt sales
advertisements   as well as company, product, and brand
                                                  images

presents a simple model that accounts for how a message is communicated from a source to a receiver. You might note that this model is similar to the operation of a telegraph—which, in fact, was its inspiration. The *source* of the communication determines which information is to be conveyed, *encodes* the message (translates it into appropriate symbols), *transmits* it (sends it over some medium, such as a telegraph wire), to a *receiver* (consumer) who must *decode* it (interpret the symbols/comprehend the message) and take appropriate *action* (perhaps purchase).

Figure 18–3 also shows the relevant agents and stimuli involved in each of these stages and the major activities that occur at each stage. Although each stage is important to the success of promotion strategies, two are especially critical. The first occurs when the marketer/source creates *(encodes)* the promotion message to convey a particular meaning. The second critical stage occurs when consumers are exposed to the promotion message and interpret *(decode or comprehend)* it. A huge amount of research has addressed each of these stages and activities in the communication process. We can only briefly touch on some of it below.

Source Effects

The **source** of a promotion message influences its effectiveness.[13] For instance, salespeople whom customers perceive as credible, trustworthy, and similar to themselves are often more effective.

---

[13]Brian Sternthal, Ruby Dholakia and Clark Leavitt (1978), "The Persuasive Effect of Source Credibility: Tests of Cognitive Response," *Journal of Consumer Research* (March), pp. 252–260.

FIGURE 18–3   **A General Model of the Communication Process for Promotions**

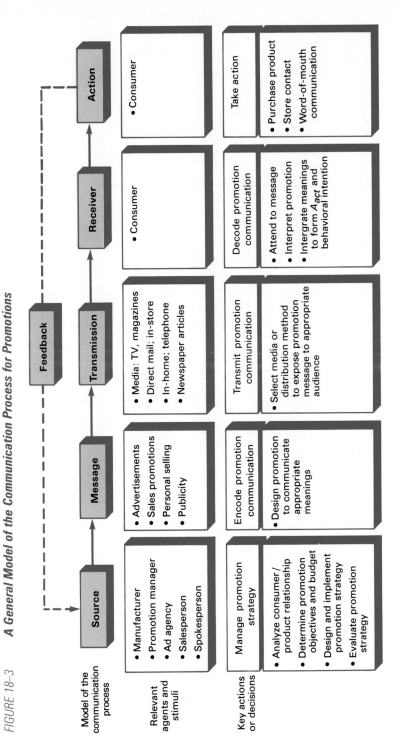

Source: Adapted from Henry Assael (1984), Consumer Behavior and Marketing Action, 2nd Edition, Boston, MA: Kent Publishing, p. 523.

AT&T. The reason you've always taken long distance services for granted.

Whenever you wanted to feel close to someone faraway, when you wanted to share a smile or just felt like a chat, you gave them a call. You didn't worry about the call. Because you took for granted that you could reach wherever you wanted, and that you'd get a clear long distance connection.

AT&T's Long Distance services have always been there for you to call upon. In fact, few things are as reliable, as dependable as AT&T.

Only AT&T has over 35,000 long distance operators to offer any assistance you may need.

Only AT&T lets you reach out anywhere you want. Not just coast-to-coast, but also to over 250

countries and faraway locations worldwide.

What's more, all these services come with savings. Dial direct state-to-state Sunday-Friday from 5pm-11pm and save 40% off AT&T's Day Rate. Friday from 11pm-Sunday 5pm and nightly from 11pm-8am, save 60%. (Different discounts apply to Alaska.)

Plus, AT&T has special programs and plans that can help your long distance dollars go farther.

You know with AT&T you can continue to take these services for granted. Because there's someone we'll never take for granted: you. **Reach out and touch someone.**

© 1985 AT&T Communications

AT&T
The right choice.

Courtesy AT&T Communication

An effective celebrity spokesperson.

Celebrity spokespersons are often hired to appear in TV and radio ads where they serve as the source for promotional messages about the product. After extensive research, AT&T selected actor Cliff Robertson from among 20 potential celebrities to help the company retain its dominance in the $45 billion U.S. long-distance telephone service business against MCI, GTE/Sprint, and other competitors. According to AT&T's di-

HIGHLIGHT 18–5   **Star Power**

In 1985, approximately 10 percent of the ad dollars spent on TV went for celebrity ads. Despite the obvious success of certain celebrity spokespersons such as Linda Evans for General Foods' powdered soft drink Crystal Light or Cliff Robertson for AT&T, however, there seems to be little to celebrate in celebrity advertising.

First of all, it isn't cheap. Actor Bill Cosby pulled down an estimated $1.5 million in 1985 as company spokesperson for Coca-Cola and Jell-O pudding—more than the salary of either company's chief executive officer. And, for all the money, advertisers don't always get a stirring testimonial. Pepsi-Cola USA paid an estimated $5 million each to get Michael Jackson and Lionel Richie to appear in blockbuster commercials, yet neither singer praises or even drinks the product. Instead, they dance and sing about the "new generation" of Pepsi drinkers.

Evidence suggests that consumers often don't believe what a star says, anyway. According to a 1984 survey, about half of 1,000 adult TV viewers assumed that the celebrity was just "doing it for the money." Perhaps Bill Cosby's claim that he liked the new-formula Coke better than the original he had been hawking for four years seemed a bit strained to some consumers.

What can celebrity ads do? Some advertisers consider star spokespersons as zap insurance in the increasing clutter of TV ads. "What you get from a celebrity at bare minimum," says an ad agency executive, "is audience attention." Perhaps this explains using sequin-clad actress Suzanne Somers in Ace Hardware ads. But research shows that only 40 percent of TV ads using celebrities had better-than-average brand awareness scores—and only half of those produced increases in brand attitudes.

However, when used skillfully, celebrities can do more than command attention. Consider the following advantages:

- When a star is used as an entertainer (Lionel Richie in the Pepsi ads), watching the ad is more enjoyable.
- An exceptionally credible spokesperson can lend trustworthiness to the ad, the product, and the company. Every advertiser's ideal is Walter Cronkite, former anchor on the "CBS Evening News," who thus far has not appeared in any ad.
- A close matching of celebrity and product can make an ad convincing, as has Miller Lite's campaign using beer-loving retired athletes.
- Sometimes a celebrity can give a warm, human dimension to an abstract product, e.g., Cliff Robertson's work for AT&T long-distance services.
- Some celebrities generate huge amounts of free publicity, as Geraldine Ferraro, the 1984 vice presidential candidate, did when she appeared in a commercial for Diet Pepsi.

Source: Stratford P. Sherman (1985), "When You Wish Upon a Star," Fortune *(August 19), pp. 66-73.*

rector of advertising, "We see Cliff as a solid, reliable, dependable person who will stand up and say directly what he thinks." Robertson accounts for his believability by saying, "I have to say the copy in a way that's effective and that doesn't deter from my beliefs. I don't try to sell. I just try to say it with conviction."[14] But many other celebrity spokespersons don't seem to have this type of easygoing warmth, credibility, or effectiveness (see Highlight 18–5).

Message Effects

The actual informational content of the promotion influences its effectiveness. The larger the print ad, the higher the coupon value, the bigger the sweepstakes or contest prize, the more attractive the cereal-box premium, the more effective the promotion strategy is likely to be, all other things being equal. In general, marketers must trade off making the promotion *attractive* enough to stimulate sufficient consumer response, against making it *small* enough that the costs don't outweigh the benefits.

Media Effects

Promotional strategies can be delivered via a variety of media, each of which has an influence on the effectiveness of the promotion. Advertisements, for example, can be placed in many different media, each with distinct advantages and disadvantages, as shown in Figure 18–4. As another example of how the method of transmitting a promotion strategy influences its effectiveness, Figure 18–5 presents redemption rates for coupons distributed in different ways.

Receiver Characteristics

The success of a promotion will be affected by the characteristics of the consumers who receive it. Foremost among these factors are the consumers' knowledge about and enduring involvement with the product or brand being promoted. Another important receiver characteristic is consumers' **deal proneness**—their general inclination to use promotional deals such as buying on sale or using coupons.[15] Some consumers are highly involved in using coupons, and may even belong to clubs in which coupons are traded

---

[14]Jennifer Pendleton (1985), "Robertson Believe-Ability: Star Presenter Oozes Honesty," *Advertising Age* (May 2), pp. 5, 49.

[15]P. S. Raju and Manoj Hastak (1980), "Consumer Response to Deals: A Discussion of Theoretical Perspective," in *Advances in Consumer Research*, Vol. 7, Jerry C. Olson (ed.), Ann Arbor, Mich.: Association for Consumer Research, pp. 296–301; Robert Blattberg, Thomas Biesing, Peter Peacock and Subrata Sen (1978), "Identifying the Deal Prone Segment," *Journal of Marketing Research* (August), pp. 369–397.

FIGURE 18–4 **Advantages and Disadvantages of Various Advertising Media**

	Advantages	Disadvantages
Newspapers	Almost any ad size available. Impact of black against white (still one of the most powerful color combinations). Sense of immediacy. Quick response; easy accountability. Local emphasis. Changes possible at short notice.	Loss of fidelity, especially of halftone illustration. Too many ad-format variations among newspapers. Variance in column widths. Difficulty in controlling ad position on page.
Magazines	High-quality reproduction. Prestige factor. Accurate demographic information available. Graphic opportunities (use of white space, benday screen, reverse type). Color.	Size not as large as those of newspapers or posters. Long closing dates, limiting flexibility. Lack of immediacy. Tendency to cluster ads. Possible difficulties in securing favorable spot in an issue.
Television	Combination of sight and sound. Movement. A single message at a time. Viewer's empathy. Opportunity to demonstrate the product. Believability: "What you see is what you get."	No time to convey a lot of information. Air clutter (almost 25 percent of broadcasting is nonprogramming material). Intrusiveness (TV tops list of consumers' complaints in this respect). Capricious station censorship.
Radio	Opportunity to explore sound. Favorable to humor. Intimacy. Loyal following (the average person listens regularly to only about two stations). Ability to change message quickly.	Lack of visual excitement. Wavering attention span (many listeners tune out commercials). Inadequate data on listening habits (when is the "listener" really listening?) Fleeting nature of message.
Direct mail	Graphic and production flexibility, such as use of three-dimensional effect (folding, die-cuts, pop-ups). Measurable. As scientific as any other form of advertising. Highly personal.	Damper of state, federal, and postal regulations on creative experimentations. Censorship often unpredictable. Formula thinking encouraged by "proven" direct-mail track records.
Posters	Graphic opportunities. Color. Large size. High-fidelity reproduction. Simple, direct approach. Possibility of an entirely visual message.	Essentially a one-line medium with only a limited opportunity to expand on the advertising message. Inadequate audience research, especially in transit advertising.
Point of sale	Opportunities for three-dimensional effects, movements, sound, and new production techniques.	Difficulty in pinpointing audience. Failure of retailers to make proper use of material submitted to them.

Source: Stephen Baker (1979), Systematic Approach to Advertising Creativity, *New York: McGraw-Hill, p. 154.*

and promotion deals are monitored and discussed. Such consumers are much more likely to respond favorably to sales promotions than are consumers who consider coupons a waste of time.

Actions

Although the key consumer action of interest to marketers is purchase of the promoted product or brand, other behaviors may also be the targets of promotion strategies. For instance, some promotions are intended to generate store contact. Some grocery stores offer a "double coupon" strategy (each coupon is worth twice its face value) in an effort to build store traffic. Other promotions may attempt to stimulate word-of-mouth communications between consumers. (This topic will be discussed later.)

FIGURE 18–5   **Redemption Rates for Grocery Product Coupons Distributed Using Different Methods**

	Average redemption rate	
	1984	**1982**
Daily newspaper		
R.O.P. solo	2.6%	2.9%
Co-op (all)	2.7	3.2
Free-standing insert	4.2	—
Sunday paper		
Free-standing insert	4.5	4.6
Supplement	2.1	2.3
Magazine		
On-page	2.0	2.5
Pop-up	4.7	5.2
Direct mail		
	8.1	9.3
In/on package		
Regular in-package	16.6	18.1
Regular on-package	13.3	12.7
Cross in-package	5.8	6.8
Cross on-package	5.1	4.1
Instant on-package	27.9	—

Source: Curt Schleier (1985), "Marketing Image Plots Turnaround," Advertising Age *(August 15), p. 16; data from A. C. Nielsen Co.*

Managing Promotion Strategies

Developing and implementing effective promotion strategies is a complex, difficult task. Although no single approach or "magic formula" can guarantee an effective promotion mix, the model presented in Figure 18–6 identifies the key activities in managing promotion strategies.

Analyze Consumer/Product Relationships

Developing effective promotion strategies begins with an analysis of the relationships between consumers and the products or brands of interest. This requires identifying the appropriate target markets for the product. Then, marketers must identify consumers' needs, goals and values, their levels of product and brand knowledge and involvement, and their current attitudes and behavior patterns. In short, marketers must strive to understand the *relationship* between their target consumers and the product or brand of interest.

When dealing with a new product or brand, marketers may have to conduct considerable marketing research to learn about the consumer/product relationship. This research could include interviews to identify the dominant means-end chains that reveal how consumers perceive the relationships between the product or brand and their own self-concepts. Other methods might include focus group interviews, concept tests, attitude and use surveys, and even test marketing. For existing products and

FIGURE 18–6   **Managing Promotion Strategies**

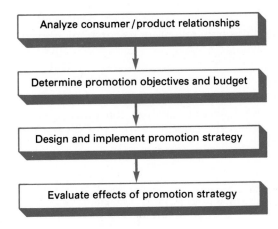

FIGURE 18–7   **The Foote, Cone & Belding Grid for Analyzing Consumer/Product Relationships**

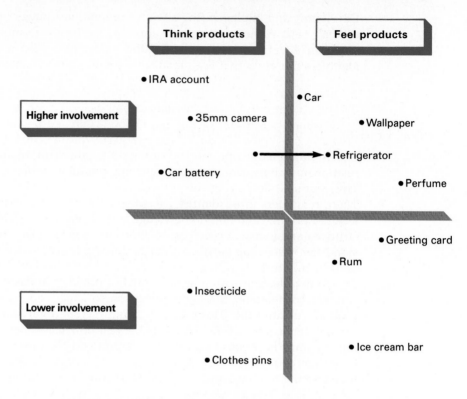

Source: David Berger (1986), "Theory Into Practice: The FCB Grid," European Research (January), p. 35.

brands, marketers may already know a great deal about consumer/product relationships. Perhaps only follow-up research might be necessary here.

The FCB Grid

Figure 18–7 presents a simple grid model used by Foote, Cone & Belding, a major advertising agency, to analyze consumer/product relationships.[16] The figure also shows the typical locations of several different products,

---

[16]See David Berger (1986), "Theory into Practice: The FCB Grid," *European Research* (January), pp. 35–46; and an earlier paper by Richard Vaughn (1980), "How Advertising Works: A Planning Model," *Journal of Advertising Research* (October), pp. 27–33.

based on extensive consumer research conducted around the world. The FCB grid is based on two concepts you studied in earlier chapters: consumers' *involvement* and their *salient knowledge, meanings,* and *beliefs* about the product.

Consumers have varying degrees of felt involvement (enduring plus situation involvement) with a product or brand, denoted as lower or higher involvement in the grid model. Moreover, various types of knowledge, meanings and beliefs may be activated when consumers evaluate and choose among alternative products or brands. Some products are considered primarily in terms of rational factors, such as the functional consequences of using the product. These are termed **think products** in the grid model. Included in this category are such products as investments, cameras, and car batteries—all products purchased primarily for their functional consequences.

In contrast, **feel products** are considered by consumers primarily in terms of nonverbal images (visual or other types of images) and emotional factors, such as psychosocial consequences and values. For instance, products purchased primarily for their sensory qualities—ice cream, soft drinks, cologne—as well as products for which emotional consequences are dominant—flowers or jewelry—are feel products in the FCB grid.

Because the consumer/product relationships are quite different in the four quadrants of the grid, the FCB grid also has implications for developing promotion strategies—including developing creative advertising, measuring advertising effects, and selecting media in which to place ads. The

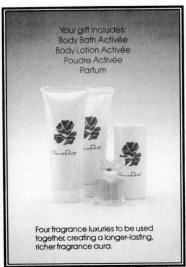

Courtesy Parfums Stern, Inc.

Scent strips allow consumers to experience "feel" products.

HIGHLIGHT 18–6   **Promoting "Feel" Products**

How do you promote a product such as perfume or cologne—definite "feel" products? Market research shows that consumers are more likely to buy products that they have sampled. The way you sample a scent is by smelling it. But getting customers to the perfume counters in department stores is difficult and expensive. Enter *scent strips,* which can be placed on advertisements that can be seen (and smelled) by millions of consumers.

Scent strips appear to be a very effective promotion device in the crowded $3.8 billion perfume market. According to Sunny Bates, beauty advertising manager for *Elle,* the U.S. version of the French fashion magazine, "Scented strips make sampling easier and a lot less expensive." Small vials used for sampling perfumes cost about 30 cents each, but scent strips cost only about a nickel.

Although no public marketing research study has quantified the impact of scent strips, many perfume manufacturers consider the phenomenal success of Giorgio, an expensive perfume launched in 1981 and promoted almost exclusively through scent strips, as sufficient evidence that this sampling method works well. Giorgio sold $2.5 million in 1982 and topped $100 million in 1986.

Now everyone is trying to do what Giorgio did. Scent strips are getting so popular that the average issue of *Vogue* smells like the perfume counter at Bloomingdale's. Interestingly, some advertisers (and some magazine readers) have begun to complain about the odoriferous advertising. Because too many scents spoil the magazine, most publishers refuse to carry more than three scent strips per issue.

Source: Lisa Gubernick (1986), "The Nose Knows," Forbes (January 13), pp. 280-281.

appropriate promotion strategy depends on the product's position in the grid (see Highlight 18–6). Sometimes, a product can be "moved" within the grid, like the refrigerator in Figure 18–7, which was shifted from a "think" to a "feel" product by the following strategy. A South American client of FCB once had a problem: 5,000 ugly green refrigerators in inventory were not selling while the competing brands offered desirable product features such as ice makers. High-involvement products such as refrigerators tend to be sold in terms of functional consequences; but in this case there was no rational benefit to promote. So, FCB designed a promotion strategy to move refrigerators from the "think" quadrant to the "feel" quadrant. They created ads that featured Venezuelan international beauty queens and termed the refrigerators "another Venezuelan beauty." The 5,000 refrigerators sold out in 90 days. In general, FCB has found that traditional *think* products often can be marketed successfully using *feel* advertising promotion strategies. In sum, the FCB grid model illustrates how a careful analysis of the consumer/product relationship can help in the development of effective promotion communications.

Determine Promotion Objectives and Budget

Promotion strategies can have both behavior and cognitive effects on consumers. Thus, promotions may be designed to meet one or more of the following objectives:

- *to influence behaviors:* change or maintain consumers' specific behaviors concerning the product or brand—usually purchase behaviors.
- *to inform:* create new knowledge, meanings or beliefs about the product or brand in consumers' memories.
- *to persuade:* change consumers' beliefs, attitudes, and intentions toward the product or brand.
- *to transform knowledge structures:* subtly modify the images, feelings, and emotions that are activated when consumers consider the product or brand.
- *to remind:* increase the activation potential of the brand name or some other product meaning in consumers' memories.

Before designing a promotion strategy, marketers should determine their specific promotion objectives and the budget available to support it. The long run objective of most promotion strategies is to influence consumer behaviors, especially store patronage and brand purchase. Shopping malls sponsor auto, boat, or home-builder shows to build consumer traffic. Many promotions are designed to directly and quickly affect consumer purchases of a particular brand. The rebate programs and low-interest financing offered by automakers are intended to stimulate short-run sales of certain brands and models. Finally, many promotions have multiple objectives. Frito-Lay frequently uses a sales promotion strategy of placing coupons on the package. This promotion is designed to stimulate immediate sales and to encourage repeat sales, with the long-run goal of creating more brand-loyal consumers.

Some promotions are designed to first influence consumers' *cognitions* in anticipation of a later influence on their overt *behaviors.* When a new product or brand is introduced, a primary objective for advertising promotions may be to create awareness of the product and some simple beliefs about it. Marketers also try to generate publicity for new products for these reasons, as well as to create a favorable brand image. These cognitions are intended to influence sales behaviors at some later time.

Design and Implement Promotion Strategy

Designing alternative promotion strategies and selecting one to meet the promotion objectives is based largely on the consumer/product relationships that have been identified through marketing research. Implementing the promotion strategy may include creating ads and running them in various media, designing and distributing coupons, putting salespeople to work, and developing publicity events. Many of these tasks may be done with the aid of an advertising agency or a promotion consultant.

Designing Promotion Strategies

Consider the various consumer segments portrayed in Figure 18–8. These groups are defined by consumers' purchase behavior and attitudes toward a brand. Consumers who dislike the brand and never buy it are not likely to be persuaded by any promotions and can be ignored. On the other hand, consumers who never buy the brand but have a favorable (or at least

FIGURE 18–8   **An Analysis of Consumer Vulnerability**

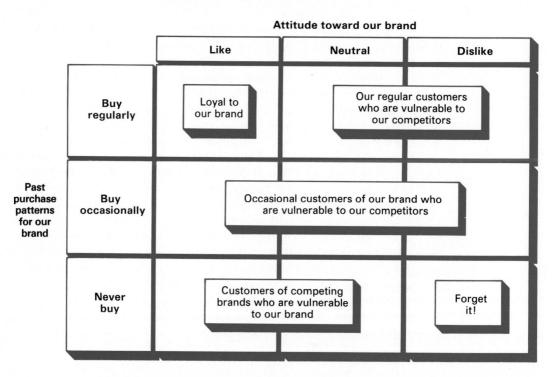

Source: Adapted from Yoram Wind (1977), "Brand Loyalty and Vulnerability," in Consumer and Industrial Buying Behavior, A. G. Woodside, J. N. Sheth and P. D. Bennett (eds.), New York: North Holland Publishing, pp. 313-320.

neutral) attitude toward it are vulnerable to the company's promotions. Free samples, premiums, contests, or coupons may encourage these consumers to try the brand and move them to an occasional user segment.

Occasional purchasers of the brand are vulnerable to the promotion strategies for competing brands. In that situation, a promotion objective might be to encourage repeat purchases of the brand. A purchase plan such as offering a free dozen donuts after the consumer has bought 12 dozen, or a premium for saving proofs of purchase may be effective strategies. Or a firm might try to demonstrate the superiority of its brand over competing brands. For example, Burger King and Pepsi-Cola have used **comparative advertising** to "prove" that their brand is better than McDonald's and Coca-Cola, respectively.[17]

Finally, brand-loyal consumers who like a company's brand and purchase it consistently can be influenced by promotions designed to keep them happy customers. The airlines have used a phenomenally successful promotion, commonly called *frequent flyer programs,* to reinforce the attitudes and purchase behavior of their frequent customers. Consumers rack up mileage on flights taken with the airline and receive free trips when sufficient mileage has been accumulated. The programs are supposed to be limited to frequent flyers, usually defined as those taking 12 or more plane trips per year. However, in 1984 an estimated 7 million Americans were enrolled in frequent-flyer programs, many more than the estimated 1 million frequent flyers. In fact, more than a third of air travelers are enrolled in four such programs—not exactly what the airlines had in mind when the promotion was begun![18] In any case, these incentive programs have seemed so successful that they are being copied by other types of companies (see Highlight 18–7).

Phone calls by salespeople to "check up on how things are going" may reinforce past customers' attitudes and intentions to rebuy when the need arises. Joe Girard, the top car salesman in the United States for 11 years in a row, sends out over 13,000 cards to his customers each month, wishing them Happy New Year from Joe Girard, Happy St. Patrick's Day, and so on.[19] Finally, promotions can inform current consumers of new uses for existing products. Advertising campaigns promoted Saran Wrap for

---

[17]George E. Belch (1981), "An Examination of Comparative and Noncomparative Television Commercials: The Effects of Claim Variation and Repetition on Cognitive Response and Message Acceptance," *Journal of Marketing Research* (August), pp. 333–349; William L. Wilkie and Paul W. Farris (1975), "Comparison Advertising: Problems and Potential," *Journal of Marketing* (October), pp. 7–15.

[18]Coleman Lollar (1984), "From Sales Gimmick to Global Reality," *Frequent Flyer* (November), pp. 75–85.

[19]Thomas J. Peters and Robert H. Waterman, Jr. (1982), *In Search of Excellence: Lessons from America's Best-Run Companies,* New York: Warner Books, p. 158.

HIGHLIGHT 18–7   **Rewarding Customer Purchase Loyalty**

For airlines, the concept of rewarding loyal customers with free flights has worked like a dream. American Airlines considers its frequent-flyer program, "the single most successful marketing tool we've ever had." Now an increasing number of companies from banks to retailers to car rental agencies are trying to mimic the airline's success with frequent-buyer programs of their own. Under these plans, customers accumulate points, usually based on dollars spent, that can be cashed in for prizes or discounts.

Lester Wunderman, chairman of Young & Rubicam's direct marketing group, finds the trend refreshing. "The history of American marketing has been to breed disloyalty to get someone to try something new," he says. "These frequent-purchase programs are just the opposite. American business is beginning to understand the enormous profit leverage in loyalty."

But these clone programs may not be as successful as the frequent-flyer programs. Airlines can award free flights at minimal expense because planes often fly with vacant seats. Companies in other industries must devise rewards that tantalize consumers and figure ways of handling the record-keeping without breaking the bank.

Neiman-Marcus, the up-scale Dallas-based retailer, started its InCircle program in 1984 to differentiate itself from competitors such as Saks Fifth Avenue. Neiman offers relatively modest rewards. For $3,000 in annual purchases, customers receive periodic deliveries of chocolates. They get caviar for spending $12,000. The costs for administering the program are modest too, because almost all participants use the Neiman charge card and thus are on its computer system. The program seems to be working—more InCircle customers remain high spenders than was true before the program was instituted.

Source: John Paul Newport, Jr. (1985), "Frequent-Flyer Clones,' Fortune (April 29), p. 201.

use in microwave cooking and Static Guard to eliminate static electricity from carpets around computers.

These brief examples illustrate three important points. First, appropriate promotions depend on the type of relationship consumers have with the product or brand, especially their level of enduring involvement. Second, promotion methods vary in their effectiveness for achieving certain objectives. Personal selling, for example, is usually more effective for closing sales; advertising is more effective for increasing brand awareness among large groups of consumers. Third, promotion objectives will change over a product's life cycle as changes occur in consumers' relationships with the product and the competitive environment. The promotion strategy that worked well when the product was introduced is not likely to be effective at the growth, maturity, or decline stages.

Courtesy The Dow Chemical Company

Promoting a new use for an existing product.

Developing Advertising Strategies

A number of factors must be considered in developing advertising strategies. One model of advertising strategy identifies five key elements, presented below:

- *Driving force:* the value orientation of the ad strategy; the end goal or value on which the advertising is focused.

- *Consumer benefits:* the key positive consequences for the consumer that are to be communicated in the ad, either visually or verbally.

- *Message elements:* the concrete or abstract product attributes or features that are to be communicated in the ad, either verbally or visually.

- *Leverage point:* the specific way in which the value or end goal is linked to the specific features of the ad; the "hook" that activates or taps into the driving force.

- *Executional framework:* all the details of the advertising execution— models, clothes used, setting—as well as the overall scenario or action plot; the ad's overall theme or style; the vehicle for communicating the means-end message.[20]

Each of these ad strategy factors requires many decisions by marketing and ad agency personnel. As we have seen, the first step in developing an advertising strategy is to analyze the consumer/product relationship. Means-end measures of consumers' knowledge structures are useful for this purpose.[21] From a means-end perspective, the end goals or values that consumers seek to achieve are the key to developing effective advertising strategies. The marketer must select the key value, end state, goal, or benefit to be communicated in the ad. Then, the marketer must determine how the ad will communicate that the product can achieve or satisfy this end goal or value.

The attribute, consequence, and value levels of product knowledge in a means-end chain are directly related to three of the major decision elements of advertising strategy. Knowing consumers' salient product attributes helps marketers decide which *message elements* to include in an ad. (Should ads for Ruffles potato chips emphasize their flavor, crunchiness, or ridges?) Data about the important functional consequences consumers perceive can help identify the key *consumer benefits* to be communicated. (Are Ruffles chips for dipping or an accompaniment for sandwiches?) Values or end goals are directly related to the *driving force* of the ad strategy.

Finally, developing the *executional framework* and the *leverage point* requires selecting and putting together the specific executional aspects of an ad—the product attributes mentioned or shown, the models used, the

---

[20]Jerry C. Olson and Thomas J. Reynolds (1983), "Understanding Consumers' Cognitive Structures: Implications for Advertising Strategies," in *Advertising and Consumer Psychology,* Larry Percy and Arch Woodside (eds.), Lexington, Mass.: Lexington Books, pp. 77–90.

[21]Material for this section is derived from Olson and Reynolds (1983), "Understanding Consumers' Cognitive Structures."

camera angles, the plot, the various cuts to different scenes, etc.—to effectively communicate the connection between the product and the basic goals and values the consumer is seeking. These decisions require creative imagination that can be guided by means-end data. We hasten to emphasize that this approach does not make developing advertising strategies or creating specific ads easy or foolproof. Instead, this is a convenient framework that organizes and gives focus to the many decisions. Generally, it should produce more coherent and effective advertising that communicates complete means-end meanings.

Developing Personal Selling Strategies

The process of developing a personal selling promotion strategy is illustrated in Figure 18–9.[22] The model is referred to as ISTEA, which stands for impression, strategy, transmission, evaluation, and adjustment. This model suggests that salespeoples' influence depends on their skills at performing five basic activities: (1) developing useful *impressions* of the customer; (2) formulating selling *strategies* based on these impressions; (3) *transmitting* appropriate messages; (4) *evaluating* customer reactions to the messages; (5) making appropriate *adjustments* in presentation should the initial approach fail.

According to this model, the personal selling process works as follows:

> In the first activity, the salesperson combines information gained through past experience with information relevant to the specific interaction to develop an impression of the customer. Salespersons can derive information about their target customers by examining past experiences with this and other customers, by observing the target customer during an interaction, and by projecting themselves into the target customer's decision-making situation.
>
> In the second activity, the salesperson analyzes his/her impression of the customer and develops a communication strategy which includes an objective for the strategy, a method for implementing the strategy, and specific message formats.
>
> Having formulated the strategy, the salesperson transmits the messages to the customer. As the salesperson delivers the messages, she/he evaluates their effects by observing the customer's reactions

---

[22]Barton W. Weitz (1978), "Relationship between Salesperson Performance and Understanding of Customer Decision Making," *Journal of Marketing Research* (November), p. 502. Also see Barton W. Weitz (1981), "Effectiveness in Sales Interactions: A Contingency Framework," *Journal of Marketing* (Winter), pp. 85–103.

FIGURE 18–9   **A Model of the Personal Selling Process**

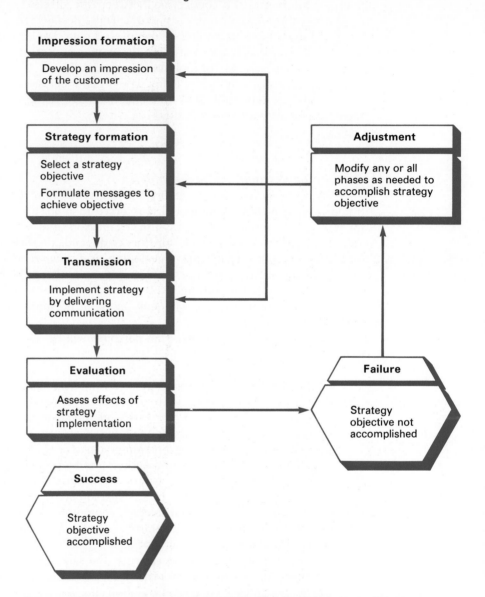

Source: Adapted from Barton A. Weitz (1978), "Relationship between Salesperson Performance and Understanding Customer Decision Making," Journal of Marketing Research (November), p. 502.

Alan Carey/The Image Works

Would the ISTEA approach be useful in this personal selling situation?

and soliciting opinions. On the basis of these evaluations, the salesperson can make adjustments by either reformulating the impression of the customer, selecting a new strategic objective, or changing the method for achieving the strategic objective, or the salesperson can continue to implement the same strategy.[23]

---

[23]Weitz, "Effectiveness in Sales Interactions."

Although this model was developed for industrial (business-to-business) marketing situations, it is consistent with the communication approach to consumer promotion discussed above.[24] The model emphasizes analysis of the customer as the starting point for strategy development. Research confirms that impression formation (consumer analysis) and strategy formulation by salespeople improved their sales performance.[25] Similarly, research on sales transactions in retail sporting goods stores suggests that successful salespeople adapt their communication style to interact appropriately with customers.[26]

Evaluate Effects of Promotion Strategy

Evaluating the effects of a promotion strategy involves comparing its results with the objectives. While this might seem like a simple task, determining promotion effects can be quite difficult. For example, clearly stated cognitive objectives such as "increase brand awareness by 25 percent" are not easily evaluated. Different methods of measuring awareness may give different results. Moreover, it is often difficult to determine whether a change in brand awareness resulted from the promotion strategy or from something else, such as word-of-mouth communications. Similarly, promotion objectives stated in behavior terms—"increase sales by 10 percent"—are often hard to evaluate. It is often difficult to determine what factors caused a sales increase. Increases in competitors' prices, opening new territories and outlets, changes in consumers' attitudes, and various other factors may be responsible for the increase in sales. Likewise, if sales decrease or remain the same during the promotion period, it is difficult to determine whether the promotion strategy was ineffective or whether other factors were responsible.

In other cases, however, evaluation of promotion effects can be relatively straightforward. Sales promotion tools such as coupons are used to stimulate short-term sales, and coupon redemption rates can give a good idea of effectiveness. The dollar amounts sold by salespeople can also be compared to determine their relative effectiveness. Experimental approaches (such as BehaviorScan) and other research (surveying target consumers' recall and recognition of ads and brands) can also be used to

---

[24]Also see Richard W. Olshavsky (1975), "Customer-Salesman Interaction in Appliance Retailing," *Journal of Marketing Research* (May), pp. 208–212.

[25]Harish Sujan (1986), "Smarter versus Harder: An Exploratory Attributional Analysis of Salespeople's Motivations," *Journal of Marketing Research* (February), pp. 41–49.

[26]See Kaylene C. Williams and Rosann L. Spiro (1985), "Communication Style in the Salesperson-Customer Dyad," *Journal of Marketing Research* (November), pp. 434–442.

examine the effects of advertising.[27] In sum, while measuring the effectiveness of promotion strategies may be difficult, marketers do have methods for estimating these effects.

Measuring Advertising Effects

Because the major impact of advertising tends to be on consumers' cognitions, measuring its effects is often difficult. Given that the costs of advertising are very high (about $65 billion in 1982), marketers have tried to develop measures of the communication effectiveness of ads. This is usually called **copy testing.**[28] Two types of measures are most common: *recall* and *persuasion (belief and attitude change)*. Recall measures have been attacked for not really measuring the important impacts of ads.[29] For certain types of ads (reminder or image ads) recall may be an important objective, however. Some ads are intended to create high levels of awareness, and a measure of top-of-mind awareness such as brand name recall may be quite appropriate.

The Promotion Environment

The **promotion environment** includes all the promotion strategies marketers create to influence consumer cognitions and behaviors: advertising, sales promotions, personal selling, and publicity. The promotion environment also includes the physical and social environment in which the promotions are experienced. Many of these factors can affect the success of a promotion. In this section, we discuss three environmental factors that can influence advertising and sales promotion strategies—clutter, level of competition, and types of advertising executions.

---

[27]For a review of various measures of advertising effectiveness, see David W. Stewart, Connie Pechmann, Srinivasan Ratneshwar, John Stroud and Beverly Bryant (1985), "Advertising Evaluation: A Review of Measures," in *Marketing Communications—Theory and Research*, Michael J. Houston and Richard J. Lutz (eds.), Chicago: American Marketing Association, pp. 3–6.

[28]See Benjamin Lipstein and James P. Neelankavil (1984), "Television Advertising Copy Research: A Critical Review of the State of the Art," *Journal of Advertising Research* (April–May), pp. 19–25.

[29]Lawrence D. Gibson (1983), "Not Recall," *Journal of Advertising Research* (February–March), pp. 39–46.

HIGHLIGHT 18–8   **Clutter and the 15-Second Commercial**

At one time, believe it or not, the 60-second commercial was the most common on TV. Over the years, marketers had collected a body of research data that established benchmarks of effectiveness for these longer ads. Then, in the late 1960s, a crisis came along. All of this research was jeopardized by the introduction of 30-second commercials. At the time, it was thought that the shorter ads, and the extra "clutter" they would create, would cause havoc with advertising effectiveness and measurement. It didn't happen, and the 30-second ad is now the standard.

But a new crisis is looming: 15-second ads. What will their effect be?

Preliminary evidence provided by a large-scale comparison of 30 15-second and 5,221 30-second ads suggests that the new ads won't wreak havoc, either. When the average 30-second commercial was scored 100 for communication performance, the average 15-second ad scored 78. The 15-second ads also scored well on a measure of the number of ideas in the ad played back later by the viewer—2.6 versus 2.9 for the 30-second ads. Finally, both ad lengths scored about the same in terms of the sense of importance of the main idea created by the commercial. Yet the 15-second ad costs only slightly more than half as much money to run.

So, will the 15-second ads be a problem? Probably not. Remember, it is not the length per se that makes an ad effective or ineffective. If an ad establishes a reason—a reward—for viewing it in the first few seconds, consumers are likely to pay attention and comprehend its meaning, no matter how long it is.

Certain communication goals are more difficult to achieve with 15-second ads: a feeling of newness, a multistep process, a sense of variety, creating a mood or emotion, and humor. But the very same problems were mentioned for the 30-second ads, and we know how that turned out.

Source: Robert Parcher (1986), "15-Second TV Commercials Appear to Work 'Quite Well'," Marketing News (January 3), pp. 1 and 60.

Promotion Clutter

A key promotion objective is to increase the probability that consumers come into contact with, attend to, and comprehend the promotion message. In recent years, however, competition has so increased that the effectiveness of any given promotion strategy may be impaired by **clutter**—the growing number of competitive strategies in the environment. Advertisers have long been worried that the clutter created by multiple ads during commercial breaks and between TV programs will reduce the communication effectiveness of each ad (see Highlight 18–8).[30]

---

[30]See Peter H. Webb and Michael L. Ray (1979), "Effects of TV Clutter," *Journal of Advertising Research* (June), pp. 7–12.

Clutter also affects other types of promotion strategies, especially sales promotions. Over the past decade, marketers have dramatically increased their spending on sales promotions. Traditionally, *couponing* has been the most popular form of sales promotion, and its use has grown every year. Approximately 95 percent of major U.S. consumer-goods companies used coupon promotions in 1984. The sheer number of coupons distributed yearly is staggering: 163 billion in 1984, up 14 percent from 1980. Coupon redemption rates have not kept pace, though. Across all methods of distribution (see Figure 18–5) only about 3.8 percent (or 6.3 billion) of coupons were redeemed.[31] Some marketers wonder whether this clutter will cause couponing to become a victim of its own success.

Level of Competition

The **level of competition** is a key aspect of the promotion environment for a product category. As competition heats up, marketers' use of promotions usually increases. We saw this in the large number of promotions tried by the airlines when deregulation created a more competitive environment. Moreover, the *types* of promotion strategies change as competitive pressures increase. Comparative advertising, featuring direct comparisons with competitive brands, may become more common. Sometimes miniature "wars" are fought through TV commercials. In one notable example, Pepsi "challenge" ads claimed taste preference superiority over Coke, and Coca-Cola retaliated with taste tests that showed consumers preferred Coke. In fiercely competitive environments, promotion often becomes the key element in the marketer's competitive arsenal. Marketers may develop complex promotion mixes that include couponing, premiums, advertisements, price reductions, and publicity.

Advertising Content

Marketers have studied a great many content characteristics of advertisements. These include such factors as fear, humor, sexual content, one- and two-sided arguments, size of print ads, length of broadcast ads, strong visual images, specific claims, celebrity spokespersons, multiple repetitions, subliminal stimuli (see Highlight 18–9) and many others. Few generalizations have been gained from this research, however. Partly this is because the effects of any ad are a function of the knowledge and involve-

---

[31]These data are from Curt Schleier (1985), "Marketing Image Plots Turnaround," *Advertising Age* (August 15), pp. 15–16.

HIGHLIGHT 18–9   **Subliminal Advertising**

Although most advertisers pay little or no attention to the topic, **subliminal persuasion** in advertising just won't go away. Writers like Wilson Key keep turning out widely read books that claim subliminal advertising is all around us. Key claims that marketers intentionally embed subliminal stimuli—usually sexual objects, symbols, or words—in advertisements. Moreover, he claims that these hidden, subliminal stimuli affect us in powerful ways of which we are unaware.

What do we know about the effects of subliminal stimulation? First, it is clear that stimulation below the level of a person's conscious awareness *can* be shown to have measurable effects upon some aspects of that person's behavior. That is, people can respond to stimuli without realizing that the stimuli exist. But these stimuli are not necessarily subliminal—that is, they are not necessarily presented at intensities below our perceptual threshold. They just tend not to be consciously noticed as consumers go about their business. As we have seen throughout this text, a great deal of cognitive activity occurs "automatically." Thus, consumers often are not able to report the existence of a stimulus or an awareness that some cognitive process has occurred.

With regard to Key's claims about sexual embedding, two issues are in question. First, are subliminal embeddings being made in advertisements as a matter of course, as Key claims?

Virtually no evidence exists that this is so. Certainly, sexual stimuli are found in a great many advertisements, but not in subliminal embeds. Second, could subliminal stimuli affect goal-directed behaviors like purchase choices?

A key finding in cognitive psychology that we have emphasized throughout this text, is that the meaning of a stimulus does not reside in the *stimulus*. Rather, meanings are *constructed by consumers* in active and sometimes complex ways as they come into contact with the stimulus. Most stimuli have little or no influence on our cognitions or behaviors when presented at a recognizable level. Why, then, should they suddenly have a strong effect when presented subliminally? Key claims that humans have two processing systems, one of which operates on a completely unconscious level and immediately picks up on the alleged subliminal embeds. However, no psychological theories or data support such a system of cognition.

None of this is to say that ads may not have effects on consumers' meanings at a subconscious level—but the stimuli don't have to be subliminal for that to occur.

Source: Jack Haberstroh (1984), "Can't Ignore Subliminal Ad Charges," Advertising Age *(September 17), pp. 3 and 42; Timothy E. Moore (1982), "Subliminal Advertising: What You See Is What You Get,"* Journal of Marketing *(Spring), pp. 38-47.*

ment of the consumer audience and the environment in which exposure takes place. Thus, it is likely that fear appeals or humor or sex might be effective in one situation but not in another.

One content characteristic of current interest concerns the dominant theme or type of information in the ad. Different types of advertising have different impacts on consumers' knowledge, meanings, and beliefs about a product, including their moods, emotions, and image meanings. Most frequently, informational, factual, or reason-why ads are contrasted with transformational, emotional, or image ads. If attended to and comprehended at a deep, elaborate level, **informational ads** are thought to create new semantic knowledge or beliefs about the product, its attributes, and consequences.[32] On the other hand, **emotional and image ads** are thought to create different types of meanings.[33] They make consumers feel differently about themselves and perhaps about their relationship with the product. Such meanings may affect product purchase, especially for "feel" products.

A particularly interesting issue concerns the ability of so-called **transformational ads** to influence consumers' interpretations of their product use experiences.[34] Transformational ads create images, feelings, meanings, and beliefs about the product that may be activated when consumers use it.[35] These meanings then "transform" consumers' interpretations of product usage. Consumers then experience the product differently than if they had not been exposed to the ad. This is more common than you might think. Consider your reaction to a movie you saw after someone told you the plot and described several key scenes. You probably reacted quite differently to the film than you would have if you had been an uninformed viewer. The effects of transformational ads have not been heavily researched as yet; but their likely impacts on consumers' product-use experiences are consistent with our view of consumer cognition.

Promotion Cognitions

Promotion cognitions concern all of the cognitive processes and knowledge, meanings, and beliefs that we discussed in Section Two. *Interpretation processes* (attention and comprehension) and *integration processes* (especially

---

[32]See Morris B. Holbrook (1978), "Beyond Attitude Structure: Toward the Informational Determinants of Attitude," *Journal of Marketing Research* (November), pp. 545–556.

[33]Julie A. Edell and Richard Staelin (1983), "The Information Processing of Pictures in Print Advertisements," *Journal of Consumer Research* (June), pp. 45–61.

[34]Christopher P. Puto and William D. Wells (1984), "Informational and Transformational Advertising: The Differential Effects of Time," in *Advances in Consumer Research*, Vol. 11, Thomas C. Kinnear (ed.), Ann Arbor, Mich.: Association for Consumer Research, pp. 638–643.

[35]Ibid.

attitude formation) are of critical importance. As we discussed, consumers' comprehension processes vary in depth and elaboration, depending on their levels of knowledge and involvement. Thus, exposure to a promotion communication—whether an ad, a coupon, or a sales presentation—may produce meanings that vary in number (elaboration), level of abstraction (semantic versus sensory), and interconnectedness. Consumers also may form inferences about product attributes or consequences, or the marketer's motivation. In this section, we will examine several other cognitive concepts that are relevant to understanding the effects of advertising. They include consumers' attitudes toward ads and persuasion processes.

Attitude toward the Ad

Advertisers have long been interested in measuring consumers' evaluations of advertisements.[36] Recently, researchers have become interested in the affective and evaluative meanings associated with the ad itself—consumers' **attitude toward the ad.** Research suggests that consumers' attitudes toward the *ad* can influence their attitudes toward the advertised product or brand.[37] That is, ads that consumers like tend to create more positive brand attitudes and intentions than ads they don't like.

Persuasion Processes

Persuasion refers to changes in consumers' beliefs and attitudes caused by promotion communications. Current research suggests that there are two "routes" or types of cognitive processes by which advertising persuades: central and peripheral.[38]

---

[36]Mary Jane Schlinger (1979), "A Profile of Responses to Commercials," *Journal of Advertising Research* (April), pp. 37–46.

[37]See Andrew A. Mitchell and Jerry C. Olson (1981), "Are Product Attribute Beliefs the Only Mediator of Advertising Effects on Brand Attitude?" *Journal of Marketing Research* (August), pp. 318–332; Meryl Paula Gardner (1985), "Does Attitude toward the Ad Affect Brand Attitude under a Brand Evaluation Set?" *Journal of Marketing Research* (May), pp. 192–198; Richard J. Lutz, Scott B. Mackenzie and George Belch (1983), "Attitude toward the Ad as a Mediator of Advertising Effectiveness: Determinants and Consequences," in *Advances in Consumer Research*, Vol. 10, R. Baggozi and A. Tybout (eds.), Ann Arbor, Mich.: Association for Consumer Research, pp. 532–539.

[38]Richard E. Petty, John T. Cacioppo and David Schumann (1983), "Central and Peripheral Routes to Advertising Effectiveness: The Moderating Role of Involvement," *Journal of Consumer Research* (September), pp. 135–146.

Central Route

The central route to persuasion involves the classic deep, elaborate comprehension processing that we described in Chapter 6. In the **central route,** consumers focus on the key product message communicated in the ad. Central processing forms semantic beliefs about the attributes and consequences of a product or brand. If these beliefs are activated and used in integration processes, they may affect consumers' brand attitudes and purchase intentions. In sum, in central cognitive processes, consumers *(a)* interpret the ad message and form beliefs about product attributes and consequences and *(b)* integrate these meanings to form brand attitudes and intentions.

Peripheral Route

The **peripheral route** to persuasion is quite different. Here consumers are not motivated to process the ad message about the product. But they may still pay attention to the ad, perhaps for its entertainment value. (Soft-drink ads featuring pop singers seem to encourage this type of processing.) In peripheral processing, nonproduct features of the ad are given greater attention. Based on their meanings and beliefs about the ad, consumers may form attitudes toward the *ad,* but not toward the product. Interestingly, though, evidence is mounting that attitude toward the ad may influence attitudes toward the brand, thus causing some indirect persuasion.[39]

Whether consumers engage in central or peripheral processing depends largely on their goals during exposure to the ad. If exposure occurs while the consumer is actively considering purchase of the product, central processing is likely. If exposure occurs when the consumer is uninterested in the product (low enduring and situation involvement), peripheral processing is more likely.

Promotion Behaviors

Ultimately, promotions must affect not only consumers' cognitions, but also their *behaviors.* A firm's sales, profits, and market share objectives can be accomplished only if consumers perform a variety of behaviors, including purchase of its product. Different types of promotions can be used to

---

[39]Julie A. Edell and Marian C. Burke (1984), "The Moderating Effect of Attitude toward an Ad on Ad Effectiveness under Different Processing Conditions," in *Advances in Consumer Research,* Vol. 11, Thomas C. Kinnear (ed.), Ann Arbor, Mich.: Association for Consumer Research, pp. 644–649.

influence the various behaviors in the purchase/consumption sequence. Because we have already discussed purchase behavior in this chapter and throughout the book, we focus here on two behaviors that are critical to the success of promotion strategies: information contact and word-of-mouth communication with other consumers.

Information Contact

Consumer contact with promotion information is critical to the success of a promotion strategy. **Information contact** with promotions may be *intentional* (as when consumers search the newspapers for food coupons); but probably is most often *incidental* (the consumer just happens to come into contact with a promotion when engaging in some other behavior). Sometimes, promotion contact can even trigger the purchase decision process, as might occur in coming across a sale or an incentive promotion. As a practical matter, the marketer must place the promotion message in the target consumer's physical environment to maximize chances for exposure, and design the promotion so that it will be noticed (attended to). This requires knowledge of the media habits of the target market.

Placing information in consumers' environments may be easy when target consumers can be identified accurately. For example, catalog marketers can buy lists of consumers who have made mail-order purchases in the past year. Then they can send promotion materials directly to these target consumers. Of course, sending coupons or a sweepstakes promotion through the mail does not guarantee that consumers will open the envelope and read its contents.

Contact for personal selling promotions can be achieved through "cold calls" on consumers. But referrals and leads (or consumers contacting salespeople during their search process) are likely to be more successful. Marketers sometimes encourage referrals by offering gifts in return for the names of potential customers. Telephone contact or **telemarketing** is an increasingly popular method of personal selling. State Farm Insurance, for example, has used a telemarketing approach in which consumers are called and asked what time of the year they pay their homeowners' and automobile insurance premiums. Then, just prior to that time, rate information is sent to these consumers to encourage a switch to State Farm's insurance products.

Exposure to promotion messages is not enough, however. Consumers must also *attend to* the promotion messages. Promotions that generate high levels of situation involvement (large discounts, big prizes) are likely to be noticed and receive higher levels of attention. How well the promotion interacts with such consumer characteristics as enduring involvement and existing knowledge also affects the level of attention. For instance, the effectiveness of price-reduction promotions depends largely on consumers' price sensitivity.

Jean-Claude Lejeune

Word-of-mouth communication can be a powerful influence on consumer behavior.

Word-of-Mouth Communication

Marketers may want to encourage consumers' **word-of-mouth communication** about a promotion. This helps to spread awareness beyond those consumers who come into direct contact with the promotion.[40] Consumers may share information with friends about good deals on particular products, a valuable coupon in the newspaper, or a sale at a retail store. For example, a consumer may phone a friend who is looking for tires to say that Sears is having a great sale. Consumers sometimes recommend that their friends see a particular salesperson who is especially pleasant or well informed, or who offers good deals on merchandise. Consumers often pass on impressions of a new restaurant or retail store to their friends. As these examples illustrate, simply by placing information in consumers' environment, marketers can increase the probability that the information will be communicated to other consumers. And because personal communication

---

[40]Barry L. Bayus (1985), "Word of Mouth: The Indirect Effects of Marketing Efforts," *Journal of Advertising Research* (June–July), pp. 31–39.

from friends and relevant others is a powerful form of communication, marketers may try to design promotions that encourage word-of-mouth communication.

Back to the Case

The case described three different sales promotion strategies, each of which was quite successful. In this chapter, we have discussed many of the factors that affect the success of such promotion strategies. Promotions are complex strategies designed to affect consumers' cognitions and, especially, their behaviors. Marketers have a large number of promotion options from which to choose. It is important that promotion strategies be carefully designed to fit the relationship that the target consumers have with the product and to communicate the appropriate meanings to consumers. All of the concepts we have discussed about consumers' cognitions, behaviors, and environment are relevant for developing effective promotion strategies.

Summary

This chapter presented an overview of how knowledge about consumers' cognitions, behaviors, and environments can affect marketers' decisions about promotion strategies. We began by considering the four types of promotion methods—advertising, sales promotions, personal selling, and publicity. Then we reviewed a basic communication model. Next, we focused on developing a managerial model for designing and executing promotion plans. We then discussed three elements in the promotion environment—clutter, level of competition, and advertising content. Attention was also given to promotion cognitions including attitudes toward the ad and persuasion processes. We concluded by discussing two promotion behaviors—information contact and word-of-mouth communication.

Additional Readings

David A. Aaker and Donald E. Bruzzone (1981), "Viewer Perceptions of Prime-Time Television Advertising," *Journal of Advertising Research* (October), pp. 15–23.

Michael J. Baker and Gilbert A. Churchill, Jr. (1977), "The Impact of Physically Attractive Models on Advertising Evaluations," *Journal of Marketing Research* (November), pp. 538–555.

George E. Belch (1982), "The Effects of Television Commercial Repetition on Cognitive Response and Message Acceptance," *Journal of Consumer Research* (June), pp. 56–65.

Joe A. Dodson, Alice M. Tybout, and Brian Sternthal (1978), "Impact of Deals and Deal Retraction on Brand Switching," *Journal of Marketing Research* (February), pp. 72–81.

Christopher H. Lovelock and John A. Quelch (1983), "Consumer Promotions in Service Marketing," *Business Horizons* (May–June), pp. 66–75.

George P. Moschis and Roy L. Moore (1982), "A Longitudinal Study of Television Advertising Effects," *Journal of Consumer Research* (December), pp. 279–286.

Jerry C. Olson, Daniel R. Toy and Philip A. Dover (1982), "Do Cognitive Responses Mediate the Effects of Advertising Content on Cognitive Structure?" *Journal of Consumer Research* (December), pp. 245–261.

Marsha L. Richins (1983), "Negative Word-of-Mouth by Dissatisfied Consumers: A Pilot Study," *Journal of Marketing* (Winter), pp. 68–78.

Robert E. Smith and William R. Swinyard (1982), "Information Response Models: An Integrated Approach," *Journal of Marketing* (Winter), pp. 81–93.

Gary F. Soldow and Gloria Penn Thomas (1984), "Relational Communication: Form versus Content in the Sales Interaction," *Journal of Marketing* (Winter), pp. 84–93.

Daniel R. Toy (1982), "Monitoring Communication Effects: A Cognitive Structure/Cognitive Response Approach," *Journal of Consumer Research* (June), pp. 66–76.

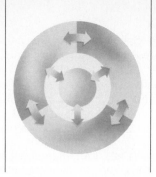

Chapter Nineteen

Pricing Strategy and Consumer Behavior

A Pricing Puzzle

Vinnie Bombatz is a construction worker who makes $12 per hour. While he could work overtime on Saturday at $18 per hour, he takes off two consecutive Saturdays to go fishing.

Vinnie is a heavy drinker . . . of Diet Pepsi. On the morning of his first Saturday off, he walks two blocks to a convenience food store to purchase a 12-pack for his fishing trip. The price is $5 plus 5 percent sales tax. Vinnie complains about the high price and is told by the clerk: "I don't set the prices. Take it or leave, Jack!" Vinnie is more than a little upset, but he pays the money because he's in a rush to get to the lake. He vows to himself never to get ripped off like this again. He walks home. The whole trip has taken 10 minutes.

On the next Saturday, Vinnie again needs a 12-pack of Diet Pepsi for his fishing trip. Remembering his previous experience at the convenience store, he decides to get in his car and drive six miles to the discount supermarket. He is pleasantly surprised that Diet Pepsi is on sale for $2.99 a dozen plus tax. Although the store is a bit crowded and it takes him a while to get through the checkout, he drives home feeling good about the purchase and the money he saved. This shopping trip takes a total of 45 minutes.

On which Saturday did Vinnie get a better price?

In several ways, *price* is the most unusual element of the marketing mix. For one thing, it is the only one that generates revenues; all of the other elements, as well as marketing research, involve expenditures of funds by organizations. Another difference is that although price may seem tangible and concrete, it is perhaps more intangible and abstract than other elements of the marketing mix. For example, in the product area, consumers often have a tangible product to examine, or at least information about a service to evaluate. In the promotion area, consumers have magazine and newspaper ads and information from salespeople to see, listen to, and evaluate. In the distribution area, consumers have malls and stores to experience. However, the price variable is a rather abstract concept which,

FIGURE 19–1   **The Wheel of Consumer Analysis: Pricing Strategy Issues**

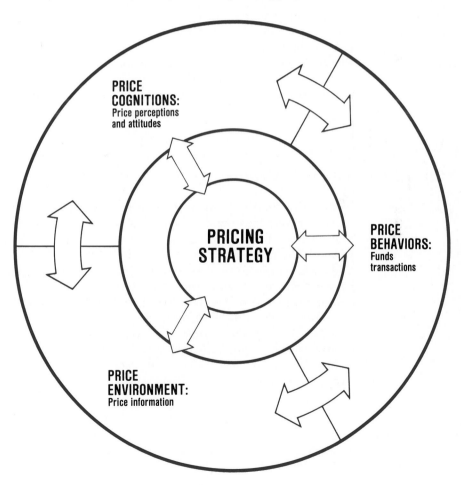

while represented as a sign or tag, has relatively little direct sensory experience connected with it. Perhaps because of this, basic research on pricing issues in marketing has been relatively modest compared to work done on the other marketing mix elements.

These differences should not lead you to underestimate the importance of price to marketing and consumer behavior, however. For example, Rao states:

> The effects of price changes are more immediate and direct, and appeals based on price are the easiest to communicate to prospective buyers. However, competitors can react more easily to appeals based on price than to those based on product benefits and imagery. It can be argued that the price decision is perhaps the most significant among the decisions of the marketing mix (strategy) for a branded product.[1]

In this chapter, we focus on some important relationships among consumer cognitions, behaviors, and the environment as they relate to the price variable of the marketing mix. These variables and relationships are shown in Figure 19–1, which provides an overview of the topics to be discussed. We begin our discussion by offering a conceptual view of the role of price in marketing exchanges. We then discuss pricing strategy, the environment and consumer cognitions and behaviors, in that order.

Conceptual Issues in Pricing

From a consumer's point of view, **price** is usually defined as what the consumer must give up to purchase a product or service. Research typically views price only in terms of the dollar amount asked or paid for a particular item or service. Because we believe that price is a pivotal element in the exchange process, we offer a conceptual view of price that encompasses more than dollar amount or financial cost to the consumer. Our discussion is intended to help you better understand the role of price in marketing strategy development.

Figure 19–2 offers a general model of the nature of marketing exchanges and highlights the role of price in this process. Although we will focus on for-profit organizations, the model could be developed and discussed in terms of nonprofit marketing. The major differences in nonprofit

---

[1]Vithala R. Rao (1984), "Pricing Research in Marketing: The State of the Art," *Journal of Business* (January), p. S39.

exchanges are that (1) while nonprofit organizations may seek money from consumers, they (at least in theory) do not seek surplus funds beyond costs, and (2) the value derived by consumers in nonprofit exchanges is often less tangible.

Figure 19–2 identifies four basic types of consumer costs: money, time, cognitive activity, and behavior effort. These costs, when paired with whatever value or utility the product offers, are a convenient way to consider the meaning of price to the consumer. While we do not argue that consumers finely calculate each of these costs for every purchase, we do believe they are frequently considered in the purchase of some products.

In Figure 19–2, we have also divided marketing costs into the four categories of production, promotion, distribution, and marketing research. Most business costs and investments could be attributed to one or another of these categories. These costs, when paired with the desired level of profit a firm seeks, offer a convenient way to consider the marketing side of the exchange equation. Basically, the model implies that products must usually cover at least variable costs and make some contribution to overhead or profits for the offering to be made to the marketplace.

For marketing exchanges to take place, the price consumers are willing to pay must be greater than or equal to the price at which marketers are willing to sell. However, while this may seem simple enough, a number of complex relationships need to be considered when pricing is viewed from this perspective. Of major importance is the nature of consumer costs

FIGURE 19–2   **The Pivotal Role of Price in Marketing Exchange**

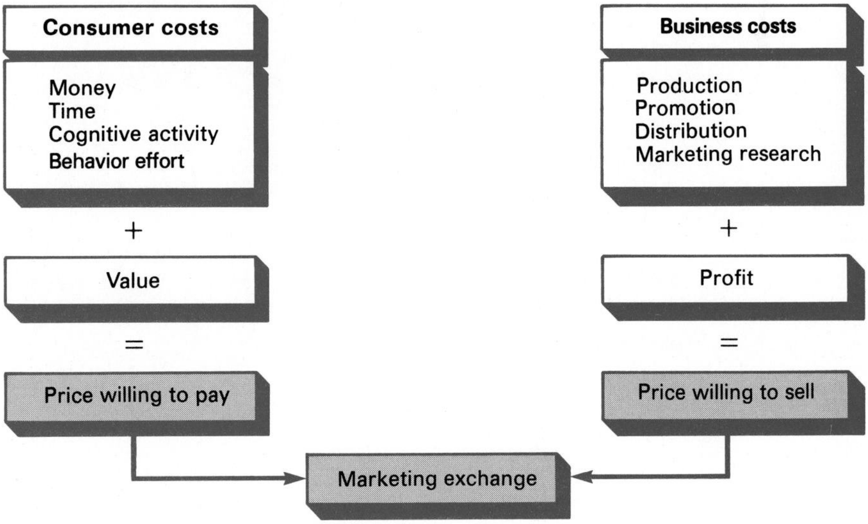

Courtesy Avis Rent A Car System, Inc.

A marketing strategy to reduce several consumer costs.

and the relationships between them. What should become clear is that the dollar price of an item may often be only a part of the total price of an exchange for the consumer.

Money

As we have noted, most pricing research has focused only on the dollar amount a consumer must spend to purchase a product or service. This research has recognized that the same dollar amount may be perceived differently by different individuals and market segments, depending on income levels and other variables. However, several important aspects of the dollar cost of offerings are not always considered. One of these concerns the *source* of funds for a particular purchase. We suspect that money received as a tax rebate, gift, interest, or as gambling winnings has a different value to many consumers than does money that is earned through work. Consequently, the dollar price of a particular item may be perceived differently by the same individual, depending on what sources of funds are used to pay for it.

Similarly, the "actual" price of a credit-card purchase that will be financed at 22 percent for an extended period is much different than the price if cash is used. To consumers who are accustomed to carrying large credit-card balances, this difference may be irrelevant; to others, the difference may forestall or eliminate a purchase. In addition, the type of work consumers do may affect how valuable a particular amount of money is to them—as well as affecting their willingness to spend that money on particular products and services.

There are also a number of ways to reduce the dollar amount spent for a particular item, although they often involve increasing other costs. For example, time, cognitive activity, and behavior effort are required to clip and use coupons or mail in for rebates. Shopping around at different stores seeking the lowest price involves not only time, cognitive activity, and behavior effort, but also increases other dollar costs such as transportation or parking.

Time

The time necessary to learn about a product or service and to travel to purchase it, as well as time spent in a store, can be important costs to the consumer. Most consumers are well aware that convenience food stores usually charge higher prices than supermarkets. Many convenience food stores are very profitable, for most consumers purchase from them at least occasionally. Clearly, these consumers often make a trade-off of paying more money to save time, particularly if only a few items are to be purchased. Time savings may result because the convenience outlets are located closer to home and thus require less travel time or because less time is required in the store to locate the product and wait in line to pay for it. Given the high cost of operating an automobile, it might even be cheaper in dollar terms to shop at stores that are closer to home, even if they have higher prices! Thus, bargain hunters who travel all over town to save 25 cents here and 50 cents there may be fooling themselves if they think they are saving money.

However, we should not treat time only as a cost of purchasing. In some situations, the process of seeking product information and purchas-

HIGHLIGHT 19–1   **Some Short-Term Price Reduction Tactics**

1. *Cents-off deals:* "Package price is 20¢ off."
2. *Special offers:* "Buy one, get one free"; "Buy three tires and get the fourth free."
3. *Coupons:* store or manufacturer coupons in newspaper, magazines, flyers, and packages.
4. *Rebates:* mail in proof-of-purchase seals for cash or merchandise.
5. *Increase quantity for same price:* "2 extra ounces of coffee free."
6. Free installation or service for a limited time period.
7. Reduce or eliminate interest charges for a limited time: "90 days same as cash."
8. Special sales: "25 percent off all merchandise marked with a red tag."

ing products is a very enjoyable experience—rather than a cost—for consumers. Many consumers enjoy Christmas shopping and spend hours at it, for instance. Some consumers enjoy window-shopping and purchasing on occasion, particularly if the opportunity cost of their time is low. In areas that allow shopping on Sunday, some consumers prefer going to the mall and shopping rather than sitting at home watching football games. Similarly, some consumers enjoy spending hours looking through catalogs of their favorite merchandise. Thus, while in an absolute sense consumers must spend time to shop and make purchases, in some cases this may be perceived as a benefit rather than a cost.

Cognitive Activity

One frequently overlooked cost of making purchases is the cognitive activity involved. Thinking and deciding what to buy can be very hard work. For example, suppose it is 1984 and a consumer is trying to decide which car to purchase. A number of dealers have been contacted, a number of cars looked at, and a number of ads have been seen and heard. The consumer, after many hours of deliberation, narrowed the choice to either a Ford Thunderbird or a Chevrolet Citation. In that model year, counting the different combinations of engines, transmissions, and optional accessories, the consumer had more than 69,000 varieties of Ford Thunderbirds and 32,000 varieties of Chevrolet Citations to assess! Now, we are not arguing that consumers would ever make all of these comparisons; but consider the cognitive activity that would be required to make even a small fraction of them. Clearly, it would not only take a lot of time, but would be very taxing in terms of cognitive work.[2] Yet, if even only a few comparisons are made, some cognitive effort must be expended.

In addition to all of the cognitive work involved in comparing purchase alternatives, the process can also be quite stressful. Some consumers find it very difficult and dislike making purchase, or other types of, decisions. To some, finding parking spaces, shopping in crowded malls and stores, waiting in long checkout lines, and viewing anxiety-producing ads can be a very unpleasant experience emotionally. Thus, the cognitive activity involved in purchasing can be a very important cost.

As you learned in Chapter 8, the cost involved in decision making is often the easiest one for consumers to reduce or eliminate. Simple decision rules or heuristics can reduce this cost considerably. By repeatedly purchasing the same brand, consumers can practically eliminate any decision making within a product class, for example. Other heuristics might be to purchase the most expensive brand, the brand on sale or display, the brand mom or dad used to buy, the brand a knowledgeable friend recommends, or the brand a selected dealer carries or recommends.

On the other hand, there are some situations in which consumers actively seek some form of cognitive involvement. Fishing enthusiasts frequently enjoy comparing the attributes of various types of equipment, judging their relative merits, and assessing the ability of different equipment to catch fish. We suspect that while consumers may enjoy periods in which they are not challenged to use much cognitive energy or ability, they may also seek purchasing problems to solve as a form of entertainment.

Behavior Effort

Anyone who has spent several hours walking around in malls can attest to the fact that purchasing involves behavior effort. In fact, when large shopping malls were first developed, one of the problems they faced was that consumers had long walks from the parking lot and considerable distance to cover within the mall itself. Many consumers were not physically comfortable with this much effort, and some avoided malls or shopped in only a small number of the stores available. Benches and chairs were placed in malls primarily to overcome this problem by giving consumers places to rest while shopping.

As with time and cognitive activity, behavior effort can also be a benefit rather than a cost. For example, walking around in malls and stores

---

[2]For a model and approach to measuring this cost, see Steven M. Shugan (1980), "The Cost of Thinking," *Journal of Consumer Research* (September), pp. 99–111.

is good exercise and is sometimes done as a source of relaxation. Some malls have started early-morning mall-walking programs for senior citizens. These programs may create a positive image for malls and bring in potential buyers.

Perhaps the most interesting aspects of behavior effort is the willingness of consumers to take on some marketing costs in order to reduce the dollar amount they spend and to make trade-offs among various types of costs. In some cases, consumers will perform part of the production process to get a lower dollar price. For example, consumers may forgo the cost of product assembly for bicycles and toys and do it themselves to save money. Heathkits produces a large line of electronic gadgets that are cheaper but must be assembled by the consumer.

There are also cases in which consumers will take on at least part of the cost of distribution to lower the dollar price. At one time, for example, it was common for milk to be delivered to the home; now, most consumers purchase it at stores. Consumers with access to a pickup truck frequently "deliver" their own furniture and appliances rather than pay a store for delivery. Catalog purchases require the consumer to pay the cost of shipping directly, yet may be less expensive than store purchases. If they are not, the consumer at least saves shopping time and effort in order to have the product delivered to the home. As we noted earlier in the text, consumers will also perform promotion and marketing research for firms to receive lower prices or other merchandise "free."

A final trade-off of interest in terms of pricing concerns the degree to which consumers participate in purchase/ownership. Consumers have several options with regard to purchase: (1) they can buy the product and enjoy its benefits as well as incur other costs such as inventory and maintenance; (2) they can rent or lease the product and enjoy its benefits but forgo ownership and often reduce some of the other costs, such as maintenance; (3) they can hire someone else to perform whatever service the product is designed to perform and forgo ownership and other postpurchase costs; (4) they can purchase the product and hire someone else to use and maintain it for them. For many durable goods, such as automobiles, appliances, power tools, furniture, and lawn mowers, at least several of these options are available. Clearly, as we stated at the beginning of the chapter, price is a lot more than just dollars and cents!

Value

To this point, we have discussed four aspects of price from the consumer's point of view. We have suggested that consumers can sometimes reduce one or more of these costs, but this usually requires an increase in at least one of the other costs. Purchases can be viewed in terms of which of the elements is considered a cost or a benefit and which is considered most

The Best Value in Lodging
Just Got Better.

Spring Break Sale.

Now's the time to take your spring break while TraveLodges across the country offer special spring rates...many as low as $25. You can always count on comfort and convenience at more than 450 locations coast to coast. So check-in to today's TraveLodge and check-out with the best value in lodging.

TRAVELODGE

MOTELS & MOTOR HOTELS

For the TraveLodge location
at your next destination, call toll free: **800 255-3050**

A member company of the TRUSTHOUSE FORTE GROUP WORLDWIDE

Courtesy Travel Lodge Motels & Motor Hotels

Creating perceptions of value.

critical for particular purchases. However, regardless of what cost trade-offs are made, it seems that whatever is being purchased must be perceived to be of greater *value* to the consumer than merely the sum of the costs. In other words, the consumer perceives that the purchase offers benefits greater than the costs, and is willing to exchange to receive these benefits.

While this view of price is useful, we want to restate that consumers seldom (if ever) finely calculate each of these costs and benefits in making brand level decisions. Rather, for many types and brands of consumer packaged goods, the amounts of money, time, cognitive activity, and behavior effort required for a purchase are very similar. For these goods, choices between brands may be made on the basis of particular benefits or imagery, although price deals may be important.

For some purchases, all of these costs and trade-offs may be considered by consumers. Yet, the major importance of our view of price is not the degree to which consumers actively analyze and compare each of the costs of a particular exchange. Instead, this view is important because it has direct implications for the design of marketing strategy, as we explain in the next section.

Pricing Strategy

Pricing strategy is of concern in three general situations: (1) when a price is being set for a new product, (2) when a long-term price change is being considered for an established product, (3) when a short-term price change is being considered. Marketers may change prices for a variety of reasons, such as an increase in costs, a change in the price of competitive products, or a change in distribution channels.

Many models have been offered to guide marketers in designing pricing strategies.[3] Most of these models contain very similar recommendations and differ primarily in terms of how detailed the assumptions are, how many steps the pricing process is divided into, and in what sequence pricing tasks are recommended. For our purposes, we have developed a six-stage model, which is shown in Figure 19–3. Our model differs from traditional approaches primarily in that greater emphasis is placed on consumer analysis and greater attention is given to the four types of consumer costs in developing pricing and marketing strategies.

The six stages in our strategic approach to pricing are discussed below. Although consumer analysis is not the major focus in all of them, our discussion is intended to clarify the role of consumer analysis in pricing and to offer a useful overview of the pricing process.

---

[3]For example, several of the models are compared in Kent B. Monroe and Albert J. Della Bitta (1978), "Models for Pricing Decisions," *Journal of Marketing Research* (August), pp. 413–428. Also see Rao, "Pricing Research"; and Philip Kotler (1984), *Marketing Management: Analysis, Planning, and Control*, 5th ed., Englewood Cliffs, N.J.: Prentice-Hall, chapter 16.

Analyze Consumer/Product Relationships

Pricing strategy for a new product generally starts with at least one given: the firm has a product concept or several variations of a product concept in mind. When a price change for an existing product is being considered, typically much more information is available, including sales and cost data.

Whether the pricing strategy is being developed for a new or existing product, a useful first stage in the process is to analyze the consumer/product relationships. Answers must be found for questions such as: How does the product benefit consumers? What does it mean to them? In what situations do they use it? Does it have any special psychological or social significance to them? Of course, the answers to these questions depend on which current or potential target markets are under consideration.

A key question that must be answered honestly is whether the product itself has a clear differential advantage that consumers would be willing to pay for—or whether a differential advantage must be created on the basis of other marketing mix variables. This question has important implications for determining which of the four areas of consumer costs (time,

FIGURE 19–3   **A Strategic Approach to Pricing**

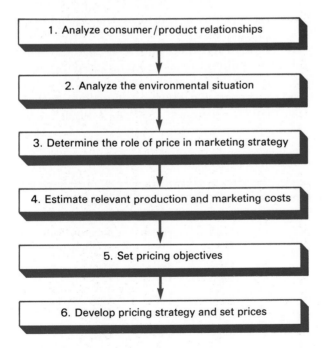

1. Analyze consumer / product relationships

2. Analyze the environmental situation

3. Determine the role of price in marketing strategy

4. Estimate relevant production and marketing costs

5. Set pricing objectives

6. Develop pricing strategy and set prices

money, cognitive activity, or behavior effort) can be appealed to most effectively.

Suppose a firm is considering marketing pizza for home consumption and is analyzing consumer/product relationships. The firm is considering three forms of pizza and, after considerable research, has developed Figure 19–4. This type of analysis illustrates several important concepts. First, it is clear that consumers of the three types of pizza make trade-offs in the costs they are willing to incur. Consumers of pizza made from a mix are willing to spend a greater amount of time, cognitive activity, and behavior effort to save money, and may get a poorer tasting pizza. Consumers of pizzeria pizza, on the other hand, are willing to pay a higher dollar price to reduce these other costs and may get a better tasting pizza.

Second, this analysis has clear implications for segmentation. It is important to determine the size of the markets for the different forms, their demographic profiles, and the degree of market overlap. That is, are these different consumer groups or are they the same consumers who eat different types of pizza in different situations?

Third, while this analysis has a number of implications for all facets of marketing strategy, our focus is on the implications for pricing. Clearly, the question of what pizza means to consumers is critical for determining appropriate pricing strategies. For example, the pizza-mix market is apparently very price sensitive. Thus, while a reduction of the other types of consumer costs or an increase in value (taste) may offer market opportunities, the dollar price of the mix would likely have to remain low. Perhaps the consumer/product relationship could be summarized as "Pizza is a low-dollar-cost, filling meal."

The frozen-pizza consumer apparently values having the product on hand—and while willing to make some trade-offs, wants a better tasting pizza. This market is not as price sensitive as the pizza-mix market and likely considers preparation effort an important cost. Thus, within the frozen-pizza market, consumers may pay a higher dollar cost for better

---

FIGURE 19–4　　**Relative Consumer Costs for Various Pizza Product Forms**

Cost	Pizza Mix	Frozen Pizza	Pizzeria Pizza Home Delivery
Money	Low	Middle	High
Time	High	Middle	Low
Cognitive activity	High	Middle	Low
Behavior effort	High	Middle	Low
Value: Taste	Worst	Middle	Best

tasting pizza or pizza that can be prepared more quickly and easily (e.g., microwave pizza). Perhaps the consumer/product relationship could be summarized as "Pizza is a quick meal or relatively tasty snack."

The consumer of home-delivered pizzeria pizza likely focuses strongly on taste and convenience and is not highly price sensitive. Thus, taste, ingredients, and fast delivery time are worth a higher price. Note, however, that even a price of $10 to $15 is inexpensive for a family meal when compared to the price of going to a nice restaurant. Perhaps the consumer/product relationship could be summarized as "Pizza is a delicious meal, and it sure beats cooking."

This brief example illustrates an approach to evaluating the relationships between consumers and products. One of the important outcomes of this analysis is an estimate of how sensitive consumers are to various dollar prices, other costs being relatively the same. In economics, this is called **price elasticity**, which is a measure of the relative change in demand for a product for a given change in dollar price. Once the firm has a clear idea of these relationships and opportunities, it can then focus attention on other aspects of the environment.

Analyze the Environmental Situation

There is no question that a firm must consider elements of the environment—economic trends, political views, social changes, and legal constraints—when developing pricing strategies. These elements should be considered early in the process of formulating any part of marketing strategy and should be monitored continually. By the time a firm is making pricing decisions, many of these issues have already been considered. While this may also be true for competitive analysis, consideration of competition at this point is critical for developing pricing strategies.

In setting or changing prices, the firm must consider its competition and how that competition will react to the price of the product. Initially, consideration should be given to such factors as:

1. Number of competitors.
2. Market share of competitors.
3. Location of competitors.
4. Conditions of entry into the industry.
5. Degree of vertical integration of competitors.
6. Financial strength of competitors.
7. Number of products and brands sold by each competitor.
8. Cost structure of competitors.
9. Historical reaction of competitors to price changes.

HIGHLIGHT 19–2   **Some Things to Know for Pricing Decisions . . .**

Know your customers and markets
Know your product and competitive products
Know your costs and objectives
Know your environment and situation

. . . And Some Pricing No-Nos

Price fixing—conspiring with competitors to fix prices
Deceptive pricing—pricing practices that mislead consumers, such as marketing items with a fictitious price, crossing this price out, and then putting on the normal price as though it were a bargain
Predatory pricing—setting prices low to drive out competitors and then raising prices
Price discrimination—charging similar, competing channel members different prices, which lessens competition or tends to create a monopoly

Courtesy 375 Spirits Company

A pricing strategy for positioning a prestige product.

Alternative Terms	What Is Given in Return
Price	Most physical merchandise
Tuition	College courses, education
Rent	A place to live or the use of equipment for a specific time period
Interest	Use of money
Fee	Professional services: for lawyers, doctors, consultants
Fare	Transportation: air, taxi, bus
Toll	Use of road or bridge, or long-distance phone rate
Salary	Work of managers
Wage	Work of hourly workers
Bribe	Illegal actions
Commission	Sales effort

Source: Thomas C. Kinnear and Kenneth L. Bernhardt (1983), Principles of Marketing, *Glenview, Ill.: Scott, Foresman, p. 561.*

Analysis of these factors helps determine whether the dollar price should be at, below, or above competitors' prices. However, this analysis should also consider other consumer costs relative to competitive offerings. Consumers often pay higher dollar prices to save time and effort.

Determine the Role of Price in Marketing Strategy

This step is concerned with determining whether the dollar price is to be a key aspect of positioning the product or whether it is to play a different role. If a firm is attempting to position a brand as a bargain product, then setting a lower dollar price is clearly an important part of this strategy. Barbasol shaving cream positions itself as just as good as but half the price of the other brands, for example. Similarly, if a firm is attempting to position a brand as a prestige, top-of-the-line item, then a higher dollar price is a common cue to indicate this position. Chivas Regal scotch has long used this approach, for example. Of course, the success of these types of strategies also depends on analyzing the trade-offs with other elements of consumer costs.

In many situations, dollar price may not play a particularly important positioning role other than in terms of pricing competitively. If consumers enjoy greater convenience in purchasing (e.g., free delivery), or if the product has a clear differential advantage, the price may be set at or above that of the competition but not highlighted in positioning strategy. In other cases, when the price of a product is higher than that of the competition but there is no clear differential advantage, the price may not be explicitly used in positioning. For example, premium-priced beers do not highlight price as part of their appeal.

Estimate Relevant Production and Marketing Costs

The costs of producing and marketing a product effectively provide a very useful benchmark for making pricing decisions. The variable costs of production and marketing usually provide the lowest dollar price a firm must charge to make an offering in the market. However, there are some exceptions to this rule. These exceptions typically involve interrelationships among products. For example, a firm may sell its cameras below cost to sell a greater volume of film; or a grocery store may sell an item below cost (i.e., a loss leader) to build traffic and increase sales of other items.

Set Pricing Objectives

Pricing objectives should be derived from overall marketing objectives, which in turn, should be derived from corporate objectives. In practice, the most common objective is to achieve a target return on investment. This objective has the advantage of being quantifiable. It also offers a useful basis for making not only pricing decisions but also decisions on whether to enter or remain in specific markets. For example, if a firm demands a 20 percent return on investment, and the best estimates of sales at various prices indicate that a product would have to be priced too high to generate demand, then the decision may be to forgo market entry. Other types of pricing objectives are listed in Figure 19–5.

Develop Pricing Strategy and Set Prices

A thorough analysis in the preceding stages should provide the information necessary to develop pricing strategies and set prices. Basically, the meaning of the product to the consumer and consumer costs have been analyzed. The environment has been analyzed, particularly competition. The role of price in marketing strategy has been determined. Production and marketing costs have been estimated. Pricing objectives have been set. The pricing task now is to determine a pricing strategy and specific prices that are (1) sufficiently above costs to generate the desired level of profit and achieve stated objectives; (2) related to competitive prices in a manner consistent with the overall marketing and positioning strategy;

(3) designed to generate consumer demand based on consumer cost trade-offs and values.

In some cases, prices may be developed with a long-run strategy in mind. For example, a **penetration price policy** may include a long-run plan to sequentially raise prices after introduction at a relatively low price; or a **skimming price policy** may include a long-run plan to systematically lower prices after a high-price introduction.

However, most price changes occur as a result of a change in consumers, the environment, competition, costs, strategies, and objectives. A dramatic example of the relationships among these variables can be found in the pricing of air fares.

Prior to deregulation, prices were set by the Civil Aeronautics Board.

FIGURE 19–5   **Some Potential Pricing Objectives**

1. Increase sales
2. Target market share
3. Maximum long-run profits
4. Maximum short-run profits
5. Growth
6. Stabilize market
7. Desensitize customers to price
8. Maintain price-leadership arrangement
9. Discourage entrants
10. Speed exit of marginal firms
11. Avoid government investigation and control
12. Maintain loyalty of middlemen and get their sales support
13. Avoid demands for "more" from suppliers—labor, in particular
14. Enhance image of firm and its offerings
15. Be regarded as "fair" by ultimate customers
16. Create interest and excitement about the item
17. Be considered trustworthy and reliable by rivals
18. Help in the sale of weak items in the line
19. Discourage others from cutting prices
20. Make a product "visible"
21. "Spoil market" to obtain high price for sale of business
22. Build traffic
23. Maximum profits on product line
24. Recover investment quickly
25. Decrease demand in periods of supply shortages

Source: Adapted from Alfred R. Oxenfeldt (1973), "A Decision-Making Structure for Price Decisions," Journal of Marketing *(January), pp. 48–53.*

Courtesy People Express Airlines

A marketing strategy promoting low money costs.

Price increases were the result of petitions to this agency based on evidence of increased costs of operation. Thus, price was not a very important competitive weapon, as all carriers charged the same fare for the same routes. After deregulation, however, price became a most critical competitive tool—and in fact, in some periods, up to 25,000 price changes are

> Increase price for same quantity and quality
> Maintain price for less quantity
> Maintain price for less quality or auxiliary services
> Reduce or eliminate price deals
> Increase interest rate and charges

made in a single day! Major carriers attempt to compete with low-price, "no-frills" airlines by lowering the price on competitive routes and raising the price on routes the low-price airlines do not serve. In addition, the major carriers have engaged in efforts to cut costs to try to be more competitive with the no-frills airlines. Consumers have a basic choice between attempting to minimize dollar cost by spending more time shopping for low prices, foregoing some flexibility in departure times and dates, and giving up some additional services versus paying full fare and receiving these benefits. Often, business travelers may pay the higher full-fare price, while leisure travelers spend the time and effort necessary to get cheaper fares.

This example illustrates how a change in the environment (deregulation) led to a change in competitors (entrance of no-frills airlines), which led to a change in pricing strategies (price cuts for some seats but overall attempts to maximize revenues per flight) and cost-cutting efforts. Many consumers also changed as they became more involved in the purchase of airline tickets and perhaps even traveled more by plane as dollar prices fell, at least in the short run.

Price Environment

As we stated at the beginning of the chapter, price is perhaps the most intangible element of the marketing mix. From an environmental perspective, this means that the price variable typically offers very little for the consumer to experience at the sensory level, although it may generate considerable cognitive activity and behavior effort. In the environment, price is usually a sign, a tag, a few symbols on a package, or a few words spoken on TV, or radio, or by a salesperson in a store or on the phone. The price variable also includes purchase contracts and credit-term information.

One area that has been the subject of consumer research on price information in the environment is unit pricing. Unit pricing is common for grocery products and involves a shelf tag that indicates the price per unit for a specific good. For example, a 13-ounce can of Hills Brothers Electric Perk Coffee that sells for $3.69 might include a shelf tag that indicates it costs $.284 per ounce. This information is designed to help shoppers make more informed purchases in comparing various brands and package sizes.

One interesting study of unit pricing replicated a previous study that was conducted 10 years earlier in two Safeway stores in the Washington, D.C. area.[4] This study found an increase in the use of unit-pricing information by consumers over the 10-year period, in both a city and a suburban store. In the city store, usage of unit prices increased from 24.8 percent of consumers to 33.1 percent; in the suburban store, usage increased from 37.6 to 59.9 percent. Thus, while usage of unit-price information increased over the 10-year period, considerably more suburban shoppers used unit prices than did city shoppers. Differences were also found between awareness and comprehension of unit pricing in the suburban versus the city store, as well as the use of that information to compare and switch between package sizes and brands. This study demonstrates that there are differences in the effects on consumer cognitions and behaviors of various types of price information in the environment.

How price information is communicated also has an effect. For example, the advent of scanner checkout systems has reduced price information in the environment for many grocery products, because prices are no longer stamped on each package or can. A study by Zeithaml found that having each item marked increased consumers' certainty of price recall and decreased errors in both exact price and unit-price recall.[5] The study also found some differences in the effects of shelf price tags, supporting the idea that not only the price itself but also the method by which price information is communicated affects consumer cognitions and behaviors.

Price Cognitions

As we noted, there is typically little sensory experience connected with the price variable. Yet information about prices is often attended to and comprehended, and the resulting meanings influence consumer behavior. For some purchases, consumers may make a variety of price comparisons

---

[4]David A. Aaker and Gary T. Ford (1983), "Unit Pricing Ten Years Later: A Replication," *Journal of Marketing* (Winter), pp. 118–122.

[5]Valarie A. Zeithaml (1982), "Consumer Response to In-Store Price Information Environments," *Journal of Consumer Research* (March), pp. 357–368.

among brands and evaluate trade-offs among the various types of consumer costs and values.

There have been several attempts to summarize the research on the effects of price on consumer cognitions and behavior, but these reviews have found few generalizations to offer.[6] For example, it has long been believed that consumers perceive a strong relationship between price and the quality of products and services. Experiments typically find this relationship when consumers are given no other information about the product except dollar price. However, when consumers are given additional information about products (which is more consistent with marketplace situations), the price-quality relationship is diminished.

In general, all of these reviews conclude that research on the behavioral effects of pricing has not been based on sound theory, and that most of the studies are seriously flawed methodologically. Thus, it should not be surprising that there is little consensus on basic issues of how price affects consumer choice processes and behavior.

Price Perceptions and Attitudes

Price perceptions are concerned with how price information is comprehended by consumers and made meaningful to them. One approach to understanding price perceptions is information processing, which has been advocated by Jacoby and Olson.[7] An adaptation of this approach is outlined in Figure 19–6.

This model illustrates an approach to describing price effects for a high-involvement product or purchase situation. Basically, it suggests that price information is received through the senses of sight and hearing. The information is then comprehended, which means that it is interpreted and

---

[6]Rao, "Pricing Research"; Jerry C. Olson (1977), "Price as an Informational Cue: Effects on Product Evaluations," in *Consumer and Industrial Buyer Behavior*, Arch G. Woodside, Jagdish N. Sheth and Peter D. Bennett (eds.), New York: Elsevier-North Holland Publishing, pp. 267–286; Valarie A. Zeithaml (1984), "Issues in Conceptualizing and Measuring Consumer Response to Price," in *Advances in Consumer Research*, Vol. 11, Thomas C. Kinnear (ed.), Provo, Utah: Association for Consumer Research, pp. 612–616; Kent B. Monroe and R. Krishnan (1983), "A Procedure for Integrating Outcomes across Studies," in *Advances in Consumer Research*, Vol. 10, Richard P. Bagozzi and Alice M. Tybout (eds.), Ann Arbor, Mich.: Association for Consumer Research, pp. 503–508.

[7]Jacob Jacoby and Jerry C. Olson (1977), "Consumer Response to Price: An Attitudinal, Information Processing Perspective," in *Moving Ahead with Attitude Research*, Yoram Wind and Marshall Green (eds.), Chicago: American Marketing Association, pp. 73–86. Also see Jerry C. Olson (1980), "Implications of an Information Processing Approach to Pricing Research," in *Theoretical Developments in Marketing*, Charles W. Lamb, Jr. and Patrick M. Dunne (eds.), Chicago: American Marketing Association, pp. 13–16.

made meaningful; i.e., consumers understand the meaning of price symbols through previous learning and experience.

The stated price for a particular brand may be considered a product attribute. This knowledge may then be compared with the dollar prices of other brands in a product class, other attributes of the brand and other brands, and other consumer costs. Finally, an attitude is formed toward the various brand alternatives.

For a low-involvement product or purchase situation, dollar price may have little or no impact on consumer cognitions or behaviors. For many

FIGURE 19–6   **Conceptual Model of Cognitive Processing of Price Information**

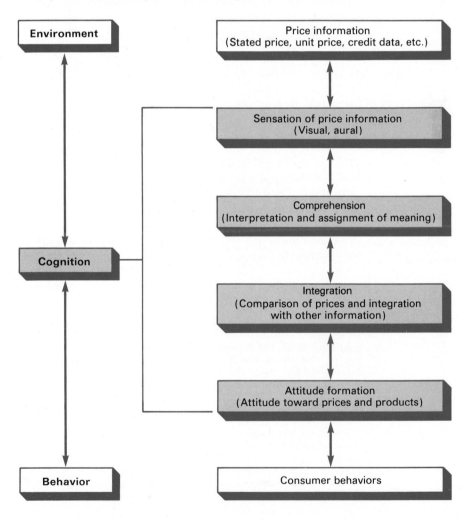

products, consumers may have an implicit price range; and as long as prices fall within it, price is not even evaluated as a purchase criterion. Similarly, some products are simply purchased without ever inquiring as to the price but simply paying whatever is asked for at the point of purchase. Impulse items located in the checkout area of supermarkets and drugstores may frequently be purchased this way, as might other products for which the consumer is highly brand loyal. In the latter cases, consumers may well make purchases on the single attribute of brand name without comparing dollar price, other consumer costs, or other factors.

In other cases, price information may not be carefully analyzed because consumers have a particular price image for the store they are shopping in. Discount stores such as Venture or Shopko may be generally considered low-priced outlets, and consumers may forgo comparing prices at these outlets with those at other stores.

Price Behaviors

Depending on the consumer, the product and its availability in various stores and other channels, and other elements of the situation, price could affect a variety of consumer behaviors. Two types of behaviors are of particular relevance to the price variable: funds access and transaction.

Funds Access

One source of embarrassment for most of us as consumers is to arrive at the point in the purchase process where we have to produce funds for an exchange and realize that we do not have sufficient funds available. Not having enough money at the grocery checkout counter and having to replace several items can be embarrassing, particularly when the total amount of money needed is quite small! Similarly, it is embarrassing to bounce a check, or to have a credit-card purchase refused because we have exceeded our limit, or to be refused a purchase because of a poor credit rating. For these reasons, most of us are likely to do some type of planning to access funds and to ensure that sufficient funds are available when we go shopping.

As we have noted previously, there are many ways consumers can access funds. First, many consumers carry a certain amount of cash to pay for small purchases. This cash supply may be replenished as needed for day-to-day activities. Second, many consumers also may carry checkbooks (or at least a few blank checks) in case a need arises for a larger amount of money. Third, millions of Americans carry credit cards to handle pur-

HIGHLIGHT 19–5   **U.S. Credit Card Data**

Card	Number Issued in the United States	Billings on Card in 1984 (in $ billions)
Visa	77,200,000	$60.6
MasterCard	60,000,000	49.7
American Express	15,000,000	36.6
Sears	60,000,000	13.6
Issued by Citicorp		
Visa, MasterCard	6,000,000	6.8
Diners Club	2,200,000	4.9
Carte Blanche	300,000	.4
Choice	1,000,000	.7

Source: Estimated from the Nielsen Report *as reported in Monci Jo Williams (1985), "The Great Plastic Card Fight Begins," Fortune (February 4), pp. 28–33.*

chases. Although the interest rates on credit cards may be high, this method of accessing funds is very popular.

We suspect that credit-card purchases and payments are not only convenient for the consumer but also may make the purchase seem less expensive. This is because consumers do not see any cash flowing from their pockets or a reduction in their checkbook balances, but merely need to sign their names and not even think about payment until the end of the month. In one sense, if no balance is carried over on the credit card, the purchase is "free" for the time between the exchange and the payment. We suspect that while many consumers may keep tabs on their checkbook balance, they may be less concerned throughout the month with their credit card balances—unless, of course, they are close to their credit limits.

Credit cards also facilitate purchasing because little effort is required to access funds. Even going to a bank to cash a check before shopping requires more effort than using a credit card. Thus, overall, the use of credit cards may reduce consumers' time, cognitive activity, and behavior effort costs.[8]

---

[8]For additional discussion, see Gillian Garcia (1980), "Credit Cards: An Interdisciplinary Survey," *Journal of Consumer Research* (March), pp. 327–337.

Transaction

The exchange of funds for products and services is typically a relatively simple transaction. It usually involves handing over cash, filling out a check, signing a credit slip, or signing a credit contract and following up by making regular payments.

However, as we have emphasized throughout this chapter, consumers exchange much more than simply money for goods and services. They also exchange their time, cognitive activity, and behavior effort—not only to earn money, but also to shop and make purchases. Thus, analysis of these elements, and of the value consumers receive in purchase and consumption, may provide better insights into the effects of price on consumer behavior.

Back to the Case

When considering only the money cost of the Diet Pepsi, at first glance it may appear that the supermarket price is better: $2.99 plus $.15 tax, which equals $3.14—versus $5 plus $.25 tax, which equals $5.25 in the convenience store.

Now let's consider the cost of operating Vinnie's car. Assume that it costs $.20 per mile; driving 12 miles thus equals $2.40. The supermarket purchase now costs Vinnie $3.14 plus $2.40, which equals $5.54—which is more than the convenience store price of $5.25.

Next, it seems reasonable to estimate the cost of Vinnie's time. Several rates could be considered. While his market value for this time is $18 per hour, when considering taxes and other deductions, Vinnie does not take home the full amount. Let's assume he takes home $9 per hour and agree that this is the value of the time to Vinnie.

The convenience-store trip had a time cost of 10 minutes @ $9 per hour, which equals $1.50, for a total of $5.25 plus $1.50, which equals $6.75. The supermarket trip has a time cost of 45 minutes @ $9 per hour, which equals $6.75, for a total of $5.54 plus $6.75, which equals $12.29. The convenience store trip now appears to be a real bargain!

Finally, let's consider how Vinnie felt about the two trips and what he experienced. In terms of cognitive activity, the convenience store trip was clearly stressful and unpleasant and likely required more behavior effort than the trip to the supermarket. However, the exercise may have been good for him physically. On the other hand, the supermarket trip was pleasant, and Vinnie felt very good about the purchase.

So, which was the better price? To Vinnie, it was the price paid at the supermarket, for he ignored other costs. However, if one accepts the economic assumptions involved in valuing Vinnie's automobile operating costs and time, an outside observer might conclude that the convenience store price was a better buy. Depending on how the cognitive activity and behavior effort are evaluated, either of the two may be considered to be the better purchase.

Finally, consider the fact that Diet Pepsi was on sale at the convenience store for $2.79 plus tax on the same day that Vinnie went to the supermarket and paid $2.99 plus tax. Had he known this, Vinnie could have walked to the convenience store and saved both money and time.

Which was the better price? It depends on whether we consider the question from Vinnie's point of view or from that of an outside observer with perfect information. In addition, it depends on whether we analyze only the dollar price of the item or also consider the other dollar costs, time, cognitive activity, and behavior effort involved.

Summary

This chapter presented an overview of pricing decisions and consumer behavior. Initially, the chapter focused on developing a conceptual framework for considering pricing decisions that included discussion of four types of consumer costs—money, time, cognitive activity, and behavior effort. These elements, when coupled with value, provide a framework for examining price from the consumer's point of view. Next, a pricing strategy model was developed for use in determining appropriate prices for new products as well as for making price-change decisions. Finally, the price environment, consumer price cognitions, and several price-related behaviors were discussed.

Additional Reading

Eitan Gerstner (1985), "Do Higher Prices Signal Higher Quality?" *Journal of Marketing Research* (May), pp. 209–215.

Joseph P. Guiltinan (1976), "Risk Aversive Pricing Policies: Problems and Alternatives," *Journal of Marketing* (January), pp. 10–15.

Kent B. Monroe (1979), *Pricing: Making Profitable Decisions,* New York: McGraw-Hill.

Thomas Nagle (1983), "Pricing as Creative Marketing," *Business Horizons* (July–August), pp. 14–19.

———(1984), "Economic Foundations for Pricing," *Journal of Business* (January), pp. S3–S26.

David J. Reibstein and Hubert Gatignon (1984), "Optimal Product Line Pricing: The Influence of Elasticities and Cross-Elasticities," *Journal of Marketing Research* (August), pp. 259–267.

Chapter Twenty

Channel Strategy and Consumer Behavior

IBM

A bear when it sells big computers to corporations, IBM is a Bambi of a storefront retailer. In the early 1980s the company began opening grandly decorated computer stores called IBM Product Centers in high-rent business districts all over America. While the first 81 stores had sales estimated at $100 million in 1983, IBM shelved plans to expand the chain to 100 stores.

The centers sell IBM's Personal Computer (PC) and typewriters, along with add-on gear and software made by IBM and others. Burdened with start-up costs and high overhead, the stores made far less than the 20 percent per year IBM is accustomed to earning on invested capital.

Glimpsing the chance to sell typewriters to small businesses and branch offices of big companies without costly door-to-door calls, IBM had opened three Product Centers by mid-1981. Then, when the PC burst on the scene, the company decided to plunk stores down in every metropolitan area. However, most of the 1,600-odd independent stores that carry the firm's PC and competing makes have done a better job of selling the target clientele. The rival stores belong mostly to big chains such as ComputerLand, Entré Computer Centers, and Sears Business Systems Centers.

IBM made mistakes right off the bat. Although it is a major producer of sophisticated point-of-sale computer systems to centralize billing, inventory, and sales audits—with 1983 sales estimated at $125 million—the company forced its own salespeople to record transactions on Stone Age carbon-paper invoices. At the end of each day, clerks typed the information into a computer in the back room. Result: mistakes galore in record-keeping and billing.

In choosing the Product Centers' decor, IBM revealed retailing naiveté. Anxious not to appear cold and remote, it abandoned its traditional icy blue and decorated the centers bright red. "Red doesn't just irritate bulls," remarked Warren Winger, chairman of CompuShop, a Dallas-based chain, "it makes salesmen hostile and alarms customers." To keep its stores classy, IBM eschewed the usual tacky trappings of computer retailing—flashy in-store displays, brochures, and racks of impulse items near the cash registers. "The in-store merchandising—we never realized how important it was," confessed Jim Turner, the IBM vice president in charge of the centers. IBM also staffed the stores entirely with its own career salespeople, few of whom had retailing experience. Consumer research by a large New York ad agency showed that the staff intimidated first-time customers. In interviews the customers revealed that they expected more of IBM Product Centers than of other computer stores, but came away disillusioned.

Product Center chief Turner hints that in the future the centers may concentrate on selling full-blown office automation systems. While he insists that IBM has no plans to close up shop, there's some question whether the company ought to be in the retail jungle at all. The margins are low, competition is fierce, and the other animals are quick and crafty and know the terrain.

Source: Excerpted from Peter Petre (1984), "IBM's Misadventures in the Retail Jungle," Fortune *(July 23), p. 80.*

From an economic perspective, channels of distribution are thought of as providing form, time, place, and possession utilities for consumers. **Form utility** means that channels convert raw materials into finished goods and services in forms the consumer seeks to purchase. **Time utility** means that channels make goods and services available *when* the consumer wants to purchase them. **Place utility** means that goods and services are made available *where* the consumer wants to purchase them. **Possession utility** means that channels facilitate the transfer of ownership of goods to the consumer.

While this view of channels is useful, it perhaps understates their role in our society. Channels of distribution have a very important impact on consumer cognitions and behavior. The locations of malls, shopping centers, and stores, as well as specific products and other stimuli within these environments strongly influence what consumers think and feel and what behaviors they perform, such as store contacts, product contacts, and transactions. In return, consumer actions at the retail level determine the success or failure of marketing strategies and have an important impact on the selection of future strategies.

In this chapter, we focus on the relationships among consumer cognitions, behaviors, and environments at the retail level. Our primary focus

Courtesy Kohler Co.

An example of form utility.

is on these interactions for store retailing rather than for nonstore retailing, because some form of store is involved in about 95 percent of product sales to the consumer and in the majority of service sales. Some noteworthy areas of nonstore retailing, such as mail-order sales and direct-to-home retailing, will not be treated in detail in this text,[1] nor will developments in in-home computer-assisted shopping systems.[2]

[1]For a discussion of the essentials of nonstore retailing, see Barry Berman and Joel R. Evans (1983), *Retail Management: A Strategic Approach,* 2d ed., New York: Macmillan, pp. 104–112. For a discussion of consumer resistance to catalog shopping, see Maggie McComas (1986), "Catalogue Fallout," *Fortune* (January 20), pp. 63–64.

[2]For a discussion of this type of retail system, see Joel E. Urbany and W. Wayne Talarzyk (1983), "Videotex: Implications for Retailing," *Journal of Retailing* (Fall), pp. 76–92.

Figure 20–1 provides a model of the basic relationships among cognition, behavior, and the environment at the retail level and the role of channel strategy. We begin this chapter by discussing some basic channel strategy issues and then discuss store environment, consumer store-related cognitions, and consumer store-related behaviors, in turn.

Channel Strategy Issues

Marketing managers have many decisions to make in designing effective channels of distribution. For example, decisions must be made as to

FIGURE 20–1   **The Wheel of Consumer Analysis: Channel Strategy Issues**

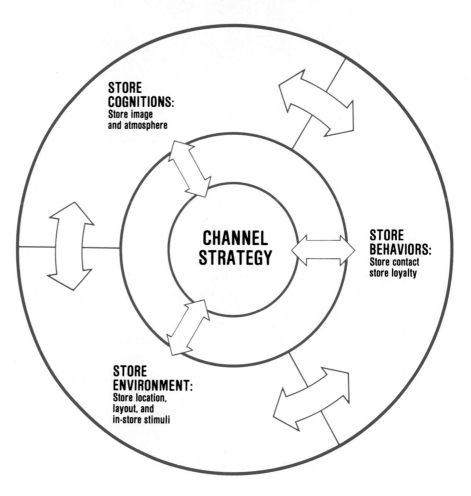

Buying—purchasing a variety of products and components, usually for assembly and resale

Selling—promoting the product to potential consumers through advertising, personal selling, sales promotion, and publicity

Assorting—assembling a collection of products for potential consumers

Financing—offering credit to potential consumers to facilitate transactions, and providing funds to other sellers in the channel to aid distribution flow

Transporting—physically moving merchandise through the channel to the consumer

Sorting—breaking bulk items into amounts desired by consumers

Risk taking—absorbing business risks associated with inventories, obsolescence, and bad debts

Research—accumulating information such as sales volumes, fashion trends, expected sales, and consumer profiles

Storage—warehousing the product and maintaining inventories to provide better customer service

Grading—judging and classifying products on dimensions such as size and quality

whether to market directly to the consumer through company-owned or franchised stores or indirectly through combinations of middlemen, such as independent retailers, wholesalers, and agents. Decisions must be made as to whether to use store retailing or nonstore retailing or some combination of the two. Decisions must be made about plant and warehouse locations, and how products will be delivered to consumers. Decisions must be made concerning who will perform what marketing functions within the channel.

In some cases, manufacturers market products in their own stores. For example, Sherwin-Williams paint company owns and operates more than 1,400 retail outlets, and Hart, Shaffner & Marx, a clothing manufacturer, operates over 275 specialty clothing stores.[3] The majority of manufacturers sell through independent retailers and retail chains, however.

Selling through independent retailers can lead to a conflict in objectives for the two types of marketing institutions. That is, while *manufacturers* are concerned with developing consumer brand loyalty (repeated purchase of their brand), *retailers* are concerned with developing consumer store loyalty (repeated patronage of their stores). Retailers may not be highly concerned with which brand of coffee the consumer buys, as long as it is purchased in their particular stores, for instance. This situation has

---

[3]Berman and Evans, *Retail Management*, pp. 66–67.

led many manufacturers to put a large portion of their marketing budgets into trade promotions directed at retailers (e.g., 1 case free for every 10 purchased by the retailer). **Trade promotions** may influence retailers to put up special displays, give more shelf space to a brand, lower prices to consumers, and sponsor local advertising of the brand for the manufacturer.

Our discussion highlights the fact that different members of a distribution channel may be primarily concerned with influencing different consumer behaviors. This is an important point; the role of retail management is often overlooked in discussions of marketing and consumer behavior. Retailers affect consumers most directly, and perhaps most influentially, for many types of products and most services. As a result, in this part of the chapter, we view channel strategy from the manufacturer's perspective and consider criteria for selecting channel members, particularly retailers.

As with the other elements of the marketing mix, the starting point for designing effective channels is an analysis of consumer/product relationships. At least six basic questions must be considered:

1. What is the potential annual market demand? That is, given a particular marketing strategy, how many consumers are likely to purchase the product and how often?
2. What is the long-run growth potential of the market?
3. What is the geographic dispersion of the market?
4. What are the most promising geographic markets to enter?
5. Where and how do consumers purchase this and similar types of products?
6. What is the likely impact of a particular channel system on consumers? That is, will the system influence consumer cognitions and behaviors sufficiently to achieve marketing objectives?

While these questions emphasize that consumers are the focal point in channel design, the answers require an analysis of a variety of other factors. As suggested in Figure 20–2, these factors must be analyzed both in terms of their relationships with and impact on the consumer, and in terms of their relationships with the other variables. We briefly discuss each of these factors, starting with commodity.

Commodity

By **commodity,** we mean the nature of the product or service offered to the consumer. Different products and services vary in their tangibility, perishability, bulkiness, degree of standardization, amount of service required, and unit value. These factors influence whether it is effective to market the commodity directly to consumers (as is done with hair-styling services) or indirectly through a number of middlemen (as is done with designer jeans).

Key consumer-related questions in considering the nature of the product or service are (1) What consequences or values does the product or service provide the target market? (2) How much time and effort are target market consumers willing to expend to shop for, locate, and purchase the product? and (3) How often do target-market consumers purchase the product? Thus, it is the *relationships* among consumers, the commodity, and the channel that are critical, rather than the analysis of these factors in isolation.

Conditions

Conditions refer to the current state of and expected changes in the economic, social, political, and legal environments in which the firm operates. This information is critical in channel design, because channels typically

---

FIGURE 20–2   **Channel Design Criteria**

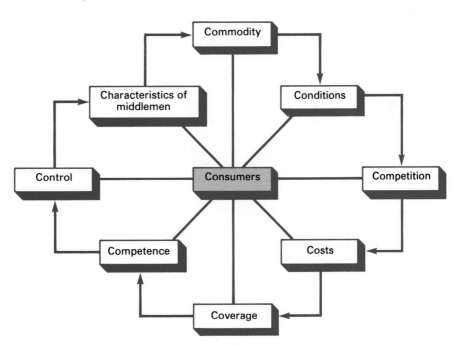

involve long-term commitments by the firm that may be difficult to change. For example, one of the major problems that led to the dramatic loss of market share and consolidation of A&P supermarkets was that A&P had long-term leases for many small stores in inner cities. Consumers were moving to the suburbs and purchasing in the larger, well-stocked, conveniently located suburban stores of competitors. Thus, situational analysis of the macro environment is critical in channel design in order to respond to potential problems and to exploit opportunities.

Competition

The size, financial and marketing strengths, and market share of a firm's competitors are major concerns in designing effective marketing strategies. For channel decisions, a key issue concerns how major competitors distribute products and how their distribution system affects consumers. In some cases, emulating the channels of major competitors in the industry is the only feasible alternative. For example, many convenience goods require intensive distribution to all available retailers.

In other cases, a differential advantage can be obtained by selecting nontraditional distribution methods. The traditional channel for record albums is to produce original records and then sell them in record shops and discount stores, using radio as the primary promotion medium. Yet K-tel found a more effective approach resulting in a 37-nation, $170 million record empire. K-tel puts out 15 LPs each year made up of singles that have already been released by other companies. Between 30 and 90 days after a particular tune has peaked on the record charts, K-tel obtains production rights from the label that originally recorded it. When it has enough such singles to make a "Best of" or "Greatest Hits" album, it hires a manufacturing company to press the new LP and blitzes the TV airwaves with commercials. K-tel uses a nonconventional distribution system, in that it distributes records not only to record stores and discount chains but also to drugstores, supermarkets, and department stores totaling over 25,000 outlets.[4]

Costs

While channel strategies seek to provide form, time, place, and possession utilities for the consumer in order to affect consumer cognitions and be-

---

[4]Howard Reich (1983), "Hooked on K-tel," *Marketing News* (September 16), p. 4.

HIGHLIGHT 20–2　**What Intermediaries Add to the Cost of a Record Album**

Vinyl and pressing	$ .48		
Record jacket	1.02		
American Federation of Musicians dues	.09		
Songwriter's royalties	.25		
Recording artist's royalties	.82		
Freight to wholesaler	.07		
Manufacturer's advertising and selling expenses	.70		
Manufacturer's administrative expenses	.69		
Manufacturer's cost	$4.12		
Manufacturer's profit	.62		
Manufacturer's price to wholesaler		4.74	
Freight to retailer		.03	
Wholesaler's advertising selling and administrative expense		.15	
Wholesaler's cost		4.92	
Wholesaler's profit		.30	$3.65
Wholesaler's price to retailer			$5.22　(intermediaries)
Retailer's advertising, selling, and administrative expenses			.84
Retailer's profit			2.33
Retailer's price to consumer			$8.39

Source: Thomas C. Kinnear and Kenneth L. Bernhardt (1983), Principles of Marketing, *Glenview, Ill.: Scott Foresman, p. 331.*

havior, these strategies are constrained by the cost of distribution. In general, a basic goal is to design a distribution system that facilitates exchanges between the firm and consumers but does so in a cost-efficient manner. Distribution costs include transportation, order processing, cost of lost business, inventory carrying costs, and materials handling. Thus, costs can be viewed as a constraint on the firm's ability to distribute products and services and to serve and influence consumers. In general, firms seek distribution systems that minimize total distribution costs at a particular level of customer service.

Coverage

There are two separate meanings of the term **coverage** in channel strategy. First, there is the idea that seldom can every member of a selected target market receive sufficient marketing coverage to bring about an exchange. Because of cost considerations, even major consumer-goods companies often cannot afford to distribute their products in outlets that do not serve a relatively large population.

Second, *coverage* also refers to the number of outlets in a particular geographic area in which the product or service will be sold. Distribution coverage can be viewed along a continuum ranging from intensive, through selective, to exclusive distribution. Figure 20–3 explains the basic differences in these three alternatives.

FIGURE 20–3   ***Exclusive, Selective, and Intensive Distribution: Market Coverage***

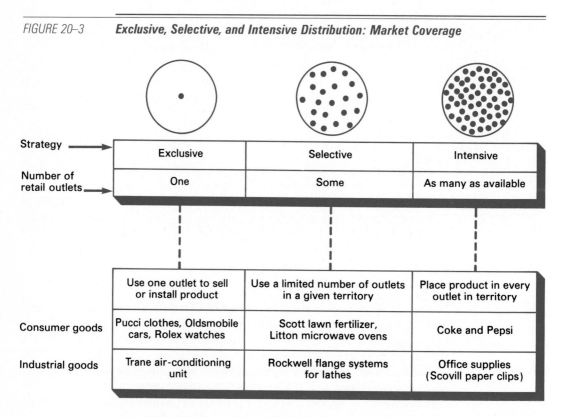

Strategy	Exclusive	Selective	Intensive
Number of retail outlets	One	Some	As many as available

	Use one outlet to sell or install product	Use a limited number of outlets in a given territory	Place product in every outlet in territory
Consumer goods	Pucci clothes, Oldsmobile cars, Rolex watches	Scott lawn fertilizer, Litton microwave ovens	Coke and Pepsi
Industrial goods	Trane air-conditioning unit	Rockwell flange systems for lathes	Office supplies (Scovill paper clips)

Source: Thomas C. Kinnear and Kenneth L. Bernhardt (1983), Principles of Marketing, *Glenview, Ill.: Scott, Foresman, 1983, p. 348.*

Competence

A frequently overlooked criteria in designing channels is the firm's **competence** to administer the channels and to perform channel tasks at all levels to ensure effective distribution to the consumer. Both financial strength and marketing skills are crucial, but many production-oriented firms seriously underestimate the importance of marketing and overestimate their marketing abilities. Further, many manufacturers do not have a sufficiently large product line to develop their own retail stores. These firms opt for intermediaries, such as Sears which sells 75 percent of its merchandise under its own label, or J. C. Penney, which sells 85 percent private-label merchandise. Finally, marketing skills for one market are not always transferable to other markets. For example, many of the failures in international marketing have resulted from firms not adapting their products and marketing strategies to foreign markets.

Critics of marketing frequently point out that marketing intermediaries increase the cost of products, because the profits these wholesalers and retailers make add to the cost of the product to the consumer. These critics generally do not understand that intermediaries are used because they can perform some marketing functions more efficiently and more cheaply than can the manufacturer.

Control

An important managerial criterion in designing channels is the **degree of control** desired for effective marketing of the product to the consumer. In general, there is greater control in direct channels, because no intermediaries are involved. Franchised channels also involve greater control than indirect channels, because the franchiser typically places strong contractual constraints on the operations of the franchisee. This control is quite important in delivering the major benefit of franchises to the consumer (i.e., standardized products and services).

Characteristics of Middlemen

A final but extremely important consideration in designing channels concerns the characteristics of the intermediaries that are available and willing to handle the manufacturer's product. If no acceptable middlemen are available, then the firm must either market direct, encourage the development of intermediaries, or forego entering a particular market.

In addition to such factors as the size, financial strength, and marketing skills of intermediaries, *consumer perceptions* of intermediaries can be crucial in channel strategy. For example, many consumers view discount

AVAILABLE AT
BERGDORF GOODMAN
  New York, NY
NEIMAN-MARCUS
  Dallas, TX
I. MAGNIN
  San Francisco, CA
GRACE JONES
  Salado, TX
JOHN BALDWIN
  St. Petersburg, FL
JULIAN GOLD
  San Antonio, TX
BALLIET'S
  Oklahoma City, OK
BEATON'S
  Phoenix, AZ
CHARLES SUMNER
  Boston, MA
AUER'S
  Denver, CO
M.M. COHN
  Little Rock, AR
MELODY ANN FASHIONS
  Hallandale, FL
And other specialty stores

Courtesy Ned Gould

A selective distribution strategy.

stores as places to purchase good-quality merchandise, but not necessarily prestige items. Manufacturers of prestige products (such as Calvin Klein jeans) may lower the image of their products by selling them in discount stores. Thus, manufacturers (and retailers) must consider the consumer/store relationships, i.e., the relationships among the store environment, consumer cognitions, and consumer behaviors.

Store Environment

As we noted previously, retail stores are relatively closed environments that can exert a significant impact on consumer cognitions and behavior.

In this section, we will consider three major decision areas in designing effective store environments: store location, store layout, and in-store stimuli.

Store Location

Although not part of the internal environment of a store, store location is a critical aspect of channel strategy. Good locations allow ready access, can attract large numbers of consumers, and can significantly alter consumer shopping and purchasing patterns. As retail outlets with very similar product offerings proliferate, even slight differences in location can have a significant impact on market share and profitability. In addition, store location decisions represent long-term financial commitments; and changing poor locations can be difficult and costly.

Research on retail location has been dominated by a regional urban economics, rather than a behavioral approach. Thus, it is not surprising that many of the assumptions upon which the models are based offer poor descriptions of consumer behavior. For example, these approaches generally assume that consumers make single-purpose shopping trips from a fixed origin. Considerable behavioral research suggests, however, that 50 to 60 percent of all shopping trips are multipurpose. The regional models also assume that consumers have equal levels of knowledge about different stores; and they often ignore the impact of store advertising and promotion on consumers. Although recent work has begun to integrate behavioral variables such as store image into location models, the models still place primary emphasis on economic variables and assumptions and on *predicting* rather than *describing* consumer behavior. Consumers are considered primarily in terms of demographic and socio-economic variables, and in terms of traffic patterns and distances to various locations.

Despite these criticisms, many retail location models are quite sophisticated and can deal with a variety of criteria. While we will not review all of the approaches available for selecting trading areas, business districts, shopping centers, and optimal store sites,[5] we briefly discuss four general approaches to store location. These include the checklist method, analog approach, regression models, and location allocation models.[6]

---

[5]For excellent discussions of these topics, see C. Samuel Craig, Avijit Ghosh and Sara McLafferty (1984), "Models of the Retail Location Process: A Review," *Journal of Retailing* (Spring), pp. 5–36; J. Barry Mason and Morris L. Mayer (1984), *Modern Retailing: Theory and Practice*, 3d ed., Plano, Tex.: Business Publications, pp. 767–806.

[6]The information in this section on store location is based heavily on the discussion in Craig, Ghosh and McLafferty, "Models of Retail Location," pp. 20–27.

Checklist Method

The **checklist method** attempts to systematically evaluate the relative value of a site compared to other potential sites in the area. Essentially, it involves an evaluation of various factors that are likely to affect sales and costs at a site. Marketing managers then make decisions about the desirability of the site based on these comparisons. Checklists commonly include information about socioeconomic and demographic composition of consumers in the area, level of consumption, and consumer expenditure patterns. Site-specific factors, such as traffic count, parking facilities, ease of entry and exit, and visibility are often considered, also.

Analog Approach

The **analog approach** first identifies an existing store or stores similar to the one that is to be located. Surveys are used to observe the power of these analog stores to draw consumers from different distance zones. The ability of the analog stores to attract consumers is then used to estimate the trading area and the expected sales at alternative sites. The site with the best expected performance is then chosen for the new store.

Regression Models

Regression models are commonly used to investigate the factors that affect the profitability of retail outlets at particular sites. Retail performance has frequently been studied in regression models as a function of store location, store attributes, market attributes, price, and competition. In most of the studies, performance has been found to be affected by population size and socioeconomic characteristics of consumers in the store's market area, as well as by service factors such as local promotion and advertising.

Location Allocation Models

While the above approaches are most commonly used to evaluate store location sites, **location allocation models** typically have been used to assess an entire market or trading area. Location allocation models generally involve the simultaneous selection of *several* locations and the estimation of demand at those locations in order to optimize some specified criteria. These models allow the investigation of the effects on profitability of one store in a chain if another store is added in the same trading area, and can be used to systematically consider the effects of possible changes in the future marketing environment, such as competitive reactions.

Store Layout

Store layout can have important effects on consumers. At a basic level, the layout influences such factors as how long the consumer stays in the store, how many products the consumer comes into visual contact with, and what routes the consumer travels within the store. Such factors may affect what and how many purchases are made. There are many types and variations of store layouts; two basic types are the grid and free-flow layouts.

Grid Layout

Figure 20–4 presents an example of a **grid layout** common in many grocery stores.[7] In a grid, all counters and fixtures are at right angles to each other and resemble a maze, with merchandise counters acting as barriers to traffic flow. The grid layout in a supermarket forces customers to the sides and back of the store where items such as produce, meat, and dairy products are located. In fact, 80 to 90 percent of all consumers shopping in supermarkets pass these three counters.

In a supermarket, such a layout is designed to increase the number of products a consumer comes into visual contact with, thus increasing the probability of purchase. In addition, because produce, meat, and dairy products are typically high-margin items, the grid design can help channel consumers toward these more profitable products. Similarly, the location of frequently purchased items (such as bread and milk) toward the back of the store requires consumers, who may be shopping only for these items, to pass many other items. Because the probability of purchasing other items is increased once the consumer is in visual contact with them, the grid layout can be very effective in increasing the number of items purchased.

The grid layout is more likely to be used in department and specialty stores to direct customer traffic down the main aisles. Typically, these retailers put highly sought merchandise along the walls to pull customers past other merchandise to slow-moving merchandise areas. For example, sale merchandise may be placed along the walls not only to draw consumers to these areas, but also to reward consumers for spending more time in the store and shopping carefully. This may increase the probability of consumers returning to the store and following similar "traffic patterns" on repeat visits. Expensive items can be placed along the main aisles to facilitate purchases by less price-sensitive consumers. The grid layout is commonly found on the main floors of multilevel department and specialty stores, and mass merchandisers.

Free-Flow Layout

Figure 20–4 also presents an example of a **free-flow layout.** Here, the merchandise and fixtures are grouped into patterns that allow unstruc-

---

[7]The figures and part of the discussion of store layout are based on Mason and Mayer, *Modern Retailing,* pp. 680–682.

FIGURE 20–4   **Basic Store Layout**

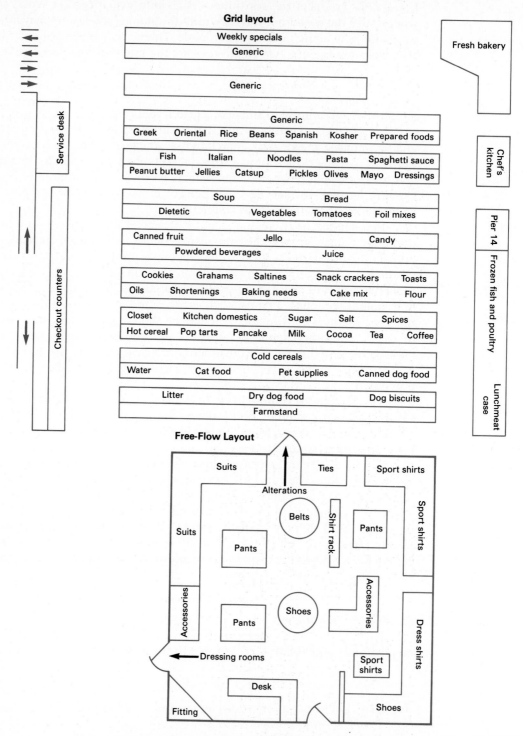

Source: J. Barry Mason and Morris L. Mayer (1984), Modern Retailing: Theory and Practice, 3d ed., Plano, Tex.: Business Publications, p. 681.

tured flow of customer traffic. Merchandise is divided on the basis of fixtures and signs, and customers can come into visual contact with all departments from any point in the store. A free-flow arrangement is often used in specialty stores, boutiques, and apparel stores. This arrangement is particularly useful for encouraging relaxed shopping and impulse purchases. It may also be useful for aiding store salespeople to move consumers to several different types of merchandise. For example, it may aid in selling a collection of different items, such as a suit, shirt, tie, and shoes in a clothing store, thus increasing the total sale. Figure 20–5 presents a summary of the major advantages and disadvantages of the grid and free-flow layouts.

In-Store Stimuli

In most environments there is an endless number of stimuli that could affect cognitions and behavior. A retail store is no exception. Stores have many stimuli that affect consumers: the characteristics of other shoppers and salespeople, lighting, noises, smells, temperature, shelf space and displays, signs, colors, and merchandise, to name a few.

Although the effects of some in-store stimuli have been studied extensively, much of this research is proprietary. (It is not available in the

---

FIGURE 20–5   **Advantages and Disadvantages of Grid and Free-Flow Layouts**

Grid

Advantages	*Disadvantages*
Low cost	Plain and uninteresting
Customer familiarity	Limited browsing
Merchandise exposure	Stimulator of rushed shopping behavior
Ease of cleaning	Limited creativity in decor
Simplified security	
Possibility of self-service	

Free-flow

Allowance for browsing and wandering freely	Loitering encouraged
Increased impulse purchases	Possible confusion
Visual appeal	Waste of floor space
Flexibility	Cost
	Difficulty of cleaning

Source: Robert F. Lusch (1982), The Management of Retail Enterprises, *Boston: Kent Publishing, p. 471.*

marketing or consumer research literature, because it has been conducted by firms seeking a differential advantage over competitors.) Much of the research that is available in the literature is quite dated and therefore of questionable validity in today's marketplace. In addition, of the research that is available, the results are seldom consistent, in that some studies find large effects of in-store stimuli, some find small effects, and some find no effects. Differences in findings are often attributable to methodological issues; but we believe that effects are highly situation specific and that no single in-store tactic should be expected to be effective in all cases.

With these caveats, we turn to some of the research findings concerning the effects of in-store stimuli on consumer cognitions and behavior. Four areas are discussed: the effects of signs and price information, color, shelf space and displays, and music.

Signs and Price Information

In-store signs are useful for directing consumers to particular merchandise and for offering product benefit and price information. McKinnon, Kelly, and Robison conducted an experiment that investigated the use of signs, the type of message included on the sign (price-only or product-benefit statements), and the effects of a regular versus a sale price being included on the sign.[8] The six products studied were bath towels, panty hose, ladies' slacks, men's dress slacks, men's jeans, and men's shirts. All six products were studied in varying conditions over a three-week period in three department stores.

Figure 20–6 presents a summary of the sales results obtained in the study. Based on the statistical analysis of these sales differences, the following conclusions were drawn:

1. Price influences sales more than sign type.
2. At regular prices, the addition of a price sign will not increase sales; but when the item is on sale, a price sign will increase sales.
3. Benefit signs increase sales at both regular and sale prices, but at a greater rate when the item is on sale.
4. A benefit sign is more effective than a price-only sign at both a regular and a sale price.

Overall, these results suggest that at regular prices, a benefit sign should be the only type of sign used, while at a sale price, both a price-only and a benefit sign will increase sales over a no-sign condition, with a

---

[8]Gary F. McKinnon, J. Patrick Kelly and E. Doyle Robison (1981), "Sales Effects of Point-of-Purchase In-Store Signing," *Journal of Retailing* (Summer), pp. 49–63.

FIGURE 20–6   **Sales Results for Six Types of Signs**

	Average daily sales results (units)
Regular price:	
No sign	7.66
Price sign	6.11
Benefit sign	7.81
Sale price:	
No sign	15.35
Price sign	19.07
Benefit sign	22.96

Source: Gary F. McKinnon, J. Patrick Kelly and E. Doyle Robinson (1981), "Sales Effects of Point-of-Purchase In-Store Signing," Journal of Retailing *(Summer), p. 57.*

benefit sign being the most effective. Thus, these results support the idea that signs affect consumer cognitions (consumers apparently processed different sign information) and consumer behavior (sales increased with the use of certain types of signs).

Color

Color has been shown to have a variety of physical and psychological effects on both humans and animals. Bellizzi, Crowley, and Hasty examined the effects of color on consumer perceptions of retail store environments in a laboratory experiment.[9] While noting the limitations of their study, the authors concluded that color can have customer drawing power as well as image-creating potential. A quite interesting finding was that consumers were drawn to warm colors (red and yellow), but felt that warm-color environments are generally unpleasant; cool colors (blue and green) did not draw consumers, but were rated as pleasant. The authors offered the following summary of the implications of their work for store design:

> Warm-color environments are appropriate for store windows and entrances, as well as for buying situations associated with unplanned

---

[9]Joseph A. Bellizzi, Ayn E. Crowley and Ronald W. Hasty (1983), "The Effects of Color in Store Design," *Journal of Retailing* (Spring), pp. 21–45.

FIGURE 20–7   **Percentage Increase in Unit Sales for Expanded Shelf Space and Special Display**

Product	Expanded Shelf Space	Special Display
Camay soap—bath	39%	243%
Piggly Wiggly pie shells—2 per pkg.	30	185
White House apple juice—32 oz.	16	77
Mahatma rice—1 lb.	27	103

Source: J. B. Wilkinson, J. Barry Mason and Christine H. Paksoy (1982), "Assessing the Impact of Short-Term Supermarket Strategy Variables," Journal of Marketing Research (February), p. 79.

impulse purchases. Cool colors may be appropriate where customer deliberations over the purchase decision are necessary. Warm, tense colors in situations where deliberations are common may make shopping unpleasant for consumers and may result in premature termination of the shopping trip. On the other hand, warm colors may produce a quick decision to purchase in cases where lengthy deliberations are not necessary and impulse purchases are common.[10]

Shelf Space and Displays

Research generally supports the idea that more **shelf space** and **in-store displays** increase sales. In a portion of a larger study, Wilkinson, Mason, and Paksoy examined the impact of these two variables on sales of four grocery products in an in-store experiment.[11] Comparisons were made between normal display (regular shelf space), expanded display (double the regular shelf space allocation), and special display (regular shelf space plus special end-of-aisle or within-aisle product arrangement).

Figure 20–7 presents the products studied and the percentage increases in unit sales using expanded shelf spaces and special displays. While the percentage increases varied by product, as would be expected, both tactics consistently increased sales for all of the products. Further, special displays consistently outperformed expanded shelf spaces. These results support the idea that the presentation of merchandise in store has an important effect on consumer behavior.

---

[10]Ibid., p. 43.

[11]J. B. Wilkinson, J. Barry Mason and Christie H. Paksoy (1982), "Assessing the Impact of Short-Term Supermarket Strategy Variables," *Journal of Marketing Research* (February), pp. 72–86.

It pays to have your product near the checkout in supermarkets, a chewing gum company has discovered.

In a survey of 279 stores in 22 states that do $2 billion of business yearly, it was found that the profit per square foot for the checkout-displayed products was nearly four times that of the regular shelf-displayed products.

The survey was commissioned by American Chicle, which produces gums and breath mints.

The survey results showed that checkout items take up 0.26 percent of a store's selling space, but contribute to 1 percent of a store's gross profit.

Since the survey was commissioned by a gum and mint company, it is perhaps not surprising to note that one of the results pointed out in a press release was that "the stores that allocate additional space to confectionery at the checkouts generated disproportionately higher sales and profits."

In other words, "put our stuff near the checkout and we'll both make more money."

Source: The Wall Street Journal, *January 24, 1982, p. 3.*

The study also found that in-store price reductions affected sales, but that newspaper advertising was not a strong short-term strategy variable for three of the four products. This supports the idea that in-store stimuli have very important effects on consumer behavior—and in this case, are more important than out-of-store advertising.

Music

Considerable research supports the idea that **music** played in the background while other activities are being performed affects attitudes and behavior. Music is played in many retail stores, but relatively little basic research has been conducted on its effects on consumer behavior. Milliman did examine the effects of one aspect of music—tempo—on the behavior of supermarket shoppers.[12] Three treatments were used: no music, slow music, and fast music. The basic hypotheses investigated were that these treatments would differentially affect (1) the pace of in-store traffic flow of supermarket shoppers, (2) the daily gross volume of customer purchases, and (3) the number of supermarket shoppers expressing an awareness of the background music after they left the store.

---

[12]Ronald E. Milliman (1982), "Using Background Music to Affect the Behavior of Supermarket Shoppers," *Journal of Marketing* (Summer), pp. 86–91.

The findings supported the idea that the tempo of background music does affect consumer behavior. The pace of in-store traffic flow was slowest under the slow-tempo treatment, and fastest under the fast-tempo treatment. Further, the slow-tempo musical selections led to higher sales volumes, as consumers spent more time and money under this condition. On average, sales were 38.2 percent greater under the slow-tempo condition than under the fast-tempo condition. Interestingly, when questioned after shopping, consumers showed little awareness of the music that had been playing in the supermarket. Thus, it seems likely that music affected their behavior without consumers being totally conscious of it. In terms of marketing strategy, the author suggests that:

> It is possible to influence behavior with music, but this influence can either contribute to the process of achieving business objectives or interfere with it . . . . Certainly, in some retailing situations, the objective may be to slow customer movement, keeping people in the store for as long as possible in an attempt to encourage them to purchase more. However, in other situations, the objective may be the opposite, that is, to move customers along as a way of increasing sales volume. A restaurant, for instance, will most likely want to speed people up, especially during lunch, when the objective is to maximize the "number of seats turned" in a very short period of time, normally about two hours or less. Playing slow-tempo music in a restaurant might result in fewer seats turned and lower profit, although it could encourage return visits if customers preferred a relaxed luncheon atmosphere. Again, the point is that the music chosen must match the objectives of the business and the specific market situation.[13]

Store-Related Cognitions

A variety of cognitive processes could be discussed in relation to retail stores. However, two major cognitive variables of managerial concern at the retail level are *store image* and *store atmosphere.* While the marketing literature is not clear on the exact differences between these two variables, it is clear that both deal with the influence of store attributes on *consumers'* cognitions, rather than how marketing managers perceive the stores.

---

[13]Ibid., p. 91.

Store Image

For our purposes, we will treat **store image** as what consumers *think* about a particular store. This includes perceptions and attitudes based on sensations of store-related stimuli received through the five senses. Operationally, store image is commonly assessed by asking consumers how good or how important are various aspects of a retail store's operation. Commonly studied dimensions of store image are such things as merchandise, service, clientele, physical facilities, promotion, and convenience. Store atmosphere is also often included as part of store image.

Store image research involves polling consumers concerning their perceptions of and attitudes about particular store dimensions. Typically,

Monika Franzen

Dressing salespeople as referees helps to create a sports image for this store.

HIGHLIGHT 20-4 **Models of Store Image Development**

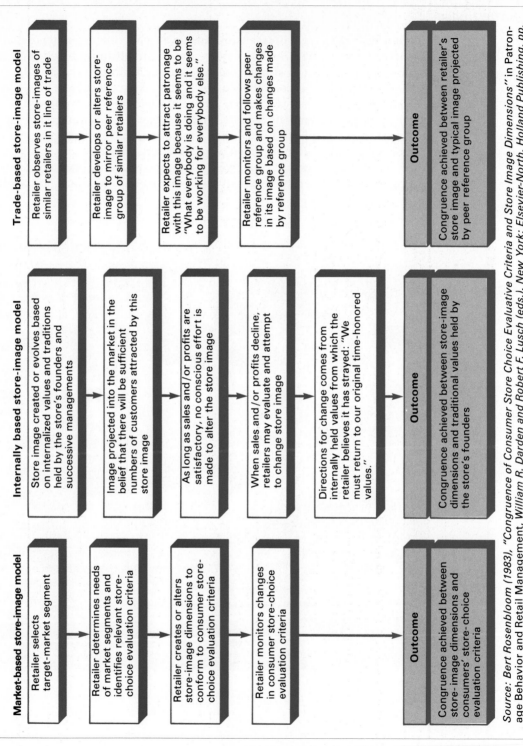

Source: Bert Rosenbloom (1983), "Congruence of Consumer Store Choice Evaluative Criteria and Store Image Dimensions" in Patronage Behavior and Retail Management, William R. Darden and Robert F. Lusch (eds.), New York: Elsevier-North, Holland Publishing, pp. 83–84.

these dimensions are broken down into a number of store attributes. For example, the merchandise dimension might be studied in terms of quality, assortment, fashion, guarantees, and pricing. The service dimension might be studied in terms of general service, salesclerk service, degree of self-service, ease of merchandise return, and delivery and credit services. Often the same attributes will be studied for competitive stores to compare the strengths and weaknesses of a particular store's image with that of its closest competitors. Based on this research, store management may then change certain attributes of the store to develop a more favorable image.

Developing a consistent store image is a common goal of retailers. This involves coordinating the various aspects of store image to appeal to a specific market segment. A number of major retailers are engaged in trying to change their images. For example, J. C. Penney spent $1.5 billion to modernize 550 of its largest stores and has done away with traditional merchandise lines such as auto repair and hardware in an attempt to create a trendier image in the minds of consumers. Penney's has added a line of women's fashion apparel, designed exclusively by Halston, to appeal to the young, affluent working woman. Penney's has eliminated fishing equipment from many of its stores, but has kept golf clubs and tennis gear as part of the attempt to break away from its homespun image. The financial objective of this image change is to increase sales per square foot from $120 to the $200 range.[14]

Store Atmosphere

Donovan and Rossiter argue that **store atmosphere** primarily involves in-store *emotional states* that consumers may not be fully conscious of when shopping.[15] Thus, many controlled studies fail to find that store atmosphere has significant effects on behavior, because these emotional states are difficult for consumers to verbalize, are rather transient, and affect in-store behavior in ways consumers may not be aware of.

The basic model underlying the Donovan and Rossiter research, shown in Figure 20–8, is taken from the environmental-psychology literature. Basically, the model posits that environmental stimuli affect consumers' emotional states, which in turn, affect approach or avoidance behaviors. **Approach behaviors** refer to moving *toward* and **avoidance be-**

---

[14]"J. C. Penney Shops for a Trendier Image" (1984), *Business Week* (February 6), p. 58.

[15]Robert J. Donovan and John R. Rossiter (1982), "Store Atmosphere: An Environmental Psychology Approach," *Journal of Retailing* (Spring), pp. 34–57.

Courtesy Drexel Heritage Furnishings Inc.

What effect might the atmosphere of this furniture showroom have on consumers?

haviors refer to moving *away from* various environments and stimuli. There
are four types of approach or avoidance behaviors related to retail stores:

1. *Physical* approach and avoidance, which can be related to store
   patronage intentions at a basic level.

2. *Exploratory* approach and avoidance, which can be related to in-
   store search and exposure to a broad or narrow range of offerings.

3. *Communication* approach and avoidance, which can be related to
   interactions with sales personnel and floor staff.

4. *Performance and satisfaction* approach and avoidance, which can be related to frequency of repeat-shopping as well as reinforcement of time and money expenditures in the store.

These authors investigated the relationships between the three types of emotional states shown in Figure 20–8 (pleasure, arousal, and dominance) and stated intentions to perform certain store-related behaviors. **Pleasure** refers to the degree to which the consumer feels good, joyful, happy, or satisfied in the store; **arousal** refers to the degree to which the consumer feels excited, stimulated, alert, or active in the store; **dominance** refers to the extent to which the consumer feels in control of or free to act in the store. The study was conducted in 11 different types of retail outlets, including department, clothing, shoe, hardware, and sporting goods stores.

The Donovan and Rossiter research found that simple **affect,** or store-induced pleasure, is a very powerful determinant of approach-avoidance behaviors within the store, including spending behavior. Further, their research suggests that *arousal,* or store-induced feelings of alertness or excitement, can increase time spent in the store as well as willingness to interact with sales personnel. They suggest that in-store stimuli that induce arousal include bright lighting and upbeat music. However, the inducement of arousal works positively only in store environments that are already pleasant; arousal may have no influence, or even a negative influence, in unpleasant store environments. Overall, then, pleasure and arousal influenced consumers' stated (1) enjoyment of shopping in the store, (2) time spent browsing and exploring the store's offerings, (3) willingness to talk to sales personnel, (4) tendency to spend more money than

---

FIGURE 20–8   **A Model of Store Atmosphere Effects**

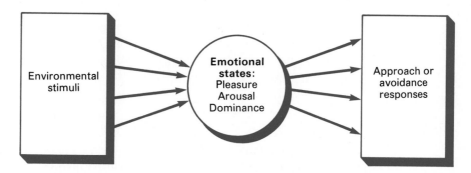

Source: Robert J. Donovan and John R. Rossiter (1982), "Store Atmosphere: An Environmental Psychology Approach," Journal of Retailing *(Spring), p. 42.*

HIGHLIGHT 20–5   **Examples of Retail Tactics Used to Influence Consumer Behavior**

Retail Design Element	Specific Example	Intermediate Behavior	Final Desired Behavior
Store layout	End of escalator, end of aisle, other displays	Bring customer into visual contact with product	Product purchase
Purchase locations	Purchase possible from home, store location	Product or store contact	Product purchase
In-store mobility	In-store product directories, information booths	Bring consumer into visual contact with product	Product purchase
Noises, odors, lights	Flashing lights in window	Bring consumer into visual or other sensory contact with store or product	Product purchase

Source: Walter R. Nord, and J. Paul Peter (1980), "A Behavior Modification Perspective on Marketing," Journal of Marketing (Spring), p. 43.

originally planned, and (5) likelihood of returning to the store. The third emotional dimension, *dominance,* or the extent to which consumers feel in control of or free to act in the store, was found to have little effect on consumer behaviors in the retail environment.

Store-Related Behaviors

Throughout this chapter we have discussed a number of cognitive and environmental variables designed to affect consumers' store-related behaviors. There are many such behaviors that marketing managers want to encourage in the retail environment. Two basic types of behavior are discussed here: store contact and store loyalty.

Store Contact

As we mentioned in Chapter 12, store contact involves the consumer locating, traveling to, and entering a store. We also noted that putting carnivals in parking lots, having style shows in department stores, and printing maps and location instructions in the Yellow Pages are common tactics to increase these behaviors. In addition, other commonly used tactics include store coupons and rebates, and local advertising.

A number of the variables discussed in this chapter are also concerned with obtaining store contacts. For example, store location decisions are strongly influenced by heavy traffic and pedestrian patterns, which facilitate store contact. Also, the visibility of the store and its distance from consumers are variables used to select locations that can increase store

Courtesy McDonald's Corporation

A strategy to initiate store contact.

contact. For many small retail chains and stores, selecting locations in the vicinity of major retail stores such as Sears, J. C. Penney, K mart, or a major grocery store may greatly increase the probability of consumers coming into contact with them. In fact, one of the major advantages of locating in a successful shopping center or mall is the store contact available from pedestrians passing by on their way to another store. From the consumers' viewpoint, such locations can reduce shopping time and effort by allowing a form of one-stop shopping.

Store Loyalty

Most retailers do not want consumers to come to their stores once and never return. Rather, repeat patronage is usually desired. **Store loyalty** (repeat patronage intentions and behavior) can be strongly influenced by the arrangement of the environment, particularly the reinforcing properties of the retail store. For example, the in-store stimuli and the attributes discussed in this chapter in terms of store image are the primary variables used to influence store loyalty.

Consider one further example of a tactic that may be used to develop store loyalty—in-store **unadvertised specials.** These specials are often marked with an attention-getting day-glow orange sign. Typically, consumers go to a store shopping for a particular product or just to go shopping. While going through the store, a favorite brand or long-sought-after product that the consumer could not afford is found to be an unadvertised special. This could be quite reinforcing and strongly influence the probability of returning to the same store, perhaps seeking other unadvertised specials. Quite likely, the consumer would not have to find a suitable unadvertised special on every trip to the store; a variable ratio schedule might well be powerful enough to generate a high degree of store loyalty. These additional trips to the store allow the consumer to experience other reinforcing properties, such as fast check out, a pleasant and arousing store atmosphere, or high-quality merchandise at competitive prices. In sum, reinforcing tactics and positive attributes of the store are used to develop store loyalty.

Store loyalty is a major objective of retail channel strategy, and it has an important financial impact. For example, it has been estimated that the loss of a single customer to a supermarket can cost the store about $3,100 per year in sales. Thus, the analysis of the store environment, and consumers' store cognitions and store behaviors are critical for successful marketing.[16]

---

[16]For further discussion of store loyalty, see Kau Ah Keng and A. S. C. Ehrenberg (1984), "Patterns of Store Choice," *Journal of Marketing Research* (November), pp. 399–409.

Back to the Case

This case demonstrates a number of points raised in this chapter and provides evidence for some of them. To start with, IBM is clearly a very effective producer and marketer of computers when selling door-to-door in the industrial market, as well as when selling through independent retailers. However, these marketing skills clearly did not transfer when the firm began selling in its own retail stores. Consider IBM's store image. Consumers initially had a very positive image, but this image changed—in the wrong direction for IBM. Also, consider IBM's mistakes in the selection of red decor, in-store merchandising, and salespeople inexperienced in retail sales.

This case is also a good example of management changing an environment based on consumer cognitions and behavior. Because their original strategy resulted in a poor store image and store atmosphere, and with store contact, product contact, and transactions at unsatisfactory levels, IBM changed the store environment.

For one thing, salespeople now receive formal training so they will be more effective in dealing with customers. A new point-of-sale computer system has been installed, and there is a new, less-forbidding store design with cozier colors, point-of-sale gimmicks, and the look of a place where you can "get a deal."

However, the stores still shrink from price cutting and avoid "bundling"—mixing and matching computer components to make up specially-priced packages. IBM's emphasis on service rather than on price and bundling has led one retail competitor to remark that the Product Centers are still "a delight to compete with."

Summary

This chapter presented an overview of channel strategy and the relationships between store environment, cognitions, and behavior. Initially, a number of criteria by which channel alternatives can be judged were discussed, and it was emphasized that it is the consumer, and the relationships between the consumer and the other criteria, that should determine the appropriate channel strategy. In terms of the store environment, three major topics were discussed, store location, store layout, and in-store stimuli. In terms of store cognitions, the two most critical for channel strategy, store image and store atmosphere, were discussed. The last part of the chapter discussed consumers' store behavior in terms of store contact and store loyalty, which are primary objectives of retail channel strategy.

Additional Reading

Danny N. Bellenger and Jac L. Goldstucker (1983), *Retailing Basics,* Homewood, Ill.: Richard D. Irwin.

Roger D. Blackwell and W. Wayne Talarzyk (1983), "Life-Style Retailing: Competitive Strategies for the 1980s," *Journal of Retailing* (Winter), pp. 7–27.

William R. Davidson, Daniel J. McSweeney and Ronald W. Stampfl (1984), *Retailing Management,* 5th ed., New York: John Wiley & Sons.

Delbert J. Duncan, Stanley C. Hollander and Ronald Savitt (1983), *Modern Retailing Management,* 10th ed., Homewood, Ill.: Richard D. Irwin.

Avijit Ghosh and C. Samuel Craig (1983), "Formulating Retail Location Strategy in a Changing Environment," *Journal of Marketing* (Summer), pp. 56–68.

Rebecca H. Holman and R. Dale Wilson (1982), "Temporal Equilibrium as a Basis for Retail Shopping Behavior," *Journal of Retailing* (Spring), pp. 58–81.

John A. Quelch and Kristina Cannon-Bonventre (1983), "Better Marketing at the Point of Purchase," *Harvard Business Review* (November–December), pp. 162–169.

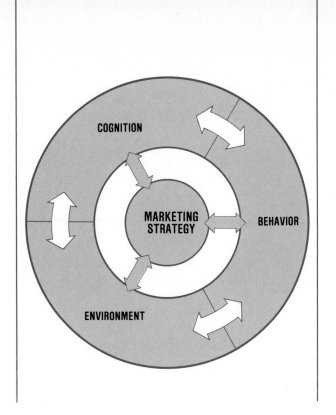

Section Six

Societal Influences on Marketing Practices

21. *Consumer Behavior, Marketing, and Social Responsibility*

Chapter Twenty One

Consumer Behavior, Marketing, and Social Responsibility

Coke and Pepsi

In that cluttered area at the end of your supermarket's soft-drink aisle, Coca-Cola and Pepsi-Cola bottlers are fighting a ferocious war. Stacked high with eight-packs and two-liter bottles and adorned with cockeyed signs that shout out the special of the week, the end of the aisle in many grocery stores looks like a listing square-rigger. Those displays, however, can account for as much as 50 percent of a store's total soft-drink volume. As Coke and Pepsi battle for space, Royal Crown, Dr Pepper, 7UP, and other second-tier bottlers are getting crushed in the fray.

Because of aggressive marketing and the success of their diet colas, Coke and Pepsi pushed their combined market share from 64.7 to 66.3 percent in 1984. That represents a $420 million gain in the $26-billion-a-year soft-drink industry. Some of the second-tier competitors lost up to .4 percent market share during the same period.

Every time a bottler loses a fraction of a percentage point of market share, it is likely to lose a little shelf space as well, because grocers generally divide up space on the basis of sales per square foot. Moans one competitor, "Pretty soon Coke and Pepsi are going to squeeze everyone else out—it's just a matter of time."

To secure the supermarkets' high-volume selling display areas, Coke and Pepsi bottlers in many parts of the United States simply pay grocers for it by giving them huge price breaks and promotional allowances. For example, it is estimated that the Kroger grocery chain was offered about $2 million worth of discounts by Coke and Pepsi in 1984 for store advertising and promotion. The second-tier soft-drink companies compete for promotional shelf space in the same way, but because their sales are far less than those of Coke and Pepsi, their clout is, too.

In desperation, some bottling companies have sued. For example, Beverage Management Inc. (BMI), which distributes 7UP in Cincinnati, asked a federal court for a preliminary injunction to stop Coke's arrangement with Kroger, contending that the cola king had unfairly restrained the 7UP bottlers' ability to compete. In court papers Coke said that its agreement—which prevented Kroger from featuring certain sizes of a competing soft drink during the same week it promoted Coke—didn't commit Kroger to reserve any time for Coca-Cola promotions. Coke maintains that Kroger was free each week to accept its offer or to take a better deal from some other company, including Beverage Management. Moreover, Coke charges that BMI brought the case because it is "losing the game" of selling soft drinks in Cincinnati. Pepsi's share of that market is 45 percent, Coke's is around 35 percent, and BMI's about 10 percent. The judge denied Beverage Management's motion for a preliminary injunction.

Some bottlers say they aren't willing to risk incurring the wrath of a big food retailer by dragging it into a lengthy antitrust case. They fear the retailers may wipe them out by slowly reallocating shelf space to other brands.

Source: Ford S. Worthy (1985), "Coke and Pepsi Stomp on the Little Guys," Fortune *(January 7), pp. 67–68.*

In this text, we have presented what we believe to be a useful description of some important relationships between consumer cognitions, consumer behaviors, the environment, and marketing strategy development. One of the major underlying premises of the text is that marketing is an important and powerful force in society; properly designed and executed marketing strategies are often effective in changing consumer cognitions and behaviors in order to achieve organizational objectives.

We have also argued that attempts to modify and control cognitions and behaviors are part of the fabric of society. In fact, we believe that the majority of social exchanges involve such attempts. Thus, even though marketing may attempt to do so in a systematic and effective manner, the majority of marketing practices are not unethical per se.

Further, we believe that marketing and free enterprise offer the best and most effective system of exchange that has been developed. For example, we believe that survival of the human species is a primary objective of any society. Given the development and marketing of a variety of products and services, life expectancies and the quality of life have been dramatically improved for many people. There is also no question that marketing can be used to encourage a variety of socially desirable behaviors, such as reduction in littering, smoking, pollution, and other behaviors.

This is not to say that marketers always perform in a manner that is good for society, however. There are clear examples where marketers have misused their power to affect consumer cognitions and behaviors. Thus, the purpose of this final chapter is to discuss the responsibility of marketing to society.

The Rights of Marketers and Consumers

Both marketers and consumers are granted certain rights by society, and both have a degree of power. Overall, many people believe that marketers have considerably more power than consumers. Several years ago, Professor Philip Kotler provided the following list of rights granted to marketers (sellers):

1. Sellers have the right to introduce any product in any size, style, color, etc., so long as it meets minimum health and safety requirements.
2. Sellers have the right to price the product as they please so long as they avoid discrimination that is harmful to competition.
3. Sellers have the right to promote the product using any resources, media, or message, in any amount, so long as no deception or fraud is involved.
4. Sellers have the right to introduce any buying schemes they wish, so long as they are not discriminatory.
5. Sellers have the right to alter the product offering at any time.
6. Sellers have the right to distribute the product in any reasonable manner.
7. Sellers have the right to limit the product guarantee or postsale services.[1]

While this list is not exhaustive, it does serve to illustrate that marketers have a good deal of power and latitude in their actions.

Since the Consumer Bill of Rights was issued in the early 1960s, consumers have been typically granted at least four basic rights: to safety, to be informed, to choose, and to be heard. While this list may appear to grant the consumer considerable rights and protection, it has an important weakness: most of these rights depend on the assumption that consumers are both capable of being and willing to be highly involved in purchase and consumption. In fact, however, many consumers are neither. Young

---

[1]Philip Kotler (1972), "What Consumerism Means for Marketers," *Harvard Business Review* (May–June), pp. 48–57.

children, many elderly people, and the uneducated poor often do not have the cognitive abilities to process information well enough to be protected.[2] Further, even those consumers who do have the capacity often are not willing to invest the time, money, cognitive energy, and behavior effort to ensure their rights.

The right to choose is also predicated on the assumption that consumers are rational, autonomous, knowledgeable cognitive processors and decision makers. While we believe that most consumers are capable of being so, evidence suggests that consumers often do not behave this way.[3] Further, the right to choose ignores the power of marketing to influence attitudes, intentions, and behaviors. Consumers' needs, wants, and satisfaction can be developed through conditioning and modeling processes used by marketers, for instance. Thus, the assumption of consumer autonomy is not easily supported.

Finally, no matter how much effort consumers exert to ensure they are choosing a good product, they cannot process information that is not available. For example, consumers cannot be aware of product safety risks that are hidden from them.

Overall, then, if there were no other forces in society, marketers might well have more rights and power than consumers do. This is not to say that consumers cannot exert countercontrol on marketers or that consumers do not vary in the degree to which they are influenced by marketers. However, as our society and system of government and exchange evolved, a number of constraints or societal influences on marketing activities have also developed. As shown in Figure 21–1, these include legal, political, competitive, and ethical influences.

Before discussing each of these societal influences, three points should be noted. First, as we stated earlier, we believe that marketing and the free enterprise system offer the best and most effective system of exchange that has ever been developed. This does not mean that the system could not be improved. For example, there is still a large group of poor, uneducated, hungry people in our society who have little chance of improving their lot.

Second, while marketing usually receives the brunt of society's criticism of business, marketing managers are no more or less guilty of wrongdoing than are other business executives. Corporate responsibility to

---

[2] See, for example, Deborah L. Roedder (1981), "Age Differences in Children's Responses to Television Advertising: An Information Processing Approach," *Journal of Consumer Research* (September), pp. 144–153; Gerald J. Gorn and Marvin E. Goldberg (1982), "Behavioral Evidence of the Effects of TV Food Messages on Children," *Journal of Consumer Research* (September), pp. 200–205.

[3] For example, see Richard W. Olshavsky and Donald H. Granbois (1979), "Consumer Decision Making: Fact or Fiction?" *Journal of Consumer Research* (September), pp. 93–100.

FIGURE 21–1   **Major Sources of Consumer Protection**

society is a shared responsibility of all business executives, regardless of functional field. In addition, marketing executives are no more or less ethical than most other groups in society.[4] Similarly, while business, particularly big business, is commonly singled out for criticism, there is no question that other fields—including medicine, engineering, and law—also have their share of societal problems. Some consumers could also be criticized for the billions of dollars of merchandise that is shoplifted annually, as well as for other crimes against businesses and society.

Third, while some critics of marketing focus on the field in general, many of the problems are confined to a relatively small percentage of firms and practices. Figure 21–2 presents a list of some of the most commonly cited areas of concern, divided into product, promotion, pricing, and distribution issues. Many of these practices are subject to legal influences or constraints.

---

[4]For empirical support of this statement, see Shelby D. Hunt and Lawrence B. Chonko (1984), "Marketing and Machiavellianism," *Journal of Marketing* (Summer), pp. 30–42.

Charles Gatewood/The Image Works

Like corporations, consumers should respond in a socially responsible manner.

Legal Influences

Legal influences are federal, state, and local legislation and the agencies and processes by which these laws are upheld. Figure 21–3 presents a list of major federal legislation designed to protect consumers. Some of this legislation is designed to control practices in specific industries (such as textiles or toys); others are aimed at controlling functional areas (such as packaging and labeling, and product safety).

FIGURE 21–2 **Some Problem Areas in Marketing**

Product Issues
Unsafe products
Poor-quality products
Poor service/repair/maintenance after sale
Deceptive packaging and labeling practices

Promotion Issues
Deceptive advertising
Advertising to children
Bait-and-switch advertising
Anxiety-inducing advertising
Deceptive personal selling tactics

Pricing Issues
Deceptive pricing
Fraudulent or misleading credit practices
Warranty refund problems

Distribution Issues
Sale of counterfeit products and brands
Pyramid selling
Deceptive in-store selling influences

A variety of government agencies are involved in enforcing these laws and investigating business practices. In addition to state and local agencies, this includes a number of federal agencies, such as those listed in Figure 21–4.

One marketing practice of major interest to the Federal Trade Commission is deceptive advertising—advertising that misleads consumers. One FTC approach to dealing with this problem is **corrective advertising.** Corrective advertising requires that firms which have misled consumers must rectify the deception in future ads.[5] Profile bread advertising led consumers to believe it was effective in weight reduction; Domino sugar advertising led consumers to believe it was a special source of strength, energy, and stamina; Ocean Spray Cranberry Juice Cocktail misled consumers about food energy; and Sugar Information, Inc., misled consumers

---

[5]For an excellent, comprehensive discussion of corrective advertising, see William L. Wilkie, Dennis L. McNeill and Michael B. Mazis (1984), "Marketing's 'Scarlet Letter': The Theory and Practice of Corrective Advertising," *Journal of Marketing* (Spring), pp. 11–31.

FIGURE 21–3   **Consumer Oriented Legislation**

Pure Food and Drug Act (1906). Prohibited adulterations and misbranding of foods and drugs sold in interstate commerce. Amended in 1938 and 1962.

Federal Meat Inspection Act (1906). Provided for government inspection and certification of meat in interstate commerce. Designed to upgrade slaughtering, packaging, and canning practices. Amended in 1967 to require states to match federal meat inspection standards.

Federal Trade Commission Act (1914). Declared all unfair methods of competition unlawful. Established the Federal Trade Commission. Amended in 1937 by the Wheeler-Lea Act to provide FTC regulatory powers over the advertising of food, drugs, cosmetics, and therapeutic devices.

Federal Food, Drug and Cosmetics Act (1938). Established the Food and Drug Administration and empowered it to seize products found unfit for consumption and to prosecute persons or firms held in violation. Amended in 1958 to provide for regulation of food additives, and in 1962 to require pretesting of drugs to assure safety and efficacy.

Wool Products Labeling Act (1939). Required wool-products labels to include percentages of wool, reprocessed wool, and reused wool. Amended in 1949 and 1953.

Fur Products Labeling Act (1951). Stated mandatory specifications for labeling, invoicing, and advertising of fur products.

Flammable Fabrics Act (1953). Prohibited marketing of highly flammable materials for clothing. Amended in 1968 to include household products, fabrics, and materials.

Poultry Products Inspection Act (1957). Provided for government inspection of poultry products used in interstate commerce. Amended in 1968 to provide federal support for improving state-level regulation of the poultry industry.

Textile Fiber Products Identification Act (1958). Required percentage labeling of textile fiber content and regulated usage of names of synthetic fibers. Also required identification of producer or distributor and country of origin, if foreign.

Hazardous Substances Labeling Act (1960). Required warning labels for toxic, corrosive, irritating, or flammable products used in household applications.

Fair Packaging and Labeling (Truth-in-Packaging) Act (1966). Specified contents, name, and size or weight labeling requirements for many household products. Contained a section encouraging voluntary standardization of package sizes.

Cigarette Labeling Act (1966). Required cigarette producers to label packages: "Caution: Cigarette smoking may be hazardous to your health." (See Public Health Smoking Act.)

Child Protection Act (1966). Banned sales of hazardous toys and articles intended for children.

National Traffic and Motor Vehicle Safety (Traffic Safety) Act (1966). Provided a national safety program and provided for establishment of national safety standards for motor vehicles.

Consumer Credit Protection (Truth-in-Lending) Act (1968). Required disclosure of credit, terms, and annual percentage rates for consumer loans and installment purchases.

FIGURE 21–3   *(concluded)*

Radiation Control for Health and Safety Act (1968). Provided for recall of faulty electronic products.

Child Protection and Toy Safety Act (1969). Increased coverage of Child Protection Act. Specified prohibited electrical, mechanical, and thermal hazards.

Public Health Smoking Act (1970). Banned cigarette advertising on radio and television and revised the caution label on cigarette packages to read: "Warning: The Surgeon General has determined that cigarette smoking is dangerous to your health."

An Amendment to the Federal Deposit Insurance Act (1970). Prohibited issuance of unsolicited credit cards, limited a consumer's liability for credit card loss to $50, specified certain credit bureau practices, and provided consumers with access to their credit files.

The Fair Credit Report Act (1971). Designed to protect consumers against the circulation of inaccurate or obsolete information. Aimed to insure that consumer reporting agencies exercise responsibilities in a manner that is fair and equitable to consumers.

Consumer Product Safety Act (1972). Established a Federal Consumer Product Safety Commission with authority to create federal standards for products which may pose an injury risk for consumers.

The Fair Credit Billing Act (1974). Requires a creditor to take certain steps if a debtor, within 60 days of the report of a bill, complains that the billing is in error.

Real Estate Settlements Law (1974). Requires disclosure of all costs to buyers and borrowers prior to the consummation of a real estate transaction.

Magnuson-Moss Warranty—FTC Improvement Act (1975). Warranties on goods costing $5 or more must disclose the terms of the warranty in simple and readily understood language. If a product costs more than $15, the warranty must be labeled "full" or "limited."

The Equal Credit Opportunity Act (1977). To ensure that credit is made available fairly and impartially. Prohibits discrimination against any applicant for credit because of race, color, religion, national origin, sex, marital status, or age, or because the customer is on public assistance or because he or she has exercised rights under consumer credit law.

The Consumer Leasing (Trust-in-Leasing) Act (1977). Requires leasing companies to provide information about total costs and terms of the contract.

Source: Frederick D. Sturdivant (1985), Business and Society: A Managerial Approach, *3d ed., Homewood, Ill.: Richard D. Irwin, pp. 384–386.*

about sugar benefits. Figure 21–5 presents the text and number of ads required for correcting these deceptions.

Legal influences and the power of government agencies to regulate business and marketing practices grew dramatically in the 1970s; but so far, the 1980s have witnessed a decrease in many areas of regulation. In

FIGURE 21–4   **Some Important Federal Regulatory Agencies**

Agency	Responsibilities
Federal Trade Commission (FTC)	Enforces laws and develops guidelines regarding unfair business practices
Food and Drug Administration (FDA)	Enforces laws and develops regulations to prevent distribution and sale of adulterated or misbranded foods, drugs, cosmetics, and hazardous consumer products
Consumer Product Safety Commission (CPSC)	Enforces the Consumer Product Safety Act— which covers any consumer product not assigned to other regulatory agencies.
Interstate Commerce Commission (ICC)	Regulates interstate rail, bus, truck and water carriers
Federal Communications Commission (FCC)	Regulates interstate wire, radio, and television
Environmental Protection Agency (EPA)	Develops and enforces environmental protection standards
Office of Consumer Affairs (OCA)	Handles consumer complaints

Source: E. Jerome McCarthy and William D. Perreault, Jr. (1984), Basic Marketing, *8th ed., Homewood, Ill.: Richard D. Irwin, p. 131.*

fact, deregulation of business has been the major thrust in this period and government agencies have considerably reduced their involvement in controlling business practices.[6] Thus, while legal constraints are an important form of consumer protection, it appears that this influence, at least at the federal level, has diminished somewhat.

Political Influences

By **political influences** we mean the pressure exerted to control marketing practices by various consumer groups. These groups use a variety of meth-

---

[6]See Christine Dugas and Paula Dwyer (1985), "Deceptive Ads: The FTC's Laissez-Faire Approach Is Backfiring," *Business Week* (December 2), pp. 136–140; John Wilke, Mark N. Vamos and Mark Maremont (1985), "Has the FCC Gone Too Far?" *Business Week* (August 5), pp. 48–54.

FIGURE 21–5   **Examples of Corrective Ads**

Profile Bread

"Hi, (celebrity's name) for Profile Bread. Like all mothers, I'm concerned about nutrition and balanced meals. So, I'd like to clear up any misunderstanding you may have about Profile Bread from its advertising or even its name.

"Does Profile have fewer calories than any other breads? No. Profile has about the same per ounce as other breads. To be exact, Profile has seven fewer calories per slice. That's because Profile is sliced thinner. But eating Profile will not cause you to lose weight. A reduction of seven calories is insignificant. It's total calories and balanced nutrition that count. And Profile can help you achieve a balanced meal because it provides protein and B vitamins as well as other nutrients.

"How does my family feel about Profile? Well, my husband likes Profile toast, the children love Profile sandwiches, and I prefer Profile to any other bread. So you see, at our house, delicious taste makes Profile a family affair."

(To be run in 25% of brand's advertising, for one year.)

Amstar

"Do you recall some of our past messages saying that Domino Sugar gives you strength, energy, and stamina? Actually, Domino is not a special or unique source of strength, energy, and stamina. No sugar is, because what you need is a balanced diet and plenty of rest and exercise."

(To be run in one of every four ads for one year.)

Ocean Spray

"If you've wondered what some of our earlier advertising meant when we said Ocean Spray Cranberry Juice Cocktail has more food energy than orange juice or tomato juice, let us make it clear: we didn't mean vitamins and minerals. Food energy means calories. Nothing more.

"Food energy is important at breakfast since many of us may not get enough calories, or food energy, to get off to a good start. Ocean Spray Cranberry Juice Cocktail helps because it contains more food energy than most other breakfast drinks.

"And Ocean Spray Cranberry Juice Cocktail gives you and your family Vitamin C plus a great wake-up taste. It's . . . the other breakfast drink."

(To be run in one of every four ads for one year.)

Sugar Information, Inc.

"Do you recall the messages we brought you in the past about sugar? How something with sugar in it before meals could help you curb your appetite? We hope you didn't get the idea that our little diet tip was any magic formula for losing weight. Because there are no tricks or shortcuts; the whole diet subject is very complicated. Research hasn't established that consuming sugar before meals will contribute to weight reduction or even keep you from gaining weight."

(To be run for one insertion in each of seven magazines.)

Source: William L. Wilkie, Dennis L. McNeill and Michael B. Mazis (1984), "Marketing's 'Scarlet Letter': The Theory and Practice of Corrective Advertising," Journal of Marketing (Spring), p. 13.

FIGURE 21–6   **Some Political Groups Concerned with Consumerism**

Broad-Based National Groups
Consumer Federation of America
National Wildlife Federation
Common Cause

Smaller Multi-Issue Organizations
National Consumer's League
Ralph Nader's Public Citizen

Special-Interest Groups
Action for Children's Television
American Association of Retired Persons
Group against Smoking and Pollution

Local Groups
Public-interest research groups
Local consumer protection offices
Local broadcast and newspaper consumer "action lines"

Source: Adapted from Paul N. Bloom and Stephen A. Greyser (1981), "The Maturing of Consumerism," Harvard Business Review *(November–December), pp. 130–139.*

ods to influence marketing practice, such as lobbying with various government agencies to enact or enforce legislation or working directly with consumers in redress assistance and education. Figure 21–6 lists some organizations that are designed to serve consumer interests. These are but a few examples; one tally found over 100 national organizations and over 600 state and local groups that are concerned with consumerism.[7]

Bloom and Greyser argue that consumerism has reached the mature stage of its life cycle and that its impact has been fragmented.[8] Yet they believe consumerism will continue to have some impact on business, and they offer three strategies for coping with it. First, businesses can try to accelerate the decline of consumerism by *reducing demand* for it. This could be done by improving product quality, expanding services, lowering prices, and toning down advertising claims.

Second, businesses can *compete* with consumer groups by having ac-

---

[7]Ann P. Harvey (1980), *Contacts in Consumerism: 1980–1981,* Washington, D.C.: Fraser/Associates.

[8]Paul N. Bloom and Stephen A. Greyser (1981), "The Maturing of Consumerism," *Harvard Business Review* (November–December), pp. 130–139.

tive consumer affairs departments that offer redress assistance and consumer education. Alternatively, a business could fund and coordinate activities designed to "sell" deregulation and other probusiness causes.

Third, businesses can *cooperate* with consumer groups by providing financial and other support. Overall, most of these strategies would likely further reduce the impact and importance of political constraints. However, to the degree that following these strategies leads business firms to increase their social responsibility activities in the long run, the consumer could benefit.

Competitive Influences

Competitive influences refer to actions of competing firms intended to affect each other and consumers. These actions can be taken in many ways.

Peter LeGrand: Click/Chicago

Obtaining shelf space is a competitive struggle.

For example, one firm might sue another firm or point out its alleged fraudulent activities to consumers. Johnson & Johnson frequently took competitors to court to protect its Tylenol brand of pain reliever from being shown in competitive ads. Burger King publicly accused McDonald's of overstating the weight of its hamburgers.

Perhaps the most important consumer protection generated by competition is that it reduces the impact of information from any single firm. In other words, in a marketing environment where there are many active competitors, no single firm can dominate the information flow to consumers. In this sense, conflicting competitive claims, images, information, and offers may help consumers from being unduly influenced by a single firm or brand. Conversely, it may also lead to information overload.

Consumers may also benefit from the development and marketing of better products and services brought about by competitive pressure. Current merger trends and the concentration of various industries may lessen these competitive constraints and societal advantages, however.

Ethical Influences

Perhaps the most important constraints on marketing practices are ethical and involve **self-regulation** by marketers. Many professions have codes of ethics (see Highlight 21–1), and many firms have their own consumer affairs offices that seek to ensure that the consumer is treated fairly. In addition, some companies have developed a more positive image with consumers by emphasizing consumer-oriented marketing tactics such as offering toll-free hot lines for information and complaints, promoting unit pricing, and supporting social causes.

A difficult problem in discussing ethical constraints is that there is no single standard by which actions can be judged. Laczniak summarizes five ethical standards that have been proposed by various marketing writers:

1. *The Golden Rule:* Act in the way you would expect others to act toward you.

2. *The Utilitarian Principle:* Act in a way that results in the greatest good for the greatest number.

3. *Kant's Categorical Imperative:* Act in such a way that the action taken under the circumstances could be a universal law or rule of behavior.

4. *The Professional Ethic:* Take actions that would be viewed as proper by a disinterested panel of professional colleagues.

5. *The TV Test:* A manager should always ask: "Would I feel comfortable explaining to a national TV audience why I took this action?"[9]

Following these standards could result in many different interpretations of an ethical marketing practice. If you doubt this, try applying them

The party begins.

I can drive when I drink.

2 drinks later.

I can drive when I drink

After 4 drinks.

I can drive when I drink.

After 5 drinks.

I can driv when I drive

7 drinks in all.

I can drwedn dr...

The more you drink, the more coordination you lose. That's a fact, plain and simple.
Still, people drink too much and then go out and expect to handle a car.
When you drink too much you can't handle a car. You can't even handle a pen.

The House of Seagram

For reprints please write Advertising Dept. PL-782, The House of Seagram, 375 Park Ave., N.Y., N.Y. 10152. © 1973 The House of Seagram

Courtesy The House of Seagram

A classic example of corporate social responsibility.

HIGHLIGHT 21–1   **Code of Ethics of the American Marketing Association**

As a member of the American Marketing Association, I recognize the significance of my professional conduct and my responsibilities to society and to the other members of my profession:

1. By acknowledging my accountability to society as a whole as well as to the organization for which I work

2. By pledging my efforts to assure that all presentations of goods, services, and concepts be made honestly and clearly

3. By striving to improve marketing knowledge and practice in order to better serve society

4. By supporting free consumer choice in circumstances that are legal and are consistent with generally accepted community standards

5. By pledging to use the highest professional standards in my work and in my competitive activity

6. By acknowledging the right of the American Marketing Association, through established procedure, to withdraw my membership if I am found to be in violation of ethical standards of professional conduct

Source: The American Marketing Association, Chicago.

to the scenarios in Figure 21–7 and then comparing your answers with those of other readers.

Overall, then, what constitutes ethical marketing behavior is a matter of social judgment. Even in areas such as product safety, what constitutes ethical marketing practices is not always clear. While at first blush it might be argued that all products should either be completely safe or not be allowed on the market, deeper inspection reveals questions such as, How safe? and For whom? For example, bicycles often head the list of the most hazardous products, yet few consumers or marketers would argue that bicycles should be banned from the market. Much of the problem in determining product safety concerns the question of whether the harm done results from an inherent lack of product safety or unsafe use by the consumer.

---

⁹Gene R. Laczniak (1983), "Framework for Analyzing Marketing Ethics," *Journal of Macromarketing* (Spring), pp. 7–18.

FIGURE 21–7　　**Marketing Scenarios That Raise Ethical Questions**

Scenario 1

The Thrifty Supermarket Chain has 12 stores in the city of Gotham, U.S.A. The company's policy is to maintain the same prices for all items at all stores. However, the distribution manager knowingly sends the poorest cuts of meat and the lowest quality produce to the store located in the low-income section of town. He justifies this action based on the fact that this store has the highest overhead due to factors such as employee turnover, pilferage, and vandalism. *Is the distribution manager's economic rationale sufficient justification for his allocation method?*

Scenario 2

The Independent Chevy Dealers of Metropolis, U.S.A. have undertaken an advertising campaign headlined by the slogan: "Is your family's life worth 45 MPG?" The ads admit that while Chevy subcompacts are *not* as fuel efficient as foreign imports and cost more to maintain, they are safer according to government-sponsored crash tests. The ads implicitly ask if responsible parents, when purchasing a car, should trade off fuel efficiency for safety. *Is it ethical for the dealers association to use a fear appeal to offset an economic disadvantage?*

Scenario 3

A few recent studies have linked the presence of the artificial sweetener, subsugural, to cancer in laboratory rats. While the validity of these findings has been hotly debated by medical experts, the Food and Drug Administration has ordered products containing the ingredient banned from sale in the United States. The Jones Company sends all of its sugar-free J. C. Cola (which contains subsugural) to European supermarkets because the sweetener has not been banned there. *Is it acceptable for the Jones Company to send an arguably unsafe product to another market without waiting for further evidence?*

Scenario 4

The Acme Company sells industrial supplies through its own sales force, which calls on company purchasing agents. Acme has found that providing the purchasing agent with small gifts helps cement a cordial relationship and creates goodwill. Acme follows the policy that the bigger the order, the bigger the gift to the purchasing agent. The gifts range from a pair of tickets to a sporting event to outboard motors and snowmobiles. Acme does not give gifts to personnel at companies which they know have an explicit policy prohibiting the acceptance of such gifts. *Assuming no laws are violated, is Acme's policy of providing gifts to purchasing agents morally proper?*

Scenario 5

The Buy American Electronics Company has been selling its highly rated System X Color TV sets (21, 19, and 12 inches) for $700, $500 and $300 respectively. These prices have been relatively uncompetitive in the market. After some study, Buy American substitutes several cheaper components (which engineering says may slightly reduce the quality of performance)

FIGURE 21–7   (concluded)

and passes on the savings to the consumer in the form of a $100 price reduction on each model. Buy American institutes a price-oriented promotional campaign which neglects to mention that the second-generation System X sets are different from the first. *Is the company's competitive strategy ethical?*

Scenario 6

The Smith & Smith Advertising Agency has been struggling financially. Mr. Smith is approached by the representative of a small South American country which is on good terms with the U.S. Department of State. He wants S & S to create a multi-million dollar advertising and public relations campaign which will bolster the image of the country and increase the likelihood that it will receive U.S. foreign aid assistance and attract investment capital. Smith knows the country is a dictatorship which has been accused of numerous human rights violations. *Is it ethical for the Smith & Smith Agency to undertake the proposed campaign?*

Source: Gene R. Laczniak (1983), "Framework for Analyzing Marketing Ethics," Journal of Macromarketing *(Spring), p. 8.*

Back to the Case

This case illustrates a number of issues discussed in the chapter. First, it highlights the tremendous power of firms with large market shares and their ability to capture even greater market shares. In this instance, market power is used to influence the retail environment to gain sales to consumers.

Second, there is no question that—at least in the short run—consumers benefit by getting lower prices on soft drinks. In many areas, supermarkets routinely put soft drinks on special for just a penny and a half per ounce, which is less than it cost 10 years ago. Consumers now purchase and drink more soft drinks than any other beverage, including milk, beer, and coffee.

Third, the case illustrates one form of competitive influence, that of taking a competitor to court. Although BMI was not successful, at least the issue was brought to society's attention and a judgment could be made. If the second-tier soft-drink companies are eliminated from the market, however, at least a portion of the competitive constraint will be removed.

Finally, while the success of Coke and Pepsi may be viewed as a marketing victory, it is also worth considering the position of the firms with smaller market share. From an economic point of view, some of these firms may be less efficient than the larger-share firms; but our society traditionally has valued having a number of competitors in each industry. Note that the problem with these brands is not a function of poor quality, but an inability to compete with the industry giants. If these firms are eliminated from the market, consumers will likely have fewer brands from which to choose.

Summary

In the final chapter of the text, we have discussed some of the important relationships among marketing, consumer behavior, and social responsibility. Overall, while society offers marketers considerable power and latitude in performing marketing tasks, marketers also have a variety of constraints placed on their behavior. In addition to consumer countercontrol and individual differences in consumers, these include legal, political, competitive, and ethical influences.

Additional Reading

David A. Aaker and George S. Day (1982), *Consumerism: Search for the Consumer Interest,* 4th ed., New York: Free Press.

Paul Busch (1976), "A Review and Critical Evaluation of the Consumer Product Safety Commission: Marketing Management Implications," *Journal of Marketing* (October), pp. 41–49.

Robert G. Harris and James M. Carman (1984), "Public Regulation of Marketing Activity: Part II: Regulatory Responses to Market Failures," *Journal of Macromarketing* (Spring), pp. 41–52.

Patrick E. Murphy and Gene R. Laczniak (1981), "Marketing Ethics: A Review with Implications for Managers, Educators and Researchers," in *Review of Marketing 1981,* Ben Enis and Kenneth Roering (eds.), Chicago: American Marketing Association, pp. 251–266.

Terence A. Shimp and Ivan L. Preston (1981), "Deceptive and Nondeceptive Consequences of Evaluative Advertising," *Journal of Marketing* (Winter), pp. 22–31.

Kenneth C. Schneider and Cynthia K. Holm (1982), "Deceptive Practices in Marketing Research: The Consumer's Viewpoint," *California Management Review* (Spring), pp. 89–96.

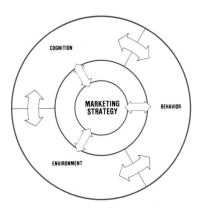

Cases

America's Movie Theaters
Black & Decker
Cub Foods
General Foods
Hallmark Greeting Cards
Hasbro Bradley Inc.
Hershey Foods
McDonald's Corporation
Nike
Timex Corporation

America's Movie Theaters

The price of admission to many of America's movie theaters buys an experience sensible people would pay to avoid. The blackened and musty carpet in the lobby could be a relic from the silent screen era. The $1.25 bucket of popcorn—that's the small size!—holds 10 cents worth of corn covered with a strange liquid, perhaps derived from petroleum. Beneath the broken seats, sticky coats of spilled soda pop varnish the floor. The screen is tiny, the sound tinny, and the audience is rude. Oh, and one more thing—the picture stinks.

Many theater owners bought into the business at low prices after 1948, when antitrust rulings forced the major Hollywood studios, which had previously owned the leading theater chains, to give up their movie houses. The new owners got a great deal. They owned the only show in town (sometimes literally), and the studios promoted the movies. As the easy profits rolled in, many exhibitors lost contact with their customers. They milked the business and let their theaters deteriorate.

But the success of video cassette rentals and cable TV during the early 1980s converted many moviegoers to stay-at-homes. These changes forced exhibitors to recognize their folly at last. By 1985, theaters were no longer the only show in town. Attendance dropped 12 percent over 1984 figures. The $5-billion-a-year American movie theater industry was fighting for survival.

Now the theater owners were in a bind. To regain the loyalty of their customers, they had to pour money into refurbishing, rebuilding, and restoring the glamour of moviegoing. But at the same time they are being hurt by the new technologies that compete with them.

To survive during these changes, exhibitors had developed a couple of temporarily successful strategies. One was to develop their lobby concession stands as a source of revenues. To keep some of their customers, theaters had kept prices fairly low—the average was about $3.50 to $4—prices that lagged behind inflation. Once inside, though, moviegoers were a captive market for the popcorn, soda, and candy sold at stupendous markups ranging to 500 percent or more. A well-run concession stand generates at least $1 of sales and as much as 75 cents of profit per ticket buyer. Exhibitors found that they could survive by charging ever more outrageous prices for popcorn.

The other strategy was the multiscreen theater. During the 70s exhibitors began chopping up their grand old theaters into smaller ones that many moviegoers have come to hate. Individual exhibitors did great, though (as long as they were the only show in town). A theater with four

Source: Excerpted from Stratford P. Sherman (1986), "Back to the Future," Fortune (January 20), pp. 909–994.

screens, about the national average, is four more times likely to book a hit picture. The exhibitor then showed the hit in the largest room and lesser movies in the smaller theaters.

But on a larger scale, more seats were the last thing the industry needed. The total number of tickets sold annually remained constant at about 1 billion, a number that hasn't varied much for 25 years. But when the growing population is considered, this translated into a 24 percent per capita decline in moviegoing. As a writer for *Variety* said, "Filmgoing used to be part of the social fabric. Now it is an impulse purchase." During the 1980s, the population was aging and the prime moviegoing segment of under-30-year-olds was declining. When the damage done by VCRs and cable TV was added . . . well, you get the picture.

To survive into the 1990s, exhibitors must relearn how to woo moviegoers. There is something special about seeing a terrific film in a great theater with an appreciative audience. And by using technologies such as widescreen 70-millimeter projection and wraparound Dolby sound, theaters can create a sense of spectacle that no TV set can match. Theater owners can make their theaters clean and comfortable again, maybe even palatial. In fact, many exhibitors began to remodel their old elegant theaters and restore them to their former grandeur. Moreover, new construction was being upgraded. One successful exhibitor coddled customers in specially designed $130 seats, costing twice the national average.

Another exhibitor says, "We have to upgrade the quality of the moviegoing experience." His newest theaters have granite-floored lobbies with painted murals, spacious auditoriums, and first-rate sound and projection. But the higher construction costs pay off in more customers at higher than average ticket prices, and a splendid $1.35 per ticket take at the concession stand. However, such theaters are still rare.

As the drama of change pervades the movie exhibition industry, the major beneficiary is likely to be the long-suffering moviegoers. When consumers enter the theater of the future, they may not encounter a marvel of technology, but at least they won't stick to the floor.

Discussion Questions

1. Back before VCRs, made-for-TV movies, and movie cable channels, people had alternatives to going to the movies. What were they? How have these alternatives changed over the years?

2. How have changes in consumers' environments, cognitions, and behaviors contributed to the long-term decline in moviegoing?

3. Why do consumers buy high-priced snacks at concession stands in movie theaters? Analyze the environmental, cognitive, and behavioral factors that are operating in that situation.

4. Why do consumers go to the movies? What are the key attributes, consequences, and values that are relevant for two prime market segments: teenagers and young adults under 30?

5. Analyze consumers' decision processes at three levels: product class (Do I want to go to the movies versus something else?); product form (What type of movie do I want to see?); and brand (What specific movie should I go to?).

Black & Decker

At the end of 1985, Black & Decker was about halfway through the biggest brand name swap in marketing history. The company, once best known for its power tools, bought General Electric's small-appliance business in 1984 for $300 million. Black & Decker had until mid-1987 to bring all of GE's 150 or so appliance products under its own logo.

By renaming the GE appliances, B&D did for its competitors something they could not possibly have accomplished for themselves—eliminated the best-known brand name in the small-appliance business. But these other companies—including Sunbeam, Rival, Hamilton Beach, and Norelco—did not show much gratitude. Sensing confusion in the market and weakness in their competitor, they increased their advertising budgets and introduced new products in an attempt to intercept the GE customer before they got to Black & Decker. In return, Black & Decker unleashed a new-product blitz of its own and began a $100-million advertising and promotion campaign, the largest ever in the small-appliance industry.

For years GE had been the best-loved name in the appliance game. They still were in 1985. In one survey, consumers were asked to name small-appliance makers: GE came up a remarkable 92 percent of the time, Sunbeam was a distant second at 41 percent, and Black & Decker was mentioned only 12 percent of the time. In fact, another 1985 survey showed that most consumers didn't know GE had left the game.

Kenneth Homa, vice president for marketing, directed the complex Black & Decker strategy to make GE's name its own. The company broke the changeover process for each product into about 140 steps to be completed over a 14-week period. According to Black & Decker, the process went so smoothly that they stepped up the timetable to be complete by the end of 1986.

Black & Decker decided to launch each product as if it were new. For some products, they made alterations ranging from simple changes in color to major redesigns. For instance, GE's under-the-cabinet Spacemaker products—including a coffee maker, a toaster oven, and a can opener—were remodeled into sleeker units. Black & Decker also doubled the warranty period for every GE product to two years.

One big question for Black & Decker was whether to use its own brand name alongside GE's in the initial promotion and advertising. They decided not to for most appliances. Research had revealed that consumers associate the same qualities with Black & Decker—among them reliability and durability—that they did with GE. So Black & Decker tried to keep consumer confusion to a minimum by making a clean switch—the Black &

Source: Excerpted from Bill Saporito (1985), "Ganging Up on Black & Decker," Fortune *(December 23), pp. 63–72.*

Decker name for GE. For instance, the popular Spacemaker was remarketed without a reference to GE. TV commercials emphasized the Spacemaker brand name and ended with the tag line, "Now by Black & Decker."

Competitors, of course, did not stand still while the brand name switch took place. In particular, Sunbeam wanted consumers to forget both GE and Black & Decker. It increased its 1985 advertising budget to $42 million, four times what had been planned, to take advantage of the confusing situation.

Irons are a very important part (about 25 percent) of Black & Decker's small-appliance business. Thus, the company delayed conversion until it had experience with other lines. Research showed that 40 percent of customers go into a store intending to buy a particular brand of iron (usually GE). Therefore, Black & Decker modified their "clean switch" strategy. They included GE's name next to their own in print ads for irons and in promotional materials in the stores. On TV, however, it was more difficult to explain the switch. So, Black & Decker promoted the irons under its own name in television commercials.

The short-run concerns with the name change are not the only problems that Black & Decker must face. Most appliance sales are to people replacing their worn-out items, rather than to first-time buyers. Therefore, in any given year, only about 10 percent of the small-appliance market turns over. This means that most consumers who now own GE products won't buy new ones until after the GE name is long gone from the small-appliance scene. What will they think when they go into the store and find no GE products?

Discussion Questions

1. Describe the cognitive processes and knowledge structures that were involved in consumers' confusion over the GE name change to Black & Decker.

2. What types of strategies could Sunbeam use to try to derail the Black & Decker strategy? How can Black & Decker counter each of these?

3. How does the corporate image of Black & Decker or General Electric affect consumers' beliefs and attitudes toward the products and brands that they make?

4. What types of means-end chains (attributes—consequences—values) do people consider when they make purchase choices of small appliances such as a toaster oven?

5. Analyze the pros and cons of Black & Decker's decision not to mention the GE name in their changeover campaign. Discuss the pros and cons of their decision to feature the GE name for irons.

Cub Foods

Leslie Well's recent expedition to the new Cub Foods store in Melrose Park, Illinois was no ordinary trip to the grocery store. "You go crazy," says Wells, sounding a little shell shocked. Overwhelmed by Cub's vast selection, tables of samples, and discounts as high as 30 percent, Wells spent $76 on groceries—$36 more than she planned. Wells fell prey to what a Cub executive calls "the wow factor"—a shopping frenzy brought on by low prices and clever marketing. That's the reaction Cub's super warehouse stores strive for—and often get.

Cub Foods has been a leader in shaking up the food industry and forcing many conventional supermarkets to lower prices, increase services, or—in some cases—to go out of business. With Cub and other super warehouse stores springing up across the country, shopping habits are changing, too. Some shoppers drive 50 miles or more to a Cub store instead of going to the nearest neighborhood supermarket. Their payoff is that they find almost everything they need under one roof, and most of it is cheaper than at competing supermarkets. Cub's low prices, smart marketing, and sheer size encourage shoppers to spend far more than they do in the average supermarket.

The difference between Cub and most supermarkets is obvious the minute a shopper walks through Cub's doors. The entry aisle, called by some "power alleys," is lined two stories high with specials, such as bean coffee at $2 a pound and half-price apple juice. Above, the ceiling joists and girders are exposed, giving "the subliminal feeling of all the spaciousness up there. It suggests there's massive buying going on that translates in a shopper's mind that there's tremendous savings going on as well," says Paul Suneson, director of marketing research for Cub's parent, Super Valu Stores Inc., the nation's largest food wholesaler.

Cub's wider-than-usual shopping carts, which are supposed to suggest expansive buying, fit easily through Cub's wide aisles, which channel shoppers toward high-profit impulse foods. The whole store exudes a seductive, horn-of-plenty feeling. Cub customers typically buy in volume and spend $40 to $50 a trip, four times the supermarket average. The average Cub store has sales of $800,000 to $1 million a week, quadruple the volume of conventional stores.

Cub Foods has a simple approach to grocery retailing: low prices, made possible by rigidly controlled costs and high-volume sales; exceptionally high quality for produce and meats—the items people build shopping trips around; and immense variety. It's all packaged in clean stores that are

Source: Excerpted from Steve Weiner and Betsy Morris (1985), "Bigger, Shrewder and Cheaper Cub Leads Food Stores Into the Future," The Wall Street Journal *(August 26), p. 17.*

twice as big as most warehouse outlets and four times bigger than most supermarkets. A Cub store stocks as many as 25,000 items, double the selection of conventional stores, mixing staples with luxury, ethnic, and hard-to-find foods. This leads to overwhelming displays—88 kinds of hot dogs and dinner sausages, 12 brands of Mexican food, and fresh meats and produce by the ton.

The store distributes maps to guide shoppers. But without a map or a specific destination, a shopper is subliminally led around by the arrangement of the aisles. The power alley spills into the produce department. From there the aisles lead to highly profitable perimeter departments— meat, fish, bakery, and frozen food. The deli comes before fresh meat, because Cub wants shoppers to do their impulse buying before their budgets are depleted on essentials.

Overall, Cub's gross margin—the difference between what it pays for its goods and what it sells them for—is 14 percent, six to eight points less than most conventional stores. However, because Cub relies mostly on word of mouth advertising, its ad budgets are 25 percent less than those of other chains.

Discussion Questions

1. List at least five marketing tactics Cub Foods employs in its stores to increase the probability of purchases.

2. What accounts for Cub's success in generating such large sales per customer and per store?

3. Given Cub's lower prices, quality merchandise, excellent location, and superior assortment, what reasons can you offer for why many consumers in its trading areas refuse to shop there?

General Foods

In 1984, General Foods' Post cereal division suffered a drubbing at the hands of Kellogg, the market leader. Kellogg had begun to turn up the competitive heat in the early 1980s by increasing advertising expenditures and introducing a stream of new cereal products. During 1984, Kellogg increased its market share by 2 percent (up to 40 percent), while number-three-ranked GF dropped 2 percent (down to a 14 percent market share). The number two company, General Mills, held on to about a 20 percent market share, which had not changed significantly since 1980. These were not small changes. The ready-to-eat cereal market is a $4 billion market, so each share point was worth about $40 million in sales.

Post did have one hugely successful product in 1984, Fruit & Fiber, which cleverly satisfied two potentially contradictory desires of adult cereal consumers—a healthful cereal that tastes good. On the negative side was the costly failure of Smurfberry Crunch that fizzled early despite very heavy advertising promotion. The heavy ad expenditures on these two brands had left little for promoting the other Post brands. So, while Kellogg was gearing up for its ad blitz, Post actually reduced ad spending by 24 percent to $44 million. Instead, GF spent additional promotional dollars on cents-off coupons and discounts to grocers. This strategy encouraged one-time sales, but didn't build long-term loyalty the way advertising does. In 1984, the disparity got worse. Kellogg increased its advertising spending by 49 percent to $160 million, while GF's rose only 16 percent to $52 million. At the same time Post's share sank from 15.5 to 14.6 percent.

But a different strategy was being planned at GF. Management decided to increase ad spending to match Kellogg's—but not over all its 14 brands. Instead, it would concentrate its dollars on five core brands—Raisin Bran, Grape Nuts, Fruit & Fiber, Super Golden Crisp, and Pebbles—which together account for 75 percent of Post's cereal sales. They increased ad expenditures by 40 percent in 1984 and again in 1985. But dollars alone don't do the trick in the cereal business. According to David Hurwitt, who runs GF's $500-million Post cereal business, "It costs just as much to run a lousy commercial as a good one." In fact, one of the reasons Post ad spending had decreased in 1983 was because GF (and their ad agencies) couldn't come up with the right advertising strategies and campaigns. Why spend money to show ineffective advertising?

More than most products, cereal is what marketers call "marketing sensitive." Dollars spent on mediocre marketing simply fall into the void—they have no noticeable effect. The same amount of money, however, spent on a well-designed communication strategy can dramatically increase

Source: Excerpted from Pamela Sherrid (1985), "Fighting Back at Breakfast,"
Forbes (October 7), pp. 126–130.

sales. For instance, Post's Grape Nuts campaign—with its tag line "Are you right for Grape Nuts?"—offended many people. However, sales increased about 10 percent, compared to industry growth of only 3 percent.

Post's strategy was illustrated by the new campaign for Raisin Bran, launched in late 1985 at a cost of about $15 million. Hurwitt had changed the product to fit people's tendencies to eat what they think are "natural" foods. He removed the preservatives, increased the fiber, and took the sugar off the raisins. Then he hired singer John Denver—to some people the essence of all that is wholesome—for about $1 million to pitch the new product in a series of TV ads. Late in 1985, GF introduced another new cereal called Horizon, aimed at the active adult segment. The cereal is based on a "trail mix" concept, which means peanuts and grains clumped together, not in flakes.

Will Post's strategies work? The odds aren't good. Of dozens of new product entries, only a few cereals such as General Mill's Honey Nut Cheerios and Post's Fruit & Fiber have earned a sustainable 1 percent share in recent years. It's a big risk, but the potential payoffs are big, too.

Discussion Questions

1. Assume you are the brand manager for Raisin Bran. Present your arguments explaining why it is reasonable to spend $15 million in advertising on your brand even though only small (perhaps only 1 percent) shifts in market share are likely to be created. Make assumptions about the other costs that may be involved.

2. What are the relative advantages and disadvantages of using advertising and sales promotion strategies such as cents-off coupons, price reductions, and prizes and premiums to promote breakfast cereals?

3. Analyze the means-end chains that consumers might form for the new product attributes of Raisin Bran.

Hallmark Greeting Cards

It is one of the least likely businesses ever invented. However, Hallmark—and its main competitors, American Greetings and Gibson Greetings, plus an assortment of upstart alternative card companies—make a very good living selling sentiment to American consumers. In fact, greeting cards are one of the most profitable things that can be made with paper and ink. Consider Hallmark's classic pansy card:

> Pansies always stand for thoughts—
> At least that's what folks say,
> So this just comes to show my thoughts
> Are there with you today.

Since 1941, Hallmark has sold 22 million of these cards. Each card costs an estimated 7 cents to manufacture and retails for about 40 cents. Assuming a 100 percent markup at retail, Hallmark would receive about 20 cents at wholesale, for a 200 percent profit. With these financial numbers, Hallmark has grown at a compounded rate of 17 percent each year for the last 76 years. In 1985, their annual revenues approached $2 billion. Although nearly 50 percent of Hallmark's revenues come from ancillary products such as gift wrap, stuffed animals, and paper plates, greeting cards are still the most profitable line.

The costs of a card reflect not so much the paper or even the artwork, but the organized distribution system. Hallmark produces about 11 million cards per day which are sent to 37,000 outlets, most independently owned. The company has invested millions in computers to keep track. "We know which card is four rows up and five rows over, and how long it's been there," says a company representative. Reorders are shipped from two enormous automated warehouses, based on the past sales of each card. Because 90 percent of the cards are replaced with new designs each year, records must be constantly updated. Currently, Hallmark has some 32,000 card types to keep track of.

Hallmark didn't invent the commercial greeting card. Well-to-do Americans exchanged expensive Christmas cards with friends as long ago as the 1870s. This genteel custom was popularized by two marketing-oriented men—Jacob Sapirstein for American Greetings and Joyce Hall for Hallmark. Between them, they convinced consumers to buy graduation cards, wedding cards, sympathy cards, and cards for many other occasions.

Source: Excerpted from Robert McGough (1986), "Pansies Are Green," Forbes *(February 10), pp. 898–892.*

The card business is treacherous and highly competitive. There are three main companies: Hallmark has 40 percent of the market, American Greetings has 30 percent, and Gibson Greetings has 10 percent. Hallmark is in the nerve-racking position of being the front runner in a race where the pace of change has been accelerating. Moreover, "alternative" cards (risque or goofy) are becoming a serious threat. For instance, Recycled Paper Products, with sales of $60 million in whimsical animal cards, has been growing at a rate of 30 percent a year. Several small companies are thriving by making cards for niche markets that Hallmark leaves alone—such as cards for gays.

"The big segment of the market is what we deal in," says Irvine Hockaday, president of Hallmark. However, in 1982 Hallmark did introduce a "Lite" line of cards ("A third less serious than regular greeting cards"). More recently, they introduced cards to compete with the alternative lines. While not exactly salacious—"I'd like to tell you how much I love you. Have you got all night?"—these cards are not what you'd send to Aunt Tillie.

What is the allure of greeting cards? They certainly are not a convenience item. "It takes more time to drive down to the village and pick out a card than to write a letter," says a sociology professor. The greeting-card business is a triumph of marketing, which has convinced consumers that they need to send greeting cards.

Discussion Questions

1. What environmental factors affect the greeting-card business? (*Hint:* What about situational factors?)

2. What cultural factors are relevant to the greeting-card business? What trends do you see that will affect this industry?

3. What is the attraction of greeting cards? What needs do they serve? What symbolic meanings do greeting cards have for consumers? What happens to the consumer who sends or receives a greeting card?

4. What niche markets might Hallmark wish to pursue? What strategy do you recommend that Hallmark follow in trying to expand its market share?

5. Discuss the tangible versus the intangible aspects of greeting cards. Which factors are most important?

6. What types of consumers would you expect to be heavy users of greeting cards? What types of consumers do not send cards?

7. What changes in the social environment that might affect the sales of greeting cards should Hallmark monitor?

Hasbro Bradley Inc.

Coleco's Cabbage Patch dolls set a toy industry record in 1983 with $60 million in sales. This sales record lasted for only a single year, however, as Hasbro Bradley Inc. marketed the most successful toy introduction in history and obtained sales of over $100 million in 1984. Hasbro Bradley's product, called Transformers, consists of a variety of robot characters with both good and evil personalities. The toys are small and can be changed from vehicles to larger robots.

There are about 500 manufacturers in the U.S. toy industry. Traditionally, toys were manufactured and marketed with little attention to marketing research and R&D. And less than 1 percent of the 3,000 to 4,000 toys introduced each year succeeded.

In recent years, however, toy manufacturers have invested heavily in marketing research and R&D. Focus group interviews, concept fulfillment, and other directional studies involving children as young as five years of age are becoming commonplace in the industry. Hasbro Bradley spent $8.8 million on R&D in 1983 and $6.5 million in the first half of 1984. Overall, industry sales in 1984 increased 20 percent to a record $12 billion; and except for 1983, increases have ranged from 11 to 27 percent since 1978.

A major competitor for Transformers is Tonka Toys' Gobots. Gobots attained $82 million in sales in 1984 and surpassed Transformers in unit sales. These two toys set a precedent in the development of what the industry calls "boy dolls," in that personalities are developed for each of the good and evil characters. Hasbro Bradley executives believe that the development of personalities for the toy characters played a major role in the success of Transformers; but the personality development is sketchy enough that the children can fill in the details and actions.

One controversial method involved in promoting Transformers and a variety of other toys is the development of animated TV programs featuring these characters. The TV programs help develop the characters' personalities and story line, but critics see them as simply commercials designed to sell the featured toys. The number of toy-based shows jumped from 14 in 1983 to 40 just two years later.

While Hasbro Bradley has made extensive use of this TV promotional vehicle, the company downplays its importance. Their vice president of marketing says that the program "doesn't really sell at all. It's way down the line in importance in developing a product personality."

Sources: Kevin T. Higgins (1985), "Research, Marketing not Playthings for Toymakers," Marketing News *(July 5), p. 1; John Wilke, Lois Therrien, Amy Dunkin and Mark N. Vamos (1985), "Are the Programs Your Kids Watch Simply Commercials?"* BusinessWeek *(March 25), pp. 53–54; "Toys for '85,"* Fortune *(March 18, 1985), p. 9–10.*

Other marketing experts, however, argue that the practice is quite profitable, and that in addition to selling toys, it helps to build brand loyalty to the featured characters, making generic alternatives unacceptable. Critics of product-based programming to children argue strongly against this practice. The president of the National Association for Better Broadcasting charges, "It's deceptive and cynical, because kids can't tell when they are being pitched." The president of Action for Children's Television, a consumer advocacy group, argues, "Toy companies say they turn products into shows out of a need to give the toys a personality, but they're really doing it to move the products off the shelves."

Discussion Questions

1. What is the role of reference group and family influence in the purchase of a collection of toy characters?
2. What factors account for the success of Transformers?
3. What societal problems are involved in the use of product-based programming with children?

Hershey Foods

U.S. consumers spend about $8 billion a year on candy. Throughout the 1970s, Mars Candy Company was the candy king and by the end of that decade had pushed its market share to 14 percentage points ahead of competitors. However, in the 1980s, Hershey Foods caught up with Mars, and the two companies now share market leadership. The two companies together control 70 percent of the candy-bar market and make all 10 of the best-selling candy bars (five for Hershey's and five for Mars). Peter Paul Cadbury, maker of Mounds and Almond Joy, sells about 9 percent of the U.S. candy bars. Nestlé, maker of Nestlé Crunch, sells about 6 percent.

One reason for Hershey's success in the 1980s is that it has been very active in introducing new products. In fact, almost 20 percent of its candy sales came from new products in 1984, versus 7 percent in 1979. Hershey's research shows that most people who walk up to the candy counter will choose from 6, maybe as many as 12, items that are acceptable. Hershey's has 17 of the 60 best-selling candy bars; Mars has only 9 in this group.

Many of Hershey's brands are targeted to adults—the baby-boom grown-ups. While children under 12 are still a very important market, people over 18 eat 55 percent of all candy sold. Hershey's strategy is to carefully target to mothers, because it reasons that mothers determine children's early taste in candy. This strategy has made Hershey's the top seller in food stores, where half of candy dollars are spent. Because Mars' single bars sell faster than Hershey's, however, Mars is number one at newsstands and vending machines. Mars' Snickers bar is the number one U.S. candy, with 1984 sales of about $400 million.

Targeting to adults led to several successful changes in marketing strategy. Two candy bars, Take Five and Skor, were introduced with less chocolate and less sugar than in children's candies. Skor, a chocolate-covered toffee bar, now sells more than the traditional Heath bar. In December 1983, Hershey raised wholesale prices enough to push up the retail price of a standard candy bar to 35 cents. While this was very profitable for Hershey's (particularly because adults are likely to be less price sensitive than children), it could adversely affect competitive brands aimed at kids. Hershey also introduced the Big Block line—larger, 2.2-ounce candy bars selling for 50 cents that appeal to adult males. Golden Almond and Golden Pecan bars weigh 3.2 ounces, sell for $1.19 at retail, and contain a smoother blend of chocolate and whole (rather than chopped) nuts. These bars are designed to appeal to adult consumers as a higher-quality product. These products, along with New Trail granola bars, bring in about $100 million in annual sales.

Source: Excerpted from Steve Lawrence (1985), "Bar Wars: Hershey Bites Mars," Fortune (July 8), pp. 52–57.

In addition, traditional brand sales have done very well. A national ad campaign led to Hershey's Kisses tripling its sales between 1977 and 1984; and a contest on the package led to double-digit increases in sales of Reese's Peanut Butter Cups for both 1983 and 1984.

Finally, Hershey's chocolate milk is widely admired as a marketing coup: the familiar brown and silver labels on the milk cartons double as small advertising billboards for chocolate bars in almost every supermarket in the country.

Discussion Questions

1. What are the advantages of targeting candy bars to adults rather than to children?

2. Does targeting to adults require a change in image for candy products?

3. Describe your most recent purchase of a candy bar in terms of relevant cognitions, behaviors, and environments.

4. What means-end chains might different consumers have for candy bars?

McDonald's Corporation

McDonald's Corporation has achieved greater sales and profits from burgers than any company in history. In 1983, McDonald's had sales of $8.7 billion, compared to $3.1 billion for Burger King and $1.9 billion for Wendy's. In 1984, systemwide sales rose to $10 billion, and international sales were up 20 percent to nearly $2 billion. McDonald's is not only the largest hamburger chain but the largest food-service operator in the world, accounting for nearly 40 percent of all fast-food hamburgers sold.

McDonald's corporate motto is QSCV: Quality, Service, Cleanliness, and Value. Interestingly, while the company has sold billions of burgers, research suggests that consumers are not really wild about their taste. When a former Burger King executive was asked how McDonald's stays number one in spite of this problem, he replied, "Do they have great French fries? Yes. Is the service quick? The fastest. Are the restaurants clean? Immaculate. You have to give McDonald's credit for knowing exactly what they're doing."

Much of McDonald's growth can be attributed to expansion in the number of restaurants in both domestic and foreign markets. For a number of years, McDonald's achieved its objective of opening at least 500 new restaurants per year. In recent years, about one third of these have been in foreign markets; and this figure is expected to increase to 50 percent by the end of the decade. In the United States, McDonald's has played the growth game by looking for nooks where it can squeeze in new restaurants. McDonald's first laid claim to the suburbs, then spread to smaller towns. It has continued expansion into big cities and what it calls its semicaptive markets. These include toll roads, military bases, museums, hospitals, and universities where there are lots of people—and almost no place else to eat. These markets have been very profitable. The McDonald's restaurant at Camp Pendleton, for example, grossed $3 million in its first year of business.

While expansion into new markets accounts for some of the sales growth, it is not the whole story. In 1984, average sales per restaurant increased 8 percent, from $1.169 million to $1.264 million. In this same year, advertising and marketing expenditures were $600 million, or 6 percent of systemwide sales. About 80 percent of this was spent domestically.

McDonald's also test marketed a variety of new products in recent years, some of which have been extremely successful. Chicken McNuggets account for at least 8 percent of sales, and one month after the national launch of this product, McDonald's became the second-largest chicken

Sources: Scott Hume (1985), "After Strong '84, Big Mac Stays on Track," Advertising Age (May 27), p. 6; Monci Jo Williams (1984), "McDonald's Refuses to Plateau," Fortune (November 12), pp. 34–40.

retailer, behind Kentucky Fried Chicken. The company is very enthusiastic about Chicken McNuggets, for it believes this product does not cut into hamburger sales and brings new customers to the restaurants. Other new product tests included a one-third-pound gourmet burger, salad bars, pre-packaged salads, a cheeseburger with lettuce and tomato, and a sandwich version of chicken cordon bleu called Chicken McSwiss. For several years McDonald's tested McRib, a pork sandwich that oozed barbeque sauce, even moving it into a 3,500-store test. Many consumers tried the sandwich once but didn't like the sloppiness or the taste.

Many analysts speculate that McDonald's will eventually have to diversify into other areas of business besides restaurants to maintain growth. In fact, there was some speculation in 1984 that McDonald's would buy Walt Disney Productions. When asked about this acquisition, however, McDonald's chief executive responded: "My view is that we can maintain a growth rate in the teens through this decade. And if you believe that, it makes the question of diversification beside the point."

Discussion Questions

1. What factors account for the overall consumer acceptance of McDonald's? In other words, why do you eat at McDonald's?

2. What threats are there to McDonald's continued success in the fast-food industry?

3. If McDonald's were paying you a consulting fee of $3,000 per day, what recommendations would you make to improve the company's sales, profits, and market share in the long run?

Nike

By mid-1985 the signs were clear—after years of mystique and spectacular growth, jogging was finally puffing into middle age. For instance, in the previous year, unit sales of running shoes were down 17 percent, and dollar sales were off 15 percent. Nike, the market leader, sold about $270 million worth of running shoes in 1983 (for a 31 percent market share), but only $240 million in 1984 (for a market share of 26 percent). The industry was beginning to engage in sporadic price cutting as Nike and competitors fought to hold on to their market share. The discounting and larger advertising and promotion expenditures necessary to move inventory reduced Nike's net profit margins from 6.6 to 4.4 percent. Profits dropped from $57 to $41 million.

Finally, the market for running shoes had become highly segmented—a sign of a mature market. According to the director of the National Sporting Goods Association, "We've probably reached pretty close to the maximum participation in running." Part of the reason is demographic. A primary market for running gear is the baby boomers—ages 25 to 40. But that market had been saturated. (Nearly everyone who wanted to run had tried it.) As the leading age of this group pushed toward 40, lacing up the shoes for a five-mile run began to seem less adventurous than it did at age 24.

Running develops the legs and the cardiovascular system. But many runners had begun to notice that the rest of their bodies needed some conditioning, too. There was an increasing interest in total fitness. So, even though millions of joggers were still on the run, fewer of them doing fewer laps translated into fewer replacement shoes sold for Nike, Converse, New Balance, Brooks, and the others. As the biggest manufacturer in the business, Nike has the most to lose.

Clearly, though, the shoemakers have had a long run for their money in a market highly dominated by short-lived fads. Consider tennis, for example. Sales of tennis rackets peaked in 1976 when an estimated 8.6 million rackets were sold. Despite technological innovations and space-age materials such as kevlar, boron, and graphite, the industry sold only about 3.2 million rackets in 1984. Instead, the big boom in 1984–85 was aerobics gear and home gym equipment.

Faced with these environmental changes, Nike's strategy was to diversify. They gave shoes less-expensive technological features and sold them as fashion accessories. Also, shoes were redesigned to enter new markets—especially shoes for aerobic dancing and for basketball (the popular AirJordan). Nike also got into clothing. This was quite a switch for the

Source: Excerpted from Richard Phalon (1984), "Out of Breath," Forbes *(October 22), pp. 39–40.*

running-shoe company. They were not used to dealing with the rapidly changing fashion scene. Marketing had become much more complex than ever before, and changes (seasons, color preferences, etc.) came more quickly. In fact, the fastest growing element in the Nike mix was fashion apparel—running shorts and shirts, warm-up suits, etc. It was a new race and hard to keep up.

Discussion Questions

1. Trace the key environmental, cognitive, and behavioral changes that have affected the running/physical-fitness markets.

2. What current fads are affecting this market?

3. What types of consumer knowledge should Nike consider in developing new markets? What types of consumer segments can you identify?

4. What effects does level of involvement have on buying running shoes?

Timex Corporation

Timex Corporation was one of the first companies to offer low-cost, durable mechanical watches. These watches were completely mass-produced with hard-alloy bearings that were less costly than jeweled bearings but much longer lasting than nonjeweled watches had been before. Timex attempted to sell these watches in jewelry stores, offering a 30 percent markup. However, jewelers commonly received 50 percent markup on merchandise, and many refused to stock the Timex watches. Timex then began selling direct to drugstores, hardware stores, and even cigar stands—and at one point had a distribution system of nearly a quarter of a million outlets. This mass-distribution strategy was coupled with heavy TV advertising demonstrating the durability of the watches. For example, one ad showed a Timex watch being strapped to an outboard motor propellor and continuing to work after the engine had been run for several minutes. Such ads were used to support the contention that Timex watches could "take a licking and keep on ticking." To keep dealers and prices firmly in line, Timex limited production to about 85 percent of anticipated demand, making the watches somewhat scarce.

This strategy was extremely successful. By the late 1960s, Timex had a 50 percent market share in the United States and as much as 20 percent of worldwide sales. In 1970, Timex had aftertax profits of $27 million on sales of $200 million.

After a quarter of a century of dominance in the low-price watch market, Timex began to face serious competition in the mid-1970s. A major technological advance, which Timex executives initially judged to be unimportant, was the development of electronic watches. By the time they recognized the importance of this change and introduced an electronic watch, competitors had already developed and marketed much-improved models. In fact, the Timex electronic watches were so big and clumsy that employees nicknamed them "quarter pounders"; and prices ended up 50 percent above competitive, much more attractive watches.

By 1983, Timex's U.S. market share had plummeted to about 17 percent, and operating losses approached $100 million. Distribution had declined to 100,000 outlets. Timex ranked fifth in volume behind Japan's Seiko, Citizen, and Casio, and a Swiss combine, ASUAG-SSIH Ltd. Digital and quartz analog watches dominated the market, and even the successful Japanese companies faced increased price competition from manufacturers in Hong Kong. In fact, when the export price of the average digital watch

Source: Adapted for purposes of this text from J. Paul Peter and James H. Donnelly, Jr., (1986), Marketing Management: Knowledge and Skills, *Plano, Tex.: Business Publications, pp. 278–279.*

dropped from $5 in 1981 to less than $2, many companies were forced out of business with margins of only a few cents per watch.

Timex at this point decided to attempt to rebuild its watch market and make itself less vulnerable by diversifying into home health-care products and home computers. To rebuild its timekeeping business, the company invested over $100 million to retool and redesign its watch and clock lines. Timex's marketing vice president supported this investment by stating, "We were thick, fat, ugly, overpriced, and behind in technology." The strategy then became to produce watches that were just as attractive as higher-priced brands and to keep the major portion of the line priced under $50. Of course, this forced Timex to compete in a world already overloaded with too many inexpensive watch brands. In addition to watches from Japan and Hong Kong, Swiss manufacturers scored a big hit with a trendy timepiece called Swatch, which was brightly colored plastic and sold for $30. Sales of Swatch soared to 100,000 units per month, and the watches could not be produced fast enough.

Timex also attempted to compete in the over-$100 price range with its super-thin quartz analog Elite collection that sold in department and jewelry stores for up to $120. However, as one competitor summed up the market potential of the Timex Elite collection, "It's got one disadvantage; it's got a $12.95 name on it."

Discussion Questions

1. In what situations do consumers shop for and purchase new watches?

2. What problems and opportunities does Timex have in the low-priced watch market, and what strategy recommendations would you offer Timex?

3. What problems and opportunities does Timex have in the high-priced watch market, and what strategy recommendations would you offer Timex?

Name Index

Subject Index

*This book has been set Linotron 202, 10 point Palatino,
leaded 2 points. Section numbers are 16 point Palatino
Italic and section titles are 24 point Palatino Bold Italic.
Chapter numbers are 14 point Palatino Italic and chapter
titles are 18 point Palatino Bold Italic.*